APPLETON-CENTURY-CROFTS
SOCIOLOGY SERIES

Edited by John F. Cuber

TECHNOLOGY AND
SOCIAL CHANGE

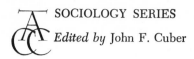

SOCIOLOGY SERIES

Edited by John F. Cuber

FRANCIS R. ALLEN, *The Florida State University*

HORNELL HART

DELBERT C. MILLER, *Indiana University*

WILLIAM F. OGBURN

MEYER F. NIMKOFF, *The Florida State University*

TECHNOLOGY
AND SOCIAL CHANGE

HM
221
T4

New York: APPLETON-CENTURY-CROFTS

DIVISION OF MEREDITH PUBLISHING COMPANY

PRINTED IN THE UNITED STATES OF AMERICA
E–02178

*This book is dedicated
to the scientific study
of social change.*

PREFACE

THERE HAVE BEEN two main reasons for producing this book—one specific and immediate, the other of broader context. The first was that no appropriate publication existed in the area of *technology and social change* for use in college and university courses. Exellent material was available which, however, had to be culled from a variety of sources. It seemed worth while to produce an up-to-date summation of knowledge in this field. It is hoped that this volume, designed for use in advanced undergraduate or graduate classes, will not only fulfill a present need but may also facilitate the development of more courses on this subject at other colleges and universities and may be of interest to general readers as well.

The broader reason for producing this volume is even more important in the eyes of the authors. We believe that the impact of technology on social change in Western society, potent for many years, has now become so crucial in various respects that greater emphasis on this whole subject is urgently needed. It is clear that this concern is shared by many other people including (indeed especially) physical and biological scientists, many of whom see great danger in such problems as that of nuclear radiation. This is evident from recent meetings of the American Association for the Advancement of Science and from articles and editorials in such journals as the *Bulletin of the Atomic Scientists*. Serious concern has been registered regarding the social aspects of science, centering on two principal considerations: (1) the place of science in society, and (2) the impact of science and technology upon society. Representatives from different branches of science have contributed valuable ideas on these subjects, but certainly discussion of the *social* aspects of science calls for the participation of social scientists. For many years social scientists have been probing the subtleties of the social structure and appraising effects of innovations upon the vast and complex array of social relationships. Some sociologists, for example, Robert K. Merton and Bernard Barber, have recently addressed themselves to the first subject mentioned above (the place of science in society), but the second one—crucial as it is in the latter 1950's—has been largely neglected. The writers of this volume—all sociologists—have therefore set themselves to fill what is to them a major gap in the literature by attempting to treat systematically the impact of science and technology upon society.

We hope that this volume may be of interest to scientists and science students of all kinds; this is intended to include the field of engineering. A recent survey sponsored by the American Society for Engineering Education has advocated increased study of social factors and effects relating to the development of science and engineering. We suggest, however, that the social sciences, just as much as the natural sciences or engineering, would do well to place greater emphasis upon this study. Sociology, for instance, has made gratifying progress during recent years in developing sharper methodological tools, in refining its theoretical concepts, and in developing certain sub-fields. It has studied a wide range of subjects with increasing thoroughness. Yet recent compilations of research projects being conducted by members of the American Sociological Society show that little attention has been paid to the enormous impact of science and technology upon society. It is a paradox that matters which vitally affect man's welfare and perhaps his survival have been mostly ignored insofar as scientific work in this field is concerned. It is hoped that this volume may stimulate systematic study and research on this subject.

Some of the problems relative to the impact of technology on social change may be major and crucial, as that of nuclear radiation or the threat of the H-bomb, long-range ballistic missile, or other war weapon, to man's urban civilization. Other problems in this sphere are less basic. The broad question has been for many years of endeavoring to derive the benefits of the constructive side of technology while at the same time controlling the destructive. At any rate, the need of solving problems of all degrees of criticalness is a consequential reason for studying the subject.

The real emphasis of the present volume, however, is on presenting the panoramic picture of change—the steady, cumulative, all-pervasive flow of change in all departments of human life—the persistent, all-round transformation of the social environment. There is no wish to concentrate on the spectacular and sensational any more than the field of meteorology devotes all its attention to the hurricane.

Present college and university students, having a stake in the future, have much to gain from this study. Assuming that they will have in the United States an expectation of life of around fifty years on the average after graduation from college, they will witness and be affected by countless changes of importance. No matter what their specific vocational interest may be, they will find themselves concerned with social trends, processes of change, and expectations with regard to major occurrences during coming years. The recording of unique events needs to be supplemented by this broader understanding of the process of change.

A view of the present volume is that it is more satisfactory to appraise the phenomenon and problems of social change in an over-all way than to divide up the study into many small segments. Some may believe that changes in community life should be exclusively studied by the community specialists, changes in family living by the marriage and family experts, population changes by the population experts, changes in race relations exclusively by the race specialists, and so on. It may be suggested that in this piecemeal fashion the whole subject will finally be covered. Although specialists are bound to have such interest in their own specialty, we hold that to "segmentize" or "atomize" the subject of social change is faulty on at least two important counts. First, it must be recognized that many different aspects of change often have identical underlying causes. The most destructive war weapon and the new life-saving medical innovation may stem from the same basic development in pure science. To fail to appreciate the common ancestry of seemingly distant and unconnected events is to miss a major point of the process of change. One needs to have the perspective of the whole forest, not a narrower focus on a clump of trees. Second, to fail to grasp the interrelatedness of different social phenomena, aside from the matter of common origin, is a major error in sociology. As Professor Ogburn points out in this volume, elements of the social system comprise a network and they affect each other. A modification in one part of the system may bring the need of adjustment in another part; however, if one is concentrating on a narrow segment of the field, he may miss this completely.

"Segmentizing" in this subject may be compared to that in a medical study of cancer. Here, too, some "segmentizing" will be inevitable: skin cancers will be studied by the dermatologists, lung cancers by the chest specialists, stomach cancers by the gastrointestinal specialists, and so on. Yet there is no question as to the advisability of having over-all study of the cancer problem, and institutes for cancer research have been established for that purpose.

Finally, this text maintains a definite point of view toward the subject of social change: it holds that technology and applied science constitute a dominant and crucial force in causing change in modern Western society. This may be regarded as the basic underlying theme of the work. This influence rests to a large extent on the constant accumulation of knowledge in the basic sciences. There are other important influences causing social change too, such as migrations and other forms of population change, social movements and other types of collective behavior, changes in natural resources, the development of new ideologies, and other social influences. Sometimes these influences are notable in causing change. In general, they are not thought to be as large or as decisive a factor as that of technology and applied science. Sometimes these other causes of social change will be rooted in the technological factor anyhow, for migrations may be related to industrial opportunities (which may have resulted from technological advances); or a trend of gradual aging of population may give rise to political, welfare, and other consequences (the original aging trend itself being largely due to such innovations in medical technology as vaccination).

In focusing attention on the technological influence, we do not mean to belittle other valuable social and community influences and interests— religion, education, government, race, and others. These are indeed important, and other writers will undoubtedly choose to emphasize them. Nor do we claim that man is necessarily happier because of the technological influence. We do maintain that technology has wielded a crucial influence on human affairs which must be reckoned with both for its constructive and destructive impact.

Acknowledgments. The first acknowledgment must go to the fellow authors of this volume. To a large extent the project has been a co-operative "team effort." In the initial planning stage, the sagacious advice and aid of Professor Nimkoff was most valuable. In the drafting of manuscript there was considerable critical reading of chapters written by other authors, which led to improvement and to better integration of the volume. Deepest appreciation is especially extended to Professors Ogburn and Hart, distinguished leaders in the study of social change, for being most generous with their time in reading chapters of the younger authors and for contributing in many ways from their wealth of knowledge and rich experience. A cordial note of appreciation is also expressed to Professor Miller, another active member of the team, who produced efficiently and good-naturedly despite the hindrances of European travel during a part of the writing period. Even though all authors had a busy schedule, the spirit of co-operation and helpfulness was outstanding.

The authors are grateful to Professor John F. Cuber, editor of the Appleton-Century-Crofts Sociology Series, for many valuable insights and for comments that improved the book. Other acknowledgments for aid rendered are sincerely expressed to Dean Wilbur Schramm, Institute of Communications Research, University of Illinois, for critically reading and offering suggestions regarding Chapter 12; to H. Lawrence Smith, M.D., Tallahassee, Florida, for making a similar contribution to Chapter 16; and to Mr. Elmer Thompson, Director of Information, Air Transport Association of America, Washington, D. C., for aid in connection with Chapter 9. Appreciation is expressed to Sir Philip Morris, Vice Chancellor of the University of Bristol, England, for aiding Professor Miller during his stay at that university during 1954–55. This made available much information on social change in England and otherwise in Europe. Appreciation is also extended to Dr. Charles M. Grigg and his staff of the Center for Social Research, Florida State University, for assembling the composite index (using IBM machines) after authors had made separate indexes for their own chapters.

Despite this considerable aid, the authors must bear sole responsibility for the product. Responsibility for the content of each chapter clearly rests with the stated author.

Francis R. Allen

Tallahassee, Fla.

CONTENTS

CONTENTS

PART I

Processes and Theories of Social Change

CHAPTER 1

THE MEANING
OF TECHNOLOGY

■ *William F. Ogburn*

> TECHNOLOGY is like a great mountain peak. It looks different according to
the side from which one views it. From one vantage point only a small part
may be seen, from another the outlook is clouded; yet we may get a clear
view from still another side. Few of us see it from all its sides; so each of us
is likely to have a very limited conception of its nature. It is desirable, then,
to look at technology from various points of view; for in this way we get a
less narrow picture.

DIFFERENT VIEWPOINTS TOWARD TECHNOLOGY

Technological schools. To many young students who have not thought
very much about it, technology is understood as something that is taught at
an institute of technology or something they learn about in a technological
high school. It has to do with engineering, mechanics, electricity, chemistry,
laboratories, shop work, and various studies that one does not find in the
curriculum of a liberal arts college or an ordinary secondary school. Graduates of these technological schools get jobs with engineering companies in
construction work, or go out to develop new countries, or are associated
with architectural firms. To them, technology is very definitely not a social
science such as history, economics, or politics.

Gadgets and push buttons. An even more narrow view is found among
those who think of technology only as the source of the many gadgets that
are finding their way into our homes, offices, restaurants, automobiles, and
other places frequented by the mass of the people. These gadgets may be
radio sets, pipes for radiant heat, deep-freeze lockers, automatic gear shifts,
microfilm readers, tape recorders, copying machines, electric blankets,
automatic door openers, or ultra-violet-ray lamps. Hundreds of such gadgets
are being placed at our disposal for our convenience and comfort. These are
the products of technology with which we come in daily contact, their new-
ness forced upon our attention by advertisements. Thus it is natural that we

3

should think of technology as something that furnishes the mechanical devices which appeal to us as aids; although sometimes they may appear to some of us as nuisances.

Destroyer of artistic skills. The great flowering of technology as we know it today, based on metals and mechanical power, succeeded an era of handicrafts based upon wood and muscle. The age of handicrafts was one of great individual skill, and it resulted in productions of charm and artistic merit. A single craftsman would fabricate a whole product—a chair, a clock, a costume, or a curtain. We may suppose that he derived a certain joy in his creation, much as an artist does in painting a picture. But as the machine age replaced handicrafts, the individual worker created only part of a product. His skill and the joy that went with it were destroyed. In their place came routine, monotony, and toil, with a workman assigned only a fragment of a complete job, for example, sawing a piece of wood, winding a wire, sewing a buttonhole, or unfolding a bolt of cloth. This repetition daily, monthly, and yearly meant utilizing only a minute part of man's great capabilities. Thus the workman and the artist tend to view technology as the destruction of an artistic and humanly wholesome way of life and a replacement of these by long hours of monotonous toil in a factory.[1]

Technological unemployment. To some observers, technology suggests unemployment and little else. To them the social implications of technology, particularly in the 1920's and the 1930's in the United States, were the loss of a job and the replacement of men by machines.[2] There was a good deal of unemployment in these decades, and the idea that it was caused by technological innovations was widely spread in writings and discussions in newspapers, magazines, and books. Other influences of technology were only dimly seen at the time, and technology came to signify this social problem of unemployment. Since the prosperous years of the 1940's and 1950's, marked by a scarcity of labor, little has been heard of technological unemployment.

Aid to non-industrial peoples. Another aspect of technology has been introduced to the popular mind in the 1940's and the 1950's. It is that technology will raise the standard of living of peoples who are as yet without much industrialization.[3] This idea was presented to the general public as the fourth point in a program submitted by President Truman to the Congress. "Point Four" came to symbolize technological aid to less-developed countries. World War II made Americans more familiar with many distant peoples. Soldiers and travelers were impressed with the rudimentary nature of the tools used, for example, in parts of the Far East, as compared with those

[1] John Ruskin, *The Crown of Wild Olive* (Philadelphia, H. Altemus, 1895).

[2] Corrington Gill, *Unemployment and Technological Change,* Report to the Temporary National Economic Committee (Philadelphia, Work Projects Administration, 1940).

[3] "Factors of Economic Progress," *International Social Science Bulletin,* Vol. VI, No. 2 (1954), Part I, pp. 159–294.

in the United States and in Western industrial countries. If an iron plow could replace a wooden one, the productivity of a farm worker could be increased, and his labor lessened. To do something to help the so-called "backward" peoples appealed to the imagination of Americans who had been forced by war to kill and destroy. The exportation of machinery and tools no doubt appealed to our businessmen, for raising the incomes of these peoples would create a better market. But experience had taught that it was not enough to export equipment to peoples who would not know how to make the best use of it or repair it. So there arose the necessity of exporting "know-how" as well as the implements. Thus was technology to be exported. The idea was also in line with the ameliorative aims of other organizations such as UNESCO. Teams of technicians were, therefore, sent to the different peoples to teach them the best ways to use these new tools and machines. In this manner, then, Americans began to learn another influence of technology: its capability of raising the standard of living of slightly-industrialized peoples.

Maker of wealth. Technology can not only improve the material well-being of peoples with low per capita incomes, but it can also raise the standard of living of highly industrialized peoples. The standard of living of the people of the United States in 1950 is twice as high as it was in 1900. This doubling of per capital income in dollars of the same purchasing power is due largely to developments in technology and applied science.[4] There are valid reasons to think that, short of destructive war, the already high incomes in the United States will be increased even more during the second half of the twentieth century as a result of continued inventions and discoveries in science. A mechanical cotton picker now exists which can do the work of twenty-three laborers picking by hand. Today we are discussing the coming of automatism in industry when only a few will be needed in a factory to push buttons, to run the machinery that will manufacture products without further assistance from human beings. Nearly automatic factories will greatly increase productivity per worker and our standard of living will be raised, for national income is a function of the rate of production. Technological development, thus, may be seen as the force which raises the standard of living of peoples of any level.

Materialization versus spiritualization. The peoples who were to benefit from "Point Four" programs in material wages and standards of living generally had a set of values which emphasized religion, the life of the spirit, or such human values as happiness. New and better tools brought material advantages, but they did little or nothing to help the human spirit in its search for sustaining philosophies.

In the highly industrialized countries of the West, technology brought about an increased emphasis on material things that seemed relatively to de-

---

[4] W. F. Ogburn, "Technology and the Standard of Living in the United States," *American Journal of Sociology*, Vol. LX, No. 4 (January, 1955), pp. 380–386.

emphasize spiritual values. Many religious and moral groups see this aspect of technology, namely, that it is a force seemingly antagonistic to the life of the spirit. To them, technology stands for the secularization of life. One goes to a school of technology now instead of to a school of theology as in former times. To these followers of the spirit, technology is a false god. They resent the sight of our young people with no higher aim than material success.

Machine the master. The view of technology as a tempter which leads us away from the true values of the good life changes rather readily into the view that technology is a dictator that controls our lives. When the factory whistle blows, we must be up and at work. The railroad runs on a time table that we must follow and obey. The automobile maims and kills. We listen to the radio and watch television, but we seem to be unable to do anything to improve their programs.[5] Factories close down in a business depression, and we lose our jobs. The assembly line moves by, and the workers must keep up with its speed. The typist works for a typewriter which makes her sit before it for eight hours a day. To those groups of people whose temperament is tinged with rebelliousness, or who love the open road or the ways of nature, technology dictates a schedule that takes away freedom and makes daily life a routine.

Technology as a worker of miracles. By contrast, technology appears as a mechanical slave to do our bidding. It helps us do the things we want to do. It makes for us the things we want.[6] An automobile is ours to command, to take us anywhere at any time we wish. The airplane enables us to fly over mountains and over seas, and with it we can travel around the world in two or three days. By means of radio we can speak instantly to millions of people on the other side of the world. We can measure the distance to the sun and tell the composition of distant stars. A block of wood can be made into silken stockings, and one element can be changed into another. A lump of coal will yield dyes of more colors than are found in nature. We can record a symphonic concert on coiled wire no bigger than a spool of thread. From this viewpoint technology is a servant, but it is more. With its aid we can work miracles undreamed of by the ancients. It will continue in the future to give us power to do things that we now cannot even imagine. To these observers, technology is a great boon because it extends the capabilities and powers of men.

A precipitator of change. A banker once defined an invention as that which made his securities insecure. The securities of the railroads fell with the invention of the motor truck and the airplane, and the nitrate industry of Chile lost its market in the United States when nitrate was made from the nitrogen of the air. Inventions in technology bring profits and prosperity to

[5] Siegfried Giedion, *Mechanization Takes Command* (New York, Oxford University Press, 1948).

[6] Waldemar Kaempffert, *Modern Wonder Workers: A Popular History of American Invention* (New York, Blue Ribbon Books, 1931).

some, woe and destruction to others. Technology is seen, at any rate, as a cause of changes for better or worse.[7]

The range of inventions is wide, and changes are occurring in many different phases of life.[8] To agriculture, oil and electricity have brought the power revolution. Warfare is mechanized and the great powers among nations are reranked. Science is changing the forms and nature of religious beliefs. These changes may or may not be progress, but the new replaces or is added to the old. So to many, technology is viewed as a disturber of the status quo, a destroyer of peace and quiet by precipitating unanticipated changes. These changes may offer prospects for new business or opportunities to make the world a better place in which to live, or they may bring threats that we feel we should oppose.

A changing environment to which we adjust. Like other animals, man adjusts to his environment; otherwise he does not live. Man's material environment, however, unlike that of the lower animals, does not consist only of land, water, air, fauna, flora, temperature, and pressure. It also consists of buildings, tools, clothing, fire, vehicles, books, schools, clocks, churches, munitions, writing materials, medicines, contraceptives, machines, prime movers, and the various objects that we call material culture. These are the products of technology and applied science.[9] The natural environment in any one place is quite stable except for diurnal and seasonal changes, but the technological environment in recent years is a whirling mass of change. This change in modern material culture is partly owing to inventions and scientific discoveries. Technology may thus be viewed as a changing environment of mankind.

The natural environment changes from winter to summer, to which a man must adjust as he also does when he goes from, say, the arctic to the tropics. Likewise, man has had to adjust as his technological environment changes. The life of a farmer differed from that of a hunter. The way of life in a city is different from life in the open country. In recent years we have changed our habits as we use television. We read less; we stay at home more; we go to motion pictures less frequently; our children play at athletic sports less. We make similar adjustments to the automobile and the airplane. And just now we are concerned with what adjustments we must make to the atom bomb and the thermonuclear bomb. The harnessing of atomic energy for peaceful purposes will occasion still other adjustments. We have, then, a technological environment which is changing rapidly and to which we must make continuous adjustments.

Creator of cultural lags. Adjustment to a changing environment is difficult for many reasons. One is that the change in the technological environment is

[7] Lewis Mumford, *Technics and Civilization* (New York, Harcourt, Brace, 1934).

[8] M. D. C. Crawford, *The Influence of Invention on Civilization* (New York, World Publishing Company, 1942).

[9] Stuart Chase, *Men and Machines* (New York, Macmillan, 1929).

seldom foreseen, and preparation for it is rarely ever made. The automobile was first thought not to be practical; and the railroads, much of whose business was taken away by automotive vehicles, made no prior adjustment to it. City streets were not widened in anticipation; nor were through highways constructed in time. That airplanes carrying bombs would bring war to the civilian population and would find great cities ideal targets was not foreseen, nor have adjustments to this yet been made. That the hydrogen bomb would change international relations, make alliances more difficult, and increase the tendency toward neutrality was not anticipated.

There are delays and lags in adjusting to new technological developments, and during this period of lag man's adjustment is generally worse than it was before the technological change.[10] Thus cities in a farming area draw families to higher-paying jobs, and mothers leave crowded quarters to work away from home. Their unsupervised children join city gangs of youngsters with thieving and juvenile crime as a result, a worse adjustment for children than on the farms and in the villages. There are some groups who make a quick adjustment and profit thereby. Such are the business groups who make money out of new inventions, for instance, motion pictures, metals, and mowing machines. However, in some situations, adjusting is more difficult than inventing. Thus making atomic bombs was quicker and less difficult than is the abolition of war, the dispersal of cities, the formation of a one-world government, or the effective prohibition of the manufacture and use of atomic bombs. From this standpoint, technology is seen as the generator of social problems because of lags in adjustments to new mechanical inventions.

TECHNOLOGY AS A BROAD CONCEPT: ITS INTERRELATIONS WITH SOCIOLOGY

From the foregoing it is apparent that "technology" may be variously conceived by different observers. We shall, however, use the term in a very broad sense. A strict definition of technology is that it is the study of technics. Technics, though, covers a very great range of material objects. Indeed, it is so comprehensive as to include all the objects of a material culture. Technology would thus encompass the making of a great variety of objects, such as bows and arrows, pottery, harness, plows, dynamos, engines, jewelry, and nylon. Technology therefore goes far beyond the curriculum of an institute of technology, which necessarily is limited.

Exploring further the concept of technology, we may inquire into the relationship of science to technology. Is technology different from applied science? It may be said that the making of mechanical objects rests upon the application of science, though in cases the science may be very crude and simple, as in the making of a trap or a spear by primitive hunters. Technology may therefore include the applied science that aids in making ma-

[10] W. F. Ogburn, *Social Change* (New York, The Viking Press, 1950).

terial objects. A good deal of applied science, for instance, goes into the making of a radio receiving set.

In popular language we often find word symbols that are roughly equivalent to the term *technology*. The word *machine* is an abbreviated symbol that stands in a rough way for technology. So also is *factory* or the *factory system* as a referent for the technology that has developed since the invention and use of the steam engine.

From these comments it can be seen that the purposes of the studies which follow are best suited by using the broadest concept of technology. The purpose of these studies is to explore the social aspects of technology. The significance of technology lies in what it does. For example, we are interested in a telephone only for what it does. The wires, the current, the transmitter, the receiver are of no concern in themselves. Their significance lies in their use in transmitting sounds for long distances between persons. It is the function of the structure that gives it importance, and the function of the products of technology is use by human beings. Technology is therefore essentially social.

We do not ordinarily think of technology as sociological. Rather we consider it as mechanical and belonging to the physical sciences. To the degree that technology is concerned with the making of physical objects, it lies in the realm of the physical sciences. The curricula of colleges of technology are largely devoted to the physical sciences and deal little with the biological or the social sciences. Producing the objects of technology is, then, not in the field of social science. But since the meaning of these technological objects lies in the field of the social sciences, it is strange that the social sciences are treated as if they have no concern with technology. They discuss behavior, motivations, relation of the individual to the group, and institutions such as the family, the church, and government as if they existed independently of a material culture. So, too, teachers in technological schools instruct their students in how to make this and construct that; and though these fabrications are to be used by society and have an effect upon social life, such matters appear to be of no concern to technologists. It is as if there were a great wall separating technology and sociology.

One of the objectives of the chapters in this book is to break down this artificial wall which has been erected and tends to separate two disciplines that are inherently closely interwoven.

The interrelationship of sociology and technology is of two kinds. One is in the sociological situation that gives rise to invention and discovery and to their uses by society. The other is in the effects upon society of the uses of invention and discovery.

It is true that technological work does not take place in a vacuum but generally in response to a social demand. So the origin is sociological. Yet those who learn the techniques of fabrication or apply them in construction are essentially concerned with physical properties of the materials used and not with the social conditions that originated the work. The men who make a prime mover are concerned mainly with making one that is more efficient or less costly or more durable or that occupies less space. They do not think very much about the reasons for this demand. With the social background of this social demand, however, we shall not be much concerned in the pages which follow.

It is with the social effects of technology that we shall deal. These effects were the concern of those who held the various views of technology described in the preceding paragraphs. Thus some were concerned with the effect of technology on unemployment, others with its influence on raising the standard of living, or in giving us more power to do the things we want to do, or in making us change our habits in adjusting to new situations which technology creates.

Sociology deals with the interrelationship between the individual and the group, and between one group and another, as they are manifested in habits and institutions. Groups, habits, and institutions are all being altered by technological developments. The technology of early agriculture increased the size of groups from small wandering bands of hunters to larger stabilized villages. Domesticated animals and plows brought about communities with larger populations, making possible many kinds of small organizations not possible in a hunting culture. The steam engine changed the large family which was an economic institution producing a variety of goods into a small one producing little or nothing, with the members of the family becoming producers in other economic institutions. The invention of contraceptives had the effect of lowering the birth rate, of reducing the number of children in a family, and hence of affecting the personality of children; for a child with no brothers or sisters to play with, or with only one, has a personality different from a child reared with many playmates. Inventions in communication and transportation, coupled with conquest, have made possible larger governments, and made them more centralized. The practice of war has been changed frequently by inventions: when gunpowder replaced arrows and lances, when tanks replaced cavalry, and when Flying Fortresses brought destruction to civilians. So the materials with which sociology deals—groups, habits, institutions—are being changed from time to time, indeed in modern times continuously, by technology. So it is proper that the fences which separate technology and sociology be removed.

As a first step in this effort, we turn in the next chapter to consider in some detail the process by which technology changes groups, habits, and institutions.

ANNOTATED BIBLIOGRAPHY

BEARD, Charles A., ed., *Whither Mankind* (New York, Longmans, Green, 1929). A stimulating account of speculations as to the future course we are likely to take in our various activities and institutions, written by different specialists. Written many years ago, the forecasts and emphases may be compared with what has happened since.

BURLINGAME, Roger, *Engines of Democracy* (New York, Scribner, 1940). A quite readable account of some of the relationships between machines and society, with especial emphasis upon the democratic process, capitalism, and mechanical power. It is not a systematic account so much as an exposition of interest in a field in which few enter.

FORBES, R. J., *Man the Maker* (New York, Schuman, 1950). This summary is valuable for its brevity and selection. It stresses the heroic theory of invention rather than the social forces.

HOPKINS, John A., *Changing Technology and Employment in Agriculture* (Washington, Government Printing Office, 1941). Agriculture is being subject to new forces not evident in the adoption of power machines in the late nineteenth and early twentieth centuries. The later emphasis is upon chemistry, particularly in fertilizers and in insecticides.

KAEMPFFERT, Waldemar, *Science: Today and Tomorrow* (New York, Viking Press, 1939). A brilliant account of the selected developments in recent science, particularly in basic science.

President's Research Committee, *Recent Social Trends in the United States* (New York, McGraw-Hill, 1933). An encyclopaedic account of trends since the beginning of the century across the whole range of civilization in the United States. The technological influence is evident in many of the studies. The report was made under the auspices of Herbert Hoover, President of the United States.

STAMP, Sir Josiah, *The Science of Social Adjustment* (London, Macmillan, 1937). An excellent appreciation by an able statistician and statesman of the general idea of the impact of science upon society.

THORNTON, Jesse E., *Science and Social Change* (Washington, The Brookings Institution, 1939). A series of descriptive chapters setting forth how various developments in applied and basic science have been related to social movements and social changes.

CHAPTER 2

HOW TECHNOLOGY CAUSES SOCIAL CHANGE

■ *William F. Ogburn*

THAT TECHNOLOGY is considered a cause of social change is indicated by various expressions often heard. Gunpowder destroyed feudalism. Railroads created cities. The steam engine increased divorce. The automobile is moving the department store and the supermarket to the suburbs. The airplane reranked the great military powers.

To explain how inventions cause social changes is not a simple task. We must first come to an agreement on what is meant by *cause,* for the word has different meanings to different users. Then we shall describe the process by which inventions cause social changes.

THE NATURE OF CAUSATION

Concomitant Variation Essential in Causation

The key to an understanding of cause is variation. Whenever a result occurs, something has varied. A fall in the death rate is a variation from higher to lower. The decrease in the death rate is a result caused by something that has also varied, say, an increase in the use of vaccines. There are at least two variables involved, a result and a cause, and since these vary together, their variation is called concomitant.[1]

A result may be extremely great variation from nonexistence to existence, as when something is created. Thus when a telephone is first created, there is a variation from nothing, that is no telephone, to a telephone. Causes may, too, vary from absence to presence, as when vaccination is first introduced.

The fact that variation is concomitant does not in itself establish causation. Thus the price of milk may rise at the same time that attendance at football games is increasing, without there being any causal connection.

The causal connection may be established, in various ways, from infor-

[1] Karl Pearson, *The Grammar of Science,* 3rd ed. (London, A. and C. Black, 1911).

12

mation not necessarily derived from the particular measurement of concomitant variation. Though tall sons generally have tall fathers and short sons generally have short fathers, this concomitant variation does not tell us which is a cause of the other. So far as the concomitance of the variation is concerned, tall sons may cause tall fathers. But common knowledge of age and of biology tells us that the variation in fathers causes the variation in the sons and not vice versa.

Similarly, if increased use of fertilizer is followed by larger crops, this concomitant variation does not prove that more fertilizer increased the crops. The causal connection lies in our knowledge of plant life and the chemicals required for growth. However, the causation could be established without understanding it, that is, without knowing about plant growth and chemicals, by showing the concomitant variation when variation in all other influences (such as temperature, moisture, light, quality of seed, parasites) is eliminated.

This causal connection can sometimes be shown with a very small number of cases or made highly probable with only one case. Thus two seeds of the same genetic quality may be planted in the same soil growing side by side in the same light, moisture, and temperature, with the same spraying and cultivation, but with one plant being fertilized and the other not. If the experimental plant produces more than the control, the influence of the fertilizer has been demonstrated.

A Result Cannot Be Explained by a Constant

Since cause and effect are always variables, then, an effect cannot be explained by something that has not varied.[2] Yet it is commonly said that war is caused by the pugnacious instinct in man. But an instinct is inherited, and in, say, the population of the United States in the first half of the twentieth century the instinct of pugnacity has not varied; that is, it has been a constant. But during these fifty years, there have been two wars; twice, a variation from peace to war. The pugnacious instinct could not therefore have been a cause of either war, for a variable cannot be explained by a constant. The activity of the instinct may be greater at one time than another. But the variation in its activity is not due to any change in the instinct, which is hereditary, but to variation in outside influences playing on the instinct. Actually, since inborn tendencies of human beings are modified by conditioning and other types of learning, use of the term *drive* is preferred by present-day psychologists and sociologists.

The pugnacious tendency is, though, a factor in war, but not a factor in changing from peacetime conditions to a war. A factor *related to* a phenomenon does not have to be a factor *in a change* in that phenomenon. Temperature is a factor in the growth of a plant, but in the aforementioned ex-

[2] W. F. Ogburn and M. F. Nimkoff, *Technology and the Changing Family* (Boston, Houghton Mifflin, 1955), Ch. 2.

periment with fertilizers on plant growth, temperature was not a factor in the change in the growth of the plant. The cause of a phenomenon and the cause of a change in the phenomenon may be different.

This principle is sometimes forgotten because the same factor may be variable in one situation and at the same time a constant in another. The resulting confusion leads to erroneous analysis. For instance, we may explain the settlement of America in the sixteenth century by the hardiness of bold and adventuresome men. In this instance, the adventurous character of men is a variable. Some men in a large population are bold and others timid. The timid stayed at home; the bold crossed the seas. But the character of man does not explain why America was settled in the sixteenth century and not in the fifteenth century. There is no reason to think that the distribution of boldness and timidity was any different in the men of the fifteenth century from what it was in the sixteenth century. Thus boldness is likely to be a constant from one century to another in a large population, but it is also a variable at one time among the men within a large population. The *settlement* of America in the sixteenth century was caused by adventurous men, but the settlement of America in *the sixteenth century* was not caused by adventurous men, though adventurous men were a factor in the settlement. Some other factor was the cause of this change from no settlement to settlement.

Such are, then, the conceptions of cause and effect that will be used in showing how technology causes social changes, which we hope the reader will bear in mind even though he may be accustomed to somewhat different usages. These conceptions stress the following:

1. Cause and effect are to be seen in terms of variables.
2. Concomitant variation does not necessarily show cause and effect.
3. Concomitant variation, if adequately shown, may prove causation but it does not explain the nature of the causation, which must be understood from outside sources of knowledge.
4. A variation cannot be explained by something that does not vary, hence an effect cannot be explained by a constant.
5. A factor in a phenomenon may be different from a factor in the change of the phenomenon.
6. The same factor may be a variable in one situation and a constant in another.

PSYCHOLOGICAL ASPECTS OF CAUSATION

Inanimate Objects and Human Beings as Causes

That the automobile created a new type of hotel, called the motel, is a common observation. But it may be asked, How can an inanimate object such as an automobile create anything? Must not all cultural objects, as a motel, be created by human beings? Men are not the creators of objects of nature such as mountain ranges, but they are the creators of the objects of material culture such as a motel. In other words, a motel would not be created by nature, or it would not exist at all if there were no men. How then can it be said that the automobile creates motels? What is meant by the statement is that the human beings who use the automobile create motels; they created a demand for them that led to their creation by construction workers.

We say that the automobile creates motels, though actually it is the human beings who do the creating, because the variable is the automobile and not the human beings. The effect we are trying to explain is the new existence of motels. At one time there were no motels, at another time there were. This variation from no motels to motels must be explained by a variable, which was the automobile and not the drivers or users. Potential drivers and users existed before motels and after motels. They were always there in large numbers, hence are denoted as a constant. So we do not say it was the users of automobiles but rather the automobile that created motels; although a factor in their creation was human beings.

The foregoing analysis could be extended. A few automobiles will not lead to the construction of motels along the highways. There must be enough users of the automobiles to make the construction and operation of motels profitable. If such refinement of analysis is needed, then the number of automobiles becomes a variable and is a cause.

The analysis may be pursued even further. If, in a populous country, towns and villages are close together and there is sufficient space for parking near the local hotel, the usual hotels may be adequate and there is no need for motels. In this analysis we are trying to explain not why motels are constructed, but why they are constructed in country A but not in country B. The variable in this case is the sparseness of towns and villages.

From these illustrations, it is seen to be quite proper to call the use of an inanimate invention a cause of social change, though it could not be a cause without the active manipulation of it by a human being.[3]

The Individual as a Cause of Unique Events

When a specific result can be traced to the actions of an individual, the individual is often considered to be the cause. Thus Columbus discovered America; no other cause is given. One reason is that the single individual is compared implicitly with others. It was Columbus and not Amerigo Vespucci or other explorer who made the discovery. The variable is individuals. If we wish to consider different individuals, that is, individuals as varying, then properly we attribute the discovery to Columbus. But such is only one view of why a result occurred. Why was America discovered in 1492 and not in earlier centuries? In earlier centuries, sailors could not sail into the wind and hence stayed close to the land. The stars had not been charted ac-

[3] Leslie A. White, *The Science of Culture* (New York, Farrar, Straus, 1949).

curately. The compass was not available. Boats were small. The variable then becomes the means of navigation.

If courageous and adventurous sailors were found in a sizable proportion of the seagoing population in the fourteenth, thirteenth, and other centuries, then this fact is not an effective variable from one century to another as an explanation of why America was discovered in the fifteenth century. If Columbus had not lived, would not some other courageous and adventurous sailor, given the large sailing vessel and the navigation knowledge of the era, have discovered America?

Social Forces

It may be further said that the response of persons to those new means of navigation was a social force that led to the settlement of America.[4] Most general histories are written records of the achievements of individual leaders in war, in government, and in social movements; the record is in terms of these actors rather than in terms of social forces. This is quite adequate if we think in terms of the variability of individuals.

In preliterate history, as revealed by archaeologists, the names of the chief actors are unknown. Nor are they known in the accounts of the development of primitive cultures. Since we do not know who discovered that seeds could be planted and that plants could be cultivated with a digging stick, we cannot attribute the transformation of the hunting economy into agriculture to a great man, but we can attribute it to invention.

The Supply of Ability

It is obvious that the material culture of an area—that is, the technological equipment of a people—varies from time to time, though among early primitive peoples it must have changed very slowly; in the Stone Ages it must have remained the same for centuries and perhaps for millennia. But in modern times it changes more quickly. Thus railroads existed in the nineteenth century but not in the eighteenth. It is this great variability of technology that makes it possible for it to be a cause of social change.

But is not the supply of great men from era to era highly variable too? It would seem so, if we define greatness in terms of achievement. For instance, Columbus was a great man because he discovered America. But in judging the supply of great men as a cause of change we cannot define greatness in terms of achievement, that is, change. For achievement is what we are trying to explain. If we are trying to explain why X varies, and if $X = Y$, then we cannot say Y causes a variation in X, for that is the same as saying X causes a variation in X. If achievement is a definition of greatness, then since achievement varies from century to century, *ipso facto,* greatness must

---

[4] W. F. Ogburn, "The Great Man versus Social Forces," *Social Forces,* Vol. 5 (December, 1926), p. 226.

vary from century to century. To inquire into the question of whether greatness varies from era to era, we must have some other test of greatness.

Greatness can be defined in terms of heredity, that is, in terms of inherited ability. In a large population a certain proportion will have a given degree of inherited ability.[5] This proportion will hardly change from century to century, for that could only occur through selection or mutations, both of which are slow processes, the latter having in the past been very slow indeed.[6]

Greatness can be defined in terms of learned ability. Einstein's greatness depended upon his learning. He no doubt inherited the capacity for greatness, but this capacity could not have produced the famous equation $E = mc^2$ if he had not learned mathematics and physics; he would not have learned the latter if he had been born among the Greeks who did not have algebra. The average school child in Greece today can do computations which Aristotle could not do. Obviously, acquired ability varies greatly in modern times from era to era. Two hundred years ago we knew nothing about electricity; today our abilities in electricity are great. This variation in acquired abilities over the years is caused by the variation in what is learned, namely, in our culture. Is it not, then, a variation in cultural forces rather than in individuals that causes the change in supply of great men from century to century?

We are not accustomed, though, to seeing the causal forces that underlie great achievement. Rather we see achievement as the result of actions on the part of individuals—Edison, Lincoln, Churchill, Gandhi—without pursuing the causes of these efforts. For these reasons, a few illustrations are desirable.

For instance, the invention of the steamboat is credited by Americans to Robert Fulton, whereas six others invented the steamboat at about the same time. If Fulton had never lived, it would have been invented. Even if the seven inventors had never lived, given the boat and the steam engine and the demand for a boat that could move without the wind or against the current, would not someone have put a paddle wheel turned by steam on a boat and thus have made the steamboat? There are hundreds of similar instances where two or more individuals made an invention or discovery acting independently of each other, at about the same time.[7]

The invention of the steamboat might well be better attributed to the steam engine than to a great man, in much the same way as the discovery of America was due to new means of navigation rather than to a particular individual. The point may be further illustrated by the supremacy of Britain among nations in the nineteenth century, which is commonly attributed to

5 W. F. Ogburn and M. F. Nimkoff, *Sociology,* 2nd ed. (Boston, Houghton Mifflin, 1950).

6 Robert H. Lowie, *Culture and Ethnology* (New York, P. Smith, 1929), Ch. 2.

7 William F. Ogburn and Dorothy L. Thomas, "Are Inventions Inevitable? A Note on Social Evolution," *Political Science Quarterly,* Vol. XXXVII, No. 1 (1922), pp. 83–98.

her great leaders—Nelson, Wellington, Palmerston, Gladstone, Disraeli. These men certainly made great achievements. But it should be remembered that Britain was first in ships and was the first to acquire the factories, steel mills, and iron-hulled ships that arose from the inventions of steam and steel. If these great ministers and generals had never lived, might not there have been other great men who would have led Britain with her advanced technology to these achievements? We cannot be certain, as in the case of the steamboat. But we may note that Churchill was a leader quite in a class with Britain's best, yet dominance in steam and steel in the twentieth century are not Britain's as it was in the nineteenth; and her priority as a power among nations has passed to another despite the able leadership of Churchill.

Choice versus Technology as a Cause

When we say that an invention caused a social change we seem to negate any will of man, and such a negation is sometimes resented. Thus if we say that in the Civil War in the United States in 1860–64 the victory was won for the North by their factories and mills, we feel that this statement neglects the role of human effort; it fails to recognize and appreciate the heroism of the soldiers who died for their country. However, if we say that automobiles caused more injurious accidents last year than the year before, we do not insist that it was the drivers who caused the injuries. The fact that we call them "accidents" takes them out of the realm of will power.

We must, then, examine the relation of choice to technological influence. Some view an invention as merely an instrument for man to use as he wills. Thus one may state that a knife does not determine any particular result; the result is determined by how man chooses to use the knife. He may use it to kill, to prepare food, to make furniture, to save a life by surgery. We may further observe that for these uses it is not the same knife. The knife used to take a life is a different instrument from the knife used to save a life as in surgery. But there are instruments which may be used for a variety of purposes without any alteration in their form. Thus a radio receiving set may be used to listen to classical music, folk songs, hymns, speeches, or news. Or it may not be used at all if one prefers to read, or to talk, or to sleep. It is the individual and not the invention that determines the use to which it is put, within the limit of the capacity of the instrument. Certainly the invention does not determine to which use it will be put. The variable is the person; the invention is a constant.

But granting that we may choose to use a radio receiving set in several different ways, if enough people use a radio to listen to music, then it may be said that a radio has a social effect upon our musical enjoyment. If enough choose to listen to reports of the news, then broadcasting has a social effect upon our civic education. Without radio broadcasting, these effects would not have occurred so extensively. Hence the fact of choice does not prove that a mechanical object cannot be a cause of social influences.

Freedom to choose is affected by various influences. If outside factors influence our choices, it may be asked whether our choices are freely made. Are we not responding, some in one way and some in another, to outside stimuli? If many respond in the same way, are not the outside stimuli the cause?

An illustration is the decline of Chester, England, as a port and the growth of the nearby port of Liverpool. Chester is somewhat inland on the mouth of a river and is a port suitable only for small vessels, whereas Liverpool has facilities for large ships. We, therefore, say that the change in the size of ships caused the rise of Liverpool and the decline of Chester. Shippers and travelers had, of course, the right to choose whether to use small ships or big ships. They chose big ships; hence it presumably could be claimed that it was the human choice and not the invention that caused the decline of Chester and the rise of Liverpool. But since shippers and travelers generally chose big ships, it may be that choice was the result of factors such as the desires for space, speed, safety, and economy. Since all chose big ships, the attitudes of the people were not a variable; whereas the change in the size of the vessels obviously was.

Concluding the discussion of the relation of choice to technological influence, we observe that insofar as factors affect our choice of whether to use or not to use an invention, then these factors may be said to be causes. Sometimes, some of these factors are technological. If we think rarely of the technological factors that affect our choice, then adequate account is not given of technology as a cause. But if enough people choose, irrespective of reasons, to use an invention one way or another, then the invention has social effects.

INVENTIONS AND THE PROCESS OF SOCIAL CHANGE

Having examined the concepts of causation and having shown how inanimate objects such as inventions can cause social changes through the media of active human agents with capacity for choices, let us outline the processes by which technological changes produce social changes.

Direct Effects

Inventions to be used must first be produced. Some scientific discoveries, such as a vaccine for poliomyelitis, must also be produced. Hence agencies of production are created and usually result in some economic changes, for example, the creation of factories. Similarly, when new inventions are made available to consumers, the habits and customs of consumers are changed. Thus a person rides in an automobile instead of in a horse-drawn vehicle or in a railway car.

These changes, arising from the making and using of inventions, are called direct effects of an invention. They are sometimes called immediate effects because they are not postponed as long as others are, as indicated later. However, the occurrence of these effects is related to the time required in production and in distribution. Then, too, the extent of this direct social effect is dependent on the number of users. The number of users of the telephone is still increasing, though this invention has been in some use for nearly three quarters of a century. Hence the direct social effects of the telephone continue to spread. The direct effects of an invention are commonly recognized, since it can be readily seen that they change the customs of production and consumption.

The Derivative Effects

The effect of an invention does not end with the change in the habits of users and makers,[8] for these changed habits in turn cause other changes. Thus when automobiles were able to carry passengers, there was a reduction in the number of passengers traveling via railroad. Another derivative effect of the invention of the automobile was to reduce the number of makers of horse-drawn vehicles. These are first derivative effects.

The influence of an invention does not always end with its first derivative effects.[9] For the derivative effect may become in turn a cause of a second derivative effect. Thus the loss of passengers on railroads because of the use of automotive vehicles may lead to a reorganization of a railroad, and abandonment of short-haul tracks off the main line, or a modernization of equipment—all second derivative influences of the invention of the automobile. Or the diminished demand for horses and mules occasioned by automotive vehicles may bring about an increase in the planting of wheat and corn as more food for human beings, a second derivative effect.

The process is not unlike the play on the billiard table. Energy from the cue in one's hands is imparted to the cue ball, which is set in motion. The cue ball strikes another ball, which in turn hits another ball.

The impact of an invention may continue through many derivatives. Thus the steam engine is used in factories, which draw (1) work and workers from the home which lessens (2) the authority of the head of the house, which (3) increases the liberty of wives, who (4) attain various legal rights not held before. The impact of an invention produces a chain reaction. An effect is at the same time a cause, that is, a cause of another effect which is also a cause, and so on, like the links of a chain.

In general, the derivative effects, being somewhat far removed from the original impact of an invention, are often not readily seen as an influence of that invention. But the derivative effects are nonetheless real and are widely spread. We see how the improvement in the technique of navigation of the

---

[8] Sir Josiah Stamp, *The Science of Social Adjustment* (London, Macmillan, 1937).
[9] W. F. Ogburn, "The Pattern of Social Change," *Proceedings of the 14th International Congress of Sociology,* Vol. III (1951).

seas increased travel and transportation, but we do not see that this improvement led to the discovery and settlement of America, a derivative effect.

Convergence

The perception of derivative causes is also hindered because several derivative causes may operate conjointly to produce an effect. For example, we have said that the employment of the husband and father away from home lessened in practice his authority as the head of the family. But there are other causes of the decline of his authority than employment away from home. Attendance at school is also a cause of the decline of the authoritarian family, for the authority of the father over the children is shared to some extent with the teachers. Too, the employment of wives and daughters away from home decreases the authority of husband and father. The employer acquires some of this authority, which accrued to the husband and father in the first place because he was an employer of the members of his family. Police and public health authorities, sanitary inspectors, building codes and various government agencies also take away some of this authority of the head.

The decline of the authority of the head of the family is, then, not due solely to his employment away from home, but to many different causes: employment of wives and daughters, school attendance, and growth of government authority. These various causes converge to produce the result, the loss of authority by the head of the family. This pattern of convergence is somewhat like that of a wheel, where the spokes converge on the hub.

Convergence is very common. That such is the case is shown by the scarcity, in social phenomena, of a correlation of 1, which would be found if there were only the one cause in the correlation.[10]

The correlation coefficient showing the relationship between the stature of fathers and the stature of sons is no more than, say, .5, because there are other causes, for instance, the stature of the mother. Then, too, income, nutrition, and disease are factors affecting the stature of sons as well as heredity. It is generally more accurate, then, to speak of *a* cause rather than of *the* cause.

Diminishing Influence Through Successive Derivatives

The conception of causation as a chain of derivatives is an oversimplification. As an illustration, we may observe the following linkages: Airplanes change (1) warfare since they are highly efficient weapons of offense which (2) widens the gap between large powers and small powers, since only the large powers can maintain an adequate supply of airplanes, which in turn changes (3) the nature of international relationships and organizations.

Considering the first link in this chain, we note that the influence of air-

[10] W. F. Ogburn, "Social Effects of Technology in Industrialized Societies," *International Social Science Bulletin*, Vol. IV, No. 2 (Summer, 1952).

planes on warfare is only one of many factors, of which three others may be mentioned: armored tanks, rockets, and bombs. And, in the second link, the changed nature of war is not the only factor in making the big powers more powerful and the small powers relatively less so. We mention two others: population and income. Finally, for the third link, the reranking of the powers is not the only factor affecting international relations. Three others are the communication and transportation systems, trade and investment, and ideological aspirations.

It is true that the airplane has an effect upon international organization, through war and power relations; but it shares influence with many other factors. In the foregoing analysis, the airplane is one of four factors affecting war, one of seven affecting power relations, and one of eleven affecting international organization. The more remote the derivative effect, the larger the number of other factors. The influence of an invention diminishes through successive derivative effects, on the principle that the more variables there are, the lower the correlation with any one.

The process we have pictured may be looked at either from the beginning or the end of the linkages. From the beginning, we see causes producing effects. From the end, we see effects produced by causes. Looking at the process from the end, the further back we go in the linkages searching for causes, the more we find. So we readily see that international organization is affected by many more factors than airplanes, and the influence of airplanes on international organization seems to be less than on war.

Dispersion

The process describing how technology causes social change is not complete without noting that some inventions have not just one effect but many. Thus the effects of the airplane disperse in many directions. The airplane affects war, transportation, government, commerce, agriculture, tourism, medicine, archaeology, meteorology. These influences flow out from an invention much as the spokes of a wheel radiate out from the hub. The phenomenon of dispersion is the opposite of the phenomenon of convergence.

Causation a Network

We earlier noted that causes and effects are related like the links of a chain. Then we saw that a link, as an effect, may have resulted from several causes converging on it. In the preceding paragraph we observed that a link, as a cause, may have had several dispersed effects radiating from it. The resulting pattern of causation is like that of a network, rather than that of a single chain.[11]

This conception of a network is quite in conformity with the idea that civilization is a mass of interrelationships. Government is related to educa-

11 W. F. Ogburn and M. F. Nimkoff, *Sociology,* 2nd ed., Ch. 26.

tion, to industry, to family, and family to church, and so on. Some relationships are quite close, for instance, transportation and production. Others are quite remote, for instance, poetry and geology. It is not surprising, then, that a great invention like printing or the internal combustion engine should have influences affecting many different parts of civilization.

The illustration of a network makes the problem of tracing causes appear to be difficult and complex because everything seems to be connected. But, as previously observed, some of the relationships are slight. Then, too, not all parts of the network are in equal activation at any one time. The appearance of energy from the nucleus of the atom sets in motion connections related to mechanical power, to medicine, and to war, whereas agriculture remains relatively unaffected. Changes in religious beliefs are not so many and so frequent as nearly a century ago when a discovery of the origin of species was launched upon a believing world.

The picture of the process is one where a new invention or scientific discovery is made; and, if adopted or accepted, effects are soon felt by users and producers, sometimes in many different areas. These are followed by successive derivative effects in other parts of society which are also being affected by changes coming from various other sources. So that the effect of the new invention or discovery tends to be lost sight of eventually in the distant parts of our culture amidst the various other changes that are occurring.

Cultural Lags

Not all changes occur easily. An invention often meets resistances which delay or prevent resulting changes. Thus the use of contraceptives is resisted by some religions. Schools are slow to adopt the new communication inventions and hence to experience their effects. The impact of the communication and transportation inventions on trade and travel is resisted by barriers and policies of nationalism. It was a long time before the discoveries of Pasteur were accepted by medicine, longer still before their effect was felt on the general population. Because of these resistances, one may conclude too hastily that the limits of the effects of an invention are more restricted than they will ultimately prove to be. Religions are now effectively opposing birth control, but it is not certain that such will be the case in the future. The effect of a new technological development is thus more fully seen after a considerable lapse of time, when the lags will have disappeared.

Clusters of Inventions

Inventions vary from one to another as to their social effects. Some are quite negligible in their effects, for instance, a new type of safety razor blade. The great majority of inventions have slight use and little social significance. A few inventions such as television will have many far-reaching social influences. Indeed, the most extensive and assured effects come from a group of converging inventions. There are many different inventions, for example that converge to produce the suburbs of a modern city, namely, the electric street car, the autobus, the private automobile, the commuter railway train, the telephone, the motion pictures, and the chain store. Their influences are additive.[12] In other words, the influence of a cluster of inventions is greater than the influence of one. Another illustration is the increased comfort and attractiveness of a family dwelling as a result of electrical inventions. The electric light adds to the attractiveness of the home, but this is only one invention of many. Others are the electric fan, the thermostat, the air conditioner, the refrigerator, radio, television, and phonograph.

The most discussed cluster of modern times is that which produced the Industrial Revolution; this includes all those inventions which use the steam engine, steel and other metals, and the various production inventions that flow therefrom. Frequently this magnificent cluster is referred to merely as the steam engine, or as steam and steel. One may ask how this idea of a cluster of inventions fits into the conception of the process of technological influence on social change as a network? The cluster is merely convergence, but one of such size as to compose an appreciable portion of the network.

Sometimes such a cluster is the converging of several influences that may come through several derivatives from many dispersed effects of a single invention complex. Thus of the various influences converging to lessen the authority of the male head of the family—the working of men away from home, the employment of women outside the home, the removal of occupations from the dwelling, the expansion of education beyond the confines of the home—many are influences that come from various dispersed effects of the steam engine. The steam engine placed men in factories, gave jobs to women away from home, and transferred occupations out of the home. In instances where the dispersed effects of an invention pull together in a convergence, the influence of a single invention is very great indeed.

CONCLUSION

In describing how technological developments cause social changes, we have noted that change takes place over a period of time. Hence any account of why a change takes place must explain why it took place in one period of time and not at some other.

If we attribute the cause of the change to leaders, then we imply that there were no such leaders at a prior time. We cannot define such a leader as one who produced the change, for that is defining the cause in terms of the result—which is what we wish to explain.

If we define leaders in terms of heredity and maintain that such hereditary

---

[12] W. F. Ogburn and M. F. Nimkoff, *Technology and the Changing Family,* Ch. 2.

capability exists year after year, then leaders cannot be regarded as a cause; for a variable cannot be explained by a constant.

To the extent that leadership acquired through learning and experience varies from period to period, then leaders may be a cause. But if the learned leadership is a result not of a changing heredity but of the changing social environment, then the leaders whose numbers vary over time become media through which the forces of a changing social environment operate. Some of the forces of this changing social environment are technological.

Technological forces in the changing social environment are obscured by descriptions in terms of human behavior. These descriptions are common in newspapers, in histories, in conversation. We thus tend to see change in terms of the actors: Lincoln freed the slaves. Similarly the role of technology is not appreciated when, in making choices, we do not think in terms of the factors that affect our choices.

How technological changes cause social changes depends on an understanding of the nature of causation, and is seen to be a process. Basic to the process is the fact that a technological influence does not always stop at its first direct effect upon users and producers, but often has a succession of derivative effects which follow one another like the links of a chain. These are often not recognized, because an effect is generally not the result of one cause alone but of several converging causes. Also, since the impact of an invention may have several effects dispersed in different directions, the process is more like a network than a chain.

The chainlike nature of technological effects and the easy recognition of the first, the direct effect, has meant that we often do not credit technology with being a cause of the derivative effects. This lack of recognition of technological change as a cause of derivative effects is made more frequent because there are also other causes of derivative effects than that of particular inventions, some of which are not caused by technology.

This chapter does not, of course, claim that all social changes are caused by technological changes, nor does it claim that any definite proportion of such changes are caused by mechanical invention and scientific discovery. Its purpose has been to outline the process of how technology causes social change.

ANNOTATED BIBLIOGRAPHY

BEARD, Charles A., *Toward Civilization* (New York, Longmans, Green, 1930). Another symposium by experts on what is to be expected in our evolution toward a better society.

GILFILLAN, S. C., *The Sociology of Invention* (Chicago, Follett, 1935). A widely quoted analysis of invention in general in a social setting, written with great insight and knowledge. There is especial emphasis on the nature of invention and on the social conditions that give rise to them.

HART, Hornell, *The Technique of Social Progress* (New York, Holt, 1931). An early book on many aspects of social change, with emphasis on rates of change. This book foreshadows some of Hart's later researches. Much light is thrown on the ways and means of change.

MUMFORD, Lewis, *Technics and Civilization* (New York, Harcourt, Brace, 1934). An exciting book with many insights, dealing with the social implications of some early and significant inventions.

OGBURN, William F., *The Social Effects of Aviation* (Boston, Houghton Mifflin, 1946). An attempt to trace out the many social changes that will be caused in the future by this great invention of aircraft. There are two chapters on how social effects of invention are studied.

————, and NIMKOFF, Meyer F., *Technology and the Changing Family* (Boston, Houghton Mifflin, 1955). An attempt to study forces affecting changes in a single social institution, with the conclusion that many of these forces derive from inventions and scientific discoveries.

PEARSON, Karl, *The Grammar of Science*, 3rd. ed. (London, A. and C. Black, 1911). A standard book on the relation of concomitant variation to causation, and a necessary treatise for those who would analyze social changes and causes.

ROSEN, S. McKee, and ROSEN, Laura, *Technology and Society* (New York, Macmillan, 1941). A general treatise on the status of this subject at the beginning of World War II. Told clearly with due regard for emphasis for those who want an introduction.

U. S. Department of Agriculture, *Technology on the Farm* (Washington, Government Printing Office, 1940). A dramatic account of how new inventions will affect farming, and rural life in terms of particular inventions and discoveries.

CHAPTER 3

ACCELERATION IN SOCIAL CHANGE

■ *Hornell Hart*

ACCELERATION IN CULTURAL CHANGE HAS BEEN DAWNING ON THE SCIENTIFIC MIND

THE REALIZATION that social change has been taking place faster and faster, over the broad sweep of time, has gradually been dawning on social scientists.[1] As long ago as 1877, Lewis H. Morgan, the anthropologist, wrote:

Human progress, from first to last, has been in a ratio not rigorously but essentially geometrical (slowest in the first period, and most rapid in the last). This is plain on the face of the facts: and it could not, theoretically, have occurred in any other way. Every item of absolute knowledge gained became a factor in further acquisitions. . . .

In 1912, James Harvey Robinson, the historian, said:

Man's progress was . . . well-nigh imperceptible for tens of thousands of years, . . . but it tends to increase in rapidity with an ever accelerating tempo.

In 1917, Robert H. Lowie, another anthropologist, put it more vividly:

We may liken the progress of mankind to that of a man 100 years old, who dawdles through kindergarten for 85 years, takes 10 years to go through the primary grades, then rushes with lightning rapidity through grammar school, high school and college.

In 1922, William F. Ogburn, the sociologist, wrote:

A brief perspective of the growth of culture[2] from its beginnings shows that the

[1] For sources, and a fuller analysis of such statements, see *American Sociological Review,* Vol. 11 (June, 1946), pp. 279–281. Since the publication of that article, similar opinions by a number of additional students of social change have been noted, including statements by H. G. Wells in 1908, by Ernest R. Groves in 1922, by J. C. Flugel in 1930, by Alfred Korzybski in 1933, by Gustav Spiller in 1935, by Howard W. Odum in 1937, and by Stuart Chase in 1948.

[2] In ordinary conversation, when one speaks of "a cultured person," one means that he is well educated, talks grammatically, appreciates literature, music, and art, is versed in the history and the customs of various peoples, and the like. Culture in that sense implies something akin to refinement. But Dr. Ogburn was using the word in a

change was quite slow in very early times. Based on the finds in stonework, the development of the material culture of the Chellean period to the Acheulean and the Acheulean to the Mousterian required an interval of about 25,000 years each. . . . From neolithic times to the historic period and from the historic period on, the changes in material culture have been much more rapid. At the present time both the change and the accumulation of material culture are quite rapid and may be measured in such brief intervals as generations or even decades. . . .

In 1928, F. Stuart Chapin, the sociologist, wrote:

Culture elaborates, accumulates, piles up, at what appears to be an ever-accelerating rate. . . . Particularly since the advent of writing and the use of iron, has cultural growth shot up.

In 1931, the present writer summed up a large assortment of anthropological and historical data in the following generalization:

Man's power to control his physical environment has been increasing with accelerating speed, with only temporary and local set-backs and stagnations.

The six foregoing quotations on acceleration in cultural change illustrate the fact that social thinkers, in various fields of inquiry, have (in various ways) reached this same conclusion: social change is taking place faster, and faster, and faster. This crucial fact, and its bearings on the problems of the Atomic Age, is clearly revealed in a series of outstanding examples.

SOME EXAMPLES OF TECHNOLOGICAL ACCELERATION

Some Preliminary Definitions

The terminology of sociology has grown up in a rather haphazard manner. The term *social change* came into use as a substitute for the perhaps misleading phrase, *social evolution*. Without employing any biological analogy, or assuming that the process had to be progressive, *social change* referred generally to alterations in social structures and social processes which take place through time.

Then the term *culture* became popular, borrowed from the social anthropologists. *Cultural change* referred to alterations in human behavior patterns and in the patterns of artifacts, rather than merely or primarily alterations in social organizations and activities.

But culture came to be divided into material and nonmaterial culture. Material culture includes the patterns of tools, utensils, clothing, buildings, vehicles, and other physical objects. Technology is the branch of cultural

---

special sense which has been developed by anthropologists and adopted by sociologists. To these social scientists, culture means all those patterns of behavior which are learned by imitation and tuition, rather than merely inherited biologically through the genes. To a sociologist, profanity is as much a part of culture as is poetry: alcoholism is as much a part of culture as is symphonic music. When sociologists speak of *cultural acceleration,* they mean the underlying tendency of discovery, invention, and diffusion to take place faster and faster, in steeper and steeper surges.

Acheulean
About 100,000 B.C.

Magdalenian
About 8500 B.C.

Machine Age
About 1915 A.D.

Chellean
About 300,000 B.C.

Solutrean
About 13,500 B.C.

Bronze
About 2000 B.C.

Cromerian
About 500,000 B.C.

Aurignacian
About 13,500 B.C.

Neolithic
About 5000 B.C.

Sub-Red Crag
About 1,300,000 B.C.

Mousterian
About 50,000 B.C.

Mesolithic
About 7000 B.C.

THE EVOLUTION OF CUTTING BLADES

anthropology concerned with the study of material culture. It has come to mean particularly the processes by means of which man manipulates and controls his physical environment. *Technological change* thus means change in man's behavior patterns as related to industrial, transportational, and extractive arts and sciences. Often it is extended to biological arts and sciences, as in agriculture and medicine. By a further extension, it may include applied science in general.

The area in which the acceleration of cultural change has been most obvious is with respect to technology. The title of this book, *Technology and Social Change,* points to the fundamental nature of this relationship. Our more detailed consideration of acceleration may therefore well begin with the acceleration of change in technology.

A Million Years of Acceleration in Cutting-Tool Efficiency

Museums contain vast collections of the chipped flints which were the cutting blades of prehistoric man—the stone knives, axes, spear points, and arrow heads used by our ancestors for hundreds of thousands of years in the past. Flints do not rot away like baskets or huts or wooden spoons, and they last longer than even bones. Therefore, the various series of flint tools in our museums, stretching back into the past, serve as the clearest long-range index of prehistoric human power to grapple with the physical environment.

A representative selection of typical cutting blades is illustrated on page 29. The reader is invited to look at this chart and ask himself: How does the progress during the more than 1,000,000 years from Sub-Red Crag to Acheulean blades compare with the progress during the 8,000 years from Mesolithic to Machine-Age tools? The answer would seem to be evident: advances in cutting-tool efficiency have speeded up tremendously.

This obvious acceleration can be reduced to quantitative terms if we measure cutting-tool efficiency against five criteria: (1) keenness of cutting edge; (2) durability; (3) differentiation and specialization; (4) effectiveness of mechanisms employed to apply the blade to the materials to be cut; and (5) utilization of auxiliary power. When prehistoric tools are rated with respect to these five factors, the combined index confirms the qualitative impressions gained from an inspection of the chart. Man's technological competence in the cutting and shaping of materials has increased as much in the last 3,000 years as it did in the previous million years.[3]

Man's Accelerating Mastery of Physical Power

The prehistoric ages of human culture have customarily been divided in accordance with the materials and techniques man has used to produce tools.

[3] For details on the quantitative rating of prehistoric cutting tools, see Hornell Hart, *The Technique of Social Progress* (New York, Holt, 1931), p. 61. Many of the sources for this and the next two sections of the present chapter will be found in that book, pp. 49–84. See also "A Million Years of Evolution in Tools" (with Mildred Fairchild), *Scientific Monthly,* Vol. 28 (January, 1929), pp. 71–79.

The Old Stone Age was the epoch of stone tools sharpened by chipping; the New Stone Age was the epoch of stone tools sharpened by grinding; the Copper, Bronze, and Iron ages were differentiated by the types of metals used in making tools. But even more fundamental than the materials from which man has shaped his tools have been the various types of power by which he has driven them. When we analyze prehistory and history from that aspect we obtain even clearer evidence of accelerating mastery in man's technological culture.

The age of merely muscular energy stretches back thousands of times farther than do the more recent phases of power. Throughout the Old Stone Age, the power applied to tool-driving was derived entirely from human muscles. Rudimentary progress was made in the more effective utilization of this power: the handles applied to stone axes and the bows employed to drive drills and shoot arrows were not merely for the purpose of imparting and directing the desired motion but also for the sake of applying more energy. The spear-thrower, which appeared in Magdalenian times, was another device for augmenting the force of the human arm.[4]

Domestication of beasts of burden and enslavement of human beings were late elaborations of the Age of Muscular Power. Neolithic domestication of animals brought power reinforcement. Four-wheeled wagons, drawn by asses and oxen, were used in Mesopotamia about 3300 B.C., and India had bullock carts about 3000 B.C. It was not until after the Hyksos invaders brought him horses that the ancient Egyptian fastened to his hoe the attachments which turned it into the first known beast-drawn plow.

The ancient Egyptians seem also to have been the first to harness water power, by mooring in midstream a boat with millstones geared to paddle wheels. The ancient Romans worked their millstones by horse power, slave power, and probably water power. The early Anglo-Saxons drove their mills by donkey power before 500 A.D. In the eighth century they probably used water power. Windmills began to be used in England as early as 833 A.D., and the Middle Ages show progressive minor improvements in wind and water mills. Wind power was harnessed to saws in England about the beginning of the thirteenth century. Germany had water-power saws as early as 1322. A trip-hammer run by water power was introduced in England in the seventeenth century.

The developments reviewed above occupied the overwhelming majority of man's past time on earth. To acquire the aid of any tool-wielding power beyond their own muscles was a task which took our ancestors more than a million years. The age of horse and sail transportation and of slave and

[4] "A unique and exceedingly useful implement is the spear-thrower, a V-shaped and often concave piece of hard wood about two feet long, tapering at one end to a narrow handle and at the other to a blunt point to which is attached by a tenon a short sharp wooden point. This fits into a hollow in the end of the spear and propels it with much greater force and leverage than the arm alone could impart."—George Peter Murdock, *Our Primitive Contemporaries* (New York, Macmillan, 1934), p. 34.

water-wheel work power lasted from approximately 3000 B.C. to about 1800 A.D.—a period of nearly 5000 years. Then came the Industrial Revolution.

Watt's first patent on his steam engine was granted in 1765. From then onward, the use of coal power began to expand, later supplemented by petroleum and hydroelectric power. In comparison with the almost unimaginably long stretches of time during which man's mastery of power was elementary, the electrical, internal-combustion, and jet-engine phase of power evolution has been exceedingly brief, occupying less than the last 100 years.

It was not until 1871 that the first reliable statistics on power production in the United States became available. In the 80 years from 1873 to 1953 the per capita production of power in this country was multiplied more than sevenfold. Today we are witnessing the gradual dawn of atomic power. The swiftness of acceleration in man's mastery of his material world could hardly be more clearly demonstrated than by this spectacular upsurge in the physical power at his command.

The Speed-Up of Human Speeds

How fast have human beings been able to move, parallel to the surface of the earth, at various periods of history and in various years of recent decades? How have the speed records been changing, as the thousands of years—and then the centuries, and the decades, and finally the years—have gone by?

The chart on page 33 illustrates the acceleration of human speeds. It is based on one which appeared in successive editions of Ogburn and Nimkoff's *Sociology;* and that, in turn, was based on one which was first published in Hart's *Technique of Social Progress,* in 1931. We may well begin our survey of the speed-up of speeds by reviewing some of the facts on which this chart was based.

The earliest date shown on the chart is 1750. At that time, man's fastest method of travel was on horseback. A searching inquiry has failed to reveal any mode of travel which human beings used before 1750 that could carry them faster than on horses.[5] Horses first broke into history about 1700 B.C. when the Hyksos invaders brought them to Egypt. We can imagine the chart extended to the left to 1700 B.C. It would increase in width approximately 4 feet. Horses were probably domesticated first in Central Asia. Four-wheeled wagons drawn by asses and oxen are slower than horses; so, going back from 1700 B.C., a gently downward sloping line would represent speeds of travel by ox, donkey, and perhaps other animals, until the chart got back to the remote time at which human beings first substituted some beast of

[5] The question arises whether ice boats might not have attained high speeds before 1800. They had no need of steam power nor of electricity. Actually, however, until 1879, the best ice boats were mere boxes on runners, incapable of the fine maneuvering necessary to outsail the wind. The world record of 31 miles per hour for a 20-mile course was not made until 1907. (See *Encyclopedia Americana* (1946), Vol. 14, p. 624.)

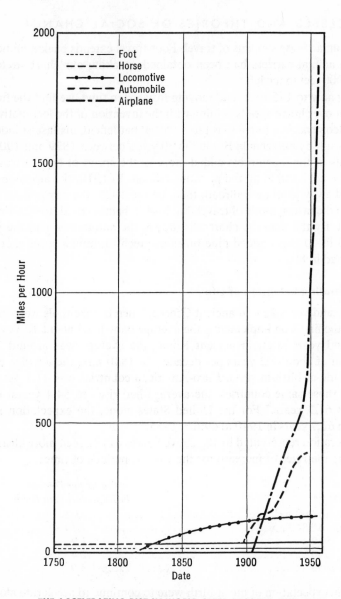

THE ACCELERATING RISE IN WORLD SPEED RECORDS, 1750–1956

burden for human legs as means of travel. Foot-travel extends back a million years before animal carriers had been obtained—making our chart stretch more than 1000 feet to the left.

Returning now to 1750 A.D. and moving forward in time, we find the first improvement over horse speeds coming with the invention of the locomotive. When Napoleon was in a hurry to get to a crucial battlefield, his fastest mode of travel was still by horseback. But in the 80 years between 1829 and 1909, improvements in the locomotive added more to the speed of human travel than had been achieved in all the previous million. In 1910, the automobile took the lead away from the railroad; then, before 1921, the airplane, in its turn, became the fastest mode of travel that human beings could (for the time being) attain. By the time the chart was drawn, the automobile and the jet airplane had in 40 years added nine times as much to human speed as the locomotive had in 80.

Man's Accelerating Extension of Life

Four thousand years ago, in ancient Greece, when bronze tools were giving place to the first iron implements, the average baby lived about 18 years. Two thousand years later, in ancient Rome, the average was around 22 years—a gain of about .02 years per decade.[6] In 1840 A.D., the average expectation of life at birth in seven Euro-American countries was 41.1 years. By 1910, in those same countries, the average had risen to 54.4 years. By 1940, it was 61.7 years.[7] For the United States alone, the expectation increased from 63.7 years in 1940 to 69.6 in 1955.[8]

The acceleration represented by the above figures can be seen more clearly by comparing the rates of increase for the various periods of time:

Dates	Gains per Decade in Expectation at Birth
2000 B.C. to 200 B.C.	.02
200 B.C. to 1840 A.D.	.79
1840 to 1910	1.9
1910 to 1940	2.4
1940 to 1955	3.9

If increases in expectation of life at birth were to continue to accelerate along the trend indicated by the above figures, the average expectation of American babies born in the year 2000 would be approximately 100 years.[9]

The increase in expectation of life has been grouped in this section as one of four examples of technological acceleration. But it is actually far more than that. Decreasing death rates do reflect man's increasing conquest of physical matter, with a corresponding increase in real income, including food,

[6] Metropolitan Life Insurance Company, *Statistical Bulletin* (October, 1947), pp. 1–3.
[7] Hornell Hart and Hilda Hertz, "Expectation of Life as an Index of Social Progress," *American Sociological Review*, Vol. 9 (December, 1944), p. 612.
[8] *Statistical Bulletin*, passim.
[9] See Chapter 19 for further details.

clothing, shelter, medical care, and other needs. But it reflects also his increasing knowledge of the causes of disease and accidents. And it reflects increasing success in solving the problems of human co-operation, achieving efficiency in local, state, and national governments, developing international co-operation in health problems, and building up voluntary co-operative agencies to reduce death hazards.

EXAMPLES OF ACCELERATION IN NONMATERIAL CULTURE

The proposition that culture in general tends to change acceleratingly is not universally accepted. A. L. Kroeber remarks: "Science, and in the main technology, are evidently accumulative by nature, while philosophy, religion, art—and empire and nationalism too—tend strongly to be substitutive: a new product replaces an old one."[10]

The evidence for acceleration in nonmaterial culture is, however, clear. That the principle of more and more rapid increases in man's power to carry out his purposes is valid in psychological and sociological matters as well as in mechanical inventions will become evident in subsequent chapters of this book. The swift acceleration in the number of persons graduating from high schools, colleges, and universities will be discussed in Chapter 21. The slower (but unmistakable) acceleration in man's power to govern will be illustrated in Chapter 17, in terms of the maximum areas controlled from any given capital. Acceleration in the volume of social research will be demonstrated in Chapter 21. Kroeber concedes that science is accumulative by nature. But if science is accumulative, accelerating progress may take place in any subject which is studied scientifically. Not only in technology, but also in every field in which mankind works systematically to carry out purposes, the power to achieve those purposes tends to increase faster and faster.

ACCELERATING POWER TO KILL AND TO DESTROY

The acceleration of cultural change has just been summarized in terms which show the faster and faster increases, over the long range of history, in the power of man to carry out his purposes. The illustrations thus far presented have involved constructive purposes. But human beings are also moved—and exceptionally powerfully—to destroy their enemies. The accelerating working out of this drive may be studied in terms of several different variables.

Past Acceleration in Size of Killing Area

The most reliable quantitative index of destructive power, reaching back through the history of the Western world into prehistoric times, consists in the range of projectiles. As used here, the phrase *record-breaking range of*

[10] A. L. Kroeber, *Anthropology* (New York, Harcourt, Brace, 1948), p. 303.

projectiles will be taken to mean, for any given date, the longest nonstop distance, from base to target, over which a missile intended to destroy life or demolish structure has been hurled or piloted through the air. The term *killing area* will be taken to mean the maximum area within which lives and property may be destroyed by such projectiles. The table following, based on the best information which the present writer has been able to discover, lists records that conform to the foregoing definitions.

**WORLD-RECORD-BREAKING RANGES OF PROJECTILES,
1,000,000 B.C. to 1954 A.D.**

Date	Type of Projectile	Maximum Range in Miles	Killing Area in Square Miles
	From before 1,000,000 B.C. to at least 200,000 B.C., nothing better than rock missile, thrown club, or simple javelin	.01	.0003
	Period between javelin and arrow	.03	.005
	Starting sometime between 75,000 B.C. and 10,000 B.C., bow and arrow	.10	.09
	From about 500 B.C. to 1453 A.D., catapult and ballista	.35	.8
1453	Cannon	1.0	3
1670	Cannon	1.1	4
1807	Rocket	2.0	13
1830	Coast artillery	3.0	28
1859	Armstrong's breach-loading rifle gun	5.0	78
1900	Coast artillery	6.3	125
1910	Coast artillery	10.2	326
1912	Coast artillery	11.4	408
1915	Zeppelin raid on London	200	126,000
1918	Bombing plane	280	246,000
1938	Average European bombing formation	750	1,761,000
1943	Bombing plane	1,200	4,480,000
1944	Bombing plane	2,050	12,900,000
1945	Bombing plane	2,500	19,000,000
1948	Bombing plane	3,900	45,000,000
1949	Bombing plane	5,000	69,000,000
1954	Bombing planes refueled from air . .	12,500	197,000,000

SOURCE: Through 1945, same as for corresponding items in Table 5, *American Sociological Review*, Vol. 11 (June, 1946), p. 288; for 1948, "B-50 Flies Record 8,000 Miles with Five-Ton Load," by Charles Corddry, U.P. dispatch, *Durham Sun*, May 20, 1948, p. 7B; *New York Herald Tribune*, March 21, 1948, p. II 9; *New York Times*, March 6, 1949, p. E1, col. 5; *Science Digest*, Vol. 26 (Dec., 1949) pp. 23–27; the 1949 record is based on a 10,000-mile flight with full load by B-36. The 1954 record takes account of the world-circling possibilities of bombers refueled while in flight.

That the range of projectiles has been increasing at accelerating rates is evident when the historic and prehistoric records are studied. During the early part of lower Paleolithic times no hafted weapons were available, and killing beyond arm's reach depended upon hand-hurled rocks and clubs, with ranges which may safely be assumed to have been less than the modern record for the shot-put, that is, about .01 mile. Sometime between this stage and the development of the bow and arrow, stone-pointed spears and then spearthrowers came into use, presumably with ranges comparable to those

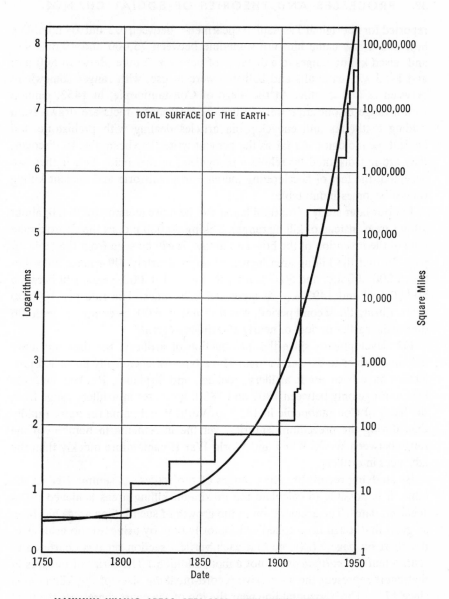

MAXIMUM KILLING AREAS, 1750–1950, WITH FITTED TREND

reported for aboriginal Tasmanian spearmen—between .02 and .04 mile. The bow and arrow came into use sometime between 75,000 and 10,000 B.C. and raised killing ranges to a distance of not over .2 mile. Between 500 B.C. and 1453 A.D. catapults and ballistae were in use, with ranges somewhere between .2 and .5 mile. At the Siege of Constantinople, in 1453, cannon with a range of one mile were in use. These general facts are drawn from leading textbooks and encyclopedia articles dealing with prehistoric and ancient technologies. As far as the present writer has been able to discover, they are not disputed by scholars recognized in this field. Yet, if they are accepted, the fact of accelerating increase in prehistoric and ancient killing ranges becomes indubitable.

For our later study of cultural lag, it will be more meaningful to talk about killing areas instead of killing ranges. Taking 50,000 B.C. as the approximate date of the invention of the bow and arrow, it will be seen from the table on page 36 that the killing area increased approximately .09 square miles between 200,000 B.C. and 50,000 B.C., that is, in 150,000, years. But between 50,000 B.C. and 1493 A.D., it increased 2.90 miles. The rate per 100,000 years, during the second period, was thus nearly 6.00, as compared with .06 during the earlier period, or nearly 100 times as great.

For developments since the introduction of artillery, the data are more definite, both as to date and range. Three types of chemically propelled projectiles have been used: artillery, rockets, and airplanes. Rockets held the lead in range only between 1807 and 1830. Increases in artillery range from the Siege of Constantinople in 1453 to World War I came far more rapidly than during the preceding centuries, yet the increments in bombing-plane range between World War I and World War II came more quickly than the advances in artillery.

By studying record-breaking ranges of projectiles, as summarized in the table, it is possible to calculate the maximum killing areas achieved up to specified dates. The acceleration in the growth of such killing areas has been so great that it can be graphed satisfactorily only by using a ratio grid, as in the chart on page 37. (Note that each vertical section on this chart represents a tenfold *multiplication,* not a mere addition.) The series of terraces in that chart represent the successive record-breaking sizes of the killing area since 1750. The horizontal line near the top of the chart represents the total area of the earth. The curved line represents a fitted mathematical trend.[11] But it requires no mathematical subtlety to observe the accelerating growth of the killing area, as represented by the terraced line. There should have been no essential difficulty in realizing, long ago, that this killing area was about to engulf the total surface of the earth.

[11] The formula is: $\text{Log } A_d = .49 + 10^{.1168} + .01135 \ (d - 1880)$ where d is any assigned date during the period for which the formula is valid, and A_d is the calculated killing area for that date.

Accelerating Progress in Aiming Devices

The power of projectiles to destroy has other dimensions in addition to range. The effectiveness of projectiles may be measured by five factors: (1) range (and consequent killing area); (2) accuracy with which projectiles can be aimed at the crucially important targets within the area being attacked; (3) number of tons which can be brought to bear in the target area in a given length of time; (4) destructive power per ton; and (5) speed and other factors which enable the projectile to evade or penetrate interception.

Accuracy of aiming is too complex to be reduced to any single index. But if we consider some of the recent developments in this field, we shall see accelerating efficiency revealed here, as in the other dimensions of destructiveness. Up through World War I, a number of fairly important improvements had been made in accuracy of aiming. Smooth-bore cannon were very inaccurate; and rifling of barrels was developed to make the shells rotate on their axis of flight, with great improvement in marksmanship. Sights on rifles were developed which provided accurate allowances for range while aiming. Telescopic sights, both for rifles and for artillery, and telescopic range finders improved aiming. The theory of ballistics was developed, making it possible to solve complicated aiming problems more and more accurately. These changes developed rather slowly, during the course of more than a century.

Important as these developments were, they were far overshadowed by the swift improvements in aiming accuracy which were achieved as bombing planes and rockets took the lead over artillery. One of the famous military secrets of World War II was the Norden bombsight. An even more important development was radar. The proximity fuse was another spectacular invention, consisting of a radio transmitter and receiver built into an explosive shell in such a way that when the shell gets near enough to an enemy plane to destroy it, reflected radio waves trigger the explosion. The automatic calculating devices for aiming guns on bombing planes are examples of still more complicated developments. Unpiloted rocket bombs which will seek out targets having high temperatures (such as blast furnaces) are said to be under development. Indeed, the development of guided missiles has become a complex branch of military engineering. Such improvements of aiming accuracy as these have taken place with unprecedented swiftness during and since World War II. It seems evident that in this, as in other dimensions of destructiveness, sharp acceleration has been occurring.

Parenthetically, this matter of improvements in aiming provides a striking illustration of how spotty the ability to forecast social trends has been in times past. In 1914, just before World War I, H. G. Wells wrote a prophetic novel called *The World Set Free*. Building on the discovery of radioactivity by the Curies, Wells foresaw the coming of the atomic bomb and pictured it as the crucial weapon in a world war. But he pictured the bomb as being heaved over the side of an open airplane by hand, and he told of the aviators communicating with each other by shouting through megaphones!

More and More Tons Per Raid

Of the five dimensions of projectile destructiveness, we have considered two: (1) range (and consequent killing areas); and (2) accuracy of aiming. The third dimension to be considered is the number of tons of bombs thrown into the target area.

Data on bomb tonnages do not go back beyond World War I. The best available index is the maximum number of tons of bombs dropped in any single raid up to given dates. The figures are as follows:[12]

Month	Tonnage
June, 1918	10
November, 1940	450
May, 1942	3,000
March, 1944	3,360
October, 1944	5,040
March, 1945	5,600
August, 1945	6,000

The acceleration which occurred in the ability to drop bombs into target areas is evident if we compare the increase per year from 1918 to 1940 with that from 1940 to 1945:

Time Interval	Increase, Tons per Year
June, 1918, to November, 1940	20
November, 1940, to August, 1945	1190

The increase per year from 1940 to 1945 was nearly 60 times as great as from 1918 to 1940. Of course, the immense increase in the 1940's was achieved under the pressure of war. But remember that the highest figure achieved under the pressure of World War I was 10 tons. The increase in recent years genuinely reflects the stupendous acceleration which has occurred in the industrial power to manufacture means of destruction.

The Long-Time Rise in the Killing Power of Explosives

The fourth dimension of the destructiveness of projectiles is the power, per ton of explosives, to kill and to demolish. Long before the military men learned to use TNT, the chemists were developing such explosives as fulminate of mercury (1800), guncotton (1838), and blasting gelatin (1875). Each of these broke all previous records for explosive power. Fulminate was 1.7 times as powerful as gunpowder. Blasting gelatin was about three times as

[12] Hornell Hart, "Technological Acceleration and the Atomic Bomb," *American Sociological Review*, Vol. 11 (June, 1946), p. 289.

powerful as fulminate. If this trend had continued, chemical explosives might have been expected to become more and more powerful. Indeed a U.P. dispatch from Freehold, New Jersey, published on January 9, 1948, mentioned cyclamite, described by Army authorities as 22 times as powerful as black gunpowder.

Even these increases in non-atomic explosive power show marked acceleration. Since 1875, from blasting gelatin to cyclamite, the percentage increase per year was 5 times as great as the gain per year for the previous five centuries. But these increases sink into relative insignificance compared to atomic explosive power.

In 1896 Röntgen's discovery of x-rays opened the way to knowledge of radioactivity and of atomic energy. From 1905 onward, Einstein's Theory of Relativity was developed, leading to his basic equation $E = mc^2$, which revealed the basic transformation of mass into energy. On December 2, 1942, at the University of Chicago, the first self-sustaining chain reaction of nuclear fission was established, and atomic energy became accessible. The resulting sequence of actually or prospectively developed explosive power has been summarized by Joseph Alsop:[13]

Date	Type of Bomb	Explosive Power (in tons of TNT)
1945	Hiroshima A-bomb	20,000
1951	Trigger for H-bomb	250,000
1952	Primitive H-bomb	4,000,000
1954	Full-scale H-bomb	8,000,000

The fundamental shift of gears in our accelerating destructiveness produced by atomic energy is shown graphically in the chart on page 42. The curve near the bottom of the chart, running from 1840 to 1944, represents the trend in the power of explosives, as demonstrated in laboratory tests, taking the power of black gunpowder as 1.0. The steep curve in the upper-right-hand corner of the chart represents the trend of explosive power as shown in tests of A-bombs and preliminary H-bombs. The chemical trend showed a 22-fold increase in 600 years; the nuclear trend showed a 500-fold increase in 9 years.

The preceding paragraphs deal with explosive power in the laboratory, measured by effects on a block of lead, or in experimental field tests. Explosive power may also be measured in terms of deaths per ton. Gunpowder was first used in battle in 1346. It was the most deadly military explosive until 1902, when TNT was introduced. During World War I, the Germans

[13] Joseph Alsop, "Taxes and H-Bombs," *Durham Morning Herald*, August 25, 1953, Sec. 1, p. 4, col. 4. Hanson W. Baldwin reported the explosive power of the 1952 H-bomb as equal to more than 5 million tons of TNT (*New York Times*, September 6, 1953, p. E5, cols. 1–2).

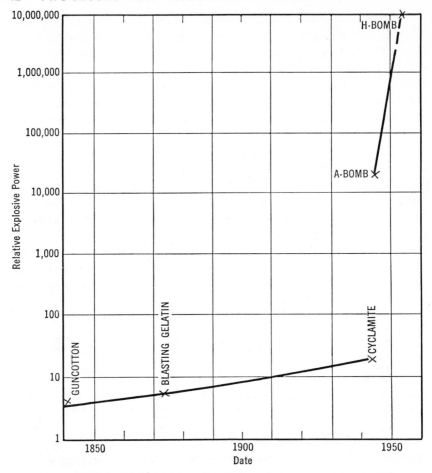

THE ACCELERATING INCREASE IN EXPLOSIVE POWER HAS SHIFTED GEARS

raided London repeatedly with TNT, killing about 3 people per ton of bombs dropped.[14]

The most deadly raid with pre-atomic explosives was that made on Tokyo, on March 9, 1945. The explosive used was TNT, combined with a new and highly effective type of incendiary bomb. That raid killed 50 people per ton of bombs used.[15]

Then, on August 6, 1945, an air force was able, for the first time, to make use in battle of a small fraction of the theoretical explosive power which had been discovered by atomic physicists six years earlier. When the atomic bomb was dropped on Hiroshima, the lives of 75,000 people were snuffed

15 *Ibid.* Other factors beside explosive power entered into this death rate, including the character of Japanese cities and the developed techniques of massive bombing.

14 Hornell Hart, "Technological Acceleration and the Atomic Bomb," *American Sociological Review,* Vol. 11 (June, 1946), p. 277.

out. That meant about 10,000 persons killed per ton of normal bomb load for the B-29 which made the raid.[16]

The Hiroshima bomb is now known as "Model T." Its blast damaged an area of 7 square miles. The improved A-bomb, exploded in 1950, had a blast-damage area of 25 square miles. The hydrogen bomb exploded in 1952 had a blast area reported as 160 square miles. It was estimated that the improved H-bomb, which was next to be dropped would have a blast-damage area of over 250 square miles. After the actual drop had occurred, in March, 1954, it soon became known that the blast-damage and incendiary power of the older and smaller bombs had been far transcended by the fall-out of deadly radioactive dust. In February, 1955, the Atomic Energy Commission reported that fall-out from the 1954 H-bomb blast at Bikini, if it had occurred over a land area, would have spread radioactive contamination lethal enough to threaten all unprotected human life in an era covering 7,000 square miles.[17]

What had happened was thus that the accelerating increase in destructive technology had moved once more into a new dimension of expansion. While the 1954 H-bomb was reputed to have the power of 8 million tons of TNT, it was reported in January, 1956, that both the United States and Soviet Russia would soon have bombs equivalent to 50 million tons.[18]

From the facts about explosive power which have just been reviewed, the following conclusions seem to be fairly clearly established:

1. The five centuries from 1346 to 1875 saw several times as much increase in explosive power as had been achieved in the previous million years.

2. The 70 years from 1875 to March, 1945, saw several times as much increase in explosive power as the previous five centuries.

3. The discovery of atomic power is merely a tremendous intensification of the swiftly accelerating increase which had already been manifested.

Radiological, Chemical, and Bacteriological Warfare

The development of explosive projectiles is only one area in which technological progress has been producing accelerating power of destruction. Closely related to atomic and hydrogen bombs is the development of radio-

[16] *New York Times*, June 30, 1946, p. 21; *United States Strategic Bombing Survey, Summary Report* (Pacific War) July, 1946, pp. 23–24. Tons of bomb per plane were 6.0 in the Tokyo raid, and 6.5 in the mean of 93 urban attacks of March 9, 1945. Norman Cousins has reported (*Saturday Review of Literature*, September 17, 1949, p. 10) that the actual deaths from the Hiroshima bombing were over 210,000, instead of the 75,000 figure accepted by the Bombing Survey.

[17] Stewart Alsop and Dr. Ralph Lapp, "The Inside Story of Our First Hydrogen Bomb," *Saturday Evening Post* (October 25, 1952), p. 150; cf. *New York Times Magazine*, May 17, 1953, p. 34. See also Los Alamos Scientific Laboratory, *The Effects of Atomic Weapons* (Washington, Atomic Energy Commission, June, 1950), p. 374. For discussion of the 1954 effects, see Ralph Lapp, "Radioactive Fall-Out," *Bulletin of the Atomic Scientists*, Vol. 11 (February, 1955), pp. 45–51.

[18] *Facts on File*, 1956, 3 D–E 3.

active dusts, which have been shown to have destructive potentials even greater than the bombs themselves. At the extreme of radioactive destructiveness is the hypothetical cobalt bomb, which theoretically might wipe out life on the entire globe.[19]

Military technology also includes the extremely important subjects of chemical warfare, bacteriological (germ) warfare, use of guided missiles, and other less traditional weapons. Since these subjects are discussed elsewhere in this volume,[20] they will not be considered in detail here. All the war weapons exhibit an acceleration in growth of destructive power which, along with the inability of nations thus far to control war, has brought a major crisis in world affairs.

Interceptibility

The first four factors in the destructive power of explosive projectiles—range, accuracy of aiming, quantity, and explosive power—have all shown highly accelerating trends of increase. The fifth factor is the power to evade or to penetrate interception.

It has often been said, in the past, that offense and defense keep seesawing back and forth, with neither winning a permanent advantage. Against the increasingly deadly spear, arrow, bullet, artillery shell, and bomb, the defense developed shields, battlements, body armor, dugouts, and reinforced-concrete shelters. Against the bombing plane was developed the fighter plane; against the swifter-than-sound V-bomb is developing the automatic interceptor. Interception is the process in which science works for the defense. But has it been a stand-off? Has the defense always come up with an answer which neutralizes the rising menace of accelerating destructive technology? The ultimate test is to be found in war casualty rates.

The Harvest of War Deaths

During World War I, Zeppelin airships dropped explosives on London, and Allied planes dropped some bombs on German cities. As a result, somewhat less than three persons were killed for every 100,000 of population in England and Germany. But during World War II, the V-bombs rained death on English cities while great fleets of Allied bombers demolished German cities with TNT and fire bombs. Almost 300 persons were killed for every 100,000 of population in the two countries. More accurately, the best available data indicate the following rates: World War I, 2.4; World War II, 287.5.[21]

[19] James R. Arnold, "The Hydrogen-Cobalt Bomb," *Bulletin of the Atomic Scientists,* Vol. 6 (October, 1950), pp. 290–292.

[20] See Chapter 15, *The Influence of Technology on War.*

[21] Based on data in the following: *United States Strategic Bombing Survey, Overall Report,* September 30, 1945, p. 101; Edward M. Earle, "The Influence of Air Power upon History," *Yale Review,* Vol. 35 (Summer [June], 1946), p. 583; *Encyclopaedia Britannica* (1929), Vol. 1, p. 461.

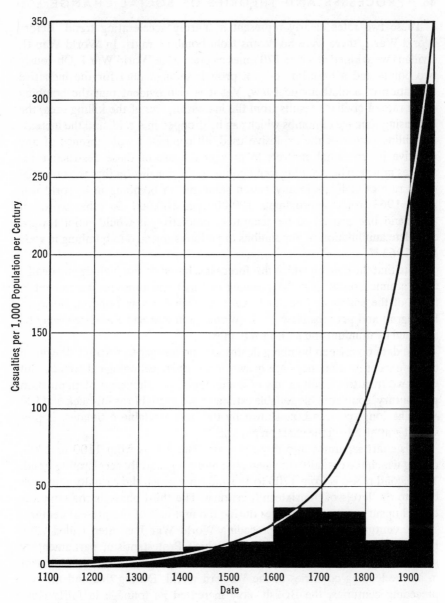

THE ACCELERATING INCREASE OF WAR CASUALTIES, 1100–1950

These two rates clearly represent a sharply accelerating trend. Before World War I, there were no deaths from bombing raids. In World War II, civilians were killed at a rate 120 times as great as in World War I. Obviously two points and a base line do not provide enough data for the inductive derivation of a mathematical law. Yet it is also evident that the bombing death rate of civilians results from the increasing size of the killing area, the increasing tonnage of bombs which can be dropped in a raid, and the increasing killing power of the explosive used, all combined with absence of any effective international controls to prevent the use of these destructive resources in war. The resulting trend points to the conclusion that the potential death rate of civilians in any nation subjected to bombing in a world war about 1963 would approximate 100,000 per 100,000. In other words, if this trend line proved to be accurately predictive, it would point toward complete annihilation of populations in nations subjected to bombing in wars after 1963.[22]

Note that the data on which this forecast is based do *not* include any deaths from atomic bombs. But the meaning of this trend must be interpreted in terms of the nearer and nearer threat that such cities as London, Moscow, Leningrad and perhaps New York, Washington and San Francisco, may be smashed by uranium and hydrogen bombs.

The data on civilian bombing deaths are too meager to warrant drawing a trend, except as inferences are drawn from other technological trends. But when we turn to casualty rates of combatants, per thousand of population per century, some roughly reliable estimates are available as far back as 1100 A.D. The long-run trend, as shown by the best available estimates, is presented graphically in the chart on page 45.[23]

This chart separates into three periods. The first is from 1100 to 1700, during which the casualty rate increased along a generally accelerating trend. The second phase is from 1700 to 1914, during which the casualty rate sank back to the levels of the sixteenth century. The third phase is the unprecedented upsurge of war casualties during the first half of the present century.

The century of peace just preceding World War I is often called "Pax Britannica." It was the period during which Protestantism, parliamentary government, and popular education were reaching high levels of development in all the leading countries of the Western world. During this and the two preceding centuries, the British navy increased its tonnage in fairly close conformity to a logistic curve, which it followed from 1600 to 1885. This 285-year trend was interrupted by the British-German naval race which got under way about 1890.

[22] The curve might, of course, approach, but never reach, complete annihilation.

[23] The chart is based on a revision of Sorokin's data for Europe in *Social and Cultural Dynamics* (New York, American Book, 1937), Vol. III, p. 341; cf. p. 337; *ibid.*, summarized in Quincy Wright, *A Study of War* (Chicago, University of Chicago Press, 1942), Vol. I, p. 656, supplemented by the Metropolitan Life Insurance Company's estimate of casualties in World War II.

This Pax-Britannica period may be regarded as an experiment which ultimately broke down. In the seventeenth century, the war casualty rate had risen to more than twice that of any previous century. Pax Britannica lowered it again to half its peak. But the two world wars carried the death rate from battle up to nearly six times what it had ever been before.

The conclusion seems, then, to be clear-cut. Hiroshima and Nagasaki are merely new highs in the runaway acceleration in growth of destructive power. The burst of the atomic bomb has not been an isolated, freak fact, suddenly disrupting an otherwise safe and secure civilization. Rather, explosive power is only one of several series of measurements, each tending to confirm the others, and all pointing toward the one basic fact: If present trends continue, the annihilation of entire populations by raids from beyond national frontiers will become possible within a very few years.

Conceivably, all mankind might be exterminated within a decade or two from now. This might, perhaps, result from uncontrollable epidemics started by bacteriological warfare. Or it might result from deadly radioactivity created by atomic warfare. On the other hand, effective atomic bombardment of the major cities of Western civilization would rapidly put out of operation the steel, coal, petroleum, and other basic industries, the railways, airplanes, automotive, and other transportation systems, the electrical generating systems, and the organized agencies for repairing such damages. Famine, pestilence, anarchy, and local violence would kill off further portions of the population. The resulting disorganization might paralyze the power for further large-scale destruction.

The ominous trends, it will be noted, are not based primarily upon the discovery of the atomic bomb. They are the outgrowth rather of the age-long acceleration in the range of deadly projectiles. Ever since our illiterate ancestors substituted bows and arrows for spears, human power to kill has been increasing more and more rapidly. The public was somewhat upset, temporarily, by the spectacular jump in explosive power represented by the atomic bomb. The thing to remember is that this increase is merely a dramatic expression of a tendency which has been evident for centuries and which is now culminating in a world-threatening uprush of destructive power.

WHY CULTURAL CHANGE ACCELERATES

The above illustrations indicate something of the nature of acceleration in cultural change. First, it was shown that the efficiency of man's cutting tools has been improving at an accelerating rate which has persisted through more than a million years of the prehistory revealed by archaeology. Second, accelerating increase in the physical power employed per person was shown. Third, the more and more rapid increase in world speed records was presented. Fourth, the accelerating increase in expectation of life was summarized. Fifth, some illustrations of nontechnological acceleration in cultural change were cited. Finally, the accelerating increases in various aspects of man's power to kill and to destroy were set forth in some detail.

The above list does not by any means exhaust the evidences that man's power to carry out his purposes in the material world has been increasing faster and faster. The reality of acceleration in technological growth can scarcely be doubted by any intelligent person who is acquainted with the facts.

The faster-and-faster trend of change, in various fields, is unmistakably clear. But what are the underlying causes of this trend? The present section seeks to develop the major causal factors in some detail in the light of accumulated factual data.[24]

The Nature of Invention

The basic fact which underlies acceleration in cultural growth is that every invention consists of a new combination of old elements. For example, an airplane is a combination of a box-kite, a windmill, a gasoline engine, a pilot, and the atmosphere, each of these (except the atmosphere) being adapted by various modifications. Similarly, the automobile is essentially a carriage, plus a gasoline engine, plus a driver, plus a road, plus a filling station, plus a repair shop. A telegraph is essentially an electromagnetic circuit, plus sending and receiving keys, plus two telegraphers, plus a Morse Code.

Mechanical inventions may seem at first to be merely combinations of physical parts, such as raw or prefabricated materials, plus an environment, plus properly trained operators. However, even mechanical inventions always include also certain *ideas* which enter into combinations with these other factors. In some kinds of inventions the crucial part played by ideas becomes even more obvious. For example, Galileo's telescope was not merely a combination of lenses and certain other physical parts, but also—and crucially—a combination of the laws of optics (as understood by Galileo) and the problem of seeing heavenly bodies more clearly. A slide rule is a combination of two rulers, the matched-lumber principle, a mathematician, and, crucially, the principles of logarithms.

Quite often the decisive factor in a new invention is the precedent created by a previous invention. For example, the discovery that certain molds in the earth secreted a chemical called penicillin, which killed off certain kinds of disease germs, provided a key idea that led to the discovery of a whole series of antibiotics.

Not only machines, scientific instruments, and healing drugs are invented by new combinations of old elements. This same principle holds true in the invention of social institutions. When the Constitution of the United States was being drafted, Thomas Jefferson and the other inventors of our form of democratic government were putting together a combination of various pre-

[24] For previous treatments of this question, see references in footnote 1 in the present chapter.

existing organizations (such as courts of law, legislative bodies, executive officers, and the like) with certain ideas and ideals (such as the ultimate sovereignty of the people, equality of voting rights, balance of power, equality before the law, and the like). All of these examples are seen thus to illustrate the one principle—that inventions consist in new combinations of old elements.

In the light of this principle of invention by combination, it becomes clear that the speed of cultural change depends upon five factors: (1) the number of culture elements from which new inventive combinations can be made; (2) the speed and completeness with which new inventions and discoveries are made known and made available to those who can make use of them; (3) the amount of improvement which each element is able to contribute; (4) the degree to which scientific methods are applied to the problems of cultural change; and (5) the ity of the need or desire for the solution of various proble

T⎺ rts to Combine

mines the number of culture elements available to be w combinations? To seek an answer to this question, let us cave dweller and look over the elements which he had available into new inventions. He had, of course, his own body, with ıse organs, its brain, and the like. He had also clay, water, s, and stones of various kinds. More than a million years ago, loreover, he was surrounded by various sorts of living plants Primitive inventions emerged out of combining these simple ith his hands the cave man knocked stones together, and graduıed to turn sharp fragments into knives and axes. With his stone ıdually learned to cut down green saplings, to kill animals, and to ıes. Combining his stone tools and hides, he learned to make leather ı combined his chipped flint with a straight piece of wood and a ıme strong fiber to make a stone-headed spear. After hundreds ı s of years of working with these materials, he combined thongs ıingy length of wood to make a bow, then combined his bow with ıre spear, and thus achieved the bow and arrow.

w let us jump suddenly from the cave-man inventor to the modern ıarch team at work in its laboratory. Instead of a limited variety of sticks, ıes, hides, and mud, the modern man has at his command practically all ı hemical elements in purified form and a nearly endless variety of chemiı mpounds, plastics, textiles, metal alloys, cutting tools, machines to conı mperature, sources of almost limitless energy, and instruments for almc...ı unlimited magnification of his sensory powers. Whereas cave men had no written language, the modern inventor has access to hundreds of thousands of books and scientific articles, elaborately indexed, and quickly available through the aid of reference experts.

The above paragraph brings out one fundamental reason for accelerating social change, namely, the immense increase of the variety of elements available to be combined into inventions. At first sight, this increase might seem to be due merely to the accumulation of inventions. When something useful is invented, the inventor and those who see him benefiting by his discovery may treasure his new prize, and it may become part of the cultural heritage. Some inventions become obsolete and drop into disuse—like flint knives or horse-drawn artillery. But the additions vastly outnumber the subtractions, and the cultural heritage becomes richer and richer.

Yet this is not by any means the whole of the story. Certain inventions and discoveries are specially prolific in giving birth to other inventions. For example, fire became the means by which men cooked, heated their huts, smelted iron, made glass, and carried out various chemical reactions. Each of these inventions in turn became the ancestor of multitudinous progeny. Glass gave birth to costume jewelry, drinking goblets, window panes, lenses, Crookes tubes, x-ray tubes, electric light bulbs, photo-electric tubes, radio and television tubes, and various other products. Lenses in turn gave birth to eyeglasses, simple magnifying glasses, telescopes, compound microscopes, cameras, range-finders, searchlights, and the like.[25] In other words, just as a prolific couple gives birth to descendants who may multiply geometrically, so a pregnant invention often brings forth a geometrically increasing number of descendants. Both through simple accumulation and geometrical multiplication, therefore, the number of elements available to combine into new inventions increases faster and faster.

Faster and Faster Diffusion

There is still another major reason why the number of factors ready to be combined into new inventions increases more and more rapidly, namely, the greater and greater ease and swiftness of communication. Today hundreds of millions of people speak the English language in areas covering a considerable fraction of the entire globe. Back in prehistoric times, these same areas were inhabited by hundreds of different tribes, using hundreds of mutually unintelligible languages. Every prehistoric invention had not only to struggle against rock-ribbed conservatism in the tribe in which it was born but, before it could be widely adopted, it had also to traverse wall after wall of foreign language and of aversion to the "outlandish." Moreover, the

[25] Similarly, the following elements have each entered into many different inventions: leather thongs, pottery, the bow spring, cloth, the domestication of plants and animals, the lever, the wheel, the screw, the alphabet, iron smelting, wire drawing, formal logic, geometry, algebra, Arabic numerals, the experimental method, money, gunpowder, printing, newspapers, treaties, logarithms, slide rules, calculus, the steam engine, internal-combustion engines, the electromagnet, the electric dynamo-motor, the correlation coefficient, the telephone, radio, electric light, photoelectric tubes, the airplane, machine guns, and atomic power.

acceleration of invention of devices for more and more swift and adequate communication has speeded diffusion.

The speed-up in the rate of culture transmission may be illustrated by three examples:[26]

Date	Invention	Diffusion Rate in Miles per Year
16,000 B.C.	Pottery making	.25
1440 A.D.	Printing	12.5
1925 A.D.	Insulin	12,000

This table shows that pottery making, in the Early Neolithic Age in Europe, took 400 years for each 100 miles that it spread from community to community, whereas insulin, invented in Canada in 1925, spread throughout the world in less than a year.

Inventions Become More and More Powerful

We have just seen that the rate of invention increases acceleratingly because the number of elements ready to be combined keeps multiplying in geometric ratio. Again, this is not the whole story by a great deal. The modern team of inventive engineers not only works with a vast arsenal of materials and possible parts as compared to the meager assortment available to the inventor of even a hundred years ago, but the units which the modern engineer combines are each of them vastly more powerful than the units with which the primitive or even the early modern inventor had to work. Take, for example, the men who have pioneered for progress in travel. Those daring innovators who first had the courage to leap onto the backs of wild horses and tame the first steeds were able to add 10 or 15 miles per hour to the speed of travel. But a modern engineer has the energy of ten thousand horses tied up in one engine. He calls on high-powered mathematics to design wings a thousand times as great as those of a bird, and when a test pilot climbs into the cockpit of the newly invented sky chariot, he and his fellows may be adding hundreds of miles per hour to human speed.

Take another example. Thousands of years ago, some early Egyptian or Assyrian (who was part inventor, part artisan, and probably part dreaded wizard) produced a little batch of glass. Some of the glass happened to be formed into a small, clear globe. Perhaps the artisan was deliberately trying to produce beads, and one of them happened to turn into a lens. In any event, this wizard-artisan-inventor chanced to look through his little blob of clear glass and saw that the pores and the hairs on the back of his hand, or the script on a scrap of papyrus, looked twice as large as usual. In the true spirit of the inventor, this early genius seized upon this fact and became a cultural ancestor of all spectacle makers. He helped toward adding two or three diameters to the power of the human eye to see details. But the modern

[26] See Hornell Hart, *Technique of Social Progress,* 1931, p. 680.

engineer, using magnets to bend streams of electrons, multiplies the power of previous microscopes by hundreds or by thousands.

Illustration after illustration could be given of this third basic reason for cultural acceleration: that the modern inventor is combining elements each of which is vastly more powerful than the elements with which his predecessors had to work. Hence each forward and upward leap attained by a modern invention is many times as large as the steps taken by earlier innovations. Once again we see that, by the very nature of things, when the processes of invention have an opportunity to work themselves out, man tends to progress faster and faster toward whatever goals he systematically seeks.

Methods of Inventing Become More and More Efficient

A fourth great reason why social change accelerates is that the methods of making inventions are themselves a part of the culture and that, like the other parts, these methods tend to improve faster and faster. The better the method, the faster and greater will be its achievements. Hence this improvement in inventive techniques tends to increase acceleration.

To see this development at work, turn back in imagination to the Old Stone Age. For hundreds of thousands of years, men knocked stones together, blindly at first and then intentionally, and used for knives the flints thus sharpened. When the stone-chippers had once found the way to make a useful knife, they clothed this method with defensive taboos and clung to it tenaciously for generation after generation. Stone-chipping methods stayed the same for thousands of years. Back in those prehistoric times, the method of invention was "fumble and succeed." The fumbling had to be done in little, isolated societies, where the old methods were sacred and where the innovator was likely to be regarded with frightened aversion.

From these prehistoric times of darkness, let us leap ahead to Charles Goodyear in the year 1830. He was interested in India rubber. He thought the stuff might be used to make waterproof cloth. The trouble was that when this crude rubber got warm it turned into a sticky gum. For ten years Goodyear blundered along by trial and error, recklessly attempting experiment after experiment, with failure after failure in his search for a process to cure rubber. He borrowed money; he went bankrupt; he was sent to jail for debts; he sold his children's schoolbooks to get money for further tests. At last, when he was experimenting with India rubber mixed with sulphur, he accidentally dropped some on a hot stove. When he grabbed it up in chagrin, he noticed that a layer of the rubber between the burned part and the still sticky part had been "vulcanized." The crucial step in producing useful rubber was thus an accident. Such were the methods by which a large fraction of our early modern inventions were achieved.

A major advance beyond this blind groping for a lucky combination has been the method of trying out systematically all the possible combinations. For example, when Edison was seeking the right combination of factors to produce a good storage battery, he tried more than 9,000 experiments. A friend remarked what a shame it was that he had done so tremendous an amount of work with no results, but Edison retorted, "Why, man, I have gotten a lot of results. I know several thousand things that won't work."

When the factors to be combined are many, and when each factor varies through a long range, the number of combinations becomes so huge that exploring all of them is quite impossible. That is where scientific theory comes in. The modern chemist, for example, working on the synthesis of some drug which may save millions of lives, does not have to try all the possible combinations blindly. Scientific knowledge of the structure of molecules enables these leaders of the laboratory to focus their efforts on the processes where results can be attained relatively swiftly.

Science consists in the systematization and increased efficiency of the process of truth-seeking. Underlying principles are discovered, by means of which the number of useless combinations to be tested can be vastly reduced. Devices for measuring and calculating are developed, so that new combinations can be described accurately and their results precisely determined. The methods of logic, of statistics, and of experiment are themselves systematically improved. Thus the acceleration of progress is raised to a still higher power.

Our survey of pertinent facts has thus confirmed the insight which Morgan expressed in 1877, in the quotation cited early in this chapter. Acceleration of social change is inherent in the very nature of human culture and of its growth processes. It is as natural for culture to accelerate as it is for a baby to grow into an adult. We have seen that this is true for four reasons: (1) the elements ready to be combined into new inventions become more and more numerous, faster and faster, because inventions breed inventions; (2) the inventions of all the world are more and more pooled, as the barriers of communication progressively break down; (3) the elements being combined are becoming not only more and more numerous but also more and more powerful; and (4) the methods of defining the problems to be solved, collecting the elements to be combined, and working out the most effective combinations of those elements, are all being improved more and more swiftly as our methods of invention become more and more scientific.

The Motivation of Invention

The four factors summarized above account largely for the fact that culture in general is accelerating. But a fifth factor remains to be considered, namely, the intensity of the desire for the solution of problems—the urgency of the need which given inventions or discoveries meet and the keenness of the pleasure which their use provides. Inventors and reformers are likely to concentrate energy on problems for whose solution an intense demand exists. The lures of fame, fortune, and personal interest stimulate the quest for progress in such fields. When an invention is made, the keener the public demand, the more likely is that innovation to be widely adopted and to be further developed. Insofar as improved communication and better scientific knowledge of human needs and desires develop, this factor contributes to the acceleration of social progress in general.

But the play of motivation is even more significant in determining the *relative* speeds of social change in various fields—and in particular, the excessive acceleration in the development of weapons of death and destruction. During the whole course of evolution, each living animal has had two imperative tasks to perform. First, it has had to get its own breakfast (or have it gotten by some convenient servant). Second, it has had to make sure not to be someone else's breakfast. To fail in the first of these tasks, on a given morning, is likely to be uncomfortable; it is not likely to be fatal. But any animal who failed once to avoid becoming the breakfast of another animal was thereby eliminated permanently from the survival stream. To be afraid—or preferably to be discreetly, intelligently, and courageously cautious—was an imperative requirement for becoming an ancestor of the present human race. Self-defense, both by individuals and by groups, thus became the most urgent of all motives.

In prehistoric times, the need to get breakfast and the need not to become breakfast were both promoted by the same spear, bow, and arrow. But about the time that written history dawned, the art of killing human enemies became differentiated from the art of killing game. The vital urgency of preserving oneself and one's group from slaughter and from enslavement made inventors, and the patrons of inventors, pay the keenest attention to improvements in the weapons and the arts of war. These strivings were marked "passed" or "failed" in one of the most effective of all performance tests— survival in battle. In the light of these facts, it is not surprising that almost the steepest of all accelerations has been that relating to weapons.[27]

PROGRESS IS NOT INEVITABLE

The preceding section discusses a number of the causes which have accounted for the fact that technological progress—and even nonmaterial forms of cultural change—have shown a pervasive tendency to accelerate. These causes appear to be inherent in the very nature of invention and of diffusion. If the facts and principles summarized above told the whole story, we might find ourselves back in the stage of social thinking which characterized many sociologists in the Victorian Age, that is, the belief that progress was inevitable.

However, the history of culture shows many examples of stagnation and

[27] The only case of cultural acceleration found thus far which may have accelerated more rapidly than destructive power is the speed of long-distance communication. Radio broadcasting (after a circuit has been established) takes place with the speed of light, whereas before 1800 such communication was limited to the speed of horsemen, signal fires, and drum telegraphs.

of deterioration in culture. The well-known phenomena of the rise and decline of empires illustrates this. It is only over the long run, and on the whole, that cultural change can be said to accelerate persistently.

These setbacks and stagnations in social change become more significant when we recognize two facts. First, it seems evident that the acceleration of developments in technology, in science, and in other forms of culture has been predominantly characteristic of the Western world and has not been uniformly true in such countries as China and India. Second, there seems to be no inherent reason why the maladjustments, disasters, and breakdowns which have brought stagnations and setbacks in cultural change might not vary in their intensity—and might not conceivably become so gigantic as to destroy the great bulk of modern culture, to make large portions of the earth uninhabitable, or even to destroy life entirely on this globe.

These counter-factors, which must be taken fully into account if cultural change is to be thoroughly understood, will be discussed in detail in later chapters of this book—particularly in Chapter 17 on cultural lag, and in Chapters 19, 20, and 21, which deal with social planning.

ANNOTATED BIBLIOGRAPHY

CHAPIN, F. Stuart, *Cultural Change* (New York, Century, 1928). Another pioneering exploration of the laws of cultural acceleration.

CHASE, Stuart, *The Proper Study of Mankind* (New York, Harper, 1956), Ch. 13, "Some Laws of Social Change," pp. 129–140. A stimulating popularization of Ogburn's theories, with some exploration of related ideas.

HART, Hornell, *The Technique of Social Progress* (New York, Holt, 1931). This was an early attempt to explore factually—and, as far as possible, quantitatively—the basic principles of social change.

———, "Technological Acceleration and the Atomic Bomb," *American Sociological Review,* Vol. 11 (June, 1946), pp. 277–293 (bibliography). This was a formulation intermediate between Hart's earlier book and the present chapter.

MERRILL, Francis, and ELDREDGE, H. W., *Culture and Society* (New York, Prentice-Hall, 1952), pp. 105–122, 583–587. This is one of the very few textbooks in sociology which has made any really serious attempt to assimilate the available scientific facts about cultural acceleration and the underlying laws of social change.

OGBURN, William F., *Social Change* (New York, Viking Press, 1922 and 1950), pp. 73–79, 103–118. The first major introduction of the acceleration principle into sociological theories of social change, though Ogburn cited the idea from Robert H. Lowie's *Culture and Ethnology* (1917).

CHAPTER 4

OBSTACLES TO INNOVATION

■ *Meyer F. Nimkoff*

A STUDY of the obstacles to change is a significant part of the total study of social change, for if it were not for the obstacles, the rate of change would be different. Ours is an age of rapid change, which implies that obstacles are being overcome. Indeed, over the long span of time, the rate of social change in general has been accelerating, as demonstrated in the preceding chapter. This means that the obstacles to inventions and scientific discoveries are either becoming fewer and fewer or less and less effective.

The obstacles to innovations are of two large kinds: (*a*) the difficulties in making inventions and scientific discoveries, and (*b*) the resistances to their use. The first is the problem of the acquisition of new knowledge, and the second is the problem of its diffusion. These are distinct, although inter-related, problems.

DIFFICULTIES IN ADDING TO KNOWLEDGE

Students[1] of social change have shown that innovations depend on (*a*) mental ability; (*b*) demand; and (*c*) existing knowledge.

Man is the only animal with the requisite mental ability to develop a substantial culture, that is, to accumulate a stockpile of inventions and discoveries. Since man has such a stockpile, is his mental ability an obstacle to innovation?

It may be helpful to consider mental ability in both its inherent and acquired aspects. It is very likely that the inherited or genetic intelligence of mankind has not changed appreciably during historic times, whereas man's knowledge has grown markedly. Since inherited intelligence is a constant factor, it cannot be a cause of change in culture. Man's inherited intelligence appears to be adequate for continued cultural growth. It is therefore not an obstacle to cultural innovation. To be sure, if man's basic intelligence were greater, if he were to become a superman, he might become capable of solving problems which now remain unsolved. But there is no immediate

[1] William F. Ogburn and M. F. Nimkoff, *Sociology,* 2nd ed. (Boston, Houghton Mifflin, 1950), Ch. 25.

prospect of an increase in the intrinsic intelligence of man. So while man's innate intelligence sets limits to his achievements, these limits are difficult to determine; and man does not yet appear to be approaching his cultural limits, as he appears to be approaching his physical limits, for example, in the time of running the 100-yard dash. Man's inherited intelligence does not appear to be an effective obstacle to cultural innovation in the foreseeable future.

Incompletely Utilized Mental Ability

Of those with the requisite mental ability to invent or discover, only a small percentage actually contribute new knowledge because most are not trained to be inventors or discoverers. Among the 18,000 superior engineers in *Who's Who in Engineering,* only 10 per cent are listed as inventors,[2] although some of those not so listed may have contributed some inventions. A study of the childhood, age, and education of a group of inventors[3] shows that inventive ability manifests itself earlier than some other kinds of ability. The peak productive age of physical scientists is 35 to 39 years, and the age period for highest quality of work is close to that for greatest quantity.[4] In general, poets and physical scientists are most productive at an earlier age than social scientists. Since inventive ability is manifested early, it could be spotted and trained; yet the writer does not know of a single class in invention (as a subject) in any school anywhere in the world. If inventive ability were diagnosed early and cultivated, the number of inventors and discoverers would be increased, as would also presumably the number of inventions and discoveries. There are economic and other reasons why this is not done. Perhaps the plan of special classes in invention in colleges, institutes, and universities is not so practical as the present practice of encouraging inventions in industrial research laboratories and other places. In any event, there appears to be an insufficient demand for special classes in invention. If there were more demand for such classes, steps would be taken to supply them. This leads us to a discussion of demand, the second factor in the supply of innovations.

Lack of Effective Social Demand

If there is little or no demand for a given invention or discovery, the chances of its being made are greatly reduced. Contrariwise, a strong social demand for an innovation is a potent stimulus to its production. For instance, there is little organized or effective demand at the present time for knowledge

[2] J. Rossman, "Engineers as Inventors," *Patent Office Society Journal,* Vol. 13 (1931), pp. 376–383.

[3] J. Rossman, "A Study of the Childhood, Education, and Age of 710 Inventors," *Patent Office Society Journal,* Vol. 17 (1935), pp. 411–421.

[4] Harvey C. Lehman, *Age and Achievement* (Princeton, N. J., Princeton University Press, 1953).

which will make possible the control of the sex of the child. There are a good many individual parents who, if they had a choice, would prefer a boy to a girl or vice versa; but in the United States there is evidence[5] that most parents are satisfied as to the sex of their children. Most parents prefer a balanced family, with children of both sexes; and the probabilities in general favor getting balanced families. The lack of organized sentiment in behalf of research which would make sex control possible is probably a factor in the dormant state of research in this field. In 1946, a biologist[6] indicated his reasons for believing that it might be technically feasible to control the sex of the child. He pointed out that the X-chromosome is slightly larger than the Y-chromosome and contains more chromosomal material, hence is more dense. He stated his belief that a special centrifuge could be constructed for the separation of these two kinds of cells. Since it has been hypothesized for some time that the child's sex is determined by the type of sperm cells involved, with the union of two X-chromosomes producing a female and the union of an X- and a Y-chromosome producing a male, the mechanical separation of the two types of sex cells would make control of the sex of the child possible. Harvey thinks there is about a fifty-fifty chance for the separation of the sex cells by the method he describes, yet he has not pursued these experiments, nor has anyone else, to the writer's knowledge. There are other approaches to sex control on which some work is being done, but not much. The principal reason seems to be that the effective demand for sex control is not great.

On the other hand, work on more satisfactory methods of birth control is proceeding with vigor, especially efforts to produce a physiological contraceptive, say a pill, which will achieve its objective without disturbing physical side-effects or serious interference with the balance of the endocrine system. There is also considerable work under way on more effective chemical contraceptives. Numerous experiments are being performed, using hormones, anti-hormones, anti-enzymes, immune bodies, modified media, symbiotic organisms, dietary factors, and special agents. The attack is on many fronts and it is impressive. Why so much effort? A prominent reason certainly is the great demand for an improved, economical contraceptive, especially in nations with a large and growing population, like India, where the pressure of population on the food supply is a matter of official concern. Proposals have also been made for the experimental use of the rhythm method in a country like India where extreme poverty and lack of plumbing and other facilities make mechanical and chemical methods of birth limitation impractical. The rhythm method of fertility control is, of course, a scientific discovery of consequence; and an effective plan for the use of this method

[5] Jeanne E. Clare and Clyde V. Kiser, "Social and Psychological Factors Affecting Fertility. XIV. Preference for Children of Given Sex in Relation to Fertility," *The Milbank Memorial Fund Quarterly,* Vol. XXIX (October, 1951), pp. 440–492.

[6] E. Newton Harvey, "Can the Sex of Mammalian Offspring Be Controlled?" *Journal of Heredity,* Vol. XXXVII (March, 1946), pp. 71–73.

among a large population of limited wealth and education would be a social invention of no small importance.

Lack of Essential Knowledge

Where a strong demand exists for an invention or a discovery, failure to produce it may usually be ascribed to a lack of the knowledge which is needed to make the innovation possible. In the case of cancer, for example, the demand for a cure is very great indeed. Many millions of dollars are invested in cancer research, and many hundreds of persons are engaged in the quest for a cure. Little by little, the knowledge that is needed for the understanding and possible conquest of the disease is being accumulated. The demand for a cancer cure is probably intensified in turn by the growing body of knowledge regarding the nature and causes of cancer. The demand for a cancer cure has probably also been increased by the increased need for a cure; that is, by the increase in the incidence of cancer in the United States, in part because of the aging of the population.[7] Demand is, then, somewhat related to the prospect for achieving a goal or objective. If there is not much chance of getting what the group wants simply because what the group wants is not available, then the demand for it is likely to be small. There is considerable demand for a cure for cancer because (a) the need is great and (b) the prospects for a cure in the near future are bright.

The prospects are bright because considerable knowledge concerning the origin and control of cancers has been accumulated. There was a time when the nature of all cancers was a complete mystery. No amount of social demand for the control of cancer could then have been of any avail. With the discovery of viruses and the identification of certain cancers with viruses, a new area of investigation opened up. Earlier the causes of diseases had been identified with bacteria. Now a new cause of disease was discovered—a chemical cause, not a microbe. It was then possible to study a wide range of chemical substances to see which substances when applied to tissue produced an irritating effect which led to tumors. Thus it was, for instance, discovered that certain coal tars like those found in nicotine, when applied to tissue resembling that of the human lung, resulted in cancer in experimental animals. Also experience had shown that early detection of cancer is important, for once the cancer cells have spread in the body they are difficult to check. Physical examinations at frequent intervals were recommended and were desirable, but a hidden cancer in its early stages might escape detection by this method. The search for a simple and more efficient method of diagnosis has led to the study of the blood, since a spreading cancer breaks through tissue walls and invades the blood stream. An effective test of cancer

---

[7] The cancer death rate rose from 65.0 per 100,000 population in the United States in 1900 to 139.8 in 1950. *Vital Statistics-Special Reports,* "Leading Causes of Death —United States and Each State, 1950," Vol. 37, No. 15 (December 16, 1953) (Washington, National Office of Vital Statistics, Department of Health, Education, and Welfare).

via the blood sample has had to await the accumulation of knowledge regarding the behavior of cancers, and the chemistry of blood. Now medical science is hopeful that early detection of cancer through simple blood tests may soon be possible.

If knowledge is essential to innovations, it follows that the more the knowledge that is available, the larger the supply of possible new knowledge. Our primitive forebears of the Paleolithic Age had relatively few inventions and discoveries with which to work: flint implements, wooden handles, bone implements, fire, painting and carving, and religion. With so few tools, progress was slow; and many tens of thousands of years were required before Neolithic man, before the dawn of history, achieved polished stone, the bow and arrow, pottery, domesticated animals, weaving, and the use of the hoe. With the dawn of history came the plow, copper, iron and bronze, writing, the calendar, and smelting, while modern man has added printing, firearms, glass, steel, electricity, chemistry, the steam engine, wireless communication, the internal combustion engine, synthetic materials, and atomic energy. At first the supply of knowledge was meager and the rate of progress slow; as the stockpile of knowledge increased, the rate of progress increased. As shown in Chapter 3, it has become faster and faster. Since a new idea is often a combination of two existing ideas, the greater the supply of available ideas, the greater the opportunities of creating new ones.

RESISTANCES TO DIFFUSION OF KNOWLEDGE

Once it has been made, an innovation encounters obstacles to its spread which may be of an economic, technological, psychological, or social nature, or a combination of these factors.

Economic Factors

In the case of a mechanical invention, public acceptability depends in part on the adequacy and cost of the invention. The first models of an invention are often inadequate in some particulars. Thus the first radios were crude crystal sets which required earphones and delicate tuning by hand, which involved locating a sensitive spot on a mica crystal. It is a far cry from these crude first radios to the push-button FM radios of the present. The technical deficiency of the early radio was, then, a factor limiting its general appeal.

Cost is also a factor affecting the acceptability of a new invention. For example, there is a machine, a facsimile printer, which can be installed in one's living room and which makes it possible to print a daily newspaper in your own home. Pictures and diagrams are reproduced as well as words. Facsimile operates like a television camera, scanning the original page and transmitting the signal to the home receiver which reassembles the characters on a sheet of special paper. But why spend several hundred dollars on this machine when the daily newspaper can be purchased for five or ten cents and when the price includes delivery of the paper to your front lawn which is not far removed from the living room? Facsimile has the advantage of making possible more recent news, but this advantage is offset by the availability of frequent newscasts by radio. Radio makes possible more up-to-the-minute news but at the expense of details and analysis such as a newspaper can supply. Frequency of news is then at the sacrifice of fullness of the news. That is one of the more important reasons, in all probability, why radio has not displaced the newspaper, as some early observers thought it might. The radio is not a complete or nearly complete substitute for the newspaper, as the newspaper is for facsimile in the home. We conclude that a new invention is not likely to be well received when an existing invention meets the same need at lower cost.

In the case of the radio it is not difficult to see the almost inevitable imperfections of the early models and the successive stages by which, taking place over time, improvements have since been made. In the case of mechanical inventions, we are likely to understand the process of progressive improvement with use and accumulating knowledge. In the case of social inventions, we do not so readily allow for possible improvements with use and experience; and we are often less tolerant of early imperfections. For instance, nationalized health insurance in England in the late 1940's had, when it was first introduced, many shortcomings. A nationalized medical service is, of course, a social innovation. The initial costs of the program in England were very heavy, heavier than had been anticipated, in part because the demand for special services like dentures and eyeglasses was very great. Many doctors were hostile to the program, and the quality of medical care was in many instances lowered. But these difficulties were in part early imperfections which have since been corrected. After the initial run on opticians, the demand for glasses diminished because those who needed them had been provided for, and the novelty of getting free glasses, whether needed or not, wore off; they were there to be had if one needed them, and it was not necessary to anticipate the need. So in subsequent years the demand for special services dropped, and accordingly also the cost of this phase of the program. Also adjustments were made in the contracts with the British Medical Society which are said to have left the doctors better satisfied. The program was initially conceived by the Liberal party, put into operation by the Labor party, and maintained by the Conservative party. The early difficulties with compulsory health insurance in England were then presumably not due to an unworkable and unrealistic conception but rather to the imperfections of the initial plan. If the innovation has merit, successive plans show improvement as there is more and more experience with the program and as new knowledge is acquired, much as in the case of material inventions; although the test of adequacy of performance is not so simple and objective in the case of social inventions as in the case of material ones.

The deficiencies in an innovation may, of course, be greater than just imperfections as to details. The proposal may be unsound in principle or it may be unworkable and unrealistic. An illustration is the Townsend Plan, proposed during the dark days of the depression of the 1930's, to pay all persons over 65 years of age a state pension of $100 a month. There was not money enough in the state treasuries to finance such a plan, and attempts to provide a pension of this size would have led to bankruptcy.

If the necessary knowledge exists and if there is a considerable demand for an invention and there is no satisfactory substitute, the probabilities are very great that the invention will be made and, in time, systematically improved. A good illustration is the helicopter, which appears to have a bright future. Progress has been relatively slow since the first workable models were introduced. There have been many technical difficulties. The helicopter has been expensive; and it has been difficult to operate, much more difficult than an ordinary airplane. But expense can be reduced by mass production induced by increased public demand. Operation can be simplified by automatic controls and additional safety features. The future of the helicopter is assured because it has no effective substitute and because it meets important needs. Unlike conventional aircraft, it can take off in the vertical position, it can hover in one spot, it can go forward or backward, and it can land on a small space no bigger than a tennis court. Airports are generally located some distance from the traveler's destination in the city he is visiting; but the helicopter can land on the roof of the building in which he has business to transact, if the roof is suitable. The helicopter has proved useful in moving mail from the post office to the airport and in transporting passengers from one airport to another, serving as a kind of interurban taxi service where the cities are not far apart. More spectacular have been the uses of the helicopter in rescue work and in evacuating the wounded from the field of battle. The helicopter may also be useful to the high command in observing battle lines at a forward position more fully than can be done by other means.

Psychological Obstacles[8]

We next consider resistances to innovations based in the attitudes and habits of the members of the society into which the innovations are being introduced. Hugo Munsterberg when teaching at Harvard University resorted to the following pedagogical device to drive home to his students the tenacity of habit formation. He would write the word *habit* on the blackboard, then erase the "h." "Observe," he would say, "you still have 'a bit of it' and you still have a 'bit' of it when you remove the 'a.' Even when you wipe out the 'b' you still have 'it.' " Habits, once formed, resist change. The customs of a society are collective habits; and especially where sentiment pervades custom, custom is slow to change when challenged by new ideas and practices. To cite but a single illustration, innovations in housing have

[8] Donald G. Marquis, "Psychology of Social Change," *Annals of the American Academy of Political and Social Science,* Vol. 249 (January, 1947), pp. 75–80.

been but slowly adopted, in part because we grow up in houses to which we become sentimentally very strongly attached. When we leave our parental home and establish a home of our own, we tend to perpetuate our childhood home which has become a symbol of "home." We tend to keep the white frame Cape Cod Cottage with green shutters, despite the availability of more durable, modern, new building materials like steel, aluminum, glass, and glass brick.

Affection for the familiar and the old is matched by fear of the new. There may be curiosity as to the new which makes it attractive, while at the same time there is uncertainty as to the new which leads to distrust and fear. There are many who are afraid to travel by air, although the statistics on accidents are reassuring. When there is no apparent danger, as in the use of the telephone, fear will not be a factor in the diffusion of the innovation, although it is reported that the late Queen Mary of England never used the telephone during her lifetime. The opposition to compulsory, tax-supported health insurance in the United States is in part due to the uncertainty as to how the program will work and a fear that it may result in the lowering of the quality of medical services.

Fear of the new is often based on ignorance, or more precisely on erroneous ideas as to the nature of the innovation or how it will work. For instance, when the cast-iron plow was first introduced by Jethro Wood in 1814, farmers resisted it because they thought it would poison the soil, an erroneous idea. Some of the opposition to Pasteur and immunization was the result of the fear of introducing germs into the body, a baseless fear when the germs are properly prepared. When the tomato was first introduced, it was widely regarded as poisonous.

Erroneous ideas do not always serve as obstacles to innovations. They may facilitate the adoption of an innovation, especially an ideological innovation, if the error leads not to fear but to confidence in the new ideas. As judged by scientific tests, ideas like those asociated with astrology and numerology are erroneous; but these ideas have a large following among those who want simple answers to difficult questions. These persons do not, of course, recognize the ideas as erroneous.

Ideas as well as emotions may be powerful obstacles to innovations, especially when systematized, organized, and widespread, as in the form of ideologies. Emotions, of course may become attached to ideas; and ideas may be developed to rationalize our emotional biases. Prejudices, when extensive, are a special form of ideology; and since they prejudge the situation, they almost automatically are hostile to new ideas that go counter to the existing ideologies. Thus there was the opposition of Gandhi and his numerous following to the industrialization of India. Gandhi, using the spinning wheel as a symbol of his social movement, was interested in quickening the nationalistic fervor of his countrymen and thought his objective could be accomplished by emphasizing the native handicrafts rather than Western technology. Gandhi was also opposed to birth control except by means of sexual abstinence, perhaps because his ideology was one of self-denial and self-discipline and perhaps also because as a realist he recognized that existing artificial contraception was not economically feasible in a country as impoverished as India. The opposition of the Catholic Church to contraceptives is, of course, an opposition based on an ideology, that is, on moral principles.

The sentiments and habits of individuals which impede social change are derived from social experience and can often be modified most effectively by using a group approach to the problem. An illustration of this relates to our food habits, which are among the earliest and most persistent habits we establish. New foods, when greatly different from those to which we are accustomed, are introduced into our diet with great reluctance. In one experiment with six different groups of Red Cross volunteers in home nursing, the groups, ranging from thirteen to seventeen members, were encouraged to eat more beef hearts, sweetbreads, and kidneys in the interests of better nutrition. In one group where this information was presented by the lecturer, who told about the use of these foods in her own family only 3 per cent of the women who heard nothing but the lecture served one of the new meats. But where the diet was discussed by the group as a whole, 32 per cent of the members used the new foods.[9]

Social Obstacles

Ideological obstacles to social change are also social obstacles, since ideologies are held by groups. We discuss the group aspects separately because, in addition to a clash of ideas produced by innovations, we often have also a clash of group interests or some disruption of the existing societal pattern by the innovation. Innovations may also meet resistances from the group where no ideologies are involved.

One form of group resistance to innovation is inertia. Earlier we saw that where there is lack of demand, inventors and discoverers are dissuaded from working on inventions or discoveries. Lack of social demand may likewise be a deterrent to the diffusion of an innovation. Esperanto, for example, is a social invention which has not had much appeal, even though it has more followers than any of the other dozen or so universal languages that have been developed.[10] In a world that is shrinking in size, so to speak, because of more rapid transportation and communication, and where mobility is on the increase, the need for a universal language to overcome the barriers of national and ethnic groups would appear to be great. But the obstacles in the way of a universal language like Esperanto are numerous and formidable. There is no body of tradition in Esperanto, no literature, history, science, or

[9] Kurt Lewin, "Group Decision and Social Change," in Theodore M. Newcomb, Eugene L. Hartley, and others, *Readings in Social Psychology* (New York, Holt, 1947), pp. 330–344.

[10] *Encyclopaedia Britannica* (1949), Vol. 22, p. 861.

philosophy as there is in, say, German, French, or English. Esperanto has to contend with other universal languages as well as with the effort to establish English as the international language. French has long been the language of international relations, and the publications of UNESCO are in English and French. In addition, there are partial substitutes for Esperanto and other universal languages aimed at reducing the language barrier to international understanding, namely, (1) simultaneous interpretation equipment for use at international conferences; and (2) a beginning in machine translation of written material. The first system operates from soundproof booths in which interpreters listen to an address transmitted to them from the speaker's microphone via a wired system leading to their headphones. While listening, the interpreters provide a simultaneous running translation which is carried, in one system, over separate wired circuits to every seat in the room, each seat being equipped with headphone and a selector switch, as in the UN headquarters in New York, where translations are made into English, French, Spanish, Russian, and Chinese. A second system, not using wires, provides each individual with a lightweight radio receiving set equipped with earphones and with an aerial lodged in the shoulder strap, enabling the listener to move about freely within the auditorium if he chooses. The translating machine, developed early in 1954, is a giant electronic computer which has translated, from Russian into English, brief statements about politics, law, mathematics, chemistry, metallurgy, communications, and military affairs. The machine is still far from being able to receive a Russian book at one end and produce an English translation at the other, but he would be a rash person who would deny that it may be done.

National sentiment favorable to one's own mother tongue, the resistance to learning a new language, and the limited utility of a universal language known by only a relatively small group of persons are some of the principal social obstacles to the spread of a universal language, as are also the mechanical inventions which facilitate translations.

Social Dislocations

A society is an organization of many parts with a functional unity, that is to say, there is usually a state of harmony or balance or adjustment existing among the parts, a condition which Sumner described as a "strain toward consistency." This harmonious relationship among the parts of a culture is especially noticeable in preliterate societies where the rate of change is low and where there has been time to work out satisfactory adjustments around basic values. When a new invention or discovery is introduced into a society, it changes the existing pattern to some degree; and if the innovation is of major proportions, its dislocating effect on the society may be great.

There is, accordingly, a tendency for the group to resist change that brings social dislocations. A simple example is the resistance to calendar reform. A calendar has two principal functions: to fix dates and to furnish an instrument for the measurement of equal intervals of time. Our present calendar is deficient in both. As evidence of the fact, the relation between "month-day" and "week-day" fluctuates constantly. As evidence of the second, Easter may be as early as March 22 or as late as April 25, a range of thirty-five days. So there is demand for calendar reform. In 1923 the League of Nations Committee of Inquiry on Calendar Simplification considered some 185 calendar reform proposals and recommended two plans as most meritorious: the Cotsworth Calendar and the World Calendar, shown below. The Cotsworth Calendar consists of thirteen identical months, each month consisting of

The Cotsworth Calendar. Contains thirteen identical months like the above. The extra day of the common year would be Year Day, coming at the end of the thirteenth month. The extra day of leap year would be Leap Day, coming at the end of the six months.

Sun.	Mon.	Tues.	Wed..	Thurs.	Fri.	Sat.
1	2	3	4	5	6	7
8	9	10	11	12	13	14
15	16	17	18	19	20	21
22	23	24	25	26	27	28

SOURCE: W. E. Castle, "Calendars and Calendar Reform," *Scientific Monthly*, Vol. 56 (February, 1943), pp. 163–168.

four full weeks. The additional month, which is inserted between June and July, is made by combining the last thirteen days of June and the first fifteen days of July. The "World Calendar" consists of twelve months as at present, but each quarter has a first month of 31 days and two others of 30 days each. The calendar is the same year after year. December 30 is always Saturday and is followed by "Year Day," a second December 30. Each of the twelve months has 26 business days.

The World Calendar. Contains four quarter-years, all exactly like the one above, with Year Day and Leap Day as in the Cotsworth Calendar.

Days of the Week	First Month					Second Month					Third Month			
Sunday	1	8	15	22	29		5	12	19	26		3	10	17	24
Monday	2	9	16	23	30		6	13	20	27		4	11	18	25
Tuesday	3	10	17	24	31		7	14	21	28		5	12	19	26
Wednesday	4	11	18	25		1	8	15	22	29		6	13	20	27
Thursday	5	12	19	26		2	9	16	23	30		7	14	21	28
Friday	6	13	20	27		3	10	17	24		1	8	15	22	29
Saturday	7	14	21	28		4	11	18	25		2	9	16	23	30
91 Days Per Quarter	5 Sundays 26 Week days					4 Sundays 26 Week days					4 Sundays 26 Week days			

SOURCE: W. E. Castle, *op. cit.*

Objections to the thirteen-month calendar are that 13, being a prime number, is not divisible exactly into halves or quarters. Also this calendar would increase business costs by requiring statements to be issued 13 times a year instead of 12, meters to be read 13 times instead of 12, and so on. Objections to both the thirteen-month calendar and the "World Calendar" are that new and old dates would be difficult to harmonize and that the sequence of religious holidays would be disturbed.

It would be a mistake to think that innovations that bring social dislocations are always resisted. On the contrary, such innovations may be enthusiastically received and promoted. The reason is that the dislocations caused by innovations are not always anticipated. The innovation may be desired for its own sake and its disrupting influence may not be evident until some time has elapsed. Thus the steam engine and steel tools were desired because they meant more production and increased production meant a higher economic standard of living. But steam and steel, and associated inventions, brought urban civilization; and life in crowded cities brought an increase in crime, disease, and mortality. This was the first phase of man's experience with industrialization, and further experience has led to improved adjustment. But the point to be made here is that resistance to innovations is likely to occur only when the disorganization they produce is anticipated.

A further qualification is that resistance to innovation is not likely to be great even when serious social dislocations are anticipated, if the alternative to the innovation is thought to entail the risk of even greater social disorganization. Here the atom bomb provides a good example. With the atom bomb have come considerable adjustments in budget, military strategy, types of armaments, emphasis on military intelligence and civilian defense, stockpiling of raw materials, and decentralization of some industries. The group is willing to cope with these appreciable changes because the question, at the time of writing, is not whether the world is to have nuclear weapons, but rather which nation or combination of nations is to have supremacy in such weapons. The social consequences of achieving strength in nuclear weapons, despite the burdens entailed, may be less damaging or disorganizing in the long run than the consequences of *not* developing strength in such weapons and adjusting to them.

It is worthy of note that the decision to build the first atom bomb was made by a relatively few persons; and while many thousands of individuals were employed in the project, the nature of the undertaking in which they were engaged was kept secret from them. It was a distinct surprise to the public generally when the announcement was made by President Truman that an atom bomb had been exploded over Hiroshima. In this instance, the atom bomb was manufactured by a monopoly, the goverment of the United States, and a secret monopoly at that. The great mass of the people could not have registered an objection to the atom bomb, assuming they might have wished to do so, which is probably not the case. After the bombs were exploded over Japan, some groups, especially groups of atomic scientists, urged that controls be established to make atomic bombing impossible; but these appeals were ineffective in the absence of an international agreement concerning the atom bomb. The protestations of the atomic scientists and other groups can scarcely be considered effective obstacles to the invention and improvement of atomic weapons.

Vested Interests

Innovations bring changes that affect the interests of groups differently. Some gain, others lose. One man's meat, we say, is another man's poison. A particularly potent obstacle to change is the opposition to innovation by strong, organized groups that stand to lose by the change. Such organized groups that exert pressure to prevent change were called *vested interests* by Thorstein Veblen, since they have a vested interest in maintaining the status quo; and the phrase has come into wide use. A realistic inventory of the sources of resistance to social change needs to give prominence to vested interests.

The introduction of the diesel engine may be used to illustrate the role of vested interests in resisting change. The shift from coal-burning engines to diesels led to a reduced demand for coal, which in turn threatened coal mines with loss of work and pay. The organized coal miners through their unions fought dieselization and brought pressure on the railroads to retain their steam locomotives. Diesels made longer trains possible and threatened the jobs of railroaders who through their unions sought to limit the length of trains and to increase the number of workers required to man a train. These pressures, raising costs, would serve as obstacles to the diffusion of diesel engines.

Since dieselization of locomotives has continued apace, with some railroads now 100 per cent dieselized, it is plain that the effect of the opposition of the groups named above and of other similar groups has been to impede change rather than to prevent it altogether. This despite the fact that the effect of the change has been disastrous for some groups. Thus the introduction of the diesel locomotive has brought economic and social ruin to some towns which were division points on the railroad.[11] These towns, watering and service stops for the steam locomotives, were converted into ghost towns by the diesels.

A reason why the will of vested groups does not always prevail is that in a society as vast and complex as ours, there are hundreds of powerful organized groups, sometimes with divergent interests; and the pressures exerted by some of them cancel out or offset the pressures exerted by others. Thus the railroads are organized into a trade association which is active in promoting the interests of the owners. Diesel engines mean greater economy of operation and therefore greater profits. Also the weight of general public opinion would be felt in behalf of dieselization, since it results in less pollution of the air, although this public opinion is not organized.

It is clear that vested interests promote changes which are to their ad-

---

[11] W. F. Cottrell, "Death by Dieselization, A Case Study in the Reaction to Technological Change," *American Sociological Review*, Vol. 16 (June, 1951), pp. 358–365.

vantage as well as oppose changes which they believe are not to their advantage. The railroads, for example, have opposed the growth of the trucking industry, just as earlier the turnpike and stagecoach companies fought the railroads. But the railroads have promoted innovations in engines and passenger cars, as well as improvements in organization of services although, it must be added, not without the prodding of competition from the autobus, truck, and airplane. Monopolies would have less incentive to make improvements, but even in monopolies there is the incentive to make improvements which will result in greater profits.

The opposition to change by vested interests is usually emphasized by writers on social change and not the promotion of changes by vested interests, perhaps because in part opposition to change is more dramatic than support of change. The changes that vested interests make are mainly improvements in existing practices, whereas the opposition they show is directed against major innovations.

It may be noted that vested interests exist in a variety of fields, not merely in business. Divorce lawyers constitute a vested interest and have fought efforts to reform the divorce laws; that is, they have opposed efforts to substitute for the present adversary procedures of the divorce trial a system of scientific inquiry by trained social workers into the causes of divorce, with a view to reconciling the couple when possible and desirable. So, too, certain groups of doctors have furnished organized opposition to proposals for compulsory tax-supported health insurance. And in the colleges, the newer disciplines like sociology have had to make their way slowly against the opposition of the established subjects, like history and politics. In an earlier period, when history was being introduced into the curriculum, history in turn had to contend with the hostility of the classics and other established subjects.

The efforts of vested interests to prevent change are evident, but how effective are such efforts? Opposition to change may in certain instances actually promote change by dramatizing the issue. This is apparent in the case of, say, the enhanced appeal and popularity of a banned book or motion picture. We have already seen that the effect of opposition is generally to delay change rather than to prevent it altogether, at least in minor matters. It would be difficult in a complex society like ours, with so many competing interest groups, to find a group powerful enough to prevent major innovations in its segment of the culture. Monopolies or cartels may, of course, do so. Dictatorial governments, being political monopolies, have such power, in theory. Thus the Communist party in Russia, a monopolistic vested interest group, has succeeded in preventing the two-party or multi-party system from being established, which is linked to an innovation we call democracy. But even where vested interests do no more than delay change, an appreciable delay in a change may be very expensive to those wishing to effect the change.

There are a surprising number of inventions and discoveries which we take for granted today that were vigorously opposed when they were first made.

Scientific discoveries, if valid, are demonstrable, but not to the closed mind. When Pasteur announced his discovery of germs, some eminent scientists refused to look into the microscope because, as they put it, it just could not be so. Harvey's discovery of the circulation of the blood in the first part of the seventeenth century was likewise opposed. Harvey claimed that no man over 40 accepted the doctrine when he first presented it.[12] At least twenty anatomists wrote against it, nearly all of them invoking the authority of Galen.[13] It is interesting to note that the appeal in many such instances is to authority rather than to evidence.

Opposition to scientific discoveries is likely to be of shorter duration than opposition to social inventions, because scientific discoveries are subject to the test of evidence, whereas social inventions involve values about which there is likely to be more dispute. So it is easier to understand why there should be more difference of opinion as to the possible benefits of a proposed social invention and why so much time should have been required for certain proposals to be adopted. It took decades to adopt the progressive income tax, the direct election of senators, workmen's compensation, women's suffrage, and similar reforms. Some proposals like national prohibition of the sale of liquor have been accepted and then rejected, presumably because in part at least they have been unworkable. And still other proposals, like Judge Lindsey's plan of companionate marriage[14] as a solution to some of the problems of youth, were never taken seriously enough to be put into effect.

Today there are many proposals for social reform concerning matters of fundamental importance, proposals to which there is strong opposition in some quarters. Such proposals have to do, for example, with world government as a solution to the problem of war, and with a compulsory tax-supported program of health insurance in the United States as a solution to the problem of the costs of illness. Are these proposals unrealistic and will they ultimately be abandoned? Or, if they are likely to bring us great benefits, as have some of the proposed reforms of the past, are we being denied these benefits because of the present opposition to them? Proposed innovations and the obstacles to these innovations are not without serious consequences to all of us.

SUMMARY

Obstacles to cultural innovation are (*a*) the difficulties in making innovations, and (*b*) the resistances to their use. For the world as a whole and in the long run, the rate of social change is probably affected more by the former than by the latter.

[12] Robert Willis, translator, *Introduction to the Works of Harvey* (London, Sydenham Society, 1847), p. xlvii.

[13] Bernhard J. Stern, *Social Factors in Medical Progress* (New York, Columbia University Press, 1927), p. 47.

[14] Ben Lindsey, *Companionate Marriage* (New York, Boni and Liveright, 1927).

Demand is a factor in invention, but more important is the knowledge that is necessary to make an invention. No amount of demand will produce an invention if the culture is not ready for it; but an invention can be made even if there is little or no demand for it, although such an invention will be little used.

An innovation may be resisted because of cost, initial imperfections, the fear of the new, existing sentiments, prejudices, and ideologies, inertia, anticipated social disorganization, and the opposition of vested interests. Many of the advantages we now enjoy and take for granted were bitterly resisted when they were first proposed. An interesting question is which, if any, of the social innovations now being proposed will be regarded as a blessing fifty years from now.

ANNOTATED BIBLIOGRAPHY

BARNETT, H. G., *Innovation: The Basis of Cultural Change* (New York, McGraw-Hill, 1953). An attempt to formulate a general theory of the nature of innovation and to analyze the conditions for, and the immediate social consequences of, the appearance of novel ideas. Part IV is entitled: "Acceptance and Rejection." The approach is socio-psychological.

HART, Hornell, *The Technique of Social Progress* (New York, Holt, 1931). A pioneer study. Obstacles to change are treated in a comprehensive manner in pp. 607–632, 653–658.

MEAD, Margaret, ed., *Cultural Patterns and Technical Change* (New York, Columbia University Press, 1954). Experts from various countries suggest ways of introducing technical changes with a minimum of social disorganization.

OGBURN, William F., *Social Change* (New York, Viking Press, 1950), new edition with supplementary chapter. This book contains a chapter on resistances to inventions and a special one on the nature of cultural lag.

STERN, Bernhard J., "Resistances to the Adoption of Technological Innovations," *Technological Trends and National Policy,* National Resources Committee (Washington, Government Printing Office, 1937). A running account of the resistances which have developed to the adoption of successful mechanical inventions, such as the railroads, the coach, and so on. A readable and almost unbelievable account of resistances to inventions which have proved of great benefit to society.

———, *Social Factors in Medical Progress* (New York, Columbia University Press, 1927). An analysis of all types of resistances to a few significant medical discoveries that have proved to be of great value to the human race. One of the earliest studies in this field and still a valuable source.

VEBLEN, Thorstein, *Vested Interests and the State of the Industrial Arts* (New York, B. W. Huebsch, 1919). This book, which originated the term *vested interests,* points out their tremendous power regarding the phenomenon of economic change.

WOLFE, A. B., *Conservatism, Radicalism, and the Scientific Method* (New York, Macmillan, 1923). One of the few studies on the nature of conservatism and radicalism with reference to social change. The value of the scientific approach is especially emphasized.

CHAPTER 5

THEORIES OF SOCIAL CHANGE

■ *Delbert C. Miller*

THE UNDERSTANDING of social change has been a persistent challenge of man. He has searched every corner of his universe for an explanation—finding it sometimes in the pleasure of the gods, sometimes in the vicissitudes of the physical world, in the mysteries of his own mind and body, or in the social world of his own time. With all of his science and technology, modern man is still confounded by the complexity of the old challenges: How and why does society change? What is the direction of society?

This chapter describes some of man's more recent efforts to find answers to these questions. To understand why these questions are so difficult for the modern social scientist, it is first necessary to appraise the problem of observation and the identification of changing patterns in a society.

THE PROBLEM OF ANALYZING SOCIAL CHANGE AND FORMULATING SOCIAL THEORY

Problems of Observation

Position of the observer relative to space. *Social change refers to a pattern of social relationships, in a given social setting, which exhibits change over some defined period of time.* The student of social change faces a number of initial difficulties in identifying a changing pattern. The first of these are difficulties owing to his position. The observer of society, like the observer of the physical world, always stands in some position relative to space and time. What he sees is usually a small part of the universe of data and his records are reliable only to the extent that he has sampled a representative segment of society. Most theories of social change, for example, are largely reflections based on Western society, inasmuch as the observers and their data are products of Euro-American thought and culture.

Position of the observer relative to time. Time is also an elusive dimension. What is a "long time"? What is "fast"? Such concepts as length of time and rate of time constantly appear. When the statement is made that the present epoch is a period of rapid social change, it signifies that over some current time span a large number of social relationships may be observed to change rapidly, that is, compared with such other rate records as are available to the observer. The phenomena of social change may take place at an instant in time or it may encompass all of man's cultural history. Sociologists have devoted attention to problems of social change along this full continuum of the time dimension.

Position of the observer relative to values. Special problems of validity also arise.[1] What any observer sees of the world depends partly on the position from which he observes and partly on the ideas which have been inculcated in him. The social observer has an especially difficult task of disciplining his observations so that his own valuations do not intrude into the data which he sees and interprets. He must not forget, if he is looking at his own society, that he is himself a living product of it. He must see just as clearly those changing parts which he prefers would remain fixed as he sees those which he would like to change. Thus, the question of what parts of society are changing and how fast they are changing depends on the representativeness of the sample data, time specifications, and the objectivity of the observer.

The Identification of Patterns of Social Change

Order and change. The identification of social change implies an ability to separate changing relationships from those that are stable or changing very slowly. As one writer has put it, "Sociology propounds the infinite flexibility of culture. At the same time, it looks for constants in the flow of social change that will submit to generalization."[2] In one sense, all is change. Society can be observed as a dynamic equilibrium of changing relationships with each day different from the one preceding. Variations between societies reveal marked differences. But focus on the persistence of uniformities within a culture area and social stability emerges as the dominant characteristic.

Distinction between cultural and social change. Culture signifies the social heritage—all that a given people has created or preserved, including artifacts, customs, their technological system, social institutions, art, ideas, and weapons. Cultural forms often have a long history and exhibit persistence and continuity. Political, economic, or social revolutions may bring great changes in social relationships, yet culture may remain but little changed. New élites appear, social classes change, populations die or are killed off— these are the kind of social changes which are of large magnitude and are readily observed. In our era when change seems so fast and pervasive, it is important to appraise the stable relationships as carefully as the changing ones. A high degree of stability is built into society by a number of factors. The first of these is the constancy of man's biological needs[3] and

[1] George A. Lundberg, *Social Research* (New York, Longmans, Green, 1946), Ch. II.

[2] Svend Reimer, "Empirical Training and Sociological Thought," *American Journal of Sociology,* Vol. LIX (September, 1953), p. 107.

[3] Edwin G. Boring, Herbert S. Langfeld, and Harry P. Weld, *Foundations of Psychology* (New York, Wiley, 1948), pp. 114–124.

certain common social motives, such as a desire for association, recognition, and approval.[4] Men everywhere build institutional practices around their need for making a living, satisfying sex desire, the need for companionship, the desire for religious worship, and the need for play and relaxation.[5] Moreover, environmental conditions may remain with but little change over hundreds of years. All of these conditions describe constants that are of special importance to the social scientist. One of his tasks is to identify cause-and-effect connections in changing social relationships. If all relationships were changing rapidly, the task would be enormously magnified. The fact that many patterns of social relationship remain relatively stable simplifies the problem. Yet it is still true that the determination of social causation is fraught with unusual difficulty in the present stage of sociological knowledge.[6] Many of the theories of social change have been born from social philosophy rather than from social research. They are largely deductions from premises and gross observations rather than inductions based on the collection of primary source data. Moreover, they are based on a concept of society as a totality and refer therefore to all human society. The history of social-change theory until very recently has been largely a description of attempts to discover from historic records the laws presumed to be inherent in the social evolution of human society.

The scope of modern theory. Modern sociologists still are searching for an understanding of changes that spread across human society, but research work has demanded that much smaller segments be selected for study and that shorter time spans be examined. New standards of rigor have been introduced by the logic of the scientific method and the statistical knowledge of sampling, correlation, and tests of significance. This chapter will attempt to delineate both historic theory and modern thought. It will deal, therefore, with both the long-run questions of societal change as well as the shorter-run questions of measuring specified changes within a given society.[7]

The Major Theoretical Tasks

Identification of cause and effect. *The Meaning of Functional Relationship.* When anything changes, it may be called a variable. A phenomenon to be explained is called a *dependent variable* because the change is dependent

---

[4] These motives must be learned and are not necessarily universal but are commonly derived from early interaction with the social norms of group life in most societies.

[5] Kingsley Davis has stressed that there are societal necessities which are universal to every kind of society from insect to man. These are: (1) maintenance of the population; (2) division of function among population; (3) solidity of the group; and (4) perpetuation of the social system. See K. Davis, *Human Society* (New York, Macmillan, 1949), pp. 28–31.

[6] Cf. R. M. MacIver, *Social Causation* (Boston, Ginn, 1942), Chs. III and IV.

[7] The importance of this distinction is best described by Talcott Parsons, *The Social System* (Glencoe, Ill., Free Press, 1951), pp. 481–486.

upon (or caused by) a change in another variable or variables. These latter variables are called *independent*. Thus an increase in school enrollments (dependent variable) may result directly from an increase in the birth rate (independent variable). A change is caused by another change and never by a *constant,* as was pointed out in Chapter 2.

Those parts of man's biological nature or of external environment which remain unchanged are not included in the equation of forces which cause a change. The problem is to ascertain the nature of the relationship between an independent and dependent variable by observing the variations in the dependent variable as changes occur in the independent variable. Sometimes the two variations occur together or one occurs after a lag. Thus an increase in a demand for producer goods such as machine tools is usually accompanied by an increase in demand for consumer goods such as autos, clothing, and food. This is because expansion of the economic system tends to increase total purchasing power among all the consuming groups in the society. Not all such concomitant variations have a causal connection. For instance, between 1940 and 1950 there was a marked rise in the number of persons attending church as well as a large increase in national income. We cannot conclude that the increase in church attendance was due to the increase in national income. A connection must be established beyond the mere concomitance of the variation. We must derive our knowledge of cause from logical grounds as further evidence is screened. When two variables change simultaneously over a period of time and no direct causal connection can be established between the two variables, there is a strong presumption that there is some indirect connection through a third variable. In the case of the increased church attendance and increased national income, the connection is through the impact of World War II and its aftermath.

Four Manifestations of Causes. It was pointed out in Chapter 2 that causes may manifest themselves in a *sequence,* as a *convergence* or cluster, as producing *dispersion* effects, or as a *complex network.*

1. Causes may occur in a *sequence* like the links on a chain. Some of these causes are direct and immediate, others are indirect and remote. Thus, a decline in worker motivation and sense of personal responsibility may be due to the direct fact that much labor is performed in the large corporation on highly repetitive jobs; the remote causes are the factory system and mass market which, in turn, were brought about by the steam engine, the electric motor, and machine tools.

2. Several causes may *converge* to produce a change. Thus, electric power and several transportation and communication inventions have converged to augment the decentralization of industry. These converging causes are often called a cluster.

3. The effects of a single cause may be *dispersed* outward into many different sectors of a society. Thus, the average increase of formal education

which is being acquired by Americans has many different effects on the family, church, community, military organization, and labor relations.

4. The phenomena of convergence and of dispersion may be tied in with the phenomena of sequence to produce a *complex network* of causes. This is a very common manifestation, but the complexity can be simplified by recognizing that causes vary in importance, and important causes may be identified which account for a large part of the effects observed.

Identification of an Important Cause. An important cause is one which accounts for a large part of the variation in some observed effect. If the independent and dependent variables can be expressed in measurable terms, a correlation statistic can be derived. The correlation coefficient is a measure of variation between two quantitative variables. If the coefficient is 1.0 and the variables are causally related, there is only one cause. The multiple correlation coefficient enables the researcher to measure the variation between a dependent variable and a number of independent variables. Since most changes are due to multiple causes, the social researcher is constantly trying to find the most important ones and to measure them. He rarely expects to get a correlation of 1.0 unless the pattern of cause and effect is a very simple one and he can hold all the other variables constant. A multiple correlation of 0.8 is usually very notable in prediction of social variables, since this means that the factors identified account for 64 per cent of the variation in the dependent variable. If the correlation is small, say 0.2, it is not very important (only 4 per cent of the variation is explained).

In the absence of measured factors, we must make approximations. Most of the theories of social change rest upon approximations which are inferred from observation or general knowledge and related through insight and logic. The analysis is thus essentially qualitative in nature. Important causes are sought by identifying a cluster of related variables such as population growth, urbanization, or closing of the frontier. Important causes are most often found as clusters because of the phenomenon of convergence. The Industrial Revolution is a particularly important cause and can be observed as a cluster of mechanical and social inventions which converged to bring about mass production, the factory system, urban concentration, the modern corporation, mechanized warfare, new social classes, and numerous other effects. Factor analysis is one of the newer tools in statistics which exists to identify the common factor in those clusters of related variables which may be reduced to measurement. The inability to get many of the important variables in quantitative form is both the source of frustration and of challenge to the social scientist. Qualitative approximations are poor substitutes for the rigorous manipulation which is possible when variables can be measured in standard units. Error is introduced by qualitative analysis, and at best it is difficult, if not impossible, to check the reliability and validity of insight or random observations. Yet there is no immediate way out of this dilemma. Statistics alone do not demonstrate causation. Moreover, vast areas of social data have never been reduced to quantitative measurement. Many social scientists believe that there are variables which are not susceptible to measurement at all. Others take an opposite view and say that it should be possible to measure all of the changing relationships in a system of cause-effect variations. This is not the place to argue this controversy. For the moment, it is enough to acknowledge that qualitative and quantitative analysis should continue, and the skills of each may be employed to probe the complex problem of functional relationships in social change.

THE SEARCH FOR CAUSATIVE FACTORS

The problem of social causation has long been of central interest to sociology. Numerous factors have been singled out as having the primary or most important role in determining social change. These causative factors have been located within the range of the main classifications which were set forth —the geographic, biological, group, and cultural influences. In an effort to explain social change, social theorists have commonly assumed one-sided causation. The history of social theory is largely a series of statements asserting that some one factor is the sole cause of social change. These notions have been called determinisms. To say that the stars determine the course of men and nations is to assign sole weight to *one* factor. It is characteristic of these notions of determinism, and they are many, to assert that the sole factor operates according to its own inherent laws independently of all factors including man's will and desires. The simplicity of this conception has had a wide appeal. The most common determinisms and sub-branches are as follows:

1. Geographic determinism, which explains the character of culture and social life in terms of climate, rainfall, soil, or other geographic facts. (High civilizations develop only in the temperate zones where the vitality of the people is great.)
   a. Physical determinism, which explains social phenomena in terms of physical forces—stars, electricity, sunspots, atomic dust, etc. (Sunspots determine the outbreak of wars and revolutions.)
2. Biological determinism which holds cultural differences between groups to be expressions of innate individual differences in intelligence, capacities, and abilities. (It is the family blood that determines the character of the man.)
   a. Racial determinism, which explains societal characteristics as expression of innate differences in racial stock. (Race determines the capacity of a man and a nation to make high achievements.)
   b. Psychological determinism, which explains social reality in terms of innate tendencies, instincts, libido, temperament, or capacities. (Everything men do and have created can be traced back to sexual impulses.)
   c. Social Darwinism, a doctrine holding that struggle is part of the law of life which has been always the same from the beginning—ceaseless and inevitable struggle and competition, ceaseless and inevitable selection and rejection, ceaseless and inevitable progress. Kidd said that war is

part of this endless struggle.[8] (War and competition bring out the best in men and remove the weak and incompetent nations.)

3. Cultural determinism, which explains that society is a social product produced by such parts of culture as the folkways, mores, and institutions which reside in the culture base.

   a. Religious determinism, which explains social characteristics as the result of religious ideals and practices. (The moral life of the community is determined by the church.)

   b. Political determinism, which explains the distinctive quality of a society as the result of political ideals and practices. (Everything boils down to politics. The politicians are responsible for social change.)

   c. Economic determinism, which holds that the economic factor molds the social institutions. (The big financiers make the important decisions which determine the direction of society.)

   d. Technological determinism, which stresses that society is a product of the technology which operates within it. (The steam engine was the most important element in creating modern civilization.)

   e. Familial determinism—The family is the basic social institution which determines the quality of the culture. (The character of all institutions rests upon the family, the basic institution.)

These forms of determinism do not exhaust the list of single-factor theories of social change. A comprehensive inventory can be found in such books as N. L. Sims's *The Problem of Social Change*[9] or Pitirim Sorokin's *Contemporary Sociological Theories*.[10] The tremendous effort to define causes of social change is testimony to the intensity of interest in this subject. All of it stands as a monument to the variety of factors which interplay in society. It has become abundantly clear that no one factor is responsible for all social phenomena. Modern thinking embraces a pluralistic conception of many factors interacting to produce specific patterns. In mathematical terms, a dependent variable is a function of one or more independent variables ($y = f(x)$). In a purely methodological way, it is necessary in the beginning to isolate a definite social variable and then to study its functional relationship to those phenomena which are believed to be causally related to it, thus $y = f(x_1 \ x_2 \ . \ . \ . \ x_n)$. The emphasis is upon important factors with which dependent variable is most highly correlated. It will be recalled that an "important factor" is one to which a large part of the variation in a dependent variable may be attributed.

The concept of functional relationship presents the possibility of treating any factor as a variable and trying to find with what phenomena it is correlated and to what extent. Where marked interdependence is suspected, the function may be inverted from $y = f(x)$ to $x = f(y)$, that is, taking an "independent" variable and treating it as a dependent variable. For instance, the economic factor may be presumed to be an independent variable and it may be studied to find out to what extent it is correlated with certain re-

[8] Benjamin Kidd, *Social Evolution* (New York, Macmillan, 1894), p. 9.
[9] N. L. Sims, *The Problem of Social Change* (New York, Crowell, 1939).
[10] Pitirim Sorokin, *Contemporary Sociological Theories* (New York, Harper, 1928).

ligious phenomena. In another case, religious phenomena may be assumed to be an independent variable which is correlated with certain economic phenomena. Two outstanding social theories are constructed on these different interpretations of the function between these two variables. Karl Marx took the economic factor as an independent variable and traced correlations with religious and other institutional variables. Max Weber took the religious factor as an independent variable and related it to changes in the economic system.[11]

In this section we have elected to trace the theories which relate the economic and technological factors to such aspects of society as its social institutions, its division of labor, and its dominant habits of thought and action. Most of the theorists who are described hold either that the economic factor is the primary one which determines all the others or that it is the most important one among many which influence the social processes. Primacy may mean either (a) that this factor is the first in a causal chain which determines all the other social phenomena, or (b) that its influence upon social phenomena is far greater than that of other factors (say, correlates 0.90 in a functional relationship with a dependent variable, thus accounting for 81 per cent of the variation). This leaves 19 per cent of the variation due to other factors. The first usage of primacy bases interpretation on the conception of a single-factor determinism and of irreversible causal relations; the second embraces a functional conception of a system of interacting variables. Most of the theorists discussed below have accepted primacy in the first sense, that is, as the determiner of all other social phenomena in the causal chain.

Theory of Economic Materialism

The quest for laws of social change began among the Greeks and Romans and persists to the present time. Physical and biological scientists have demonstrated in numerous discoveries that the world of nature moves according to many principles of order. Newton's discovery of the universal law of gravitation and Darwin's discovery of the laws of biological evolution awakened suppositions that society must itself have similar laws underlying its growth and development. One of many men who sought the key to history

[11] Max Weber, *The Protestant Ethic and the Spirit of Capitalism,* trans. by Talcott Parsons (London, George Allen & Unwin, 1930). This study is part of a much broader analysis of capitalism and of religion. It attempts to show that the attitudes of capitalist mentality derived from the ethics of Calvinistic Protestantism. Religious influence is explained as one of the significant influences (independent factor) in the rise of capitalism (dependent factor).

Other important references include: *From Max Weber: Essays in Sociology,* trans. by H. H. Gerth and C. W. Mills (New York, Oxford University Press, 1946); Max Weber, *The Theory of Social and Economic Organization* trans. by T. Parsons and A. M. Henderson (London, Hodge & Co., 1947), pp. 8–55; R. Bendix, "Max Weber's Interpretation of Conduct and History," *American Journal of Sociology,* Vol. I (May, 1946), pp. 518–526.

was Karl Marx (Ger., 1818–83). Marx's own summary of his theoretical position throws light on the way he came to rest his entire thinking on the factor of economic organization. He wrote this summary of his views:[12]

> The general conclusions at which I arrived and which, once reached, continued to serve as the leading thread in my studies, may be briefly summed up as follows: In the social production which men carry on they enter into definite relations that are indispensable and independent of their will; these relations of production correspond to a definite stage of development of their material powers of production. The sum total of these relations of production constitutes the economic structure of society—the real foundation, on which rise legal and political superstructures and to which correspond definite forms of social consciousness. The mode of production in material life determines the general character of the social, political and spiritual processes of life. It is not the consciousness of men that determines their existence, but, on the contrary, their social existence determines their consciousness.
>
> At a certain stage of their development, the material forces of production in society come in conflict with the existing relations of production, or what is but a legal expression for the same thing—with the property relations within which they had been at work before. From forms of development of the forces of production these relations turn into their fetters. Then comes the period of social revolution. With the change of the economic foundation the entire immense superstructure is more or less rapidly transformed. In considering such transformations the distinction should always be made between the material transformation of the economic conditions of production which can be determined with the precision of natural science and the legal, political, religious, aesthetic or philosophic—in short ideological forms in which men become conscious of this conflict and fight it out. Just as our opinion of an individual is not based on what he thinks of himself, so can we not judge of such a period of transformation by its own consciousness; on the contrary, this consciousness must rather be explained from the contradictions of material life, from the existing conflict between the social forces of production and the relations of production. No social order ever disappears before all the productive forces, for which there is room in it, have been developed; and new higher relations of production never appear before the material conditions of their existence have matured in the womb of the old society. Therefore, mankind always takes up only such problems as it can solve; since, looking at the matter more closely, we will always find that the problem itself arises when the material conditions necessary for its solution already exist or are at least in the process of formation. In broad outlines we can designate the Asiatic, the ancient, the feudal, and the modern bourgeois methods of production as so many epochs in the progress of economic formation of society. The bourgeois relations of production are the last antagonistic form of the social process of production—antagonistic not in the sense of individual antagonism, but of one arising from conditions surrounding the life of individuals in society; at the same time the productive forces developing in the womb of bourgeois society create the material conditions for the solution of that antagonism. This social formation constitutes, therefore, the closing chapter of the prehistoric stage of human society.

[12] Karl Marx, *A Contribution to the Critique of Political Economy,* trans. by Stone (New York, International Library Publishing Co., 1904), pp. 11–13.

Here we have an *economic interpretation of history*. To this interpretation Marx coupled a doctrine of class struggle. In 1847 *The Communist Manifesto* written with Friedrich Engels proclaimed:[13]

The history of all hitherto existing society is the history of class struggle.

Freeman and slave, patrician and plebeian, lord and serf, guildmaster and journeyman, in a word, oppressor and oppressed, stood in constant opposition to one another, carried on an uninterrupted, now hidden, now open fight, a fight that each time ended either in a revolutionary reconstitution of society at large, or in the common ruin of the contending classes. . . . The modern bourgeois society that has sprouted from the ruins of feudal society, has not done away with class antagonisms. . . . Society as a whole is more and more splitting up into two great hostile camps, into two great classes directly facing each other: Bourgeoisie and Proletariat.

Here we can see how Marx has joined *an economic interpretation of history*[14] with a doctrine of *class struggle*.[15] Such is the essence of Marx's theoretical position. There is a belief in the evolution of society. This evolution is said to rest upon the mode of production which determines the character of all other social institutions. It is alleged that the antagonisms reflected in class struggles have been inherent in all other forms of production.[16] These antagonisms are to pass away when communism appears.

Economic Theory of Socialization

Thorstein Veblen (1857–1929), an American social economist, has greatly influenced contemporary thought by relating economic institutions to the social motives and habits which are interiorized in personality. We saw that for Marx the causal series began with changes in the techniques of produc-

[13] K. Marx and F. Engels, *The Communist Manifesto* (Chicago, Charles H. Kerr, 1940). There is a very large literature dealing with Marxian philosophy. Some of the most important works by Karl Marx include his *Capital* (Chicago, Charles H. Kerr, 1909); *The Poverty of Philosophy* (Chicago, Charles H. Kerr, 1910); *Der Historische Materialismus* (Leipzig, Alfred Kroener Verlag, 1932).

[14] In two letters written in 1890, Friedrich Engels, the lifelong collaborator of Marx, opposed the dogmatic interpretation: "Marx and I are ourselves partly to blame for the fact that the younger writers sometimes lay more stress on the economic side than is due to it. We had to emphasize this main principle in opposition to our adversaries, who denied it, and we had not always the time, the place, or the opportunity to allow the other elements involved in the interaction to come into their own rights."— Karl Marx and Friedrich Engels, *Selected Correspondence, 1846–1895* (New York, International Publishers, 1942), pp. 472–473, 477.

[15] Cf. Harold W. Pfautz "The Current Literature on Social Stratification, Critique and Bibliography," *American Journal of Sociology,* Vol. LVI (January, 1953), pp. 391–418.

[16] Bendix and Lipset point out that Marx thought of social class as a condition of group life which was constantly generated by the mode of production. Essential to its formation was the existence of a common "class enemy." Awareness of the enemy was an indispensable element, but he believed that this awareness would inevitably arise along with the growing contradictions in capitalism. See Reinhard Bendix and Seymour Martin Lipset, *Karl Marx' Theory of Social Class,* Reprint No. 52 in the Publications of the Institute of Industrial Relations (Berkeley, University of California, 1954), pp. 31–33.

tion (independent variable) which initiated changes in the economic structure of society (dependent variable). In turn, the economic structure (now an independent factor) shaped the "general character of these social, political, and spiritual processes of life" (dependent variables). Whereas Marx was more directly concerned with the relation of production to economic structure including implications of class struggle and political dynamics, Veblen was interested in the direct relation of the economic institutions to the habits of life and thought which are produced through socialization.[17] He said,[18]

Any community may be viewed as an industrial or economic mechanism, the structure of which is made up of what is called its economic institutions. These institutions are habitual methods of carrying on the life process of the community in contact with the material environment in which it lives. When given methods of unfolding human activity in this given environment have been elaborated in this way, the life of the community will express itself with some facility in these habitual directions.

Change in the community was seen to come chiefly from economic forces, because it was pecuniary pressure which brought about a readjustment of institutions in the modern industrial community. This was so because changes in the conditions of life come from altered methods of dealing with the environment. Such changes are not equitable throughout the group. An advance in technical methods, in population, or in industrial organization, will require at least some of the members of the community to change their life.[19]

Wherever the institution of private property is found, the economic struggle is characterized by a struggle between men for the possession of goods. This struggle for wealth is not substantially a struggle for subsistence in the modern economy. The motive that lies at the root of ownership is emulation. Wealth becomes the conventional basis of esteem and becomes also a requisite to self-respect. The individual within a community should possess as large a portion of goods as others with whom he is accustomed to class himself; otherwise, he shall have no peace of mind. If the standard changes toward a higher possession, then this gives rise to a new standard of sufficiency and a new pecuniary classification of himself as compared with his neighbors. The process is an invidious comparison of valuating persons with

17 Alvin Johnson writes of him: "In college Veblen read the standard textbooks on economics . . . but there is no evidence that then or at any later time orthodox economics appeared to him anything better than an apology for the dominant order. Nor was he drawn toward Marxism. A Kantian by training and instinct, he had little interest in the Hegelian dialectic either in its original idealistic form or in the materialistic adaptation by Marx. The Marxian antithesis of capitalist and proletariat, both defined in strictly economic terms, unsupported by any convincing sociological and psychological analysis of the character of these classes, appeared to Veblen too simple and abstract to be useful. . . . He had no interest in programs of reform."—*Encyclopedia of the Social Sciences* (New York, Macmillan, 1934), Vol. XV, p. 234.

18 Thorstein Veblen, *The Theory of the Leisure Class* (New York, Macmillan, 1912), p. 193.

19 *Ibid.,* p. 195.

respect to worth. The accepted end of human effort becomes the achievement of a favorable comparison with other men. Property becomes the most easily recognized evidence of success as distinguished from heroic or signal achievement. Purposeful effort comes to mean, primarily, effort directed toward the acquisition of more accumulated wealth. There is a restless straining to place an ever widening pecuniary interval between himself and the average standard.[20]

Man seeks in every act the accomplishment of some concrete end. He senses merit in serviceability or efficiency and demerit in futility, waste, or incapacity. This propensity may be called the instinct of workmanship.[21] The habitual comparison of one person with another in efficiency brings out an emulative or invidious comparison of persons. Esteem is gained by putting one's efficiency in evidence. In a predatory culture of exploit, the taking of life is honorable in the highest degree. Arms are honorable. Working with tools in industry is held in low esteem. The emergence of a leisure class coincides with the beginning of ownership. These two institutions result from the right to hold private property. In a superior pecuniary class, diligence and thrift become secondary to the demands of pecuniary emulation. Conspicuous leisure becomes a mark of esteem. Conspicuous expenditure, whether of goods or of services or human life, also becomes a mark of esteem if it is an expenditure of superfluities. The leisure class is the conservative class. They are not required by changes in industrial technique to forfeit their habits of life or their theoretical views of the external world. The conservatism of the wealthy class becomes recognized as a mark of respectability.[22]

The effect of the pecuniary interest and the pecuniary habit of mind is seen in those institutional enactments that make for security of property. The pecuniary classes not only act to conserve the accepted social scheme but also to shape industrial processes. The effect of the leisure class is felt not only upon social structure but upon individual members of society. The bases of esteem originated by this class become norms shaping habits of thought. The effect is brought about partly by a coercive educational adaptation and partly by repression or selective elimination of those who cannot adapt to the accepted scheme. The principles of pecuniary emulation thus become erected into canons of life which coerce men to their ends.[23]

Division-of-Labor Theory

Emile Durkheim (1858–1917), a French sociologist, identified division of labor as an important variable in determining the character of society. His study of social differentiation, *De la Division du Travail Social,* is a careful study of social solidarity. He treats division of labor as both an independent

---

[20] *Ibid.,* pp. 24–34.

[21] Thorstein Veblen, *The Instinct of Workmanship and the State of the Industrial Arts* (New York, Macmillan, 1914), pp. 1–37.

[22] Veblen, *The Theory of the Leisure Class,* p. 199.

[23] *Ibid.,* p. 210.

and dependent variable. In his first analysis, he tries to correlate the impact of division of labor on society. The changes in the division of labor are identified as ranging from a very slight division, such as occurs in many primitive societies, to the intense divison of modern industrial societies. Societies with a slight division of labor are said to be possessed of a "mechanist solidarity" based on homogeneity of individuals. The tie which binds them in one solid unity is strong unanimity of public opinion, based on mental and moral homogeneity. Tradition dominates and there is a lack of individuality. The differences brought into society are due only to differences in the heredity of the members. Communal property becomes the basis for economic organization and important social affairs and acts of justice are enacted by the whole body of the group in the public meetings of its members. Local and tribal patriotism are strong sentiments. Religious belief centers in impersonal totemic force free from personality.[24]

The division of labor increases with the process of time. This is a historical trend which can be observed in societies with an advancing technology. When division of labor becomes great, vast changes are observed in human behavior, in law, in social solidarity, in political regime, economic organization, and in religion and ideology.[25]

When division of labor becomes great, it brings about an "organic solidarity" with the following changes:

1. There is a decrease of tradition and the increase of individuality in tastes, beliefs, opinions, and morals.
2. There is an increase of individual freedom and increase of contractual law and relationships based on free agreement of parties.
3. Solid unity of a group is based on non-self-sufficiency of heterogeneous individuals caused by division of labor. They now "need" one another and cannot exist without co-operation, because everybody does only a special part of the work. Thus is "mechanistic" solidarity transformed into the "organic."
4. Political functions become more specialized and there is an increase of contractual relationships between government and citizens.
5. The economic organization of society is characterized by private property, economic individualism, and contractual co-operation. The "open door" system which permits everybody to enter any occupation prevails.
6. There is an "individualism" and "personalization" of God which is accompanied by a universalization of religion.
7. Local and tribal patriotism wanes and there is an increase of cosmopolitanism or internationalism.[26]

[24] Emile Durkheim, *On the Division of Labor in Society,* trans. by George Simpson (New York, Macmillan, 1933).
Cf. Howard Becker, "Constructive Typology in the Social Science," *American Sociological Review,* Vol. V, No. 1 (February, 1940) pp. 40–55; reprinted in Harry Elmer Barnes, Howard Becker, and Frances Bennett Becker, eds., *Contemporary Social Theory* (New York, Appleton-Century, 1940), Part I.
[25] For a thorough analysis of Durkheim's works, see Talcott Parsons, *The Structure of Social Action* (New York, McGraw-Hill, 1937), pp. 301–470.
[26] Cf. Ferdinand Tönnies, *Gemeinschaft and Gesellschaft,* 1st ed., 1887, translated and edited by Charles P. Loomis as *Fundamental Concepts of Sociology* (New York,

Social-Differentiation Theory

Among modern American sociologists, MacIver and Page have emphasized the role of differentiation in social change. Like Durkheim, they find in differentiation the "clue" to an evolutionary process in history. This process is not to be regarded as a unilineal sequence in which specific institutions of the simpler societies pass by similar processes into specific institutions of the more advanced societies. Such a view overlooks the fact that differentiation may take a multitude of forms, in many different social systems. They caution against drawing tight parallels between biological and social evolution. With these reservations, social evolution is seen as an all-embracing social process in which society may be observed as undergoing increasing specialization of organs or units within a social system. This differentiation is not to be understood as though it meant or implied progress. Nor is there anything inevitable about such an increasing specialization. It is simply asserted that a process of differentiation does manifest itself in the following ways:

a. A greater division of labor, so that the energy or more individuals is concentrated on more specific tasks and so that thereby a more elaborate system of co-operation, a more intricate nexus of functional relationships, is sustained in the group.

b. An increase in the number and the variety of functional associations and institutions, so that each is more defined or more limited in the range or character of its service; and

c. A greater diversity and refinement in the instruments of social communication, perhaps above all in the medium of language.[27]

The main line of social evolution may be traced from primitive societies to modern "advanced" societies. It reveals a coherence of successive stages from

Communal Customs
   The fusion of political-economic-familial-cultural usages, which pass into
Differentiated Communal Institutions
   The distinctive forms of political, economic, familial, religious, cultural procedures which become embodied in
Differentiated Associations
   The state, the economic corporation, the family, the church, the school, etc.

American Book, 1940). Translation of the Gemeinschaft and Gesellschaft concepts into a sociometric rating scale has been made and applied in an analysis of rural organization. For this interesting scientific application, see Charles P. Loomis and J. Allan Beegle, *Rural Social Systems* (Englewood Cliffs, N.J., Prentice Hall, 1950).

See also C. H. Cooley, *Social Organization* (New York, Scribner, 1929). The rapid transition of our society from a predominantly rural to a predominantly urban society has challenged many social theorists. Von Wiese and Becker see the transition as from a sacred to a secular society; MacIver as from communal to associational, and Shaler as from sentimental to rational.

[27] Robert M. MacIver and Charles H. Page, *Society: An Introductory Analysis* (New York, Rinehart, 1949), p. 527.

The passage from one stage to another is accompanied by a momentous transformation of the social structure. Although there are many social changes which may seem undirected and inconsequential, there are others which clearly fall within an evolutionary process. This indicates that there are great persistent forces underlying many social changes which may seem to be mere events in the historical flux.[28]

Socio-Cultural Theory of Social Change

A socio-cultural theory of social change is probably the most widely accepted theory among social scientists today. The systematic analysis of culture may be said to stem from the work of E. B. Tylor and William Graham Sumner.[29] A large literature has now been accumulated in which the anthropologist has contributed a substantial body of field work on primitive societies.[30] There is little doubt that the greatest contribution using this approach to social change has been made by William F. Ogburn.[31] His theoretical conception of the subject is fully stated in his classic volume published in 1922, with additions made in the 1950 edition of the book and in Chapter 2 of the present volume. The major elements of his theory of social change may be briefly summarized as follows: (1) Social change is largely explained by changes in culture, other causes of change (for example, geographical and biological) being of lesser significance. (2) The chief factors that explain cultural change or evolution are invention, accumulation, diffusion, and adjustment. Of these factors, invention is the central one. (3) In the making of inventions, several influences are of especial importance, namely, mental ability, demand, and the existence of other cultural elements out of which an invention may be made (the latter being known in the aggregate as the *culture base*). (4) Inventions and discoveries are frequently made inde-

[28] *Ibid.,* p. 598.

[29] William G. Sumner, *Folkways* (Boston, Ginn, 1906); E. B. Tylor, *Primitive Culture* (New York, Holt, 1889).

[30] Clark Wissler, *Man and Culture* (New York, Crowell, 1923); Robert H. Lowie, *An Introduction to Cultural Anthropology* (New York, Rinehart, 1940); Alexander A. Goldenweiser, *History, Psychology and Culture* (New York, Knopf, 1933); Ralph Linton, *The Study of Man* (New York, Appleton-Century-Crofts, 1936); M. J. Herskovits, *Acculturation: The Study of Culture Contact* (New York, J. J. Augustin, 1938); George Peter Murdock, "The Cross-Cultural Survey," *American Sociological Review* (June, 1940), pp. 361–370; A. L. Kroeber, *Configurations of Culture Growth* (Los Angeles and Berkeley, University of Southern California Press, 1944); Bronislaw Malinowski *The Dynamics of Culture Change* (New Haven, Yale University Press, 1945); Ralph Linton, ed., *The Science of Man in the World Crisis* (New York, Columbia University Press, 1945); H. G. Barnett, *Innovation, The Basis of Cultural Change* (New York, McGraw-Hill, 1953); Margaret Mead and Rhoda Metraux, eds., *The Study of Culture at a Distance* (Chicago, University of Chicago Press, 1954); A. L. Kroeber, ed., *Anthropology Today: An Encyclopedic Inventory* (Chicago, University of Chicago Press, 1953); Leslie A. White, *The Science of Culture* (New York, Farrar, Straus, 1949).

[31] Ogburn, *Social Change* (New York, B. W. Huebsch, 1922; Viking Press, 1950). In the 1950 edition Part VI, "Social Evolution, Reconsidered," has been added.

pendently by two or more persons, which shows a common dependence on the same culture base. (5) The size of the existing stock of cultural items (the culture base) bears an important relation to the rate of cultural change; when the culture base is small, inventions tend to be few; when it is large, inventions are many. (6) Adjustment to an invention takes note of the fact that culture is a network of interrelationships, hence many customs and institutions will often need to "adjust" to an invention if the latter is important. Adjustment to an invention may sometimes take the form of the creation of a new social invention. (7) Much factual evidence exists to substantiate the generalization that the rate of cultural change is accelerating. While earlier emphasized by Ogburn, this principle has been further discussed and illustrated by developments of the 1950's in Chapter 3 of the present volume. And (8) other subjects of importance to cultural change—for example, the phenomena of *dispersion* (the dispersing effects of inventions) and of *convergence* (the results which have developed from combined effects of different social factors including inventions)—have been discussed in Chapter 2 of the present volume.[32]

Extended comment on these major elements of Ogburn's theory of social change are not made here since they receive much discussion, often with citing of examples, elsewhere in this volume. For example, the hypothesis of cultural lag is discussed in Chapter 17, and many examples of the dispersing effects of inventions are presented in the chapters which follow directly after this one.

THE SEARCH FOR PATTERNS OF CHANGE WITHIN SOCIETY

The Description of Trends

A basic effort in building scientific knowledge of social change is the establishment of reliable social trends. Much of the intelligent direction of human affairs depends on the careful collection and analysis of data to reveal the magnitude and changes exhibited by such selected social variables as birth, deaths, school enrollments, accidents, and wages.[33] Time-series analysis has been developed in statistics as a way of depicting an arrangement of data in accordance with its time of occurrence. The analysis of the time series consists of the description and measurement of the various changes or movements as they appear in the series during a period of time. The most common changes or movements may be classified as:

[32] Other ideas introduced in Ogburn's early volume (1922) included the following: the subject of resistances to inventions (discussed in the preceding chapter of the present volume), and the adjustment of human nature and culture (which is in part discussed in Chapter 18 of the present volume).

[33] "Recent Social Changes Issue," *American Journal of Sociology,* Vol. XLVII (May, 1942). This entire issue is given over to recent social changes. See *Recent Social Trends in the United States* (New York, McGraw-Hill, 1933).

1. Secular trend or long-time growth or decline over a period of perhaps ten years or more. (Patterns of technological change, scientific advance, growth of population, etc.)

2. Seasonal variation of the more or less regular movement within a twelve month period. (Seasonal unemployment, births, deaths, suicides, types of crimes.)

3. Cyclical movement refers to the rise and fall of some series of data. This movement varies in time, length, and intensity. (Business activity, style changes, cycle in the life of a nation or culture.)

4. Random or accidental variations including such unusual movements as disasters, fads, or strikes.

A wide range of social data has been subjected to time-series analysis by demographers, economic statisticians, and many other research workers. The analysis shows that various types of curves may be derived from different series of data. The most frequent are the straight line and the ogive or normal growth curve. Fitting data to curves is an important tool of analysis, because such a technique often defines the nature of variables which were formerly obscure. Moreover, as these variables are identified, it is possible to make assumptions about future change and to project trend lines on these assumptions.[34]

The Forecast of Change

The researcher often seeks to forecast future change in some social variable. Hypotheses help him in selecting the relevant factors which influence the predicted variable. They underly his choice of assumptions (future conditions of maximum likelihood). If his hypotheses prove valid and his grounds for prediction do match future events, his prediction will approximate the actual variation. An illustration of a time-series analysis and a forecast of population and enrollment trends is depicted in the work of Calvin F. Schmid and associates. These workers attempted to assess as precisely as possible student enrollment in kindergarten, elementary and secondary schools, and in various types of institutions of higher learning in the State of

[34] Bross has pointed out three types of prediction which may arise from knowledge of the variation in a single variable. These are persistence prediction, trajectory prediction, and cyclic prediction. *Persistence prediction* means nothing more than the prediction that there will be no change and is based on stable characteristics which persist over a period of time (as would be shown by a straight line without slope); *trajectory prediction* is based on a changing variable, but the extent of the change is stable (secular trend, growth curve, seasonal variation); and *cyclic prediction* assumes cycles or patterns of events that are stable. The method has been used in predicting the return of comets, the occurrence of sunspots, insect plagues, high and low agricultural yield, weather, stock prices, and the course of civilization. "In going from Persistence to Cyclic Prediction there is a utilization of more and more data. The former needs only the most recent occurrence of the event, while in the latter the available historical information is used."—Irvin D. J. Bross, *Design for Decision* (New York, Macmillan, 1953), pp. 34–36.

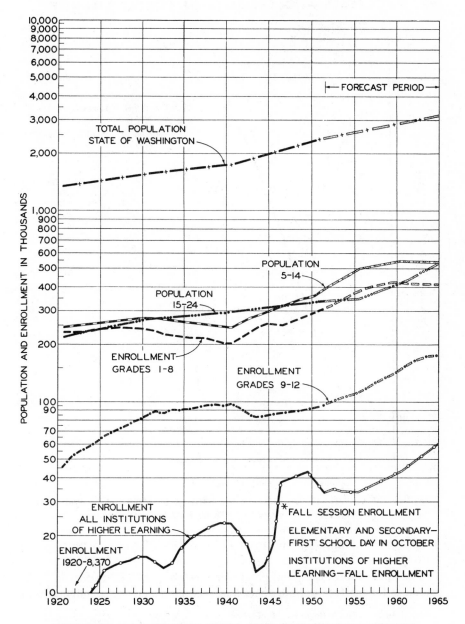

POPULATION AND ENROLLMENT TRENDS, STATE OF WASHINGTON, 1920–1965

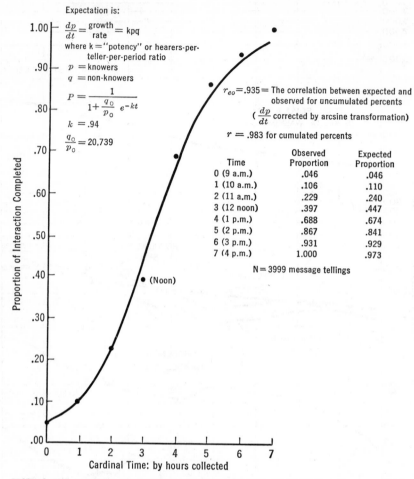

Expectation is:

$$\frac{dp}{dt} = \frac{\text{growth}}{\text{rate}} = kpq$$

where k = "potency" or hearers-per-
teller-per-period ratio

p = knowers
q = non-knowers

$$P = \frac{1}{1 + \frac{q_0}{p_0} e^{-kt}}$$

$k = .94$

$\frac{q_0}{p_0} = 20{,}739$

$r_{eo} = .935$ = The correlation between expected and
observed for uncumulated percents

($\frac{dp}{dt}$ corrected by arcsine transformation)

$r = .983$ for cumulated percents

Time	Observed Proportion	Expected Proportion
0 (9 a.m.)	.046	.046
1 (10 a.m.)	.106	.110
2 (11 a.m.)	.229	.240
3 (12 noon)	.397	.447
4 (1 p.m.)	.688	.674
5 (2 p.m.)	.867	.841
6 (3 p.m.)	.931	.929
7 (4 p.m.)	1.000	.973

N = 3999 message tellings

Proportion of Interaction Completed

(Noon)

Cardinal Time: by hours collected

TESTING THE LOGISTIC HYPOTHESIS FOR THE GROWTH OF DIFFUSING BY THE INTER-ACTING OF A GROUP OF PERSONS TO EACH OTHER

Washington during the period from 1955 to 1965. The chart on page 89 portrays the past trends from 1920–54 and the forecasts for 1955–65.[35]

This kind of forecasting has great value to school administrators in making plans for the future. Many decisions rest upon such data, ranging from

[35] Calvin F. Schmid, Earle H. MacCannel, and Vincent A. Miller, *Enrollment Forecasts, State of Washington* (Seattle, State Census Board, 1954). Forecasts are based on past trends and on the following assumptions: (*a*) Economic conditions will continue on approximately the same level as those existing at the present time; (*b*) a yearly average of net immigration in the total population of approximately 25,000; (*c*) a slightly declining trend in mortality and fertility; (*d*) there will be no war; and (*e*) Selective Service policies will remain as they were in the fall of 1954.

This example is associative prediction because it uses the data from other events (enrollment in elementary and secondary schools) to predict a second type of event (enrollment in higher institutions). See Bross, *op. cit.,* p. 36.

the planning and location of buildings, the recruiting of staff, and the revision of curricula, to methods of school finance.

The Search for Principles of Social Change

Social scientists often set out a theory or a hypothesis predicting the shape of a distribution, hoping to arrive at a general statement or principle of social change which holds under given conditions. Data are gathered to test the distribution of one or more variables. When predicted and observed data coincide, the scientist has a proof for his hypothesis.[36] The advance of sampling methods which economize research effort has greatly stimulated this kind of research endeavor. In Chapter 3 were cited various types of data which support the principle of acceleration of social change. The work of Stuart C. Dodd on testing the diffusion of a message over time is another example of this search.[37] The chart on page 90 illustrates the use of a mathematical model based on the hypothesis that a message diffuses among a group of interacting persons according to an S-shaped growth curve. The data plotted on the graph are from an experiment in which 184 persons were motivated in a prize contest to interact by trading messages. The correlation index between the observed data and the logistic expectation in distribution form was .94 (and .99 in cumulative form). It may be concluded that the logistic hypothesis was confirmed under the conditions specified.

The Search for Universal Processes of Change

Social changes may be observed to occur in similar forms of social interaction or *processes*. A social process refers to continuous change taking place in a *definite manner* through the operation of variables within some sociocultural system. The most common among many social processes which have been identified are competition, co-operation, conflict, accommodation, and assimilation. Change is often observed to occur in particular sequences of these processes. For example, two nations may be observed to be simply trade *competitors* until some new element enters and they enter into hostile *conflict*. Cold war gives way to a shooting war. Then, as war becomes increasingly disagreeable, a surrender is arranged and a treaty signed. The conflicting parties work out an *accommodation* of their interests, and per-

[36] This is analogue prediction. It sets up a correspondence between two sets of events. One of the sets is simple, or at least familiar, and consequently predictions can be made for the set of events. The analogues of these predictions are then made from the second set. A mathematical analogy (or model) may be constructed as shown in the illustrated case and the performance of the model is predicted. *Ibid,* pp. 37–38.

[37] This experiment is one in a series of experiments made by S. C. Dodd to test the interactance hypothesis. The full report may be found in "Controlled Experiments on Interacting," as read to the Sociological Research Association at Atlantic City, September 2, 1952. The report is available from the Washington Public Opinion Laboratory, University of Washington, Seattle.

haps, in time, begin to *co-operate* as they face a common enemy together. They begin to exchange ideas and resources in a common cause and *assimilate* the different parts of their separate cultures. The unity of the culture continues and competition remains at a low level until new changes cause them to struggle for wants that each greatly desires.

George Simmel (Fr., 1858–1918) and Leopold von Wiese (Ger., 1876–) are most closely associated with the development of a systematics of social process. Simmel held that the proper object of sociology, as a specific science, is the study of the *forms* of social interaction as contrasted with its *contents*. The content and form represent quite separate phenomena or views of the phenomena. The same forms of human relationship may have different social content; the same social content may have different forms of social relationship. Each of the forms of social interaction (domination, subordination, competition, imitation, division of labor, conflict, etc.) is found in such diverse social groups as a business organization, family, a criminal gang, a religious community, or a mob. The central task of sociology is to analyze and describe the various forms and processes in which social phenomena reveal themselves.[38]

Like Simmel, von Wiese accepted this definition of sociology and proceeded to identify about 650 forms of human relationship.[39] He made two main divisions of these forms by discriminating between interindividual relations and intergroup relations.

A brief outline follows:

INTERINDIVIDUAL RELATIONS
1. *Toward*   *each other*
        Contact, approach, adaptation, combination, and union.
2. *Away*   *from each other.*
        Competition, opposition and conflict
3. *Mixed*   *form*
        (Relations partly toward, partly away).

INTERGROUP RELATIONS
1. *Differentiating processes*
   Social promotion, degradation, domination, subordination, stratification, selection, and individuation.
2. *Integrating processes*
   Uniformization, stabilization, crystallization, and socialization.
3. *Destructive processes*
   Exploitation, corruption, formalization, commercialization, radicalization, spoliation.
4. *Modifying-constructive processes*
   Institutionalization, professionalization, liberation.

[38] N. J. Spykman, *The Social Theory of Georg Simmel* (Chicago, University of Chicago Press, 1925).
[39] Leopold von Wiese, *Allgemeine Sociologie* Teil I (Munchen, Beziehungslehie 1924), Chs. I and II. For a description in English, see von Wiese, *Systematic Sociology,* adapted and amplified by Howard Becker (New York, Wiley, 1932).

The classification of von Wiese is probably the most systematic effort yet made to define social processes. Sociologists have submitted many of these processes to various tests and have found that they commonly suffer from ambiguity and overlapping. Their utility is definitely limited when lifted from the content of the social phenomena which they seek to explain. However, when used as a conceptual tool for qualitative analysis of specific social content, some of these social forms have been most helpful in understanding patterns of change. Almost every introductory text in sociology retains the concepts of competition, co-operation, conflict, accommodation, and assimilation.[40] In addition, there will be found such concepts from human ecology as centralization and decentralization, invasion, succession, specialization, and segregation.[41] Each of these ecological processes has helped to relate social changes to both space and time.

THE SEARCH FOR THE DIRECTION OF SOCIETY

The theory relating to direction of specific changes within society has been reviewed. There remains the ever challenging question of whether there are over-all changes in human society which take place in a specific direction and according to some underlying law. Many theorists have believed that there are such over-all laws of societal direction. These may be identified as linear, successive stage, and cyclical theories.

Linear Theories

The characteristic feature of linear theories is the positing of a total movement which constantly advances toward a definite goal. Social thought of the second half of the nineteenth century was marked by such linear conceptions. The drawing of parallels between biological evolution and social change produced a conviction that human progress was the normal quality of social change.[42] The notion took hold in the nineteenth century, that regardless of periodic setbacks, the evolution of society was always toward a "better" life.[43]

Modern social thought is critical of all analogies between biological evo-

[40] A thorough description of social processes may be found in Joyce O. Hertzler, *Society in Action* (New York, Dryden Press, 1954).

[41] R. E. Park, E. W. Burgess, and R. D. McKenzie, *The City* (Chicago, The University of Chicago Press, 1925). Original statement of the zonal hypothesis of the city (pp. 47–58) and ecological processes observed in the growth of a city. For a thorough review of the ecological processes, see A. B. Hollingshead "Human Ecology" in Alfred McClung Lee, ed., *New Outline of the Principles of Sociology* (New York, Barnes and Noble, 1946), pp. 66–118.

[42] Morris Ginsberg, *The Idea of Progress, A Revaluation* (London, Methuen, 1953), p. 1. Cf. Herbert Spencer, *The Study of Sociology* (New York, D. Appleton and Co., 1895).

[43] Carl Becker, "Progress," *Encyclopedia of Social Science,* Vol. 12 (New York, Macmillan, 1933), pp. 495–499; C. Becker, *Progress and Power* (Stanford, Stanford University Press, 1936); J. O. Hertzler, *Social Progress* (New York, Century, 1928); A. J. Todd, *Theories of Social Progress* (London, Macmillan, 1928); Hornell Hart, *The Technique of Social Progress* (New York, Holt, 1931).

lution and social change.[44] It is believed that social phenomena follow their own distinctive patterns. The idea of progress has been shown to be an ethical concept and that the residing notions of "happier," "wealthier," and so on, are relative to individual and group valuations. As goals or ends they lie outside the realm of science. An acceptable theory may speak only of a relative trend or tendency. The impact of modern technology is a central interest of many modern theorists. There is wide consensus that the major problems of modern society are either initiated by or at least strongly affected by technological change. The American cultural anthropologist Ralph Linton comes to a similar conclusion and presents a modern linear theory. He suggests that the culture content of any society may be divided into three categories. The first of these includes *Universals,* the learned responses that are common to all sane adult members of the society. To this category would be assigned such elements as use of a particular language, modes of dress and housing, and common ideals or values. Second, *Specialties,* those elements of culture which are shared by certain recognized groups of individuals and are created because of the division of labor in the society. Behavior and technics of the different occupational groups fit this category. Although the elements of the Specialties are not shared by the entire society, the benefits arising from them are shared, and the entire society knows about the benefits which come from the end products of each activity. The *Alternatives* are traits which are shared by certain persons and groups but which are not common to all members of the society or even to all members of any one of the socially recognized categories. Different ways of thinking and acting fall into this category.[45] In our culture these could be illustrated by the patriarchal, matriarchal, and democratic patterns of family life, the wide range of religious thought and habit, or the use of different forms of communication and transportation.

Linton explains that:[46]

. . . all cultures consist of two parts, a solid, well-integrated and fairly stable core, consisting of the mutually adapted *Universals* and *Specialties,* and a fluid, largely unintegrated, and constantly changing zone of *Alternatives* which surrounds this core. It is the core which gives a culture its form and basic patterns at each point in history, while the presence of the fluid zone gives it its capacity for growth and adaptation.

A constant interchange takes place between Alternatives and the core traits. Alternatives which prove more satisfactory may pass into the core and replace a core trait. The core trait is drawn into the Alternatives and may

[44] An able review of the evolutionary ideas and their impact on American sociology is found in Robert E. L. Faris, "Evolution and American Sociology," in Stow Persons, ed., *Evolutionary Thought in America* (New Haven, Yale University Press, 1950), pp. 160–180. An interesting modern statement of social evolution is V. Gordon Childe, *Social Evolution* (London, Watt & Co., 1951).

[45] Ralph Linton. *The Study of Man,* pp. 272–274.

[46] *Ibid.,* p. 282.

finally drop out of the culture. Watching fashions in dress would give an observer an opportunity to see this occur rather quickly and frequently.

The proportion between Alternatives and the core of Universals and Specialties may vary widely. The presence of Alternatives competing for entry into the core and a balanced rate of interchange is helpful. This is the precondition for a dynamic society. But there is real danger in a competing zone of Alternatives that grows proportionately larger than some optimum relationship to the core. As new traits are accepted, they draw out certain traits which were formerly Universal and Specialties. As the core is reduced, the culture increasingly loses pattern and coherence. In a rapidly changing society like our own, the danger is that Alternatives which are introduced at an increasing rate will reduce the core below a level sufficient for common participation in the culture. A group of people function as a society only as the elements which form the core of their culture enable them to share in a community of habits and ideas. So far as this does not exist, the possibility of co-operative behavior is reduced and finally eliminated. The breakdown of small local units and the rise of ever greater urban masses has impeded the assimilation of new traits to pre-existing patterns. Urban life emphasizes anonymity and individuality, and as such increases patterns of life based on *Alternatives*. Linton predicts that, "We are rapidly approaching the point where there will no longer be enough items on which all members of the society agree to provide the culture with form and pattern."[47]

These linear theories of the increasingly differentiated society have been interpreted in terms of their consequences for the development of personality:[48]

In the more advanced social system, with its specializations, its cultural diversities, its numerous groups and associations, its mingling of many elements into a complex whole, we cannot expect to find the all embracing solidarity of a simpler society. A nation has inevitably a type of unity different from that of a clan or a tribe. The individual has to choose his cultural loyalties, to maintain his own values, to decide his own attachments, in far greater measure. He must seek for the *common* to which he really belongs, the common to which his individuality responds. The unity of the social group is not to be identified with that of one cultural community. He can share in both kinds, but he has to adjust for himself the one loyalty to the other. *Society no longer integrates all his values for him*—that becomes the task of his own integrating personality.

Successive-Stage Theories

Many anthropologists and sociologists have suggested that every society must develop through a series of growth stages.

1. August Comte (Fr., 1798–1857) is often called the father of sociology, for it was he who defined the specialization of interest which led to the express development of sociology as a specific social science. Comte formulated a conception of society based on a belief in a law of three stages. Society was

[47] *Ibid.*, p. 284.
[48] MacIver and Page, *op. cit.*, pp. 634–635.

regarded as a dynamic social unity fulfilling itself through a series of evolutionary stages, the theological, metaphysical, and positive. Each stage was seen as a dominant thought form. It was this thought form, not merely the type of economic or political organization, which expressed the fundamental principle of social solidarity in each epoch. By assembling an array of historical evidence, Comte proceeded to show that man began to seek answers to his questions through a theological explanation; that this explanation gradually lost its essential theological elements and was at length supplanted by metaphysics. Metaphysics represented an attempt to discover through the process of reason the essence of phenomena. Comte said metaphysics was now giving way in Western society to the final or positive stage in which the mind would abandon its search for essences and absolutes and content itself with the discovery of relationships between phenomena, that is, with the construction of sciences.[49]

This conception has proved stimulating to the development of scientific methods in social science. However, Comte's three stages have not been shown to be stages of society but modal tendencies in the development of human attitudes. As such, the three stages remain as useful constructs in a sociology of knowledge. It is interesting to note that Comte believed the positive stage would be crowned by a spiritual or intellectual unification of society.

2. Lewis H. Morgan in America set out a sequence of so-called "ethical periods" and formulated criteria by which the position of any observable society in the sequence could be recognized. Three periods were designated Savagery, Barbarism, and Civilization, with subdivision of lower, middle, and upper "status." He said each society has been guided by a natural law.[50] His position was like that of E. B. Tylor in England who said, "Human institutions, like stratified rocks, succeed each other in series substantially uniform over the Globe, independent of what seems the comparatively superficial difference of race and language, but shaped by similar human nature."[51]

3. In Germany F. Müller-Lyer set forth his own statement of culture stages and showed how economies evolved from hunting and gathering as the earliest stage, followed by herding, agriculture, commerce and industry.[52]

4. Karl Marx based his theory of economic materialism on a successive-stage theory based on four distinct productive regimes and their social orders. He claimed that history had been marked by the Asiatic, ancient, feudal, and modern bourgeois regimes. These four are antecedents of a fifth, a final

[49] August Comte, *Cours de Philosophie Positive,* trans. by H. Martineau, 3rd ed. (London, Trubner, 1893), 2 vols.

[50] L. H. Morgan, *Ancient Society* (New York, Kerr, 1887).

[51] E. B. Tylor, as quoted by V. G. Childe, *op. cit.,* p. 5.

[52] F. Müller-Lyer, *History of Social Development,* Eng. trans. (London, Allen & Unwin, 1920), pp. 245–253, 319–339.

form which was to be the socialistic regime. He foresaw two stages of this regime, the first of which was "the dictatorship of the proletariat," and the second communism. Under the dictatorship, the state would remove all traces of the bourgeois (capitalist) mind and its institutions. Then under communism, the state is to wither away, classes disappear, and the "ascent of man from the kingdom of necessity to the kingdom of freedom." The end is Utopia, wherein the process comes to rest.[53]

All of these successive-stage theories and others have intrigued social scientists seeking general laws of social change, but they do not have many supporters today. The reason for this is that upon examination of many instances, negative cases showed up. Karl Marx would have been surprised to learn that his predicted dictatorship of the proletariat would occur in one of the least industrialized countries of Europe and Asia. According to the theory, the revolution should have occurred in a highly industrialized country like Great Britain or Germany. But just as in all the single-factor theories, these particularistic stage theories in their sweeping generalizations exclude man as creator and critic and substitute a rigid doctrine of immutable direction for society.

Lynd has described the dangerously deceptive trap of cultural determinism:[54]

Beginning with the useful discrimination between the culture (or the institution) and the person, we then proceed by imperceptible shifts in emphasis to treat culture as something *apart from* the persons who live by it; next, we slide over into the acceptance of culture as *independent* of the persons who live by it; and then we are tempted to move on to acceptance, overt or tacit, or *cultural determinism,* viewing culture as a self-contained force, operating by inner laws of its own to coerce and to shape people to its ends.

Temporal classifications of cultural growth, when viewed as *tendencies* but not laws, have significance in interpreting the role of technology. Mumford's classification is a good example.

5. Lewis Mumford has provided a framework of successive stages (originally coined by Patrick Geddes) with which he interprets the history of technology and the development of social organization. The four stages are described as follows:[55]

Eotechnic—Refers to the dawn age of modern technics: an economy based on the use of wind, water and wood as power, with wood as the principal material for construction. Dominant in Western Europe from the tenth to the eighteenth

[53] M. M. Bober, *Karl Marx's Interpretation of History* (Cambridge, Harvard University Press, 1927), pp. 260–261; Karl Marx, *op. cit.,* Ch. I; F. Engels, trans. by E. Aveling, *Socialism, Utopian and Scientific* (Chicago, Kerr, 1908).

[54] Robert S. Lynd, *Knowledge for What?* (Princeton, N. J., Princeton University Press, 1939), pp. 22–23.

[55] Lewis Mumford, *The Culture of Cities* (New York, Harcourt, Brace, 1938), pp. 495–496. These stages are described in detail in his *Technics and Civilization* (New York, Harcourt, Brace, 1934).

century. Marked by improvements in navigation, glass-making, and the textile industries, from the thirteenth century on: by widespread canal-building and increased utilization of power and power-machines in the later phase.

Paleotechnic—Refers to the coal and iron economy, which existed as a mutation in the eotechnic period (blast furnace and primitive railway) but began in the eighteenth century, to displace the eotechnic complex, and became a dominant between 1850 and 1890. Key inventions: steam engine, railroad, steamship, Bessemer converter, various automatic devices in spinning and weaving. Up to the last quarter of the nineteenth century, the eotechnic economy remained as a recessive.

Neotechnic—Refers to the new economy, which began to emerge in the eighties, based on the use of electricity, the lighter metals, like aluminum and copper, and rare metals and earths, like tungsten, platinum, thorium, etc. Vast improvements in utilization of power, reaching its highest point in the water-turbine. Destructive distillation of coal; complete utilization of scrap and by products. Growing perfection and automatism in all machinery. Key inventions; electric transformer, electric motor, electric light, and electric communication by telegraph, telephone, and radio; likewise vulcanized rubber and internal combustion engine. At the present time, the eotechnic complex is a survival, the paleotechnic is recessive, and the neotechnic is a dominant.

Biotechnic—Refers to an emergent economy, already separating out more clearly from the neotechnic (purely mechanical) complex, and pointing to a civilization in which the biological sciences will be freely applied to technology, and in which technology itself will be oriented toward the culture of life. The key inventions, on the mechanical side, are the airplane, the phonograph, the motion picture, and modern contraceptives, all derived directly, in part, from a study of living organisms. The application of bacteriology to medicine and sanitation, and of physiology to nutrition and daily regimen, are further marks of this order: parallel applications in psychology for the discipline of human behaviour in every department are plainly indicated. In the biotechnical order the biological and social arts become dominant: agriculture, medicine, and education take precedence over engineering. Improvements, instead of depending solely upon mechanical manipulations of matter and energy will rest upon a more organic utilization of the entire environment, in response to needs of organisms and groups considered in their multifold relations: physical, biological, social, economic, esthetic, psychological.

This theoretical framework provides the basis for Mumford's *Technics and Civilization* (1934) and *The Culture of Cities* (1938). He does not regard these stages in history as following any immutable laws but rather as a classification of technic ways which form culture complexes. These complexes are then assumed to provide a set of influences which spread (dispersion effects) over the entire culture and produce a number of social and psychological effects. Any modern culture can be observed to be an overlay of all these technic strata. In Mumford's terms, a society with an advanced technology is neotechnic in its dominant mode but exhibits an increase of biotechnic traits. Paleotechnic recessives and eotechnic survivals can be observed as remnants of earlier technological orientation. As conceptual tools, these stages have high utility. An adaptation of this framework is used in Chapters

11 and 14 to help explain the influence of technology on industry and agriculture respectively.

Cyclical Theories

Perhaps the oldest conception of social change is that which conceives society as following a cyclical course.[56] Rythmn is a pervasive manifestation of life. It is exhibited in human physiology as heartbeat, breathing, hunger and satiation, and finally as a process of organic growth and decline. The life of every species is a closed cycle of birth and death forever repeated until the extinction of the species. In the social world, one of the most universal observations concerning history is that in certain respects it often repeats itself. Speculations have ranged from depictions of history as exactly reproducing itself in time, through ideas of statistical, regular recurrences of phenomena, to notions of random recurrences. In recent times, such historians as Oswald Spengler (*The Decline of the West*) and Arnold J. Toynbee (*Study of History*) have commanded attention with theories explaining the rise and fall of civilizations. Sociologists usually discard the concept of civilization and look for cultural unities. The theories of Pitirim Sorokin and F. Stuart Chapin illustrate recent conceptions of two sociologists who conceive of societal change as cyclical in form.

1. Sorokin's theory of cyclical change. Sorokin's theory is based on a classification of "socio-cultural systems." *Social and Cultural Dynamics* is based upon his detailed study of the Greek, Graeco-Roman, and Western culture from about 600 B.C. to 1920 A.D., with cursory references to Egyptian, Hindu, and Chinese cultures. He identifies three main types of socio-cultural supersystems as distinct patterns, each capable of surviving for several centuries. These are the "ideational" system, the "sensate" system, and an intermediate or mixed system called "idealistic." The ideational system is characterized as one in which the elements are based on faith (sacred). The sensate system is composed of elements based on empirical science and rationality (secular). The idealistic system is a combining of these two forms and is characterized by more emphasis upon the creative activity of the human mind in art, literature, and thought. Sorokin draws upon the fields of painting, music, literature, science, technology and invention, philosophy and law, deriving therefrom statistics out of which he has constructed a series of graphs. Using these graphs he claims to show that cyclical fluctuations have occurred in the creative achievements of Western man from the dawn of history. He relates these cultural activities to the ideational, idealistic, and sensate systems and charts growth and decline. This brings him to this question: Does the total culture of a given area change all together as one

---

[56] For a list of cyclical theories, see Pitirim A. Sorokin, *Society, Culture, and Personality, Their Structure and Dynamics* (New York, Harper, 1947), Ch. XLV.

system or do its various elements change independently from one another?

Sorokin maintains that cycles of total culture and of the various elements of culture are directed by a sort of logical principle residing in the total culture. He writes:[57]

From the moment of its emergence, any empirical socio-cultural system is a self changing and self directing unity that bears in itself the reason for its change, the nature of its functions, the phase of its unfolding, and the essentials of its destiny. As such, it has always a margin of autonomy from all the force external to it.

The direction of these systems is described as that of variable recurrence.[58] Culture change may tend to conform to a linear form and then owing to changes within it, change its direction, and a new form appears. The new form may be again linear, or cyclical, perhaps oscillatory. The valid conceptions is that of an "incessant variation of the main recurrent themes."[59] In the course of many irregular changes, culture may partially return to a condition approximating but never identical with a former state. Thus, the culture completes the nearest thing to a cycle that may be expected in the history of human society.[60]

2. Chapin's theory of synchronous culture cycles. In Chapin's theory, cycles belong in three orders: the order of material culture, the order of non-material culture, and the order of larger cultural composites.[61] Each higher order fluctuates more slowly than the preceding order. Within each order, there are cycles of major and minor degree.

The following hypotheses are proposed: (1) Every cultural form has its own law of change, with the qualification that for certain classes of social phenomena there may be some basic and common law of change. (2) The law of each cultural form is probably cyclical and may be periodic. (3) It is possible to discover and express quantitatively the law of its life cycle or periodic function. (4) When the cycles or periods of a number of cultural forms of the first and second order are synchronous, we have the era of maturity of the cultural nation or groups in which the culture traits are found.[62]

There is, in these conceptions of Sorokin and Chapin, a belief that certain classes of phenomena fluctuate together and that a cyclical form emerges.

3. Kroeber's test of the cultural creativity hypothesis. This question of synchronous fluctuation has been studied by the anthropologist A. L. Kroeber, who examined a number of cultural fields such as philosophy,

[57] Pitirim A. Sorokin, *Social and Cultural Dynamics* (New York, American Book, 1937), Vol. IV, p. 73.

[58] *Ibid.*, Vol. I, p. 186.

[59] *Ibid.*, Vol. IV, p. 732.

[60] For a critical examination, see Robert K. Merton, *Social Theory and Social Structure* (Glencoe, Ill., Free Press, 1949), pp. 226–236.

[61] F. Stuart Chapin, *Cultural Change* (New York, Century, 1928), pp. 201–223.

[62] *Ibid.*, pp. 210–211.

science, philology, sculpture, painting, drama, literature, and music. He began by observing that men who were evaluated by subsequent periods as being great seemed to appear in clusters. He hypothesized that such clusters indicated periods of maximum cultural creativity of highest cultural quality. Using a panel of judges to identify the "great" men in the various fields of culture, Kroeber noted the periods when they seemed to cluster and then attempted to analyze the significance of the cultural phenomena they expressed. The analysis covered a time span ranging from early Greek civilization to the present day and included all European nations and many Asiatic countries. He found that clusters of "great" men did indicate the flowering of some culture pattern and that intervals without great men occur. He believed that these periods of culture defined certain directions of cultural activity or "opportunity." His central conclusion is as follows:[63]

I see no true law in the phenomena dealt with; nothing cyclical, regularly repetitive, nor necessary. There is nothing to show either that every culture must develop patterns within which a florescence of quality is possible, or that, having once so flowered, it must wither without chance of revival.

CRITICISM AND INTERPRETATION

These many conceptions of social change are suggestive of the thinking which theorists have followed in attempts to find causes of change and the direction of society. Today, single-factor theories as all embracing independent factors are discredited. Most sociologists have long since abandoned the evolutionary perspective which assumed a neatly arrayed development of culture in universal stages from lower to higher forms. Linear, successive-stage, and cyclical theories purporting to explain a fixed direction for society remain unproved.[64] One outstanding conclusion of all theories of social change must indeed be that history holds no laws which can deliver the final sentence to man's hopes and possibilities.

Sociological interest is now primarily structural and functional rather than historical. The sociologist is restricting his examination of culture to more specific traits and patterns within a given society and is drawing parallels between societies with great caution. He is aware that culture does not develop in a single linear pattern and that any internal-development process in a society can be profoundly influenced by diffusion of elements from other societies. He has found that social change results from a multitude of causes,

[63] A. L. Kroeber, *Configurations of Cultural Growth* (Berkeley, University of California Press, 1944), p. 761.

[64] Lundberg cites the principal reasons for this inconclusiveness as (1) the inadequacy of the historical data which have been relied upon in nearly all these studies; (2) the difficulty or impossibility of applying sufficiently rigorous scientific methods to the data available to permit reliable generalization; and (3) the incomparability of the concepts, methods, and data employed by different students which prevents both corroboration and comparison of their results.—G. A. Lundberg, *Foundations of Sociology*, (New York, Macmillan, 1939), pp. 511–512.

often proceeds in a given society in more than one direction, and takes on more than one kind of form. Some changes are fitful, some "lunge and lapse,"[65] some are cumulative, some are cyclical and spiral, some are pulsating, and some are serial. The sociologist continues to seek out the uniformities and regularities which mark the changing phenomena of social structure and processes. A new body of scientific theory based on a network of limited hypotheses is slowly growing and appears destined to replace much of what was widely believed only a half century ago.[66] Thus runs the course of social change.

CONCLUSION

Social-change theory, until very recently, has been largely a description of attempts to discover all-embracing laws of history.

There is increasing recognition that a general theory of the processes of change of social systems is not possible in the present state of knowledge.

The work of modern sociologists is directed toward a theory of particular subprocesses of change *within* a particular society, not of the over-all processes of change of the society as a totality.

Many theories of societal change have been propounded. These include linear, stage, and cyclical conceptions. Many of these have been discredited; others remain unproved. The most useful theories are those which enable an observer to appraise changes in parts of the culture.

A new body of scientific theory based on a network of limited hypotheses is slowly growing and appears destined to replace much of what was widely believed only a half-century ago.

Social theory and social research have come closer together. New knowledge of experimental design, sampling methods, statistics, and sociometric scales provide the technics for the acquisition of more reliable data for the building of more adequate theory.

ANNOTATED BIBLIOGRAPHY

CHAPIN, F. Stuart, *Cultural Change* (New York, Century, 1928). Analyzes the processes operating in cultural change with especial attention to the historic role of invention.

DODD, Stuart C., *Systematic Social Science* (Seattle, University of Washington Book Store, 1948). Presents a theory for a quantitative analysis of social forces and processes. Points the way to future advances in measurement.

[65] Stuart C. Dodd, *Systematic Social Science* (Seattle, University of Washington Bookstore, 1948).

[66] Parsons concludes, "A general theory of the processes of change of social systems is not possible in the present state of knowledge. The reason is very simply that such a theory would imply complete knowledge of the laws of process of the system and this knowledge we do not possess. The theory of change in the structure of social systems must, therefore, be a theory of particular sub-processes of change within such systems, not of the overall processes of change of the systems as systems.—*The Social System*, (Glencoe, Ill., Free Press. 1951), p. 486.

DURKHEIM, Emile, *On the Division of Labor in Society,* trans. by George Simpson (New York, Macmillan, 1933). Emphasis on the division of labor as the causative factor in determining social solidarity of a society.

LINTON, Ralph, *The Study of Man* (New York, Appleton-Century-Crofts, 1936). The cultural theory of change is described with careful attention to invention and diffusion. Linton brings extensive anthropological research to the support of his conclusions.

MACIVER, Robert M., and PAGE, Charles H., *Society, An Introductory Analysis* (New York, Rinehart, 1949). A major part of this book is devoted to a theoretical analysis of social change. Technological factors are carefully reviewed and the theories of Marx and Veblen are given special attention.

MARX, Karl, *A Contribution to the Critique of Political Economy,* trans. by N. I. Stone (Chicago, Charles H. Kerr and Co., 1913). Contains the central ideas in Marx's theory of economic materialism and the role of class struggle in history.

MUMFORD, Lewis, *Technics and Civilization* (New York, Harcourt, Brace, 1934). Describes the history of technology and analyzes patterns of technical elements as eotechnic, paleotechnic, neotechnic, and biotechnic stages of society. The sequence of change from each technological pattern is correlated with numerous social changes in all parts of the society.

OGBURN, William F., *Social Change* (New York, Viking Press, 1950). The concept of culture lag was introduced by Ogburn in this book. There are numerous illustrations of the thesis that various parts of modern culture are not changing at the same rate and that a rapid change in one part requires readjustments in the various correlated parts of culture.

SIMS, Newell L., *The Problem of Social Change* (New York, Crowell, 1939). A survey of theories dealing with social change. There is a discussion of the processes of social change as automatic, purposive, and revolutionary. Contains a large bibliography.

SOROKIN, Pitirim, *Contemporary Sociological Theories* (New York, Harper, 1928). A comprehensive description of sociological theories which is organized around various schools of sociological thought such as mechanistic, sociologistic, social-psychological, etc. Gives excellent coverage to European as well as American thought.

————, *Society, Culture, and Personality* (New York, Harper, 1947). Summarizes Sorokin's theory of socio-cultural cycles and presents his research evidence for the "sensate," "ideational" and "idealistic" cultural super systems.

VEBLEN, Thorstein, *The Theory of the Leisure Class* (New York, Macmillan, 1912). Brings together most of the concepts with which Veblen examined society. Included are such concepts as pecuniary emulation, conspicuous consumption, conspicuous leisure, and pecuniary standards of taste.

PART II

The Social Effects of Selected Major Inventions

CHAPTER 6

THE AUTOMOBILE

■ Francis R. Allen

THE THESIS that technology exerts a major influence on social change is well illustrated in the instance of the automobile. As one considers the various social effects of this invention, it is clear that the latter has been the cause of hundreds of social changes. This is particularly true in the United States, less so in other nations. In the automobile, indeed, we behold an invention which has become an important factor in the day-to-day living patterns of the American people and has had a tremendous and all-pervading influence on their social and economic life. In its social impact it is, in truth, one of the great inventions of all time.

William F. Ogburn declared in the late 1930's that "the inventor of the automobile has had more influence on society than the combined exploits of Napoleon, Genghis Khan, and Julius Caesar."[1]

Allen Sievers states that ". . . the automobile is the broadest symbol of our time both because its production typifies modern industrial and business organization and because, more than any other single contribution of modern technology, it has transformed the average man's way of life—at least here in the United States, . . ."[2]

Development of the Automobile

Although the "horseless carriage" or automobile of the 1885–1900 period was hardly an impressive vehicle compared with the car of today, the important facts were, first, that the early car *did run* and, second, that from this time onward it was continually improved. As mechanical improvements were made, the average citizen saw it less as a toy of the rich (the first view) and more as a desirable vehicle for his own transportation. As automobile sales increased, there was an increased emphasis on improving roads. All told,

[1] William F. Ogburn, *Machines and Tomorrow's World,* Public Affairs Pamphlet, No. 25 (New York, Public Affairs Committee, 1938), p. 3.
[2] Allen Sievers, *General Economics: An Introduction* (Philadelphia, Lippincott, 1952), Ch. 1, "The Automobile," p. 5.

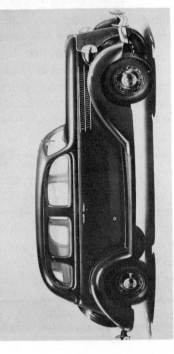

Courtesy of Ford Motor Company

**EVOLUTION OF THE FORD CAR,
1906–1922–1936–1957**

both the automobile itself and driving conditions were improved tremendously between 1900 and around the mid-1930's. Wilfred Owen distinguishes three fairly distinct periods of automotive history:[3] (1) *the formative period,* approximately until World War I, during which time high costs and low standards of service were the rule; (2) *the growth period,* roughly from 1919 until the mid-1930's, when the demand for cars was heavy, significant improvements in the vehicle were made, and a phenomenal expansion of the highway system occurred; and (3) *the period of maturity,* from approximately the mid-1930's to the present, when there was a leveling-off in growth and an emphasis on maintaining the high standard of service which had been earlier achieved.

Certain occurrences in the development of the motor vehicle may have interest for different people. These include the freeing of automotive production from a restrictive patent (amounting almost to a monopoly) in 1911; the application of mass-production techniques to the automotive industry in 1913, led by Henry Ford; the invention of the self-starter by Charles F. Kettering in 1911; and the innovation of buying cars on the installment plan (57 per cent of cars were so purchased in 1952; 59 per cent in 1953; and 62 per cent in 1954).[4] One may observe also that various conditions in the United States favored the production and use of motor vehicles. This was a nation which possessed abundant resources for production (such as a well-developed steel industry, considerable inventive talent, manufacturing skill, and business initiative); it had a high per capita income as compared with other nations, hence many people could afford to buy cars; and it comprised a large land area on which a highway vehicle would be useful.[5]

The main fact so far as social results are concerned was that a large proportion of the American population did own and drive motor cars. In early 1955, surveys indicated that approximately 35 million U. S. families, or 71 per cent of all families, owned an automobile—sometimes more than one.[6] Over 48 million passenger cars were registered in the United States in 1954. Motor-vehicle traffic in this nation was estimated to be close to 561 billion vehicle-miles during this year—or an average of 7,800 miles per driver. Motor vehicles consumed a total of 44,365,465,000 gallons of gasoline during 1954.[7]

During the remainder of this chapter, attention will be focused upon the

[3] Wilfred Owen, *Automotive Transportation: Trends and Problems* (Washington, The Brookings Institution, 1949), pp. 63–65.

[4] Automobile Manufacturers Association, *Automobile Facts and Figures,* 35th ed., 1955, p. 19.

[5] Lawrence H. Seltzer, "Automobile Industry: The United States, Manufacture and Sale," article in the *Encyclopaedia of the Social Sciences* (New York, Macmillan, 1930), Vol. II, pp. 322–326; Charles F. Kettering, "Automobile," article in the *Encyclopaedia Americana* (1946), Vol. II, pp. 643–657.

[6] *Automobile Facts and Figures,* 1955, p. 68.

[7] *Ibid.,* pp. 21, 36–37.

motor-vehicle influence on living habits, on social institutions, and on the American way of life generally. Although the social effects of the use of the automobile are so numerous and diverse as to be almost incalculable, effort will be made to include at least the large number of major effects.[8]

SOCIAL EFFECTS

In considering social effects which have resulted from use of the motor vehicle, it is desirable to distinguish between (a) effects which have been significantly related to use of this vehicle but which would have occurred to a lesser extent with other transportation vehicles, and (b) effects which would not have occurred at all without the automobile. Both kinds will be noted on the pages that follow. One may also observe that some effects are of major importance, whereas others are of relatively minor moment.

On Transportation

There seems to be no disputing the conclusion that the motor vehicle has brought more efficient, more enjoyable, quicker road transportation for millions of people—for purposes of business or pleasure. In short, it revolutionized land transportation for great masses of people. Generally the use of the private automobile is especially important in medium- and small-sized communities—less so in large cities where subways, interurban railway, or other transportation may be available.[9] Yet as one considers other types of vehicles in use, such as buses, trucks, and vans, it is clear that the motor vehicle (all around) exercises an important function in all sizes of community. Moreover, cars make pleasureable vehicles for recreational trips—picnics, jaunts to mountains or seashore, swimming and camping trips, hunting and fishing expeditions, visits to relatives or friends.

On Population Distribution

A major influence of the use of the automobile has been its effect on population distribution in communities. The railroads had much to do with the original location of many cities; the automobile has brought an outward expansion of people toward the peripheries and suburbs. This trend of outward expansion was begun with the use of electric trolleys and it was aided by other inventions too, such as the telephone. Nevertheless, the motor vehicle is believed to be the greatest influence by far associated with the out-

---

[8] In this chapter the term *automobile* includes such related vehicles as truck, bus, taxicab, van, ambulance, etc.

[9] This is shown in the car ownership figures in relation to city size. In U. S. cities of 500,000 or more population, 57 per cent of families owned a car; in cities of 100,-000 to 500,000 size, 74 per cent owned a car; in cities of 10,000 to 100,000 size, 73 per cent owned a car; in cities of size under 10,000, 80 per cent owned a car; while in farming areas 78 per cent owned a car.—*Automobile Facts and Figures*, 1955, p. 67. The above figures are based on sampling surveys during a recent year.

ward move. People were no longer required to live close to their place of work. They could live in the more quiet and spacious suburbs. This in turn influenced city real-estate values and caused the settlement of many residential areas on the fringe of cities.

The result of this outward expansion of city people was to form what are known as metropolitan areas; since 1950 the U. S. Census Bureau has used the phrase *standard metropolitan area*. The Census Bureau found that between 1940 and 1950 the 168 Standard Metropolitan Areas of the nation had an increase in population amounting to 13.9 per cent within the central cities; outside the central cities the increase amounted to 35.5 per cent on the average.[10] For some sample metropolitan areas the contrast is as follows:

POPULATION INCREASE BETWEEN 1940 AND 1950

City	Per Cent Increase Inside Central City	Per Cent Increase Outside Central City
Akron, Ohio	12.2 per cent	43.1 per cent
Atlanta, Georgia	9.6	57.8
Baltimore, Maryland	10.5	72.9
Boston, Massachusetts	4.0	11.5
Buffalo, New York	0.7	33.1
Chicago, Illinois	6.6 per cent	31.2 per cent
Cincinnati, Ohio	10.6	20.8
Cleveland, Ohio	4.2	41.6
Dallas, Texas	47.4	73.7
Denver, Colorado	29.0	73.4

One may well conclude that the differential increase in the population of central city as contrasted with outside sections of these metropolitan areas is based in a major way—though not entirely—on the use of the motor vehicle. Commuting by railway has also been a significant factor.

On Mobility

The use of the motor vehicle has been largely instrumental in making the American people highly mobile—forever "on the go." Here we do not have in mind mere commuting between suburb and central city, but rather longer trips for all sorts of purposes. One man may hear of a job opportunity in a neighboring state. Another may drive one hundred miles or more to witness an athletic event or political rally. Parents may visit a son or daughter in college or a son in an army camp. A family member may be driven to some medical specialist or clinic. Many families will think nothing of driving a thousand miles or more on a vacation trip. In short, man has placed at his disposal a vehicle that enables him to travel about his area at will, to satisfy

[10] Bureau of the Census, *U. S. Census of Population: 1950*, Vol. I, Number of Inhabitants, Ch. 1: U. S. Summary (Washington, Government Printing Office, 1952), pp. 69 ff.

his every transportation wish and whim, just as long as he is able to operate the vehicle and can maintain it financially.

On Vacation Patterns

As a result of the development of mobility, a new vacation pattern has been established for many people, namely, a "keep moving," touring pattern instead of the former "stay put" vacation at the seaside or mountain resort. This new automobiling pattern has brought a highly lucrative tourist trade to California, Florida, and other "tourist" states. The number of these states, however, may be surprising to some. In 1952, indeed, a total of twenty-six states of the United States ranked travel among their three largest industries.[11] It was further estimated that 80.7 per cent of vacation trips in 1951 were made by automobile. The American Automobile Association made the following summary in 1955:[12]

It is estimated that twenty-four million automobiles, with an average of three passengers each, carry a total of seventy-two million persons on their vacation trips. The average car covers 1,400 miles in twelve days of travel or an aggregate of 11.5 billion miles in the pursuit of pleasure. Each occupant is estimated to spend an average of $165, bringing the total of automobile vacation expenditures to $11.2 billion.

The increasing tendency of the American people, then, seems to stress "on the move" vacations. The average tourist is likely to visit attractions and points of interest several hundreds of miles or more from his usual place of residence; he is less likely to remain at one vacation hotel or lodge for the whole vacation, although many people do that. The modern motorist is likely to stay in an area just so long as he and his family like it—and no longer.

On Business and Industry

Use of the automobile and associated vehicles has had a tremendous impact, all told, on business and industry. First, the invention of the automobile has given rise to the development of a huge industry (automobile production) as well as various allied industries. This is especially the case in the United States; it is to a lesser extent true in England, France, Germany, Russia, and Italy. In the United States upwards of 143 million motor vehicles (passenger cars, trucks, and buses) have been built during the fifty-five year period 1900–1954 inclusive. During 1954 a total of 7,964,360 passenger automobiles were built in all nations of the world; 5,558,897, or 70 per cent, of these were built in the United States.[13] In 1954 the U. S. motor-vehicle retail business had a volume of $29,961,000,000, exclusive of parts and accesso-

[11] *Automobile Facts and Figures,* 33rd ed., 1953, pp. 38–39.
[12] Michael Frome, American Automobile Association, Washington, D. C., letter to F. R. Allen dated May 31, 1956.
[13] *Automobile Facts and Figures,* 1955, pp. 4, 15.

ries sales.[14] This industry included within its ranks the largest, third largest, and fifth largest of American industrial corporations.[15]

It has been estimated that a total of 9,800,000 persons are currently employed in the highway transport industries in the United States. *This comprises one out of every seven persons employed.*[16]

The motor truck business is a huge one in itself. There were 30,300 truck dealers and 5,137,000 full-time truck drivers in the United States on January 1, 1951.[17] The following table shows the growth of truck registrations in this country:[18]

Year	No. Privately-Owned trucks	Percentage of Total Private Motor Vehicles
1904	700	1.3 per cent
1910	10,123	2.2 per cent
1920	1,107,639	12.0 per cent
1930	3,518,747	13.3 per cent
1940	4,590,386	14.3 per cent
1950	8,272,153	17.0 per cent
1954	9,444,394	16.3 per cent

There were in 1954 a total of 21,058,357 truck registrations in the world, which was more than 2.5 times the world figure for registrations in 1940 (8,320,432).[19]

The importance of truck transportation is suggested by two sets of figures which are illustrated here by those for the year 1949. During that year motor trucks hauled 8.3 billion tons of freight in the United States, comprising 75 per cent of all freight hauled; the railroads hauled 1.5 billion tons, or 14 per cent of all freight.[20] This, taken by itself, tends to overemphasize, however, the role of trucking in the total transportation business. To express freight hauling in terms of ton-miles hauled is also advisable, since the railroads are

[14] *Ibid.,* p. 18.

[15] See 1955 ranking of U. S. industrial corporations by *Fortune* magazine based on net sales. The General Motors Corporation was the leading industrial corporation; its sales were approximately double that of the second largest industrial corporation. The Ford Motor Company ranked third; Chrysler Corporation ranked fifth. *Fortune,* Supplement (July, 1956), "The Fortune Directory of the 500 Largest U. S. Industrial Corporations," p. 2.

[16] *Automobile Facts and Figures,* 1955, p. 64.

[17] "Motor Truck Facts" (pamphlet), 1951 ed. (Detroit, 1951), p. 25. This pamphlet was published by the Motor Truck Committee of the Automobile Manufacturers Association.

[18] *Ibid.,* p. 20; *Automobile Facts and Figures,* 1955, p. 21.

[19] *Automobile Facts and Figures,* 1955, p. 28.

[20] "Motor Truck Facts," 1951 ed., pp. 28–29, 39–41, 46. To cite further details, trucks hauled 97 per cent of the milk supply from farms to initial market, 94.6 per cent of shell eggs to thirteen major markets, 99.1 per cent of live poultry to ten major markets, 75.1 per cent of total livestock to 63 major markets (1950), 48.1 per cent of fruits and vegetables to thirteen major markets, and 99 per cent of the tobacco crop to markets.

especially used for long-distance shipments.[21] During 1949 trucks hauled 122 billions of ton-miles of freight or 11 per cent of the total, while the railroads hauled 569 billions of ton-miles or 49 per cent of all freight hauled; the waterways hauled 345 billions of ton-miles or 31 per cent of total. It is nevertheless clear that the truck transportation business has considerable volume.

The bus industry has grown significantly. There were in 1925 a total of 17,808 privately-owned buses registered in the United States; in 1954 the number had grown to 140,003. The total number of privately and publicly owned buses registered amounted to 248,346 in 1954; this excluded military vehicles.[22]

The volume of the bus transportation business in the United States is indicated by the facts that a total of 1,638 companies were engaged in city and suburban bus service in 1950, while an additional 2,858 companies were engaged in intercity service. The operating revenue during that year amounted to $791,879,000 for the city and suburban service and $512,747,-000 for the intercity service.[23] Also, a total of 120,976 school buses were in use in the United States in 1950. The grand total of buses of all types in operation in the U. S. was 228,815 in 1950.[24]

The taxicab business has grown considerably. In 1951 a total of 78,764 taxicabs in the United States carried 1,577,781,044 passengers an aggregate distance of 4,876,650,266 miles, according to the records of the organized taxicab companies. Gross revenue of the business during that year amounted to the sum of $881,841,464.[25]

The auto rental business has consistently increased. During 1953 a total of 159,745 passenger cars were operated by 2,140 rental and "you-drive-it-yourself" companies. Nearly 98,000 cars were rented on "long-term lease," that is, leased for periods in excess of thirty days.[26]

Business in parts and accessories amounted to $1,682,000,000 in 1951 in the United States.[27] For instance, a total of 45,457,870 tires were sold during 1952 as replacements for worn-out tires on passenger cars; this amounted to 65 per cent of tires for passenger cars produced during that year. In addition to this, over 8,800,000 tires were sold as replacements for

[21] Trucks tend to engage predominantly in short hauls. See D. Philip Locklin, *Economics of Transportation*, 3rd ed. (Chicago, Irwin, 1951), pp. 678–680.

[22] *Automobile Facts and Figures*, 1955, p. 21.

[23] "Motor Truck Facts," 1951, p. 16. Original source was "Bus Transportation," February, 1951.

[24] *Ibid.*, p. 13.

[25] *Automobile Facts and Figures*, 1952, p. 13. These figures include taxicabs operated by regularly organized companies, not those operated by individual persons. Source is Cab Research Bureau, Inc., affiliated with the National Association of Taxicab Owners.

[26] *Automobile Facts and Figures*, 33rd ed., 1953, p. 12. Original source was "A Rental Automobile Survey," May, 1953, Defense Transport Administration.

[27] *Ibid.*, 1952, p. 39.

trucks and buses. And more than twenty-two million auto batteries were shipped out during 1952 as replacements for worn-out batteries. Other industries affected by the production of accessories for automobiles are those producing radios, heaters, cigarette lighters, and seat covers. In 1954 over four million radio sets for automobiles were produced; 75.2 per cent of U. S. automobiles were equipped with a radio in 1953–54. A total of 96 per cent of the 1953–54 model cars also provided a heater; 41 per cent had seat covers; and 94 per cent had turn indicators.[28]

Other basic industries have been affected by motor-vehicle production. For example, the American Iron and Steel Institute has estimated that the automobile industry consumed 11,792,989 tons of steel during 1954. This represented 18.7 per cent of all steel used in the United States.[29] Substantial amounts of plate glass, rubber, nickel, lead, and other materials were also used.[30] Various agricultural products are also used in motor-vehicle production, such as cotton (over 460,000 bales were used during 1952), wool, corn, mohair, cattle hides, hogs, flaxseed, tung oil, and turpentine.[31]

The sale of gasoline and lubricants has grown to vast proportions. As enumerated in the 1947 Census of Manufacturers, there were a total of 188,253 gasoline filling-stations in operation in the United States at that time. This did not include retail gasoline outlets where some other type of product was the main source of income, as in the twelve thousand or more general stores which sell gas and oil. The total volume of the gas and oil retail business in the U. S. amounted to $11,445,000,000 in 1954; it had been slightly over $9 billion only three years before.[32] This business also includes some of the largest of American industrial corporations: Standard Oil of New Jersey, Gulf, Socony, Standard Oil of Indiana, Texas Company, and Shell.[33]

A new business to develop with the growth of automobiling was that of automobile storage and parking. This is especially important in large cities

[28] *Ibid.,* 1955, pp. 10–11.

[29] *Ibid.,* 1955, p. 36.

[30] Current accurate estimates of use by the automobile industry are not available, according to Stanley S. Roe, Statistical Department, Automobile Manufacturers Association, Detroit, Michigan, letter to F. R. Allen dated October 22, 1953.

Mr. Charles F. Kettering stated for the year 1939 that the automobile industry used 80 per cent of the rubber supply of the United States, 69 per cent of the plate glass, 90 per cent of the gasoline, 25 per cent of the nickel, 33 per cent of the lead, and 40 per cent of the mohair. Kettering, "Automobile," article in the *Encyclopaedia Americana* (1946), Vol. II, note esp. pp. 655–657.

[31] *Automobile Facts and Figures,* 1953, p. 39.

[32] *Ibid.,* 1952, p. 36; *ibid.,* 1955, p. 18.

[33] According to *Fortune* magazine's ranking of U. S. industrial corporations in 1955 on the basis of net sales, Standard Oil of New Jersey was the second largest U. S. industrial corporation; Gulf Oil ranked eleventh; Socony ranked thirteenth, Standard Oil of Indiana fourteenth, Texas Company fifteenth, and Shell sixteenth. See *Fortune,* Supplement (July, 1956), p. 2.

and has gradually increased in volume as the vast number of automobiles made it difficult for people to find free parking places. In 1948 a total of 8,533 storage and parking places (including lots) were reported in the U. S. Census of Business. Receipts of the business reached the total of $190,347,-000 for that year; 25,618 people were reported to have been employed.[34]

It is clear that the total impact of all these enterprises on the U. S. economy is powerful. Admittedly motor-vehicle production, production of accessories, and sale of gas and oil are the most significant items—especially the former. So great, indeed, is this influence that that barometer of economic well-being —the stock market—may experience a decline in prices if the giant automotive industry is in a slump. Low auto sales are likely to bring, in turn, cuts in motor-vehicle production, lessened demand for steel and other raw materials, labor layoffs, reduction in general purchasing power, and other results. Decline in the automotive industry has been an influential factor in causing a downward trend in general stock prices before and it will undoubtedly happen in the future.[35] If the industry is prospering, it may wield an influence in the opposite direction.

Business and industrial adjustments of varying import have also been made to the automobile age. For instance, the restaurant business has certainly existed for a long time, but increasingly restaurants have been located along main highway routes; and the new "drive-in" restaurant has gained vogue. This may be an establishment which serves a full-course meal or it may be a short-order place or "hamburger stand." Or the establishment may specialize in ice cream, milk, milkshakes, or frozen custards (the dairy bar); fruit juices; or other foods or beverages.

Another effect of use of motor vehicles was the partial relocation of retail merchandising establishments in cities. As people increasingly bought automobiles and lived farther out from the center of the city, they found it more difficult to find parking places near the downtown stores. Store executives endeavored to adjust to the automobile age in various ways. First, many stores provided parking lots, often free of charge. Second, branch and chain stores were located away from the town center; ample parking space was provided around these decentralized stores. The stocks of chain stores were usually replenished by use of trucks and vans. Third, large department stores inaugurated the trend of establishing branch stores in suburbs. Grocery stores also were located in the suburbs. Supermarkets were often established, also providing abundant parking space. The older neighborhood grocery was no longer sure of receiving the bulk of trade in its section of the community. People would drive several miles if necessary in search of good bargains or

[34] Bureau of the Census, *Statistical Abstract of the United States: 1952* (Washington, Government Printing Office, 1953), pp. 911–912. Then there is in addition the parking meter business—these meters being found in practically all U. S. cities having 25,000 and over population.

[35] See *New York Herald Tribune*, Financial Section, June 10, 1956.

what they considered good merchandise. Another recent development is the community shopping center, located in the suburbs. Many people do the bulk of their daily shopping in these centers. Jonassen found, in a study of consumer practices and attitudes in Columbus, Ohio, that his sampling of people preferred downtown stores for purchase of sixteen out of a total of twenty-three shopping items. Among the most frequent *disadvantages* of shopping in the downtown area, as listed by the Columbus residents, were problems related to use of the automobile: "difficult parking" and "congested traffic." "Too crowded" was also mentioned.[36]

Another business adaptation to the auto age has been the development of motor courts or motels. Again, hotels and inns have provided for the traveler's lodging for centuries, but it was perhaps inevitable that as the automobile age developed more convenient accommodations would be developed for the many motorists. The volume of business of the motel industry is indicated by the fact that in 1948 there were a total of 25,919 tourist courts and camps in the United States. Total receipts of these courts during that year amounted to $195,505,000.[37] Growth of motor courts was such that in September, 1953, the *American Motel Magazine* estimated that there were close to 50,000 motels in operation in this country.[38] It was only in 1925 that the word *motel* was first used.[39]

Another adaptation to the automobile age occurred with respect to the motion picture business. The "drive-in" motion picture theatre was introduced. Families can attend a movie as a group in their own car, as can courting couples, friends, and others. In January, 1952, there were believed to be 3,483 "drive-in" theaters in operation in the United States, as compared with 820 of these theaters in 1948.[40] On the basis of an average capacity of 500 cars with 2.7 persons per car, the 3,483 theaters thus had a total capacity of 4,702,050 people. The trend during recent years has been toward building larger theaters—having a capacity of one thousand or more automobiles. A further innovation has been the provision of de luxe patios in the "drive-in" for patrons who wish to eat dinner while watching the motion picture.[41]

Another business adaptation to the automobile age was an innovation in banking, namely, the establishment of "auto windows" as a service to patrons

[36] C. T. Jonassen, *Downtown versus Suburban Shopping,* Bulletin No. X–58, Bureau of Business Research, Ohio State University (Columbus, Ohio, 1953), pp. 29–35; note especially Tables 6, 7, 8, 9, and 11.

[37] Bureau of the Census, *Statistical Abstract of the United States: 1952* (Washington, Government Printing Office, 1953), pp. 910–911.

[38] *American Motel Magazine,* September, 1953, p. 6.

[39] Donald E. Lundberg and C. Vernon Kane, *Business Management: Hotels, Motels and Restaurants* (Tallahassee, Fla., Peninsula Publishing Company, 1952), p. 11.

[40] *Motion Picture and Television Almanac, 1952–1953,* ed. by Charles S. Aaronson (New York, Quigley Publications, 1952), p. v.

[41] *Boxoffice,* The Pulse of the Motion Picture Industry, Vol. 63, No. 12 (July 18, 1953), p. 14.

who often had difficulty parking their car near the bank. This was especially helpful for simple banking errands in which the patron could remain in his car and have a check cashed or deposit made.

The invention and widespread use of the motor vehicle had crucial effects on industries which comprised alternate forms of transportation. Certain older industries, notably wagon and buggy production, were generally supplanted. This was inevitable. As the more efficient form of transportation increased in usage and was integrated in American culture, the older, less-efficient vehicle was less in demand. Then, the development of the automobile and associated vehicles (truck, bus, trailer, and van) has unquestionably been associated with increasing financial difficulties for the railroads. A significant diversion of traffic from railroads to motor vehicles and other forms of transportation has occurred, especially on the short-haul trade; railroad revenues have unquestionably declined because of this. There is no way of knowing, says Locklin,[42] the losses of the railroads due to diversion of traffic to the truck and van carriers and private trucks, and also to the reduction in rail rates which have been made in order to prevent diversion of traffic to the highways. While some railroads have experienced serious financial difficulties because of this competition, it may also be pointed out that many railroads have, on the other hand, gained considerable revenue due to the automobile industry. It has been estimated that during 1952, for example, the automobile industry shipped by rail motor vehicles, parts, tires, gasoline, oil, iron and steel, lumber, rubber, and other goods amounting to $821,000,000.[43] The automobile industry has, therefore, provided both heavy competition and a sizable amount of business for the railroads.

As a final industrial effect, it may be observed that not only is the peace-time production of motor vehicles notable, but in time of war this immense production may be converted to the output of tanks, jeeps, and other machines of war. Thus the motor-vehicle industry is able to serve the nation in time of crisis. As noted in Chapter 15, war has become increasingly mechanized. During World War II, the United States was called the "arsenal of democracy." Although all industries play a part in war production, the automobile industry's contribution is especially significant. An available supply of millions of trained workers, of expert managerial talent versed in motor-vehicle production, and of mechanics and truck drivers is indeed of no little importance to a nation in time of war.

On Government

Widespread use of the automobile has made necessary the creation of highway organizations at all governmental levels. The Bureau of Public Roads deals with highway activities at the (U. S.) national level. In the

[42] Locklin, *op. cit.*, p. 691.
[43] *Automobile Facts and Figures,* 1953, p. 20.

various state governments, the organization is called the Department of Highways in thirty-six American states; in the remaining twelve states maintenance and control of highways is vested in a Highway Commission.

Road construction became a major interest as the number of automobiles increased rapidly. At first road-building was performed by communities. Later the counties undertook the work, usually with state subsidies. When this was regarded as unsatisfactory, because of the large number of motor vehicles in use and the consequent need for a well-planned system of highways, the states took over responsibility. Today the building and maintenance of principal highways in all states are the work of the state governments, which act in close co-operation with the Bureau of Public Roads. In general, the states administer the main trunk lines, the counties the bulk of rural roads, and the municipalities the city streets. In North Carolina, Virginia, West Virginia, and Delaware, the state government has control of rural roads as well. Beginning with the Federal Aid Road Act of 1916, the national government has sought to shape state and local road policy through a system of grants-in-aid. Minimum standards have been set. One objective of national aid has been to create a nation-wide net of arterial highways.[44]

Use of the motor vehicle has also brought into being another unit of state government generally called the Bureau of Motor Vehicles. This bureau has charge of licensing the operators of vehicles and the vehicles themselves. It, along with the state police, is also in charge of enforcing the motor-vehicle laws. Many laws and regulations have been passed governing the operation of vehicles. For example, revocation of the license to drive is mandatory in forty-three states if the driver has been convicted of manslaughter while operating a motor vehicle; in forty-five states, upon conviction of drunken driving; in thirty-eight states, if a person is convicted of a felony in the commission of which a motor vehicle was used; in thirty-five states, upon conviction of successive charges of reckless driving; and in forty-two states, upon conviction of hit-and-run driving.[45] Many other state and local laws have been passed regulating speed of driving, parking, and other matters.

The finances of federal, state, and local governments have been notably affected by the use of motor vehicles—chiefly by the construction of highways and bridges. Also, a large number of motor vehicles are owned and operated by the various branches and levels of government in the United States. Highway and bridge construction has resulted in huge costs. State expenditures for highways were in 1949 the second largest of any per-capita

[44] Concerning the various levels of governmental highway organization, see William H. Young, *Ogg and Ray's Introduction to American Government,* 11th ed. (New York, Appleton-Century-Crofts, 1956); W. Brooke Graves, *American State Government,* 4th ed. (Boston, Heath, 1953), pp. 439–444, 757, 827–830; William Anderson and Edward W. Weidner, *State and Local Government* (New York, Holt, 1951), pp. 663–670; and Charles A. Beard, *American Government and Politics,* 10th ed. (New York, Macmillan, 1949), Ch. 22.

[45] Graves, *op. cit.,* p. 443.

expenditures by the state governments.[46] Expressed in round figures, governmental outlays for highways since around 1915 have reached almost astronomical figures. The original Federal Aid Road Act of 1916 provided for appropriations rising by stages to the sum of $25,000,000 for the one year 1921. The sum granted to each state had to be matched by that state.[47]

In 1930 a total of $2,194,000,000 was expended for highways by the federal government, by the forty-eight states, and by local communities. In 1950 the grand total of $4,161,000,000 was spent on highways at the various governmental levels.[48] The cost of bridges may be illustrated by the fact that the Golden Gate Bridge which crosses the entrance to the harbor of San Francisco cost $35,000,000 to build; this is the longest single-span bridge in the world (4,200 feet). The Triborough Bridge in New York City cost $60,000,000 to build.[49]

Because of the high expenditures involved in highway and bridge construction, one effect of the motor complex has been to increase spoils politics and political corruption in some communities. It has been observed that with the letting of large contracts, the purchasing of expensive equipment, the condemning of land for a right-of-way, and the hiring of unskilled seasonal employees, there is the opportunity for playing spoils politics in each of these steps.[50]

Political pressures have also been exerted with regard to routing highways through certain towns, as well as to taking certain routes through a town or city. Paving and surfacing contracts and similar items have also become matters for partisan politics. If an alderman can obtain the paving of a street in his district at general city expense, he can expect more support at the next election. If a legislator secures a rerouting of a state highway so that it favors the interests of some of his more powerful constituents, he will likely receive aid during the coming political campaigns.[51]

Use of the motor vehicle has been a factor causing changes in conducting political campaigns. The modern political aspirant, riding in a motor vehicle and using a loud-speaker, tends to travel over his whole area of jurisdiction and so make an appearance before the voters. Often a whirlwind tour over the state or other area is made by a fast-traveling motorcade or "political

---

[46] Anderson and Weidner, *op. cit.*, p. 89. Note Figure 4. Expenditures for schools ranked highest.

[47] Ogg and Ray, *op. cit.*, 7th ed., p. 109.

[48] *Automobile Facts and Figures,* 1952, p. 55. Figures are those of the Bureau of Public Roads.

[49] *The World Almanac: 1952* (New York, New York World-Telegram, 1952), p. 458. Source of data is the Chief of Engineers, U.S. Army, and other official data.

[50] Anderson and Weidner, *op. cit.*, p. 663. They venture the opinion that "with the exception of police administration, no field of government has had a greater tendency to corruption than highway administration."

[51] *Ibid.,* pp. 664, 666.

caravan" of the candidate and his advisers and supporters. This kind of a political campaign is often effective because it provides the opportunity for many people to see and shake hands with the candidate. The personal contact—"I shook hands with Mr. X"—frequently makes stout converts and is therefore the politician's delight.

Another effect on politics has been the fact of millions of automobile workers swelling the ranks of labor which has had a considerable influence on pressure politics. The Auto Workers' Union is in itself a powerful pressure group. In struggles with the forces of big business and in stating its positions before the general public, the hand of labor has been immeasurably strengthened by the millions employed by the automobile and allied industries.

Law enforcement has been considerably affected by the development of the automobile. Police departments have made good use of motor vehicles as patrol wagons, runabout squad cars, and motorcycles. These have provided fast pursuit for criminals and other law breakers who have, however, also made use of motor vehicles. While one bandit is robbing the bank cashier or filling-station his crony is likely to be at the wheel of a car with motor running for a rapid get-away. Use of the automobile and truck has, indeed, been generally integrated into the whole realm of crime—from holdups to smuggling goods to murder. The latter has frequently been committed by a person in a standing or moving automobile. Moreover, to commit a murder, gangster style, has often been to take the victim "for a ride."

Motor vehicles have, in addition, become prominent objects to be stolen. Automobile thefts now assume large proportions. The Federal Bureau of Investigation has reported that during 1940–52 upwards of 150,000 automobiles *every year* have been stolen in this nation. Estimates show that for each year more than 90 per cent of the stolen automobiles were later recovered. In 1952 a total of 215,310 automobiles were estimated to have been stolen; 92.4 per cent were later recovered.[52]

Another community service which has been affected by use of the motor vehicle has been that of public health protection. The various levels of health organizations, especially the state and local health departments, have provided mobile health clinics of various sorts—for example, the tuberculosis x-ray units, dental clinics, veneral disease clinics, clinics for examination of school children, diabetes clinics, and cancer clinics. These traveling clinics perform a valuable service in locating cases of diseases which are readily communicable (for example, tuberculosis and veneral disease) or where early detection is important (as in cancer). In bringing the clinical service right to the neighborhood of the citizen, many cases are diagnosed which otherwise would not be found until the disease had reached an advanced stage. Both the individual concerned and the community benefit greatly from this service.

[52] *Automobile Facts and Figures,* 1953, p. 21.

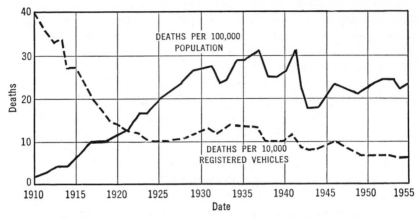

SOURCE: *Accident Facts,* 1953 ed. (Chicago, National Safety Council, 1953), p. 9.

TRENDS IN MOTOR-VEHICLE DEATHS AND RATES

On Individual Health

The automobile has affected the health of individual people in various ways. The habit of automobiling may be correlated, to some extent at least, with a decrease in walking and bicycling—which provide good exercise. Devotees of the vigorous life often criticize the American people as being too physically "soft"; frequent riding in automobiles is sometimes associated with this. It is held that the increasing American tendency is to drive along mountain highways rather than to actually climb the trails—and generally to ride instead of walk whenever one can. Needless to say, other influences of the machine age (as television) have brought forth the same charge. However, any alleged decrease in exercise (due to the automobile) such as would affect a large number of people has never been objectively proven so far as this writer is aware. Many people, on the other hand, drive their car to the golf course, tennis courts, beach, or gymnasium for the very purpose of exercising.

Most of the early health prejudices against the automobile which were current during the early 1900's are properly forgotten. These include the notions that automobiling "interferes with the freedom of the nasal passages"; that exposure to wind currents would inflame the sinuses, "the individual developing an automobile face"; that automobiling, even at a speed of about 20 miles per hour, was undesirable for delicate females who would suffer undue nervous excitement and circulatory disturbance.[53] The latter sentiment is especially dated—strictly a reflection of the cultural ideas of around 1900.

[53] David L. Cohn, *Combustion on Wheels, An Informal History of the Automobile Age* (Boston, Houghton Mifflin, 1944), pp. 58–60.

The most notable, all-too-true effect of the motor vehicle on health and well-being at present results from the occurrence of auto accidents. Despite hundreds of safety campaigns and other community measures, the "slaughter on the highways" has continued. Accidents have become the fourth leading cause of death in the United States, and deaths from *automobile accidents* comprise more than one-third of all accidental deaths. They constitute the greatest single type of accidental death. During 1950 motor-vehicle accidents were responsible for a total of 34,763 deaths in the nation; this amounted to a death rate of 23.1 per 100,000 population.[54] Besides this there is the staggering total of injuries yearly. The National Safety Council estimated that during 1952 a total of 1,400,000 people in the United States were injured in motor-vehicle accidents. Of this number approximately 38,000 died, 110,000 were "permanently injured" (meaning anything from a permanent stiffening of a joint to permanent, major crippling), and 1,250,-000 had temporary disabilities; the latter were, however, all disabling beyond the day of the accident. Property damage resulting from motor-vehicle accidents amounted to an estimated $1.5 billion during 1952.[55]

The total deaths in the United States from the use of the motor vehicle is approximated in the table on page 124, which shows the deaths from auto accidents from 1903 to 1955. For these fifty-three years the total number deaths was 1,149,724. This toll from automobile driving compares with total battle deaths of U. S. military forces, from the American Revolution up to and including the Korean War of 1950–53, of 469,458 men.[56] Deaths from auto accidents (1903–55) are thus more than twice as numerous as battle deaths of U. S. military forces during all the wars of American history.

Another effect of use of the automobile concerns medical care. It is clear that physicians can get around much faster in visiting bedridden patients and are able to make many more calls. Also, less-seriously-sick patients can get down to the physician's office more easily with use of automobile or bus. In rural areas, medical care has especially been improved because of better transportation. If needed, the physician can readily drive to the rural home; this would have been much more difficult and time-consuming during horse-and-buggy days. Use of an ambulance if needed also brings drastic improve-

[54] "Deaths and Death Rates for 64 Selected Causes: The United States and Each State, 1950," *Vital Statistics—Special Reports*, Vol. 37, No. 10, National Office of Vital Statistics, Department of Health, Education, and Welfare (September 11, 1953), pp. 252–265, esp. pp. 258, 265.

[55] *Accident Facts*, 1953 ed. (Chicago, National Safety Council, 1953), pp. 4, 13. Estimates were based on figures of the National Office of Vital Statistics, state traffic authorities, and other sources.

[56] General George C. Marshall has stated the number of battle deaths of U. S. forces from the American Revolution to and including World War II. See his report, *The Winning of the War in Europe and the Pacific* (New York, Simon and Schuster, 1945), p. 107. To this total figure has been added the estimated U. S. battle deaths of the Korean War from its beginning in 1950 until the time of the armistice in July, 1953, namely, 25,000 deaths.—*New York Times*, July 27, 1953.

NUMBER OF DEATHS FROM AUTOMOBILE ACCIDENTS, 1903–1955

Year	Motor Vehicle Deaths
1903–1907 ave	400
1908–1912 ave	1,900
1913–1917 ave	6,700
1918–1922 ave	12,500
1923–1927 ave	21,700
1928	28,000
1929	31,200
1930	32,900
1931	33,700
1932	29,500
1933	31,363
1934	36,301
1935	36,369
1936	38,089
1937	39,643
1938	32,582
1939	32,386
1940	34,501
1941	39,969
1942	28,309
1943	23,823
1944	24,282
1945	28,076
1946	33,411
1947	32,697
1948 (5th Revision)	32,259
1948 (6th Revision)	32,259
1949	31,701
1950	34,763
1951	37,300
1952	38,000
1953	38,300
1954	36,000
1955	38,300
TOTAL	1,149,724

SOURCE: *Accident Facts,* 1955 Edition (Chicago, National Safety Council, 1955), p. 12; *New York Times,* February 2, 1956 (release of 1955 figures by National Safety Council).

ment for the rural dweller who is seriously sick. "With good roads, automobiles, and ambulances, a patient can now be transported thirty miles more safely than he could be carried three miles in the days of dirt roads and buggies."[57]

Unquestionably many lives are now saved which formerly would have been lost because of this factor of motor-vehicle transportation and good roads.

[57] F. M. Reck, "A Car Traveling People" (booklet) (Detroit, Mich., Automobile Manufacturers Association, undated but published after 1942), pp. 9–10.

On the Family

In considering effects upon the family it is well to remind ourselves, first, that the automobile has been integrated with the daily activities of most American families.[58] This means that the bulk of family activities—carrying on a job by the breadwinner, shopping, carrying the children to school, and so on—tend to assume the use of an automobile. The typical American family would be hard put to it if use of an automobile were suddenly removed from the round of activities.

Use of the automobile has a considerable effect on the family budget. In view of the importance of an automobile to family life, most families in the United States demand a car—which must be kept in proper running condition. The combination of initial cost plus gasoline and oil expense, periodic lubrication jobs and checkups, repair bills, and tire and battery replacements, and insurance adds up to no little financial item. Since the median income of persons with money incomes was estimated at $2,300.00 in 1952,[59] which was declared to be the highest in the nation's history, this suggests that automobile costs must constitute a sizable item in the average family budget. It also explains why many families purchase their automobile on the installment plan.

The automobile has the effect of both disuniting and uniting family members. The automobile seems to be at times a notable means of isolating and disuniting family members as it implements the varying outside interests of husband, and wife, and perhaps teen-age children. Indeed, many family arguments may center around the question as to who shall have the car at some time or another. On the other hand, the family may be united during an automobile vacation trip, picnic, or other outing as on almost no other occasion.

On Sex Customs and Morals

Use of the automobile has had a significant effect on sex customs and morals—both premarital courtship behavior and postmarital activities.

Granted that such behavior as "necking," "petting," and other romancing did not originate during the automobile age, there seems to be little doubt that the present, widespread use of automobiles has given people much easier opportunity for courtship activities involving sex play. A short ride takes the young couple out of the realm of parental supervision; they are then on their own as to conduct. There seems little reason to doubt that freedom from primary-group controls has brought an increase in preliminary sex play. The development of the "drive-in" movie theatre has provided another easy opportunity for such activity for those so inclined.

[58] It has been noted earlier that 71 per cent of American families were estimated to have owned an automobile during early 1955. It is probable that, except for families living in large cities, the automobile may be regarded as "almost a necessity."

[59] Bureau of the Census, *Current Population Reports,* Series P-60, No. 14, December 31, 1953, "Consumer Income."

Moreover, premarital sex relations (that is, the act of coitus as contrasted from preliminary sex play) may have increased due, in part, to use of the automobile in getting away from the family scene. The development of the motel, again, provides a convenient opportunity for the practice of sex immorality, although it is not necessarily believed that use of a motel for such purposes is greater than use of a hotel. Some operators have taken measures to prevent local couples from registering at the motel. Local residence is taken to mean residence within the county, which can be determined from the automobile license.

If preliminary sex play and premarital sex relations may have increased in this nation, it should be made clear that many factors are related to this phenomenon in addition to use of the automobile. Certainly the liberalizing of sex discussion, the increasing secularization of ideas and decline of the religious influence, the general overemphasis on sex in American culture, and the development and dissemination of knowledge of contraception are all directly related. It is believed that the chief influence of the automobile has been, again, in providing *easy opportunity* to escape the watchful parental eye and to evade the local community mores.

On Rural Life

Use of the automobile has had a terrific impact on rural life. The day-to-day living patterns of farmers have been virtually transformed. First of all, perhaps most important, the loneliness and feeling of being isolated on the farm have been reduced. The farmer and his family are now able to get away from the former pattern of "living alone, seldom seeing anyone, seldom going any place. Just plowing, washing and ironing, cooking, and milking from dawn to dark; then tumbling into bed, sleeping the sleep of exhaustion, and getting up the next morning to face the same round of work."[60] The farmer and his family can now avail themselves of their car for a trip to town in order to shop, receive advice concerning crops, attend church, secure medical attention, have recreation, or just chat. Moreover, the farm agent, home-demonstration agent, minister, salesman, and friend can easily drive out to the farm. The farmer's children can ride in a bus to the consolidated school. All this was possible but more difficult during the horse-and-buggy era.

The increasing mobility of farmers and their pilgrimages to the city and the contrariwise automobiling of city people to the country has probably brought about an improved understanding between city and rural dwellers. There is doubtless an improved perception of the other's problems. Interaction with urban dwellers, coupled with an extension of the radio, TV, and other inventions to the rural scene, has tended to urbanize some of the rural dweller's attitudes.

It also seems reasonable to conclude that automobile travel has similarly brought improved *regional* understanding within the United States. It is not

[60] F. M. Reck, *op. cit.,* p. 12.

contended that harmony or mutual admiration has always resulted. As the New York City or Chicago dweller motors to Missouri, Alabama, or Massachusetts, or vice versa, the traveler may not like what he sees. He may conclude that the area visited is not as attractive as he had imagined; and he may criticize X, Y, and Z items in the environment. On the other hand, the resident of whatever area may not entirely approve of the traveler and his behavior either. Although tourists at times encounter disagreeable experiences, furthermore, it is nevertheless believed that a net improvement in *understanding* between people of different regions tends to result from travel. Travelers may sometimes be critical of other regions and may ethnocentrically regard the new area in terms of their home region. On the other hand, travelers are also often generous in their appreciation of new patterns of living and may place a high valuation on new sights and different customs.

On Attitudes

Use of the motor vehicle has tended to influence various attitudes of people in addition to those related to communities and regions. Since cars have brought a more efficient mode of transportation, it is assumed that the ways in which people are affected relate especially to speed and mobility. Use of the automobile, supplemented by other influences, has increased the tempo of life. Thus if one were to compare community life around 1880 in the United States with life in a similar-sized community around 1950, it is suggested that speed of movement would be one of the significant differences observed. Not only would the speed of transportation vehicles be faster in 1950 (in miles per hour), but the whole accent would emphasize greater speed during the later year. For example, the phrases "step on the gas," "step on it," and "get going" may be regarded not only as extensions of language but also as verbalisms which express the typical spirit of the automobile age. Conversely, a somewhat impatient attitude is likely to be manifested toward slow-moving things—depreciatively regarded as "horse-and-buggy" activities. In short, frequent automobile driving at high rates of speed is thought to gear us to a more rapid tempo in other pursuits. Speed has become one of the cultural emphases of the automobile age.

The attitude of restlessness may be similarly related, in part, to use of the automobile. One occasionally hears reference to "American restlessness"; almost never to "American contemplation." Such a relationship, if true, is doubtless of the intangible and elusive sort, and hence would be difficult to prove. Conditioned to speed as the American people are, urged to "get going" and "keep moving," goaded by advertisements and other cultural phenomena to drive to Florida during the winter, visit the Wisconsin lakes or the Maine woods during the summer, see the Mardi Gras or Washington cherry trees at other times, drive to this or that place—being "on the move" is, again, an emphasis in American culture; it is probably more related to use of the automobile than to any other transportation vehicle.

Considerable caution needs to be exercised, on the other hand, in attempting to correlate other attitudes with auto driving. For example, has impoliteness increased because of the automobile influence? It is suggested as more likely that rude or inconsiderate driving behavior (such as unnecessary horn-blowing) merely reveals a trait of rudeness developed earlier in life. Similarly one may inquire if selfishness and recklessness have been increased owing to use of the motor vehicle. To assess the role of the automobile as a cultural innovation in relation to such traits would indeed be difficult. Again, it is likely that the automobile merely provides an opportunity for persons to reveal themselves as "road hogs," chance-takers, and the like. At the age when most people begin to drive a motor vehicle, such traits would presumably be well developed—if they are going to develop.

Other Effects

This chapter does not attempt to discuss all the known effects which have resulted from the use of the motor vehicle. Some other effects may be briefly listed. *Effects on housing*—especially the development of the "home on the move" (the trailer), of which about 700,000 were in use in the United States in 1953;[61] *effects on education*—such as the use of school buses which, especially in rural areas, enabled the consolidation of many schoolhouses; also the development of the "field trip" in various studies and the "study-tour," both of which are usually made in automobiles or buses; *effects on library service*—especially the development of the "traveling library" or "bookmobile" in rural areas;[62] effects on various community services not previously mentioned, such as the *improvement of fire protection* with use of modern fire engines which replaced the earlier horse-drawn "pumper"; *effects on mail service,* including more rapid delivery and collection (especially in rural areas) and also use of the "auto mail collection box" outside of post offices so that motorists may mail letters without alighting from their car; *effects on churches*—such as the development of the "traveling minister" who preaches to several congregations on Sundays; also the consolidation of churches (like schools) because people can drive to a centrally-located church; *effects on recreation*—including the touring vacation pattern, jaunts to the mountains, hunting and fishing areas, seashore, national and state parks;[63] the development of auto racing; and the rise of that recreational

---

[61] Estimate of the American Automobile Association for that year. Eleanor Kelly, Department of Public Relations, American Automobile Association, Washington, D. C., letter to F. R. Allen dated November 25, 1953.

[62] Katherine Tappert, "The Automobile and the Traveling Library," *Annals of the American Academy of Political and Social Science,* Vol. CXVI (November, 1924), pp. 66–68.

[63] For example, during the travel year ending September 30, 1951, a total of 1,904,174 persons visited the Great Smoky Mountains National Park (N.C.-Tenn.) using a private automobile; a total of 1,326,862 visited the Shenandoah National Park (Va.) by use of automobile; a total of 1,173,065 persons traveled by automobile to the Rocky Mountain National Park (Colo.); and a total of 1,149,278 persons traveled

specialty of teen-agers, "hot-rod" auto driving; *effects on language and vocabulary*—including additions to the language of such words as *sparkplug, generator, octane, synchromesh,* and *streamline,* and such phrases as "step on the gas" and "they were given the green light to . . .";[64] and finally, *effects on social status*—a main item here being the provision of another criterion of social status: possession of this or that kind of automobile. Thus Jones is known in part as "the person who owns a Cadillac." In some cases the status level may carry with it, rightly or wrongly, notions of social fitness for some activity.

Unquestionably many other social effects of the use of the motor vehicle could be listed. It is hoped that enough effects have been discussed or briefly mentioned in this chapter to indicate the wide range of effect which this invention has had in bringing changes to the American social environment.

CONCLUSION

1. The social effects resulting from the use of the automobile in the United States are so numerous as to be almost incalculable. They relate to virtually all social institutions and to nearly all life activities in one way or another, causing hundreds of social changes. The automobile has been well integrated in the American way of life. For most American families, especially those living in small communities and rural areas, use of the automobile may be considered as almost a necessity. Because of the diversity and importance of these social effects and the large number of people affected, the automobile is believed to be, in its social significance, one of the most important inventions of all time.

2. It is recognized that some of these effects involve changes of major importance, while other effects are of much less consequence. The creation of the huge automotive industry, one of America's foremost, is clearly of major import for the nation's economy. The industry's effects on other businesses, on millions of stockholders, and on the lives of millions of automotive workers and their families are of prime importance. As a source of employment (approximately one-seventh of the total American labor force) and as a tremendous producer of wealth, the motor vehicle and highway in-

---

by automobile to the Yellowstone National Park (Wyo.-Mont.). These were the four leading national parks in order of visitors during 1951 who traveled by private motor vehicle. The visitors who traveled to national parks in 1951 *by automobile* comprised 96.5 per cent of all visitors.—*Automobile Facts and Figures,* 32nd ed., 1952, p. 68. Original source of data is the National Park Service, Department of the Interior.

[64] As Chapple and Coon point out, American culture, in which the automobile complex is prominent, has enough names of parts of the automobile and aspects of automobiling to fill a good-sized book. On the other hand, our American vocabulary has only one word for *camel.* The Arab culture, in which camels assume a place of prominence, has an enormously rich vocabulary dealing with camels. The Arabs, in contrast, have only one word for automobile, "tomobil." See Eliot D. Chapple and Carleton S. Coon, *Principles of Anthropology* (New York, Holt, 1942), p. 581.

dustries clearly occupy a place of prominence in the nation's economic affairs.

Other major effects, in the opinion of this student of the automobile and its social influence, are the bringing of immeasurable benefit and enjoyment to millions of citizens in the many, diverse activities of life—the daily round of human activities; the outward expansion of population with respect to the pattern of city life (the suburban trend); the high mobility and more-cosmopolitan-mindedness of the American people; the huge governmental expenditures for highway construction; the benefits which have accrued to rural dwellers, with specific mention of the effects on rural schools and medical service; the potential importance of production of the automobile industry in time of war; the generalized effects on human attitudes of the automobile age's emphasis on speed and restlessness; and, finally, the large number of deaths and injuries resulting from motor-vehicle accidents. The latter would seem to be the greatest single negative result of the development and use of the motor vehicle.

Other effects seem to be, on the other hand, of relatively minor importance. Among this group may be mentioned the development of "auto windows" at banks and of "auto mail boxes" outside post offices—which, helpful as they are, hardly qualify as developments of great moment; the use of the "bookmobile" in rural counties, although this may be potentially important; the use of motor vehicles in parades and other community celebrations; the occurrence of auto races; and the rise of "hot-rod" driving among teenagers. Such effects as these doubtless have value and/or are matters of interest to some people; they can hardly be viewed as major developments in the life and culture of the nation.

3. It is recognized that some effects of use of the automobile would have occurred anyway with other forms of transportation, *though to a lesser extent*. Other effects would not have occurred at all without the automobile. As examples of the former type of effect, one may cite the outward expansion of population living in cities, the rendering of various community services, and the building of highways. As examples of the latter type, one may mention the creation of the motor-vehicle industry, the high mobility of the American people (outside their home community), and the resulting extension of horizons and more cosmopolitan character of the people; also the occurrence of motor-vehicle accidents, the development of automobile insurance, and development of the motel industry are specifically related to use of the motor vehicle.

4. Human adjustment to the development of the motor vehicle must be regarded as not yet complete. The toll of highway accidents is still too high, even though the motor-vehicle death rate as expressed in number of deaths per 10,000 registered vehicles has notably declined. For most American communities of moderate size or larger every day, surely every weekend, produces its list of motor-vehicle crashes. In large cities the courts are

crowded with automobile-accident cases. Traffic jams in cities are frequent, and the parking problem is likely to be difficult. Arterial highways are often crowded, and means of alleviating the problem involve fantastic expense. Despite frequent widening of roads and building of four- and six-lane highways, the gap between traffic needs and available highways is sizable. Basic to the general problem has been the huge increase in motor-vehicle registrations. Thus various lags exist in relation to the automobile invention; further adaptations need to be made.

5. Various derivative effects of use of the automobile have been noted: Effects on industry (as bringing the chain stores, neighborhood shopping centers, motel industry), effects on government, health, housing, education, church attendance, courtship behavior, recreation, and other areas. Further derivative effects are to be expected in the future. Coming effects are likely to result from the combination of many converging factors. The theoretical possibilities of new derivative effects would seem to be almost unlimited. Recognizing that other cultural forms and innovations will be related to future effects, one should take care not to claim too much for the influence of the automobile itself. Excessive claims of this nature would be indeed foolish, since the *bona fide* effects of motor-vehicle travel have been of great importance—and will doubtless continue to be so.

ANNOTATED BIBLIOGRAPHY

Automobile Manufacturers Association, *Automobile Facts and Figures* (Detroit, Mich.). Helpful annual statement of general automobile facts. Sources of data are U. S. government and other reliable organizations.

———, "One Hundred Million Motor Vehicles" (booklet), 7th printing (Detroit, Mich., 1953). Shows many social effects of use of the automobile, with pictures. Booklet was written to commemorate the production of one hundred million motor vehicles in the United States between 1893 and 1948.

COHN, David L., *Combustion on Wheels, An Informal History of the Automobile Age* (Boston, Houghton Mifflin, 1944). Light-vein but perceptive discussion of the automobile age. Author, a non-sociologist, is well informed with regard to pertinent sociological literature.

LOCKLIN, D. Philip, *Economics of Transportation,* 3rd ed. (Chicago, Irwin, 1951). Chapters 28–29 of this widely-recognized text deal with highway transportation. Well worth reading.

NEVINS, Allan, with Frank Ernest Hill, *Ford: The Times, the Man, the Company* (New York, Scribner, 1954). Henry Ford, the man who brought lower prices and mass production to the automobile industry, warrants attention. An important and interesting volume; industrial history at its best.

OGBURN, William F., "Machines and Tomorrow's World," Public Affairs Pamphlet, No. 25 (New York, Public Affairs Committee, 1938). A valuable pamphlet, written by America's leading authority on subject of social change. Has much material relative to the automobile.

OWEN, Wilfred, *Automotive Transportation: Trends and Problems* (Washington. The Brookings Institution, 1949). A concise summary of many aspects of automotive transportation, including the cost, highway, and parking problems.

RECK, Franklin M., "A Car Traveling People—How the Automobile Has Changed the Life of Americans" (pamphlet) (Detroit, Mich., Automobile Manufacturers Association, undated but apparently written about 1944). Worth reading.

SIEVERS, Allen M., *General Economics: An Introduction* (Philadelphia, Lippincott, 1952), Ch. 1, "The Automobile." Sievers begins his economics textbook with discussion of the automobile, its economic importance and social influence. An ably-written chapter.

CHAPTER 7

MOTION PICTURES

■ *Delbert C. Miller*

THE PROCESS of social change as it occurs through communication involves answers to a complex question. "*Who* communicates *what* to *whom* by *what medium,* under *what conditions,* and with *what effects?*"[1] Technology in the twentieth century has added the movie, the radio, and television to modern life. Each of these communication devices spreads ideas from some point outward toward a mass audience. They may be contrasted with such point-to-point communication media as the letter, the telephone, the telegraph, and the two-way radio.

Point-to-point devices usually involve one person communicating at a given time with another person. The mass-communication devices are used to reach audiences. It is theoretically possible for one person to communicate by radio to all persons in the world at one time. The motion picture and television have almost equal possibilities under certain conditions. Obviously, these mass-communication devices have great potential power to influence not only complete locality groups such as towns and cities but entire nations as well. No other single institution can compete with the institutions of communication in numbers of persons who are reached. In America, the church or church school touches perhaps 30 million, the school and college reach something like 50 million, but the movies attract as many as 85 million a week. Terry Ramsaye has said that "being a basic, primitive implement, the film reaches low and deep, with an order of authority to the senses enjoyed by no other form of expression."[2]

DEVELOPMENT AND CHARACTERISTICS OF MOTION PICTURES

Rise of the Motion Picture Theater

The first screening of a motion picture took place at Koster and Bials Music Hall at Broadway and Thirty-fourth Street, New York City, in 1896,[3]

---

[1] Douglas Waples, "Communications," *American Journal of Sociology,* Vol. 47 (May, 1942), p. 907.

[2] Terry Ramsaye. "The Rise and Place of the Motion Picture," *Annals of the American Academy of Political and Social Science,* Vol. 254 (November, 1947), p. 1.

[3] Mae D. Huettig, *Economic Control of the Motion Picture Industry* (Philadelphia, University of Pennsylvania Press, 1944), p. 10.

as an added attraction to the vaudeville program. The pattern of vaudeville and pictures was very successful in attracting patrons and it was extended. Into the theater came a new class of amusement buyers—the customers of the arcades, the peep shows, and the dime museums. Storerooms were converted to house the growing number of men, women, and children who sought to see the movies.

In 1905, the vaudville and pictures pattern was broken. A real estate operator in Pittsburgh took a vacant storeroom and produced a motion picture theater by the simple expedient of putting in a movie projector, a piano, and ninety-nine seats. The film shown was *The Great Train Robbery;* admission was five cents.[4] The response was instantaneous. *The Great Train Robbery* marked a turning point in the history of the movies. It created the nickelodeon which swept the country. By 1907, there were five thousand of them[5] and the demand for film mounted.

By 1913, the motion picture theater was established as a part of the community on the Main Streets of America. The movies had become respectable. In 1953, there were over 15,000 motion picture theaters in the United States and admissions numbered over 2 billion.[6] The "flickers" had all but dealt the death blow to vaudeville, the legitimate stage, and the lecture bureau. Alone among the arts, the motion picture was handed upward from the masses, and not downward from the intelligentsia.[7]

Characteristics of the Motion Picture

Produced for a large, general audience. Films possess a number of characteristics which distinguish them from other forms of mass communication. Perhaps, the most significant characteristic is that they are made for a large, general audience. The movie audience is part of a mass market which forms and disbands for each motion picture. The movie producer must sell his movie to this mass market which is characterized by a magnitude and heterogeneity unknown to the universe of print or radio. A public of at least 100 million must be sought for the showing of a feature film, and it will be judged as *one* movie, and not as simply one product from, let us say, Paramount Pictures. This is in contrast with a newspaper, which is judged by the total aspect of its news stories and editorials day after day. The movies, unlike the press and radio, have no local identity. A newspaper or radio station reflects the ideas or aspirations of all or part of the community and builds up a "public." The Hollywood-made movie must straddle the varieties of political and social philosophies of its national and international market. It

[4] *Ibid.*, p. 21.

[5] Will Hays, *See and Hear* (New York, privately printed, 1929), p. 17.

[6] See Motion Picture Theaters—Number of Theaters, Admissions and Receipts by Regions: 1948 and 1953, *Statistical Abstract of the United States, 1955* (Washington, Government Printing Office, 1955), p. 876.

[7] Benjamin B. Hampton, *A History of the Movies* (New York, Covici-Friede, 1931), pp. 7–10.

must serve all peoples and all classes. Its costs are such that it can be generally supported only by massed buying power of majorities. Many minorities cannot be served as they are by the less expensive media of radio, stage, newspaper, book, or magazine.

Audience must be physically assembled. Once a movie audience is formed, it differs from most other audiences in that the members must be physically assembled in one place in order to consume the product. Printed matter is read by one person at a time, the radio or television is listened to or watched by one or a few people, but a motion picture is viewed in a group situation by an audience ranging from 50 to 5,000 people. The audience reaction is itself an integral part of the social setting in which the film communicates.

Audience must pay for the whole product. Advertising supports radio, TV, magazines, and the newspaper, but ordinarily the full cost of the movie must be met through ticket admissions. This makes the movie a relatively expensive form of entertainment. This fact, in turn, greatly influences what is produced, for the product must be attractive enough to induce large numbers of patrons to leave the radio, television, magazines, and books which may be available in their homes.

Production methods differ greatly from those of other media. The production methods in the making of a radio program, a television broadcast, or an issue of a daily newspaper are much simpler and far less expensive than the making of a film. The film takes much longer to produce, it is much more expensive, and the technical problems are more involved.[8] The Grade-A picture from Hollywood will cost a million dollars or more.[9] A new radio station can be erected for anywhere between $25,000 and $125,000. A large metropolitan newspaper will sell for between $5,000,000 and $15,000,000. It should be emphasized that "*one* motion picture costs twice as much to produce as it takes to purchase a large radio station, lock, stock, and barrel, and that the output of any studio in Hollywood for a period of three or four months involves enough capital to purchase a metropolitan newspaper."[10] The media of print or radio derive little, if any, revenue from overseas, but a movie company may depend on foreign markets for as much as one-half of its sales revenue. In many instances, the United States market pays for the cost of production, and the foreign market represents the profit.[11] A single

[8] Cf. Robert W. Wagner, "Motion Pictures in Relation to Social Controls," in N. B. Henry, ed., *Mass Media and Education,* Fifty-third Yearbook, National Society for the Study of Education, Part II (Chicago, University of Chicago Press, 1954), esp. pp. 54–56.

[9] *Newsweek,* April 26, 1954, p. 20, reported that Warner Bros. spent $5 million on a remake of "A Star Is Born."

[10] Leo C. Rosten, "Movies and Propaganda," *Annals of the American Academy of Political and Social Science,* Vol. 254 (November, 1947), p. 117. See also Bruce Smith, Harold D. Lasswell, and Ralph D. Casey, *Propaganda, Communication, and Public Opinion* (Princeton, N. J., Princeton University Press, 1946), p. 12.

[11] Rosten, *op. cit.,* p. 122.

scene which offends the political or moral sensibilities of a nation or a cultural group may result in serious monetary losses.

CONTENT OF THE MOTION PICTURE

Dorothy B. Jones analyzed 100 Grade-A and Grade-B films released during the film season of 1941–42. Using a scheme of "wants" or values of the leading characters as a criterion of the chief aim of the motion picture, the author reported that 68 per cent wanted love; 26 per cent wanted fame, reputation, or prestige; 16 per cent wanted "safety," that is, health and economic security; 14 per cent wanted a "way of life"; 10 per cent wished for money or material goods; 9 per cent desired to do their duty. These percentages are overlapping, that is, some characters had more than one dominant want.[12]

Edgar Dale made an analysis of 500 feature films appearing between 1920 and 1930 and found similar themes, with love and sex predominating.[13]

Dale has pointed out that the most important conclusion which he derives from his data on movie content is the fact that,

in large measure the characters, the problems, and the settings are remote from the lives of the persons who view them. This remoteness is seen in the emphasis placed on romantic love, a problem which nearly all individuals must meet and face in some way but not in the manner or to the degree indicated in the motion pictures on which we have presented data. It is seen also in the emphasis on wealth and luxury which serves neither to point a desirable ideal nor to offer methods by means of which the mass of the people can attain that ideal.[14]

CHARACTERISTICS OF THE MOVIE AUDIENCE

Age

Age is the most important personal factor by which the movie audience is differentiated. The movies strongly attract young people, defined as those under 30 years of age. The 1950 Film Daily Yearbook provides the following age estimates:[15]

Years of Age	Percentage of Total Attendance
5–11 years	10%
12–17	20
18–30	35
31–45	20
Over 45	15

[12] "Quantitative Analysis of Motion Picture Content," D. B. Jones, *Public Opinion Quarterly,* Vol. 6 (1942), pp. 411–428.

[13] Edgar Dale, *The Content of Motion Pictures* (New York, Macmillan, 1935), p. 17.

[14] *Ibid.,* p. 224.

[15] *1950 Film Daily Yearbook of the Motion Pictures* (New York City, Film Daily, 1501 Broadway, 1950), p. 81.

These estimates compare closely with a survey made by Paul Lazarsfeld and C. Wright Mills in a Midwestern city of 60,000. They found that 70 per cent of their sample reported attending movies with a regularity ranging from a few times a year to many times a week. The decline of frequent movie attendance with increasing age was shown to be very sharp.[16]

The Hulton Survey of 1953, based on a representative sample of Britons, showed similar age patterns for movie-going in the British Isles.[17]

Since youth compose the greatest regular attendants of the movies, the content of pictures is to a great extent aimed at satisfying them. Seldes points out that

as Americans pass through the stage of courtship and begin married life, as they go to work, break from the protection and discipline of their parents, and begin to establish families of their own, the need for the particular satisfactions given by the movies becomes less acute.[18]

Income

Lazarsfeld reports that income and education matter little in distinguishing attendance at the movies.[19] The Hulton survey in Great Britain, however, found that a higher percentage of the lower income groups went regularly. Yet when the proportions of *all* cinema-goers is examined, including those who go occasionally, it is obvious that there is very little difference in income and social class.[20]

	Class AB*	Class C	Class D
Go Regularly to Cinema	29.8%	36.8%	43.4%
Go Occasionally	57.2%	48.8%	38.0%
All Cinema-Goers	85.0%	85.6%	81.4%
Never Attend	15.0%	14.4%	18.6%

*Class AB refers to professional and businessmen with incomes in excess of £650; Class C refers to lower middle class composed of skilled workers, small tradespeople, and the important clerical workers with incomes between £400 to £648; Class D refers to the great bulk of manual workers with incomes between £225 to £399.

Sex

All studies show that men go to the movies as often as women at all age levels.[21] It is well known that people usually go to the movies in company

16 Paul F. Lazarsfeld, "Audience Research in the Movie Field," *Annals of the American Academy of Political and Social Science,* Vol. 254 (November, 1947), p. 164.

17 Hulton Research, *Hulton Readership Survey of 1953* (London, Hulton Press, 1953).

18 Gilbert Seldes, *The Great Audience* (New York, Viking Press, 1950), p. 12.

19 Lazarsfeld, *op. cit.* p. 165. Lazarsfeld reports that rural people go to the movies considerable less often than urban people.

20 Hulton Research, *Patterns of British Life* (London, Hulton Press, 1950), p. 139. The table is an adaptation of the original data.

21 Based on Lazarsfeld and Hulton surveys.

with others. In the Lazarsfeld-Mills sample, 91 per cent reported that they went to the last movie in the company of others, in most cases with their family, and in other cases with their friends. The typical attendance unit consists of two people. The act of movie-going, therefore, must be regarded as a product of group decision rather than of individual decision.

Film Discrimination

When asked whether they went to see a certain picture or primarily just to go to the movies, 60 per cent of the Lazarsfeld-Mills sample replied they chose a picture; 21 per cent just wanted to see whatever was available; and 19 per cent checked both reasons. It is believed that a substantial core of regular movie-goers habitually attend once or more a week, and probably go to the same theater. They accept whatever program is provided, good or bad, comedy or tragedy.[22] With the competition of TV, more people may select films before attending the picture.

USES OF MOTION PICTURES

The largest investment in the movies is for the production of commercial entertainment films. However, a growing use of non-theatrical film is found in education,[23] religion,[24] industry,[25] military organization[26] and in a variety of community groups.[27] It is estimated that between 500 and 1,000 non-theatrical films are now being produced each year.

The film has a wide range of uses, many of them still untapped. They can be used in scientific work, in therapy, in art, and in teaching.[28] The filming of textbook material has begun.[29]

The statistics on the production of film by various producers is revealing. In 1947 the production of film was being carried on as follows:[30]

[22] Lazarsfeld, *op. cit.* p. 164. A study made in 1946 in England showed that almost a quarter of the people who go to watch films once a month or more often generally visit the same cinema regardless of program.—Kathleen Box, *The Cinema and the Public,* Social Survey Report, No. 106, 1946.

[23] James W. Brown and A. W. VanderMeer, "School Use of Audio-Visual Instructional Materials," in N. B. Henry, ed, *Audio-Visual Materials of Instruction,* Forty-eighth Yearbook, National Society for the Study of Education, Part I (Chicago, University of Chicago Press, 1949), p. 42.

[24] Gloria Waldron, *The Information Film* (New York, Columbia University Press, 1949).

[25] Henry C. Gipson, *Films in Business and Industry* (New York, McGraw-Hill, 1947).

[26] Charles F. Hoban, *Movies That Teach* (New York, Dryden Press, 1946).

[27] Gloria Waldron, *op. cit.,* p. 159.

[28] Paul Rotha, *Documentary* Film (New York, Norton, 1939); The Arts Enquiry, *The Factual Film* (London, Oxford University Press, 1947); Gloria Waldron, *op. cit.;* Forsyth Hardy, ed., *Grierson on Documentary* (New York, Harcourt, Brace, 1947).

[29] McGraw-Hill Book Company has a Film-Text Department.

[30] Bureau of the Census, *Statistical Abstract of the United States, 1953* (Washington, Government Printing Office, 1953), p. 839 (Table 1003). Original source of data: 1947 Census of Manufacturers.

Type of Production	Number of Establishments	Number of Employees	Total Cost of Work Done
Theatrical Film Producers	100	27,549	$383,082,000
Non-Theatrical Film Producers	127	2,445	18,359,000
Laboratories and Other Service Organizations	50	4,805	58,702,000

Roger Manvell, Director of the British Film Academy, believes that four main forms of film making will dominate the motion picture industry. These are:[31]

Films for TV, using the familiar TV screen size.

Films for science, industry, or education using current screen sizes and perhaps introducing stereoscopic techniques.

Wide screen films for popular entertainment.

Films for selected theaters on huge curved screens filling the greater part of your range of vision, so that you feel that you are taking part in the action.

SOCIAL EFFECTS OF MOTION PICTURES

The Motion Picture Theater as a Social Institution

The local motion picture theater is a social institution which serves many different social-psychological needs. The motives of the movie-goer have been described as follows:[32]

I go to be distracted (or "taken out of myself"); I go when I don't want to think; I go when I do want to think and need stimulus; I go to see pretty people; I go when I want to see life ginned up, charged with unlikely energy; I go to laugh; I go to be harrowed; I go when a day has been such a mess of detail that I am glad to see even the most arbitrary, the most preposterous, pattern emerge; I go because I like bright light, abrupt shadow, speed; I go to see America, France, Russia; I go because I like wisecracks and slick behaviour; I go because the screen is an oblong opening into the world of fantasy for me; I go because I like a story, with its suspense; I go because I like sitting in a packed crowd in the dark, among hundreds riveted on the same thing; I go to have my most general feelings played on. These reasons, put down roughly, seem to fall under five headings; wish to escape, lassitude, sense of lack in my nature or my surroundings, loneliness (however passing), and natural frivolity.

From such motives and others, the box office demand is built. To the exhibitor, the supplying of films to satisfy such motives is a business service through which he makes his living. As such he is a sensitive financial barometer. He watches the box office and talks with patrons. The exhibitors' willing-

[31] Bristol Evening World, November 17, 1954, p. 7.

[32] Elizabeth Bowen, in Charles Davey, ed., Footnotes to Film (London, Lovat Dickson, Ltd., 1937), p. 205.

ness to pay higher film rentals indicates to the producer that he has sensed the trend of public entertainment wants.[33]

Rarely does a studio venture to produce a feature picture unless it believes it will be a real money maker.[34] Occasionally, a studio will deliberately produce a picture for prestige purposes. However, with production costs more than doubled in the last ten years the picture must usually be selected for its money-making possibilities.[35]

Role of the Movies in Recreation

Trends in the use of leisure time reflect changes in our economic and social structure. At the turn of the century, the list of leisure activities would have included church suppers, lodge nights, and other entertainment by fraternal organizations, fairs, bazaars, horse races, and strawberry festivals. The twentieth century has brought many new developments in recreation such as:

1. A great expansion of pleasure travel, chiefly by means of the automobile.
2. Universal popularity of the movies, radio, and television.
3. A growing interest in competitive sports, both as participants and spectators.
4. Widespread development of public recreational facilities.[36]

The most significant change is the vast growth of organized and commercial recreation made possible by the shortening of working hours, increased leisure time, and a rising standard of living. The motion picture theater has risen on these trends. During the years of World War II, the movies had a virtual monopoly of the entertainment business. With national employment at an all-time peak, transportation blocked, and radio converted in large part to the dissemination of war news, the movie theaters enjoyed an automatic attendance limited only by the hours of the day and their seating capacity. With the end of the war, movie attendance declined.[37] The table below shows movie attendance for 1945–53 and gives some corresponding figures for television's growth.[38]

[33] Charles P. Skouras, "The Exhibitor," *Annals of the American Academy of Political and Social Science, op. cit.,* p. 123.

[34] Leo C. Rosten, "Movies and Propaganda," *Annals of the American Academy of Political and Social Science, op. cit.,* p. 123.

[35] Floyd B. Odlum, "Financial Organization of the Motion Picture Industry," *Annals of the American Academy of Political and Social Science, op. cit.,* p. 22.

[36] J. Frederick Dewhurst and Associates, *America's Needs and Resources, A New Survey* (New York, The Twentieth Century Fund, 1955), Ch. 11.

[37] John Houseman, "Hollywood Faces the Fifties," *Harper's* (April, 1950), p. 50.

[38] Source: Standard and Poor's Industry Surveys: *Motion Pictures, 1953.* The figures for the number of cinemas are complicated by the growth of drive-in cinemas which are included and estimated to have grown from 800 in 1948 to 4,000 by the end of 1952. The number of normal type cinemas closed down during the last few years thus runs to probably 5,000 or more.

MOVIE AND TELEVISION TRENDS IN THE UNITED STATES

Year	Average Weekly Movie Attendance (Millions)	Number of Television Sets in Use (End of Year) in Millions	Number of Motion Picture Theaters (End of Year)
1945	98	—	21,550
1946	98	—	20,300
1947	90	—	19,200
1948	88	1	20,100
1949	70	3	19,300
1950	60	10	19,800
1951	54	15	19,000
1953*	41	28†	15,504*

* SOURCE: Department of Commerce, Bureau of the Census, 1953 Report on Motion Picture Theaters.
† SOURCE: *The World Almanac,* 1956, p. 790.

The effect of this decline has been to throw many theaters out of business. The number of admissions to motion picture theaters in the United States in 1948 was 3,351,778,000; in 1953, 2,120,012,000—a drop of 36.7 per cent.[39]

Whatever may be the other causes for the decline in movie attendance, television cannot be discounted as the chief rival. By 1956 more than two out of three homes in America had a television set. A *New York Times* survey of 100 TV areas across the country places the drop in movie attendance at from 20 to 40 per cent in those localities. By 1960 it is expected that television will be in almost all homes throughout the United States. Even if this estimate is not reached, it is obvious that the movies have a challenge the like of which they have never faced in the half-century of their birth and growth. The impact of television on Derby, England, may be taken as representative. The researchers who made the study of movie-going and television were careful to see that the television-owning and non-television-owning groups which they compared were matched for sex, social class, and age. This matching, in turn, provided an approximate balance for occupation and education. The results are shown in the table below.

MOVIE-GOING AND TELEVISION (DERBY): SPRING, 1953

	People in Homes with Television	People in Homes Without Television (Balanced Sample)
Number interviewed	345 = 100%	500 = 100%
Proportion going to the movies	%	%
Once or more a week	17	29
1–3 times a month	15	17
Less than once a month	34	35
Never	34	19

[39] See *Statistical Abstract of the United States, 1955* (Washington, Government Printing Office, 1955), p. 875.

The table reveals a sharp drop among television homes in the proportion of people who go to the movies every week, and an increase in the proportion of those who never go at all. An analysis made of visits during the seven days before interview showed a fall of about a third in movie attendances by people in homes with television when compared with attendances by the people in homes without a set.[40]

The movies have added color, three-dimensional images with larger screens, and directional sound. Movie-going has incorporated such accompanying activities as outdoor movies, bank nights, and popcorn eating. And today, in the face of television, it continues to hold an important place in the lives of millions of Americans and foreigners who see the American films.[41]

General Effects on Social Behavior

The movies as a reflector of social values. The movies may transmit traditional values, reinforce "idealized values," or create new cultural values. As entertainment, the movies function primarily on the emotional level through their production of daydreams. Certain "idealized" values are greatly emphasized. For example, there is an almost obsessional emphasis on "romantic love." Love is presented as the goal of existence. Making money, work, friendships, and one's place in the world are all given a secondary place. The emphasis on love is commonly coupled with sex themes. It is often impossible to make any distinction in the films between the two—in fact, sexual attraction is commonly presented as "love."

The real world has crime and violence in it. The movie world takes themes of crime and builds them into elaborate emotional pictures of personal and social deviation. The just and happy ending of the plot vindicates the validity of the moral principles: "Be good and you will be blessed."

The Movie Heroine. Within these two major themes of romantic love and crime, the movies create characters which reflect traditional and idealized values of life. The supporting players are often cast in more genuine portrayals of the roles enacted in real life. The hero and heroine are more often idealized to fit current styles of romantic love. Wolfenstein and Leites point out that the modern Hollywood heroine may be called a "good-bad girl."[42] The old style vamp of the twenties, who used her sexual appeal

---

[40] T. Cauter and J. S. Downham, *The Communication of Ideas* (London, Chatto and Windus, 1954), p. 130.

[41] The following advantages are claimed for the motion picture: (1) Provides an audience experience for the movie-goer, a satisfaction only partly attainable for the small group around a television receiver. (2) The large screen provides a much larger picture of better quality than is possible in television. (3) The movie is a planned, carefully photographed (often in vast exteriors) and elicited product in contrast with the television product which captures a live action on the spot, as it happens (like a sports event), or photographs its staged events on a very small set and close up for transmission on the small television screen.

to fascinate men and lead them to ruin, has been replaced by this good-bad girl. The vamps were dangerous women.

The "good-bad girl" type tends to combine the satisfactions of profane and sacred love. Freud has said that the difficulty of choosing between a good and bad girl is one of the major problems in the love life of Western man. The difficulty arises in associating two impulses with the same woman. There are sexual impulses which a man may feel to be bad and which he may therefore find difficult to associate with a woman whom he considers "good." A good girl is the sort a man should marry, but she may not be sexually stimulating. The "good-bad" girl resolves this dilemma on the screen because she satisfies every need. This stereotype reflects trends in American culture. The ideal of monogamy persists and calls for affectionate impulses which are evoked by women who resemble the man's mother or sister, that is, "good" women. Hedonistic demands point to the "bad" girl who excites and pleases the senses. The combination of monogamy and hedonism leads to the expectation of finding one person who will satisfy every wish. The high divorce rate is, in part, an index of the failure to find these almost impossible expectations in the same woman.[43]

The Movie Mores. The Institute of Propaganda Analysis in 1938 listed the following samples of value judgments common in the movies:[44]

1. That the successful culmination of a romance will solve most of the dilemmas of the hero and heroine.
2. Catch the criminal and you solve the crime problem.
3. War and the preparation for war are thrilling, heroic, and glamorous.
4. The good life is the acquisitive life, with its emphasis upon luxury, fine homes and automobiles, evening dress, swank, and suavity.

The Movie Taboos. The taboos of society have been especially imposed upon the film industry. Inglis says that

no pressure coming from outside the industry has been more powerful or persistent than that concerned with the moral effects of motion pictures. Since the earliest beginnings of the movies, women's, civic, welfare, and religious groups have worried about the effect of movies upon children; upon the mentally, emotionally, or morally retarded; and upon the whole society.[45]

Inglis declares that the usual response of the motion picture industry has been to evade the morality issue whenever possible but yield when necessary. Self-regulation through a Production Code has been industry's method of fulfilling its obligations with reference to the moral content of films. Since

42 Martha Wolfenstein and Nathan Leites, "An Analysis of Themes and Plots," *Annals of the American Academy of Political and Social Science, op. cit.*, p. 44.
43 It is granted that there are many different reasons for divorce.
44 *Propaganda Analysis* (New York, Institute for Propaganda Analysis, 1938).
45 Ruth A. Inglis, *Freedom of the Movies* (Chicago, University of Chicago Press, 1947), pp. 1–2.

the code is a list of prohibitions which have emerged as the result of societal judgments, it is a reasonably accurate portrayal of the active taboos in modern society.[46] The principal restrictions are defined as:

1. *Crimes against the law*. These shall never be presented in such a way as to throw sympathy with the crime as against law and justice or to inspire others with a desire for imitation.

2. *Sex*. The sanctity of the institution of marriage and the home shall be upheld. Pictures shall not infer that low forms of sex relationship are the accepted or common thing.

3. *Vulgarity*. The treatment of low, disgusting, unpleasant, though not necessarily evil, subjects should be guided always by the dictates of good taste and a proper regard for the sensibilities of the audience.

4. *Obscenity*. Obscenity in word, gesture, reference, song, joke, or by suggestion (even when likely to be understood only by part of the audience) is forbidden.

5. *Profanity*. Pointed profanity and every other profane or vulgar expression, however used, is forbidden.

6. Numerous restrictions are set forth regarding *costume, dances, religion, national feelings, titles, and repellent subjects*.

The movies as a creator of values. The role of the motion picture in creating values has been an object of much philosophic reflection, but little is known of its possibilities. The use of film as a vehicle of entertainment has almost excluded the use of film as a social medium of public enlightenment. However, there is general agreement that the screen's power to influence is tremendous. Eric Johnston, President of the Motion Picture Association, list the following assets:[47]

We know that a motion picture based on a classical novel will induce thousands of people to read or reread the book; we know that the introduction of a classical musical composition into a motion picture story will stimulate the demand for recordings of that composition. We know—almost as a matter of common knowledge—that great numbers of the American people are better informed as a result of attending motion pictures, and here I include the newsreels, which record history in the making. We know that the motion picture has contributed hugely to breaking down the cramping boundaries of provincialism with the United States. What we do not yet know, but what I think we shall realize in the days ahead, is that the motion picture can also break down barriers of misunderstanding among nations as readily as it has broken down lesser barriers within this country.

The role of the motion picture in creating values depends on the function it serves. Three principal views can be observed:

1. The function of the motion picture is to provide "pure" entertainment.
2. The function of the motion picture is to provide mature presentation of serious subjects and all sides of controversial questions.

[46] *Ibid.*, pp. 206–209.
[47] Eric Johnston, "The Motion Picture as a Stimulus to Culture," *Annals of the American Academy of Political Social Science, op. cit.*, p. 98.

3. The function of the motion picture is to serve as a positive instrument in reinforcing democracy and opposing totalitarianism.

These three views raise questions of policy and the place of all mass media in the total society. Such questions are outside the scope of this chapter. The pertinent scientific question is, "To what extent can film content actually serve as stimuli for changes in attitude, belief, and act?" It is important to remember that almost all "effects" derive from the (theatrical) motion picture industry which now functions mainly to provide the public with "pure" entertainment.

General Impact on Knowledge and Habits

Two effects may be identified as applying to large groups of persons who are influenced by the motion pictures or by ideas generated through them. They are (a) the homogeneity effect, and (b) the reinforcing effect.

The homogeneity effect. This effect is seen in the ability of a film to convey behavior which is adopted by the participants. Countless examples can be drawn from influences involving clothing, speech, hair style, manners, and love-making. Lazarsfeld specifically asked the sample of women drawn from the Midwestern city the following: "Have you ever happened to get any ideas on what kind of clothes to wear or how to fix your hair from the movies you see." Twenty-six per cent answered in the affirmative,[48] and it can be inferred that others were influenced but were not conscious of it.

Dale has made a study of the clothing worn by leading characters and the patterns of love-making shown in one sample of films. He concludes that film characters are used as behavior models and that their patterns are imitated. He points out that motion picture producers have been intensely aware of the screen as an advertising medium. Clothing copied from that worn by the stars is sold in department stores, sometimes so as to fit in with the time the picture is released. Advertising may also be arranged through screen magazines.[49] J. F. Dewhurst believes that the radio and movies are probably the most powerful influences in standardizing the attitudes, tastes, and consumer demands of the bulk of the United States population. To their influence is ascribed the erasing of many elements of heterogeneity that have characterized our population in the past.[50]

The reinforcing effect. In the area of public opinion toward controversial issues, the most conspicuous effect of communications is a reinforcement of existing opinions. The most competent studies of the various media of communication have, in general, minimized the social effects of propaganda, except when it coincides with strong predispositions and is made convincing

[48] Paul S. Lazarsfeld, *op. cit.* p. 168.
[49] Edgar Dale, *The Content of Motion Pictures* (New York, Macmillan, 1935), pp. 67–68.
[50] Dewhurst, *op. cit.*

by the short-run trend of current events.[51] This reinforcing effect places prime importance upon social background and personality. If the person is responsive to the patterns observed, he may on occasion use ideas and techniques seen at the movies.[52]

Now people have to be reached if changes are to take place, and it has been repeatedly observed that people avoid those controversial values with which they do not agree.

Every laboratory experiment has shown that an educational film or radio program increases greatly the knowledge of lower educated people. But the same people for whom these experiments show great change would not under ordinary circumstances, be the ones who would listen to the program or see the film.[53]

Moreover, there is considerable consensus that the motion pictures stress values that are "typically those which make no contribution to the process of social change."[54]

If the traditional values are emphasized at the exclusion of alternatives, then the motion picture remains as a conservatice force. Failure to use the film as a medium for the presentation of controversial issues restricts its influence to entertainment and to traditional values. The threat of governmental repression is sometimes given as a reason for not presenting controversial issues on the screen. Darryl Zanuck, the movie producer, has made this claim in *Treasury for the Free World*:[55]

Let me be blunt. The fear of political reprisal and persecution has been a millstone about the neck of the industry for many years. It has prevented free expression on the screen and retarded its development. The loss has not been merely our own. It has been the nation's and the world's.

While Darryl Zanuck of the private film industry fears governmental reprisal and gives it as a reason for abstaining from the production of controversial films, Paul Rotha, a foremost English producer of documentary film, claims that private industry cannot support the serious film:[56]

[51] Douglas Waples, *Print, Radio, and Film in a Democracy* (Chicago, University of Chicago Press, 1942).

[52] Paul G. Cressey, "The Motion Picture Experience as Modified by Social Background and Personality," *American Sociological Review*, Vol. 3 (August, 1938), p. 517.

[53] Paul F. Lazarsfeld, "Communication Research and the Social Psychologist," in Wayne Dennis, ed., *Current Trends in Social Psychology* (Pittsburgh, University of Pittsburgh Press, 1951).

[54] Muzafer Sherif and Stansfeld Sargent, "Ego Involvement and the Mass Media," *Journal of Social Issues*, Vol. III (Summer, 1947), p. 16. Cf. Paul Lazarsfeld, *Current Trends in Social Psychology* p. 253; see also Douglas Waples, Bernard Berelson, and F. R. Bradshaw, *What Reading Does to People* (Chicago, University of Chicago Press, 1940); Paul F. Lazarsfeld, "The Effect of Radio on Public Opinion," in *Print, Radio, and Film in a Democracy, op. cit.*

[55] Quoted by Inglis, *op. cit.*, p. 17.

[56] Paul Rotha, *op. cit.*, Cf. M. Ernst, *The First Freedom* (New York, Macmillan, 1946). Ernst points out that the major American movie studios own a large part of the more important movie houses all over the country. It is therefore, difficult for experimental movies to develop in America because it would be difficult to get them exhibited.

The fact is that under the limits defined by the present economic system, entertainment cinema cannot possible hope to deal either accurately or impartially from a sociological point of view with any of the really important subjects of modern existence. It is my contention, moreover, that whilst developed under the demands of financial speculation alone, cinema is unable to reach a point where its service to public interest amounts to anything more valuable than an emotional catharsis.

Institutional Effects

Recreation. The movie audience is usually a society of strangers, but there are latent bonds of common experience among the members. All of the wants encouraged by modern life reside in the personalities assembled. The movie patron, having gained admittance to this temporary society by payment of a fee, secures a place among other people like himself and the illusion of intimate contact with the exciting and the beautiful people of the screen. If he is lonely, he secures the euphoria of social contact. If he is beset with anxieties, he escapes from the tensions of an immediate world. If he is gay, he may laugh through his idle hours.

In the emotional atmosphere created by dramatic situations, suggestive cues initiated by an audience member are particularly apt to be stimulating to other members. Something like a chain reaction of response can be observed, and sometimes this feeds back and causes a heightening of response through circular stimulation. Studies of audience laughter reveal that the frequency and length of audience laughter is highly correlated with the size of the audience.[57]

The movie experience may be seen as largely socially directed by the film, but is combined with the significant fact of audience participation.

The movie experience may variously (1) provide the essential satisfaction of fantasy; (2) blunt the individual's powers of emotional response; or (3) narcotize the person so that personal and social problems are avoided.

1. People go to the cinema because they receive something that supplements their daily life. Fantasy provides an essential part of the life of the individual. In the main, the interests of people center on love problems and the struggle for bread, money, and position. The lifelike presentation in the motion picture satisfies the imagination of many persons better than books and lectures. One psychologist explains:[58]

I am perhaps not greatly mistaken in saying that the vicarious satisfaction of sexual and aggressive tendencies, providing compensation for what concrete life has not given to the individual—love, happiness, appreciation, success, position, supremacy—constitutes the main gift which the "movies" are able to present,

[57] Jack Morrison, "Audience Laughter," *Sociometry*, Vol. III (April, 1940), pp. 179–185.
[58] Samuel Lowy, *Man and His Fellowmen* (London, Kegan, Paul, Trench, Trubner, 1944). A summary of thought and research on origins and prevalence of hostility may be found in Robin M. Williams, Jr., *The Reduction of Inter-group Tensions* (New York, Social Science Research Council, 1947), pp. 47–77.

with such variation and regular frequency, with such appeal to individuals of all types, on a scale which has apparently been approached by nothing else yet known in social history. The overwhelming majority of people feel more or less frustrated, feel more or less a tendency toward revenge and aggression under the influence of the particular conditions of our life. And there is no doubt about the satisfaction-value of the cinema-plays on this point. By the process of identification with the actors of the play the spectators gain a temporary satisfaction of their own ambitions and of their tendencies to revenge.

Still more obvious is the temporary satisfaction and compensation for subjective deficiencies in that other sphere of human life, love, and sex. I have used the expressions compensation and satisfaction. For these are, in fact, two different thirsts that can be quenched through the enjoyment of the "pictures."

Franklin Fearing concurs in the view that the films provide a great deal of emotional catharsis in releasing aggressions and inhibitions and affording a vicarious outlet for the tensions of modern living.[59]

2. J. Mayer concludes from his study of British movie autobiographies that the films may lead to a degree of emotional exhaustion from regular overstimulation of the more violent feeling which run through a large proportion of current output. He believes that the long-run effect may be to make the person increasingly incapable of sensitive reactions in real life.[60]

3. Norman Woelfel sees the movie as the real "opiate of the people";[61]

At the cinema, for a pittance, boys and girls and men and women are enabled truly to live outside themselves for a few hours. Here they may laugh, cry, be mystified, horrified, thrilled, entertained, educated, informed, saddened. They can go on an emotional spree at will. . . . There can be little wonder at the increasing failure of people to be interested in how they are governed, how they are educated, how they are made secure in the Four Freedoms, how they should regard institutions like the church and the law, how they can achieve democracy and international peace, when escape to synthetic romance and adventure is so near at hand in the neighborhood motion picture theatre.

Delinquency and crime. *Alleged Injurious Effects of the Movies.* The movies have been frequently under attack for their alleged influence on delinquency and crime. Mortimer J. Adler has summarized the injurious effects that the movies are alleged to produce. The effects include injury to health, morals, education, and public manners.[62]

Of these assorted effects, two firm statements can be made. First, it can

[59] Franklin Fearing, "Influence of Movies on Attitude and Behavior," *Annals, of the American Academy of Political and Social Science, op. cit.,* pp. 75–77.

[60] J. Mayer, *Sociology of the Film* (London, Faber and Faber, 1945), p. 168.

[61] Norman Woelfel, "The American Mind and the Motion Picture," *Annals of the American Academy of Political and Social Science, op. cit.,* p. 92. One group of critics accepts the fact that the movies should always play a significant role as an instrument of diversion, but point out that there are many themes that can recreate far better than escape dramas. They suggest that the movies can lead in showing ways of life that have consequences for the political, economic, and artistic consequences of the people. See Roger Manvell, *Film* (London, Penguin, 1946).

[62] Mortimer J. Adler, *Art and Prudence* (New York, Longmans, Green, 1937), p. 151.

be said that nearly everyone—social scientists, movie-makers, and laymen —seems to agree that there are profoundly important relationships between motion pictures and human behavior. Secondly, very little in the way of research exists to demonstrate how these relationships are formed and how they influence attitudes and behavior. The best systematic body of research which exists is that obtained in a series of studies conducted by a number of sociologists and psychologists under the aegis of the Motion Picture Research Council and financed by the Payne Fund. The results of these studies, usually known as the Payne Fund Studies, were published as a series of monographs in 1933.[63]

More than twenty years have elapsed, and few other studies on the effects of movies on conduct have been made.[64]

The film industry, fifth largest industry in the United States, has sponsored very little systematic research on its product or the factors influencing the acceptance of the product.[65]

However, the behavior mechanism by which movie content becomes a stimulus source is known. The definition of "cause" is the crucial problem.

The Defining of Cause. The question of cause arises when the attempt is made to attribute some definite form of behavior—for example, juvenile delinquency—to the specific influence of the movies. It has been pointed out by various writers that there are two distinct levels to be recognized in interpreting the influence of the motion picture.[66] We must differentiate between (1) the *content* of motion pictures as a stimulus source for patterns of thought, feeling, and behavior; and (2) the study of its *net contribution* in terms of the total social situation in which it is experienced by a given person.

The study of the motion pictures as a source focuses attention upon the content of films and the hypothetical reaction of viewers to that content. It cannot be assumed, however, that the film has some specific effects on an audience that is more or less inert or in some manner especially impression-

[63] Following is a list of these monographs. All of them were published by Macmillan, New York, 1933, except two by Edgar Dale in 1935 as noted. Herbert Blumer, *Movies and Conduct;* Herbert Blumer and Philip M. Hauser, *Movies, Delinquency and Crime;* W. W. Charters, *Motion Pictures and Youth; A Summary;* Edgar Dale, *Children Attendance at Motion Pictures* (1935); Edgar Dale, *How to Appreciate Motion Pictures;* Wendell Dysinger and Christian A. Ruckmick, *The Emotional Responses of Children to the Motion Picture Situation;* Perry Holaday and George D. Stoddard, *Getting Ideas from the Movies;* Mark A. May and Frank K. Shuttleworth, *The Social Conduct and Attitudes of Movie Fans;* Charles J. Peters, *Motion Pictures and Standards of Morality;* Samuel Renshaw, Vernon L. Miller, and Dorothy Marquis, *Children's Sleep;* L. L. Thurstone and R. C. Peterson, *Motion Pictures and the Social Attitude of Children.*

[64] Readers interested in a psychological interpretation should examine *Movies, A Psychological Study,* by Martha Wolfenstein and Nathan Leites (Glencoe, Ill., Free Press, 1950). Cf. J. Mayer.

[65] Franklin Fearing, "Influence of the Movies on Attitudes and Behavior," *Annals of the American Academy of Political and Social Science, op. cit.* p. 71.

[66] Paul G. Cressey, *op. cit.,* p. 517.

able, and hence may be affected or swayed in a given direction. This is a simple one-directional view which implies that the film has stimulus values that are alone responsible for subsequent attitudes or behavior patterns. Much of the thinking which describes harmful behavior to films is based on this unilateral cause-effect chain.

Social scientists reject this explanation of causation. They recognize that the motion picture is not a fixed pattern of meanings or ideas which are received by a passive mind. They believe the individual reacts selectively, that is, what he "gets" is determined by *his social background* and *his needs*. How he organizes them depends upon the particular configuration of the needs which the individual brings with him. How he expresses them in conduct will depend to a great extent on the social groups in which he participates. The study of the motion picture becomes an extraordinarily complex process of isolating the net contribution of the film to a given person within a total social situation.

Influence of Movies on Conduct. Herbert Blumer undertook to appraise the influence of the movies on the conduct of youth by evaluating the "motion picture autobiographies" of 1,823 young Americans of varying race, color, and religion. He found that the adolescent is particularly *prone to daydreaming,* with 66 per cent of the high school students acknowledging this experience as a result of seeing films. A high proportion of the fantasies described were concerned with wealth, luxury, social ambition, and success of various kinds. The fantasy was often enjoyed for its own sake and was generally unaccompanied by any overt behavior. However, *imitation* of some kind was reported by 62 per cent of high school students. The usual imitations were in the area of clothes, mannerisms, and methods of love-making. *Emotional possession* was frequently reported. Films evoke measurable reactions of children to two types of scene—love and danger. The experience of fright seems to be common in witnessing certain kinds of motion pictures according to reports of children, high school, and college students.[67] A few children at the age of 9 years react to erotic scenes in motion pictures, and this reaction occurs in increasing numbers of children until its climax among the 16- to 18-year-olds and thereafter falls away probably through the influence of adult discount.[68] Both boys and girls reported that, in some instances, love pictures made them *more receptive to love-making* and *induced relaxation of ordinary controls.* One youth reported that "I generally pick the movies we attend with that point in mind—the girl's emotional state can be regulated and used to what may be either advantage or disadvantage."

In the area of crime, the movies were found to be stimulating for those predisposed to delinquent or criminal patterns of behavior. The study concludes that crime and sex pictures are an aggravating influence on de-

[67] These conclusions are drawn from H. Blumer, *Movies and Conduct.*
[68] Dysinger and Ruckmick, *op. cit.*

linquents. They *stimulate daydreaming and provide techniques for crime and sex delinquency.*[69]

Blumer's interpretation[70] is that the:

motion pictures may challenge what other institutions take for granted. The schemes of conduct which they present may not only fill gaps left by the school, by the home, and by the church, but they may also cut athwart the standards and values which these latter institutions seek to inculcate. What is presented as entertainment with perhaps no thought of challenging established values, may be accepted as sanctioned conduct and so enter into conflict with certain of these values. This is peculiarly likely in the case of motion pictures, because they often present the extremes as if they were the norm. For the young movie-goer little discrimination is possible. He probably could not *understand* or even *read* a sophisticated book, but he can *see* the thing in the movies and be stirred and possibly misled. This is likely to be true chiefly among those with least education and sophisticated experience.

Education. *Educational Implications of Theatrical Films.* A number of findings from research reveal the significance of theatrical films as an educative force. These include such findings as:

1. Any film, regardless of its character—documentary, musical, western, or realistic—has some measurable effects on the specific attitudes of those exposed to it and provided the audience is sufficiently interested to give it sustained attention.[71] There are striking individual differences. There are clear differences in reaction in terms of age.

2. Children even of the early age of 8 see half the facts in a picture and remember them for a surprisingly long time. The second- and third-grade children at the end of six weeks remembered 90 per cent of what they knew on the day following the show.[72] The effect of films on adult learning has been reported as marked.[73]

3. Children of all ages tend to accept as authentic what they see in the movies unless it is flagrantly incorrect.[74]

4. The attitude of children toward a social value can be measurably changed by one exposure to a picture. The effect of similar and continued exposure is cumulative.[75] Effect on opinion is reported as less marked for adults than changes in factual knowledge.[76]

5. Sleep patterns are often affected by the movies. Renshaw, Miller, and Marquis studied 163 children in nine experiments. Normal sleep patterns were ascertained in terms of motility. The children were exposed to the movies, and then changes were observed in the sleep patterns after attendance. Beneath the

[69] Summary of Blumer and Hauser's study in W. W. Charters, *op. cit.,* pp. 54–55.

[70] H. Blumer, *op. cit.,* pp. 196–197.

[71] F. Fearing, *op. cit.,* p. 79.

[72] P. W. Holaday and George D. Stoddard, *Getting Ideas from the Movies, op. cit.*

[73] Carl I. Hovland, Arthur A. Lumsdaine, and Fred D. Sheffield, *Experiments on Mass Communication* (Princeton, N. J., Princeton University Press, 1949), p. 254.

[74] Holaday and Stoddard, *op. cit.*

[75] Ruth C. Peterson and L. L. Thurstone, *Motion Pictures and the Social Attitudes of Children, op. cit.*

[76] Hovland and Lumsdaine, *op. cit.*

bed of each child was attached a hypnograph unit which caused an electrical contact to break whenever the occupant of the bed moved slightly. This motility of the child was automatically recorded on a polygraph unit. Increase in motility following the movies ranged from 0 to 90 per cent. On the average, boys showed 26 per cent and girls 14 per cent greater hourly motility after movies than in normal sleep.[77]

6. The influence of movies on conduct is due to the factor of emotional possession which is especially strong in children because they have not developed in marked degree the emotional detachment and discount which characterizes adult viewing. The motion picture plays a role in the informal guidance of children. The movies have been observed to influence play patterns. The movies stimulate ambitions, and develop ideals. There is great individual variation in the conduct patterns which result from given movies.[78]

7. Films express basic meanings inherent in the relationships of human beings to each other and to the society of which they are a part. Films assist the individual in structuring his world—of making some intelligible arrangement out of his life.[79]

Educational Implications of Nontheatrical Films. Considerable research has been devoted to the effectiveness of films in teaching. Some of the research findings may be stated as follows:[80]

1. In a number of knowledge areas, films enable students to learn more quickly and to retain learning longer than they otherwise would. In one study the film-using group averaged 38 per cent higher in terms of retained information than did the control group.

2. Use of films conclusively motivates heightened interest in pupils.

3. Movies dealing with people, causal relationships, and social and economic relations were more valuable than those concerned with dates and events sequences.

4. Film-using groups make more intelligent judgments and interpretations and more readily grasp interrelationships.

5. Motion pictures do not, of themselves, develop critical thinking, but they provide experiences particularly rich in opportunity and material for such development. The kind of critical thinking developed on the basis of film usage is likely to be more realistic and more functional in the lives of students than that developed on the basis of verbal experience alone.[81]

6. Motion pictures portray social customs, actions, and behavior graphically. Retained impressions affect not only the critical thinking of children but also their attitudes and actions.

[77] Renshaw, Miller, and Marquis, *op. cit.*

[78] See Charters, *Motion Pictures and Youth, op. cit.*, pp. 35–44. The Wiggie Test is now used to choose films for the Children's Film Library. Two trained observers post themselves inconspicuously in the side aisles of the little theatre where they can watch the facial expressions and uninhibited body movements of the 60–80 boys and girls. A recording of behavior is made under eight classifications. See Henri Storck, *The Entertainment Film for Juvenile Audiences* (Paris, UNESCO, 1950), pp. 231–237.

[79] F. Fearing, *op. cit.*, pp. 75–78.

[80] The summary is by Walter A. Wittich and John G. Fowlkes, *Audio-Visual Paths to Learning* (New York, Harper, 1946). Cf. the summary in Dale, Finn, and Hoban, *op. cit.*, p. 255.

[81] Charles Hoban, Jr., *Movies That Teach* (New York, Harper, 1946). Cf. Franklin Fearing, *Motion Pictures as a Medium of Instruction and Communication* (Berkeley, University of California Press, 1950).

Industry. A questionnaire was sent out to five hundred film purchasers from the Office of Education inquiring into the value and effectiveness of films. Both industrial and educational users were in agreement that increased interest, improved instruction, resulted in greater compre- nd improved quality of workmanship. However, 73 per cent of the users thought the films shortened training time, whereas only 52 e educational users thought so.

onclusion which is agreed upon by both industrial and educa- s that films are not helpful in and of themselves but only if they de and well used. We do not yet know very much about the tech- mmunication with films for educational purposes.[82]

organizations. Social psychologists conducted research on the ome of the army orientation films during World War II by testing ation and attitude changes. These researchers report the follow- ary of results:[83]

films had marked effects in the men's knowledge of factual material g the events leading up to the war. Highly effective presentation meth- ssible with this type of film.

e films also had some marked effects on opinions where they specifically the factors involved in a particular interpretation, that is, where the test item was prepared on the basis of film content analysis and anticipated change from such analysis. Such opinion changes were, however, less t and, in general, less marked than changes in factual knowledge.

e films had only a very few effects on opinion items of a more general na- had been prepared independently of film content, but which were con- e criteria for determining the effectiveness of the films in achieving ntation objectives.

e films had no effects on items prepared for the purpose of measuring on the men's motivation to serve as soldiers which was considered the te objective of the orientation program.

ternational relations. The manufacture of motion pictures in America esults in the production of about 300 to 400 films of feature length each year. These films are shipped to movie theaters in most parts of the world. It is estimated that there are between seventy-five and eighty thousand motion picture theaters in operation around the world. The weekly attendance is calculated to be in the vicinity of 235,000,000.[84] To the millions who see American-made films, the fictitious portrayals become real symbols of Amer- ican life. The American and foreigner alike interpret them according to their understanding of the behavior shown and make a judgment of its prevalence in the national life. No other mass media has the power of influencing ideas about America that the motion picture has in its impact on foreigners. (What

[82] F. E. Brooker, *Training Films in Industry,* Office of Education Bulletin, No. 13 (Washington, Government Printing Office, 1946).
[83] Carl I. Hovland, Arthur A. Lumsdaine, Fred D. Sheffield, *op. cit.,* pp. 254–255.
[84] Terry Ramsaye, *op. cit.,* p. 1.

we send abroad is commonly regarded as a true picture of life in the United States.) Foreign audiences are particularly sensitive to incorrect movie portrayals of them or of their history and classics.[85] Since World War II many nations, great and small, have striven to establish their own motion picture industry, often for propaganda or business reasons of their own.

SUMMARY

The motion picture is a mass-communication medium which reaches a world-wide audience. A public of at least 100 million must be sought for the showing of a feature entertainment film.

The history of the motion picture is one that is encompassed within the past fifty years; it reflects increased technical and artistic improvement. Alone among the arts, the motion picture was handed upward from the masses and not downward from the intelligentsia.

The distinctive characteristics of the motion picture include: (1) its production for a large, general audience; (2) the audience must be physically assembled; (3) the audience must pay for the whole product; (4) production methods are greatly different from those of other mass media.

The motion picture features entertainment developed around such prevailing themes as love, crime, and sex.

The movie audience is composed predominantly of young people under the age of 30. There is very little difference in sex, income, or social class of movie-goers. There is considerable difference in the discrimination of movie-goers in selecting the film.

Nontheatrical film is being widely used in education, religion, government, industry, military organization, and in a variety of community groups.

The motion picture theater is a local recreational institution which provides vicarious experience appropriate to certain psychological needs. The movies may transmit traditional values, reinforce ideal values, or create new cultural values. The general effect has been to transmit traditional values and avoid controversial subjects.

Two specific effects on group behavior are the homogeneity effect and the reinforcing effect.

Recreational effects of movies on various persons may include: (1) providing the essential satisfaction of fantasy; (2) blunting of emotional response; (3) narcotizing the person so that personal and social problems are avoided.

Movie attendance is being reduced by television and other recreational interests.

The impact of the movies on conduct depends upon selective perception which rests on the individual's social background and his psychological needs. Crime and sex pictures can be an aggravating influence on delinquents.

---

[85] Luigi Luraschi, "Censorship at Home and Abroad," in *ibid.*, p. 149.

Any film has some measurable effects on the specific attitudes of those exposed to it provided the audience is sufficiently interested to give it sustained attention. As an educational tool, it helps students learn more quickly and to retain learning longer in a number of knowledge areas.

The motion picture film carries an impression of national life wherever it is shown. As such it represents powerful influence in the shaping of attitudes toward other nationality groups.

ANNOTATED BIBLIOGRAPHY

Annals of the American Academy of Political and Social Science, Vol. 254 (November, 1947). This issue is devoted to a consideration of the motion picture from the viewpoint of the producer, the exhibitor, the clergyman, the economist, the sociologist, the educator, the anthropologist, and others, each of whom discusses the medium in a different light.

CHARTERS, W. W., *Motion Pictures and Youth* (New York, Macmillan, 1933). A summary of the conclusions of the Payne Fund Studies of the effect of motion pictures upon children and youth.

HARDY, Forsyth, ed., *Grierson on Documentary* (New York, Harcourt, Brace, 1947). John Grierson's writings, as compiled in this book, reflect the thinking of an important producer of documentary films.

HENRY, Nelson B., ed., *Audio-Visual Materials of Instruction,* Forty-eighth Yearbook, National Society for the Study of Education, Part I (Chicago, University of Chicago Press, 1949). A thorough survey of the educational uses of film including a summary of research on audio-visual materials.

———, *Mass Media and Education,* Fifty-third Yearbook, National Society for the Study of Education, Part II (Chicago, University of Chicago Press, 1954). A symposium on mass communication organized around three questions: What are the mass media for? How does mass communication work? What can the schools and public do about mass media?

HOVLAND, Carl I., LUMSDAINE, Arthur A., and SHEFFIELD, Fred D., *Experiments on Mass Communication* (Princeton, N. J., Princeton University Press, 1949). Describes research appraisal of the effectiveness of films on soldier audiences conducted during World War II.

INGLIS, Ruth A., *Freedom of the Movies: A Report on Self-Regulation from the Commission on Freedom of the Press* (Chicago, University of Chicago Press, 1947). The author sketches the social role of the film, examines the provisions of the Production Code, and discusses the many pressures—economic, social, and legal—which attend the process of making motion pictures.

JACOBS, Lewis, *The Rise of the American Film* (New York, Harcourt, Brace, 1939). A thorough, historical coverage of the development of the motion-picture industry up to 1939.

MAYER, J. P., *Sociology of the Film* (London, Faber and Faber, 1945); and his companion study, *British Cinemas and Their Audiences* (London, Dennis Dobson, Ltd., 1948). Studies of the effect of films on children and adults in Great Britain largely through a case-study approach.

POWDERMAKER, Hortense, *Hollywood, The Dream Factory* (Boston, Little, Brown, 1950). A study of movie producers, writers, directors, and actors based on nine hundred interviews by an anthropologist. The central hypothesis of the study is that the social system in which the movies are made significantly influences their content.

ROSTEN, Leo C., *Hollywood, the Movie Colony, the Movie Makers* (New York, Harcourt, Brace, 1941). Deals with the manners and mores of Hollywood and discusses movie producers, actors, directors, writers. Interesting and useful statistical data are included in the appendix.

ROTHA, Paul, *Documentary Film* (London, Faber and Faber, 1952). Analyzes the documentary film and traces its historical development. The author explores its possibilities as a positive instrument of education.

SCHRAMM, Wilbur, ed., *The Process and Effects of Mass Communication* (Urbana, University of Illinois Press, 1955). A synthesis of theory and research by some of the ablest researchers in the field of mass communication.

SELDES, Gilbert, *The Great Audience* (New York, Viking Press, 1950). Deals with the mass media and places the motion picture in its perspective in relation to the radio and press.

WOLFENSTEIN, Martha, and LEITES, Nathan, *Movies: A Psychological Study* (Glencoe, Ill., Free Press, 1950). An analysis of film content to discover its psychological role in the life of the viewer.

CHAPTER 8

RADIO AND TELEVISION

■ *Delbert C. Miller*

THE RISE OF RADIO AND TELEVISION BROADCASTING

Radio

Radio was developed originally by physicists and engineers as a means of point-to-point communication. Prior to 1920 it was used for ship-to-shore contact, for military communication, and as a way of sending messages to specific receivers. Only a few foresaw, at first, the development of radio as a medium of mass communication. Early "broadcasts" were largely improvisations by wireless operators. A lonely engineer might play phonograph records to a friend at another station. Nonprofessional eavesdroppers would "listen in" with their newly-contrived tube or crystal sets. Soon, the radio manufacturers became aware of the advertising possibilities, and began sending out broadcasts of records and news as a means of stimulating the sale of parts, and later, of completely-assembled receiving sets. As receivers increased, the number of transmitting stations also increased. Almost spontaneously a mass medium was born.[1]

The rapid rise of radio was initiated by a historic event. In 1920 station KDKA in Pittsburgh, Pennsylvania, broadcast the results of the presidential election of that year. The event fired the imagination of the public and the demand for radio receiving sets soon outraced supply.

The increase of broadcasters was likewise rapid. Three radio stations existed in 1920; by the end of 1923 nearly 600 were in operation. This can now be compared with the 2,873 commercial AM stations and the 555 commercial FM stations and 129 educational FM stations which were authorized by the Federal Communications Commission in July, 1955.[2] It is known that about 98 per cent of American homes are equipped with radio receiving sets, and a majority of homes have more than one. In addition, more than 35 million of American automobiles are radio equipped and

[1] Giraud Chester and Garnet R. Garrison, *Television and Radio,* 2nd ed. (New York, Appleton-Century-Crofts, 1956), pp. 20–41.
[2] As released by the FCC. *World Almanac* (New York, New York *World Telegram,* 1956), p. 790.

10,000,000 sets are available in restaurants, offices, stores, and other places away from home.[3]

Television

The growth of television in the United States has been very rapid during the past five years. The table below shows the growth of television and makes a comparison with radio.[4]

GROWTH OF RADIO AND TELEVISION IN THE UNITED STATES

Year	Number of Homes with Television Sets in Use	Number of Homes with Radio Sets
1946	8,000	35,000,000
1947	250,000	37,000,000
1948	900,000	40,000,000
1949	3,250,000	45,000,000
1950	9,800,000	45,850,000
1951	15,000,000	46,000,000
1952	21,000,000	48,000,000
1953	27,600,000	50,000,000
1956	36,900,000	52,000,000

It was estimated in 1956 that 68 per cent of America's families owned a television set.[5] The history of television broadcasting in the United States began in 1941 when the first station was authorized for commercial use. There were six stations on the air at the end of World War II. On July 31, 1955, there were 584 commercial stations and 34 educational TV stations authorized by the Federal Communications Commission.[6]

Color television is confidently expected to become widely distributed in the near future. Regularly scheduled, experimental transmission of color television was begun by the Columbia Broadcasting System on May 28, 1941. Commercial color television was inaugurated in 1954 with scheduled programs by the major networks. It is estimated that approximately 10,000 color sets were in actual use in early 1955 in the United States. More and more television stations have been equipped to originate color and others to broadcast color programs.[7]

Meanwhile intensive research on color television continues. Black-and-white-TV is expanding its physical facilities. Coaxial cables now cross the

[3] Chester and Garrison, *op cit.*, p. 5.

[4] *World Almanac* (1956), p. 790 and *Information Please Almanac*, 1956, p. 298. Figures relate to December of each year. England is experiencing a marked increase, but set ownership is not as widely distributed. Twenty per cent of the homes in Great Britain now have television sets; almost 90 per cent of British homes are able to listen to B.B.C. sound programs. See T. Cauter and J. S. Downham, *The Communication of Ideas* (London, Chatto and Windus, 1954), p. 140.

[5] *Statistical Abstract of the United States, 1956* (Washington, Government Printing Office, 1956), Table No. 621, p. 515.

[6] *World Almanac* (New York, 1956), p. 790.

[7] *Keesings Contemporary Archives*, Vol. IX (July 10–17, 1954), p. 13671.

United States and are knitting the country into a common grid. Four national networks are operating. The present system provides assignments for the building of over 2,000 stations over the nation.[8] It is possible to place television within reach of every household in the United States.[9]

CHARACTERISTICS OF RADIO AND TELEVISION AS MASS MEDIA

Cheapness and Easy Availability

The most common motive for turning on the receiving set is to be entertained. From the very outset "listeners accepted radio broadcasting as manna from heaven. It came to them without money and without price, entertainment that was free as air."[10] The notion that listeners pay nothing for their radio and television services is an illusion, but at least no direct payment is involved either by way of tax or subscription.[11]

The availability of radio is well known. Radio is found in the home, factory, beer tavern, school, and club. It is installed in auto, bus, train, and depot. So ubiquitous is the radio and television that the definition of listening needs revision. The concept of secondary listening has been coined to refer to that listening which is done while the individual is engaged in other tasks. It has been reported that secondary listening may be higher than direct primary listening.[12] A very similar pattern of secondary viewing is reported for television in a recent audience study.[13] The omnipresence of sound has been the source of poetic lines by Carolyn Kizer:[14]

[8] Federal Communications Commission Mimeo #37460, FCC 49–948.

[9] Paul A. Walker, Chairman of the FCC, in Carroll V. Newsom, ed. *A Television Policy for Education* (Washington, American Council on Education, 1952), p. 29. Under the new plan, 70 ultra high frequency channels were added to the previously existing 12 channels in the very high frequency bands. This provides for a potential accommodation of 2,053 stations in 1,290 communities.

[10] Gleason Archer, *Big Business and Radio* (New York, American Historical Society, 1939), p. 64.

[11] C. A. Siepmann, *Radio, Television and Society* (New York, Oxford University Press, 1950), pp. 71–73. Only 50 per cent of a representative cross-section of the listening public in the United States were aware that government has anything to do with the operations of radio stations. The writer points out the significance of this to programming.

[12] The B.B.C. made an analysis of listening at meal times and during peak evening listening hours. Fifty-seven per cent of the listeners admitted they were doing something else at the same time—domestic duties, reading, writing, etc. Cited by T. Cauter and J. S. Downham, *op. cit.*, p. 144.

[13] Forty-six per cent of television viewers apparently do something else while watching television. These activities include sewing, knitting, household chores, baby care, eating, drinking, and even reading. A quarter of all television viewers reported reading at some time while watching television. Cited by C. A. Siepmann, *Television and Education in the United States* (Paris, UNESCO, 1952), p. 36.

[14] Excerpts from a poem by Carolyn Kizer, "O Silence, Silence," *Harper's* (November, 1952), p. 47.

The air is continually humming, humming
. . . Over meals and deals, ringing
In the pillow at nightfall,
. . . Everlasting
Sound is around the mind, murmuring, humming.

Speed

Lazarsfeld has pointed out that the major technical aspect of radio is its *speed,* in contrast to the major technical aspect of print, which is permanence. He speculates that radio's main influence is not so much in the intellectual sphere but in the sphere of action. "The pilot talking to the ground crew is the symbol of radio just as the scholar studying the ideas of other scholars transmitted to him in print is the symbol of the printed media."[15] Radio can flash news and instructions to a population almost instantaneously.[16] In addition, radio broadcasting is a relatively indestructable system of communication. It is true that radio and television stations can be destroyed, but field transmitters may be as mobile as the moving person, the truck, or the airplane on which they are placed.

Power to Influence

Radio also has demonstrated that it can excite mass action. A spectacular instance was the effect of a dramatic script entitled *War of the Worlds* which was broadcast on a national radio network during the evening of October 30, 1938. Hadley Cantril, who studied the effects of this broadcast, describes what happened:[17]

Long before the broadcast had ended, people all over the United States were praying, crying, fleeing frantically to escape death from the Martians. Some ran to rescue loved ones. Others telephoned farewells or warnings, hurried to inform neighbours, sought information from newspapers or radio stations, summoned ambulances and police cars. At least six million people heard the broadcast. At least a million of them were frightened or disturbed.

The power to influence has been recognized by politicians who have used radio and television to command attention for themselves and their ideas.[18] The use of radio by Adolf Hitler for hour-long addresses illustrates how a political leader can convey his ideas to a national audience. It is apparent that communications emanating from a single source, and potentially capable of reaching a vast audience, introduce a new problem of social control. A single individual or agency may determine the content of communication

---

[15] Paul Lazarsfeld in W. Dennis, ed., *Current Trends in Social Psychology* (Pittsburgh, University of Pittsburgh Press, 1951), p. 253.
[16] Delbert C. Miller, "How Our Community Heard About the Death of President Roosevelt," *American Sociological Review,* Vol. X (October, 1945), pp. 691–694.
[17] Hadley Cantril, *The Invasion from Mars* (Princeton, N. J., Princeton University Press, 1940) p. 620.
[18] Also see discussion in Chapter 12.

for millions of persons. Psychologists and sociologists have produced knowledge of human interests, motivations, and learning habits which now enables the unscrupulous manipulator to sway thought and emotion by well-tested propaganda devices.[19]

CONTENT OF RADIO AND TELEVISION PROGRAMS

It is estimated that over 99 per cent of all programs are broadcast by commercial radio stations and less than 1 per cent by educational radio.[20] The content of radio and television programs might be grouped into three kinds of program classes: entertainment type, information type, and orientation type. The categories are based on the manifest intent to entertain, to impart information, and to affect attitudes and values respectively. An industry estimate of commercial station program content (made in 1946) showed that 76 per cent of all *radio* time in that year was of entertainment type, 16 per cent of information type, and 8 per cent of orientation type.[21]

The content of *TV* programs is similar to radio. If advertising time is disregarded, entertainment type programs make up about 75 per cent of broadcast time, information type programs slightly less than 20 per cent, and orientation type about 5 per cent.[22]

THE RADIO AUDIENCE

General Character

The radio audience is made up of numerous publics which vary, on the one hand, with the time of day and the availability of a radio to the listener and, on the other hand, with the age, interest, and disposition of the listeners.

In homes that have both radio and television receivers, the people listen to their radios an average of 1 hour and 45 minutes per day *in addition* to their television viewing; in homes without television, people listen to the radio an average of 4 hours and 5 minutes per day. Radio, with its unique ability to entertain and inform individuals while they are engaged in some other activity, has become the "companion" of the American individual, following him from room to room, to public places, and on the highway.[23]

[19] Leonard Doob, *Public Opinion and Propaganda* (New York, Holt, 1948).

[20] D. W. Smythe, "The Content and Effects of Broadcasting" in N. B. Henry, ed., *Mass Media and Education,* Fifty-third Yearbook, National Society for the Study of Education, Part II (Chicago, University of Chicago Press, 1954), p. 196.

[21] *Ibid.,* p. 196. A comparison with B.B.C. sound programs in 1952 and 1953 would seem to show that 70 per cent was of entertainment type, 20 per cent of information type, and 5 per cent of orientation type. See Cauter and Downham, *op. cit.,* p. 142.

[22] *Ibid.,* p. 200. A comparison with B.B.C. television programs appears to show 70 per cent of an entertainment type, 25 per cent of an information type, and 5 per cent of orientation type. See Cauter and Downham, *op. cit.,* p. 143.

[23] Chester and Garrison, *op. cit.,* p. 5.

Shared Attitudes

A majority of listeners use the radio as a reliable and convenient source of the news. Seventy-four per cent like to listen to the news in the evening hours; 44 per cent use radio, rather than newspapers as their main source of news. Comedy and variety programs are of equally general appeal. Music ranks high in popularity, with 76 per cent of listeners expressing like for some kind, though tastes differ widely.[24]

Social Differentiation

Lazarsfeld suggests that a mass-communication audience may be classified on the basis of *primary characteristics,* such as education, age, and sex; *psychological characteristics,* as shown by personality tests or attitudes on a variety of issues; and *communication habits,* such as reading, movie-going, or TV viewing.[25]

Primary characteristics. 1. *Education.* It has been shown that the poorer and less educated the listener, the more he tends to listen to the radio, though he listens less to the more serious programs.[26] Taking public-affairs discussions and classical music as the most typical representatives of serious programs, the relation of education may be clearly shown by two national samples polled by the National Opinion Research Center. The following table is based on a survey taken at two different times in which people were asked to select their favorite radio programs from a long list.

PROPORTION OF RESPONDENTS PICKING THE TWO TYPES
OF PROGRAMS AMONG THEIR FAVORITES

| | Public Affairs | | Classical Music | |
Education	1945	1947	1945	1947
Less than high school	33%	35%	21%	22%
High school	40%	43%	32%	27%
College	55%	63%	54%	54%

Other data are available to confirm the relationship between education and interest in matters of citizenship.[27] The significance of this relationship is that many other factors are interrelated such as economic level, class consciousness, and life outlook.

[24] Paul Lazarsfeld and Patricia Kendall, *Radio Listening in America* (Englewood Cliffs, N. J., Prentice-Hall, 1948), pp. 34–35, 122–123.

[25] P. Lazarsfeld, in W. Dennis, ed., *op. cit.,* p. 236.

[26] Lazarsfeld and Kendall, *op. cit.,* pp. 25–28; for a fuller treatment see Lazarsfeld, *Radio and Printed Page* (New York, Duell, Sloan and Pearce, 1940), pp. 15–47.

[27] See P. Lazarsfeld, B. Berelson, and H. Gaudet, *The People's Choice* (New York, Columbia University Press, 1944). Contains striking evidence of the effect of educational and economic status on political outlook. Lazarsfeld and Kendall report from their 1947 study of Radio Listening that "programs of serious music and discussions of public issues are selected as favorites twice as frequently in the college group as in the grade-school group."—*Radio Listening in America,* pp. 25–26.

2. *Age.* There are striking differences between listening habits and age differentials. People under age 30 differ significantly from older age groups in their preference for popular music, and for their lesser interest in religion and public affairs.

3. *Sex.* Women show considerably less interest in public affairs and more interest in fictional material. Women compose the vast majority of the daytime radio audience. Some 20 million women regularly tune in on daytime serials; as many as eight to ten such dramas may be followed daily.[28] The need for emotional catharsis growing out of frustrations in the woman's role is suggested by this listening pattern. It is also possible that daytime radio tends to reinforce the difference in the interests of men and women which the social and economic structure of our society has developed.[29]

Psychological characteristics. The results of efforts to determine the relation of personality characteristics to communication patterns has so far revealed practically no correlation. It is believed that differences may exist and that they may be identifiable. It is known, for example, that about half the women at home during the day are avid fans of the "soap opera." The other half dislike these programs. At one time or another, every conceivable personality test has been applied to these two types of women. The results have been negative.

Interest differences have been repeatedly shown, but it may be that these are more *social* than psychological differences. Self-selection of audiences plays a considerable role. People listen to the political candidates who express their own convictions, they look for more information on topics with which they are acquainted. In general, it can be said that people do not look for new experiences in the mass media, but for a repetition and an elaboration of their old experiences into which they can more easily project themselves.[30]

Communication habits. Radio habits are interlocked with other communication habits. If education and other primary factors are kept constant, many marked relationships still remain. For example:

People who listen to news commentators on the radio are also more likely to read news magazines and, in smaller towns, to subscribe to the Sunday edition of metropolitan newspapers. Women who are interested in the "true fiction" type of magazine are also more interested in daytime serials and prefer the more romantic type of movies. People who never go to the movies at all are also likely to listen less to the radio.[31]

[28] Rudolf Arnheim, in Frank Stanton and Paul Lazarsfeld, eds., *Radio Research, 1942–3* (New York, Duell, Sloan, and Pearce, 1944), p. 35.

[29] And H. M. Beville, Jr. "The ABCD's of Radio Audiences," *Public Opinion Quarterly,* Vol. IV (1940), pp. 195–206.

[30] Lazarsfeld, in W. Dennis, ed., *op. cit.,* p. 243.

[31] *Ibid.,* p. 245. Cf. Cauter and Downham, *op. cit.,* pp. 205–235.

These findings demonstrate the mutual reinforcement of the mass media and suggest that a number of basic factors may distinguish audience members. A general factor of "seriousness" may be separating those inclined to listen to public affairs, popular science, and so on, from those who are mainly interested in fiction material. Another general factor may be related to those who prefer individual participation to those who like mass participation. A musical factor may distinguish the preferences of listeners for music or for verbal programs. At the present time, little work has been done on identification of such factors and what is known rests on a few preliminary studies.[32]

THE TELEVISION AUDIENCE

The size and composition of the television audience is changing as a rapidly increasing number of television sets are acquired by America's families. There is a progressive trend toward increased purchases by people in lower income groups.[33] The lower income groups are not only the heavier purchasers but also the most enthusiastic viewers. As with radio listening, television viewing increases as you descend the socioeconomic scale.[34]

There are more young children in television families and interest in television is on the increase in children under 10. Professor Paul Witty, of Northwestern University, in his fifth annual study of television viewing by elementary and high school students in the Chicago and Evanston, Illinois, areas, discovered that elementary school children averaged 21½ hours of viewing per week, while high school students averaged 17 hours.[35]

Early checks showed that men showed most interest in television.[36] (It now appears that the proportion of women viewers in relation to men is tending to increase.) A recent study in Derby, England, showed that women, on the average, were listening and watching longer than men.[37]

According to the A. C. Nielsen Co., television sets in American homes were viewed in 1956 on the average of 6 hours and 2 minutes per day. Television viewing has clearly assumed the role of America's favorite leisure-time pursuit for men, women, and children.

[32] W. S. Robinson, "Preliminary Report on Factors in Radio Listening," *Journal of Applied Psychology,* Vol. 24 (December, 1940), pp. 831–837.

[33] Siepmann, *Radio, Television and Society,* p. 339. Of all set owners in 1949 only 11 per cent were in the top income group. The middle brackets accounted for 76 per cent, and 13 per cent of all set owners were in the lowest income group.

[34] A control group study of five main socioeconomic groups (A, B, C, D, E) in Britain showed that the two highest income groups accounted for only 30 per cent of the TV viewing while 65 per cent of the viewing was concentrated in socioeconomic groups C and D. Reported by Siepmann in *Television and Education in the United States.*

[35] Paul Witty, "Televiewing by Pupils, Parents, and Teachers," in *School and Society,* Vol. LXXIX (May 15, 1954), pp. 150–152.

[36] Siepmann, *Radio, Television and Society,* p. 340.

[37] Cauter and Downham, *op. cit.,* p. 154.

USES OF RADIO AND TELEVISION

Entertainment

The major use of radio and television is, by any measure, for entertainment. It will be recalled that estimates of commercial radio and TV broadcast time (advertising excluded) show that three-fourths of it falls within the entertainment category. Even noncommercial AM stations devoted 53 per cent of their program time in 1949 and 59 per cent in 1950 to entertainment.[38]

Advertising

Network advertisers in 1954 spent approximately $320 million for network television time and $137 million for network radio time, exclusive of money spent on talent, programs, and commercial production costs. One advertiser alone, Procter and Gamble Company, spent over $36 million on radio and television network advertising.[39] A Class "A" hour (6:00–11:00 P.M., Monday through Friday) over the basic line-up of 55 NBC affiliated stations in 1956 cost $68,275.[40]

Television boasted some 23,000 advertisers in January, 1950, and its revenue was rapidly rising.[41] One writer reports that the cost of providing a nation-wide system of television broadcasting by advertising alone indicates conclusively that it will be necessary for advertisers to spend more money on advertising in television than they spend today on radio, magazines, and outdoor advertising put together.[42]

Education

Radio and TV have a number of major opportunities in education both for students within schools and colleges as well as with the out-of-school audience. The opportunities embrace classroom instruction, extra-classroom education for students, after-classroom education for adults, information and training for citizenship, and cultural and practical benefits.[43]

Commercial stations have a mandate from the Congress of the United States to provide programs of public service. Sixteen per cent of program time was being given to information-type programs when the most recent industry estimates of commercial station program content was made in 1946. Of this time, 13 per cent was given over to news and commentators, 2 per

[38] Dallas W. Smythe, *op. cit.*, p. 197.
[39] Chester and Garrison, *op. cit.*, p. 100.
[40] *Ibid*, p. 96.
[41] Siepmann, *Radio, Television, and Society*, p. 329.
[42] Bernard B. Smith, in *Journal of the Association for Education*, Vol. 9 (February, 1950).
[43] Educational Television Institute Report in Carroll V. Newsom, ed., *A Television Policy for Education*, pp. 141–144.

cent to farm programs and 1 per cent to homemaking.[44] TV content shows similar proportions.

The more than 100 educational radio stations on the air provide less than 1 per cent of the total broadcast time available to the public. While numerically small, they do provide a greater amount of information content in their programs. The noncommercial AM stations devoted 37 per cent of their broadcast time in 1949, and 32 per cent in 1950, to information-type programs.[45] The United States government has recently made the ultra high frequencies in the radio spectrum available exclusively for educational purposes. These frequencies are considered suitable for broadcasting in local areas, and many large cities have established their own stations.[46]

There is much interest in the educational use of television. Tele-courses have been offered to the public by college and university instructors with some instances of remarkable acceptance. Television has shown itself useful as a tool of instruction in communicating skills and techniques such as are found in arts and craft. It has been used in social studies courses with success. The use of television for training teachers has received much attention, since the medium provides a way of presenting master teachers as models for study. Films made of TV programs have also proved almost as effective as the live program.[47]

Many new uses are being constantly discovered, perhaps the most dramatic of which is the teaching of surgery. The University of Kansas, the University of Chicago, and the University of Pennsylvania are using television in their medical schools.[48] In 1952 the Federal Communications Commission reserved 242 noncommercial channels for public TV broadcasting.[49] It is too early to know what financial support can be arranged for educational TV and how effectively it will be used in the schools and in adult education. One writer suggests that a pay-as-you-view system would enable educational TV to pay its own way. The technical devices to establish such a system have already been developed.[50]

Politics and Government

The use of radio and television is now fairly well established as a political and governmental instrument. Its uses include campaign speeches by candidates; broadcasting of proceedings of national political conventions; broad-

[44] Kenneth Baker, "An Analysis of Radio Programming" in Paul F. Lazarsfeld and Frank Stanton, eds., *Communications Research, 1948–49* (New York, Harper, 1949).
[45] Smythe, *op. cit.*, p. 198.
[46] J. Wayne Wrightstone, "Radio Education," in Walter S. Monroe, ed. *Encyclopaedia of Educational Research* (New York, Macmillan, 1950), p. 954.
[47] Siepmann, *Television and Education in the U. S.*, p. 123.
[48] *Ibid.*, p. 75.
[49] FCC Sixth Report and Order (52–294)—The Final Television Allocation Report, April 14, 1952.
[50] Bernard B. Smith, "Can Unsponsored TV Pay Its Way?" *Harper's* (February, 1952), pp. 97–99.

casts of governmental investigating committees; government officials explaining policies and decisions; informational broadcasting to other nations.

These uses by political and government organizations are both domestic and foreign. Domestic uses of television are markedly increasing. Each political party is allotting larger sums to radio and TV broadcasting. Commercial radio stations contribute of their own time to the presenting of controversial issues by political and governmental speakers. The use of radio to broadcast information to foreign countries rose rapidly after World War II.[51]

Religion

The broadcast of religious programs brings religious services to thousands of sick and invalid persons who would otherwise be without a direct contact with the church. Outstanding religious speakers and religious dramas have been brought into the homes of millions of listeners and viewers.

Military Organization

Radio plays a prominent role in communication on the battlefield. It is an almost instantaneous means of reaching many points simultaneously—a very important requirement for the direction of military forces. The use of walkie-talkie transmitter-receivers places mobile equipment at the disposition of moving columns. Short-wave broadcasts are effective in reaching underground resistance forces. In giving directions to civilian populations in time of war, radio is without peer. Field Marshall Lord Montgomery has said that "the mobilization system of an atomic age must be such that a national radio warning is effective in a matter of hours rather than days."[52]

Miscellaneous Uses

The uses of radio and television reach into many other fields of which only a few may be mentioned. Radio is an important aid to steamship and airship transportation; it provides news to newspapers through radio broadcasting; quicker detection of crime and criminals is made possible through police automobile patrols equipped with radio; and sports broadcasting has so magnified many audiences of sporting events as to lift many sports into the category of big business. What would professional wrestling be without TV?

RADIO AND TELEVISION AS A SOCIAL INSTITUTION

Radio and television in the United States operate within a system of free, competitive enterprise under a framework of governmental regulation. Except for a relatively few educational stations, radio and television is a private

[51] L. W. White and Robert D. Leigh, *Peoples Speaking to Peoples* (Chicago, University of Chicago Press, 1946), p. 44.
[52] *The Manchester Guardian,* October 22, 1954, p. 14.

enterprise held accountable to the public interest.[53] This fact immediately sets up a number of operating conditions. The first and obvious fact is that the station will compete for business and try to make a profit. It will broadcast the finest programs possible, but the consumer will not pay (directly) for them. The major revenue will come from advertisers, and they must be willing to sponsor the programs. The hours during which a really large audience can be reached are limited to five of the twenty-four-hour day, namely, between 6 and 11 P.M. Under these conditions, programming often comes under the control of the advertiser.

One writer has explained the command of the programming as follows:[54]

The basic fact to keep in mind is that the radio advertiser is charged a fixed sum for time, regardless of the size or nature of the audience which his program attracts, and therefore, he insists on selecting and managing the program, in order to reach the largest number of listeners. The network in effect loses control of that period of time to some one whose primary interest is not in good radio fare, but in potential customers for his products. It is much as if the editor of a newspaper had to farm out the writing of the news, page by page, to the corporations whose advertisements appeared on those pages.

One of the outstanding effects of radio and television is that a large and growing share of investment and human talent is being drawn into this industry. The capital invested in radio and TV receiving sets is approximately $10 billion. A rough estimate for the investment in stations, in equipment of manufacturing plants, and in distributive and service organizations would be between $15 billion and $20 billion. In addition to this, there is the total annual cost of physical operation of the system, including power, parts, service, and depreciation.[55]

The time devoted to radio and television listening shows that it unquestionably commands the single largest bloc of off-work time. The average viewing audience at ten o'clock on an ordinary evening in 1956 is larger than the voting electorate which chooses the President—sixty to seventy million people. Martin Mayer points out that we may remember 1956 as the year in which Americans spent as much time in a single leisure occupation as they did on their jobs. ". . . The total time involved amounted in a single year to more than 130 billion man-, woman-, and child-hours."[56] It should be re-

[53] The Communications Act of 1934 provides the basic legislation. Section 301 states: "It is the purpose of this Act among other things to maintain the control of the United States over all the channels of interstate and foreign radio transmission, and to provide for the use of such channels, but not the ownership thereof, by persons for limited periods of time, under licenses granted by federal authority, and no such license shall be construed to create any right, beyond the terms, conditions, and periods of the license."

[54] Bernard B. Smith, "Television: There Ought to Be a Law," *Harper's* (September, 1948), p. 40.

[55] Dallas W. Smythe, *op. cit.*, p. 206.

[56] Martin Mayer, "Television's Lords of Creation," *Harper's*, Vol. 213 (November, 1956), p. 25.

membered that even this figure is probably an underestimate, since additional radio and TV sets are constantly expanding the total listening and viewing time. All of this broadcast activity is serving many different audiences with many different kinds of programs.

Out of these factors, the social structure of broadcasting has been formed. It has not been the instrument for enlightened citizenship which many have envisaged. However, it must be said that the "listening public, as a whole, has thanked it for furnishing the bare room of its existence with many decorative ornaments."[57]

GENERAL EFFECTS ON GROUP BEHAVIOR

Impact on Social Values

The problem of determining effects of radio and television is similar to that posed by motion pictures.

Knowledge of just how the media affect the lives of the population is a tantalizing research frontier. It has been pointed out that the term *effect* is not a simple concept.

Mass media can affect knowledge and attitudes, opinions, and behavior of individuals. These effects can be immediate or delayed, of short duration or long lasting. Effects upon individuals might slowly become transformed into institutional changes. They can come about in simple reactions or in complicated chains.[58]

Katz and Lazarsfeld in their recent work on *Personal Influence* suggest that ideas often seem to flow *from* radio and print to opinion leaders and *from them* to the less active sections of the population.

The reflector of social values. It is generally agreed by researchers in mass communication that radio and TV reflect the existing value system of the society. In fact, Lazarsfeld goes further and says, "The only thing one can say is that at the moment the mass media tend to reinforce the status quo rather than influence changes in the institutions of this country."[59]

The reasons that might be given for such an outcome are various. It might be found partly in the commercial ownership of most facilities. The table following is an FCC analysis of business interests of television licensees, construction permit holders, and applicants:[60]

[57] Lazarsfeld and Field report that 80 per cent of the radio listeners in their survey believed that radio is doing either an "excellent" or a "good" job. Thirty-five per cent report that they never feel like criticizing when they listen. P. Lazarsfeld and H. Field, *The People Look at Radio* (Chapel Hill, University of North Carolina Press, 1946). Cf. P. Lazarsfeld and P. Kendall, *Radio Listening in America* (Englewood Cliffs, N. J., Prentice-Hall, 1948).

[58] P. Lazarsfeld, in *Current Trends in Social Psychology, op. cit.,* p. 249.

[59] *Ibid.,* p. 253. He hastens to add that this might be a temporary state of affairs.

[60] Cited by Siepmann, *Radio, Television, and Society,* p. 326.

BUSINESS INTERESTS OF TELEVISION LICENSEES, PERMIT HOLDERS, AND APPLICANTS

Type of Business	Number	Per Cent
Newspaper publishing	128	31.3
Broadcasting only	66	16.1
Motion picture theaters, etc.	27	6.6
Radio manufacturing	25	6.1
Merchants, dealers, etc.	25	6.1
Miscellaneous manufacturing	18	4.4
Real estate, insurance, etc.	17	4.2
Oil production	17	4.2
Educational institutions	10	2.4
Miscellaneous	76	18.6
Sum total	409	100.0
Information not available	26	
	435	

The role of the advertiser as the sponsor of most programs must be considered as an influence in reinforcing existing values. Perhaps what is most significant is that the content is largely of an entertainment nature. In comedy, music, and drama, the producer merely tries to provide humor, love, and sorrow so that they will be meaningful. This suggests that the content references must always be within the social values of the group.

The radio station has no message to convey and no editorial policy to project as such. Its function is to give equal time to controversial issues and to abstain from any active part in political affairs. Its purpose is, in a word, to *reflect* the community. The voluntary system of self-regulation adopted by the National Association of Radio and Television Broadcasters outlines briefly the mores of broadcasting:[61]

1. News reporting should be factual and without bias. News commentaries and political broadcasts should be identified as such. In matters controversial the principle of free speech should be honored within the terms of the laws of the land.

2. Religious broadcasts should be presented respectfully.

3. Children's programs should reflect respect for parents, for law and order, public morality, and honorable conduct.

4. In law and mystery programs criminals should be punished. Details of brutal killings and torture and the disrespectful portrayal of law enforcement officers should be avoided.

5. In accepting advertising copy, great care should be exercised not to convey information which is misleading, dangerous to health or character, distasteful, or in violation of business and professional ethics.

The disseminator of social values. Radio and TV broadcasting plays a role in spreading values and tastes to a wide audience. The effect of this

[61] Cited by Siepmann, *Television and Education in the United States*, p. 31.

dissemination has been to bring about a cultural homogeneity. The following effects have been noted.[62]

Religious differences in culture have become less pronounced.
The penetration of the musical and artistic city culture into villages and country.
Ethical standards of the city made more familiar to the country.
Distinction between social classes and economic groups lessened.
Isolated regions are brought in contact with world events.
Illiterates find a new world opened to them.
Standardization of diction and discouragement of dialects.
Aids in correct pronunciation especially of foreign words.
Cultural diffusion among nations.

Impact on Knowledge and Habits

Radio and television convey programs which add to the knowledge of the listener and which may be utilized by him in solving personal or social problems. Some of the best evidence that radio and television content can serve this function come from studies of the effects of the daytime serials on women.[63] Some 2,500 Iowa listeners who listen to daytime serials were asked the following question: Do these programs help you to deal better with the problems in your own everyday life? Forty-one per cent claimed that they were helped. Of those who consider themselves helped, two conclusions can be drawn. The less formal education a woman has, the more is she likely to consider these programs helpful to her. On all educational levels, those women who think they worry more than other people more frequently find relief in listening to serials than women who say they worry less.[64]

The interview reports show that the respondents do use the characters and the situations depicted as models by which they adjust their own behavior.

It is well known that, under certain circumstances, the individual can be directly encouraged to act. An interesting example grew out of a radio program called "Truth and Consequences." The master of ceremonies on January 23, 1943, called on the listening audience to send a penny to a mother of a nineteen-year-old boy who had recently enlisted in the United States Marines. They were to mail their letters to the mother who was instructed to buy war bonds with the money in the name of her son. One hundred and twelve sacks of mail containing 204,200 letters were delivered to the mother within a few days. The letters came from all the states within the United

[62] William F. Ogburn, "The Influence of Invention and Discovery," in *Recent Social Trends* (New York, McGraw-Hill, 1933), Vol. I, p. 153.
[63] W. L. Warner and W. E. Henry, "The Radio Day-Time Serial: A Symbolic Analysis," *Genetic Psychology Monographs,* Vol. XXXVII (1948), pp. 3–71; H. Hertzog, "Psychological Gratification in Daytime Radio Listening," in T. Newcomb and E. Hartley, eds., *Readings in Social Psychology* (New York, Holt, 1945), pp. 561–568.
[64] Hertzog, *op. cit.,* p. 562.

States, as well as from Canada, Mexico, the West Indies, and even England and North Africa.[65]

These are dramatic examples of short-run effects. What we need is more knowledge about the long-run effects. These are much more difficult to detect, since the influence of radio and TV content become intertwined with so many other experiences. A theory of accumulated stimuli would seem to fit the dynamics of long-run effects. We know that our personalities grow very slowly but firmly. Schramm has described this relation between personality and communication as follows:

> When we introduce one drop of communication into a person where millions of drops have already fallen and left their residue, we can hardly expect to reshape the personality fundamentally by that drop. If we are communicating to a child, it is easier, because the situation is not so firmly fixed. If we are communicating in an area where ideas and values are not yet determined—if our drop of communication falls where not many have fallen before—then we may be able to see a change as a result of our communication. But, in general, we must admit that the best thing we can do is build on what already exists.[66]

Social institutions represent that which already exists as social heritage. In the following section, the effect of broadcasting on relations within social institutions are reviewed.

INSTITUTIONAL EFFECTS

Family Life

Social relations in the family. There is no doubt that listening and viewing through radio and television is a central activity of the American family. What has been the effect of this activity on family life? The answer to this question can only be given tentatively. The evidence is mostly a composite of gross observation and personal judgment. A number of studies are beginning to provide some objective facts, but the novelty of television and the constant enlargement of the audience means that all data must be interpreted with caution. There is no guarantee that current habits are stabilized.

One study has inquired into the behavior patterns in televised households as of December, 1950. The general pattern of family behavior (including children aged five years or more) is graphically illustrated in the figure which follows.[67]

A B.B.C. survey of 1950 compared new viewers (people who had owned a set for less than a year) with "veteran" viewers (people with more than four years of ownership). This survey showed that the frequency of evening viewing had fallen very little with the passage of time, although a few more

---

[65] C. N. Winslow, "Sympathetic Pennies: A Radio Case Study," *Journal of Abnormal and Social Psychology,* Vol. 39 (April, 1944), pp. 174–179.

[66] W. Schramm in *Mass Media and Education, op. cit.,* p. 125.

[67] Cited by Siepmann, *Television and Education in the United States,* p. 25.

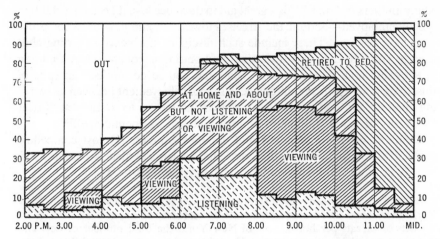

SOURCE: C. A. Siepmann, *Television and Education in the United States* (Paris, UNESCO, 1952), p. 25.

PATTERN OF BEHAVIOR IN TELEVISION HOUSEHOLDS (INCLUDING CHILDREN AGED FIVE YEARS OR MORE), MONDAYS THROUGH FRIDAYS, SEPTEMBER, 1950.

people among the veterans were likely to be listening to the radio or to be engaged in some activity about the house.[68]

A study made in Derby, England, an industrial city of 200,000, gives a good picture of age differences in listening and viewing (Spring, 1953).[69] This study showed that the popularity of radio and television is higher among those over 25 than among those aged 16–24 years. In fact, by comparing the 1950 B.B.C. survey and the Derby survey it can be said that television is least popular among young people in their late teens and early twenties. The reason is that this age group is strongly attracted to such out-of-home activities as the movies, dance hall, and youth club. After 24 years of age, home activities and responsibilities tend to become increasingly more important and television viewing increases.

Family relations are being influenced by the increase of time being given to television viewing. A study conducted in Philadelphia by a Princeton University group found 66 per cent of the respondents in the total television sample stating that it was their frank opinion that TV served to bring all the family closer together.[70] Sixty-six per cent of the people interviewed said that television keeps the children home more. Ninety-two per cent reported that their families get together often to watch the same television program.[71]

[68] R. Silvey, "Viewers, Viewing, and Leisure," *B.B.C. Quarterly* (Spring, 1952).
[69] Cauter and Downham, *op. cit.*, p. 152.
[70] Many writers question that grouping in silence around a television receiver has increased the solidarity of the family. The common experience of viewing can only reinforce family relations if it heightens social interaction and personal relations.
[71] Princeton University report, *Television* magazine (May, 1949).

Many mothers feel that TV is a great aid to them because it keeps the children quietly employed—and off the streets. However, some new behavior problems have resulted. These include such discipline problems as getting children to come to their meals on time and getting adequate sleep. Children in television homes tend to go to bed later, and so do adults.[72] In spite of this, there is no significant difference in school achievement between televiewing children and non-televiewing children (according to a study at Xavier University of 1,000 children in samples matched for mental age).[73]

Opinions on effect of crime and violence content. A most compelling problem is the influence of the crime and violence which is contained so heavily in radio and television programs. Smythe reports:[74]

In the TV programs of seven stations observed for one week in 1952 in New York, there were 2,970 acts and threats of violence, or an over-all average of 5.8 acts or threats per hour. . . . In New York, the total number of acts and threats increased 15 per cent over 1952, and the average rose from 5.8 to 6.2 per hour.

At this time there is no accurate knowledge regarding the effects of such content on the persons who listen and view. It is clear that scores of different reactions in many degrees of intensity mark the reactions of the millions who make up a given audience. There are at least *five* different opinions regarding the effects of the crime and violence content.

Opinion 1. Induces people to commit overt acts of crime. There is some evidence that this belief may be valid *under very special conditions for specified persons.* It is known that large numbers of people can be induced to carry out acts within legal bounds. The example of the sympathetic pennies sent to the mother of the enlisted marine has been cited. The Orson Welles broadcast of the "War of the Worlds" will be recalled. Another example is the achievement of Kate Smith, a beloved star of radio, who on September 21, 1943, broadcast on 65 different occasions requesting the public to buy war bonds. By the morning of the next day, $39 million war-bond pledges were registered by listeners.[75] Franklin Fearing, a psychologist, interprets these examples as evidence of specific overt behavior caused by a "congruence between content, interpreter predispositions, and situational factors."[76] He believes that these situations are likely to be relatively infrequent, since the congruent occurrence of the necessary factors is rare. He suggests that for overt and relatively immediate action to occur, the content must specifically indicate such action.

Now the fact that people can be induced to act within legal bounds is not

[72] Siepmann, *op. cit.*, p. 25.

[73] *Ibid.*, p. 104.

[74] Smythe, *op. cit.*, p. 203.

[75] Robert Merton, *Mass Persuasion* (New York, Harper, 1946).

[76] Franklin Fearing, "Social Impact of the Mass Media of Communication," in *Mass Media and Education, op. cit.*, p. 188.

predictive of illegal behavior. For a person to commit illegal acts, a set of behavior patterns (predispositions) would necessarily have to be laid down
through previous experiences in social life. The acts of violence which a
child or an adult commits probably take place only when the person's psychological or social status is disturbed.[77] Radio and TV content could only
serve as an element within a complex of pre-existing factors for which the
content could not be held solely responsible.

Opinion 2. Distorts human values and brutalizes behavior. One writer has
estimated that, with rare exceptions, every person who was 6 years old in
1938 has absorbed by now a minimum of 18,000 picture beatings, strangu-
lations, shootings, torturing to death, and blood puddles from comics alone.
No one can accurately estimate what the figure would be if TV, radio, and
movie brutalities were included. It has been charged that television writers
are fascinated by death and that in one year (November, 1950 to November,
1951) 16,932 men, women, children and animals passed away on television
programs, most of them in a sudden and violent manner.[78]

Dr. Frederick Wertham, an American psychiatrist, who has studied the
effects of comic books, represents a view which many would extend to radio
and TV programs. He says:[79]

What children get . . . is that kindness, sympathy, and regard for human
suffering are all weakness; that cunning and shrewdness are the kind of thing
that counts; and that women are not to be respected as persons but are luxury
prizes like automobiles, distinguished chiefly by sexy attributes rather than by
any high ideal of womanhood.

Parents complain that "it's not healthy the way Johnny plays. All day it's
machine guns, murder, and gangs. You can't tell me kids don't get those ideas
from radio, TV, and the movies."

The most that can be said about the effect on personal values is that the
influence will depend on the interpretations of the person who is exposed to
the content. The extent to which the heroes and villains in the vicarious world
of radio and television experience serve as models for listeners and viewers
can vary widely. It is possible that radio and TV content may create a picture of a world in which violence is *accepted* as a normal way of life, with
consequent distortion of personal values.

*Opinion 3. Narcotizes the person and removes his attention from personal
and social problems.* The view here is that the audiences may have their attention diverted *so much* to viewing and listening that they are as effectively
removed from the solution of personal and social problems as if they were
doped in their nonsleeping hours. The disproportionate absorption of time
in viewing and listening suggests that the person is utilizing the mass media

[77] *Ibid.,* p. 187.
[78] Cited by Siepmann, *TV and Education in the United States,* p. 105.
[79] *Ibid.,* p. 105.

as a vicarious means of escape from his frustrations, his inhibited aggressions, or feelings of inadequacy. There is evidence that the meaning which the content of a mass medium has for the individual is a function of his group affiliations. Rutgers University researchers studied two groups of children, those who belonged in family groups but not in peer groups, and those who belonged in peer groups.[80] The children's preferences for and interest in various types of comic strips, radio, and TV programs were compared. They found that radio and TV programs depicting violence and action are more popular with children who do not have peer group memberships than with those who do. Their sense of failure in their relations with their peers produced feelings of insecurity and inadequacy which was "highly productive of fantasies, and therefore [they] select a kind of media material, such as little animals or violent action, which would foster such fantasies."[81]

Opinion 4. Induces no harmful influence on behavior. Robert Merton has expressed the view that "it cannot simply be taken for granted that violence on the screen is emotionally damaging to the spectator." He argues:[82]

When violence becomes conventionalized, for example, as in the well-grooved patterns of the Western movie, it may not cause the least distress or damage to children who know that the noble hero will irresistibly triumph over the black-hearted villains but that, for this to happen in proper style, the good men and bad men must first work their way through a sequence of ambushes, fist fights, and gun play in which injuries and even occasional death becomes more symbolic than real.

In this connection, Dr. Paul Witty quotes a 14-year-old boy who told him:[83]

A child looks upon crime and violence as ideal adventure and excitement. . . . He has no desire to experience these things in actual form, and knows them only as fun and not in their true ugliness. The adult, on the other hand, has had actual experiences along this line and looks upon fighting and violent action as loathsome and horrid.

Dr. Loretta Bender, a child psychologist, concurs and claims that radio thrillers, on the whole, provide a healthy and harmless outlet for children's aggressive tendencies.

Opinion 5. Provides an important part of a child's education for the modern world. It has been suggested that violence in fiction has survival value in that it prepares children for life as adults through stories which present adult reality. Radio and TV violence is believed to inoculate the child against the greater shock which maturity may present them in the real world.[84]

[80] Matilda and John W. Riley, Jr., "A Sociological Approach to Communication Research," *Public Opinion Quarterly*, Vol. XV (1951) 445–460.
[81] *Ibid.,* p. 455.
[82] Robert K. Merton, *op. cit.,* p. v.
[83] Siepmann, *TV and Education in the United States,* p. 105.
[84] Smythe, *op. cit.,* p. 191.

All of these beliefs invite more research and knowledge than is now available. The most conclusive statement which summarizes these divergent views is that given by the well-accepted scientific principle,

The outcomes (effects) of exposure to particular content are extremely diverse and cannot be predicted in any particular case, except on the basis of comprehensive knowledge of the content itself, the need-value system of the interpreter, and the characteristics of the total situation as perceived by the interpreter.[85]

Recreation

Influence on time allocated to other mass media. One of the most pronounced effects of radio and television on recreation is the competition between the various media for the leisure interest of the population. The newspaper and magazine which held sole possession of the field for a long time have witnessed the advent of motion pictures, radio, and television within the last forty years. Television is initiating the most rapid changes upon the role of the other media at the present time. Radio listening is the medium most affected by television. Studies of individual radio listening and TV viewing indicate that radio listening suffers an enduring loss of about one-fourth to one-third in homes which acquire TV sets.[86] The 1950 survey of the British Broadcasting Corporation showed that in homes with a TV set, the evening peak hour television draws in almost three-quarters of the people who would otherwise have been listening to radio.[87]

It is generally reported that a greater decline in radio listening takes place when the TV set is first acquired, but within two years radio listening is partly restored by use of the radio during early evening hours and by use of the car radio in the late hours.[88] It has been suggested that a shift of functions will eventually find radio a principal medium for daytime audiences and a prominent medium for newscasts and music. Television seems likely to dominate in the field of drama and sports. As the less expensive medium, radio may come to cultivate audiences which it has not previously sought to attract.[89]

The effect of TV on reading of newspapers, magazines, and books is not yet clearly known. However, the available evidence shows that the newspaper habit appears to be relatively unaffected but the reading of books is curtailed. A study conducted in the New York metropolitan area reports that, of readers of books, 49 per cent admitted having discontinued reading entirely after the purchase of a television set, 16 per cent read less than formerly, and only 35 per cent claimed to have been unaffected.[90] In Derby, England, an analysis of reading habits of television owners and nonowners showed ab-

[85] Fearing, *op. cit.,* p. 191.
[86] Smythe, *op. cit.,* p. 208.
[87] Cauter and Downham, *op. cit.,* p. 156.
[88] Smythe, *op. cit.,* p. 208.
[89] Siepmann, *TV and Education in the United States,* p. 346.
[90] *Ibid,* p. 36.

solutely no indication of a reduced reading of newspapers and general-interest magazines among owners of television sets. However, a slight but significant drop in book reading was shown. The researchers conclude that the impact of television on reading will be concentrated on books which tend to demand consistent attention and will have little effect on newspapers and magazines which can be read at short intervals.[91]

The effect of TV on reducing movie attendance has been noted and discussed in Chapter 7.

Effect on other leisure activities. In the controlled study of TV owners in Derby we have evidence of some effects on other leisure habits.[92] The results showed that:[93]

1. There was no difference in playing or watching sports.
2. There was a lower rate of pub-going among TV owners.
3. There was no difference in the extent to which people take part in hobbies.

A study in the United States by Thomas E. Coffin at Hofstra College confirms these trends. "Sports attendance suffered only slightly while theatre going and reading declined about one-fifth, other commercial entertainment drops for about one third, while radio listening is cut nearly in half."[94]

It is reported that after a time there is a partial return to previously formed habits. As radio listening and movie attending increase, the behavior pattern becomes less routine and more selective toward listening and in the choosing of movies.

Education

The range of impacts. Radio developed for general use during the 1921–30 decade and education began to use it at this time. There was an early rise of educational stations, followed by a decline in their number owing to financial and technical difficulties. The influence of federal regulation of radio had been to strengthen commercial stations and to encourage co-operation between educators and broadcasters.[95] The Communications Act of 1934 was unique in that for the first time in American history a powerful medium of communication was deliberately reserved for use only in the public interest. The wave lengths of the air were deeded in perpetuity to the people of America. The Federal Communications Commission was charged with the responsibility of seeing that all broadcasting conformed to the "public interest, convenience, or necessity." It will be recalled that it has been estimated that about one-fifth of radio and television time is devoted to in-

---

[91] *Ibid.*, p. 160–161.
[92] Cauter and Downham, *op. cit.*, p. 155. Sex, social class, age, and education were matched in the two groups.
[93] *Ibid.*, pp. 156–161.
[94] Cited by Siepmann, *Radio, Television and Society*, p. 342.
[95] J. Wayne Wrightstone, *op. cit.*, pp. 953–955.

formation-type programs. Some of these have been broadcast directly by schools and colleges over their own stations. Some have been broadcasts made at commercial stations especially for school listening. Most have been forum and news programs which have broadcast to the adult public generally.

Ogburn's earlier list of changes resulting from the impact of radio on education is still worthy of attention. His inventory includes:

Colleges broadcast classroom lectures.
Broadcasting has aided adult education.
Used effectively in giving language instruction.
Purchasing of text books increased slightly, it is reported.
Grammar school instruction aided by broadcasting.
Health movement encouraged through broadcast of health talks.
Current-events discussion broadcast.
International relations and other important topics discussed with some social effects.
Broadcasting has been used to further some reform movements.
The government broadcasts frequently on the work of departments.
Many talks to mothers on domestic science, child care, etc.
Discussion of books aids selection and stimulates readers.
The relationship of university and community made closer.
Lessens gap schooling may make between parents and childen.
Provision of discussion topics for women's clubs.
New pedagogical methods, i.e., as to lectures and personalities.
Greater knowledge of electricity is spread.
The creation of a class of radio amateurs.

This list indicates that radio may reach the student in and out of school and carry adult education to the wider public.[96]

Effect on classroom teaching. The following claims for properly used audio-visual materials in the teaching situation are supported by research evidence:[97]

1. They supply a concrete basis for conceptual thinking and hence reduce meaningless word responses of students.
2. They have a high degree of interest for students.
3. They supply the necessary basis for developmental learning and hence make learning more permanent.
4. They offer a reality of experience which stimulates self-activity on the part of pupils.
5. They develop a continuity of thought; this is especially true of motion pictures.
6. They contribute to the growth of meaning and hence to vocabulary development.
7. They provide experiences not easily secured by other materials and contribute to the efficiency, depth, and variety of learning.

[96] William F. Ogburn in *Recent Social Trends*, Vol. 1, p. 154.
[97] Edgar Dale, D. Finn, and Charles F. Hoban, Jr. "Research on Audio-Visual Materials," in N. B. Henry, ed. *Audio-Visual Materials of Instruction* (Chicago, University of Chicago Press, 1949), p. 255.

It is reported that comparatively few teachers use radio broadcasts or recordings and that the possibilities of radio as an agency of education have only been touched as yet in the public schools.[98]

Effect on adult education. Perhaps it can also be said for adult education that the possibilities of radio and TV have only been touched. We know that the general character of programs from commercial broadcasting are affected by the primary concern of the advertiser to sell his product to potential customers, not with balanced and varied broadcast fare. Yet it must be recorded that millions of Americans listen regularly to radio and television for news, and that broadcasting has established a reputation for impartiality and reliability. The addresses of the President of the United States command huge audiences. Sustaining programs often provide sources of information not otherwise available. All in all, millions of adults are daily receiving new knowledge about events and commentary about those events. In the United States, educational and FM stations have been providing programs for minority audiences interested in art, music, and social study. It has been suggested that commercial radio will increasingly turn in this direction as one adjustment to the competition of television.

Possibilities of educational TV. The significance of television for education is not yet fully known, but some records are indicative of its future possibilities. A thirteen-week experimental series of telecasts was initiated over station KING-TV in Seattle in 1951. The purpose of the program was to stimulate children to read books. The immediate results were remarkable. By the second program the Seattle Public Library and all its branches had reported that every book by the author featured on its first program had been borrowed, and the same books were borrowed from the shelves of its 38 branches and two bookmobiles in the county.[99]

A careful study of the effectiveness of television as an instructional technique has been carried out by a research group from Fordham University for the United States Navy. Officer pilots and enlisted airmen were assigned to one of three groups to receive instruction in certain technical subjects. One group received instructions by television, another by kinescope, and the third by local instructors along conventional lines. Some of the results were:[100]

1. In half the comparisons made for both officers and enlisted men, television instruction was found to be more effective than teaching by local instructors; it was equally effective with teaching by local instructors in an additional one-fourth of the comparisons.
2. Reservists not only learned from televised instruction, but they remembered most of what they learned when retested four or six weeks later.
3. Television instruction continued to be highly acceptable to the reservists after eight weekly sessions.

98 *Ibid.,* p. 284.
99 Siepmann, *TV and Education in the U.S.,* p. 103.
100 *Ibid.,* p. 112.

On the basis of experience with educational television, a group of educational experts have listed the following significant by-products from the use of television by educational organizations.[101]

1. An improved quality of teaching is required and will result from teaching on television.
2. Constant re-examination of educational practices will result from television use.
3. Co-operation is promoted among schools, colleges, and other educational agencies.
4. Knowledge and interest of parents in the schools will increase.
5. Training in television personnel will be carried on by the schools.

Politics, Government, and International Relations

Ever since the historic night during November, 1920, when the national election returns were broadcast to the nation, political candidates have used radio extensively to wage their political campaigns. As elected officials they have explained their policies and their acts. An effective radio voice has been a special asset to politicians. The fireside chats of President Franklin D. Roosevelt revealed the capability of radio as a device for a leader to reach mass audiences directly. (It will be recalled that a large part of the press did not support the President's policies.) Governor Thomas E. Dewey of New York turned radio into a question-answering talkathon in 1950 when he answered questions over the air for hours at a time, while his constituents constantly telephoned inquiries to him. Television has added a new dimension and many candidates now attribute their elections to television appearances.[102]

The United States government supports an information service to convey accurate, factual information about the American way of life. The "Voice of America" is an overseas broadcast service which reaches most of the world over its 36 short-wave transmitters and its 15 relay stations. During 1949, fifty-six nations were beaming more than 4,000 hours of international short-wave broadcasting per week. The United Nations programs are issued steadily to world listeners from its own five short-wave transmitters.[103]

There is no available assessment of the effects of this broadcasting but it is known that ideas are now propaganda weapons, and that radio and television make it possible to reach over the heads of diplomats to the people

[101] Educational Television Program Institute Report in C. V. Newsom, ed., *op. cit.* pp. 144–146.

[102] Siepmann, *op. cit.*, p. 34. Cf. Bruce Bliven, "Politics and TV," *Harper's* (November, 1952), pp. 27–33. Section 315 of the Communications Act of 1934 provides for equal opportunity in the use of a broadcast station by all legally qualified candidates for any public office. A station is not required to make its facilities available to any candidate, but if it does it must afford equal opportunity to all other candidates for the same office.

[103] Semiannual Report of the United States Advisory Commission on Information, March, 1949.

themselves. More than one hundred thousand letters were inspired by the "Voice of America" broadcasts in 1948. Global mass communication has made psychological warfare an important part of conflict processes. The Russian government so feared the "Voice of America" that in April, 1949, it employed some 1,000 jamming transmitters to make American broadcasts unintelligible to its people. The reaction of the United States government was to pour transmitters into counteraction in such volume as to match or override Moscow's jamming.[104]

Global communication has made every word spoken or written in public of magnified significance. Siepmann writes that "the modern world, through mass communication, has become a vast whispering gallery in whose echoing corridors even the most casual remarks of public figures reverberate." The prospect of misunderstanding has increased anxieties regarding indiscretions in the public utterances of both officials and private citizens. This general tension about what is said in public today is one of the subtle, but genuinely significant, effects in which mass media play a crucial role. The concept of personal privacy for thought and act has been altered fundamentally as all primary communication has become potential secondary communication.

Business and Industry

The impact of radio and television on business and industry is reflected in a variety of changes. In the first place, radio and TV broadcasting has become a big business in its own right. The advertising agency has become a large business institution. The full impact of radio and television advertising on sales is unknown, but sales records provide concrete evidence that advertising does stimulate customer buying. Even habits can be changed. One example may suffice. After a six months' intensive advertising campaign on TV stations in Syracuse, New York, in 1951–52, tea consumption in TV homes increased 19 per cent, whereas in non-TV homes there was a nominal decrease in tea consumption. Before the advertising, 20 per cent of the persons in TV homes said they liked tea; after it, 38 per cent did.[105]

Many advertising agencies claim that TV is already the greatest advertising medium in the world today. Television is being referred to by advertisers as a *selling machine.*

Ogburn has listed the following results of radio on industry and business:[106]

In industry, radio sales led to decline in phonograph business.
Better phonograph recording and reproducing now used. (Hi-fidelity equipment is now booming.)

104 *New York Times,* August 20, 1949.
105 Smythe, *op. cit.,* p. 209. Cf. Chester and Garrison, *op. cit.,* pp. 9–11.
106 W. F. Ogburn, *op. cit.,* p. 155.

Lowering of cable rates followed radio telegraph development.

Point-to-point communication in areas without wires.

The business of the lyceum bureaus, etc., suffered greatly.

Some artists who broadcast demanded for personal appearance in concerts.

The market for the piano declined. Radio may be a factor.

Equipment cost of hotel and restaurant increased.

A new form of advertising has been created.

New problems of advertising ethics, as to comments on competing products.

An important factor in creating a market for new commodities.

Newspaper advertising affected.

Led to creation of new magazines.

An increase in the consumption of electricity.

Provision of employment for 200,000 persons

Some decreased employment in phonograph and other industries. (Until Hi-fidelity.)

Aid to power and traction companies in discovering leaks, through the assistance of radio listeners.

Business of contributing industries increased.

Miscellaneous Effects

Religion. There is a relatively large audience for religious broadcasts, and these occupy a distinct place in Sunday broadcasting. Religious programs are most popular in small towns and rural districts. Evidence indicates that the older and less-educated a population group is, the more they tend to listen to religious programs. On the other hand youth, and more particularly the "better" educated among them, appear to care less for religious broadcasts.[107] In the Derby study, TV owners showed a significant drop in church-going as compared with an equivalent group of non-TV owners.[108]

Farm life. The radio has played an important role along with the automobile in breaking down the isolation of the farmer. The urbanization of all national life is stimulated by the knowledge and standards of taste which are widely disseminated.[109] Agricultural programs and weather reports are of special interest to farms.

Community organization. There is clear evidence that television is keeping people at home.[110] The 1950 B.B.C. survey suggested that evening television had a limited effect in keeping people at home during the week, but that on Saturday evenings it kept in about a third of the people who had previously gone out. Moreover, the peak-hour television performance occupied the attention of half of all those people who would otherwise have been doing something else about the house. The Derby researchers report that, "Television owners belong to slightly fewers clubs than non-owners. The owners attend their clubs less frequently. A drop of about one-third was

---

[107] These facts are from Lazarsfeld and Kendall, *Radio Listening in America.*

[108] Cauter and Downham, *op. cit.,* p. 157.

[109] Malcolm M. Willey and Stuart A. Rice, "The Agencies of Communication," in *Recent Social Trends,* Vol. 1, p. 215.

[110] Siepmann, *Television and Education in the United States,* p. 25.

shown in the attendance pattern of TV owners.[111] Many community groups have felt the effect of television in restricting attendance at meetings. However, it is usually observed that these restricting effects tend to be lessened after the novelty of television wears away.

SUMMARY

Radio and television are new mass media which make it possible for sound and visual images emanating from a single source to reach an infinitely large audience simultaneously.

The general characteristics of these media include cheapness and easy availability to the listener or viewer, speed of communication, and power of influence.

Disregarding advertising content, three-fourths of the content of both radio and television programs is of an entertainment type, and the remainder of an information or orientation (persuasive) type.

Audiences tend to be differentiated on the basis of education, age, and sex for specific type of programs.

The major uses of the media include entertainment, advertising, education, politics and government, religion, and military organization.

A major impact of radio and television resides in the increasing size of the industry which has grown up around it, including such various businesses as radio advertising, radio and TV equipment manufacture, professional entertainment agencies, and technical operation and maintenance.

The influence of radio and TV on group behavior has been largely as a reflector and disseminator of existing social values and the reinforcement of the institutional status quo.

Radio and television are predominantly used within a family or household unit. It is known that listening and/or viewing occupy the largest single bloc of leisure time in America. The chief motive is entertainment and the effect of crime and violence content is of major concern. It is known that the content can have widely different reactions upon different individuals and at different times. The major factors include the need-value system of the personality and the total social situation as perceived by that personality.

Television has shown great power of attracting audiences of all ages. It is reducing the amount of time previously given to movie-going, radio listening, and book reading. It appears to have temporary, if not permanent, effects on many other habits such as going to church and to clubs.

Radio and television have shown great capability for adult education. It is being widely used for news information, but much less for instructional purposes.

Radio and television are playing an ever larger role in politics and government. Many candidates have attributed their election to office to television

[111] Cauter and Downham, *op. cit.,* pp. 157–158.

appearances. As a propaganda weapon in international relations, use of radio and TV has greatly accelerated, but the effects are not accurately known.

It is probable that no social institution is left unaffected by radio and TV communication. The ability to transmit any act or utterances to a mass audience changes the concept of privacy. (All primary group communication becomes potentially secondary communication.) The effect on such values as free and independent thought and action is now being carefully considered, for it appears that mass communication is an element within a growing pattern of constraint.

ANNOTATED BIBLIOGRAPHY

CANTRIL, Hadley, *The Invasion from Mars* (Princeton, N. J., Princeton University Press, 1940). A social psychological analysis of the effects caused by the radio play, *War of the Worlds*.

CAUTER, T. and DOWNHAM, J. S., *The Communication of Ideas* (London, Chatto and Windus, 1954). A study of different channels of intercommunication between people living in Derby, England, a typical industrial city of 200,000 population. The field survey consisted of 1,200 full length interviews and an additional sample of 1,800 shorter interviews.

KATZ, Elihu, and LAZARSFELD, Paul F., *Personal Influence* (Glencoe, Ill., The Free Press, 1955). A study of the part played by opinion leaders in the flow of mass communications.

KLAPPER, Joseph T., *The Effects of Mass Media* (New York, Bureau of Applied Social Research, Columbia University, 1949). Summarizes research work and compares relative effects of different media.

LAZARSFELD, Paul F., "Communications Research and the Social Psychologist," in Wayne Dennis, ed., *Current Trends in Social Psychology*, (Pittsburgh, University of Pittsburgh Press, 1951). This article outlines the field of communication research and relates research progress to the outline.

——, and KENDALL, Patricia L., *Radio Listening in America* (Englewood Cliffs, N. J., Prentice-Hall, 1948). Data in this study were collected by the National Opinion Research Center which interviewed 3,000 Americans in 1947 to ascertain their radio habits and preferences. Analysis of the data was conducted by Lazarsfeld and Kendall, who relate replies to such background variables as education, age, sex, and place of residence.

LAZARSFELD, Paul F., and MERTON, R. K., "Studies in Radio and Film Propaganda," *Transactions of the New York Academy of Sciences*, Series II (December, 1943), pp. 58–79. This article reviews the results of the author's propaganda studies made during the war.

MERTON, Robert K., *Mass Persuasion: The Social Psychology of a War Bond Drive* (New York, Harper, 1946). A social psychological analysis of the themes used by the radio star, Kate Smith, in selling some $39 million worth of war bonds over the radio in the course of one day.

NEWSOM, Carrol V., ed., *A Television Policy for Education* (Washington, American Council on Education, 1952). This book records the proceedings of the Television Programs Institute held under the auspices of the American Council on Education.

SIEPMANN, Charles A., *Radio, Television, and Society* (New York, Oxford University Press, 1950). Traces the history of radio and television as a cultural force in society and describes what has been discovered by research concerning the effects of radio and television upon tastes, opinions, and values.

————, *Television and Education in the United States* (Paris, UNESCO, 1952). A description of the television system in the United States, the television audience, and the use of television in education.

SMYTHE, Dallas W., *Inventory No. 2 of Educational Radio Programming: Analysis of 1950 Programs with Comparisons, 1949–50* (Urbana, Ill., Institute of Communications Research, 1951), and also Smythe's, *Three Years of New York Television* (Urbana, Ill., National Association of Educational Broadcasters, July, 1953. Two studies which provide valuable content analysis of educational radio and commercial television.

STANTON, Frank N., and LAZARSFELD, Paul F., *Radio Research* (New York, Duell, Sloan, and Pearce, 1941); *Radio Research, 1942–43* (New York, Essential Books, 1944); *Communications Research, 1948–49* (New York, Harper, 1949). Contains many pioneer research studies on content analysis of radio programs and research on audience composition as conducted at the Bureau of Applied Social Research, Columbia University.

United Nations Educational, Scientific, and Cultural Organization, *World Communications* (Paris, UNESCO, 1954). A graphic account of the world's facilities for communicating information and ideas by means of the press, radio, film, and television.

CHAPTER 9

AVIATION

■ *Francis R. Allen*

Aviation will play a major role in the culture of tomorrow.
WILLIAM FIELDING OGBURN (1946)

MAN'S CONQUEST OF FLIGHT

THE STORY of man's conquest of flight has been impressive and often spectacular, including as it does various early experiments in aeronautics by Cayley, Lillienthal, Langley, and others; the first human-controlled flight in a powered heavier-than-air machine achieved by the Wright Brothers at Kitty Hawk (1903); the initial flight across the English Channel by Louis Bleriot (1909); the flight to the North Pole by Richard E. Byrd and Floyd Bennett (1926); the historic, nonstop flight from New York to Paris by Charles A. Lindbergh (1927); the around-the-world jaunts of Wiley Post and Harold Gatty (1931) and others; the inauguration of the first trans-Pacific airmail service (1935); the decisive use of air power during World War II; and the frequent breaking of speed and altitude records during the post-World War II years (a special milestone here was the breaking of the sound barrier[1] in 1947). Man has become conditioned to expect wondrous exploits on the part of courageous and daring aviators. The chronology of aviation since the first uncertain flight at Kitty Hawk has been a staccato of firsts; to fly higher, faster, farther, has been the great ambition. Many people regard the ability to fly itself as one of man's supreme accomplishments. It is no doubt to be ranked among such other great achievements in human history as the use of fire, development of the wheel, use of steam power, and the development and use of nuclear energy.

The Increase in Air Travel

With increasing interest in aviation, the amount of passenger air transportation has been continually increasing. This is shown in the tables on

[1] The speed of sound is 760 to 650 miles per hour depending on altitude. In a test rocket plane piloted by Charles E. Yeager, supersonic speed was achieved for the first time. Yeager's plane actually reached a speed of over 1,000 miles per hour. *New York Times,* Sunday, October 11, 1953, Sec. 10, "Fifty Years of Aviation," p. 9.

187

pages 188 and 189. The first table indicates the increase in total number passenger-miles flown by the domestic (U. S.) airlines from 1932 to 1954. The trend is consistently upward, the change being from 127,433,000 passenger-miles flown in 1932 to 17,389,825,000 flown in 1954. These figures include both revenue and nonrevenue air travel.

The second table shows the increase in revenue passenger-miles flown during the post-World War II years, divided according to various types of service: domestic trunk-line service, local (feeder) service, insular service, and international airline service. Thus the total revenue passenger-miles flown on the Domestic (U. S.) trunk lines increased from 5,903,111,000 in 1946 to 19,205,200,000 in 1955; the total flown on the local (feeder) lines increased from 6,812,000 in 1946 to 523,300,000 in 1955; the total passenger-miles flown on the Insular lines increased from 38,033,000 in 1946 to 78,-100,000 in 1955; and the total flown on the International airlines increased from 1,100,741,000 in 1946 to 4,410,400,000 in 1955. The over-all total of passenger-miles flown on both domestic and international airlines (including local and insular) increased from 7,048,697,000 in 1946 to 24,328,000,000 in 1955.

PASSENGER-MILES FLOWN, 1932–1954

(in thousands)

Scheduled Airline Operations in U. S.

Year	Total
1932	127,433
1933	174,820
1934	189,806
1935	316,336
1936	438,989
1937	481,116
1938	560,660
1939	755,118
1940	1,157,900
1941	1,506,303
1942	1,501,279
1943	1,670,935
1944	2,211,905
1945	3,408,290
1946	6,068,315
1947	6,313,312
1948	6,245,745
1949	7,065,199
1950	8,351,745
1951	10,949,898
1952	12,996,657
1953	15,337,760
1954	17,389,825

SOURCE: Civil Aeronautics Administration, *Statistical Handbook of Civil Aviation*, 1953 (Washington, Department of Commerce, Civil Aeronautics Administration, 1953), p. 55; *ibid*, 1954, p. 60; *ibid*, 1955, p. 63.

TREND OF REVENUE PASSENGER AIR TRAVEL, 1946–1955

Revenue passenger miles (000)

Year	Domestic Trunk Lines	Local Airlines	Insular	International Airlines	Total Airline Industry (Domestic and International)
1946	5,903,111	6,812	38,033	1,100,741	7,048,697
1947	6,016,257	46,418	46,833	1,810,045	7,919,553
1948	5,840,211	87,928	52,864	1,888,997	7,870,000
1949	6,562,580	134,691	47,154	2,053,980	8,798,405
1950	7,766,008	188,782	57,746	2,206,396	10,218,932
1951	10,210,726	289,644	65,799	2,599,915	13,166,084
1952	12,120,789	339,763	67,885	3,019,810	15,548,247
1953	14,297,600	390,900	71,848	3,367,576	18,233,800
1954	16,288,400	461,200	72,700	3,743,300	20,652,700
1955	19,205,200	523,300	78,100	4,410,400	24,328,000

SOURCE: Air Transport Association of America, *Air Transport Facts and Figures*, 15th ed., 1954, p. 13; *ibid.*, 17th ed., 1956, pp. 8–9.

The development of passenger air transportation may be appropriately compared with that of the automobile. It has been pointed out that great as has been the increase in both types of transportation, there has nevertheless been a fundamental difference. The latter is that aviation has had considerable development in carrying groups of people and freight (the equivalent of the bus and truck), whereas the individual or family airplane has had only slight development.[2] On the other hand, the private automobile preceded the use of the other motor vehicles, and its use has grown to mass proportions, as noted in Chapter 6.

Speed

The outstanding achievement of the airplane is speed, especially as related to long-distance travel. The speed of the Wright Brothers' plane (1903) was recorded as 31 miles per hour. By 1910 the speed record had reached 78 miles per hour. By 1920 it had reached 188 miles per hour; by 1930, around 350; by 1940, around 470; by 1950, around 680; during early 1953, 753.[3] On November 20, 1953, a research pilot for the National Advisory Committee for Aeronautics flew 1,327 miles per hour or over twice the speed of sound.[4] This was flown at an altitude of over 60,000 feet. Charles Yeager achieved a speed of 1,650 miles per hour on December 12, 1953; Lieutenant Colonel Frank K. Everest reached 1,900 miles per hour in the Bell X-2 rocket plane in July, 1956; and Captain Milburn Apt flew the same plane in excess of 2,100 miles per hour on September 27, 1956, after which

[2] Jerome C. Hunsaker, *Aeronautics at the Mid-Century* (New Haven, Yale University Press, 1952), p. 73.

[3] *New York Times,* October 11, 1953, Sec. 10, "Fifty Years of Aviation," p. 17.

[4] *New York Times,* November 22, 1953.

his plane unfortunately crashed, resulting in his death.[5] Captain Apt's speed is the record at this date of writing.

Hunsaker points out that speed records of propeller-driven planes increased gradually, amounting to about 10 miles an hour annually on the average, but the coming of jet-propelled planes brought a revolutionary change. The latter may be regarded as a "mutation" in aeronautics; new speed trends need to be calculated on the new (jet) base.[6] The speed of the commercial transports has, in general, lagged behind the speed records by some fifteen to twenty years. When the speed record was 400 miles per hour, the air transports cruised at about 200. During 1954 the new transports cruised at around 350–365 miles per hour.[7] The lag of speed of air transports behind speed records will probably not be as great in the future, as much valuable experience has been gained concerning high-speed flight.[8] The jet plane is undoubtly most suitable for high-altitude flying—for example, for routes with stops at, say, 1,000-mile intervals and certainly for transoceanic travel.[9] For shorter flights and for carrying freight, the propeller engine is recommended.[10]

How the speed of aviation shrinks distance is indicated in the figure below. In 1929 the distance from New York to Los Angeles was covered in 48 hours, using the first trans-continental passenger service wherein travel was by plane during daytime and by railroad at night. In 1940 the distance was covered in 14 hours by airplane which made three stops. In November, 1953, the distance was covered in 7 hours and 15 minutes by a DC-7 plane flying nonstop. All of these performances were regarded as notable at the time. W. E. Beall, Vice President of Boeing Aircraft Company, has declared that within a few years new jet transport planes will cross the United States in four-and-one-half hours.[11] In September, 1955, Col. C. M. Talbott flew the 2,325 miles from George Air Force Base, California, to Philadelphia in 3 hours and 48 minutes to win the Bendix Trophy. He piloted a Super Sabre jet, the U.S.'s first supersonic combat plane.[12]

[5] *Aviation Week*, Vol. 65, No. 17 (October 22, 1956), p. 30; *New York Times*, August 3, 1956.

[6] Hunsaker, *op. cit.*, pp. 17–18. How fast will the jet travel in the future? The answer seems to be, says Hunsaker (professor of aeronautical engineering at the Massachusetts Institute of Technology): "As fast as required."

[7] Bliss K. Thorne, "Aviation: East-West," *New York Times*, July 11, 1954: also airline advertisements, *New York Times*, July, 1954.

[8] Hunsaker, *op. cit.*, pp. 28–29.

[9] A notable event was the crossing of the Atlantic by a British jet liner during December, 1955, in the time of 6 hours and 18 minutes. This flight—from Montreal to London—was the first nonstop Atlantic crossing by a jet airliner. *New York Times*, December 28, 1955.

[10] Hunsaker, *op. cit;* William F. Ogburn, *The Social Effects of Aviation* (Boston, Houghton Mifflin, 1946), pp. 102–103.

[11] Wellwood E. Beall, Interview with Editors, *U.S. News & World Report* (May 22, 1953). Such jet travel, said Beall, will be at altitudes between 30,000 and 40,000 feet, at speeds in excess of 500 miles per hour.

[12] *New York Times*, September 5, 1955.

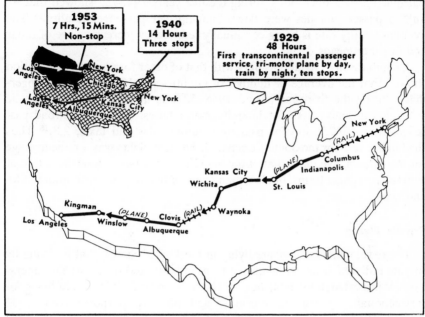

Courtesy of *The New York Times* (Oct. 11, 1953)

HOW THE AIRPLANE SHRINKS DISTANCES

Safety

People who are admittedly fearful of air crashes or accidents would do well to take note of the accident trend; the safety record of aviation is most convincing. The number of passenger fatalities per 100 million passenger-miles flown for given years in the domestic and international airline services is as follows:[13]

PASSENGER FATALITIES PER 100 MILLION PASSENGER-MILES FLOWN

Year	Domestic Airlines	International Airlines
1930	28.6	0
1935	4.8	0
1940	3.1	0
1945	2.2	3.7
1950	1.1	2.1
1953	0.6	0.1
1954	0.09	0
1955	0.78	0.04

Another way of stating the safety facts is to point out that more than 25 million airline passengers flew safely in 1952. An average of domestic (U. S.)

[13] George Lloyd Wilson and Leslie A. Bryan, *Air Transportation* (New York, Prentice-Hall, 1949), p. 443, Table 25; and (figures for 1950, 1953, 1954) Air Transport Association of America, *Air Transport Facts and Figures,* 15th ed., 1954, p. 19; *ibid,* 16th ed., 1955, p. 18.

scheduled airline operations during the five years 1948–52 showed that 95 million passenger-miles were flown annually per passenger fatality.[14] The aviation fatality rate is being continually reduced by increasing use of radar and by other means.

A comparison of aviation safety with that of other forms of transportation showed that the average of number of fatalities per 100 million passenger-miles during the five-year period 1948–52 was as follows: For domestic scheduled airlines, 1.08; for intercity motor buses, 0.19; for railroad passenger trains, 0.25; and for passenger automobiles and taxis, 2.3.[15] Thus the fatality rate for the domestic scheduled airline flights was, on the average for these years, five times that of the intercity motor buses, four times that of railroad passenger trains, but less than one-half that of passenger automobiles and taxis.

Private Flying

The development of private flying in the United States, that is, flying by private individuals as distinguished from military and transport line operations, is indicated in the table below. The trend in hours is shown of flying for instructional, commercial, business, and pleasure purposes from 1931 through 1954. The number of hours of instructional flying rose during the late 1930's, reached a very high point in 1947, and has markedly declined since that time. Commercial flying rose slightly just before World War II, increased significantly after the end of the war, has risen further during the last years recorded. The number of hours of business flying have had a trend much like that of commercial; the trend was still rising in 1954. "Pleasure and other" flying increased significantly after World War II; but has, however, tapered off since 1949. The total number of flying hours, of all four classes, was just about one-half in 1951–54 what it had been in 1947.

In general, the development of private flying in the United States has been slow and somewhat erratic. There have been waves of interest and enthusiasm, but the demand for private planes has not been sustained. Hunsaker suggests that the factor of cost has been a major one in this failure to "catch on." Between 1946 and 1952, he points out, the cost of owning and flying a plane rose at least 400 per cent.[16] Many young people who were expected to take up flying by the thousands perhaps found the cost prohibitive.

That high costs were not the sole obstacle is suggested, however, by various surveys of owners of private planes.[17] During the 1930's it was in-

[14] Jerome Lederer, "Safety in the Air," *New York Times,* Sunday, October 11, 1953, Sec. 10, "Fifty Years of Aviation." Mr. Lederer is Director, Flight Safety Foundation.
    The best measure of safety for *air* transportation, according to Wilson and Bryan, is that of "number passenger-miles flown per fatality."—*Op cit.,* p. 435.
[15] Tabulated from *Air Transport Facts and Figures,* 15th ed., 1954, p. 19.
[16] Hunsaker, *op. cit.,* pp. 61–62.
[17] Summarized by Ogburn, *op. cit.,* pp. 243–247.

dicated that time consumed in going to and from the airport and the feeling that flying was not as useful nor pleasurable as anticipated were also associated with the decline in private flying. Another survey, seeking to find out why various young people did not want to take up flying in the first place,

DEVELOPMENT OF PRIVATE FLYING IN THE U. S., 1931–1954
(in thousands of hours flown)

Year	Total Hours Flown All Purposes	Instructional Thou. Hrs.	Per Cent	Commercial Thou. Hrs.	Per Cent	Business Thou. Hrs.	Per Cent	Pleasure and other Thou. Hrs.	Per Cent
1931	1,083	307	28.3	281	25.9	152	14.1	343	31.7
1932	877	223	25.4	215	24.5	130	14.8	309	35.3
1933	795	198	24.9	200	25.2	129	16.2	268	33.7
1934	846	217	25.6	207	24.5	121	14.3	301	35.6
1935	954	292	30.6	229	24.0	132	13.8	301	31.6
1936	1,059	380	35.9	245	23.1	122	11.5	312	29.5
1937	1,173	432	36.8	227	19.4	156	13.3	358	30.5
1938	1,478	577	39.0	254	17.2	188	12.7	459	31.1
1939	1,922	755	39.3	332	17.3	246	12.8	589	30.6
1940	3,200	1,529	47.8	387	12.1	314	9.8	970	30.3
1941	4,460	2,816	63.1	511	11.5	250	5.6	883	19.8
1942	3,786	2,680	70.8	473	12.5	270	7.1	363	9.6
1943	N.A.*	N.A.	—	N.A.	—	N.A.	—	N.A.	—
1944	N.A.	N.A.	—	N.A.	—	N.A.	—	N.A.	—
1945	N.A.	N.A.	—	N.A.	—	N.A.	—	N.A.	—
1946	9,788	5,996	6.12	943	9.7	1,068	10.9	1,781	18.2
1947	16,334	10,353	63.4	1,279	7.8	1,966	12.0	2,736	16.8
1948	15,130	8,701	57.5	1,066	7.1	2,576	17.0	2,787	18.4
1949	11,031	4,187	38.0	1,449	13.1	2,615	23.7	2,780	25.2
1950	N.A.	N.A.	—	N.A.	—	N.A.	—	N.A.	—
1951	8,451	1,902	22.5	1,584	18.8	2,950	34.9	2,015	23.8
1952	8,186	1,503	18.4	1,727	21.1	3,124	38.2	1,832	22.3
1953	8,527	1,248	15	1,649	19	3,626	42	2,004	24
1954	8,772	1,061	12	1,750	20	3,918	45	2,043	23

Source: Civil Aeronautics Administration, *Statistical Handbook of Civil Aviation,* 1955 (Washington, Department of Commerce, 1955), p. 35; see also Aircraft Industries Association of America, Inc., *Aviation Facts and Figures, 1953,* edited by Rudolph Modley and Thomas J. Cawley (Washington, Lincoln Press, 1953), p. 147. Latter figures are based on those of the Civil Aeronautics Administration.
*N.A.—not available.

found out that 27.8 per cent of those interviewed were indifferent; 24.0 per cent were fearful; 18.0 per cent believed they lacked need to use planes; 13.0 per cent stated they lacked self-confidence for reasons of increasing age or physical unfitness; and a fifth group (per cent not stated) stressed the cost factor, including initial cost and upkeep. With the increased development of flying and the lowering accident rate, the factor of fear of personal safety is apparently declining; the accident rate is, however, higher for private flying than for scheduled airline flights.

Flying on the part of businessmen and farmers, especially large-scale farmers, has increased tremendously. These topics will be discussed in connection with the effects of aviation on business and agriculture respectively.

The Helicopter and the Convertiplane

As one faces the future it appears that the helicopter is likely to loom large, especially if certain mechanical improvements are made. Various observers have predicted, indeed, the "coming era of the helicopter."[18] Also other developments, such as the convertiplane, may gradually assume more prominence in the aviation picture, although the future here appears to be more doubtful in certain respects.

It is well to remember that it was only in 1939 that the first successfully-controlled helicopter was flown in the United States; the idea of helicopter-flying itself is old, even older than that of the airplane.[19] The helicopter is useful in meeting short-haul and commuter travel. In 1953 the first regularly-scheduled helicopter passenger service was inaugurated in the New York area between the La Guardia, Idlewild, and Newark airports. Helicopter mail operations in Los Angeles and Chicago have expanded. The airlines themselves are much interested in the use of helicopters for various services.[20] Then, the recent success of helicopter use by the military has been outstanding; during the Korean hostilities (1950–53), nearly all helicopter production went to the military. More extended comment on this subject is reserved for Chapter 15 ("The Influence of Technology on War"), but it may be observed here that helicopters proved to be extremely valuable in combat—moving troops and supplies, permitting commanders to view front-area conditions, and removing casualties from the front lines. The assertion is attributed to high-ranking Marine Corps officers that the helicopter was the foremost tactical innovation of the Korean War.[21] The above, moreover, has apparently increased civilian interest in the 'copter.[22]

Whether the helicopter will prove to be the "private plane of the future" or "family plane of the future" remains to be seen. It has various advantages and potential capacities: to "take off" or land in a small area (back yard, portion of flat roof top, etc.), which would be important for city use; to maneuver in any direction and to hover; to land slowly in fog or bad weather; to fly in among trees or buildings, to stop suddenly and reverse direction if necessary.

[18] See Ogburn, *op. cit.*, pp. 249 ff; Hunsaker, *op. cit.*, pp. 65, 73; *Aviation Week,* Vol. 60, No. 11 (March 15, 1954); C. Lester Walker, "Tomorrow's Helicopters," *Harper's* (May, 1953), pp. 28–35; "Up with the Helicopter," *Fortune* (May, 1951), pp. 91–95.

[19] Indeed, Archimedes toyed with the helicopter idea in the second century B.C., as did Leonardo da Vinci during the 1400's. C. Lester Walker, *loc. cit.*

[20] Aircraft Industries Association of America, Inc., *Aviation Facts and Figures, 1953,* edited by Rudolf Modley and Thomas J. Cawley, p. 142.

[21] Lynn Montross, *Cavalry of the Sky, The Story of the U.S. Marine Combat Helicopters* (New York, Harper, 1954.)

[22] Irving Stone, "Military 'Copter Success Spurs Civilian Use," *Aviation Week,* Vol. 60, No. 11 (March 15, 1954), pp. 142 ff.

It is believed, moreover, that the fundamental problems of helicopter design have been solved. Certain improvements in the machine are needed, especially relating to vibration, noise, and costs; but all of these were problems of the early automobile and were overcome. It has been pointed out that added impetus to the helicopter program might come from the federal government on the grounds that the helicopter becomes an important vehicle in event of widespread contamination from radioactive fall-out. As a rescue vehicle, the helicopter is the only one that can reach the interior of a fall-out zone without being contaminated en route.[23]

The Air Transport Association has predicted that passenger air travel between U. S. cities will double by 1970, and that helicopters will fly one-third of these inter-city passengers.[24] Others have predicted that by the year 2,000 helicopters will be in more or less mass use; they are likely to be the foremost transportation vehicle for use in traveling from one's community to destinations up to, say, 150 miles.[25] A helicopter "house trailer" has been envisioned for family trips to the beach, mountains, hunting or fishing resorts. "Heliports," special airports for use by helicopters in places where they would be landing and "taking off" in large numbers, are being planned.[26] Finally, it is possible that a "roadable helicopter" may be built which will be operated on the highways. In such an event, suggests Ogburn,[27] it may prove to be a competitor for even the automobile.

The convertiplane has the ability to rise and descend vertically like the helicopter yet travel forward with speed comparable to that of a conventional plane. According to its backers, it might combine the agility of the 'copter with the speed and range of the airplane.[28] It is recommended for medium-distance passenger travel (say, between about 150 and 600 miles).[29] Here it should maintain much greater speed than the helicopter, yet be able to land on rooftops or in other small areas.

The convertiplane is, however, viewed somewhat skeptically at present—though not by the military. Critics contend that it is not as practical as either the helicopter or the fixed-wing plane, and doubt that it is likely to be used

[23] *Aviation Week,* Vol. 62, No. 11 (March 14, 1955), "22nd Annual Inventory of Airpower," Claude Witze, p. 297.

[24] Lee Moore, " 'Copter Outlook: Third of Air Traffic by '70," *Aviation Week,* Vol. 59 (December 7, 1953), pp. 107–108.

[25] "A Bold Look at the Next Fifty Years of Flight," comments by Wernher Von Braun and C. R. Smith, *New York Times,* October 11, 1953, Sec. 10, "Fifty Years of Aviation."

[26] *Aviation Week,* Vol. 60, No. 11 (March 15, 1954), p. 142. Manhattan's (New York City) first commercial heliport was dedicated on September 26, 1956. See *New York Times* of that date.

[27] Ogburn, *op. cit.,* pp. 262, 267–268.

[28] Richard Witkin, "Convertiplanes: The Answer to Air Travel?" *New York Herald-Tribune,* Sunday, February 7, 1954, Magazine Section. For general discussion, see also "The Two-Way Airplane," *New York Times,* October 11, 1953, Sec. 10, "Fifty Years of Aviation," p. 13.

[29] It is believed that the plain helicopter is likely to monopolize air travel of less than 150 miles.

much in the future.[30] Professor Hunsaker, writing during July, 1954, observed that the convertiplane did not actually exist at that time, and he regarded the convertiplane idea as not very reasonable to an aeronautical engineer. "The compromise between helicopter and airplane design may result in the loss of peculiar advantages of each type."[31] But the military services are interested in the use of the convertiplane and are more optimistic regarding its development. It is possible, concludes Witze,[32] that the helicopter will be perfected first, and this will lead to the convertiplane as a logical next step.

With this discussion, attention is turned to the main interest of the chapter: the social effects of air travel.

SOCIAL EFFECTS OF AVIATION[33]

On Transportation

Aviation as a newer form of transportation clearly has had effects on the older established forms such as railroad, motor vehicle, and steamship travel. In the United States the railroad and highway systems are well developed—probably the most highly developed of any country in the world. The railroads have played an important part in the development of American civilization and are still basic to the economic and social system. The motor vehicle, as noted in Chapter 6, has had unprecedented use and has produced many social effects. It has provided severe economic competition for the railroads.

Since the supreme attribute of the airplane is speed of transportation over long distances, this provides further competition for the railroads as applied to distances of approximately 500 miles and more; it affects both passengers and goods. Air competition will undoubtedly be greatest for such longer distances as from New York to Chicago, Chicago to Los Angeles, New York to Florida. The rise of passenger air travel which has been observed may be assumed to bring difficulty for the railroads. On the other hand, railroad revenues from freight, which comprise four-fifths of the latter's total revenue, have not been seriously affected thus far. Freight carried by air has increased considerably as expressed in thousands of revenue ton-miles carried—from 14,433 in 1946 to 144,240 (preliminary figure) in 1954. On the other hand, cargo carried by air in 1953–54 represented only one-tenth of 1 per cent of total cargo carried by all means of transportation in the United States.[34]

[30] *Aviation Week,* Vol. 60, No. 11 (March 15, 1954), pp. 152–153.

[31] Jerome C. Hunsaker, letter to F. R. Allen dated July 30, 1954.

[32] C. Witze, in *Aviation Week,* Vol. 62, No. 11 (March 14, 1955), pp. 300–301.

[33] In previous footnotes mention has been made of Professor William F. Ogburn's volume *The Social Effects of Aviation* (1946). This definitive work has been followed in a dominant way for the remainder of this chapter. To have had the benefit of his pioneering volume has been of inestimable value.

[34] Air Transport Association of America, *Air Transport Facts and Figures,* 16th ed., 1955, p. 10; Eliot F. Tozer, Jr., "Freight by Air," *New York Times,* Sunday, October 11, 1953, Sec. 10, "Fifty Years of Aviation"; Richard Balentine, "Airfreight Faces Uphill Struggle," *Aviation Week,* Vol. 60, No. 11 (March 15, 1954), p. 182.

Thus the airlines have not comprised heavy competition in carrying freight up to this time. As air freight costs are lowered, the competition is likely to become more stringent.

With regard to the passenger competition, the railroads will be expected to improve their services, reduce costs, and otherwise endeavor to meet the air competition. The development of the light-weight, Talgo-style train since 1950 is related to this. The Talgo has been called the "train of tomorrow."

Private flying is a potential threat to the railroads just as the private automobile has already been an important competitor. But the real threat seems to be several decades or more away, as indicated previously. By this time the helicopter or roadable helicopter may be mass produced and widely used. At present businessmen and others are increasingly adopting private flying, though hardly to the extent of constituting an economic threat.

Ocean shipping is likewise being affected by air competition. To be able to fly over large bodies of water at high speed presents much time-saving; this, to many people, will be important or sometimes necessary. A new market may be tapped here, indeed, composed of people who would like to travel to Europe or other continent but who have only, say, a two- or three-week vacation. Such a trip would not be worth while by ship.[35]

Figures released by the Department of Justice, Immigration and Naturalization Service, show that the comparison of air and sea passenger travel across the Atlantic Ocean during recent years has been as follows:[36]

Year	Travel by Scheduled Airline Service	Travel by Ship
WESTBOUND (number passengers)		
1950	161,091	427,113
1951	180,465	401,243
1952	194,914	458,427
1953	251,303	397,018
EASTBOUND		
1950	135,804	296,996
1951	137,733	262,378
1952	177,432	308,654
1953	245,718	354,494

It seems likely that in coming years the steamship companies will relinquish a larger amount of the passenger trade to the airlines. This would be expected to affect notably first- and second-class passenger traffic going from northeastern United States to northern Europe.[37] This is especially likely since the international airlines inaugurated a North Atlantic tourist service on May 1, 1952. Since 1952, tourist-class travel has expanded im-

[35] Hunsaker, *op. cit.,* pp. 42–43.
[36] *Aviation Facts and Figures, 1953, op. cit.,* p. 129.
[37] Ogburn, *op. cit.,* pp. 488–492.

pressively; for example, United States traffic over the North Atlantic during 1955 showed a 22 per cent increase over that of 1954.[38]

Ocean freight is held to be much less susceptible to air competition than passenger traffic because of the low value per pound of most of the freight. Some high-value goods will undoubtedly be transported by air; most of the first-class mail is likely to be sent by air before long.[39]

The steamship companies will probably endeavor to meet the air competition by increased advertising which, ignoring speed, tends to emphasize the pleasures of the ocean voyage.[40]

In the coming years, however, the airplane's advantage of speed and time-saving when people are traveling sizable distances is likely to be crucial. The Port of New York Authority estimates, for example, that by 1970 air travel will exceed rail travel for distances between 150 and 1,000 miles, while air transport will carry practically all common carrier passengers going more than 1,000 miles.[41]

On Population

The effect of aviation on population logically follows from what has been said in the preceding section. The chief effect on population is on the *distribution* of people both within a nation and throughout the world. There is some daily commuting from home to job by plane at present, but it is uncommon; it is likely to increase during the future with greater use of private plane and helicopter. One may expect from this influence a further dispersal of homes outward from the city.[42] It is possible that commuting to the city within a 150-mile radius could be achieved. Any such commuting is likely to occur first among high-income families.

But the greater effect on distribution of population may relate to the global and regional spheres. Since the airplane's greatest use is in covering long distances quickly (requiring no track or highway), the airplane is valuable in penetrating remote regions. Aviation tends thus to aid in the distribution of population to areas which have hitherto been only sparsely settled, as Alaska, the interior of Africa, parts of South America. This is sometimes associated with mining developments or other economic opportunities in unsettled parts

[38] *Annual Report of the Civil Aeronautics Board, 1952* (Washington, 1953), p. 13; *Annual Report, 1955* (Washington, 1956), p. 8.

[39] For discussion of sending standard three-cent mail by air and current experiments in that practice, see Air Transport Association of America, *Air Transport Facts and Figures,* 16th ed., 1955, p. 6.

[40] For example, at this time of writing the advertisements of one of the largest steamship companies emphasize the theme: *"Getting there is half the fun!"*

[41] Port of New York Authority, Department of Airport Development, Airport Planning Bureau, *Air Traffic Forecast, 1950–1980: New York-New Jersey Port District* (mimeographed, 1950).

[42] Ogburn does not believe that such dispersal during the future would be as great as that caused by the automobile.—*Op. cit.*, pp. 318–319.

of the world. Aviation has already aided the development of mines in such areas as New Guinea, Australia, Honduras, Bolivia, the Belgium Congo.

Somewhat related to this is the effect of aviation in reducing differential population density in regions already settled. A transportation line connecting two unequally populated areas tends to reduce the differential in population density between them.[43] In this respect, aviation may play a part in linking more closely the Pacific Coast region with the Atlantic seaboard and Mississippi Valley. It is likely to have more effect than just adding another railroad line or highway, since new markets and other developments may be especially stimulated by aviation (because of the factor of speed). The former feeling of being isolated, which some Pacific Coast residents may have had, is reduced by the possibilities of air travel. In the air age, distance is increasingly calculated in terms of hours instead of miles. If the Los Angeles resident is now only seven to eight hours (airline transport) away from New York,[44] it stimulates contacts and trade. Probably other factors also have an effect in reducing the population density differentials between regions.

Other effects of aviation on population, as on birth and death rates, are regarded as negligible at the present time.

On Business and Manufacturing

Aviation affects business and manufacturing (industry) in various ways. For one thing, it can provide transportation service for people, goods, and mail. This may have an effect on the location or even on the organization of a business. The transport of goods may be important, as was the case with the railroad and motor vehicle as means of transportation. Freight rates for transporting air cargo are of crucial importance. As has been stated, the amount of air freight shipped has increased enormously in percentage but is still only a small fraction of total freight shipped. For selected types of manufacturing, however, the air influence may be considerable; this is no longer confined to emergency, light-weight, and luxury goods, but now includes such items as automobile parts and industrial machinery. Long-distance shipments are definitely favored for air transportation if the cost is reasonable, since much time will be saved. In cases where a manufacturing plant is located a long distance from the market or sources of supply, aviation may have a significant influence on the business. In the United States the long distance between the populous East Coast and the Pacific states may bring a considerable use of aviation in business, as in the fruit, flowers, wine, motion picture, airplane parts, and other Pacific Coast enterprises.

Business executives are increasingly using air transportation, either flying

---

[43] On this general subject, see Ogburn, *op. cit.*, Ch. 14.

[44] As of December, 1955, scheduled eastbound flights of American Airlines, Inc. and United Air Lines consumed seven and one-quarter hours while westbound flights consumed eight and three-quarters hours. Prevailing westerly winds make the eastbound flight shorter. The above flights are nonstop. See timetables of these airlines.

Wright Brothers' Plane at Kitty Hawk, 1903

Boeing 707 Jet Stratoliner

FROM THE WRIGHT BROTHERS TO THE LATER FIFTIES

Courtesy of U. S. Air Force and *Aviation Week*

Convair F-102A Jet Interceptor

their own company plane or traveling by scheduled airline flight. While the cost of operating company planes is considerable,[45] the added convenience and time saved in flying high-salaried executives is regarded by many as worth the expense. Business flying, it is asserted, is definitely increasing. The most reliable statistics on business flying that are available—those compiled by the CAA—show that during 1954 a total of 3,918,000 hours were flown by businessmen, which is nearly four times the number flown during 1946. The most flying was done by businessmen in the petroleum, manufacturing, and mining industries, according to the CAA.[46] One may, moreover, recall from the table on page 193 the increasing trend of business flying in the U. S. since 152,000 hours were flown in 1931.

It was stated in early 1956 that some 7,000 American business firms operated a total of nearly 12,000 aircraft. An additional 9,000 individually-owned planes were used primarily for business, and perhaps 14,000 more did some business flying. It was estimated that business flying during 1955 totaled about 4,300,000 hours—10 per cent more than in 1954.[47] Planners of the Civil Aeronautics Administration estimated that business flying would increase to 7,200,000 hours in 1956, and further that airplane sales to businessmen would triple between 1955 and 1965.[48] Some planes used by business executives are outfitted with desks, radio telephones, dictating machines, and other office equipment. Use of company-owned planes sometimes brings substantial savings, too. The example is given of the breakdown of an essential machine used by a construction firm. The resulting work stoppage was costing the company $1,000 every hour. But needed parts were flown in by one of the company's planes, and the plant was back in operation within two hours.[49]

Then, aviation has caused at least two important businesses to develop, namely, the manufacturing of airplanes and allied products and the air transportation (airline) business. Both of these are, at the present time, "big businesses." U. S. aircraft production has ranged from an output totaling 43 planes in 1913 to the all-time high of 96,318 planes in 1944, when American production during World War II was at its zenith point. Since 1947 military aviation production figures have been withheld for security reasons. Civilian production has leveled off at roughly 3,500 planes per year.[50]

[45] Spencer Klaw, "Twelve Thousand Company Planes," *Fortune* (January, 1956), table on p. 121. The initial cost of these planes ranged from $7,800 Piper planes to plush DC-3's (which cost more than $200,000) to the twenty-passenger-capacity Convair 340 (which costs about $750,000).

[46] *Aviation Week,* Vol. 60, No. 11 (March 15, 1954), pp. 140–141.

[47] Klaw, *op. cit.,* p. 118.

[48] Erwin J. Bulban, "Business Flying Enters 'Golden Decade,'" *Aviation Week,* Vol. 64, No. 11 (March 12, 1956), 23rd Annual Inventory of Airpower, pp. 270–271.

[49] See also "Why Executives Like Their Planes," *Aviation Week,* Vol. 60, No. 8 (February 22, 1954), pp. 16–17; "Air-Minded Executives," *Newsweek* (September 7, 1953), pp. 72–73.

[50] Civil Aeronautics Administration, *Statistical Handbook of Civil Aviation, 1953* (Washington, CAA, 1953), p. 40.

Helicopter production has risen steadily. During the seven years since the first certificated American helicopter was flown, manufacturers in the United States have produced about 3,000 helicopters; during the years of the Korean War (1950–53), these helicopters were nearly all for military use. During late 1953 six helicopter manufacturers—Bell, Doman, Hiller, Kaman, Piasecki, and Sikorsky—were producing fifteen different models.[51]

Other indices of the development of airplane manufacturing in the United States show that the *value added by manufacture* of aircraft and plane parts increased from $656,000 in 1914 to $30,986,000 in 1935 to $4,404,823,000 in 1952. Also, employment in the aircraft production industry increased from a total of 222 persons employed in 1914 to 688,889 persons in 1952.[52]

The air transportation (airline) business has likewise assumed large proportions. The domestic (U. S.) airlines may be classified according to several distinct types: (*a*) the major transcontinental lines, as American, United, and TWA; (*b*) the major intersectional airlines, as Eastern, Delta, National, and Western; (*c*) the sectional lines, as Colonial, Mid-Continent, Northeast; and (*d*) the local or "feeder" lines, as Arizona, Challenger, Iowa, Southern, West Coast.[53] Competition between airlines operating on the same or parallel routes is generally keen.[54]

The air transportation business has expanded impressively since World War II. Since 1951 total operating revenues of the industry (domestic and international airlines) have exceeded $1 billion; indeed, in 1954 they approached $1.5 billion. Total revenues had been approximately $463 million in 1946, hence they roughly tripled during the next eight years. All divisions of the airline business—domestic trunk lines, local (feeder) lines, insular, and international lines—showed marked increases in revenue between 1946 and 1954. The domestic trunk lines, for example, showed an increase from approximately $312 million in 1946 to an estimated $980 million in 1954.[55]

[51] *Aviation Facts and Figures, 1953, op. cit.,* pp. 142, 155 (note Table 7–19 on latter page).

[52] *Ibid.,* p. 21 (Table 2–2); p. 45 (Table 3–1).

Fortune magazine's rating of U. S. industrial corporations as of 1955 showed that aircraft production companies held rankings as the thirty-first, thirty-second, thirty-fifth, forty-first, and forty-sixth largest of industrials. These rankings were held by, respectively, the Douglas, Boeing, North American, United Aircraft, and Lockheed corporations. See *Fortune,* Supplement (July, 1956), "The Fortune Directory of the 500 Largest U. S. Industrial Corporations," p. 2.

[53] Wilson and Bryan, *op. cit.,* p. 176. The largest of these companies, again following *Fortune's* 1955 ratings, were American Airlines, Pan American, United, Trans World Airlines, and Eastern Air Lines. In a special ranking of the fifty largest transportation companies on basis of operating revenues, the above ranked twelve, fifteenth, sixteenth, eighteenth, and twenty-first respectively. *Fortune,* Supplement (July, 1956), p. 14.

[54] For an intensive analysis of the effects of competition on quality and price of airline service, see Frederick W. Gill and Gilbert L. Bates, *Airline Competition* (Boston, Division of Research, Graduate School of Business Administration, Harvard University, 1949).

[55] Air Transport Association of America, *Air Transport Facts and Figures,* 16th ed., 1955, p. 12.

On Cities

At present, the chief effect of aviation on cities probably pertains to urban ecology, resulting from the location of airports. Thus real estate values and residential choices are affected by nearness to an airport. A future effect of aviation on the city has already been suggested: If and when helicopters or other private planes are owned and operated in large numbers, cities will probably spread out further. Thus the ecology of the city in the helicopter age would show further decentralization of residential areas. This in turn would be likely to cause an increased urbanization of ideas and attitudes of people living near big cities. The helicopter-age city would be expected to have landing places on the flat roofs of department stores, the post office, and other buildings.

A more immediate and menacing effect of the airplane on cities is possible air attack. Coupled with the use of A-bomb, H-bomb, rocket, and guided missile, aviation may produce the destruction of the large city.[56] Urban civilization, indeed, seems threatened at the present time if a large-scale World War III should break out. Since this threat is discussed in other chapters of this volume, in Chapter 10, 15, and 20, no further comment regarding the threat itself will be made at this point.

On Health

Aviation has had various effects on health. Certain medical problems are specifically related to flying. (1) Anoxia, or altitude sickness, is caused by flight at high altitudes where there may be lack of oxygen in body tissues. The nervous system is particularly sensitive to oxygen want, and an inadequate supply of oxygen produces marked changes in the entire organism.[57] Following rapid ascents to 10,000 or more feet, people may experience respiratory difficulties, difficulty in (mental) concentration, excessive sleepiness, lassitude or indifference, headaches, and other symptoms.[58] (2) Aeroembolism, or the emitting of nitrogen quickly from the blood, may produce bubbles which hinder blood circulation. If a bubble should occur at a vital spot in the body, it might produce paralysis or even death. Use of pressurized cabins will, however, prevent aeroembolism. (3) Painful effects on the eardrum may result if inner and outer pressures on the drum are not equalized. If the eustachian tube should remain closed for some physiological or pathological reason, injury to the middle ear (otitic barotrauma) may result from changes in barometric pressure. For this reason, passengers should be encouraged to swallow just before or during the beginning of the airplane's

[56] In the future, cities could no doubt be destroyed without much use of aviation, certainly if the intercontinental guided missile is perfected. The situation would be vastly different from the attacks on London during World War II or the A-bombing of Nagasaki and Hiroshima.

[57] Ross A. McFarland, *Human Factors in Air Transportation* (New York, McGraw-Hill, 1953), pp. 682–690.

[58] McFarland, *op. cit.*, Table 15.7 on p. 684.

descent. The use of pressurized cabins is also helpful. (4) Some people may experience ordinary airsickness just as some individuals may experience auto sickness or seasickness. Studies of the Capital and Trans-Australia airlines show that children have the highest rate of airsickness (averaging about 50 children sick per 1,000 flying); women have the next highest rate (averaging about 25 sick per 1,000 women flying); and men have the lowest rate (averaging about 5 men sick per 1,000 flying). Since more men fly, however, the percentage of airsick people will average about 23 per cent men, about 60 per cent women, and about 16 per cent children.[59] The degree of turbulence of air weather will have much to do with the incidence of airsickness. (5) The effects of traveling at high speed have been studied; in general, there appear to be no special harmful physiological effects. (6) The occurrence of "blackouts," due usually to sudden change of direction or speed (as when a dive-bomber comes out of the dive) may obtain; these are not likely in "normal," certainly scheduled airline, flying. (7) Aeroneurosis, which is associated with a fear of falling, of accidents, of being grounded, and with other miscellaneous tensions related to flying, may develop. The pilot who develops this tends to have gastric, nervous, fatigue, insomnia, or other emotional symptoms. McFarland states that the cases falling in this psychological and neuropsychiatric area are numerous and are the most difficult with which an airline medical officer must deal.[60] (8) "Flying fatigue" may result from too much flying and stress. Pilots need general rest and a change from flying; otherwise they may develop aeroneuroses. Lastly (9), the effects of atmospheric changes and/or plane noises may bring certain hearing problems; temporary deafness, even permanent deafness, may result.[61]

Because of the tremendous increase in number of people who fly at the present time, including both military and civilian air transport, and because of increasing interest in such aviation health problems as the above, the new field of aviation medicine has been established. Concerned with "the effects on the human body of traveling several miles above the surface of the earth at high speed," it is the newest of the medical specialties to be recognized by the American Medical Association.[62] The Aero-Medical Association was actually founded in 1929. Although many problems in the field have been solved, one medical authority states that "just when one problem is solved, however, aircraft designers produce planes that fly faster and higher—and new problems are created."[63] In addition to health problems which have been mentioned, aviation medicine concerns itself with the selection, training,

[59] *Ibid.*, p. 677 (Table 15.5 and discussion on same page).

[60] *Ibid.*, pp. 224–229.

[61] Aside from the McFarland material as noted, the above has been largely summarized from Ogburn, *op. cit.*, pp. 375–380.

[62] "Aeromedicine Gets Specialty Status," *Aviation Week*, Vol. 58, No. 16 (April 20, 1953), pp. 46–47; Howard A. Rusk, "Nation's Supremacy in Air Tied to Medical Research," *New York Times*, April 18, 1954; Ogburn, *op. cit.*, pp. 372–374.

[63] Rusk, *loc. cit.*

and maintenance of health of flight personnel; sanitation and health in airline operations; use of air ambulances; and similar subjects.[64]

It may be noted, finally, that certain diseases may be carried by aircraft. Infectious diseases may be carried from infected to noninfected areas by insects which lodge in the plane or by passengers. The potential diseases of consequence here are yellow fever, cholera, bubonic plague, typhus fever, smallpox, and influenza. It is possible for a person to contract typhus fever in a foreign land, then board a plane for New York; since the incubation period of the disease is from five to twelve days whereas air travel is speedy, he might not know he has the disease when he embarks from the plane. The disease could then spread in the United States. Similarly, yellow fever, carried by a species of mosquito, could be spread from the endemic area of Central and South America (or even farther away). Or infected mosquitos might lodge in dark corners of planes, then bite passengers or others at landing places in America. It is not contended here that the disease would then spread rapidly, as with the severe epidemics of the nineteenth century. With modern vaccination techniques, it would be swiftly controlled in all likelihood.

Medical control measures are, however, needed at the appropriate times and places. Airliners coming from Central and South America do need to be sprayed with insecticides shortly before arrival in this country; crew and passengers are inspected upon landing and the plane is searched for insects. Communicable disease problems in the air age are international in scope, to a large degree. McFarland observes that no major epidemics have thus far been attributed to scheduled civilian air transportation, but that epidemics occur in parts of the world where air travel is very extensive. For example, a serious outbreak of cholera occurred in Egypt in 1947 and a total of 20,877 cases were reported within eight weeks; 10,265 died. A vigilant system of control is needed.[65] The Foreign Quarantine Division of the United States Public Health Service, incidentally, made a total of 215,992 aircraft inspections between 1930 and 1947. On approximately 50 per cent of the planes insects, chiefly mosquitoes and flies, were found that could have been carrying disease.

On Recreation

The airplane is having various effects on recreation. Flying, for one thing, is pleasurable in itself—is in fact something of a joy and thrill. It was observed in the table on page 193, however, that private flying for pleasure,

[64] One may say that there is an increasing realization of the importance of the human factor in aviation. It is recognized (1) that man's organic nature and modern plane travel are not necessarily compatible, and (2) that man represents a fixed biological and chemical entity while the modern airplane is constantly changing in speed and other capabilities. See *Aviation Week*, Vol. 62, No. 11 (March 14, 1955), "22nd Annual Inventory of Airpower," pp. 222–229.

[65] McFarland, *op. cit.*, pp. 641–668; Ogburn, *op. cit.*, pp. 381–385.

when expressed in number of hours flown, has receded from the high mark of the 1947–49 years; since 1950 "pleasure and other" flying has leveled off at roughly 2 million hours per year. It was much higher following World War II, nevertheless, than during the 1930's.

Aviation has an effect on recreational trips by enabling people to travel farther in short time. Instead of spending a two-week or month vacation at the nearby beach or mountain resort, one can now travel to a distant American vacation spot or to Europe, Mexico, Alaska. For economic reasons, it is likely that vacationists using the plane are of the high-income group.

In increasing the radius of travel the airplane usually tends to build up the vacation regions which railroad, automobile, and ship travel have established. Within the United States, for instance, air travel has increased vacationing in the southeastern states, Gulf area, southwest, California resorts such as Palm Springs, and similar areas. There is the likelihood that vacations will increasingly extend to more distant points—Mexico, Cuba, Nassau, the Caribbean, Central America, Alaska and northern Canada (during summer months), and North Africa. As noted earlier, European travel is increasingly made by plane.

A typical instance of the above may be seen in what has already occurred in Nassau. According to the figures of the Nassau Bahamas Development Board, tourists have visited that island resort in the following numbers between 1949 and 1955:[66]

Year	Total Number Tourists	Traveled by		Per Cent Traveled by Air
		SHIP	PLANE	
1949	32,018	10,296	21,722	67.8
1950	45,371	11,945	33,426	73.7
1951	68,502	17,700	50,802	74.2
1952	84,718	34,137	50,581	59.7
1953	90,485	34,950	55,535	61.4
1954	109,605	42,483	67,122	61.2
1955	132,434	57,136	75,298	56.9

Thus the total number of tourists to Nassau more than quadrupled between 1949 and 1955. Average of the total seven-year period discloses that a total of 62.9 per cent of all tourists to this resort made the trip by air.

The drawing power of outstanding sporting events will also be extended by air travel. The sports public interested in a championship boxing match, a World Series baseball game, tennis matches at Forest Hills or Wimbledon, intersectional football games, will increasingly be drawn from a much wider area. However, radio and TV are forces that oppose personal attendance at these events. The airplane has also widened the radius of scheduling football games and other sporting events. Since many college teams and others travel by plane, they can easily cover much longer distances than formerly.

[66] Report on Tourist Travel by Nassau Bahamas Development Board, 1956 (mimeographed), p. 5. Provided by courtesy of C. P. Bethel, Manager.

Will such an extended range of travel increasingly lead to international competition in sports? This is likely. Trips of baseball teams to Japan, further international matches in tennis, golf, boxing, and other sports should increase because of the influence of aviation. Cultural differences regarding athletics will, of course, affect this development.

In all probability the arts will be similarly affected by aviation. An increased international exchange of theater performers, concert singers, and other entertainers is likely to occur. Language is sometimes a barrier to the exchange of some types of artists, though usually not singers nor musicians. More foreign artists are likely to be used in making American motion pictures, since travel is easier and contacts more readily made. Moreover, aviation has an effect on the "shooting" of movie scenes. If the motion picture plot calls for scenes located in the Rockies, in Scandinavia, in Italy, or in Casablanca, the increasing tendency in the air age is for the cast and associated personnel to travel by plane to the designated place rather than having an artificial set built. Authentic scenes will then be featured. There may be a certain amount of expense involved in this procedure, but the construction of sets is expensive too.

On Agriculture and Stock Raising

For many years aviation has had important uses in agriculture, especially in dusting such crops as cotton, wheat, alfalfa, fruits, and vegetables. This work has long since passed the experimental stage. The contention is made that one airplane can dust more cotton in one day than one hundred of the best ground machines.[67] The airplane is also widely used in spraying fruits and truck crops. Although aerial farming of this sort is about two decades old, it was a minor business until after World War II when planes became available and many air-minded farmers returned from the armed forces.[68]

Use of an airplane in dusting and spraying brings the great advantage of speed in application. In combating such fast-working pests as the army leaf worm in cotton or in meeting emergency invasions of migratory pests as the grasshopper or white-fringed beetle, dusting or spraying from an airplane offers the best hope of protection. Equipment for dusting by planes can, moreover, be moved rapidly from one area to another. A rather dramatic example of this performed on an international scale was the incident of "Operation Locust" in Iran.[69] A call for help to check a plague of locusts was met by a flight of three transports from the United States to Iran, carrying eight small airplanes with spray equipment, nine pilots, six mechanics, and thirteen tons of a special chemical. The locusts were successfully checked.

The fact that the airplane is independent of ground conditions enables it

[67] Wilson and Bryan, *op. cit.,* p. 425.

[68] A. C. Monahan, "Farming from the Sky," *Science News Letter,* Vol. 60 (September 15, 1951), pp. 170–171.

[69] Hunsaker, *op. cit.,* p. 78.

to dust fields that often would be difficult for ground machinery. Muddy fields do not prevent planes from spraying. Neither do intertwining or tall-growing crops interfere with aerial spraying as they would with ground machinery.

On the other hand, the drift of dust has been a major handicap to airplane dusting. This may bring a considerable waste of dust or it may bring damage to, say, bees or livestock. The difficulties of turning at the ends of rows in the field have made dusting by plane practicable only on large acreages; however, a new plane for seeding and spraying, known as Ag-1, has been built at the Aircraft Research Center, Texas A & M College, under contract with the CAA. The Ag-1 is able to fly as slowly as 45 miles per hour, it can make quick turns, and can land on rough terrain with a short run.[70] Such problems as the difficulty of turning at end of the field can also be successfully met by use of the helicopter, since the latter can make quick turns, can hover over a small plot of ground, and can avoid such obstructions as tall trees or power lines.

Aerial methods constitute an inducement to increase the scale of farm operations. Like the tractor and other farm machinery, the influence of the airplane tends toward large-scale farming.

The airplane is also widely used in shipping fresh fruits, vegetables, and other agricultural products to the market. A further use is in the making of aerial surveys of soil conditions for soil conservation work. Aerial photographs are of great value in this kind of endeavor.[71]

In stock raising, too, the airplane has been useful. Especially on the large farms and ranches of the West, horseback-riding and use of trucks seem to be giving way to some extent to planes. The latter provide a quick and easy way of inspecting the livestock range. Sheep ranchers have successfully hunted coyotes in a plane; the helicopter should be even better for this activity. The plane is useful, moreover, for inspecting the condition of fences, detecting cattle rustling, and making quick trips to the market center or other city. By bringing the vast distances of the range closer to the ranch owner or manager, the airplane and helicopter generally make it possible to conduct ranching on a still larger scale.

On Forestry

Following World War I the Forestry Service of the Department of Agriculture began the use of aircraft in forestry, and it has become increasingly important. Much of the area administered by the Forestry Service, equal to

[70] A. C. Monahan, *loc. cit.* By the summer of 1956 a new plane for agricultural use—known as Ag-2—was being tested. It was designed to incorporate the best features of Ag-1 with other improvements made. *Aviation Week,* Vol. 65, No. 1 (July 2, 1956), p. 83.

[71] The reader is, in general, referred to: Ogburn, *op. cit.,* Ch. 29; Wilson and Bryan, *op. cit.,* pp. 424–431; "Business, Farm Flying Continue Growth," *Aviation Week,* Vol. 58, No. 9 (March 2, 1953), pp. 163–168.

one-tenth of the land surface of the United States, is wild land. It is often located in the high and more remote mountainous sections where transportation and communications facilities are limited and the main methods of travel have been foot and horseback. In such areas there may be, nevertheless, livestock grazing, lumbering, industry, mining, and public recreation (hiking, hunting, fishing, sightseeing).

The airplane is, first of all, valuable in detecting forest fires and in the aerial delivery of supplies to firefighters. Speed is the essence of forest fire control; the transportation of men and supplies to fires is one of the most important uses of aviation in forestry work. Before the air age, the average rate of travel in reaching a forest fire was often from one to four miles per hour. During a recent year (1952) airplanes were used by the Forestry Service to transport more than 12,000 men and approximately 2,000,000 pounds of fire supplies, of which about 1,000,000 were dropped to fire fighters working in inaccessible country.[72] Approximately 12,000 hours of flying were necessary; in addition more than 1,000 flights were made by helicopters. "Smokejumpers" (firefighters who parachute to the scene of the fire) made 1,200 jumps to 334 fires during 1952.[73] During the following year "smokejumpers" made 836 individual jumps. Airplanes were used during 1953 to transport 8,000 men and approximately 525,000 pounds of fire equipment and supplies to forest fire areas. During 1953 the transportation system of the Forestry Service included eighty-six landing fields for fixed-wing airplanes and five heliports for helicopters.[74]

The Forestry Service has also used the airplane in other ways: for aerial photography, map-making, management of wildlife (as in making estimates of big-game population), transporting seedling trees to inaccessible areas, seeding grasses by plane in burned-over forest areas. Finally, officials who administer the forest activities increasingly use air travel; and planes and helicopters are currently regarded as virtually necessary for rescuing persons lost in forest areas and in mountain-climbing. Here the helicopter is especially valuable, for it makes possible air evacuation of lost persons when the terrain is rugged.

On Mining

Mining, a basic industry upon which our industrial civilization depends, has also been considerably affected by aviation. In particular, the discovering of new mines, servicing of mines, and maintaining the mining population have been significantly influenced.

Prospecting today is far different from what it was at the time of the forty-

---

[72] *Report of Chief of the Forestry Service, 1952* (Washington, Government Printing Office, 1953), pp. 32–33.

[73] The headquarters of the "Forestry Service Smoke-jumper Corps" was established at Missoula, Montana, during the year.

[74] *Report of Chief of the Forestry Service, 1953, op. cit.,* pp. 30–31.

niners. A low-flying airplane, equipped with an aerial camera using color film, is of great value in locating sources of metals. The helicopter is also valuable for this work. Use of the airplane is helpful for another reason: Most mines in the settled areas of the world are known and are largely being worked, hence increasingly new mines are likely to be found in the more undeveloped, isolated regions. To be able to fly speedily to these oft-distant places is of real benefit. Moreover, supplies must be brought in from the outside for the miners and their families. In rough, mountainous country it is sometimes highly impractical to construct roads for the surface hauling of supplies. Under such conditions air transportation, which would normally be higher in cost than highway transport, would be recommended from the economic standpoint.

The factor of time saved is also worthy of mention. It is stated, for example, that planes loaded with freight may cross over the Andes Mountains in South America in 30 minutes, flying at an altitude of 15,000 feet. The alternative—mules trudging over jungle and ravine with the supplies—requires from around four to six weeks.[75]

An effect of the use of aviation, then, is to help promote mining in more distant and inaccessible parts of the world. Present indications are that aviation will have an increasing influence of this sort.

On Education

It would be expected that aviation, a development that is having a marked effect on man's social, economic, and political environment, would have an impact on education. This, indeed, has happened. First, significant adjustments have been made concerning the educational curriculum. Various fields of knowledge have been greatly affected by the development of aviation, especially physics, engineering, meterology, social science in general (and geography, international relations, and sociology in particular), business and commerce, and of course aeronautics. Other fields which have been partially or indirectly affected are language study, history, mathematics, biology, medicine, and geology. In fact, the all-around effects of aviation have been so great that most fields are influenced in some way.

Concerning the educational fields affected in a more major way, one may point out that physics courses have paid increasing attention to the physics of flight, both at the college and high school levels. Physical science textbooks have in some instances been recast in order to place greater emphasis on aviation.[76] The field of aeronautics is, by definition, entirely concerned with the operation of aircraft. Engineering has opened up a new branch within its field: aeronautical engineering. This is an important and highly developed field in many of the engineering schools of the United States. Meteorology,

---

[75] Ogburn, *op. cit.*, p. 538.

[76] For example, see J. G. Manzer and others, *Physical Science in the Air Age* (New York, Macmillan, 1942).

an old field, has had a new lease of life with the development of aviation. Man has long been interested in predicting the weather, but knowledge of climatology, the upper air, and other meterological subjects is nothing short of essential for the aviator. Many job opportunities have thus been created in meteorology.[77] The development of aviation is also related, in turn, to the rapid build-up of departments of meteorology in colleges and universities.[78] The meteorology program at the Massachusetts Institute of Technology, originally established in the department of aeronautical engineering in 1928, is believed to be the first professional program in meteorology offered in an American institution of higher learning.[79] The rise of meteorology programs in universities and technical schools is, at any rate, clearly correlated with the all-around development of aviation.

Social science has also been affected, especially the disciplines of geography, international relations, and sociology. Aviation has changed man's whole notion about geography. The pre-air-age barriers to travel and conquest, such as bodies of water, mountains, deserts, jungle, and extremes of temperature, do not exert much of an influence with air transportation. In times of war or peace, their significance is now minimized, perhaps entirely lost. For example, the Alps which took Hannibal two years to cross in his Roman campaign are now crossed almost hourly by airplane. The fortifications of Gibraltar and Singapore have lost virtually all their significance. Formerly they controlled sea navigation in the Mediterranean and Straits of Malacca respectively. Similarly the English Channel, once a potent barrier against attack from the continent, provides no protection in the air age. Such "barriers of distance" and much of the security based on them are lost.[80]

On the other hand, what have increased in influence in the air age are the great-circle routes of travel. New air-age maps need to be used. Mention has earlier been made of the reduction in time required to reach a certain destination (the "shrinking of distance"), also that travel distances are now better stated in terms of hours. In the age of speedy air travel all the peoples of the world are more or less "neighbors." This whole conception is far different from the older emphasis in geography that Brazil, Japan, Egypt, India, are far-away, strange places.[81] The idea of being "far away" largely dis-

---

[77] Francis W. Reichelderfer, "Career Opportunities in the United States Weather Bureau," *Weatherwise*, Vol. 6, No. 5 (October, 1953), pp. 119, 142; Major General William O. Senter, "Air Force Weather Careers," *ibid.*, pp. 122–123.

[78] "Meteorological Education in the United States: Facilities at Twenty Leading Universities," *ibid.*, pp. 126–141.

[79] "A Brief History of the Department of Meteorology at Massachusetts Institute of Technology," *Bulletin of the American Meteorological Society*, Vol. 32 (March, 1951), pp. 103–104. Meteorology was made a separate department at M.I.T. in July, 1940.

[80] Reginald M. Cleveland and Leslie E. Neville, *The Coming Air Age* (New York, Whittlesey House, 1944), Ch. 2, "Air-Age Geography" (especially p. 42).

[81] Again, one has only to refer to airline timetables in order to see the present nearness (in terms of travel time) of some of these places. For example, the Trans World Airlines (TWA) timetable as of July 1, 1956, showed that flying time between New

appears in the air age. Finally, it may not be surprising from the above that added emphasis is placed in geography on the subject of *world geography.*

It may likewise be inferred from the above that the field of international relations assumes new importance. With the former state of relative isolationism now replaced by rapid contact between countries, the relations between nations become a more vital matter. These increased contacts in the shrunken world may result in harmonious relations or in discord, possibly war. There is the possibility of a peaceful hemispheric or world community; there is the possibility, on the other hand, of atomic-germ-chemical war. Crucial, then, is this field that studies the relationship and problems between nations: Of much more consequence it is in the shrunken world of the air age than, say, in the slow-moving, isolated times of 1750 or 1850.

Social science in general, and sociology in particular, has the responsibility of pointing out the significance of the social impact of the airplane. It should assess the influence of this invention on society in comparison with other influences. It should be able to show the social influences of aviation on different parts of society—on the varied social institutions, on community life, on population, on social change. It should be able to indicate future derivative effects to be expected from the development of aviation. Such may be regarded as reasonable tasks expected of sociology. It may be argued that many sociologists have not devoted much attention thus far to the impact of this relatively new transportation field. Nevertheless a distinguished beginning has been made with Professor Ogburn's work. It is hoped that sociologists will increasingly make contributions to this dynamic and, in some ways, critical subject. It must be appreciated that aviation is far from a static field. Its further impact on society may be as momentous as has been its past influence.

The field of business and commerce has considerable interest in aviation as a new form of transportation, as a new business enterprise, as a new field for investments. The great airplane factories and airlines now each comprise billion-dollar industries. They consist of many powerful corporations, vigorous profit-making ventures, operating under regulations set by the Civil Aeronautics Board. A whole new field of business, then, has developed with the rise of the airplane. Study of the rates, records, accounts, competitive practices and other policies of this vigorous field is likely to yield worth-while results.

But other educational phenomena in addition to the college curriculum have been affected by aviation. To briefly summarize other effects, there is the general education at the high school level regarding the development and importance of aviation in our society. This is in part similar to the sociological perspective, though it emphasizes fundamental aviation facts, including

York and Paris amounted to approximately 13 hours; New York to Cairo required about 27 hours; and New York to Bombay, India, about 35 hours. This may be compared with the length of the voyage via ship.

practical social and vocational aspects, for young civilians.[82] It is stated that in the fall of 1949 at least 175 high schools in 35 states had inaugurated aviation classes.[83] Some people believe that a general education with respect to aviation and its place in modern culture should begin during the very early years. In at least one school the rudiments of aviation "and the part it plays in our lives" have been taught as early as in the second grade.[84]

There is also flying instruction given at various schools.[85] This would be likely to increase greatly if and when private flying is adopted by large numbers of people. Finally, there are miscellaneous innovations in education which are related to aviation. Teachers of adult education or extension courses frequently fly to communities where the instruction is to be given— now commonplace, in fact. Then there is the "flying classroom" experiment in instruction at Michigan State College. Beginning in 1947, aerial trips over Michigan and to Washington, D. C., and Chicago were taken to acquaint leading teachers and school administrators with social, economic, political, and educational conditions. In 1950 such a group flew to Europe and visited twelve European countries; about sixty carefully-selected adults made the trip.[86] With travel time cut to the minimum, more time was available for conferences and observation in the foreign lands.

On Government

Aviation has tended to promote various trends in American government which have already been in evidence. One of these is the trend toward increasing functions and problems of government caused by the industrialization and urbanization of the nation and aided by other inventions such as the automobile, railroad, and radio. Aviation is another industry which must be regulated in the public interest. Because of the connection between aviation and national defense, the federal government is especially interested in this industry. The government also has a stake in aviation because of providing air-mail and other services. In addition, civil flying must be regulated by government.[87] As governments take on more regulatory functions, it is granted that their influence and power will increase.

[82] William N. McGowan, "Teaching About Aviation," *National Education Association Journal,* Vol. 38, No. 8 (November, 1949), pp. 590–591; John Demeter, "A Down-to-Earth Air Education," *School and Society,* Vol. 78, No. 2014 (August 22, 1953), pp. 57–59.

[83] W. N. McGowan, *loc. cit.*

[84] "Second-Graders Try Their Wings," *National Education Association Journal,* Vol. 39, No. 2 (February, 1950), pp. 119–122.

[85] See, for example, Avery F. Olney, "The Phoenix Flying School," *National Education Association Journal,* Vol. 43, No. 1 (January, 1954), p. 45.

[86] "Michigan State College's 'Flying Classroom,'" *School and Society,* Vol. 71 (February 11, 1950), pp. 91–92.

[87] As Hunsaker expresses it, "It would be intolerable anarchy to turn loose in the air above our heads any and all who wish to risk their own necks or to sell tickets to give passengers the same opportunity. Nor can we permit unregulated use of the airspace by foreign flyers, civil or military."—*Op. cit.,* pp. 36–37.

A second trend has been that many powers and responsibilities have been transferred from local government to states and from states to the federal government. This trend began roughly about 1885–90. Many factors operated to produce this trend toward centralization, of which technological factors (especially the transportation and communications inventions) were important. The railroad and automobile had an influence in decreasing the relative importance of county government. The airplane has an influence in this same direction; it links whole regions of the nation in commerce and trade. It tends to increase the relative importance of the national government. Aviation also helps to break down regional differences between people.

The expansion of governmental functions in the United States has resulted in a greater increase in administrative activity than in legislative or judicial power. The increasing complexity of modern life and outcropping of problems has brought the need of large numbers of government agencies, staffed by experts. In the field of aviation federal regulation is performed by the Civil Aeronautics Administration (CAA) and the Civil Aeronautics Board (CAB). The former is under the jurisdiction of the Department of Commerce.

The CAA. Under the terms of the Civil Aeronautics Act of 1938, CAA activities are related to the establishment and operation of the civil airways system (including the mapping, lighting, marking, and otherwise controlling of aerial routes); enforcement of safety and other regulations established by the CAB; licensing planes and pilots; encouraging aviation education in schools and colleges; developing a national system of airports (and operating the Washington National Airport); issuing aviation statistics and information; fostering aviation research; and, in general, aiding air commerce and navigation facilities. These are, in short, executive and administrative functions.[88]

While many CAA accomplishments in relation to the above activities could be cited, one may single out for mention the opening of the 45,000 miles of ultramodern, high-frequency airways on June 1, 1952. It has been observed[89] that a new era in civil air navigation began with this date. These "Victor" airways are 10 miles wide, and each has a number of traffic levels, spaced by 1,000-foot, vertical separation. In effect, they are like a series of highways, 10 miles wide, built one above another at 1,000-foot intervals. They are numbered like highway routes.

[88] See *U. S. Government Organization Manual, 1935–1954,* Federal Register Division, National Archives & Records Service, General Services Administration (Washington, 1953), pp. 268–271; Ogburn, *op. cit.,* pp. 660–661; Wilson and Bryan, *op. cit.,* Ch. 33 (especially pp. 586–588); William H. Young, *Ogg and Ray's Introduction to American Government,* 11th ed. (New York, Appleton-Century-Crofts, 1956).

[89] *40th Annual Report of the Secretary of Commerce* (Washington, Government Printing Office, 1952), pp. 46–47.

The work of the CAA as it affects an actual flight is visualized in the following summary statement:[90]

> Let us assume we are traveling by air from New York to Washington. It may be as an airline passenger, or in one of the growing fleet of business aircraft. In either case, our safe and speedy passage will get a lot of behind-scenes-assistance from CAA. Before we ever get aboard, the pilot will have submitted a flight plan to the CAA Air Route Traffic Control Center in New York.
>
> The plan might call for the flight to be made "via Amber 7 at 6,000." Amber 7 is the route number of a Federal airway, one of the more than 100,000 miles of highways in the sky established and maintained by CAA. Radio beams, rather than asphalt or concrete, are the materials from which these aerial roads are built.
>
> The control center makes sure that no other plane has asked to fly this particular route, at this particular altitude, at this particular time. It then issues our pilot a traffic clearance. . . .
>
> In addition, our pilot must get a take-off clearance from the CAA tower, one of which controls all landings, departures and ground traffic at this and 165 other busy airports.
>
> [The pilot then follows] one of the CAA radio range beams which assures him he is on course. At intervals along his route, he will report his position to a CAA communication station. . . .
>
> We're nearing Washington now, and the weather is rather thick. Our pilot knew this in advance, of course, and is not worried. He can count on double-barreled electronic help from the CAA in piercing the overcast to an on-schedule landing. The twin aids are the Instrument Landing System, which CAA has installed at 128 terminals, and Precision Approach Radar, operating at ten airports.

The CAB. An independent agency of five members appointed by the President, the CAB has functions of rule-making (policy), adjudication, and investigation, as prescribed in the Civil Aeronautics Act of 1938. Its activities are more of a legislative and judicial character.

The CAB has four principal functions: (1) to regulate the rates for air carrier operations—transportation rates for passengers, mail, and freight; (2) to promulgate safety standards for air transportation to be known as civil air regulations; (3) to investigate air accidents, hold public hearings concerning accidents if advisable, suspend or revoke licenses if necessary; and (4) co-operate in establishing international air transportation. In general, the CAB establishes aeronautics policy.[91]

On International Relations

Reference has already been made to aviation's role in bringing quicker international contacts, in causing a "shrinking of distance," and in making

[90] Frederick B. Lee, "Aerial Traffic Cop," *New York Times,* October 11, 1953, Sec. 10, "Fifty Years of Aviation," p. 17. Lee is former Administrator of Civil Aeronautics, U. S. government.

[91] *U. S. Government Organization Manual, 1953–1954,* pp. 337–339; Ogburn, *loc. cit.;* Wilson and Bryan, *op. cit.,* pp. 588–604; Young, *loc. cit.*

more important the relations between nations; it has, indeed, brought to a virtual end the former viewpoint of isolationism.[92]

It seems likely that travel brings, on the whole, a lessening of regional and national prejudices. Admiration of travelers for a new land, and of natives toward the travelers, may not be wholehearted or complete; but it appears that attitudes are more likely to be cordial than the reverse.

Certain facts suggest that peacetime aviation contacts are more likely to cement relations among neighboring nations in the same general region than they are nations thousands of miles apart. The average length of a passenger trip on the international airlines between 1946 and 1953 ranged between 1,057 and 1,376 miles.[93] Since many flights went to Europe (well over 3,000 miles) yet the average was roughly 1,200 miles, it is indicated that the majority of flights take place in the regional orbit; the destination is a neighboring country. Aviation tends to aid the forces organizing nations into regional groups, it is accordingly believed. The supposition is held that increased contacts are likely to bring closer ties and relations all-around.

In event of war, aviation will again bring closer contacts, though unfortunately of a destructive nature. To allow for possible war in the future, big powers want a zone of security around their boundaries. They, moreover, want to have a ring of air bases surrounding them to make easier attack on an enemy. This builds up a friendly region surrounding the large power. The effect of the bomber in general is to make the big powers bigger and the little nations littler. The influence of aviation at this time is to speed the evolution of states into still larger size. In this way, aviation may help in laying the groundwork for a single world political organization. But, in order to endure, such a world organization would have to have social coherence and an *esprit de corps*.

The airplane affects international relations in yet another way. As problems between nations develop, statesmen may avail themselves of speedy air transport in the effort to reach settlements in face-to-face conference. Such aerial diplomacy would have been impossible during earlier times. Franklin D. Roosevelt, attending conferences at Casablanca, Teheran, Yalta, and elsewhere by air, was the first American president to use the airplane consequentially for purposes of diplomacy. Prime Minister Winston Churchill flew to Washington in June, 1954, for his seventh series of conferences, it is stated,[94] with an American president. Presidents Truman and Eisenhower have also been devotees of air travel—the latter's flight to the "Summit" conference of world statesmen at Geneva (July, 1955) being a good ex-

---

[92] As Professor Ogburn has phrased it, "the airplane has given the *coup de grace* to the old-time isolationism of the nineteenth century." W. F. Ogburn, "Aviation and International Relations," in Ogburn, ed. *Technology and International Relations* (Chicago, University of Chicago Press, 1949), p. 89.

[93] *Air Transport Facts and Figures,* 15th ed., 1954, p. 14.

[94] *New York Times,* June 26, 1954.

ample. Secretary of State John Foster Dulles has made many airplane trips across the Atlantic; he has shown belief in personal contacts while seeking solutions to problems, has even made several round-trips across the Atlantic within a few weeks' time.[95] Ambassadors and ministers may also fly quickly to Washington or other capitals for consultation or in order to give an immediate, on-the-spot report on some matter. Such contacts likely reduce the individual initiative of diplomatic representatives abroad; they make possible, however, a more unified policy.[96]

Thus the airplane, in war, may be a potent agent of destruction, but it may also be used by peace-minded statesmen in efforts to avert war. Aviation may be a tool to implement a world-wide regime of law and order in "one world," which concept was itself created in no small part by the influence of the airplane.

SUMMARY

The social effects wrought by aviation well illustrate the basic principle that the parts of culture are interrelated and that important changes in some major part tend to give rise to adjustments in other parts. In this instance, a major advance was made in the realm of transportation. It has been shown that aviation as developed thus far has already brought many social effects and changes in other cultural elements. There is every reason to believe that the airplane will have even more notable effects with the further passing of time, just as occurred with respect to the automobile. The effects due to aviation relate particularly to advantages of speed of travel and to the consequent ability to cover long distances quickly.

Activities or cultural elements which have been *dominantly* affected by aviation at this time include the following: (1) international relations—in which nations are brought into closer contact and nearly all nations may be viewed as "neighbors" in the air age; planes may quickly fly to other nations, carrying peace-minded statesmen, business men, travelers, or bombs; (2) education—major effects have occurred, it is suggested, in such academic fields as physics, aeronautics, engineering, meteorology, social science, and business and commerce; other disciplines have been partially or indirectly affected; (3) business and industry—two large-scale industries (airplane manufacturing and airline transportation) have resulted from the invention of the airplane; also freight is increasingly transported by plane and executives

[95] Mr. Dulles has been called variously "a new kind of secretary of state," "the diplomatic spaceman," and "America's foremost traveling salesman." According to one journalist, Secretary Dulles "appears to regard an airplane journey across the Atlantic Ocean as the equivalent of a commuter's ride to New York on the 8 A.M. special." It is stated that Mr. Dulles always has an airplane at his call for a quick trip whenever emergencies or opportunities arise. He turns his plane into a flying office and works en route. See *New York Times*, April 18, 1954; also "100,000 Miles of Diplomacy," *U.S. News & World Report*, Vol. 36 (April 22, 1954), pp. 81–83.
[96] W. F. Ogburn, *The Social Effects of Aviation*, p. 682.

are more and more using air transportation; and (4) government—aviation has aided the further extension of powers of the federal government and the trend toward centralization generally; the actual federal regulation of aviation in the public interest is performed by the Civil Aeronautics Administration (of the Department of Commerce) and the Civil Aeronautics Board.

As large numbers of people adopt private flying in future decades—using a small fixed-wing plane, a helicopter (plain or roadable), or some new form of aircraft, or combinations of the above—the influence of aviation will be expected to rise to much greater proportions. Such a mass development of individual flying is, however, not likely to come for several decades.

ANNOTATED BIBLIOGRAPHY

Air Transport Association of America, *Air Transport Facts and Figures* (Washington). Annual factual statement of air transportation resulting from operations of the certificated airlines, domestic and international. Authentic figures.

Aircraft Industries Association of America, Inc., *Aviation Facts and Figures* (Washington). Another annual compendium—also valuable—this time by the aircraft production industry. Authentic source for production figures; comprehensive.

Civil Aeronautics Administration, *Statistical Handbook of Civil Aviation* (Washington, Department of Commerce). Annual statistical summary by the CAA. A mine of official information.

HUNSAKER, Jerome C., *Aeronautics at the Mid-Century* (New Haven, Yale University Press, 1952). A valuable work which ranges over many subjects of major interest concerning aviation. "Must" reading. Author is professor of aeronautical engineering at the Massachusetts Institute of Technology.

MCFARLAND, Ross A., *Human Factors in Air Transportation* (New York, McGraw-Hill, 1953). Comprehensive work on health and sanitation aspects. Includes discussion of selection and training of flight personnel, ground crews, etc. Thorough, top-grade job.

New York Times, issue of Sunday, October 11, 1953, Section 10, "Fifty Years of Aviation." A special anniversary issue honoring the flight of the Wright Brothers in 1903. Illuminating summary of development of aviation and assessment of 1953 status from various viewpoints; expert contributors.

OGBURN, William F., *The Social Effects of Aviation* (Boston, Houghton Mifflin, 1946). Has objective of foreseeing the effects of aviation on society before those effects occur. Distinguished by careful writing and the rich interpretive contributions of a leading sociologist. Definitive. Will be valuable for many years.

Port of New York Authority, Department of Airport Development, Airport Planning Bureau, *Air Traffic Forecast, 1950–1980* (New York, 1950, mimeographed), 3 vol. Careful predictions of air traffic in the time period covered; well worth reading.

WILSON, George Lloyd, and BRYAN, Leslie A., *Air Transportation* (Englewood Cliffs, N. J., Prentice-Hall, 1949). Excellent general reference. Of wide scope, except that authors do not emphasize social effects.

CHAPTER 10

ATOMIC ENERGY[1]

■ Hornell Hart

THE ATOMIC AGE is not a sudden, isolated development; it is not an historical freak, to be considered apart from the underlying trends and basic principles of cultural change. The spectacular promise and the terrific menace of nuclear energy have suddenly made people aware of some of the vast changes in human culture which are taking place. But these changes are vast because, in our day, the age-old acceleration of social evolution has reached a pitch of headlong development which can no longer be ignored.

Fundamentally, the Atomic Age is one phase of the accelerating increase of ability to generate, accumulate, release, and apply physical energy. The evolution of man's mastery of mechanical and chemical power has been reviewed in Chapter 3. That review showed that during the past century, man has gained six times as much horsepower per capita as he achieved in all the preceding million years of technological development. It is in the perspective of this more-and-more intensified acceleration in man's mastery of power that the Atomic Age must be understood.

The current phase of the perennial acceleration in human power may be dealt with under two broad categories: (1) peaceful utilization; and (2) military effects.

PEACEFUL USES OF ATOMIC ENERGY

Present and Future Developments in Atomic Power

Long and complex debates have been going on as to the extent to which atomic energy may be expected to contribute to the future of civilization. Early exuberant forecasts that cheap atomic power would shortly abolish poverty in the world have long since been discounted. It was soon realized that capital investment rather than the cost of raw materials for fuel constitutes the major part of power costs, and that even if atomic power could be provided without any cost, it would reduce the cost of living by only a minor

[1] From a technical standpoint the term *nuclear energy* might be more accurate, but the expression *atomic energy* is so widely used that it seems preferable for the sake of easy understanding.

fraction. However, certain basic facts have begun to emerge on the positive side.

1. Atomic power plants are already in operation in submarines built for the United States government and in various pilot plants for generating electricity.

2. Experiments already under way point toward the employment of atomic power, at an early date, in locomotives, aircraft carriers, airplanes, and large electric-generating plants. The British government has announced that it hopes to generate all the nation's electricity by atomic power within 20 years.

3. The use of atomic plants to generate electricity becomes economical (Karl Cohen has calculated) when coal costs over $7.50 per ton. As more efficient methods are developed for using atomic power to generate electricity, this source will become comparatively cheaper at lower and lower levels of coal costs.

4. In many areas of the world (such as India) which lack coal, oil, and water power, the development of atomic power plants may unlock immense possibilities for industrial development and for raising standards of living.

5. As world reserves of coal and oil are more and more depleted, uranium and other atomic fuels may be expected to become more and more essential to the ongoing of industrial life.

Radioactivity as a Boon to Science

In addition to the growing effects of atomic power, the research value of radioactive isotopes, produced in atomic reactors, promises highly significant contributions to progress in the applied sciences. Radioisotopes are being used in hundreds of different ways. Before the end of 1950, the Atomic Energy Commission had sent out more than 50,000 shipments of radioactive isotopes. The following examples may illustrate their uses.

In industrial research, tires have been impregnated with radioactive substances and then have been driven along test tracks. Invisible traces of rubber worn off in the tests can be detected by Geiger counters, thus providing a sensitive and accurate technique for research in methods of reducing tire wear. Similarly, wear and friction on piston rings have been measured by radioactivity. Radioisotopes have been used to locate oil-bearing shale in dry wells, with the aid of atomic detectors. Radioactivity has been used to analyze and improve oil-cracking processes. Radioactive thickness gauges have provided new accuracy in measurements. Atomic detection has revealed defects in metal castings and welds, which would be invisible to the naked eye. Leaks in plumbing systems have been located with Geiger counters.

In biological research, atomic detectives have already uncovered invaluable clues on such problems as how green plants use sunlight to convert carbon dioxide and water into sugar and starch—how photosynthesis creates the basis of all the world's food and most of its fuel. If this research project should succeed fully, the effects on providing cheap and inexhaustible photosynthetic power might transcend the possibilities of atomic power.

Another biological possibility is the stimulation of mutations. The possible applications of this method are almost unlimited. For example, a Dutch merchant has evolved new types of tulips by radiation. Dr. Calvin F. Konzak, Brookhaven biologist, announced in November, 1953, that atomic radiation had produced resistance to rust in a susceptible variety of oats.

In a 1,000-pound cow, scientists can detect a hundred-millionth of an ounce of radioactive material. Minute quantities of isotopic tracer have been mixed into amino acids, proteins, sugars, vitamins, hormones, antibodies, anesthetics, and the like. By tracing these atomic signal flags, scientists can study how these substances get into the body, how they are used, and finally how they are broken down and eliminated.

Many of the biological uses of radioisotopes will make direct contributions to medical research. But they also have immensely important applications in the study, diagnosis, and treatment of specific diseases. One vitally important field for such research is finding out how cancer gets started and how it spreads. A substance which is known to be a cause of cancer can now be impregnated with radioisotopes and placed in the body of an experimental animal. It is then possible to follow the course of this substance as it causes the cancer. Needless to say, a great deal may be learned by this method about how cancer develops and is nourished.

Radioisotopes are also useful in locating tumors much more exactly than it was possible to do by x-ray. If, for example, a brain tumor must be located, radioactive phosphorous may be injected into the patient's body. A brain tumor growing faster than the normal healthy tissue will absorb more of this radioactive substance. By placing a counter against the head and comparing radioactivity in various parts of the brain, it is possible to determine where the tumor is.

In the treatment of cancer, isotopes can be used like x-rays or radium. Some radioisotopes are more powerful than more expensive x-ray machines or radium tubes. Some can be used internally much more effectively than can the older types of radiation. E. N. Lockard has said that in the war against cancer, "the one factor that has done the most to inspire new hope of success is the use of radioactive isotopes."

Thyroid diseases have been effectively treated by means of radioactive iodine. Heart diseases can sometimes be treated effectively by radioisotope control of thyroid activity.

Altogether, the actual and potential contributions made possible by radioisotopes, both in basic research and in practical applications, come closest to justifying the enthusiastic forecasts which have been made as to peaceful applications of atomic discoveries. If the dangers of atomic militarism can be avoided or counteracted, the knowledge which scientists are gaining through their new mastery of the atom may make vast contributions toward relieving and preventing human suffering, and toward facilitating the progressive realization of man's aspirations for higher and higher standards of living.[2]

RUSSIA'S CAPACITY TO INFLICT NUCLEAR-BLAST DAMAGE ON THE UNITED STATES[3]

Two nonmilitary effects of atomic energy have been discussed briefly in the preceding sections, namely, the peaceful utilization of atomic power and the use of radioactivity in scientific research and medical treatment. The constructive possibilities under those two heads will be chiefly of academic interest, however, unless really effective methods are developed for dealing with the critical menace created by the military destructiveness which atomic and hydrogen bombs have made possible.

The background of the military applications of nuclear energy has already been given in Chapter 3. It has been pointed out in that chapter that the crisis of the Atomic Age is simply a culmination of cultural acceleration in general, and in particular of the extreme acceleration in the growth of the technology of destruction. The emergence of weapons based on nuclear energy was there summarized. In these later sections of the present chapter, it is proposed to explore some of the practical consequences of atomic and hydrogen bombs, in terms of the damage which they might inflict on the urban civilization of the United States if Russia actually launched a large-scale attack with such weapons.

According to the most reliable nonsecret information, the blast-damage area which a Soviet raid on the United States might inflict is growing with swiftly accelerating speed. This growth is due to two basic factors: (1) the accelerating increase in the power of individual bombs; and (2) the accelerating increase in the total supply of nuclear bombs of given sizes, available to be delivered on American targets. Russia's capacity to deliver the bombs is reported to be keeping pace with her stockpile; her supply of long-range bombers, of submarines, and of guided missiles with ranges measurable at least in hundreds, and probably in thousands, of miles, is reported to be growing swiftly.

Destructive Power of Individual Bombs

The increase in explosive power is a function of the accelerating growth of destructive technology, as shown in Chapter 3. The practical effects of this growth may be illustrated by showing the swift expansion of the blast-damage

[2] Ambassador Henry Cabot Lodge, Jr., summarized the state of atomic technology in a statement before the UN Committee on Peaceful Uses of Atomic Energy (UN Press Release No. 2000, November 5, 1954).

[3] Major portions of this and of the following sections (pages 223–240) appeared as parts of an article by Hornell Hart, entitled "The Menace versus the Remedies," in the *Bulletin of the Atomic Scientists*, Vol. 10 (June, 1954), pp. 197–205.

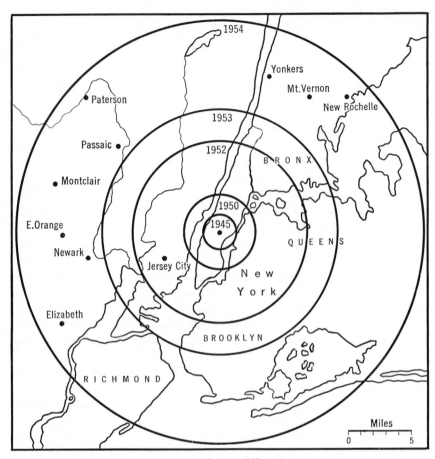

SOURCE: See footnote 3. Cf. *New York Times,* June 13, 1955, p. 16.

**GREATER NEW YORK, SHOWING THEORETICAL BLAST-DAMAGE AREAS FROM INDI-
VIDUAL BOMBS OF THE MOST DESTRUCTIVE TYPES AVAILABLE AT THE DATES
INDICATED**

area of a single explosion, at successive dates, in New York City. On the
basis of the best available estimates, the above chart has been drawn.
The meaning of this swiftly accelerating explosive power *of single bombs,* in
terms of lives and property exposed to destruction, can be seen from the following tabulation:

Year	Population Exposed	Property Value (billions of dollars)
1945	485,000	$ 3.3
1950	1,115,000	6.4
1952	5,000,000	16.5
1953	7,500,000	19.0
1954	10,000,000	24.0

But the blast area had become only part of the story by 1955. In that year the menace of radiolethal fall-out was announced. When one of the new H-bombs explodes near the ground or in water, it pulverizes great quantities of soil and building material or atomizes water in the target area. The resulting dust or spray is charged with deadly radioactivity. This death-dealing cloud is carried high into the air and then falls out over an oval area which is likely to be as large as 40 miles wide and nearly 200 miles long. The region thus dusted remains lethal for as much as a year while the deadly charge is dying down. This increases the casualty area for the H-bomb explosion from the 800 square miles assumed in the pre-1955 calculations to something like 7,000 square miles. This would mean that not only Greater New York, but also Greater Philadelphia, and an area equal to that of the entire State of New Jersey, would be within the killing range of a bomb dropped on Manhattan, if the wind were blowing from the northeast.

The above analysis is based merely upon the estimated effect of single bombs or devices, increasing in their explosive force as a result of research progress by physicists. But increasing explosive force is only one of the dimensions of the acceleration in destructive technology. A second dimension is the accelerating increase in the number of bombs available.

Soviet Russia exploded her first atomic bomb in August, 1949. The number which she is believed to have manufactured subsequently, and the numbers which she is expected to have available at specified future dates, have been "leaked" through various sources. On the basis of all the available facts, from a variety of nonsecret sources, the total number of square miles within which a blast sufficient to destroy brick buildings would occur if the Soviet military forces were able, in given years, to put all their bombs on targets in the United States, has been estimated as follows:[4]

Year	Blast Area (sq. mi.)
1953	5,910
1954	10,640
1955	18,860
1956	38,750
1957	68,500

This growth is shown graphically in the chart on page 226, which is similar to one which was published in *Bulletin of the Atomic Scientists* for June, 1954.

The above estimates are believed to be validated by numerous internal cross-checks which cannot be published here. All such estimates are, of necessity, somewhat speculative. In a situation in which no present objective verification of the facts is possible, such estimates are peculiarly liable to distortion by motives of sensationalism, of professional bias, or of political advantage, rather than expressing a pure desire for the ascertainment of scien-

[4] Hornell Hart, *op. cit.*, p. 198, Table 2.

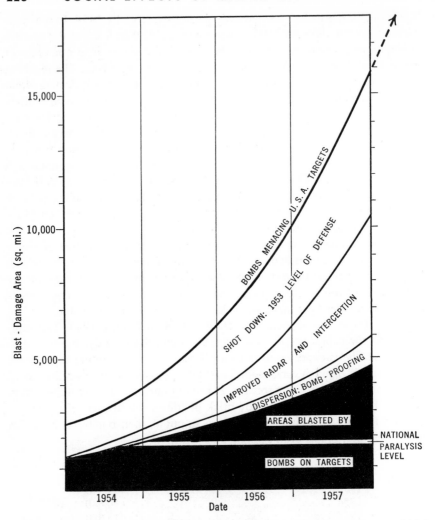

EXPECTED INCREASE IN SOVIET BLAST-DAMAGE CAPACITY DIRECTED AGAINST TARGETS IN THE UNITED STATES

The graph shows reductions claimed by advocates of improved radar warning network, dispersion, and so forth.

tific truth. But certain fundamentals are clearly established. First, the technologies of destruction have long been increasing with steeply accelerating speed in all ascertainable major respects. Second, Russia does have the atomic and the hydrogen types of bombs and she has the means to deliver such bombs on American targets. Third, Russia is devoting major resources to increasing her stockpile of such bombs and to improving her carrying devices for delivering them. Fourth, it should be borne in mind that when the basic trend indicated in the above forecast was made, it was not yet evident that the Soviet stockpile of atomic bombs could be transformed into H-bombs by using them as triggers and by adding as much as desired of such relatively cheap auxiliary nuclear-explosive materials as Uranium 238 and lithium. Fifth, the above forecast is based on blast-damage area. To take radioactive fall-out area into account would expand the killing area of the 1954-type H-bomb by more than tenfold.

In view of such facts, it seems fairly evident that the trend estimated above probably errs in being too conservative. The crucial fact was stated by President Eisenhower when, at a press conference on October 8, 1953, he announced his conclusion "that the Soviets now have the capability of atomic attack on us, and such capability will increase. . . ." Since this menace is now real and increasing, it becomes highly important to explore the probabilities as to the extent of damage which a Soviet raid might do to the United States, and the rapidity with which the menace is growing. The facts about cultural acceleration in general, about the acceleration of destructive technology, and about the accelerating growth of nuclear destructive power in particular, point toward the likelihood of a steep increase in Russia's destructive potential.

Expected Increase in Soviet Capacity to Deliver A-Bombs

On July 25, 1954, the Alsops made the following announcement in their column:[5]

In the year 1960, by the agreed estimate of the Pentagon's official analysts, the Soviet Union will fly its first intercontinental ballistic missile. . . . [This] will be an accurately guided rocket, comparable to a giant V-2, capable of carrying a hydrogen warhead over a range of 4,000 to 5,000 miles.

Further details about this "Atlas" intercontinental ballistic missile were published by Stewart Alsop in March, 1955.[6] Such a weapon (the Alsops pointed out) "will marry the ultimate in destructiveness with the ultimate in striking power." Against this ultimate weapon (said the Alsops), there will be no defense and no warning of its coming. This kind of assertion that the offense has radically outstripped defense is, however, disputed by Major Seversky.[7]

Not only will these transoceanic, supersonic missiles render obsolete the radar networks which have frantically been urged as fences across Canada to protect us, but they will carry with them the newly recognized menace of radiolethal fall-out. The menace summarized in preceding sections is therefore only a fraction as large as will confront America if and when the Soviets are ready to use H-bombs and intercontinental supersonic ballistic missiles in attacking our vital centers.

[5] *New York Herald Tribune,* July 25, 1954, Sec. II, p. 1, cols. 7–8.

[6] "Atlas," by Stewart Alsop, *Durham Morning Herald,* March 13, 1955, Sec. IV, p. 6, col. 4–6.

[7] Alexander P. de Seversky, "Lindbergh Is Wrong Again," *This Week Magazine,* December 12, 1954, pp. 6–9.

THE POSSIBLE CHARACTER OF A NUCLEAR
RAID AGAINST THE UNITED STATES

Would the Aim Be Merely to Wound—or Actually to Kill—the United States?

In World Wars I and II, the damage inflicted by bombing was localized. In World War II, various industrial plants, harbors, docks, railroad terminals, and even large sections of cities like London and Berlin were damaged and sometimes obliterated by the increasingly powerful bombs which were being dropped in greater and greater tonnages. But these bombings were analogous to wounds in the nonvital parts of a soldier's body. If a man had a finger shot off or lost a foot or even both legs, his life could normally be saved by prompt medical and nursing attention and by suitable convalescent opportunities. A large majority of all men wounded in the Korean hostilities were restored to combat effectiveness. Even quite seriously wounded men could often be rehabilitated and made economically self-supporting.

Similarly, in World War II, the obliteration of a factory, or even the wiping out of large sections of an important city, could be dealt with by civilian defense agencies with adequately trained ambulance drivers, reserve hospitals, and the like. It has taken a long time for the bombed areas in European and Asiatic cities to be restored, but the life of the respective nations has gone on, much as the life of a wounded soldier goes on so long as his wound is not a fatal one.

The difference between the bombings which took place in World War II and those likely to take place in World War III is comparable to a shift from minor wounds to fatal injuries. Our civilian defense program and other vital policies have been discussed and planned, even high up in our government, as though the crucial problem were comparable to organizing field hospitals for the care of the wounded. But if Russia should raid the United States, there is a large and swiftly increasing probability that the aim would be not to inflict a series of painful, costly, and hampering wounds but actually to assassinate the nation. Let us consider briefly, but somewhat systematically, the reasons for believing that this is so.

Could America Be Kept Unharmed for Soviet Exploitation?

Some theorists have argued that Russia would like to preserve as much of the United States intact as possible, in order to take over her factories, her mines, her farms, and her people as slaves in the Soviet regime. That objective would be attractive to the communists if it were feasible. Under the assumption that our bases for retaliation had been eliminated, it might be argued that the communists could then proceed to take us over at their leisure.

But merely to knock out our retaliatory bases would leave us still by far the strongest nation in the world. Our determination to destroy Russia would have been raised to the highest pitch. The rest of the world would be confronted with deadly danger and would be likely to join in seeking destruction of Russia. The Kremlin could not afford to take halfway measures which would leave her strongest enemies wounded but still potentially powerful enough to destroy her.

One method by which Soviet attackers might conceivably keep American cities and other physical resources intact for subsequent communistic exploitation might be to drop H-bombs in rural areas in such a pattern as to cloak the vital areas of the country with deadly radioactivity. The extent to which—and the conditions under which—such an attack might render the nation temporarily helpless to Soviet conquest, but subsequently safe for occupation, have not yet (so far as I am aware) been systematically explored.

Target Cities for a Paralysis Raid

If Russia made an attack on the United States, how would she budget the supplies of nuclear bombs whose blast areas are estimated above? Let us suppose that her plan is to produce the maximum possible immediate paralysis—primarily by casualties, panic, anarchy, and starvation. For this purpose her prime targets might presumably be of the following general types, in descending order of importance: (1) U. S. and allied strategic bombing bases, including our super-flattops; (2) our national capital; (3) population centers; (4) our sources of coal and oil; (5) crucial transportation centers and resources; (6) electric power resources; (7) financial centers; and (8) repair facilities. Obviously, the apportionment of bombs to these different types of prime targets is a highly complicated problem to which Soviet military experts would devote (and doubtless are devoting) extended study. But in order to bring out the essence of the problem which America faces, it is necessary to sketch a rough approximation of the probable distribution of the available Russian bombs.

Detailed estimates as to the objectives of a hypothetical annihilation raid by the Soviet forces against the United States have been published elsewhere.[8]

For 1957, it was estimated that 68,500 square miles of blast-area potential would be represented by the Soviet stockpile of nuclear bombs. Let us assume that half of these bombs might be held in reserve for possible subsequent raids, that one-fourth of the total might be used to neutralize our strategic bombing bases outside the United States, that about half of the bombs reaching the United States might be reserved for targets outside our leading cities, and that generous allowances are made for attackers shot down by our bombing forces and for bombs wasted by poor navigation and defective aiming. After all these deductions, a total of 5,000 square miles of nuclear blast area would remain. Let us suppose that half of this blast potential would be reserved for targets outside our leading metropolitan areas, and that the half reserved for our leading cities would be apportioned in pro-

[8] Hornell Hart, *op. cit.*, p. 203.

portion to the amount of damage to the American nation which would result from paralysis of the various cities. On that basis, the apportionments indicated in the following table have been estimated.

ESTIMATED AREAS BLASTED IN LEADING CITIES OF THE UNITED STATES, IF THE SOVIET GOVERNMENT LAUNCHED AN ANNIHILATION RAID IN 1957

Standard Metropolitan Areas	Soviet Nuclear Blast-Area Capacity (sq. mi.) Apportioned	Standard Metropolitan Areas	Soviet Nuclear Blast-Area Capacity (sq. mi.) Apportioned
New York	500	Akron	60
Chicago	290	Pittsburgh	60
Washington, D. C.	280	New Orleans	60
Philadelphia	140	Baltimore	60
Los Angeles	140	Buffalo	50
Detroit	140	Toledo	50
Cleveland	100	Cincinnati	50
St. Louis	80	Milwaukee	40
San Francisco	80	Memphis	30
Kansas City	70	Columbus	30
Boston	70	Peoria	30
Minneapolis-		Omaha	30
St. Paul	60	Total	2500

In addition to the bombs dropped on the 24 leading cities listed in the table, an approximately equal number are assigned (in the hypothetical paralysis raid) to such targets as coal-carrying railroads, strategic oil pipeline junctions and shipping ports, and supplementary locations such as would maximize the area covered by radioactive fall-out in the most populous areas of the United States.

How Much Damage, of What Kinds, Would Result?

Assuming the successful execution of the type of raid sketched above, what would be the various types of immediate and secondary damage, and how great would each be? The effects may be classified under five heads: (A) Immediate casualties; (B) demolition of vital structures; (C) paralysis of transportation and communication; (D) starvation; and (E) anarchy. Let us examine briefly the particulars under each of these five heads:

A. Immediate Casualties

1. Immediate death would come to between 10 and 30 millions of Americans, including a major fraction of the governmental, industrial, financial, transportation, medical, and educational leaders of the nation. Before the significance of radioactive fall-out had been realized, the immediate deaths from the bombing of 24 prime-target cities were estimated at 9 million.

2. Burns, wounds, or radiation poisoning would injure 10 to 30 millions more, with injuries ranging in seriousness from those calling for immediate surgery and protracted hospital care, and from poisonings certain to bring death within a few days, down to minor injuries needing only first aid.

3. Apart from the possible poisoning of the world's atmosphere, the deaths and injuries would probably amount to more than two-thirds of the populations of the central cities in the prime-target areas. Without transportation by trucks, automobiles, or railroads, how could these casualties be taken care of? A considerable fraction of all the hospitals in the country would have been destroyed—even if they could be operated without electricity, fuel, or food and drug supplies. Even to bury the 10 to 30 million dead would be quite impossible. Moreover, these casualties would include personnel essential to operating America. Can you conceive of the vital activities of the nation going forward if from half to two-thirds of the trained executives, assistants, and skilled workers in the crucial centers of the nation were dead or dying of injuries?

B. *Demolition of Vital Structures*

4. Blast-damage and fire storms would destroy the most vital buildings in each of the 24 target metropolises, including railroad terminals, electric generating plants, telephone switchboards, banks, courthouses, wholesale and retail warehouses, and other repositories of vital records.

C. *Paralysis of Transportation and Communication*

5. All railway transportation would cease immediately in the most populous northeast quarter of the United States, except for localized trips by such trains as happened to be outside blast-areas, as happened to have (for the time being) left-over stocks of fuel, and as were not immobilized by fall-out poisoning. Repair of the bombed railway terminals and junctions would of course be impossible if wrecking crews had no trucks or trains to move them and if the sources of repair materials were out of operation.

This railway paralysis would spread swiftly over the rest of the United States as existing stocks of coal and fuel oil became exhausted. The bombing of the 24 prime-target cities would paralyze the centers through which three-fourths of all the coal in the United States is wholesaled and would put out of operation the most important railroad terminals, junctions, and repair centers of the United States and the most vital telephone and telegraph switchboards. By bombing strategic points on seven railroads, 43 per cent of all coal shipments could further be doubly blocked.

6. Practically all the automobile and air traffic in the entire United States would die down, except for such remnants as might continue for the time being until local stocks of gasoline, not destroyed by the bombing, had been exhausted. Without gasoline, trucks, busses, passenger cars, and airplanes would all cease to operate. The 24 prime-target cities include the centers through which more than three-fourths of all the petroleum products sold in the nation are wholesaled. The additional bombs dropped on oil-line terminals and junctions, and upon ports from which petroleum products are shipped, would stop the flow of practically all the gasoline, lubricating oil, and fuel oil for the entire nation. It would also destroy a large fraction of all the reserve supplies of these products.

7. All telephone, telegraph, and radio communication would die down, insofar as this is dependent on electric power from major generating stations. Lack of coal and fuel oil, plus the bombing of strategic power-line centers, would paralyze the electrical industry. Electricity is essential to communication by means of telephones, telegraph, and radio. Someone has said: "Society *is* communication."

But merely this cutting off of coal, petroleum products, and railroads *would stop practically all communication* in the United States except face-to-face conversation. Short-lived exceptions would be battery-powered radios, broadcasting stations powered by small units still having reserves of fuel, and some emergency telephone and telegraph communication based on local and temporary sources of power, and routed around the devastated central switching points. For a brief period, perhaps, an emergency pony express might be operated between some points.

8. All newspaper publication would cease in the northeast quarter of the United States and in major outside population centers such as New Orleans, Los Angeles, and San Francisco, except for a few small local sheets gotten out on an emergency basis, but without any appreciable outside circulation.

D. *Starvation*

9. Virtually all major stores of food in such warehouses as were located in the major population centers would be destroyed by blast, fire, and radiation.

10. Practically all shipments of food into population centers anywhere in the nation would cease as transportation died out.

11. Farm production and transportation would be paralyzed by elimination of gasoline and oil supplies. A large majority of American farms are now operated by motorized machinery rather than by horses and mules.

E. *Anarchy*

12. Rioting and looting would develop on a huge scale on the part of tens of millions of survivors in search of food for themselves and their children. Outlaw gangs would form.

13. Unless adequate warning had been received, and full-scale evacuation achieved, the national government would be obliterated, with the death of a large majority of the top men in the executive, legislative, and judicial branches, and the destruction of the great bulk of the documents and records located in the national capital. Washington would certainly be a prime target in any such mass raid. Underground shelters inside the blast area would be deathtraps rather than lifesavers in the kind of H-bombing to which the District of Columbia would be subjected. An effective evacuation program, well designed and thoroughly rehearsed, might keep key government leaders alive temporarily. This question of evacuation will be dealth with a little later in this chapter.

14. The legal system of the nation would have been destroyed. Not only the legislative and executive branches of our national government would be gone, but the basic structure of legal authority in the country would have been smashed. The buildings and records of the leading federal courts would have been obliterated by blast and by fire. Presumably half or more of the judges and leading lawyers in the country would be dead or dying of injuries, and lack of communications would make the law ineffective in any case.

15. Smashing of the financial structure of the nation would parallel the destruction of government and law. The hypothetical raid would destroy 90 per cent of the centers through which the nation's financial transactions take place and which contain the crucial records, money reserve, bookkeeping equipment, skilled personnel, and executive knowledge and ability of the American banking world.[9]

The destruction of the governmental, legal, and financial structures of America might be likened to shooting a man through the base of his brain. But the cutting

---

[9] Some beginnings have been made toward storing, a few miles away, microfilms of vital records from New York City.

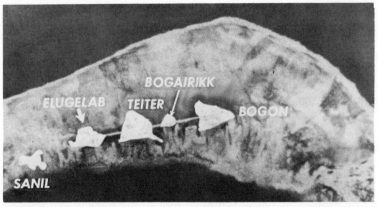

BEFORE—

DURING—

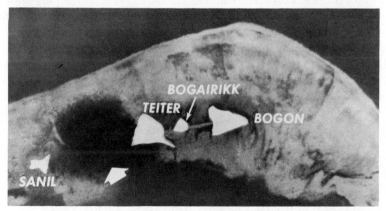

Courtesy of U. S. Air Force and Atomic Energy Commission

AND AFTER—H-BOMB DETONATION "MIKE" AT ENIWETOK ATOLL, FALL OF 1952
The white masses top and bottom are islands; the gray masses are underwater coral reefs.

off of the fuel resources of the United States would be more comparable to shooting a man through the heart. Either type of wound would be fatal to the individual; either type of destruction would be fatal to America. The vital point is that the kind of mass raid which the Soviets may be expected to be increasingly able to launch against this nation would be doubly fatal.

Could America Go Back to 1840?

One critic who read the preceding part of this chapter raised this question:

One thing which occurs to me is that in the event of a paralysis raid the American people might be reduced to rudimentary living conditions—many cities destroyed, major communications and transportation networks destroyed, the center of federal government destroyed, etc. But life was simple during the times of George Washington, too, as compared with now. Assuming that some sort of temporary, simple government would be established if the City of Washington were completely destroyed, wouldn't the U. S. exist as a nation, though at a simple level? After all, the U. S. existed in 1800.

Why not carry the idea farther and assume a national life on the level which actually was operating just before the large-scale introduction of the railroad—say 1840? Transportation and farming were then done by the horse and the mule; factories were operated by human muscles, animals (to a slight extent), and water wheels to a considerable degree. It hardly seems conceivable that national existence could be restored on this basis, even after decades had elapsed, since outside aggression on a machine-age basis could not be ruled out, and since the shocks of the demolition of our machine-age economy would not be likely to be survived.

Note, however, the contrast between the United States as it was in 1840 and the United States as it would be after a paralysis raid. In 1840 the population was growing exuberantly and its industries were developing with enthusiastic faith in progress and in the power of man to conquer the continent. The domesticated-animal population was growing along with the human population, and the supply of pasturage was ample. But after a paralysis raid, the supply of horses, mules, and cattle would be radically inadequate. The population would be reduced to a fraction of its former size, and the survivors would have standards of living adjusted (at least initially) to those of the machine age. Government in 1840 was growing up by natural social evolution, expanding in response to need, and out of the roots of the past. But after a paralysis raid, practically all existing authority beyond purely local units would be shattered. The crisis would presumably stimulate looting on a really gigantic scale, with resulting chronic civil war.

SIX FALLACIES IN CURRENT THINKING ABOUT DEFENSE
AGAINST NUCLEAR BOMBING

When the facts reviewed thus far in this chapter are taken fully into account, it becomes evident that six fallacies have been prevalent in public discussion of defense against possible nuclear-bomb attacks. Let us consider these briefly.

Static Thinking

The first of these fallacies consists in static thinking about these problems. After Hiroshima, a few leaders realized that America would certainly become vulnerable to raids with atomic bombs. By strenuous educational efforts, they sought to rouse the nation to realize that long-range bombing planes could come over America by way of the polar regions and could destroy our leading cities, unless some adequate system of advance detection and interception was developed. Only a minority of the public has fully progressed into that stage of thinking, but gradually this minority has been producing such results as the erection of radar networks across Canada, the development of civilian plane spotters, and, in a meager way, the development of the kind of civilian defense units which might have been useful if America were to have been subjected to bombing such as occurred in World War II.

Then the H-bomb was developed. Also, the possibility was demonstrated of releasing supersonic pilotless planes from mother airplanes at distances invulnerable to our defense system, and intercontinental guided missiles became more and more likely for the nearer and nearer future. These developments led a few pioneering thinkers to question whether even the best possible radar network across Canada, even when supplemented by radar ships and planes deployed in the Atlantic and Pacific Oceans, could protect us adequately. The accelerating build-up of Soviet capacity to launch mass bombing raids against us began to impress some leading thinkers with the idea that massive attacks rather than mere localized bombings needed to be planned against. But before that realization had been assimilated, the fall-out problem stupendously increased the intensity of the menace. Leaders of thought began to try to work out our defense problems to meet this new threat. Even this is being done largely without regard to future accelerating increases of the menace.

Exaggerated Evaluation of Evacuation

The second fallacy in current thinking is the delusion that mass evacuations could save the nation. To criticize this doctrine involves taking issue with the man who is probably the best-known and most competent publicist of atomic-bombing problems, namely, Dr. Ralph E. Lapp.[10] It means taking issue also with Val Peterson, Civil Defense Administrator.[11]

Belief in the efficacy of mass evacuation seems to be the result of uncriti-

[10] Ralph E. Lapp, "Civil Defense Faces New Peril," *Bulletin of the Atomic Scientists,* Vol. 10 (November, 1954), pp. 349–351; and "Radioactive Fall-out," *ibid.,* Vol. 11 (February, 1955), pp. 45–51.
[11] Val Peterson, "Mass Evacuation," *ibid.,* Vol. 10 (September, 1954), pp. 294–295.

cal acceptance of three contributing fallacies. First is the valiant but un-realistic assumption that 30 million or more people could actually be evacu-ated in advance of a mass raid. Second is the unspoken assumption that cities demolished by Soviet bombing could expect help, after the raid, from un-bombed cities. Third is the assumption that the prevention of immediate casualties would save the nation, disregarding the nation-wide breakdown of transportation and communication, the progressive starvation of the nation, and the swiftly developing anarchy which would follow such a raid. Let us examine a little further each of these supporting fallacies.

To evacuate the 30 million or more residents of the 24 target cities would mean putting the evening rush hour of each city into almost instant operation, at the raid alarm. But this rush hour would not run along the familiar chan-nels of back-home habit. It would call for moving the populations not into their nearby homes but to distances of 10 miles or more, along unfamiliar routes and into unfamiliar shelter areas. To do this successfully would re-quire at least repeated and systematic drills. Small beginnings toward such drills have been reported from a few cities. Really serious discussion of evacuation is taking place with regard to Washington, D. C., and New York City. The mass slaughter which would take place among our governmental, financial, industrial, and other leaders if Washington and New York were H-bombed would in itself be a well-nigh fatal blow. It seems conceivable that evacuation routines might be built up which would get these leaders out of these cities before the bombs fell, if several hours of warning were avail-able.

This, however, would require months of patient drill, repeated at fairly frequent intervals. Each such drill would disrupt the life of the nation's capital and of our national metropolis to a costly extent. Whether the busiest men in the nation will submit patiently and co-operate effectively in such exercises might be questioned.

On June 15, 1955, a mock hydrogen-bomb assault on 61 American cities, including Washington and New York City, was staged. It was stated that the test raid sent 15,000 federal employees, including President Eisenhower, "streaming out of Washington to secret relocation centers in a half dozen states, there to 'operate' the government through June 17." But no mass evacuation of even Washington was attempted. To what extent, then, is it realistic to suppose that mass-evacuation drills could be carried out in all the target cities? In view of public attitudes toward civil defense, does this seem politically practicable?

But suppose that evacuation of all the 24 target cities of the "paralysis raid" could actually be achieved in the brief space of two or three hours. What assurance is there that any such warning will be given? If the raid were to come in the form of relatively slow bombers, approaching over the Arctic, such a warning might be feasible. But suppose that the H-bombs were carried by supersonic guided missiles, launched from distant planes or submarines or from behind the Iron curtain. How much warning would then be available? Yet the acceleration of destructive technologies makes such methods more and more likely in the nearer and nearer future.

Let us, however, make the unlikely assumption that the 30 million people might be successfully evacuated. We must then face the fact that not merely one or a few cities would be damaged but rather that the hearts would be blasted out of 24 or more key target metropolises. Not only the central blast areas of these cities would be destroyed. Nuclear bombs create vast fire storms, in which the closely-built-up sections of the metropolitan areas around these targets would be reduced to ashes. Residential areas, stores of food, and other vital structures and supplies would be destroyed. Farms would have been paralyzed by inability to get gasoline. City water systems would be out of commission, and vast portions of the food and water supplies would have been poisoned by radioactive fall-out. No trucks or trains would be running to transport food even if it were available. Moreover, all outdoors, in the most vital areas of the nation, would have been filled with deadly radioactivity.

How, then, would the evacuated 30 millions or more be housed and fed? Note that this problem, suddenly imposed on an unprepared and paralyzed nation, would be three times as great as the problem of housing and feeding the 10 million service men and women who were under arms during World War II. Yet that smaller job required decades of experience, billions of dollars of preparatory expenditure, and organized planning by vast commissary agencies.

Even if evacuation were wholly successful, how could the nation get back into operation? Approximately half of all the manufactured products most significantly related to the replacement and repair of transportation and communication facilities (such as petroleum refining, fabricated metal products, electrical and other machinery, motor vehicles, tires, aircraft, railway equipment, ships and boats) are manufactured in the 24 target cities. Even if repair supplies and facilities were still available, how could they be transported to the points where they would be vitally necessary? Moreover, the destruction of records and the governmental, legal, and financial chaos resulting from the raids would be tremendous blocks against any effective action. As people began to starve, anarchy and violence would certainly become widely prevalent.

In brief, the fallacies of evacuation proposals may be summarized by pointing out that it is radically unrealistic to consider merely the prevention of immediate casualties, without taking account of the paralyzed condition in which the entire nation would be left by the kind of raid which the Soviets might be expected to carry out.[12]

[12] Cf. Walter Lippmann, "The Sneak Attack," *Washington Post and Times Herald,* June 23, 1955.

Dispersion and Bombproofing

The third fallacy is the idea that dispersion of industry and the erection of bombproof buildings and of shelters would solve the problem—or, indeed, would be of any major value in mitigating it. The violence and the poisonous character of the bombs is increasing with such steep acceleration that any improvements in construction cannot possibly overtake the need. Moreover, even if the entire populations of these cities were sheltered from the immediate effects of the blast, any benefit would be cancelled by the fire storms, the cutting off of transportation, and the swift coming of starvation and anarchy.

Are the basic facts of economic and industrial geography being faced by those who believe that our vital targets could be so dispersed as to make a paralysis raid impossible? The United States today, as a highly organized nation, has to have major centers of communication, of transportation, and of intensive social contacts such as dispersion would seek to eliminate. Mass production is at the very core of modern industrial efficiency, and effective dispersion would be a deadly enemy of mass production. Moreover, would not the first cost and the operating costs of anything approaching adequate dispersion so increase the costs of production as to reduce standards of living intolerably?

Civil Defense

The fourth fallacy is the idea that civil defense is likely to—or indeed can—make any major reduction of the risks we run or the damage which we suffer. Until recently, the majority of this organization's vital centers were located at the very spots which would be destroyed by a paralysis raid. This has been changed, but if highly organized industrial and transportation systems would be wrecked by such a raid, the loose and largely volunteer civilian defense organizations would certainly go to pieces. Civilian plane spotters may be of some help so long as the major menace comes from piloted bombers, and pending the time when improved radar can detect low-flying planes. But may not those two needs be expected to disappear rather rapidly?

Expecting to Avoid Nuclear War by Mutual Dread

The fifth fallacy is the idea that, if World War III comes, both sides may refrain from the use of atomic weapons because of the terrible consequences. In his address to the House of Commons on March 1, 1955, Prime Minister Churchill pointed out that it would be folly to act on any such assumption. Several considerations support his position. In a full-scale war, nuclear weapons—and particularly the H-bomb—may prove to be decisive. Indeed, the central point of the discussion of a paralysis raid is that such use of nuclear bombing could be expected to terminate permanently all effective, organized

American resistance to communism. Recognizing that fact, we can hardly be expected to hold our own nuclear weapons in reserve until we find out whether the enemy might use his. Moreover, these weapons are being integrated in detailed ways into our fire power. The resulting increase in effectiveness is the basic justification for the reduction in military manpower and for the whole present budgeting of American military expenditures.

In refutation of the oft-cited analogy between poison gas and nuclear weapons, Eugene Rabinowitch, the editor of *Bulletin of the Atomic Scientists,* said in the number for January, 1955: "Poison gas is a cumbersome, relatively ineffective weapon; atomic weapons are immensely effective, easily transportable, and potentially decisive."

The fallacy that development of terrible weapons may prevent war has misled prominent thinkers in years gone by, as well as now. In 1911, three years before the outbreak of World War I, Jack London published an article in the *Forum* magazine, in which he said: "War itself, the old red anarch, is passing. . . . Men have made for themselves monsters of battle which they cannot face in battle."

Expecting the Dictatorship Disease to Be Cured Merely by Elimination of the Soviet Government

The sixth fallacy is the assumption that all would be well if only Soviet Russia could be eliminated as an aggressive menace to the world. In his address to Parliament on March first, 1955, Winston Churchill tapped ominously on a dispatch box. He said: "A quantity of plutonium—probably less than would fill this box on the table, and quite a safe thing to store—would suffice to produce weapons which would give indisputable world domination to any great power which was the only one to have it."[13]

But one of the facts about accelerating military destructiveness is that nuclear weapons are becoming more and more accessible to more and more nations. The process of their manufacture is being simplified. Scientific knowledge about them is being disseminated throughout the world. Our international relations are on the verge of reaching the state which was prevalent in our Western frontier communities at the time when miscellaneous outlaws and desperadoes possessed revolvers, but when the sheriff was likely still to be more or less timid, slow on the draw, and lacking the support of federal troops. What kind of a world will it be when every pint-size dictator possesses bombs with which he might blow up the largest city in the world? Possibly the answer to this international Wild West situation might be similar to that which brought law and order to our Western frontier.

SOME SOURCES OF HOPE

This chapter has presented an ominous picture of the menace created by the military applications of atomic energy. These conclusions may be open

[13] *New York Times,* March 2, 1955, p. 8, col. 1.

to further exploration with respect to particular details. But as to the existence of a towering menace to the future of civilization—and even to the continuation of human life on this globe, there can be little or no doubt.

Any such threat to mankind is a challenge rather than a reason for despair. The present chapter has set forth some of the menacing facts. Constructive suggestions as to possible ways of dealing with these problems will be brought out in Chapters 20 and 21.

ANNOTATED BIBLIOGRAPHY

Bulletin of the Atomic Scientists. Current numbers and past bound volumes provide one of the richest sources of trustworthy information in this field.

BUSH, Vannevar, *Modern Arms and Free Men* (New York, Simon and Schuster, 1949). Discusses the role of science in preserving democracy.

DAHL, Robert A., and BROWN, Ralph S., *Domestic Control of Atomic Energy* (New York, Social Science Research Council, 1952). Surveys areas of profitable research in the field of atomic energy, and their implications for the social scientist.

DEAN, Gordon Evans, *Report on the Atom* (New York, Knopf, 1953). The former Chairman of the Atomic Energy Commission tells "what you should know about the atomic energy program of the United States."

HART, Hornell, "The Remedies versus the Menace," *Bulletin of the Atomic Scientists,* Vol. 10 (June, 1954), pp. 197–205. Contains some of the same material presented in the present chapter, but takes up also, in considerable detail, the inadequacies of our defenses and palliatives.

HATT, Paul·K., ed., "Energy Resources," in *World Population and Future Resources* (New York, American Book, 1952). Contains a chapter on "Atomic Energy and the World Economy" by Gordon Dean (pp. 229–238), one on "The Future of Atomic Energy" by Lawrence R. Hafstad (pp. 239–245), and one on "Solar Energy" by Farrington Daniels (pp. 246–262).

HOFFMAN, M. David, ed., *Readings for the Atomic Age* (New York, Globe Book, 1951). A collection of outstanding articles on the emotional, historical, scientific, and predictable aspects of atomic energy.

IKLÉ, Fred Charles, "The Social versus the Physical Effects from Nuclear bombing," *Scientific Monthly,* Vol. 78 (March, 1954), pp. 182–187. Based on forthcoming book by Iklé, on *The Social Effects of Bombing in Cities.* Discusses these problems in the light of World War II and Nagasaki experience.

ISARD, Walter, and VINCENT, Whitney, *Atomic Power* (New York, Blakiston, 1952). Is the widespread use of atomic power for peacetime purposes likely in the near future? Would it cause substantial changes in the location of industrial activity?

LAPP, Ralph E., *Must We Hide?* (Cambridge, Mass., Addison-Wesley, 1949). One of the best semi-popular summaries of the atomic crisis.

———, *The New Force* (New York, Harper, 1952). Evaluates atomic weapons; criticizes unnecessary secrecy.

Peaceful Uses of Atomic Energy, Report of the Panel on the Impact of the Peaceful Uses of Atomic Energy to the Joint Committee on Atomic Energy, Vols. I and II (Washington, Government Printing Office, 1956). Vol. I comprises the final, condensed report; Vol. II provides a sizable amount of background material. The combination constitutes a carefully made, top-grade appraisal of the peaceful effects of atomic energy, probably the best available as this book went to press.

ROTHMANN, S. C., ed., *Constructive Uses of Atomic Energy* (New York, Harper, 1949). This symposium, at the time it was published, was one of the most comprehensive treatments of its subject. But developments have been occurring very rapidly, and this book should be supplemented by more recent materials.

PART III

The Influence of Technology on Social Institutions

CHAPTER 11

INFLUENCE OF TECHNOLOGY ON INDUSTRY

■ *Delbert C. Miller*

INDUSTRIAL TECHNOLOGY is nothing more than the summation of man's experience with tools and techniques. The effect of technology on industry cannot be assessed without some understanding of the history of techniques and civilization. In this chapter, man's experience with technology will be telescoped. Significant phases of technological development will be selected in order to trace their influence on modern industry.

The role of technology on industry is presented in two sections. These are the influence of technology on (1) the production of goods and services; and (2) the social organization of industry.

The first section shows how man has applied tools and used raw materials to survive and to gratify his seemingly endless wants. The second section is concerned with the ways in which technology has influenced the life of the worker and the functions which large enterprise must discharge.

THE INFLUENCE OF TECHNOLOGY ON THE PRODUCTION OF GOODS AND SERVICES

A Historical View of Man and Technology

The tool maker. For roughly half of his existence on the planet, early man lived much like other animals and his existence was precarious. Man eventually achieved a dominant position over all animals largely because he learned to use his oversized brain to produce tools. *Homo sapiens* became in time, *homo faber,* the maker of tools. The bulk of technology is simply an assortment of tools, operations, and techniques which extend the power of human muscles or refine the perception of the human senses. Man began his career as a hunter. The first tool may have been a stick or a stone. The stick which was idly picked up and used as a club may have proved at once a very useful aid, and the first discoverer may have repeated its use. He may have told others of his remarkable discovery which made the arm longer and more powerful and at the same time increased the striking power of the fist.

PRIMARY MACHINE FUNCTIONS

Body Movements	Body Plus Simple Tool Movements	Sensory Functions	Miscellaneous
Pounding—steam hammer	Cutting—guillotine	Seeing—telescope	Detonating—torpedo
Crushing—rock crusher	Chipping—ingot machine	Hearing—telephone	Flying—airplane
Blowing—electric fan	Sawing—band saw	Talking—radio	Light making—flashlight
Sucking—vacuum cleaner	Splitting—rock drill	Singing—piano	Heat making—electric furnace
Digging—gang plow	Grinding—stone plane	Shouting—claxon horn	Cold making—refrigerating engine
Pushing—hydraulic ram	Boring—diamond drill	Calculating—adding machine	Pressure making—air pump
Pulling—locomotive	Drawing—kodak	Time measuring—watch	
Dancing—merry-go-round	Spraying—fire engine	Space measuring—transit	
Lifting—derrick	Sewing—sewing machine	Weight measuring—scales	
Picking—cotton gin	Writing—automatic typewriter	Temperature measuring—thermometer	
Hurling—gun		Pressure measuring—barometer	
Scraping—potato peeler		Direction measuring—compass	
Shaping—power lathe		Sound measuring—Dr. Free's machine	
Spreading—seeder			
Twisting—lathe drill			
Weaving (matting)—power loom			
Swimming—ferry boat			
Carrying—motor truck			

The improvement of clubs may be seen as a next step. Just as every basic invention breeds improved inventions, so the idea of a club was in due time supplemented by ideas of better length, diameter, balance, hardness (especially in the club head), gripping, swinging, and perhaps throwing. This thinking of the tool and the advance preparation of the tool to gain some desired object or goal is man's specialty.[1]

The maker of machines. Man is a puny source of motive power. At best he can only convert three or four thousand calories of energy a day into work and he does not do that efficiently. But he can make an engine that will absorb a hundred thousand times as much energy and deliver it with twice the efficiency. The power-driven machine tool is undoubtedly one of man's greatest achievements. The essential feature is the wheel, which does not exist in nature. Levers may be found in the limbs of all animals, but the wheel cannot be formed of bone and flesh. Man had to create it in his imagination.[2]

All machines are based on six fundamental principles. In addition to the wheel, there are the lever, the pulley, the wedge, the screw, and the inclined plane. These principles may be combined in many different ways. Stuart Chase says: "The things which, reduced to simplest terms, machines can do better than the body are many; the things which machines can do that the body cannot do, even with the aid of simple tools, are few—of which flying is perhaps the outstanding example." He has made an inventory of primary machine functions that correspond to body movements and sensory functions.[3]

The user of energy. The world is a vast reservoir of energy. No man can comprehend its magnitude. Stored within the atoms is a supply of energy that makes the abundance of land, water, and air seem to be scarce in comparison.

The discovery of the forces in nature has followed the principles of cultural growth. First the discoveries were meager. Animals were domesticated and put to work. Slaves were often forced to provide captive labor. The source was largely animate energy. Every act and movement of life involves expenditures of energy, and food is needed to sustain the available sources of animate energy. With machines, the wind and water could be harnessed. And later coal and oil were utilized. Today food, coal, and oil are the most essential energy sources, all of which are products of the sun's action. Of these three, it is coal and oil which provide the main body of mineral energy required in the world's machines. Food increasingly becomes merely the energy to sustain man as controller and operator of the machine.

In 1850, horses, mules, and oxen furnished three and half times the

[1] Ralph Linton, *The Study of Man* (New York, Appleton-Century-Crofts, 1936), p. 66. Cf. with Charles H. Judd, *The Psychology of Social Institutions* (New York, Macmillan, 1926), pp. 5–31.

[2] R. J. Forbes, *Man the Maker, A History of Technology and Engineering* (New York, Schuman, 1950), pp. 34–36.

[3] Stuart Chase, *Men and Machines* (New York, Macmillan, 1929), pp. 37–38.

amount of work energy obtained from minerals and human beings together. By 1910 we were getting more than half of the power used in production and transportation from minerals. Animals and human beings together now constitute only a negligible proportion of our total work energy supply.[4]

The builder of prime movers. The availability of energy is of no value for work output unless it can be utilized. The sun each day releases tremendous energy upon our planet, but man has not learned yet how to harness it for commercial use. The tidal movements of the sea are vast sources of hydraulic power, but they continue each day in their ceaseless rhythm without use. Coal and oil would still be buried largely intact unless man had learned how these materials could be made to do work. It was not until James Watt introduced the reciprocating steam engine in 1769 that the wide utilization of coal was initiated. Today six great prime movers produce most of our power.[5] These are:

The reciprocating steam engine
The steam turbine
The water turbine
The gasoline engine
The diesel engine
The turbojet engine

These engines are called prime movers because they furnish most of the driving power for the tools, mechanisms, and devices which make up industrialization. Five of the six are heat engines which rely on huge quantities of coal or oil. Only the water turbine, which is turned by falling water, needs no fuel. Automobile engines, in the aggregate, are the greatest prime movers in America. This is to say that far more power is transmitted in moving people and goods than in producing goods.[6]

The newest of the great prime movers is the turbojet engine. This is an internal combustion turbine which uses the expansion of burning gas (or atomized liquid fuels) directly to drive a turbine. It is now widely used in most military aircraft and will be in common use in civilian air lines by 1960.

Lilley thinks the gas turbine has promise as a stationary engine and that it may largely replace the steam turbine in power generation.[7] The gas turbine engine is already being produced commercially.

Another newcomer is the turbo-propeller engine. This is a jet engine in which the turbine is used in driving the propeller. This type of engine is proving useful for commercial airliners not requiring the attainment of very high speeds.

The ramjet engine is now in a developmental stage. This is the simplest

[4] J. Frederick Dewhurst and Associates, *America's Needs and Resources, A New Survey* (New York, Twentieth Century Fund, 1955), p. 908.

[5] R. J. Forbes, *op. cit.*, p. 310.

[6] W. S. Woytinsky and E. S. Woytinsky, *World Population and Production* (New York, Twentieth Century Fund, 1953), p. 976.

[7] S. Lilley, *Men, Machines, and History* (London, Cobbett Press, 1948), pp. 155–157.

type of jet engine there is, and it is often called "the flying stovepipe." It is also the most efficient, for there are virtually no moving parts to wear out and it delivers the greatest amount of power for the least weight of any jet engine made. Unfortunately, this engine can begin to work efficiently only when the plane gets up to 400 miles per hour. Its usefulness at present would be as a booster in multi-engined aircraft after two or more conventional jet engines had been used to get up to the necessary speed.[8]

The electric motor is often used in connection with a prime mover, and as such it may be considered a secondary mover. Electricity is generated by a dynamo usually turned by a reciprocating steam engine or a water turbine. This form of power can then be transmitted for distances of 100 miles or more (losses increase with distance) and turned into light, heat, or mechanical energy. Today current from Boulder Dam is delivered to Los Angeles, 278 miles away. Factories can be located anywhere that it is economical to place them. The rural or urban home may now use electric power for either consumption or production purposes. On the farm, the electric motor may be pumping water to the house or the barn. In the city, the motor may be at work helping to clean the living room or building furniture on a bench saw in the garage. Power is no longer where you find it but where you carry it.

The transformer of matter. The dream of the medieval chemist was to transform the baser metals like lead into precious metals like gold and silver. These transformations have not been accomplished, but something over 7,000 other transformations are achieved daily by modern chemistry.[9] The freely available materials of the earth—air, water, mineral and agricultural products, coal, petroleum, and natural gas—are being transformed into innumerable products of benefit to man. Within the last 25 years, petroleum and natural gas have become the raw materials for more than 2,500 different chemical products. Coal is also the raw material for thousands of chemicals. Dyes, drugs, and explosives are among the many products derived from the thick, tarry liquid called coal tar.

Through the science of chemistry, man can transform matter and create an artificial world. His dyes are better than any found in nature, his synthetic fibers stronger and more durable, and his plastics possess qualities hitherto unknown to nature's own products. The possibilities for reconstruction of the physical environment are literally unending. Some of the most challenging assignments for the future include refinement of certain processes now known but not carried to completion. Scientists can make gasoline from coal, cattle fodder from sawdust, and generate electricity from atomic energy, but presently the processes are not economical enough to compete with existing techniques. A large-scale attack on the nature and control of virus

[8] The operation of the jet engine, the turbine propeller engine, and the ramjet are simply described by Kenneth M. King, *The Book of Flight* (New York, Frederick Warne, 1954), pp. 7–9.

[9] *Chemical Industry Facts Book* (Washington, Manufacturing Chemists Association, 1953), p. viii.

diseases, mental disorders, cancer, heart, and circulatory diseases is perhaps the most important challenge.[10]

Modern engineering and modern medicine no longer merely adapt to nature. Engineers can create life-sustaining environments above or below ground and, to a limited extent, in the sea or air. These environments may be furnished with energy and equipped with automatic or near-automatic devices for producing goods and services, furnishing illumination, heat, and air conditioning. Modern medicine offers the prospect of germ-free enclosures and people free of contagion. In this stream of culture, the future calls for imaginative social scientists who can match the science of modern technology. Tested knowledge is needed to guide social relations so that the patterns of living are consistent, integrated, and meaningful. Adaptation to unplanned change is not enough. Creative social change is possible and becoming ever more necessary. Man, the transformer of physical and social environment, has come of age.

Technology—Measures of Its Advance

Two important indices of the advance of technology are (1) the rate of invention, and (2) the amount of energy consumed.

The rate of invention is a measure which describes the *amount of potential technical change that has been added to the technology.*

The amount of energy consumed gives a measure of the *utilization of the established technology.* If the rate of invention and the expenditure of energy are both rising, it can be concluded that technical change is pressing hard upon the social organization of society. As available energy increases, it relieves men from many tasks hitherto requiring manual and even clerical labor. The threat to vested rights in jobs and to vested financial rights in obsolete processes may become a menacing reality. The rate of invention meanwhile affects the rate of change in social habits and behavior. It can shake the entire structure of the existing economy. The automobile, for example, did both. In our day the impact of television on family life is one of the leading topics of conversation.

Rate of invention. The United States patent office has issued the following numbers of patents for each decade of the twentieth century:[11]

1901–1910	319,409
1911–1920	401,495
1921–1930	452,382
1931–1940	485,733
1941–1950	347,695

This is a picture of an increasing flow of patents. Only the intervention of World War II temporarily halted the growing volume of new invention. Post-

[10] *Ibid.,* p. 34.
[11] *Statistical Abstract of the United States, 1952* (Washington, Government Printing Office, 1953), p. 493.

war research will most surely turn the long-run trend toward greater numbers of patents. More than $4 billion are now spent annually on research in the United States. Forty per cent of the total is being spent in the electrical and chemical industries, which are investing most in the growing quest for new products. The auto and oil industry are also big spenders for research.[12] The federal government supports research on a very large scale, especially in the development of atomic energy and atomic weapons.

It must be remembered that numbers of patents issued is only an index of inventive activity, and such an index gives no clues to the significance of inventions. Lilley has selected inventions of fundamental importance from the world-wide achievements in the twentieth century. He has evaluated them as affecting a large sector of industry such as transport or manufacturing, or as affecting only one industry such as automobile or textile manufacturing.[13] Out of the list of seventy-seven fundamental inventions which he has selected, the highest score is reserved for four inventions affecting a large sector of industry. These four are the propeller-driven airplane, conveyor-belt mass production, tungsten carbide tools, and the release of atomic energy. Other "runner ups" include quality control, the gas turbine, the helicopter, and the jet-propelled airplane. The fields of radio, movie, and television have advanced greatly, but each has required a series of improving inventions rather than a single fundamental invention.

Amount of energy consumed. Two facts dominate an appraisal of energy consumption. The first is the very great increase in the use of energy, and the second is the marked shift from animate energy to inanimate energy. In the United States of 1935, the combined horsepower released from engines of all types was equivalent to some *seventy* slaves available to work for every man, woman, and child in the country.[14] The following table shows how increased use of inanimate energy has reduced the average hours of work, but has increased the net output of man hours and the national income of the labor force. Note how the working hours of 1850 have almost been cut in half. It is almost impossible to imagine that man once worked six or seven days a week and the average day might require ten or eleven hours of work. The five-day week is now conventional, and any hourly worker in industry working over eight hours a day usually receives premium pay. The four- and even three-day week may not be too far away.

Economic growth depends upon energy. The table on page 252 shows that oil and natural gas are being increasingly used as sources of energy. Bituminous coal was the dominant energy mineral until recent years. With the growing importance of the internal combustion engine on highways and farms and later with the rapid rise in the use of natural gas, the contribution of bituminous coal became less than that of oil and natural gas. The mechani-

[12] *Newsweek* (November 9, 1953).
[13] Lilley, *op. cit.*, pp. 218–220.
[14] Lilley, *op. cit.*, p. 180.

cal energy for all purposes in the United States supplied per member of the labor force increased by 116 per cent from 1900 to 1950.[15]

WEEKLY HOURS, OUTPUT PER MAN HOUR, NATIONAL INCOME, 1850–1960*

Year	Average Weekly Hours	Net Output Per Man Hour (in cents)	National Income 1950 Prices (in billions of dollars)
1850	69.8	33.7	8.8
1860	68.0	40.6	14.1
1870	65.4	42.6	17.4
1880	64.0	44.4	23.8
1890	61.9	61.1	41.3
1900	60.2	75.5	60.0
1910	55.1	89.6	82.4
1920	49.7	93.2	88.6
1930	45.9	106.9	108.2
1940	44.0	131.5	130.3
1950	40.0	193.5	217.3
1960 (Est.)	37.5	240.0	275.0

SOURCE: The table is adapted from J. Frederick Dewhurst and Associates, *America's Needs and Resources* (New York, Twentieth Century Fund, 1955), p. 40.
* Excludes governmental enterprises as well as general governmental activities.

**SOURCES OF ENERGY IN THE UNITED STATES
FOR SELECTED YEARS, 1900–1948
(percentage of total)**

Year	Coal	Oil	Natural Gas	Hydroelectric Power
1900	88.9	4.8	3.2	3.2
1910	84.9	8.1	3.5	3.5
1920	78.0	14.9	3.8	3.3
1930	62.2	25.3	9.2	3.3
1940	52.7	32.7	11.2	3.4
1948	46.6	35.1	14.3	4.0

SOURCE: United States Department of the Interior, Bureau of Mines, *Minerals Yearbook, 1948* (Washington, Government Printing Office, 1948), pp. 284–286.

Technology: Evolution of Machines

Four major stages. Four major stages in the evolution of our modern technology may be identified. These are the stages we shall call the *modern craft age,* the *machine age,* the *power age,* and the *atomic age.*[16] These are ages which may be said to have emerged at about 1400 with the modern craft age and which have succeeded one another in the sense that new key inventions have altered the ways of producing goods and services. The changes that have accompanied each age have not obliterated all traces of the preceding ages. On the contrary, vestiges of almost every technological

[15] *Statistical Abstract of the United States, 1953,* p. 515.

[16] Lewis Mumford described a three-stage evolution of technology which he calls eotechnic, paleotechnic, and neotechnic. I have drawn upon his analysis as described in *Technics and Civilization* (New York, Harcourt, Brace, 1934).

stage can be found in any community. Karl Mannheim was so impressed with this aspect of modern culture that he coined the phrase "the contemporaneity of the non-contemporaneous" to describe the simultaneous appearance of different modes of production, transportation, communication, architecture, religion, and many other aspects of social living.

Let us imagine ourselves standing at a busy street corner in a large city. Everything about us is in motion. On the left a man is laboriously pushing a barrow, on the right a horse and cart passes at a steady trot. From different directions cars and busses roll by. Somewhere in the air the hum of an aeroplane can be heard. There is nothing unusual in all this, nothing that today would call forth surprise or astonishment—barrows, drays, motor cars, and aeroplanes all represent typical means of transportation in different historical epochs and accordingly in a different historical phase of technological development. In spite of their different historical derivation, in spite of the fact that they arose in different periods, they all fit in with one another as the scene above.[17]

The chart of the four ages of technology (below) purports to show this same "contemporaneity of the non-contemporaneous." Each age has left a technical heritage which remains in various forms even as the new emerges and becomes dominant. The important elements in the technology which shape a pattern are:

Power
Tools
Work skills
Material
Transportation
Communication

Modern craft age. The modern craft age may be dated as beginning with the fifteenth century, which is often regarded as the threshold of modern civilization. Advances in navigation brought about the search for and discovery of many new lands hitherto unknown until the fifteenth and sixteenth centuries. Old trade routes were reopened. The commercial economy which flourished depended largely on goods and services prepared by the hands of skilled craftsmen. Considerable unskilled manual labor was also required to do the lifting, hauling, storing, and many other operations required in getting goods from one place to another. The muscles of animals, especially the horse and mule, were extensively employed in transportation and in agriculture. Hand tools were improved and water power was increasingly employed to turn water wheels for the grinding of wheat and the making of textiles. Wind was employed in driving sailing ships over the routes of commerce. Wood was the most commonly employed material, with iron and bronze used for the heads of tools and a limited number of products.

The machine age. The machine age may be considered as inaugurated by Watt's invention of the reciprocating steam engine and its application to the

[17] Karl Mannheim, *Man and Society in an Age of Reconstruction* (London, Kegan Paul, Trench, Trubner, 1940), p. 41.

FOUR AGES OF INDUSTRIAL TECHNOLOGY

Important Determiners of Technology in Dominant Ages	Modern Craft Age 1400	Machine Age 1785	Power Age 1870	Atomic Age 1953
Power	Muscle, wind, and water	Steam	Electricity	Atomic energy
Tools	Hand	Machine	Automatic machine	Automatic factory
Work Skills	All-around skilled craftsman—unskilled manual worker	Skilled craftsmen replaced by machine (semiskilled) operatives as a result of subdividing manufacturing processes	Skilled inspector, mechanic required as operations replace need for machine feeding or tending	Highly trained engineers as designers are required Skilled technicians required for maintenance

Material	Wood, iron, bronze	Steel, copper	Alloyed steels light alloys, aluminum	Plastics, Super alloys, Use of 32 new metals, notably magnesium and titanium
Transportation	Walking, use of animals, or sailboat via dirt road and waterway	Steam train or steamship via steel rails and ocean way	Automobile, diesel train or airplane via paved highway, railway, and air way	Jet airplane, rocket, and helicopter via stratosphere. Atomic train via railway
Communication	Word of mouth, newspaper, messenger	Mail moved faster by rail and water. Newspaper printed on steam press. Telephone, telegraph	AM and FM radio, movie, television, microfilm, magnetic tape	Televised telephone, talking book or newspaper, universal two-way radio communication, electronic machines, magnetic-tape photography, vocatypewriter

textile industry. In 1785 the steam engine was first used to drive spinning machines. Soon large factories appeared. By 1802 there were 52 textile factories in Manchester, England.[18] Other fields of manufacture waited upon the invention of machine tools such as the milling machine, the turret lathe, the automatic lathe, and the grinding machine. By 1800 the lathe was already an essential and universal tool for the manufacture of machine parts.[19] The lathe and other machine tools soon produced various product parts in quantity and with precision quality. Steam power was transmitted by a belt-and-shaft system to the machine tools. Thousands of workmen could be brought under one roof. The factory as a way of organizing work became predominant in manufacturing. Steam engines were usually fed by coal. Wherever coal could be found or transported economically, it was possible to locate steam engines. Sources of water power no longer limited the location of factories.

In a very short time, the basic principles of mass production were discovered. Mass production means, in essence, just two things: (a) The making of standard, interchangeable parts; and (b) the assembling of these parts into the completed unit with a minimum of handicraft labor.

Mass production changed the worker from a craftsman to a semiskilled machine operative. Before mass production, the worker used his new power tool in much the same way as he had a hand tool. As parts were made he continued to mate them by putting them back in the lathe or drill and scraping or drilling the parts to size. With mass production of parts, the shape-giving processes were subdivided. Each worker was assigned one or a few operations which he repeated over and over again. Patterns called jigs and various holding aids called fixtures enabled the operator to secure precision work. The skill required was increasingly transferred from the human hand to the machine. During World Wars I and II, many manufacturing industries employed persons skilled in setting up machines designed to do precision work. An operator with no more than one week's training might then be able to step into the line. In this way thousands of housewives and students were quickly brought into production.

Continuous-flow production followed the use of mass-production techniques. Continuous-flow production means that parts start to move the minute they are completed, preferably on a conveyor belt, toward a central assembly point. The Ford automobile is assembled by the use of continuous-flow production of mass-produced parts. The use of this system enables the Ford company to produce more than 9,000 vehicles a day.

Steel is the basic metal of industrial civilization. In the machine age it was almost the only suitable metal available for construction purposes. Most manufactured objects were made of it. Up to 1900, about a half-dozen metals served all of man's needs either as fabricated goods or money. Since 1900,

[18] R. J. Forbes, *op. cit.*, p. 211.
[19] *Ibid.*, p. 180.

CONTINUOUS-FLOW PRODUCTION

An overhead conveyor at Cleveland automatically switches moving engines from the main track into vacant places on the hot test stands at left. There they get gas and oil and come to life for the first time. In a Ford plant, where the assembly line can feed it more than 145 engines an hour, the system effects an important saving in the cost of each car.

the number of different metals used in commerce have tripled and alloys, a broad stream of new materials, have become available. However, the nineteenth century relied on what it knew. It knew how to make iron and later learned how to convert iron into that magnificently hard, flexible, and cheap metal called steel. Steel was to go into the new steam train and steamship, which greatly stimulated transportation and world colonization and settlement. Copper soon found a place in the telephone and telegraph wires which closed the world into a network of rapid communication.

The power age. The power age is characterized by the widespread use of electricity. Since 1870, when practical types of generators were available, industrial applications have been rapid. The first central stations began operating in a few big cities in 1880. Most electricity is still generated by the steam engine, but most factories no longer have steam engines. The cracking of belts on pulleys and shafts is no longer heard. The elaborate overhead structure has been replaced by electric motors mounted at the base of each machine tool. A flick of the switch and the low hum of a powerful motor signals that the job of producing power has been assigned to a more efficient medium. Anywhere that a wire can transmit electricity economically, electric motors can produce power for a factory. Factories can be placed again in the green valleys as the water-powered factory of the craft age was. Smoke and grease are eliminated and workers are often dressed as neatly as white-collar office workers.

Electricity is a steady, firm source of power which invites better machine tools. Multi-purpose and automatic machine tools have been added to the automatic continuous-flow conveyor belt. A multi-purpose machine tool is one that is capable of doing many operations, such as drilling, cutting, and grinding. The Studebaker Company has a machine whose 189 spindles perform automobile drilling, reaming, and tapping operations. These multi-purpose tools may be worked manually, with semi-automatic manual controls, or electronically. The most advanced form of automatic machine is coupled with an electronic machine. The electronic machine is essentially a communication machine and must "think" for the machine tool. When the electronic circuit is properly wired, a machine tool automatically proceeds to perform functions in accordance with electrical impulses (directions) transmitted to it.

The next step is to secure automatic movement of a part like a cylinder block from one automatic tool to another, in other words, to synchronize the automatic functions. Steel fingers are created to replace human ones and lever bars substitute for human arms or legs. Automatic controls are well developed. Photoelectric cells can replace the human eye. The gas detector can "smell," the microphone can "hear," the thermocouple can record "temperature," and the electric micrometer provides a measure of "touch."

"Automation" refers to the moving of a procession of parts through a series of machine operations. It differs from the assembly-line conveyor in

Courtesy of Ford Motor Company

THE AUTOMATIC FACTORY

A worker changes drills in a machine that drills 20 holes in an engine crankshaft from four different directions. Automation moves the crankshafts into place for drilling and removes them when drilling has been completed.

that it is coupled with a marvelous electric nervous system (electronic machine) that feeds, operates, and unloads the machine along its line and makes decisions that keep the flow of work running smoothly. In what is probably the most complex series of automatic machining operations in America today, the Ford engine cylinder blocks are transported automatically into and out of twenty-odd different machines that perform a grand total of 532 broaching, milling, boring, honing, drilling, and tapping operations. Virtually the only men required on the automated line are job setters, who watch the process and replace worn tools whenever a control board "toolometer" indicates that a tool is nearing the end of its life expectancy. The picture above shows a worker who is changing drills on an automated line producing auto crankshafts.

The supreme technical achievement of the power age is this automation process, the forerunner of the automatic factory and the atomic age which lies ahead. Already social changes accompanying this mechanization are taking place. Marked changes in labor requirements can be observed, and these can be expected to intensify as the atomic age advances. The introduction of machine tools decreased the need for unskilled labor and increased the need for semiskilled and skilled labor. The need for white-collar workers also increased. Under automation, the need for both unskilled and semiskilled workers declines, but the need for skilled machinists, technicians, and inspectors increases. As the power age gives way to the atomic age, these labor changes grow more pronounced. The United States Census of 1950 showed that the proportion of unskilled workers was steadily declining. While the number of semiskilled workers continued to rise, the proportionate increase was very small. The proportion of skilled workers rose between 1940 and 1950. The Census indicated an accelerated rise in the proportion of technicians and clerical workers.[20]

The power age has stimulated the use of alloys and light metals. Cheap hydroelectric power has made aluminum an abundant metal. The airplane industry, in turn, has used aluminum in great quantity. The automobile and airplane have greatly increased transportation and have cut transport time. Forty million automobiles and 25,000 airplanes daily use the highways and airways of the United States. This has built in a mobility which has changed both the character and scope of the labor market and the consuming market. Both of these markets are now almost one national market, regardless of the labor or goods available for sale.

The atomic age. The atomic age is now in its initial development. The atomic bomb signaled its arrival.[21] The atomic-driven submarine launched by the United States Navy in 1953[22] and the announcement by the Atomic Energy Commission in October, 1953, of its decision to build a commercial-size atomic energy electrical plant confirms the expected development of a new technical era. Lilley asserts that the release of nuclear energy is the most fundamental step forward in man's control of nature since he learned to control fire 200,000 years ago. He bases this assertion on the scientific basis of the discovery. To the best of our knowledge, there are three fundamentally different kinds of natural forces. These are gravitational forces, chemical or electromagnetic forces, and nuclear forces. The technical history of man has been a history of his achievements in controlling gravitational and chemical forces. Now the control of atomic energy means that man has learned to employ a third, fundamentally different, type of force. Nuclear

[20] The proportion of workers in each of the six main occupational classifications for 1940 and 1950 was as follows: professionals, 6.5 and 7.5; proprietors, managers, and officials, 17.8 and 16.3, clerical, 17.2 and 20.2; skilled, 11.7 and 13.8; semiskilled, 21.0 and 22.4; unskilled, 25.9 and 19.8.

[21] The atomic bomb was first exploded in a test at Almagordo, N. M., on July 16, 1945.

[22] The engine of the *Nautilus,* the world's first atomic-powered submarine, began operating on May 31, 1953 at the Atomic Energy Commission plant at Arco, Idaho. The first test-run of the *Nautilus* at sea was made during January, 1955.

force is far more powerful than the others. The prospect is that the release of atomic energy may eventually bring about an increase in available energy that will dwarf gravitational and chemical energy. The successful "breeding" of fissionable material, the atomic fuel, was announced in 1953 by the Atomic Energy Commission. Up to that time the use of atomic energy had been inhibited by one fundamental fact: Less than 1 per cent of the uranium that occurs in nature is the kind that can be used to generate atomic power. Atom-power development was stunted by the scarcity of fissionable material. Now, however, all ordinary uranium in the world becomes potential atomic fuel. It is believed that thorium, another element as plentiful as uranium, can be changed into atomic fuel.

The "breeder" can theoretically change ordinary uranium into fissionable plutonium at a rate equal to the rate at which U-235 is being consumed. When this happens, a reactor, or atom splitting furnace, becomes a sort of combination power station and fuel factory. It will simultaneously produce power and excess atomic fuel that can be used for other purposes.

When the process is improved so that breeding reaches this expected level of efficiency, the potentialities for vast power may be realized. Such a development is not immediately imminent. The Atomic Energy Commission says it may be five years before a breeder reactor yields as much new atomic fuel as was initially invested in it. But the blueprint is drawn. One writer has said the breeder discovery is as if the nation's scientists had discovered how to make gasoline out of the world's sea waters, so great is the potential power at stake (and indeed, the world's sea waters may be converted to energy if research work on the fusion of the atom should prove successful).

It is known that the "burning" of one pound of fissionable material releases energy roughly equivalent to that of 1,500 tons of coal. By burning ten pounds of fissionable material a day in a reactor, electric capacity equal to Hoover Dam can be produced.

Atomic power plants are now being planned and built. Besides its own plans for the construction of power plants, the Atomic Energy Commission is encouraging industry to proceed with research development. The Duquesne Light Company of Pittsburgh in 1954 signed an agreement with the AEC and spent more than $30 million in developing an atomic power plant a few miles from Pittsburgh. The North American Aviation Company, Inc., and the AEC are jointly building a reactor to be completed in 1958. A score of private companies are now conducting research on reactors. As of December, 1956, the United States had 73 nuclear reactors operating or licensed, another 118 were being built or planned. The Duquense Light Company scheduled delivery of the first commercial nuclear power in 1957.[23]

A model of the reactor designed by the North American Aviation Company is shown on page 262.

[23] *Twenty-first Semi-Annual Report of the Atomic Energy Commission* (Washington, Government Printing Office, 1957), p. xi.

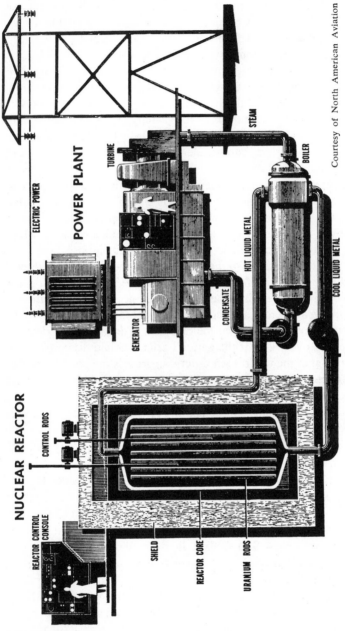

NUCLEAR REACTOR

REACTOR CONTROL CONSOLE

CONTROL RODS

SHIELD

REACTOR CORE

URANIUM RODS

POWER PLANT

ELECTRIC POWER

TURBINE

GENERATOR

CONDENSATE

HOT LIQUID METAL

COOL LIQUID METAL

STEAM

BOILER

Courtesy of North American Aviation

**SCHEMATIC OF A PROPOSED PILOT PLANT FOR GENERATION OF
ELECTRICAL POWER FROM ATOMIC ENERGY**

Heat produced by the atomic fission process in the reactor, left, would be absorbed by a liquid metal passing through the reactor core. The liquid metal is piped to a water boiler, lower center, where steam is produced. The steam would drive a turbine generator, center, producing electricity. About 8,000 kilowatts of electricity, enough to supply 2,000 average homes, could be produced for use in other atomic research with the pilot plant.

Great as is the potential of all presently utilized fuels, they are as almost infinitesimal in comparison with the energy of the sun. Two experts on energy resources estimate that our entire supply of known combustibles, including fissionable materials, are equivalent to three days of energy at the rate which we are accustomed to receive it from the sun.[24] Many experts believe that in the very long run solar energy will beat out atomic energy as the prime mover of the future world, although both are uneconomical sources at present. In the distant future we may expect the appearance of the solar age, providing man can organize his society to cope with the atomic age and the much more immediate consequences of the automatic factory.

The automatic factory is on the horizon, its full outline now before us. Automatic factories in the chemical industries already exist. Industry as a whole does not leap, of course, from hand-tending to the completely automatic. There are all manner of intermediate, semi-automatic stages in between. In the United States we now have tens of millions of automatic control systems at work—in industry, in the military establishment, in the office and in the home.[25] The homeowner is well aware of automatic controls. Most of the home furnaces in America today are operated by automatic thermostatic control. Automatic fire-control sprinkler systems may be installed in the home. The automobile may be operated by an automatic gear shift. Automatic traffic lights guide drivers and pedestrians over busy intersections and automatic signals warn him of danger on railway crossings. In turn, automatic switches guide the railroad train. Almost every industry, including its office operations, is using numerous semi-automatic or fully automatic devices. In sum, if the controls now operating in our economy were shut off, there would be chaos. The robots are here.[26]

The principle of automatic control goes back at least to the fifteenth century when men placed miniature sails on windmills to rotate the whole mill in response to changes in wind direction. Another application of a different level is the player piano of more recent times. Slots cut in a paper roll became "instructions" which "fed back" the information as to which keys were to be struck. The application of the principle to modern industry has been rapidly accelerated over the past two decades.[27] Controls may discipline all the factors of temperature, pressure, flow of gas or liquid for an entire process. The huge Oak Ridge atomic plant is run from a central control room linked to some ten miles of instrument panels, with fewer than twenty human operators to the mile. The control room in a chemical plant

[24] Eugene Ayers and Charles A. Scarlot, *Energy Sources—The Wealth of the World* (New York, McGraw-Hill, 1952).

[25] Gordon S. Brown and Donald P. Campbell, "Control Systems," *Scientific American,* Vol. 187 (September, 1952), p. 57.

[26] *Ibid.,* p. 57.

[27] Ernest Nagel, "Automatic Control," *Scientific American,* Vol. 187 (September, 1952); pp. 44–47. Cf. Wassily Leontief, "Machines and Men," *ibid.,* pp. 152–156.

Courtesy of DuPont

CONTROL ROOM IN A CHEMICAL PLANT

shown above is being increasingly duplicated in the industry. In the control room, perhaps remote from the unit, the chemical process is represented by instruments on a panel board. An operator keeps a trained eye on the flow of production, interfering only when flashing lights or clanging bells signal an emergency. The instruments serve both as a reporter and as a regulator. A meter, for example, recording the flow of a liquid sends a report to another device set to the required standard. A third instrument then turns a valve to compensate for any deviation or "error." Multiplied a hundred times over, this is the pattern of the automatic controls the operator follows on a central panel. It is estimated that over 50,000 control devices are being used in United States oil refineries alone.[28]

In manufacturing, the processes are more difficult to put under automatic operation. Human hands are well adapted to the handling of solid objects. It is difficult to make a machine that can do what the co-ordinated eyes and hands can do. In the chemical industries, which involve liquids and gases, the pumps and pipes have a great advantage over man's native endowments. A pump to transmit liquids from one place to another is far superior to anything man can do with his hands. It is not difficult to go further and measure volumes and arrange to change the output of pumps automatically.[29]

What the chemical industry has done, manufacturing industry hopes to achieve in spite of greater difficulty. Already automatic devices have come into extensive use in continuous-process industries like canneries, steel rolling mills, and especially wire and tin plate factories. They are also familiar

[28] Eugene Ayers, "An Automatic Chemical Plant," *ibid.*, pp. 82–96.
[29] "The Automatic Factory," *Fortune* (October, 1953), p. 185.

in paper factories.[30] It is the more difficult problems of manufacture and especially assembly which prevent fully automatic operation in the metals industry. A conventional factory is an aggregation of production, assembly, and handling machinery, controlled from a central position. The automatic factory will be made up of many production machines, each making a single part, one connected to another by a conveyor system, and all linked through a central master control panel.[31]

The Massachusetts Institute of Technology has constructed a milling machine which executes instructions contained on a tape which has holes punched into it by a special typewriter keyboard. By inserting a new reel of tape for each job to be performed, the milling machine can be converted from one manufacturing task to another with little more effort than is required to change a phonograph record. Once set in motion, the machine runs continuously.[32] Automatized general-purpose machine tools will eventually make possible the automatic metals-fabrication factory. Digital computers which will make possible central control are already well advanced.[33] With these machines in control, it is possible for a factory to automatically process, assemble, and finish any article of manufacture. The automatic factory is expected to develop by steps until it eventually appears *in toto*. It is believed that the possible fields to which the automatic processes may be applied are very extensive. However, they cannot be expected to penetrate where the scale of activity is small and hence uneconomical, or where work is so varied that the cost of changes would make it prohibitive. But, with these exceptions, the area of application is so vast that the resulting effects would seem to promise an industrial revolution unlike anything that man has encountered. It is a technical revolution in which the machine threatens to make the large body of available labor unnecessary in the production of goods. Moreover, the automatic devices may be extensively applied to accounting and clerical operations. The displacement of labor from both blue- and white-collar occupations is indicated.[34]

In addition to the use of atomic energy and the developments of the automatic factory, other changes are appearing. The range of materials for products is increasing. The use of plastics is growing rapidly. Meanwhile, a chemical revolution in metals is taking place. Super alloys are being employed, some of which may contain as many as twenty different metals. These super alloys are being developed for the highest stress and temperature spots in jet engines. The increased use of light metals such as aluminum, magnesium,

---

[30] Norbert Wiener, *The Human Use of Human Beings* (Boston, Houghton Mifflin, 1950), pp. 185–189.

[31] Eric W. Leaver and J. J. Brown, "Machines Without Men," *Fortune* (November, 1946), pp. 192–194.

[32] William Pease, "An Automatic Machine Tool," *Scientific American,* Vol. 187 (September, 1952), pp. 112–114.

[33] Louis N. Ridenour, "The Role of the Computer," *ibid.,* pp. 116–130.

[34] Norbert Wiener, *op. cit.,* pp. 185–189.

and titanium is well under way. Aluminum production is now running at five times its 1940 rate, magnesium is moving at twenty times 1940 production. Titanium, almost nonexistent as a pure metal four years ago, is up from nothing to 1,200 tons last year.[35] New metals which are being used increasingly include zirconium, ultrapure chromium, vanadium, molybdenum columbium, tungsten, silicon, calcium, manganese, lithium, boron, hafnium. A rising new metal is germanium, used in electronic transistors which may replace the conventional vacuum tube. A group of fifteen or so metals rather badly named rare-earth metals (they are neither very rare nor earths) possess a vast area of unknown properties and uses to be explored. To withstand the temperatures the jet engineer is striving for will probably require the development of entirely different materials. The full realization of atomic power for industrial uses demands that metals and materials withstand even higher temperatures than those encountered in jet aircraft.

The chemical and electrical industries are now striving to develop new metals, materials, and markets, moving steadily toward continuous processes, tapping ever-more-abundant sources of metals in sea water, alumina clay, and ilmenite sand.[36]

Travel by jet propulsion is here. The British have jet-propelled aircraft in commercial use. The Boeing Airplane Company has built a commercial prototype. The military fighter and bomber plane is now jet propelled. Completely automatic flying is almost a reality. Sperry Gyroscope Company has announced an automatic landing device which requires the pilot to touch the controls only as the wheels reach the ground.[37] Actually, planes already can be controlled entirely from the ground or another plane. The rocket for long-range movement and the helicopter for short-range movement have large possibilities for future travel.

In the area of communication, the televised telephone and the talking book or newspaper seem to be practical possibilities; color television is, of course, already a reality. The stereo-movie with binaural sound has arrived. In addition, ultra-high-frequency broadcasting is now being developed and expanded. Two-way radio communication may become a universal mode of point-to-point communication. Electronic photography has been demonstrated by photographing a color television program on magnetic tape. The extension of electronic communication machines to industrial and home use may be expected to affect every area of economic and social life.

Lag and Lead in Technology Between Industries

Four major ages of technology have been described, but it must not be assumed that technology moves forward in an even pace over the entire society. Some companies and some industries introduce the newest advances;

[35] Laurence P. Lessing, "The New Metals Age," *Fortune* (January, 1953), p. 157.
[36] *Ibid.*, p. 160.
[37] *Seattle Times,* October 25, 1953, p. 29.

others lag for various reasons. A lag may occur because of the high cost of replacing obsolete equipment, especially if such equipment is still in excellent condition. At Boeing Aircraft Company there is a common saying that the latest bomber model which takes to the air is already outdated. The engineers have started drawing up blueprints for a new model which will in a relatively short time replace the one for which the factory has just tooled up. The modern airplane industry must operate like a vast job shop because of a myriad of frequent changes in design. It is an industry in the machine age as far as its labor requirements for large numbers of machine operatives are concerned. However, it has adopted the light metals, the electric power, and many conveyor techniques characteristic of the power age.

The housing industry is closer to the craft age, inasmuch as houses are put up board by board, cut and fitted by a craftsman. However, the strain toward a more advanced technology can be observed in the use of precut panels and the use of power tools. Many of the largest builders have now subdivided building operations so that specialized work teams are assigned specific job functions. Each team erects various parts of the structure. Sheet rockers, painters, pipe layers, roofers, rough and finish carpenters, electricians, plumbers, and masons are among the specialists who follow in various waves like the moving of a conveyor assembly line. One large contractor makes his own cement on the building site. The prefabricated house which is cut and made ready for assembly in the factory is another step toward mass production. Both Buckmaster Fuller and the Lustron Corporation have tried to make all-metal houses for commercial sale, but both have failed to find a market. One manufacturer constructed a machine which would "lay" a hollow cement egg as large as a house. These are the searchings bursting forth from a twentieth-century technology. The housing industry will not stay put in the craft age. The automatic production of factory-built houses as a commercial success appears difficult now. But the technology points toward this end, and as problems are solved this method of manufacture can be expected. Meanwhile, the housing industry by and large is characterized by a vast technological lag.

Craft and job shops remain to do luxury and specialty work of all kinds. A mass economy strains toward mass production of standard products. This is true even in the area of services from food distribution (self-service grocery, automat), accounting service (I.B.M. equipment), education (training and TV films) to music (records). As one observes the range of processes by which goods and services are produced and distributed, he can see how widely the lag and leads of our technology are arrayed. The technic ways of the fifteenth century exist side by side with the technic ways of the twentieth century. It is interesting to think of these technic ways as being under the impact of a process which brings gradual but constant change. One is reminded of the silent movement of crushing glaciers that grind away the mountain side by imperceptible degrees. The pressure on all the vast structure of the craft, machine, and power age is a demand that it break up and give way to the forms outlined by the atomic age. Most of the structure of technology now in place is obsolete on the drafting boards of engineers who plan the future.

INFLUENCE OF TECHNOLOGY ON THE SOCIAL ORGANIZATION OF INDUSTRY

Impact of Mass Production and Mass Organization on the Worker

Modern technology opened the way for mass production and a sequence of revolutionary economic and social processes. Mass production invited mass markets and a whole host of new business organizations and technical developments within transportation, communication, banking and investment, advertising, wholesaling, retailing. No part of society was permitted complete isolation from the effects, no matter what the various prevailing local economics had been or desired to be. Markets were sought out everywhere—in the country, village, town, city, nation, and in every part of the world. The economic organization of modern society is dependent upon these far-flung markets. Karl Polanyi traces out implications of this fact:[38]

Ultimately, that is why the control of the economic system by the market is of overwhelming consequence to the whole organization of society; it means no less than the running of society as an adjunct to the market. Instead of the economy being embedded in social relations, social relations are embedded in the economic system. The vital importance of the economic factor to the existence of society precludes any other result. For once the economic system is organized in separate institutions, based on specific motives and conferring a special status, society must be shaped in such a manner as to allow that system to function according to its own laws. This is the meaning of the familiar assertion that a market economy can function only in a market society.

The modern corporation rose at the center of the market society. This new enterprise was required to organize more people than ever before—people to carry out a multitude of specialized tasks. Just as the production process became subdivided, timed, and allocated to production and assembly line stations, so workers were selected, assigned, and trained to the appropriate work positions. The mass-production principle of organizing production became in effect a huge mold, requiring that the worker fit his work to the proportions of the new form. Thus, the mass-production principle became at the same time a principle of social organization. The rising bureaucracy of the office containing the new white-collar population of clerks, technicians, and managers began to assume the organization ideology of the production line. Frederick Taylor, commonly called the father of scientific management, codified the new principles of functional analysis.[39] The principles of selection, training, and co-operation imply standardization, systematization, and

38 Karl Polanyi, *The Great Transformation* (New York, Rinehart, 1944), p. 57.
39 F. W. Taylor's paper, "The Principles of Scientific Management."

organization by which the knowledge gained by investigation and experimentation is turned to practical application.

Applied to the plant floor, these principles revolutionized the social structure of the plant society. The structure of status which arose in the craft age was based on *age* and *skill*. The youngster entered as an apprentice. He was trained to the varied tasks of the craft. He was taught to respect the skills he had learned and to look with respect upon those older workers who had risen to the rank of journeyman and master craftsman. Time and skill was required to achieve these ranks, and appropriate status and privilege were bestowed upon them. A man who entered into company with such workmen entered a fraternity. The worker spent his lifetime acquiring prestige and respect, learning as he aged and at the same time teaching the newcomers who were younger and aspired to be like him.

The mass-production principle in the machine age broke this structure wide apart. The subdividing of processes resulted in a dilution of skills. Machine operatives who could be trained in a week to run out a few repetitive motions on the machine supplanted men who had spent years learning the all-round skills. Bright-eyed youngsters found that they could turn out as much and often more than the old-timer. Equal pay for equal work was the new slogan for a social structure that had no further need or respect for the antiquated society based on age and skill. The industrial labor union (vertical type) emerged as an expression of the new plant society. Labor unions offered the individual status within a group, and it offered him a chance to rise in a new hierarchy based on his ability to represent his fellow workers. The management structure was also offering new and expanding opportunity as snappers, straw bosses, lead men, assistant foremen, inspectors, and foreman.

The mass-production principle invaded the office, but its full effects have waited upon the fuller development of office machinery. The new accounting, computing, and recording machines working on automatic principles are now beginning to make a full assault on clerical work. Stenographers and bookkeepers are likely to feel the full impact in the very near future.

The threat of technological and cyclical unemployment is always a menace to the industrial worker. As a worker who has only his labor or skill to offer, he is without the means of livelihood when he is denied access to an organization. In an industrial society, only a very small minority of artists and professional men can produce at all by themselves. All the others are dependent upon access to an organization if they are to be productive. *It is the organization,* not the individual, *which is productive in an industrial system.*[40]

Impact of Mass Production on the Role of the Large Enterprise

The worker is not the only element to feel the impact of mass production. The organization of the individual firm has had new demands thrust upon it.

[40] Peter Drucker, *The New Society* (New York, Harper, 1950), p. 8.

The significant characteristics of the current industrial scene include: (1) the emergence of the large enterprise as the representative social institution; and (2) the increase of added responsibilities as the firm discharges the triple functions of economic, governmental, and social institution.

The emergence of the large enterprise as the representative social institution. The large enterprise has emerged as the representative social institution. It is true that the great majority of the people do not work for one of the large industrial enterprises, yet their livelihood is directly dependent upon them. It is the big enterprises which occupy the strategic centers. Most small businessmen, independents, professionals and even farmers gain their livelihood largely as suppliers or as distributors for the large enterprises. It is the large enterprises which establish the price and wage policies of the nation. The pattern of union-management relations is set by the contracts drawn between big labor and big business. Governmental regulations grow up to harness and channel the economic power and practice of large enterprise. The personnel policies adopted by large industry become the models for the entire industrial society.

The large enterprise serves as a mirror, for the principles of mass production and mass organization can be utilized in their fullest proportions through the specialization which large-scale organization permits. Yet all enterprise must adapt itself to the imperatives of the market society or fail. Each must find a combination by which its advantages of size, location, and individual service can be maximized, lest it be swept aside by the large enterprise. If it cannot employ the principles of mass production and mass organization directly, then it must find ways to secure the advantages of large-scale enterprise by collaboration and co-ordination with similar firms or in conjunction with large producers, wholesalers, and distributors. It must get inside the market society or die; exceptions are reserved for a few distributors of luxury products, novelties, holders of patents, or subsistence farmers.

The triple functions of enterprise. All enterprise, large and small, has been drawn into an increasing range of responsibilities. These involve *economic, political,* and *social* functions.

As an *economic institution,* the enterprise must provide an ever higher standard of living for the worker. The worker knows that the technology is increasing his productivity and he expects to receive an increased standard of living for his labors. The firm is the organ through which the economic returns of society are distributed. It must adapt to the changing requirements of the economy. The table on page 271 shows how labor needs have drastically shifted from *producing* to *servicing, distributing,* and *co-ordinating.*

As a political institution, the business enterprise is the most influential administrative force in the daily lives of the workers. The power of managers and union leaders is a force which largely determines the size of the worker's pay, the nature of his job duties, his basic worth, and his future place in the firm. His concept of justice is derived largely from his experience with the administrative and legislative branches of the firm. The long trend has been one of increased democratization of the work plant[41] in which greater worker participation and control is exercised.[42]

OCCUPATIONAL CHANGES IN ECONOMIC FUNCTION FOR ALL WORKERS IN THE UNITED STATES, 1870 TO 1940

	1870	1940
Producing	77%	46%
Servicing	13	20
Distributing	7	23
Co-ordinating	3	11
Total Employed	100%	100%

SOURCE: C. Wright Mills, *White Collar* (New York, Oxford University Press, 1951), p. 66.

As a *social institution* the firm has attained a central position in the life of the worker. In his work plant he wins a status position that goes with him to the community. There is no factor more influential in determining a man's social position and that of his family than his occupation. Within the work plant, a complete social system arises and a plant community is established. The social life drawn from work groups must often serve as a substitute for the declining participation in family and kinship groups, neighborhood, and community. Unless the worker finds a place within a work group which is satisfying to him, he is likely to become an unstable worker. Absenteeism and turnover is likely to be markedly higher for those who are not integrated into cohesive work groups.[43] Today there is no theme more dominant at business conferences than the importance of human-relations policies in achieving the objectives of the enterprise.

The Rise of the New Middle Classes of Industry and Society

In the past eighty years there has been a vast transformation of property as industrialization has advanced. The proportion of workers who own the property from which they produce their livelihood has diminished greatly. This has brought about great changes in the composition of the labor force. The changes have been most marked in those occupations which have made up the middle class. In 1870 the United States was still predominantly rural. The farmers, businessmen, and free professionals made up the middle class. Each owned property or operated independently. By 1940 all three of these

[41] Herryman Mauer, "Management by Committees," *Fortune* (April, 1953), pp. 145–147, 191–198.

[42] See Elliott Jacques, *The Changing Culture of the Modern Factory* (New York, Dryden, 1952). This is an account of a comprehensive governing structure including the Board of Directors, the Divisional Managers, Superintendents Committee, Works Council, and Works Committee of the Glacier Metal Company of England.

[43] Elton Mayo and G. F. F. Lombard, *Teamwork and Labor Turnover in the Aircraft Industry of Southern California* (Cambridge, Harvard University Press, 1944).

groups had declined. The table below shows that the old middle class composed of farmers, businessmen, and free professionals made up 85 per cent of the middle class population in 1870; by 1940 they had declined to 44 per cent. On the other hand, a new group of white-collar workers had risen. This new middle class is made up of managers, salaried profesionals, salespeople, and office workers. The table shows how this group arose from 15 per cent of the middle class in 1870 to 56 per cent in 1940.

THE OCCUPATIONAL CHANGES OF THE MIDDLE CLASSES IN THE
UNITED STATES FROM 1870 TO 1940

	1870	1940
Old Middle Class	85%	44%
Farmers	62	23
Businessmen	21	19
Free professional	2	2
New Middle Class	15%	56%
Managers	2	6
Salaried professionals	4	14
Salespeople	7	14
Office workers	2	22
Total Middle Classes	100%	100%

Source: C. Wright Mills, *op. cit.*, p. 65.

The old middle class rested on independent proprietorship; the new middle class rests on possession of specialized abilities and skills. The possession of a specialized skill—managerial, technical, or clerical—is the basis for attachment to an organization as a wage or salary worker. The tremendous productivity of mass-production technique and the application of mass organization are the underlying reasons for this shift.

At the top of the white-collar pyramid stands the manager. Today there are more managers in every sphere of modern society, and the managerial type of man has become more important in the total social structure. The corporation increasingly relies on a corps of professional administrators who operate the firm. These administrators lean heavily on technicians which include engineers, accountants, personnel, sales, and production specialists. The vast horde of office workers make and file the paper records which coordinate the specialized and integrated processes necessary for modern mass production.

The Rewards of Mass Production and Mass Organization

Although the history of industrialization reveals a history of cyclical depressions, labor unrest, and much social protest, few persons who have enjoyed the leisure and comforts of a prosperous industrial society wish to return to a nonindustrial way of life. The average work week has been short-

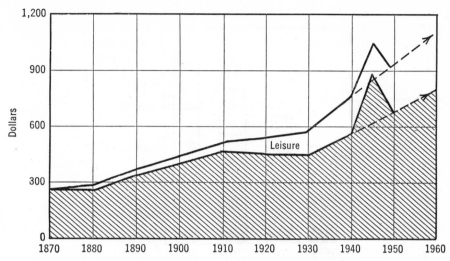

SOURCE: Wassily Leontief, "Machines and Man," *Scientific American*, Vol. 187 (September, 1952), p. 151.

INCOME PER CAPITA, MEASURED IN 1940 PRICES, AND EXCLUDING AGRICULTURE

Bottom curve is actual income per capita. Top curve is hypothetical income per capita that would have been produced on maintenance of 1870 hours of work.

ened from 67.2 hours in 1870 to 42.5 hours in 1950. Income per capita (measured in 1940 prices) increased from $230.60 in 1870 to $706.70 in 1950.[44] This means the work week was cut by more than a third while at the same time per capita income tripled in seventy years. These trends are shown in the figure above. The bottom curve is actual income per capita; the top curve is a hypothetical projection of per capita income that could have been produced by maintaining the hours of weekly work which prevailed in 1870.[45] The difference between the two curves shows the increasing leisure which is being made available by growing worker productivity.

Many observers have been impressed by the fact that the increase of per capita income has brought about a rise of a huge new moneyed middle class, that is, the burgeoning of family units with cash income after taxes of $4,000–$7,500. The number of family units with $4,000–$7,500 income has increased about 50 per cent since 1947, about 80 per cent since 1941, and about 230 per cent since 1929.[46] (Income figures are after taxes and after "inflation"; 1953 dollars are used throughout.) The figure on page 274 shows four family income groups; under $2,000, $2,000–$4,000, $4,000–$7,500,

[44] Wassily Leontief, "Machines and Man," *Scientific American*, Vol. 187 (September, 1952), p. 151.

[45] The hypothetical per capita output has been computed on the basis of the well-known Cobb-Douglass formula by Prof. Leontief.

[46] "The Rich Middle Income Class," *Fortune* (May, 1954), p. 95. Cf. Bureau of Census, *Current Population Reports*, Consumer Income Series P–60, No. 15 (Washington, Government Printing Office, April 27, 1954), p. 15.

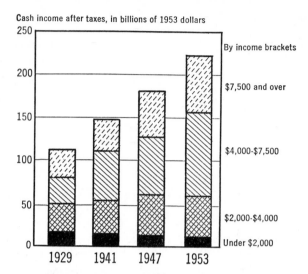

Cash income after taxes, in billions of 1953 dollars

By income brackets

$7,500 and over

$4,000-$7,500

$2,000-$4,000

Under $2,000

SOURCE: The Rich Middle Income Class, *Fortune* (May, 1954), p. 96.

INCOME COMPOSITION OF FAMILY UNITS IN THE UNITED STATES DURING 1929, 1941, 1947, AND 1953

and $7,500 and over. These respective income groups are shown for the years 1929, 1941, 1947, and 1953. The $4,000–$7,500 income class now comprises some 18 million farm and nonfarm family units and receives 42 per cent of all spendable income. This middle-income class should not be identified as the white-collar workers, for it is composed of families not only in white-collar occupations but, in fact, represents almost every occupation. This has been made increasingly possible because of higher wage returns for manual labor, and also because many of the family units (about two-fifths of the nonfarm families) have somebody in it beside the family head who is working. The occupational composition of the 15,500,000 middle-income nonfarm families is as follows.[47]

1. Nine million families headed by craftsmen, operatives, and laborers.
2. More than four million families headed by professionals, proprietors, and managers.
3. 2,400,000 family units headed by clerical and sales workers.
4. 100,000 family units deriving income from rents, royalties, annuities, stocks, and bonds.

These facts indicate that the fruits of industrialization are being widely distributed over the occupational groups in the United States.[48] Moreover,

[47] *Ibid.*, pp. 97–98.
[48] William F. Ogburn, "Technology and the Standard of Living in the United States," *American Journal of Sociology*, Vol. LX, No. 4 (January, 1955), pp. 380–386.

industry's productivity has been rising at about 3 per cent a year over the long pull. The future points to ever higher standards of living. The $4,000–$7,500 income group has a special significance, since this income class cannot only provide itself with all necessities for a high standard of living but can command many comforts or luxuries. To the businessman, this means a stability in marketing and the development of a large luxury market. To the political scientist, it means that new political appeals and voting trends may be expected. To the sociologist, it means new problems of juvenile delinquency, worker motivation and satisfaction, educational aspiration, and community organization.

Technology has with some marked exceptions (11 per cent of nonfarm families have less than $2,000 a year) made possible a comfortable life for most Americans. Twentieth-century man commands energy, goods, and leisure. With these resources he can rebuild the face of civilization. Our great technology is a two-edged sword ready to destroy man or reward him with great victories over nature. The decision rests with the puny creature with the oversized brain who rose to become tool maker.

SUMMARY

1. Man has achieved a dominant position over animals because he has learned to produce tools and techniques and to transmit his achievements from generation to generation.

2. The bulk of technology is simply an assortment of tools, operations, and techniques which extend the power of human muscles or refine the perception of the human senses.

3. The Industrial Revolution has been accomplished by the invention of prime movers and machine tools, the use of inanimate or mineral energy, and the transformation of matter by chemical processes.

4. Two important indices of the advance of technology are the rate of invention and the amount of energy consumed. Both of these indices now stand at very high levels.

5. Four major stages in the evolution of modern technology may be identified as the modern craft age, the machine age, the power age, and the atomic age. Each age has left a technical heritage which remains in various forms even as the new emerges and becomes dominant. Each age is distinguished by significant changes in power, tools, work skills, materials, transportation, and communication.

6. Future changes in technology may be predicted to rise upon the increased use of atomic energy, the development of the automatic factory, and the growing use of jet airplane, helicopter, and rocket.

7. Technological changes may be observed to occur at differential rates between industries and within a given industry creating various lags and leads.

8. Modern technology was accompanied by the invention of mass production and the creation of mass markets. Mass markets brought revolutionary changes in society. A market society emerged in which social relations became embedded in economic relations.

9. Mass production became a principle not only of organizing technical operations but also a principle of social organization. Office and factory, molded to

the requirements of scientific management, evolved into an ever larger bureaucracy.

10. The mass production principle broke up the status system based on an age-grade structure.

11. The large enterprise has emerged as the representative social institution. The principles of mass production and mass organization can be utilized in their fullest proportions through the specialization which large-scale organization permits.

12. The firm has been drawn into an increasing range of responsibilities including economic, political, and social functions.

13. A transformation of the middle class has occurred that involves a transition from property to occupation in which specialized skill—managerial, technical, or clerical—is the basis for attachment to an organization.

14. The increasing productivity of industrial organization has brought about a marked increase in the standard of living which has been widely distributed among all occupational groups.

ANNOTATED BIBLIOGRAPHY

Automation and Technological Change. Report of the Sub Committee on Economic Stabilization to the Joint Committee on the Economic Report (Washington, Government Printing Office, 1955). Reports on the social effects observed and predicted for increased automation in the United States.

AYRES, Eugene, and SCARLOTT, Charles A., *Energy Sources—The Wealth of the World* (New York, McGraw-Hill, 1952). Carefully written; a valuable reference.

BEAN, Nevin, *Soviet Machine Age, Automation in Russia* (Deadborn, Michigan, Ford Motor Company, Department of Public Relations, 1956). A first-hand report of a visit by three American engineering executives from Ford Motor Company, Westinghouse Electric Corporation, and Bendix Aviation Corporation, describing in nontechnical language advances in automation as seen in Russian factories during the fall of 1955.

CHASE, Stuart, *Men and Machines* (New York, Macmillan, 1929). This popularly written book has many suggestive insights. It is an introductory book recommended for its interesting style.

DRUCKER, Peter, *The New Society* (New York, Harper, 1950). Emphasizes mass production as the great revolutionary principle of industry and traces its influence as a technical element and as a way of organizing people to work together.

FORBES, R. J., *Man the Maker, A History of Technology and Engineering* (New York, Shuman 1950). Good coverage of the history of technology and engineering from man's earliest efforts as a maker of tools to the present.

GIEDION, S., *Mechanization Takes Command* (New York, Oxford University Press, 1948). Traces the manner in which mechanization has come to pervade the pattern of our life and discusses its impact on individual and collective living.

HOOVER, Edgar M., *The Location of Economic Activity* (New York, McGraw-Hill, 1948). Describes factors responsible for location of economic activity.

LILLEY, S., *Men, Machines, and History* (London, Cobbett Press, 1948). This history of technology singles out the most important inventions and describes their significance.

MAYO, Elton, *The Social Problems of an Industrial Society* (Cambridge, Harvard

University Press, 1945). A sociological reinterpretation of the famous Hawthorne industrial research studies which Mayo directed.

MILLS, C. Wright, *White Collar: The American Middle Class* (New York, Oxford University Press, 1951). Describes transformation of America from a rural to an urban society with accompanying changes in the middle class.

MUMFORD, Lewis, *The Culture of Cities* (New York, Harcourt, Brace, 1938). A companion volume to *Technics and Civilization* (Harcourt, Brace, 1934), this book is a history of cities and an analysis of the social processes that have attended their growth.

POLANYI, Karl, *The Great Transformation* (New York, Rinehart, 1944). The thesis set forth is that man's economy is usually submerged in his social relations but that the market economy of the 19th century produced a society which was submerged in the economic system.

A Program of Nuclear Power. Report Presented to Parliament by the Lord President of the Council, Cmd. 9389 (London, Her Majesty's Stationery Office, 1955). An authoritative statement of the governmental program for the development of nuclear power in Great Britain.

SOLOW, Herbert, "Automation: News Behind the Noise," *Fortune* (April, 1956), pp. 150–153, 160–170. A good summary of current developments in automation covering such areas as auto manufacture, various light industries, chemical industry, and electronic computation. Well-illustrated.

Special Issue on "Automatic Control," *Scientific American*, Vol. 187 (September, 1952). Various articles by experts describe the progress in the application of automatic control to industry.

WIENER, Norbert, *The Human Use of Human Beings* (Boston, Houghton Mifflin, 1950). This book by the author of *Cybernetics*, forecasts another industrial revolution based on automatic machinery and control systems.

WOYTINSKY, W. S., and WOYTINSKY, E. S., *World Population and Production* (New York, Twentieth Century Fund, 1953). This is a monumental source book of world needs and resources covering population, energy, raw materials, agriculture, industry and trade. Gives an excellent coverage of the United States followed by a treatment of each subject in other parts of the world.

CHAPTER 12

INFLUENCE OF TECHNOLOGY ON COMMUNICATIONS AND TRANSPORTATION

■ *Francis R. Allen*

> *Our generation has seen the development of moving—then moving and talking—pictures, of wireless transmission used for telegraph, telephone, and voice broadcasting; of airplane transport; of offset and color printing. Together they have changed the character of mass communication, . . . bringing the remote corners of the world within a few hours of one another.*
>
> COMMISSION ON FREEDOM OF THE PRESS, *A Free and Responsible Press* (1947)

The Communications-Transportation Revolution

Impressive as has been the technological influence on industry and on other fields (some of which will be discussed in following chapters), there is no more striking example of the effect of technology in causing social change than in the realm of communications and transportation. Changes in the latter fields have caused a basic modification of the social world in which man lives. They have brought into being entire new outlooks, have quickened the pace of living, and have made advisable or necessary many important social adjustments. Since human interaction is largely communicative interaction—in fact, social life cannot exist in the absence of communication[1] —it is not unreasonable to suppose that major changes in the communica-

[1] Edward Sapir, "Communication," article in the *Encyclopaedia of the Social Sciences* (New York, Macmillan, 1931), Vol. IV, pp. 78–80; Joyce O. Hertzler, *Society in Action* (New York, Dryden, 1954), pp. 64–65. Society itself, declared Sapir, is not a static structure but is a "highly intricate network of partial or complete understandings between the members of organizational units of every degree of size and complexity, . . ."

tions process might be followed by important changes in society itself. Much evidence on this score will be presented in this chapter.

Over the centuries the field of communication, which is generally defined as *the transmission of meanings through the use of symbols,* has had a tremendous development. Beginning with the simplest forms—the spoken or written word, gesture, grimace, intonation of voice—it has had the additional influences of the telephone,[2] telegraph, loud speaker, the press, magazines, the motion picture,[3] radio and television,[4] to say nothing of other specialized devices as blinking lights, sirens, bugle calls, and stock-exchange tickers. In its human involvement, communication extends over the range from the howling of an infant trying to attract the attention of its mother to conversations between family members; to the exchange of ideas and understandings between members of a corporation, college or university group, church, or governmental department; or to the interchange of thoughts and proposals between the representatives of nations which may affect most of the people living in the world.

The influence of technology on communications may even include developments designed to *stop* communication from occurring under certain conditions. Thus a device known as "Conelrad" (control of electromagnetic radiation) was placed in operation in 1953 in the United States. It prevents the emitting of sounds (speaking, etc.) from radiating equipment such as the radio which could be used during wartime as a "beam'" to guide enemy aircraft, submarines, or radio-controlled missiles. Such an unintended communication with hostile military forces might have disastrous consequences. Use of the "Conelrad" plan permits standard radio broadcasting stations to remain on the air—hence being able to broadcast civil defense and other official information to the public—without giving away to the enemy the locations of cities or radio-TV installations or transmitting information outside of a certain area.[5]

Transportation, also basic to social life, is frequently linked with communication, since many vehicles of transportation serve at the same time as means of communication; moreover, communication channels often provide news which suggests motivations for travel—and vice versa. The means of transportation have likewise evolved from the simple to the complex. Land

---

[2] The extent of use of the telephone in the United States, whether for life-saving or trivial purposes, is indicated in the fact that a total of approximately 186 million local telephone calls were made *every day* (on the average) during 1954; an average of over 6 million long-distance calls were made *every day* during that year. About 53 million telephones were then in use in this nation. *21st Annual Report of the Federal Communications Commission,* for the fiscal year 1955 (Washington, Government Printing Office, 1956), pp. 38–39.

[3] See discussion in Chapter 7.

[4] See discussion in Chapter 8.

[5] *19th Annual Report of the Federal Communications Commission,* 1953, pp. 25–26; *21st Annual Report,* 1955, pp. 27–28.

transportation, for example, has developed from muscle power to the use of horse, oxen, or other animal (including riding in a chariot, buggy, wagon, stagecoach, etc.); bicycle; railroad; electric streetcar (trolley); subway or or elevated trains as used in large cities; and the motor vehicle (automobile, truck, and bus).[6] The wheel, basic for many vehicles of transportation, was one of the foremost inventions of the early period of human history.[7] Water transportation has similarly evolved from the simple canoe or other small boat all the way to the modern diesel-powered ocean liner. Wiedenfeld has observed that in the total development of the various kinds of transportation, the forces of nature have gradually lost their controlling power. Of great significance for all transportation was the spanning of distances, however long, in regular scheduled operations whose duration could be calculated in advance;[8] as this was achieved one could say that distance was being conquered.

The revolution in *speed* of transportation is worthy of special mention. Comparing travel in the United States during the 1800–1815 period with that of today, one observes that at the former time a trip from Boston to New York by stagecoach (then the fastest means of land travel) consumed an estimated total of 74 hours; overnight stops were necessary at Worcester, Hartford, and Stamford. By 1825 the route had been shortened, and the journey was completed in 41 hours; one overnight stop was then required.[9] During the 1950's the same trip via railroad is made in about four hours;[10] use of automobile may require somewhat more than that depending on the driver and his automobile. A Boston-to-New York flight during early 1956 via scheduled airline travel required precisely one hour![11] Hence the time required for this trip was reduced from approximately 74 hours in 1800–1815 to one hour in 1956. Presented in chart form in Chapter 3 is the trend of maximum speed of human travel (expressed in miles per hour) since 1800.

[6] Chapple and Coon classify the means of land transportation in terms of three sources of power: (a) human muscle, (b) animal muscle, and (c) power of natural forces through the agency of machines.—E. D. Chapple and C. S. Coon, *Principles of Anthropology* (New York, Holt, 1942), p. 198.

[7] R. J. Forbes, *Man the Maker, A History of Technology and Engineering* (New York, Schuman, 1950), pp. 34–35. It was a considerable step, however, from a rolling cylinder (as a log) to an axle with a wheel attached to either end, as used on a wagon or automobile.

[8] Kurt Wiedenfeld, "Transportation," article in the *Encyclopedia of the Social Sciences* (New York, Macmillan, 1934), Vol. XV, p. 84.

[9] George Rogers Taylor, *The Transportation Revolution, 1815–1860,* Vol. IV, *The Economic History of the United States* (New York, Rinehart, 1951), p. 142.

[10] During 1954 the fastest, scheduled, Boston-to-New York run on the New York, New Haven & Hartford Railroad is stated to be 3 hours and 55 minutes. A new-style, lightweight train (the "Talgo") has made the trip in 2 hours and 30 minutes. See timetable, New York, New Haven & Hartford Railroad; also see "Railroads Eye the Talgo," *New York Times,* July 4, 1954; "Light Trains," *ibid.,* Sec. 3, Sunday, September 4, 1955; and Francis Bello, "Lightweight Trains—At Last," *Fortune* (July, 1955), pp. 110–113.

[11] Timetable, Eastern Air Lines.

The Mass Media of Communications

Just as the invention of the automobile led to the development of mass transportation, so certain technological innovations in communications introduced the phenomenon of mass communications. The term *mass media* of communications has not always been identically defined by different writers, though there is little dispute as to the principal forms of these media. Leigh has defined mass media as "communication which extends immediately beyond face-to-face contact between the two or more persons communicating. It implies for the recipients a certain disembodiment of the communicator and for the communicator an unseen audience."[12] Klapper has defined it as "all media of communication in which a mechanism of impersonal reproduction intervenes between speaker and audience."[13] In other instances the numerical connotations of the word mass are stressed, so that the chief meaning implied is that the media reach a large number of people. Schramm holds that the essential idea is that a communications organization (newspaper, broadcasting station, etc.) is the source, and the message is sent out in many identical and simultaneous copies.[14] In practical usage, in any case, the mass media are generally asumed to comprise the press, magazines, the motion picture, radio, television, and books.[15]

Exposure to the mass media. The exposure of the American public to the major mass media, excepting television, has been appraised by Berelson. He states:[16]

About 25–30 per cent of the adult population reads one or more *books* a month;

About 45–50 per cent of the adult population sees a *motion picture* once every two weeks or oftener;

About 60–70 per cent of the adult population reads one or more *magazines* more or less regularly;

[12] Robert D. Leigh, "The Mass Communications Inventions and International Relations," in William F. Ogburn, ed., *Technology and International Relations* (Chicago, University of Chicago Press, 1949), p. 126.

[13] Joseph T. Klapper, *The Effects of Mass Media* (New York, Bureau of Applied Social Research, Columbia University, 1949), Introduction, p. 3.

[14] Wilbur Schramm, letter to F. R. Allen dated January 15, 1955.

[15] For general discussion, the following are recommended: Noel P. Gist, "Communication," Ch. 19 in Seba Eldridge and Associates, *Fundamentals of Sociology* (New York, Crowell, 1950); and George A. Lundberg, Clarence C. Schrag, Otto N. Larsen, *Sociology* (New York, Harper, 1954), Ch. 13, "Mass Communication and Public Opinion."

[16] Bernard Berelson, *The Library's Public* (New York, Columbia University Press, 1949), p. 6.

See also Angus Campbell and Charles A. Metzner, "Books, Libraries, and Other Media of Communication," in Daniel Katz, Dorwin Cartwright, S. Eldersveld, and A. L. Lee, eds., *Public Opinion and Propaganda, A Book of Readings* (New York, Dryden, 1954), pp. 235–242.

About 85–90 per cent of the adult population reads one or more *newspapers* more or less regularly;

About 90–95 per cent of the adult population listens to the *radio* fifteen minutes a day or more.

It is clear that in this exposure people will differ greatly in their reactions-to and influence-derived-from the experience. They may "half read" the newspaper or "half listen" to the radio (partly preoccupied with something else), or they may intently read the news or closely follow the radio program. In some instances, reading a certain book might constitute a major event in the lives of some people; witnessing some movie or television program might possibly have prime importance for some individuals also. The differential results will be related to differences in people's intelligence, their interest in the subject presented, their education, time available, and other factors; it will also be related to the content and the quality of the media program. This was observed some years ago by Walter Lippman.[17]

Newer media; reach; accessibility; role. Certain conclusions may be made regarding the social (as apart from individual) significance of the use of mass-communications media.[18] First, the increase in types of mass media that have appeared since the development of the early hand press may be regarded as phenomenal. The advent of power printing presses, radio, motion picture, television, facsimile and other electronic devices, are remarkable developments. The process of communication has had vast changes. Second, the increasing *reach* of the new media has also been phenomenal. It has been estimated that about 15,000 persons heard Lincoln deliver in 1864 his "Gettysburg Address"—generally regarded as one of the great public addresses of all time.[19] Some seventy-five years later, however, Franklin D. Roosevelt spoke at Gettysburg before an estimated audience of 150,000 people—who heard him by means of a loud-speaker system. Indeed, it is likely that a greater proportion of the audience actually heard Roosevelt's voice (with the amplifier system used) than heard Lincoln even though the former's audience was ten times as large. But even this Roosevelt talk at Gettysburg had a small audience as compared with many of his coast-to-coast radio broadcasts. While the audiences here were unseen, it has been estimated that on each of ten occasions Mr. Roosevelt addressed a total audience of more than 40 million people.[20] Presidents Truman and Eisenhower, making addresses

[17] Walter Lippman, *Public Opinion* (New York, Macmillan, 1922; Pelican Edition published in 1946).

For more recent material on this general subject, see Wilbur Schramm, ed., *The Process and Effects of Mass Communication* (Urbana, University of Illinois Press, 1954), pp. 29–47, 56–67, 109–114.

[18] Unless otherwise stated, these are generally summarized from Leigh, *op. cit.,* pp. 130–131.

[19] W. Norwood Brigance, "Effectiveness of the Public Platform," *Annals of the American Academy of Political and Social Science,* Vol. 250 (March, 1947), p. 75.

[20] Leonard W. Doob, *Public Opinion and Propaganda* (New York, Holt, 1948), p. 481. Doob refers in turn to William C. Ackerman, "The Dimensions of American Broadcasting," *Public Opinion Quarterly,* Vol. 9 (Spring, 1945), pp. 7, 10.

over nation-wide radio and television hook-ups, have presumably had similar-sized or larger audiences. The possibility, therefore, of reaching and influencing huge audiences by use of the new mass media when delivering one address is a development of the last few decades.[21] Enormous audiences are tapped by the movies and other media too. It has been estimated that Shakespeare's play *Hamlet,* though presented, studied, and debated for more than three centuries, was probably seen by more people in the form of the movie production of 1948 (starring Laurence Olivier) than on the stage throughout its entire history.[22] The mass media, in short, reach giant-sized audiences and possess enormous potentiality for affecting people.

Related to their tremendous reach is their easy accessibility. Owing to the large number of radio and television sets in use (see Chapter 8), the delivery of daily newspaper to one's very doorstep or to nearby place where they may be purchased, to the fact that motion picture theatres are likely to be only a short ride away, it is most easy to have contact with these media if one has any interest at all.

There seems to be little doubt that the mass media have an important social role as dispensers of information. Considering the vast array of information and commentary which is issued and the extent of public exposure, this must be regarded as no small item.[23] While this statement applies chiefly to the United States, it is thought to be generally valid elsewhere in the Western world and in various other nations as well. Public-opinion researchers sometimes disclose "islands of ignorance" concerning certain subjects, and they suggest that the American public still is not particularly well informed concerning various issues of the day despite this exposure.[24] But this is believed to reflect in large part the educational level of the American people.[25] Certainly the volume of news and information presented in newspapers, magazines, over the radio, and on the TV screen is impressive and it seems beyond reasonable doubt that the state of public information has been markedly advanced as a result of this media.

Different subjects again are the importance of the mass media in relation

[21] This may be contrasted with the across-the-nation tour of President Woodrow Wilson during 1920, at which time he was seeking to promote sentiment in favor of the League of Nations. Under present-day conditions he would have undoubtedly remained in Washington and delivered one or two radio or television coast-to-coast broadcasts.

[22] Curtiss D. MacDougall, *Understanding Public Opinion* (New York, Macmillan, 1952), p. 473.

[23] Robin Williams, Jr., *American Society* (New York, Knopf, 1951), p. 267.

[24] See Bernard Berelson, "Democratic Theory and Public Opinion," *Public Opinion Quarterly,* Vol. 16, No. 3 (Fall, 1952), pp. 318–319.

[25] For example, it is reported in the Census of 1950 that 46.9 per cent of the American people age 25 and over had eight years of schooling *or less.* The *median* school years completed for all the American people age 25 and over amounted to 9.3 years.— Bureau of the Census, *U. S. Census of Population: 1950.* Vol. II, *Characteristics of the Population,* Part 1, U. S. Summary, Chapter B (Washington, Government Printing Office, 1952), p. 96.

(*a*) to the ongoing of social life and the maintenance of social controls; and (*b*) to the influence on people's attitudes and behavior. Discussion will be devoted to these subjects later in the chapter.

SOCIAL EFFECTS

On the Nature of Human Contacts

An initial observation is that the increasing use of the mass-communications inventions has brought more and more formal, impersonal, "secondary" (to use Cooley's term) contacts between people. During earlier days dominated by the primary group, life contacts were largely of the personal, face-to-face sort; one dealt mostly with people whom one knew well, often with persons whose family one had known for many years. Now, one's attention was to be increasingly drawn to persons with whom one has no personal relationship at all, often whom one had never seen: national political figures, scientific authorities, radio and television commentators and entertainers, and others. Such personalities, then, became a part of one's social world if one elected to be exposed to the media. They were sometimes imitated, especially by youth. For some individuals in large cities or elsewhere deprived of significant primary group contacts, the secondary contacts might far outweigh the volume of personal relationships of life.

On the Extension of Social Horizons

The mass-communications media, along with such transportation vehicles as the automobile and airplane, also brought a significant broadening of social horizons and of interests to many people. Before the era of mass communications and transportation, the ideas and behavior of people were largely related to the immediate local community. Their whole "social world," which gave them their interests, contacts, experiences, and possibilities of behavior, was centered in their town. In the era of radio-TV-movies-automobiles-airplanes, however, it is possible, if not probable, to have one's main residence in such a community, but, in addition have many interests, contacts, and real or vicarious experiences in other parts of the country or world. Thus millions of people will have seen press photos or motion pictures (giving an accurate or distorted account) of life in large cities, small hamlets, mountain surroundings, life on the desert; life in England, France, the tropics, Alaska, Italy, Switzerland. They will have heard radio reports or seen TV showings of meetings of world statesmen; the coronation of the Queen of England; destructive typhoons in Japan; news of a war in Korea, Indo-China, or elsewhere; crime investigations; explosion of a hydrogen bomb; and hundreds of other events. With the use of modern transportation there is an increasing chance, moreover, that they will have traveled to the area in question. Large numbers of people, in short, have become cosmopolitan-minded, less locally-oriented. There are both class and individual differences, to be sure, in exposure to the communications media and in extent of travel.[26] In the trend toward regionally, nationally, and globally oriented behavior and interests, people have become increasingly aware of nations and their inhabitants previously thought to be "far-away, strange places"—Korea, China, Turkey, French Morocco, Bolivia, the Belgium Congo.[27]

On the Growth of Public Opinion

In view of the outpouring of information and commentary on people and places coming from the various media, it should not occasion much surprise that people have more ideas and opinions regarding the happenings of the world. A related trend to the development of the mass media was the increase in schooling achieved in the United States and an accompanying decrease in illiteracy. The latter was, of course, a factor in the increase in newspaper and magazine circulations and exposure to the other media. These developments together caused an increase in the force of public opinion. For example, millions of people had seen the President of the United States—also rival political leaders—on the movie or television screen. Many had heard their speeches over the radio or read them in the newspapers. Naturally they had added interest in political occurences. Having liked (or disliked) Roosevelt, Truman, Dewey, Eisenhower, and others, they had more active opinions concerning public figures of the day. The degree of interest varied unquestionably from individual to individual; some felt swamped by the vast outpouring of daily news and became apathetic to all happenings.[28] It seems entirely reasonable to believe that the force of public opinion has vastly increased, in general, during the modern era, and that such increase may be directly explained by the remarkable growth of the press, radio, television, and other media.

On the Tempo of Life

If one were to compare an American community of given size around 1850 with one of similar size today, the latter would unquestionably have a

[26] See, for example, Paul F. Lazarsfeld, "Communications Research," in Wayne Dennis, ed., *Current Trends in Social Psychology* (Pittsburgh, University of Pittsburgh Press, 1949), pp. 233–248; Wilbur Schramm and David M. White, "Age, Education, Economic Status: Factors in Newspaper Reading," *Journalism Quarterly*, Vol. XXVI (June, 1949), pp. 155–157.

[27] There is undoubtedly a continuum of locally-oriented versus broadly-oriented behavior. Some people in every community are largely local-minded, even in the mass-communications and transportation age. It is suggested here that the proportion of locally-oriented people in the total population has tended to decrease in the modern mass-media age.

[28] Berelson, *op. cit.*, p. 319; Lundberg and others, *op. cit.*, pp. 492–493.

more rapid tempo of activities. The difference, it is suggested, would be largely owing to the influence of the modern communications and transportation inventions. On the city streets of today the influence of the motor vehicle is felt, bringing a "zip," "hustle," and "get-going" spirit which has replaced the leisurely pace of 1850 when Old Dobbin trudged along. Underground (in large cities) the subways whizz along their tracks, occasionally stopping long enough for passengers to stream out and others to dash aboard. Overhead airplanes occasionally speed by; in the case of jets one has to look quickly or the plane will have streaked across the sky and will be out of sight. The tempo-increasing qualities of the communications inventions are more indirect; but speedy telegraph and telephone service, the rapid communication of such devices as "Ultrafax," and the up-to-the-minute news flashes of radio and television all contribute to a faster pace of the modern social world. Indeed, the accelerated pace of living in large cities—the omnipresent stimuli, continued "keying-up," and inevitable development of tensions—may be regarded as a problem of modern metropolitan culture. While the rapid media "flashes" regarding what has just occurred in London, Tokyo, Buenos Aires, are no doubt as desirable as the swift-moving, motor-vehicle traffic along the boulevards, nevertheless the heightened tempo and general urban overstimulation probably needs to be kept under control somehow.

On the Rate of Social Change

Modern communications media tend, in different ways, both to accelerate and to retard social change. Just as the tempo of life has been accelerated by these media, so the diffusion of both material and nonmaterial culture traits has been increased. One may compare, for example, the slow diffusion of making and use of bronze between roughly 3500 and 1800 B.C. with the making of atom bombs during the late 1940's. The former required approximately 1,700 years in spreading from western Asia to central and northern Europe.[29] The first atom bomb, made in the United States, was exploded experimentally during July, 1945, and two bombs were used against Japan during August of that year. Spreading of the bomb-making technology (despite efforts to keep it secret) was so rapid that the Russians were able to explode an A-bomb during September, 1949; much of the base knowledge of atomic energy was the common property of all physical scientists, while some of the most secret aspects were learned by spies. This example, it is true, applies to an elite war weapon, for the production of which there was intense competition among the leading world powers. General peacetime culture items also tend to be spread rapidly during modern times, however: articles of clothing; material objects such as typewriters, automobiles, sewing machines, contraceptives; certain customs; even linguistic phrases. The larger number of modern travelers aids in this diffusion. Books, magazines, news-

[29] A. L. Kroeber, *Anthropology,* rev. ed. (New York, Harcourt, Brace, 1948), p. 700.

papers, radio, television, the movies, are important factors in the process. Present-day diffusion does not necessarily take place from one nation to adjacent ones—thanks to the radio and movies. An idea broadcast over the radio in New York may be received in Brazil, Egypt, China, or innermost Africa. Fashions broadcast from Paris may be instantly known in the United States and elsewhere. Motion pictures may especially aid in the diffusion of particular culture items, such as women's hair styles and clothing. The various media and travelers are likely to reinforce each other in causing certain items to be diffused. One should perceive, furthermore, that such an acceleration of diffusion tends, in turn, to cause an increase in the invention rate in the receiving country; this was observed in Chapter 3. On both counts the rate of social change is thus increased.[30]

It should be clear with regard to the above process that the modern use of the mass media does not merely bring an acceleration of news diffusion in relation to countries with which there has been previous contact. Entire new areas might be tapped by either communications or transportation media (for example, radio, airplane) with which there had previously been little or no contact. Hence new influences and reactions might conceivably be set in motion.

The process of change is speeded up in still another way. The rapid transmission of news events (for example, the ratification of a treaty by several nations) occurs with use of radio and other media. Consequences of the event are immediately considered by other nations. Resulting actions or moves to combat the effects of the first one may be soon formulated. If thorny problems develop, leading statesmen may fly thousands of miles for immediate conferences. Other agreements are made; other nations are likely to react to them. In such a chain of occurrences, reactions, ensuing developments, it is clear that use of the modern communications and transportation inventions brings an acceleration of the process of social change. If an important treaty had been signed in 1850, on the other hand, news of the event would scarcely have reached some parts of the world for several months. Then news of reactions to the event (if any) would have taken several months to reach other continents; immediate conferences between statesmen living in distant parts of the world would have been out of the question. The whole process would be considerably slower.

On the other hand, the observation has been rather widely made, as noted in Chapter 7, that the communications media also tend to retard social

[30] Thus one might formulate the hypothesis that the greater the number of different kinds of societies with which a given society is in contact, the greater will be the rate of social change. Or one might state that improvements in the communications and transportation media are likely to bring an acceleration in the process of cultural and social change. Or one might further hypothesize that improvements in communications and transportation will affect the rate of social change in an area more than will changes in other aspects of technology; the latter has been briefly suggested in Ronald Freedman, Amos H. Hawley, Werner S. Landecker, and Horace M. Miner, *Principles of Sociology* (New York, Holt, 1952), p. 6.

change. The reason for this is that movie, radio, and television productions are expensive, and they require large audiences if the venture is to be financially profitable. In attempting to attract mass audiences, the media have found it expedient to concentrate on majority viewpoints on social issues. Thus minority, alternative views tend to be de-emphasized or ignored. Logical as this may be from the financial viewpoint, it tends to reinforce the majority, status quo attitudes. New or alternative ideas tend to be retarded in their advancement. The net result of the mass communications and transportation inventions, in view of these accelerating and retarding influences, is probably to bring an over-all acceleration in the process of social change; but further study needs to be made of this subject.

On Migration, Internal and International

The communications and transportation media have provided the basis for one of the remarkable occurrences of modern times, namely, the large amount of migration which takes place. This is assumed to include both temporary or seasonal travel and permanent changes of residence. The means of travel are, of course, provided by the transportation vehicles. The automobile has made the American people mobile-minded. Some families, frequently on the move, live permanently in a trailer. Travel by bus and railroad has considerable volume, and long distance travel makes increasing use of the airplane, as pointed out in Chapter 9.

Motivations for wanting to migrate undoubtedly develop via the various sources of communication. There seems little reason to doubt that a close relationship exists between the tremendous amount of migration year after year in the United States and the communications and transportation facilities.[31] Permanent migrations often involve "push" and "pull" factors—dissatisfactions with the old environment, attractions of the new. Contact with the communications media is especially related to learning of the new.

International migration is similarly dependent on the communications media and on the prevailing modes of travel; between continents ship travel is naturally of more consequence, while air travel is increasing. Whether the migration be internal or international, it is fundamental in changing the number and composition of the population. This itself may be of great significance and may give rise to further changes in community facilities for youth, old people, racial groups, and others, as well to necessitate a larger water supply, extensions of police and fire protection, expansion of schools, and other services.

[31] See Warren S. Thompson, *Population Problems,* 4th ed. (New York, McGraw-Hill, 1953), Chs. 13–14; Paul H. Landis and Paul K. Hatt, *Population Problems,* 2nd ed. (New York, American Book, 1954), pp. 410–412; Rupert B. Vance, *All These People* (Chapel Hill, University of North Carolina Press, 1946), Chs. 9–10; and T. Lynn Smith, *Population Analysis* (New York, McGraw-Hill, 1948), Part IV.

Courtesy of International Cooperation Administration

ACCELERATED DIFFUSION DURING THE 1950'S

An official of the (U. S.) International Cooperation Administration (left) shows Austrian electrical engineers the rotor of a turbine generator at the General Electric Company plant, Schenectady, New York. This practice of inviting foreign experts to a nation and showing them technical processes which may then be applied in their home countries may be regarded as "the new diffusion."

On Business and Industry

The effects of the communications and transportation inventions on business and industry will be discussed briefly, since the subject has been partly covered in Chapters 6–9. First, these inventions have provided means for conducting and controlling business in large-scale ways. The factor of transportation has been mentioned in connection with urban-industrial growth. In many respects, business and industry could scarcely be conducted along modern lines if the use of such inventions as the telephone, telegraph, automobile, truck, van, dictaphone, typewriter, and other devices was suddenly withdrawn from the business world. Aviation is becoming increasingly valuable for business. Little by little, business operations have become dependent on the use of these devices; the sensitive business-industrial mechanism would be lost without them.

The mass-communications media, especially the press, radio, and television, are prominently used for business and industrial *advertising*. Although the functions and effects of advertising are many, one may at least make the minimum assertion that advertising promotes a dynamic, expanding economy. It aids significantly in the sale and distribution of goods which have been mass-produced by modern industrial methods. There is an important parallel, indeed, between the growth of advertising (and advertising media) and the growth of industry and of mass markets; this is no little subject in itself. Modern advertising constitutes a large volume of business. MacDougall[32] declares, for example, that during 1947 Americans spent $1,019,707,000 in subscribing to 10,282 newspapers and 4,610 magazines, but that this amount was only 35 per cent of the total income of these publications; the balance was derived from the sale of advertising space. With few exceptions newspapers and magazines would either cease to exist without advertising income or would be drastically reduced in size. The total volume of radio and television advertising assumes stupendous proportions.

Finally, it should not be forgotten that the developing fields of communication and transportation have included the growth of some of America's largest business enterprises. Mention has been made in Chapters 6 and 9 of the huge industrial corporations connected with producing motor vehicles, airplanes, and related commodities. Some of these corporations are among the leading ones of American industry; indeed the leader itself—the General Motors Corporation—is among the group. Other commanding corporations in the communications-transportation fields include the Bell Telephone System (and its parent company, the American Telephone & Telegraph Company[33]); various huge railway organizations such as the Pennsylvania Railroad, New York Central, Southern Pacific, Atchison, Topeka & Santa Fe, and Union Pacific;[34] many large newspaper and magazine organizations (too numerous to mention); many large book-publishing firms; large radio and television corporations such as Radio Corporation of America, Philco, and Zenith; and motion-picture giants such as Paramount, Metro-Goldwyn-Mayer, Twentieth-Century-Fox, and Warner Brothers. In many instances the above industries are also linked with other large-scale enterprises, just as automobile production is related to the gasoline, rubber, and steel industries.

On Political Behavior

It is frequently stated that the day of the "new political persuasion" has ar-arrived, meaning the use of mass-communications media. While there has

---

[32] Curtis D. MacDougall, *Understanding Public Opinion* (New York, Macmillan, 1952), pp. 655–656. The data on subscriptions was collected by *Printers' Ink*.

[33] This is the leading corporation in the utility field as of the end of 1955 as listed by *Fortune* magazine. See *Fortune,* Supplement (July, 1956), p. 16, "The Fifty Largest Utilities."

[34] These are the five leading U. S. transportation companies in the order given, rated on the basis of operating revenues during 1955 by *Fortune. Ibid.,* p. 14, "The Fifty Largest Transportation Companies."

been much discussion in the past about the power of propaganda, the propaganda menace, and so on,[35] the present-day view tends to point to both the difficulty of gauging this influence and the paucity of empirical data regarding the effects of propaganda use. It is granted that in a nation like the United States propaganda barrages bombard the people from all sides; it is apparent that 40 million people may just as easily be addressed over radio or TV by temperate, enlightened statesmen or by highly-emotional, inflamatory propagandists. The media themselves are merely neutral devices.

The rise of propaganda during modern times has apparently *not* caused any wholesale bending of attitudes and of public opinion generally to the will of propagandists. The delivery of speeches in support of (or opposed to) a certain farm policy, a regional power policy, racial segregation or desegregation, has not had the effect of mass conversion to the views of the propagandists. Thus man does not seem to be putty in the hands of skillful propagandists. On the other hand, propaganda does have some effect; it is not a negligible influence. The speeches of a Father Coughlin, a Senator McCarthy, a Hitler or Goebbels may be followed enthusiastically by millions of listeners. While listeners have often been previously conditioned toward a speaker's views, hence are already "receptive" in attitude, they may be influenced further and their active enthusiasm may be rekindled. Individuals wavering on a subject may, moreover, be influenced in one direction or another. If 40 million persons composing a media audience hear an aggression-inciting address on some subject, the net effect on public opinion *may be* considerable. Some of the listeners will themselves hold positions of power in community or nation and may wield an extra weighty influence on public opinion and on the making of decisions; this differential influence of people has been ably pointed out by Blumer.[36] Irrespective of the question of whether or not people are converted to new views (how many people, under what circumstances, etc.), it appears correct to suppose that public support is often gained for programs and social actions may be effected. This is itself an item of considerable importance.

It would not seem correct, for example, to have a low estimate of the social importance of Hitler's propaganda rantings in Germany during the 1930's. The media influence, along with use of force and other influences, did after all unite the German people under the National Socialist leadership. Germany's aggressive policy led to a large-scale war, which the German soldiers and home front did their mightiest to win; and it was only after expending tremendous cost in blood and treasure that the Allies prevented this from happening. World War II and its effects may scarcely be regarded as a trivial incident of history. While the Nazi program and beliefs were partly

[35] For example, Frederick E. Lumley, *The Propaganda Menace* (New York, Appleton-Century-Crofts, 1933).

[36] Herbert Blumer, "Public Opinion and Public Opinion Polling," *American Sociological Review,* Vol. 13 (October, 1948), pp. 542–554.

based on the earlier ideas of Hegel, Nietzsche, and other German writers, it is clear that the German mass mind was influenced by the deliberate propaganda of Hitler and Goebbels. The German people were gradually swayed and finally whipped into the war mood. As early as 1935, declares Tolischus,[37] the Nazi press hammered away at the theme that Germany was at war with a world full of enemies, and that the best defense was to attack. The mass media performed a vital part in the German war effort.

As Tolischus describes the propaganda line of the day:[38]

Now the Western powers, supposedly dominated by "Jewish international capitalism and social reactionary classes," were accused of plotting to murder Herr Hitler himself and exterminate the German people. Therefore, the German people were told, for them the war had become a question of "to be or not to be."

Hitler, moreover, was issuing such militant and inflammatory statements as the following:[39]

. . . the Jewish reactionary warmongers in the capitalistic democracies have awaited this hour for years. They had prepared and were unwilling to cancel their plans for destruction of Germany.

These warmongers want war. They shall have it.

Then followed the various German aggressions. The above attention has been paid to the Hitler regime in Germany because here, as in other totalitarian nations, it is well demonstrated how propaganda may be used to induce public support for national objectives, whether constructive or destructive.[40] The potential ability to accomplish this in other nations should not be underestimated.

The Russians are hardly amateurs in the use of propaganda either. The purpose of the mass-communications media in Soviet Russia has been ably stated by Inkeles.[41]

[37] Otto D. Tolischus, *They Wanted War* (New York, Reynal & Hitchcock, 1940), p. 101.

[38] *Ibid.*, p. 248.

[39] *Ibid.*, p. 256. The strident, bellicose propaganda was, furthermore, given differing types of expression. In addition to the charismatic addresses of Hitler, the German people could hear the more intellectual-toned utterings of a Goebbels or Alfred Rosenberg; the massive thundering of a Goering; or the crude, vulgar, spleen-venting of a Julius Streicher (especially when the latter attacked the Jews). The Nazis had, if nothing else, a change of pace.

See also Leonard W. Doob, "Goebbels' Principles of Propaganda," *Public Opinion Quarterly*, Vol. 14 (Fall, 1950), pp. 419–442.

[40] This is not to say that all of the approximately 68 million Germans of Hitler's time were converted to his views; but at least they were carried along with the Nazi program—and often enthusiastically too. Use of all the communications media saw to that—as also the staging of dramatic mass meetings, parades, and other devices to promote morale.

[41] Alex Inkeles, *Public Opinion in Soviet Russia* (Cambridge, Harvard University Press, 1950), pp. 317–318.

The Soviet Regime has developed one of the largest and most complex systems of public communication in the world. The Communist Party has forged a parallel system of control which is more elaborate and thorough than any other still in existence in the postwar [World War II] era. Both the system of communication and the control apparatus are oriented toward a single goal. They must serve as instruments through which the party and government mobilize the mind and will of the population; they must see to it that what ought to be done *is* done, what should be thought and felt *is* thought and felt. . . . The media of communication in the Soviet Union must serve "social" ends set by the party, the state, the nation. . . . The ends to which mass communication must be put are justified in terms of Marxist-Leninist theory. And that theory is interpreted by the only group with the right to interpret it in the Soviet Union —the Communist Party—as meaning that the media are to be used primarily to strengthen the party's leadership in its self-assigned role as leader, teacher, and guide of the Soviet people.

The many propaganda statements of the Russians during the 1950's which have emphasized the "hate" theme also cannot be taken lightly, since by this process roughly 200 million Russians have been in part conditioned to warlike and inflamatory policies as were the Germans under Hitler. Agitation of this sort scarcely helps the peaceful progress of world affairs. This communist "poison propaganda," as President Eisenhower termed it, may not only be accepted as valid by the Russian people but by millions of Asiatics and others as well.[42] A brazen but not unusual (during the early 1950's) instance of complete falsehood and of the "big lie" technique were the communist broadcasts at the beginning of the Korean War (1950), charging that the war had been started by the South Koreans; however, it was clear to impartial observers that the North Korean communists had launched the aggressive, military action. Such propaganda broadcasts, in this case directed particularly toward southeast Asia, cannot be assumed to be without effects.[43] Unfortunately, effects on public opinion (local or international) are made, and these have other consequences.

Leigh[44] has suggested that the mass media could be used for *positive* or *constructive* purposes—for example, for constructing a popular base for world government or the world community. This proposal in favor of positive

[42] Typical of other Russian propaganda utterances of the early 1950's was the Soviet reaction to President Eisenhower's proposal of an international plan for the peaceful use of atomic energy (1953). The President's plan, which suggested the sharing of fissionable materials under supervision of an United Nations commission so as to benefit all nations, was harshly rejected by the Russians. The latter charged that Mr. Eisenhower had "threatened atomic war," had "eulogized force," and had made a "warmongering speech." *New York Times,* December 10, 1953.

[43] More effective still, probably, were the communist propaganda efforts within Korea during 1950—when the communists had taken possession of South Korea. See Wilbur Schramm and John W. Riley, Jr., "Communication in the Sovietized State, as Demonstrated in Korea," *American Sociological Review,* Vol. 16, No. 6 (December, 1951), pp. 757–766 (esp. p. 765).

[44] Robert D. Leigh, "The Mass-Communications Inventions and International Relations," in W. F. Ogburn, ed., *Technology and International Relations* (Chicago, University of Chicago Press, 1949), pp. 138–139.

uses of the media serves as a reminder of Benoit-Levy's statement with reference to the motion picture. He wrote: "The real mission of the cinema is to show men that they are brothers. Every agency, political or cultural, that reveals or increases the basically common interest of all humanity, serves the most important purpose of our troubled times."[45]

It is possible that skillful propagandists (such as Hitler was) may in the future turn more to constructive emphases. Hopes were raised, following the "Summit Conference" of world statesmen during July, 1955, that communist propaganda might assume such an emphasis. However, even six months later considerable disillusionment had appeared in that regard in the Western world.

On Public Opinion

From the above illustrations it should be clear that the influence of communications on public opinion and propaganda may be considerable—and the ultimate effects produced, whether constructive or destructive, may be of enormous consequence. Such an influence may enable a nation to conquer new lands without actually having to engage in a war; or, as has been shown, propaganda campaigns may lead to and constitute one part of large-scale war. In domestic affairs, the influence of the mass-communications media has often been regarded as rather small insofar as influences on citizens' behavior is concerned. For instance, the Lazarsfeld-Berelson-Gaudet study[46] of voting behavior in Erie County, Ohio, indicated that group memberships of people are of basic importance in determining voters' preferences for candidates; the personal, face-to-face contacts of the people of Erie County appeared to have greater influence on their choice of candidate than the messages of the mass media. In the field of *advertising,* wherein much propaganda is used, doubt has recently been expressed in some quarters as to the real effectiveness of this alleged form of persuasion on shopping behavior.[47] Nevertheless, one must add, despite such data or contentions as the above, American political parties are eager during election campaigns to pay large sums of money for radio and television time; and "hard-headed" business executives gladly buy newspaper, radio, TV, and other forms of advertising. Presumably sales are increased. It evidently pays—or they would cease the practice. It appears that further study of this matter is likely to be of value.

On Political Leadership

A "new look" has been given to political leadership in the age of the mass media. Before this time a leader's voice, for example, was of some (though

[45] Quoted in *Annals of the American Academy of Political and Social Science,* Vol. 250 (March, 1947), p. 98.

[46] Paul F. Lazarsfeld, Bernard Berelson, and Hazel Gaudet, *The People's Choice* (New York, Duell, Sloan and Pearce, 1944).

[47] Richard T. LaPiere, *A Theory of Social Control* (New York, McGraw-Hill, 1954), p. 519.

not too much) consequence; some statesmen, as William Jennings Bryan, were aided by possessing an unusually fine voice. But during the age of broadcasting the possession of an attractive, winning voice is a *tremendous* asset. To have, on the other hand, a rasping, weak, or effeminate (in the case of a man) voice brings a severe, perhaps irreparable, handicap. With the advent of television the "new look" was extended. Now it would be enormously helpful if the leader could have a reasonably presentable appearance, indeed have all-around personality appeal. To be the diffident person, the too-unusual-looking individual, or the super-introvert was likely to bring difficulties for those with political aspirations. The man who is able to make favorable immediate impressions on others would seem to have advantages during the mass-communications age. Moreover, his contacts will no longer be confined to a small circle or to a few hundred people at one time, but may comprise millions at one media presentation.

The political uses and effects of the mass-communications media are, all in all, an excellent example of the close interaction between communications and society. One may conclude (1) that man receives his picture of reality largely from the mass media; (2) that uses of the media for political purposes have been made quickly and with important consequences, as demonstrated in Nazi Germany and Soviet Russia; and (3) that the political effects of communications media may be especially strong when used *in combination with* other forms of power—such as police, military, and economic. This point was well observed in Korea (1950) by Schramm and Riley,[48] although it applies equally to Nazi Germany and Russia. The mass media are in fact rarely used singly for political purposes, but rather as an integral part of the total society.

On International Relations

The art of diplomacy has been affected in various ways by use of the mass media. For one thing the constant prying for news on the part of representatives of press, radio, and TV seems to keep few things secret. The open atmosphere which surrounds the United States government is also created, in part, by the tremendous volume of publication performed by the Government Printing Office. As a nation the United States offers a large amount of information to all persons who want to take the trouble to read the many annual reports, statistical bulletins, and manuals. Although diplomacy is often conducted in this "goldfish bowl" atmosphere, its manner of discussion has probably not changed. In the days of prying newsmen the negotiations may increasingly take place behind closed doors; at any rate, the important decisions are likely to be made under such circumstances.[49]

It is observed, secondly, that use of the mass-communications media has

[48] W. Schramm and J. W. Riley, Jr., *loc. cit.*
[49] Leigh, "The Mass Communications Inventions and International Relations," in W. F. Ogburn, *op. cit.*, p. 141.

made it more difficult for a nation to insulate itself from foreign news and influences if it wishes to do so. The communist-dominated nations have endeavored to maintain such an insulation from foreign influence, known as the "Iron Curtain" (a phrase suggested by Winston Churchill). They have policed radio sets, jammed foreign broadcasting stations, and decreed severe punishment (sometimes the death penalty) for listening to foreign broadcasts or reading pamphlets dropped from foreign planes. The experience of World War II and of the Korean War of 1950–53 has shown that such measures greatly reduce, but do not completely cut off, clandestine radio listening or leaflet-reading.[50]

A third effect of the modern communications and transportation inventions on international relations is of a general and all-embracing nature. These inventions have brought a significant change in the whole nature of relationships between nations. *All nations are now, in effect, neighbors,* even though they may be in actual fact thousands of miles away. The ability of the airplane and other transportation inventions to cover distance and the ability of the radio and other communications inventions to transmit news quickly mean (1) that any person can travel to any part of the globe in a relatively short period of time for whatever purpose; and (2) word of occurrences, speeches, and beliefs may be dispatched around the globe almost instantaneously. Man lives in "one world" in the realm of transportation and communication; isolationism is dead. The "social world" of the present-day Cincinnati or Chicago resident is overwhelmingly different in this regard from what it was in the same city in 1900. No longer can Americans properly be indifferent to significant happenings in China, Portugal, Germany, Russia; and other nations, in the same way, should not be indifferent to important events in America.

On Language

A logical effect of the widening range of human contacts applies to the field of language. Although mankind now lives in "one world" in the realm of communications and transportation, human contacts are significantly obstructed by a barrier of language. Ease of communication and transportation is counteracted by difficulty in understanding.[51] Pei declares that there are at present 2,796 different spoken tongues, exclusive of dialects, used in the

---

[50] *Ibid.,* p. 140; also Schramm and Riley, "Communication in the Sovietized State, as Demonstrated in Korea," *loc. cit.,* p. 765. The latter pointed out that many South Koreans, while under communist domination (1950), listened by short-wave radio to United Nations broadcasts. They hid their radios in a wall or ceiling, listened a few minutes a day or even a few minutes a week. Once a broadcast or leaflet was received, its content would often be passed on through trusted friends who, in turn, circulated the word to others.

[51] This refers, of course, to understanding in personal relationships. Official dispatches and publications are likely to be translated for public use if sufficient interest or demand exists. Official governmental representatives will have use of interpreters as needed.

world; only thirteen of these have a speaking population of 50 million or more.[52] The question may be raised as to whether this use of so many languages meets the needs of the world's inhabitants in view of (1) the large amount of travel and other mobility, and (2) the technical ability of the different communications media to provide common understandings for a large proportion of the human species. Thus far the mass media have adapted themselves to the existing "language pluralities" of the world. But the influence of the modern communications media, bringing the possibility of understanding among millions of peoples (who are now essentially neighbors), would seem to be a force favoring consolidations and mergers of languages. Such may be likely to occur eventually. When communication and understanding *may* take place over large areas if not the whole world, it appears to be foolish (if not harmful) to have this possibility thwarted by people using over 2,700 different languages or even around 100 major ones.

Nevertheless, languages are established forms, and they have shown an amazing ability to persist.[53] There should be little expectation of any sudden downward revision in the number of languages used. Language mergers of even a minor sort would probably require a strong social force behind them in order to be effected. Populations tend to learn and unlearn languages with great reluctance.

The proposal of having one world language has much logic to it, in view of what has been stated. Use of one global language would, however, bring some important, though perhaps not insurmountable, difficulties.[54] As a practical measure it is hardly to be expected for a long time, and one may simply conclude that cultural lag exists in this sphere—the lag of real linguistic comprehension of the peoples of the world (caused by the use of the many different languages) behind technical advances brought by the communications inventions (which offer the possibility of the interchange of ideas on a global scale). In the meantime a regional or "area" plan has been suggested by two French phoneticians, Léonce Thommeret and Pierre

[52] Mario Pei, *The World's Chief Languages,* 3rd ed. (London, Allen & Unwin, 1949), pp. 15–16. Pei states that while there are in all 2,796 languages spoken throughout the world, over a thousand of these are American Indian languages (often spoken by a population of several hundred or less); over 500 are spoken by African Negro tribes; nearly 500 more by natives of Australia, New Guinea, and islands of the Pacific. Hence the truly significant languages of the world now number less than one hundred.

For other discussions of languages, see Edward Sapir, *Language* (New York, Harcourt, Brace, 1921); A. L. Kroeber, *Anthropology,* rev. ed. (New York, Harcourt, Brace, 1948), Ch. 6; and E. D. Chapple and C. S. Coon, *Principles of Anthropology* (New York, Holt, 1942), Ch. 24.

[53] Various local languages are good examples of this, as the Basque in Spain and the Breton in Brittany (France). See A. L. Kroeber, *op. cit.,* pp. 220–221.

[54] For example, existing languages reflect different temperaments and cultural perspectives to some extent; they do not merely provide different words for the same precise meaning. Thus one may contrast Italian with, say, German regarding the "flavor" and cultural assumptions of the language. A global language would necessarily fail to take into account such differences as the above.

Fouché.[55] This may be regarded as a compromise plan between the present system of language pluralities and use of one world language or as a first step in attempting to take up the lag. This plan divides the world into four linguistic spheres or areas. Three languages are suggested for use in each area and would be taught in all schools and colleges. The languages recommended for the various areas might overlap; English and French, in fact, are suggested for each of the four areas. Even such an "area" plan has not been seriously considered as yet, however.

On Education

The mass-communications media and related technologies have been extensively used in schools and colleges, especially in (a) audio-visual programs; (b) use of radio and television for various school purposes; (c) use of loudspeakers in school assemblies and meetings; (d) use of newspapers, magazines, and journals in such classes as journalism, English, and social science; and finally (e) use of textbooks and other books; the latter must surely not be forgotten. Many of these topics have been discussed in Chapters 7 and 8, and additional comment is unnecessary.

The use of textbooks and other books is doubtless the most important mass-media influence of all on education. This is important because (1) the basic knowledge of a field is summed up in textbooks; (2) many of these books are used widely in a nation like the United States, hence millions of high school and college students will be influenced concerning a field by this or that textbook; the aggregate influence of a textbook *can be* tremendous; and (3) the effects of knowledge may take many forms and are more or less incalculable. Books *may* have a considerable effect on public opinion, find expression in the laws, and form the basis for social movements.

The uses of the communications media which have just been mentioned have applied to *formal* education. It is likely that *informal* education has relied on these media to an even greater extent. A tremendous amount of informal education is achieved regularly through the press, radio, television, and movies. The educational influence of just one newspaper, *The New York Times,* is undoubtedly powerful in itself. The information-dispensing role of radio and television also can hardly help but be important, when one considers the many news programs, commentators' analyses of the news, and discussions by political and other leaders singly or in "Town Meeting of the Air," "University of Chicago Round Table," and other programs and forums.

On Impressions of Foreign Peoples

Another aspect of informal education is the impressions of foreign peoples that are given through the mass-communications media. Newspaper ac-

[55] See Mario A. Pei, "Six Languages for One World," *New York Times* Magazine Section, February 24, 1952.

counts, motion pictures, and the like may present reasonably accurate repre-
sentations of foreign peoples or, as is sometimes charged concerning the
movies, they may give distorted impressions. For example, it has often been
alleged that American-made motion pictures have spread the impression
abroad that this nation is a land of "whooping" cowboys, of gangsters, and of
fast-living, big-city playboys. Indeed, White and Leigh state that peoples
who have had the widest access to the means of international communication
have often had more distorted images of others than those living in relative
ignorance of the outer world.[56] Thus they noted that of misunderstandings
current about America during World War II, the most incredible were not
held by Borneo bushmen but by western Europeans who had seen dozens
of Hollywood movies.[57] Reference is made here to unintentional misrepre-
sentations of peoples; there are in addition, moreover, willful distortions of
peoples for propaganda or other purposes which are spread in the mass
media.[58]

The question of whether modern man, possessing much media information
(accurate and distorted), is less ethnocentric than his forebears appears to
be a difficult one. Has man become in part emancipated from his own cultural
emphases? It is recognized that a certain amount of ethnocentrism tends to
accompany all cultural conditioning.[59] The relationship between ethnocentric
attitudes and the influence of the mass media, it is suggested here, is a worthy
subject for further study.

On Attitudes and Opinions

Granted that the influence of the mass media on education (formal and
informal) is regarded as sizable, a related and crucial issue concerns the extent to which the use of these media brings changes in people's attitudes and
opinions. The question is more baffling than one might initially suppose. One
may begin with Berelson's undoubtedly correct generalization, namely, that
"some kinds of *communication* on some kinds of *issues,* brought to the attention of some kinds of *people* under some kinds of *conditions,* have some

[56] Llewellyn White and Robert D. Leigh, *Peoples Speaking to Peoples* (Chicago,
University of Chicago Press, 1946), pp. 2–3.

[57] It may be, however, that the situation is more complicated than at first thought.
Geis, studying with interviewing techniques the effects of American-made movies on
the people of Oslo, did not find the typical, expected influence of the films.—Gilbert
Geis, "American Motion Pictures in Norway," *Abstracts of Papers Delivered at the
48th Annual Meeting of the American Sociological Society,* Berkeley, California,
1953, pp. 61–62.

[58] For a statement of how Soviet propaganda has pictured the U. S., see Frederick C.
Barghoorn, *Soviet Image of the United States* (New York, Harcourt, Brace, 1950); also
see *Annals of the American Academy of Political and Social Science,* Vol. 295 (September, 1954), "America Through Foreign Eyes."

[59] John F. Cuber, *Sociology, A Synopsis of Principles,* 3rd ed. (New York, Appleton-Century-Crofts, 1955), Ch. 6.

kinds of *effects*."[60] In short, it is regarded as established beyond reasonable doubt that persuasion can be achieved with use of the mass media. The question is: How much? Under what conditions? With what kind of people?

On the basis of present knowledge, some hypotheses may be stated which suggest some of the power, yet also some of the limitations, of communications use. These hypotheses are as follows: (1) It is ventured that drastic events affecting one's personal well-being are always more potent in influence than any amount of the most skillful propaganda; (2) propaganda is amazingly ineffectual when used upon people who have strong convictions to the contrary;[61] (3) voting behavior is apparently *not* dominantly affected by political campaign propaganda, as demonstrated by Lazarsfeld, Berelson, and Gaudet; (4) the more personal the communications media, the more effective it is in changing opinions;[62] (5) the emotional content of the media is more effective in converting opinions than rational content; (6) communications, including propaganda, are probably more effective in influencing opinion regarding "personalities" than regarding "issues"; and (7) the less informed that people are relative to an issue, the more susceptible they are to opinion conversion through the influence of the communications media. These hypotheses need further exploration and testing, especially with regard to different kinds of people who are reacting under different types of conditions.

Evidence substantiates the view, moreover, that the new communications media are not so likely to change the behavior patterns of people as they are to be absorbed by those patterns which have been built up over the years. This is known as the phenomenon of self-selection.[63] Thus an individual tends to adopt patterns of communication behavior characteristic of his or her cultural level; if certain types of radio or TV programs, movies, or magazines do not fit into that pattern, the person will probably not participate in that communications behavior at all. If other programs are congenial to the person's behavior pattern, the person is quite likely to be exposed; and some changes in attitudes might result from the exposure. But even in such instances the likely opinion change is at present regarded as slight, whereas the deep-rooted outlook and personality conditioning which caused the interest in the first place are regarded as of greater significance. These deep-rooted personality

[60] Bernard Berelson, "Communications and Public Opinion," in W. Schramm, ed., *Communications in Modern Society* (Urbana, University of Illinois Press, 1948), pp. 171–172.

[61] The first two hypotheses are discussed in MacDougall, *op. cit.*, pp. 92–93.

[62] Thus personal conversation is more effective than a radio speech, and a radio speech tends to be more effective (other things being equal) than a newspaper account of it. Regarding this and the following three hypotheses, see Berelson, in W. Schramm, ed, *op. cit.*, pp. 172–178.

[63] Joseph T. Klapper, *The Effects of Mass Media*, Report to the Director of the Public Library Inquiry (New York, Bureau of Applied Social Research, Columbia University, 1949), Sec. I, pp. 15–17. Also see Paul F. Lazarsfeld, "The Effects of Radio upon Public Opinion," in D. Waples, ed., *Print, Radio, and Film in a Democracy* (Chicago, University of Chicago Press, 1942).

traits are the products largely of the face-to-face influences of home, neigh-borhood, and school. The person has, in other words, *already* been favorably conditioned to this or that influence—long before being exposed to the com-munications media.

Modern research, in fact, does not suggest a potent influence of the mass media on attitudes and behavior, certainly not the tremendous effect that was widely believed several decades ago. Hovland, Lumsdaine, and Sheffield concluded as follows from their experiments with U. S. Army personnel dur-ing World War II:[64] (1) that Army films had marked effects on the men's knowledge of factual material concerning events leading up to the war; (2) that the films had marked effects on opinions which were directly related to the content of the movie; (3) that the films had small effect on general-opinion items which were thought to be important in considering the effec-tiveness of the film but which were not related to direct content; and (4) that the films had no effect on items associated with motivation to serve as soldiers (an objective of the films).

Concerning the effect of having a monopoly in issuing propaganda regard-ing some subject—which is often thought to be conducive to maximum per-suasion—the same authors found that the result is related to the beginning opinions of the people.[65] They found, in a democratic nation, that the pres-entation of only one side of an issue does not lend itself to maximum persua-sion if the audience initially disagrees with the ideas of the communicator. In such a case a two-sided presentation is more likely to bring opinion change. Moreover, Lumsdaine and Janis[66] have reported that the presentation of only one side is not the most effective in cases where the audience will later be exposed to counter-propaganda arguing in favor of the opposing position. In such circumstances, communication advocating a definite position on a controversial issue is more effective in the long run if it presents and dis-cusses the opposing arguments.

Another view regarding the effect of the mass media on opinion change has been expressed by Lazarsfeld.[67] Agreeing that it has often been difficult to demonstrate the effects of the mass media on opinion change, he suggests that such may be due to the nature of the media themselves. It could be, he declares, that these media do have real effects on opinions but that research has somehow not as yet been successful in showing them. Research projects completed up to now have usually followed the design of showing a single media program (as "The Battle of Britain" film in the U. S. Army experi-ments) in which the subjects, randomly selected, are tested *before* and *after*

[64] Carl I. Hovland, Arthur A. Lumsdaine, and Fred D. Sheffield, *Experiments on Mass Communication*, Studies in Social Psychology in World War II, Vol. III (Prince-ton, N. J., Princeton University Press, 1949), pp. 254–255.

[65] *Ibid.,* p. 201–227.

[66] Arthur A. Lumsdaine and Irving L. Janis, "Resistance to 'Counterpropaganda' produced by One-sided and Two-sided 'Propaganda' Presentations," *Public Opinion Quarterly,* Vol. XVII (Fall, 1953), pp. 311–318.

[67] Paul F. Lazarsfeld, "Foreword," in Joseph T. Klapper, *op. cit.,* pp. 2–3.

the program. The effects on opinion change regarding various
shown to be meager; the films were more successful in dispens-
on. But Lazarsfeld holds that the above procedure may empha-
ge change too much, hence be inadequate for the problem.
ve effects of long-term exposure to the communications media
might, on the other hand, be considerable. Thus reading one book or viewing
one TV performance may bring little opinion change, whereas years of exposure might bring significant changes in outlook or of opinion.

Assessing the effects of the media on opinion change, then, has not proven
to be easy. Now does not seem to be the time to hold cocksure ideas on the
subject. To maintain an open-minded view until further facts are brought to
light—no doubt always desirable—is especially so regarding this particular
question.

SUMMARY

Technology has had a tremendous influence on communication and transportation. It has brought into being the mass communications and transportation media (power press, motion picture, radio, TV, etc.) which, in turn,
have caused such developments as the following: Secondary-group relationships of life have increased in volume; the social horizons of large numbers
of people have been extended; the force of public opinion has grown; the
tempo of life has been quickened; the rate of social change has been accelerated in important ways though retarded in others; business life has been
dominantly affected; political life has witnessed an increase in the use of
mass media, often for propaganda purposes; the communications media
have brought a "new look" to political leadership, the radio bringing added
importance to the leader's voice and TV emphasizing all-around personality
appeal. All in all, the communications media have been quickly applied to
the arts of politics and to maintaining social control.

International relations have been drastically influenced by the communications and transportation inventions in that (a) events occurring in one
nation are now soon known and often have repercussions in others, (b) all
the nations of the world are now essentially *neighbors* even though they may
be in actual fact thousands of miles apart, (c) statesmen and diplomats may
readily travel to other nations for conferences designed to settle pressing
international difficulties, and (d) people now have the opportunity of speedy
travel to other nations for purposes of business, of recreational or educational activities, or of dropping bombs.

Effects of the communications and transportation inventions on education and in changing attitudes and opinions have been discussed. Certain
lags related to these inventions have also been noted.

ANNOTATED BIBLIOGRAPHY

BERELSON, Bernard, "Democratic Theory and Public Opinion," *Public Opinion
Quarterly*, Vol. 16, No. 3 (Fall, 1952), pp. 313–330. The author relates the

political theory of how a democratic electorate is supposed to behave with the actuality of how public opinion researchers know it does behave in the U. S. Valuable.

HOVLAND, Carl I., LUMSDAINE, Arthur A., and SHEFFIELD, Fred D., *Experiments on Mass Communication,* Studies in Social Psychology in World War II, Vol. III (Princeton, N. J., Princeton University Press, 1949). Results of the work of the Experimental Section, Research Branch, U. S. Army Information and Education Division, during World War II. These results show significant increase in soldiers' information following the showing of army films though little change of opinions. Capably-executed researches.

INKELES, Alex, *Public Opinion in Soviet Russia* (Cambridge, Harvard University Press, 1950). Emphasizes the relationship between the mass-communications media and the social system in communist Russia. Ably-written. A major contribution.

KATZ, Daniel, CARTWRIGHT, Dorwin, ELDERSVELD, Samuel, LEE, Alfred M., eds., *Public Opinion and Propaganda* (New York, Dryden, 1954). A book of readings, edited for the Society for the Psychological Study of Social Issues, which provides a sound guide to public opinion and propaganda. A useful collection of some fifty or more articles.

KLAPPER, Joseph T., *The Effects of Mass Media,* Report to the Director of the Public Library Inquiry (New York, Bureau of Applied Social Research, Columbia University, 1949). A mountain of literature-survey seems to yield a mouse of positive statement, but this report is recommended nevertheless. A carefully-made study. Excellent foreword by Paul F. Lazarsfeld.

LAZARSFELD, Paul F., BERELSON, Bernard, and GAUDET, Hazel, *The People's Choice* (New York, Duell, Sloan, and Pearce, 1944). Survey of political propaganda and public opinion in Erie County, Ohio, during the presidential campaign of 1940. Emphasizes the importance of personal, face-to-face influences on the formation of voters' opinions.

LEIGH, Robert D., "The Mass-Communications Inventions and International Relations," in William F. Ogburn, ed., *Technology and International Relations* (Chicago, University of Chicago Press, 1949); also Leigh, *The Public Library in the United States,* General Report of the Public Library Inquiry (New York, Columbia University Press, 1950), Ch. 3. The former chapter contains many valuable and penetrating observations concerning the various effects of the mass media on international relations. The latter chapter is a high-level summary of the data assembled by Klapper (see earlier reference).

MACDOUGALL, Curtis D., *Understanding Public Opinion* (New York, Macmillan, 1952). A generally-useful, stimulating text. Written by a professor of journalism who has had major sociological orientation.

MEIER, Richard L., "Communications and Social Change," *Behavioral Science,* Vol. I, No. 1 (January, 1956), pp. 43–58. Discusses recent mathematical applications to communications such as the theoretical work of Claude E. Shannon and of Warren Weaver, also developments in cybernetics by Norbert Wiener and others. Perhaps these are bringing a great "new stage" of communications development, different in nature from that described in present chapter. Already important applications have been made to electronics, witness the versatile computer and Shannon's mechanical mouse (also his automatic chess-player).

OLIVER, John W., *History of American Technology* (New York, Ronald Press,

1956). Contains interesting and worth-while discussion of communications and transportation, written in historical perspective.

SCHRAMM, Wilbur, ed., *The Process and Effects of Mass Communication* (Urbana, University of Illinois Press, 1954). Recent articles of more than ordinary interest by leading communications authorities. Superior organizing of material and running comment by the editor. Excellent bibliography.

————, *Communications in Modern Society* (Urbana, University of Illinois Press, 1948); also Wilbur Schramm, ed., *Mass Communications* (Urbana, University of Illinois Press, 1949). Worth while. Especially recommended are the contributions by Lazarsfeld and Merton, Lazarsfeld and Kendall, C. Hovland, B. Berelson, H. Lasswell, D. Katz, and W. Schramm.

WIRTH, Louis, "Consensus and Mass Communication," *American Sociological Review,* Vol. 13, No. 1 (February, 1948), pp. 1–15. In this presidential address before the American Sociological Society, Wirth affirms the important role of the mass media in modern urban-industrial society. Discusses characteristics of the media, their importance for consensus, their use by dictators.

CHAPTER 13

TECHNOLOGY AND THE FAMILY

■ *Meyer F. Nimkoff*

THIS CHAPTER is concerned with the influence of technology and scientific discovery on change in the family. The family is the result of biological and psychological forces rather than technological ones. Men and women are attracted to each other because of deep-rooted sex drives and emotional needs, and the offspring that result from mating help to establish the family group as a more or less durable social unit. In this respect the human family is like that of other anthropoids. But in the case of man, the family very early became part of a cultural tradition. Men learned to hunt, to make stone tools, to use fire, to divide labor between the sexes, to worship supernatural beings. Later mankind learned to plant seeds and cultivate the soil, to use the hoe and then the plow, and to domesticate animals. These changes in man's culture were not without influence upon his family life. For instance, when man was a hunter his interest in his children, especially his daughters, was—from an economic standpoint—somewhat different from what it was when he became a farmer. Hunting, especially of big game, is almost exclusively a male occupation, which means that daughters were not valued so highly. On the contrary, on a farm daughters are economic assets. Even young sons are not so useful to a hunter as to a farmer, for hunting is the more highly specialized as well as the more hazardous occupation. There are more useful jobs for a young child to do on a farm than as a member of a hunting party. So children, especially daughters, are generally more highly esteemed in farming than in hunting cultures. Hunting and farming are the products of technological innovation. Thus technology, by changing the cultural base, changes the family.

Another dramatic change in the family occurred within relatively recent times, that is, within the last century or two in the West, with the invention of the steam engine and steel tools that gave rise to what is called the Industrial Revolution. Mechanical power replaced man power, and production was transferred from the home to the factory. Great aggregations of factories with their attendant social services gave rise to new cities which increased in size and number so greatly as to give us for the first time an urban civilization. The effect of the Industrial Revolution was to create a social revolution. The family, as well as the government, economic organization, and the church, underwent radical changes. With production transferred from the home to the factory, place of work and residence of the worker were separated. The father was removed from home for a longer period of time. As jobs increased, more and more wives and mothers took employment away from home. Children more than six years old in increasing numbers went to school and were not educated at home as they had been before. The demand in the cities for the labor of children was less than it had been on the farms, while the cost of rearing children increased, as did also the difficulty of rearing children satisfactorily in the environment of the city. The urban family became smaller. It also became less stable, and the divorce rate increased. So the Industrial Revolution, a technological revolution, greatly altered the family.

In this chapter we wish mainly to inquire into how inventions and scientific discoveries affect the family, that is, how they produce family changes. We are interested primarily in the manner of technological influence, although we shall also give some attention to the description of family changes.[1]

Internal Influences of Family Change

The family is a complex whole consisting of a number of interrelated parts. There are parents, children, relatives. The family is formed, it may continue through various stages, and it is dissolved eventually by death, desertion, or divorce. The family performs many functions: economic, educational, recreational, protective, religious, social psychological. Since the parts of the family are interrelated, a change in any one part results in changes in other parts. The change in the function of economic production of the family, for example, has led to changes in the relative status of husbands and wives in the family. In the farm family, the husband and father was the head because farming is a family occupation; and a business—if it is to operate successfully—generally requires a head. Policies must be formulated, and responsibilities must be assigned. The man of the house is usually the boss of the farming enterprise because the male is better suited to the heavy labor required. The subservience of the farm wife to the will of her husband is fortified by the fact that in a rural economy there are few, if any, jobs open to women other than housekeeping. The woman is therefore dependent upon a male for economic support, whether it be her father, husband, or some other male relative. In the urban, industrial society, on the contrary, there are many jobs open to women. Indeed, there are now few jobs open to men which are not also open to women, although sometimes not to the same ex-

[1] This chapter is based primarily on a study of the causes of changes in the family in the United States during the past century: William F. Ogburn and Meyer F. Nimkoff, *Technology and the Changing Family* (Boston, Houghton Mifflin, 1955).

tent. Since women have the possibility of jobs, they have an alternative to marriage and do not need to marry just in order to obtain economic security. The jobs that women get are away from home and not under the authority of their fathers or husbands. So the authority of the male is lessened, and the independence of the female is increased. The status of women has greatly changed in the direction of equality because of changes in the functions of the family, especially the economic functions of production. The changed status of women is a derivative of these changed economic roles. Here we have, then, an internal cause of family change.

External Causes of Family Change

But if we ask what caused the increase in the opportunities of women for employment, we must look outside the family for the explanation. And we find the explanation, as we have indicated, in the increase in the total number of jobs resulting from the Industrial Revolution due to technological innovations. There are new jobs, and there are many more jobs than there were before, many more than men alone can fill. Also the Industrial Revolution, by leading to the transfer of functions away from the home, has reduced the household responsibilities of wives and mothers, removing some of the obstacles to their employment. We conclude that, while the family may transmit changes from one part to another, the most far-reaching causes of family change are to be found outside the family itself. The family is a part of the total social system and is responsive to changes in that system. The family itself is a relatively stable and conservative institution and does not initiate change so much as transmit change. The more dynamic aspects of the social system are the economic and political institutions, and especially technological innovations in the former.

Multiple Causation

While this chapter is devoted to an analysis of the role of technology in family change, it is important to recognize that inventions and scientific discoveries are not the only factors in family change. We have already shown how the family itself is responsible for some family changes; that is, how some family changes induce others, because of the interrelationship of the parts of the family. Similarly, the family is itself but one institution in a large family of institutions, all of which are in a process of change and which therefore induce changes in the family. So, for example, changes in the policies of the government with respect to old-age pensions, increasing the number of occupations covered and the benefits received, affect the responsibility which children assume for the financial support of their parents in old age.

If we ask in turn what caused the government to develop the new policy of extending financial aid to aged persons, we observe that social factors are involved: (1) the mobility of modern life which separates adult children from their parents and makes it difficult for children to be held accountable for the financial support of their parents; (2) the inability or failure of many parents to accumulate sufficient savings for their old age; (3) the considerable increase in the number of aged persons in our society, making it difficult for private philanthropy to assume the total responsibility for the aged indigent; and (4) the recognition of the fact that the government is the only agency with sufficient police and tax authority to enforce a nation-wide program of compulsory insurance for old age.

An analysis[2] of the external causes of relatively recent changes in the family in the United States has shown that three categories of causes are operative: the biological, the social-psychological, and the technological. Each of these may be considered in turn.

Biological Factors in Family Change

The family involves human beings who are biological creatures, and the question therefore arises as to whether changes in the family have resulted from changes in the human constitution. Specifically, marriage is a relation between persons of opposite sex; and the family that is formed is the result of the operation of the sexual function. So we focus on the possible changes in the sexual factor as it may be related to family changes.

The division of the species into males and females is a constant phenomenon and is therefore not a factor in family change, since only a factor that changes can be responsible for other changes; and a constant factor is never the cause of any changes. The distribution of the sexes, however, is not a constant factor. In the early years of American history, when the eastern seaboard was being settled, there was a preponderance of males, for the migrants to a new region are usually young males. Likewise in the settlement of the West, there was a preponderance of males. It is usually thought that the chances for marriage are greatest when the two sexes in a community are about equal in number, but investigation[3] has shown that the marriage rate is higher where there is a slight excess of males, about 110 or 120 to 100 women, of marriageable ages. In recent years the number of women of marriageable ages in the United States has been increasing, and in the early 1950's there were more such women than men. Yet the percentage of the population married increased during these years when the percentage of marriageable women was increasing. So we say that the surplus of marriageable women was not a factor in the increase in marriage. But this is not to say that the surplus of marriageable women was without effect on the marriage rate, for if the number of marriageable women had been fewer, the marriage rate might have been still higher.

The excess of women over men in the United States is not great. In a

[2] W. F. Ogburn and M. F. Nimkoff, *op. cit.*
[3] E. R. Groves and W. F. Ogburn, *American Marriage and Family Relationships* (New York, Holt, 1928), Ch. XIII.

number of European countries following World War I and World War II, there was a considerable excess of young women because of the high casualties suffered by men. The excess of young women in Germany after World War I exceeded two million[4] and resulted in increased illegitimacy, abortion, and prostitution.

Another manifestation of the biological factor has to do with the age of biological maturity. In a good many societies, especially those that are agricultural, the lower age level at which the marriage of females is permitted is the age of puberty. Anything that affects the age of biological maturity in such societies might affect the age of marriage. There is evidence[5] that in the United States for a sample of college women who were born around 1920, the age of beginning menstruation was about one-half year less than for a sample born around 1900. During this same interval, the average age at marriage for females decreased in the United States. The increase in earlier age at maturity of American girls, if general, might then be a factor in the lowering of the average age for marriage. The earlier maturity of females is not, of course, due to any genetic change but is the result of environmental changes, specifically (*a*) the better control of disease in early childhood, and (*b*) better nutrition. Both of these environmental factors derive from inventions and scientific discoveries.

The genetic factors in man, for the historical period under review, are constant factors and therefore cannot be responsible for changes in family organization. The biological changes in man which have occurred since the beginning of history are relatively slight, hence cannot be held to be major factors in the vast changes in the family which have occurred. One of the more significant changes in the family which traces to biological changes is the increase in families with older persons, resulting from increased longevity. The increase in life expectancy is, however, attributable mainly to the same two sets of environmental causes which are responsible for the earlier maturity of females. Scientific discoveries are, then, the remote cause of these changes which are immediately attributable to biological factors.

Ideological Factors in Family Change

A second cluster of causes of changes in the family has to do with those social-psychological factors commonly called ideologies. By ideologies we mean systems of ideas which are widely held and which are integrated into guiding forces of social life. Examples in the area of government are free enterprise, socialism, and communism. Ideologies are a special category of ideas and are not to be confused with ideas per se. All inventions and discoveries begin as ideas in the minds of men. It is therefore not very helpful to ascribe social changes, and specifically family changes, to new ideas. A

[4] The League of Nations, *International Statistical Yearbook, 1926–28*.
[5] Clarence A. Mills, "Further Evidence on the Reversal in the Human Growth-Tide," *Human Biology,* Vol. 13 (September, 1941), p. 365.

more differentiated analysis is needed, in terms of types of ideas, such as ideologies, and those ideas which are capable of being embodied in techniques of doing things which we call technology, and ideas as to the nature of reality which we call scientific discovery.

As an illustration of the role of ideologies in family change, the following example may be cited. One of the prominent changes in the American family since the formation of our nation has been the increase in the status of children. Children are more highly regarded and more and more services are being provided for them. In colonial times there was a saying that children should be seen and not heard. Today they are both seen and heard.

If we ask why this change in the status of children has come about, a satisfactory answer cannot be given wholly in terms of technological changes. The new technology has made the labor of small children uneconomical, and we have child-labor laws as well as compulsory school-attendance laws to keep them from working. We can scarcely explain the higher status of children in the United States in the twentieth century by their diminished economic value. The decrease in the number of children, however, may be a factor in their higher evaluation, according to the law of supply and demand. And contraception has played an important part in decreasing the number of children. If this analysis is valid, contraceptives—compounded of inventions and discoveries—have been an indirect but influential cause of the increased status of children.

If children are economic liabilities in our time and if contraception makes it possible for mates to determine more often than otherwise whether they will have children or not, then those children that are conceived are more likely to be children who are desired for their own sakes, that is, because of the love their parents expect to bear for them. If this is correct, there has been a susbstantial change in the effective influence of love as a factor in parent-child relationships. A change in the incidence or expression of affection is probably not an ideological change, as we have defined ideology. But it is probably closely related to such an ideological change, namely, the increase in humanitarianism which appears to be an important factor in the greater emphasis on the child. To illustrate the point, in colonial times corporal punishment of children was more widespread and more frequent than it is now.[6] Punishment generally was more severe. The less harsh attitude toward children in our time is in part an expression of the greater humanitarianism. Thus more crimes were punishable by death in colonial times than now. Now we have special courts for juveniles, and punishments are more lenient than in the criminal courts for adults. Humanitarianism is an ideology which is not readily explained, and its connections with technological factors are not evident.

Another example of the role of ideologies in family change relates to

[6] Alice Morse Earle, *Child Life in Colonial Days* (New York, Macmillan, 1904), pp. 196 ff.

divorce. It is well known that the religious ideologies regarding the nature of marriage are of the utmost importance regarding the position of the church on the question of how marriages may be terminated. The Roman Catholic Church regards marriage as a sacrament, hence cannot condone divorce, which permits remarriage. The Protestant churches in the United States generally regard marriage as a holy but not as a sacred state, and so sanction divorce on certain grounds. Ideology, then, is a factor in divorce. But is it also a factor in the change in divorce in the United States during the past century; that is, a factor in the increase in divorce which has been occurring in the United States? Investigation[7] has shown that the increase in divorce in the United States has occurred without a corresponding change in the ideologies of the churches, and that therefore the ideological factor is not a cause of the rise in the divorce rate.

The origin of ideologies is varied and often obscure. Sometimes they develop out of men's hopes and fears, as in certain religious ideologies concerning the life after death. Sometimes the origins are in reactions to the abuse of power by individuals or small groups, as in the case of the growth of democracy. An ideology like monogamy seems to be an adjustment to the sex ratio and the psychological factor of jealousy. That is, it is not likely that monogamy would be so widely esteemed as a norm if the proportion of men and women was not usually about even, and if it were not easier for satisfactory adjustments to be made between one male and one female than in plural marriages. Again, in some instances ideologies may be adjustments to inventions and discoveries. Whence for example the origin of the current ideology of the equality of men and women? The sexes are more nearly equal in contemporary industrial society than they were in the earlier agricultural society, because our industrial society furnishes identical work for both sexes and permits women to obtain employment apart from their families and without the assistance of their families. If the greater economic independence of women is a factor in their status, then the technological innovations that created more jobs for women are causes of the trend toward the equality of women. The reciprocal of this view has also been propounded, namely, that ideologies may affect technological change in significant ways. Thus Max Weber[8] argued that the Protestant ethic was conducive to the development of capitalist industrial society in the West.

This chapter is devoted primarily to tracing out the influence of technological changes on changes in the family. The technological factor is not, however, the only factor in family change, although it appears to be the most significant one. Possible biological and ideological factors in family change have been considered in previous paragraphs in order to present

[7] W. F. Ogburn and M. F. Nimkoff, *op. cit.*

[8] Max Weber, *The Protestant Ethic and the Spirit of Capitalism* (New York, Scribner, 1948).

the whole picture and to provide proper perspective for the consideration of the role of invention and discovery.

INVENTION AND DISCOVERY IN FAMILY CHANGE

Dispersal and Convergence

That technological innovations and scientific discoveries have greatly changed the family is common knowledge. What is not so well known is the process by which this transformation takes place, a process which is a combination of the two subprocesses of *dispersal* and *convergence*. If, for example, we ask how the Industrial Revolution resulted in a decrease in the authority of the husband in the home, the answer may be given as follows. Mechanical power made possible by the steam engine reduced home production. It removed jobs for men from the home to the factory. It created jobs for women, with pay. It led to the growth of cities and to the growth of governmental functions. We may say, then, that there was a dispersal of the influences of this highly important technological change.

Each of these changes wrought by mechanical power in turn brought fresh changes, that is, they were causes of new effects. Certain of these new influences converged to produce a new effect, namely, the diminished authority of husbands. It is as if the rays of the sun were brought together by means of a magnifying glass to focus on one point. (1) The reduction in home production removed an enterprise over which the husband was traditionally the head. Farming and household-industry are businesses that require management, even as a factory must have a boss. (2) Jobs for men away from home left the management of the home and the children more completely in the hands of the women than before, and increased their authority, for practical purposes. (3) Jobs for women removed women from economic dependence upon their fathers or husbands and therefore from their authority. (4) The growth of cities and of governmental functions meant that more services were available to the members of the family that formerly had been supplied by the husband or father, such as protection against assault, illness, accidents, unemployment, and the like. Police, firemen, judges, and social workers, among others, are present-day rivals of husbands and fathers in the matter of exercising authority over family affairs. They represent the transfer of protective and other functions from the family to government.

Urbanism

When the influences that converge on the modern family are traced back to their sources, they are seen to originate in the city. The city is the principal locus of influences bearing on the modern family. The reason for this is that the modern city is a cluster of converging influences resulting from mechanical power, steel, modern transportation, and modern communication. These are powerful forces that have given impetus to our urban society. The city in turn is the source of the convergence of many influences upon the family. Among the more important characteristics of cities causing changes in the family are the following: (*a*) the separation of place of work from the family dwelling; (*b*) production outside the home; (*c*) the density of the population; and (*d*) the hospitality to new ideas. The significance of the first two of these for family life has been briefly explored above in connection with the diminished authority of the husband. There have been other important consequences. The absence from home, first of the father and more recently of the mother also, because of the location of production away from home, has meant a reduction in the educational, religious, and protective functions of the family. This has not been the only reason for the relative decline of the home as a center for the education of children. The social heritage, that is, the body of accumulated knowledge, has grown appreciably, beyond the point where parents are competent to transmit to their children all the knowledge and skills they may require; and the school has been designed to take over more and more of this responsibility.

The density of population in cities is a factor in the development of social services in behalf of families which has led to the reduction of protective services by the family. Where, as in cities, families live very close together, the disposal of sewage and garbage cannot so readily be left to the individual family as in the open country; and there is pressure, therefore, upon the city government, which represents all the people and has the taxing power, to assume these services of sanitation and hygiene. In addition, families in the city are able to secure water, gas, and electricity more readily and on more favorable terms than is the case where large numbers of families are not represented. It is expensive to run a power line out to an isolated farm. So in the city the family becomes the beneficiary of various services because of the density of the population—services which formerly the family either did not enjoy or had to furnish themselves.

The city is also more hospitable to new ideas and is therefore the locus of more innovations affecting family life. An illustration concerns the idea that woman's place is in the home, an old idea derived from agricultural times when the work of women was if not exclusively in the home, then close by the home. The city is more hospitable than the open country to the idea of women working away from home. This is not just because there are more jobs for married women away from home in the city. There is more freedom in the city because of the density of the population and the resulting anonymity. There are also more divergent ideas in the city, which is the crossroads of many viewpoints. This helps to make urbanites generally more liberal, farmers more conservative, in the same society.

The Industrial Revolution came first to the cities, and the influence of the accompanying social revolution on the rural areas was felt via the cities. The urban attitudes and culture traits were diffused to the surrounding countryside, and the rural population was increasingly urbanized. But in its more recent phase, the Industrial Revolution has come directly to the farm via the gasoline engine and the electric wire; and the farms are being mechanized, with consequences for farm family life comparable in some respects with the effects of mechanization on family life in the city.

Birth Control

What we have been saying in preceding paragraphs is that the impact of changing technology on the family has been mainly indirect, via the growth of industry and cities. There has been some direct effect of mechanical inventions on the family, as in the case of labor-saving devices like the vacuum cleaner and the washing machine; but the effect of these devices on family life has been relatively minor because (a) they are instruments of service and not instruments of production, and (b) they are not put to continuous use. Labor-saving devices in the home may make it easier for a married woman to combine homemaking with a job, or they may result in a higher standard of housekeeping. But they have not, of course, had the consequences for family life that machine production away from home has had.

Among the inventions and discoveries influencing the family there is one cluster that has affected it both directly and profoundly, namely, innovations in birth control. The practice of limiting the size of family is an ancient one, occurring among many primitive peoples as well as in early historical societies. In addition to infanticide and abortion, various folk methods of birth control have been utilized, as well as crude mechanical devices. So the idea of family limitation and means of achieving it are not new. What is new is the decline in the birth rate in Western nations coincident with industrialization and with the introduction and diffusion of modern contraceptives, mechanical and chemical, as well as with the discovery of the knowledge of the date of ovulation, which made possible the regulation of coitus so as to avoid conception, a practice approved by certain religious bodies to whom other methods of birth control are objectionable. It is not claimed that modern contraceptives are alone responsible for the decline in the birth rate in all Western nations, since there is evidence[9] that in Sweden an appreciable lowering of the birth rate was accomplished mainly through the use of older folk methods. It appears that the effective motive for wanting smaller families is the economic liability of children in an urban economy, since children are not economically productive as they are on farms, while at the same time the cost of rearing a child is considerably more. The difficulties of rearing a child in an urban environment are also greater. If the motive to limit the size of family is great, as it is under these circumstances, and there are available methods of limiting family size, some method of achieving the smaller size of family is likely to be utilized. Modern methods have the advantages of greater attractiveness and efficiency.

[9] *Report on the Sex Question,* translated and edited by Virginia Clay Hamilton (Baltimore, Williams and Wilkins, 1940).

Scientific Discoveries

There are other scientific discoveries beyond knowledge as to the date of ovulation in women which have been influential in changing the family. These are quite numerous when viewed in detail but may be regarded as consisting of two principal clusters. The first consists of discoveries regarding the role of learning in human behavior. Earlier, in the absence of knowledge regarding the learning process, greater significance was attached to instinct and heredity. Later came the knowledge as to the flexibility and modifiability of the human nervous system and the great importance of the learning process, especially during the early years of life, so far as emotional development is concerned. The crucial role of the mother in this early emotional development was also uncovered. A great deal of knowledge was added regarding the conditions under which learning takes place—the importance of goals, cues, rewards, reinforcements, and so on. The effects of these discoveries on the family have been mainly (a) to focus more attention on the child and to lay more emphasis on child guidance, and (b) to stress the importance of marital adjustment. As the twig is bent, so is the tree inclined. If the early years are of particular importance for personality development, the growing child must be the subject of special attention and concern. And if the most important single influence in the child's experience is his relation to his parents, and especially his mother, then satisfactory relations between mates is also highly significant, not only for the mates but for their growing children.

The second cluster of discoveries of significance for the family is important because of its influence in modifying the forms of religious beliefs that have been widely held. Religious teachings are concerned with norms of ethical conduct which are at the heart of family life, such as conceptions of marriage, attitudes toward sex, ideas regarding the optimum size of family, and policies concerning the dissolution of marriage. The scientific discoveries which have influenced religious beliefs have been derived from a variety of areas such as biology, astronomy, medicine, anthropology, psychology, sociology, some of which are not directly related to the family. The influence here has been indirect, through a modification of religious outlook which is often designated *secularization*. Discoveries regarding the origin and evolution of man, the nature of the universe, the nature of disease, and the nature of sex, to mention only a few of the more significant ones, have resulted in the partial substitution of secular attitudes and practices for sacred attitudes and practices that previously existed. For instance, in the treatment of disease there is more use of the physician and less use of the spiritual healer.

The effect of these new secular viewpoints is felt in many ways in family life. The view that marriages are made on earth and not in heaven is more widespread, and with this view goes the correlated idea that if the marriage does not succeed it may be terminated by divorce and a new marriage may be contracted.

It appears that an important function of scientific discoveries, like those just recounted, has been to remove ideological obstacles to changes in the family. Thus an effect of secularization, resulting from the impact of scientific discoveries on the pattern of religious beliefs, has been to increase the divorce rate. Couples who are unhappily married may stay together for the sake of the children or because of conviction that divorce is wrong, a conviction generally derived from church teachings. Religious teachings may favor large families, whereas secular attitudes lead to small families. So directly and indirectly secular attitudes are more likely to result in divorce, where there is marital unhappiness. Further evidence of secular influences on family stability is provided by the information that not a single major church in the United States recognizes cruelty as a ground for divorce, yet it is the most common ground on which divorces are actually granted at the present time.

TECHNOLOGY AND THE FUTURE OF THE FAMILY

The preceding discussion has been concerned with the role of invention and discovery in family change. Illustrations have been drawn from recent changes in the family, particularly in the United States.

There is interest also in the future of the family and in the influence that inventions and discoveries may have in shaping the family in the future. In part our interest is born of curiosity, in part it is due to the fact that our comfort and our happiness, and that of our children and grandchildren, will be affected by what happens to the family in the future. If the analysis of the process of social change outlined above is valid, then it should be possible for us to apply this analysis to the near future and anticipate some of the changes that lie ahead.

The discussion that follows will not deal with the family of the future but only with the probable influence of inventions and discoveries on the family, which is the subject of this chapter. The family in the future will be influenced by forces other than those of inventions and discoveries, as we have seen has been the case in the past. The approach, moreover, will not be in terms of the probable influences of particular innovations, for these are too numerous to detail; and to treat them separately would not be profitable, for, as we have seen, it is generally the convergence of many innovations on a given aspect of family life that is effective and not the influence of separate innovations. It will be more profitable, therefore, for us to consider certain important aspects of family life, recent major changes in the family, and ask how clusters of innovations are likely to affect these items in the future. Since the further ahead we try to look, the more uncertain the prognostication, we shall limit ourselves to the next twenty to fifty years, more or less. Since there is a time lag between the introduction of an innovation and the full effects that flow from it, it is highly probable that most of the changes in the family in the near future will result from inventions and discoveries that are already in existence or that are imminent.

The discussion of the future effects of innovations will be divided into two parts, first having to do with the effects of technology and the second with the effects of scientific discoveries. This is done not just as a matter of convenience because of pedagogical reasons but, as will be shown later, because of a significant difference in the aspects of family life which these two types of innovation influence.

Less Production at Home

The key to the family of the present is the decline of economic production in the home because of the rise of industrial production. It is therefore appropriate to ask what the future is likely to hold for the family in the way of production. It was steam power that moved production from the household to the factory, for the home was too small to house the steam engine and steel tools and, later, the assembly line. Since that time, electricity has become available and electricity can be run into a house through a wire. But, despite electricity, it is not expected that production will return to the home, because the home cannot compete with the economy of mass production. The net effect expected of technological innovations is that the departure of a few existing productive functions, like sewing, may be delayed and still fewer new ones added. The manufacture of ice in the mechanical refrigerator is about the only new productive function that has been recently added to the home.

Less Preparation of Food at Home

With less food grown at home, and fewer objects made at home, there is considerably more purchasing of goods by members of families than formerly, especially by women. It is expected that there will be less preparation of food at home in the future because of more processing away from home, in the form of frozen, condensed, and precooked foods. Vitamins, amino acids, and minerals will be purchased in larger quantities as supplements to the diet. The mechanical refrigerator, the deep freezer, the pressure cooker, and later the electronic stove will simplify the preparation of food.

The loss of economic production by the home has led to the loss by the family of much of its authority over its members. The family with the patriarch, who, as head of the family enterprise, ruled over its members, is a thing of the past and there is no prospect of its return.

Increasing Attractiveness of Homes

The heating of homes, with which man has had long experience, has been greatly improved by central heating, insulation, and thermostatic controls. A more recent innovation is the cooling of homes in hot weather. The knowledge exists of ways to regulate the air as to the amount of moisture, dust, mold, and pollen. At a price, practically any type of climate can be created indoors. Increasingly it will be possible to provide the kind of indoor environment desired. Furnishings using light metals, plastics, glass, and other new materials will make the interior more comfortable and, in the view of many, more attractive.

The house will especially be a place of increasing recreation, made possible mainly because of electricity. There are already the radio, television, high-fidelity phonograph, tape recorder, micro-film and micro-card viewers, photographic equipment, and workshops of considerable variety. The television set will make of the home a combined motion picture theater and legitimate theater. It appears to reduce the time spent in other ways, as in conversation between family members. It will require other adjustments in household activities on the part of viewers. But the television set is well adapted to the home.

That there will be more recreation and education for family members is indicated by two additional trends, the one toward fewer working hours and the other toward more income. The median family income in the United States in 1949 was about $3,000. In 1900 it was about $1,500 in 1950 dollars. In the first half of the twentieth century, then, the real income of American families doubled. It is estimated that before the end of the twentieth century the median family income will double again, and will be about $6,000 in 1950 dollars.[10] This gain is expected (unless prevented by destructive wars or other causes) mainly because of the increased productivity of new machines.

The increasing comfort and·recreation in the home does not guarantee more happiness or family accord. The divorce rate has been rising in most countries despite increasing comfort, leisure time, and play activities.

Redistribution of Population

The trend has been for fewer families to remain on farms and for families to increase greatly in the environs of cities, that is, in towns, villages, and small cities located near large cities, as well as in the fringes and suburbs of the cities. The population of cities has also increased, but at a lesser rate. It is expected that these trends will continue in the near future.

The effect of this redistribution of population is to accentuate different types of families. There are families with more children on the fringes of cities, more middle-aged families in the cities, as well as more older persons and more divorced, separated, and never-married persons.

SCIENTIFIC DISCOVERIES AND THE FUTURE OF THE FAMILY

Technological developments during the past century, ushering in our urban civilization, have diminished the power of the family as an institution, while increasing the power of industry and government. The economic functions of production have been largely transferred from the home, as have

[10] W. F. Ogburn, "Technology and the Standard of Living in the United States," *American Journal of Sociology*, Vol. LX, No. 4 (January, 1955), pp. 380–386.

also many of the protective functions and educational functions. Recreational activities in the home have been increasing because of the electrical inventions.

The functions remaining in the home are sex and procreation, and the provision of affection and companionship between mates, between parents and children, and among the children themselves. The preschool education of children also remains in the home. Since this is essentially a training of personality and character, we may say that the principal functions of the modern family are the personality functions.

Scientific discoveries relating to the family are significant because they affect mainly the personality functions of the family, whereas the technological innovations affect mainly the economic functions. The effect of technology on personality is largely indirect, via the changed economic and correlated functions, whereas the effect of scientific discoveries on personality is direct and therefore, all else being equal, more potent.

Conception Control and Fewer Children

Over the past century, the trend in the birth rate in the United States has been downward, and this trend is associated with the spread of birth control. Contraceptive methods now available are highly effective when properly used but are expensive and inconvenient. There is therefore a considerable demand for less expensive and more acceptable methods. One approach is improvements in contraceptive gels, using readily available, cheap ingredients like flour and salt. A newer approach is the physiological, in contradistinction to the mechanical and chemical, utilizing a variety of methods. One objective is to produce cheap and harmless antifertility compounds which can be added to the diet. But even if no new methods of control are introduced, the extension of present methods to populations in the open country, low-income groups, and certain religious groups which in the past have resisted birth control will result in a decline in the birth rate. It is expected that the drop in the birth rate will be especially marked in farm families in the future, what with the spread of farm machinery as well as birth control, although the birth rate on farms is likely to remain higher than in the cities. The differential in fertility between socioeconomic classes is also expected to be narrowed.

Fertility Promotion, Artificial Insemination, and the Preservation of Germ Cells

The spread of birth control will mean an increase in the number of wanted children. It will also entail an increase in the number of voluntarily childless couples, although the number will probably not be great, since married couples characteristically use contraception to limit and space their children rather than to remain altogether childless.

Methods are also being developed to promote fertility, which means that in the future there will be fewer couples who are involuntarily childless. Artificial insemination has been used for some time to promote fertility with semen contributed either by the husband or by a donor. A more recent development is the use of frozen semen. In 1953, three women were inseminated by physicians with semen that had been preserved for a time in the frozen state.[11] They conceived and gave birth to normal babies. If, as seems likely, semen can be preserved indefinitely without losing the fertilizing capacity, a number of interesting new possibilities are opened up. For instance, it will be possible to extend fatherhood beyond the life of the father, if his semen is preserved, and his wife is still living and able and willing to have children.

Procreation is a highly intimate function, into which even the long arm of the law is not allowed to intrude. Biological discoveries like these indicated above are therefore likely to be considered revolutionary. Artificial insemination with donor semen represents a transfer, in part, of the reproductive function from the family to an outside source. This has hitherto not been countenanced, and it will be interesting to see how the law comes to define artificial insemination with donor semen. Artificial insemination, using stored semen from men with superior heredity may lead to a renewed emphasis on eugenics by those who attach special significance to the influence of heredity. Also the separation of the physiological and psychological aspects of sex, already enhanced by birth control practices, is further emphasized by artificial insemination. These changes have the effect of raising the status of women who in addition to being regarded as the bearers of children are seen as contributors in other ways to their own happiness and the happiness of their husbands.

A Longer and Healthier Married Life for More Old People

The lower birth rate and the larger expectation of life has resulted in a larger percentage of old people in our nation, and the proportion is expected to increase. On the basis of 1949 vital statistics, white women in the United States had an average life expectancy in 1951 of 71.5 years, white men 65 years, 11 months, whereas it is estimated that a woman born in 1970 can expect to live 80 years, a man 74 years.[12] At the same time, they should be stronger, more alert, and more vigorous; and the creeping deterioration of old age should be retarded. New hormonal therapy, for instance, holds promise of modification of socio-sexual behavior. It restores virility to some persons and moderates changes in middle life.[13] A suitable diet helps to postpone aging and debilitating symptoms. The diet includes certain vitamins in heavy doses and emphasizes proteins, with the male hormone, testosterone,

[11] R. G. Bunge, M.D., and associates of the University of Iowa Medical School.
[12] Harold F. Dorn, reported in *Science News Letter*, October 27, 1951, p. 261.
[13] *Science News Letter*, September 22, 1951, p. 178.

given to help assimilate the protein; and other hormones given to help utilize sugars and starches.

Anticipated effects on family life are economic and psychological. On the economic side, better health and more physical vigor at an advanced age may mean reduced medical costs and a larger period of self-support for persons of advanced age. On the other hand, increased longevity may result in an increased period of outside support, if the aged are economically dependent. On the psychological side, more grandchildren are likely to have the opportunity to know their grandparents, with a resulting increase in family continuity. More couples will celebrate their golden wedding anniversary and experience a longer period together without children, after their children have grown up and left home.

More Knowledge About Interpersonal Relations

The personality functions of the family are concerned with affectionate relationships and companionship between (a) husbands and wives, (b) parents and children, and (c) brothers and sisters. It is expected that in the future there will be more knowledge which will contribute to harmonious and effective relationships between these members of families.

One area in which progress is likely to be made is our understanding of sex and its contribution to family welfare. A goal in marriage is mutuality in affectional and sexual response of husband and wife. In the past, mates have been hampered in achieving this goal by inaccurate ideas regarding women's sexual nature and the effects of repression on personality. Still to be unraveled are the ramifications of the relationship of sex and the sentiments, that is, precisely how sex is related to affection, and especially love of a spiritual nature. Also in need of fuller exploration is the relation of sex to happiness and the contribution that technique in sex relations may make to marital adjustment.

Research has shown that sex is a function of the total personality, and inquiry therefore leads at once from sex to the psychological factors in marital compatibility. Among the personality traits which research has shown to be conducive to marital maladjustment are emotional immaturity, narcissism, self-centeredness, inferiority feelings, rebelliousness, aggressiveness, emotional fixation on parents, extreme dominance, guilt feelings, marked insecurity, and nervousness. These findings came from studies made by psychoanalysts and others working with individual cases, as well as by sociologists and psychologists using questionnaire and interview methods with groups of married couples. The association of the traits studied with marital happiness or unhappiness has not been high, perhaps in part because in the samples used individuals with extreme deviant traits were rare, and because the methods of research were deficient. In the future it is likely that there will be research using larger and more representative samples; partial correlation and factor analysis instead of zero-order correlation:

combinations of traits instead of single traits; and pairing of traits in husband and wife. Such research should contribute new knowledge regarding the factors involved in marital adjustment. In addition, prediction tests, when greatly improved, may be used in mate selection. There is, of course, the question as to how much use will be made of such tests. If the well-adjusted persons in larger numbers marry well-adjusted persons, then more of the poorly-adjusted will marry other poorly-adjusted individuals or not marry at all. The result, however, would be to increase the proportion of harmonious marriages. For if there were, say, 100 well-adjusted men and women and 100 poorly-adjusted men and women and they were to intermarry, the result in general would be less satisfactory than if the well adjusted were to marry within their own group.

If the emotional core of personality is mainly established during the early years of life, then the most effective preparation for marriage takes place during early childhood. The problem of wholesome personality in adults becomes the problem of proper child guidance. In rearing normal children, research has shown the importance of proper doses of affection; discipline that is administered with moderation, uniformity, and understanding; identification with the parent of the same sex for the purpose of normal sextyping; confidences and congenial shared activities between parents and children.

In these areas and allied areas, having to do with interpersonal relations as they bear on the family, research is being carried on with increasing skill, resources, and vigor. Important advances in our knowledge are certain, and the demand for such knowledge will lead to its dissemination and use. It is hoped that as a result we shall have more success in eradicating undesirable personality traits and in avoiding them altogether.

SUMMARY

Changes in the family are primarily due to external factors and secondarily due to internal factors. Since the family and other parts of culture are interrelated, a change in these correlated parts induces a change in the family. The most dynamic of these correlated parts of the social system is science. It is for this reason that in this chapter we have reviewed the influences of changes in science (that is, invention and discovery) on family life.

Inventions and discoveries produce changes in certain parts of the family; and since the family is a unity of differentiated parts, a change in one part produces a change in other parts. So a change in jobs for married women changes the status of married women.

The external influences of innovations on the family operate through the mechanisms of dispersal and convergence. The effects of innovations are dispersed in many directions and affect many aspects of the total culture. These effects may, however, converge to produce a massive effect. Thus there was a dispersal of the effects of the steam engine, but many of these effects converged to produce cities. From the city in turn there flowed many effects, which converged to influence the family greatly. The influence of changing technology on the family has been mainly indirect, through the growth of cities. The factors in cities which have been especially instrumental in family change are: (1) production outside the home; (2) the separation of work and place of residence; and (3) the density of population.

Major direct effects on the family are those that influence its sex and personality functions. Birth control, a major influence, affects the size of family with important social-psychological consequences for the relationships of family members. Another important cluster of influences on the family derives from the modification in the form of the religious outlook, generally referred to as secularization. The causes of this phenomenon are complex but are generally ascribed to the influence of scientific discoveries regarding the nature of man and the universe.

The analysis of the processes of family change permits some projection of changes into the near future. In the next few decades, we anticipate that there will be no increase in economic production in the home, less processing of food at home and therefore more marketing for home consumption. Because of inventions utilizing electricity, homes will become increasingly comfortable, and attractive as places of recreation. Improved methods of birth control will probably result in more planned families. Advances in diet, medicine, and public health will lead to a longer and healthier married life. And increased knowledge contributed by the sciences of man may contribute to more effective intra-familial relationships.

ANNOTATED BIBLIOGRAPHY

NIMKOFF, M. F., "What Do Modern Inventions Do to Family Life?" *Annals of the American Academy of Political and Social Science,* Vol. 272 (November, 1950), pp. 53–58. An analysis of the direct and indirect effects of recent inventions on the family.

OGBURN, W. F., "The Changing Family," *Publications of the American Sociological Society,* Vol. 23 (1929), pp. 124–33. The first demonstration, in statistical detail, of the transference of economic, protective, recreational, educational, and religious functions of the family to outside agencies.

———, and NIMKOFF, M. F., *Technology and the Changing Family* (Boston, Houghton Mifflin, 1955). A study of the causes of changes in the family in the United States, with special reference to the role of invention and scientific discovery.

OGBURN, W. F., and TIBBITTS, C., "The Family and Its Functions," Ch. 13 in President's Committee, *Recent Social Trends* (New York, McGraw-Hill, 1933). Established the theory that increases in out-of-the-home activities are indexes of decreases in traditional functions of the family.

CHAPTER 14

IMPACT OF TECHNOLOGY ON AGRICULTURE

■ *Delbert C. Miller*

Introduction

The common roots of industrial and agricultural technologies. Modern agriculture is an industry which applies technology to the soil. Until near the end of the nineteenth century, agriculture was by far the most important industry in the United States from most points of view—economic, political, social, even psychological. The primacy of agriculture in the American economy then gave way to the growing domination of the factory and the machine. In the transition, agriculture was revolutionized by advances in technology. The culture base which brought mechanization to industry also brought mechanization to agriculture.

The similarities in technology are not apparent at first glance. Agricultural technology has distinctive characteristics and embraces a wide range of science and engineering, including farm machinery, animal breeding, insect control, and soil science.

Agricultural industry is partly the result of basic scientific discoveries and partly the result of thousands of ingenious modifications in every-day practice. The farmer cannot fully control the quantity and quality of his product. He is dependent on the structure and condition of the soil, the topography of his land, on rainfall and sunshine and the requirements of each plant. There is little room on the farm for division of labor comparable to that in industry. Unlike most industrial processes, many types of farm work cannot be carried on uninterruptedly throughout the year. The Industrial Revolution which began in the eighteenth century to mechanize manufacture did not reach agriculture until a century later. In spite of these differences between agriculture and manufacturing industry, there are marked parallels between the two technologies. The advance of farm machinery depended largely on developments in engineering and metallurgy, the sciences upon which the improvement of all machine tools rests. The automobile, which was largely responsible for the outward expansion of city population, also changed the pattern of rural life by lessening the isolation of the farm. In addition, the auto was the forerunner of the motorized tractor and the truck which are basic to modern farming. The same chemical discoveries that have given us modern plastics and invaluable drugs have served as the base for the more than five hundred or more new organic chemical compounds for use in the farmer's fields. Electricity brought the same new comforts to the farm home as it did to the urban household. And as the factory adopted this new source of power for operation of machine tools, the farm employed it for water pumping, milking, and a large number of other farm tasks.

Most persons are aware of the marked increase in the productivity of industrial workers. It is not as well known that the rate of technological progress on the 6 million family farms engaged in commercial agriculture in the United States has been almost as rapid as in manufacturing plants. Since 1910, production per employee in agriculture has progressed at about the same rate of increases as shown in industry (see the table below).

PRODUCTION PER EMPLOYEE IN AGRICULTURE AND IN INDUSTRY FROM 1910–45

Production per employee (1910–14 = 100)

	Agriculture	Industry
1910	94	97
1915	105	108
1920	118	106
1925	123	136
1930	127	150
1935	120	146
1940	151	180
1945	191	223

SOURCE: 1946 Agricultural Outlook Charts, Bureau of Agricultural Economics, December, 1945.

The efficiency of a machine is usually defined as the ratio of work output to energy input. Theodore Schultz has estimated the efficiency of agriculture by combining agriculture inputs and relating these to agriculture outputs. Inputs include such production items as labor, interest, land, taxes, maintenance, fertilizer, and operation of motor vehicles. One unit of farm input in 1950 resulted in 54 per cent more farm output than in 1910. If this improvement is averaged over the last twenty-seven years during which virtually all this improvement actually took place, it represents an average increase of 2 per cent per year.[1]

The record in agriculture is surprising, for the millions of farm operators have less favorable circumstances for adopting improvements than the larger industrial firms where financing, management, and labor functions are specialized. Technological progress in farming is due in large part to extensive research by public institutions and research and development of new products by manufacturers of farm equipment and supplies.[2]

[1] Theodore W. Schultz, *The Economic Organization of Agriculture* (New York, McGraw-Hill, 1953), p. 109.

[2] Walter W. Wilcox, *The Farmer in the Second World War* (Ames, Iowa State College Press, 1947), p. 287.

Interlocked change relationships induced by the industrial and agricultural technologies. The increased productivity of agriculture has resulted in a stream of displaced rural people who have sought employment in the cities. The cities have continued to absorb these technologically unemployed rural workers until today less than 12 *per cent* of the total experienced labor force is engaged in agricultural employment.[3] Unemployment in the cities tends to stop the flow of rural to urban migration and gives rise to dependency problems on the farms and rural communities. Depression in either the rural or urban areas of our economy soon affects the total economy adversely. Just as depression is interrelated, so is prosperity. Rural prosperity offers a strong support to urban prosperity, while urban prosperity is, in turn, the largest factor in the maintenance of good times on the farm.

Derivative technological influences affect social conditions of living as well as economic ones. The automobile, the telephone, the daily newspaper, and the magazines have increased the means of communication, bringing farmers closer to each other in time and distance and, in turn, bringing them closer to centers of population, education, and entertainment. Motion pictures, radio, and television have affected rural habits and customs.[4] The improved means of transportation and communication have broken down many provincial barriers. Urban and rural differences grow ever smaller. The suburban movement has encouraged an increasing number of urban workers to adopt a semirural pattern of living. Sociologists have called this "rurbanization," to designate a blending of dominant rural and urban personality and character traits. The future role of both the city and the farm are intimately tied to the problem of combining the industrial and agricultural technologies so that a better balance may be attained for both urban and rural populations.

In Chapter 11 the technological influence on industry was discussed. As this introduction suggests, there are many parallels between that chapter and this one. The reader will find it valuable to appraise the parallels—and the differences—that characterize the industrial and agricultural technologies. This chapter is organized in three sections. These are the influence of technology on (1) agricultural production; (2) internal organization of the farm; and (3) economic and social organization of rural life.

INFLUENCE OF TECHNOLOGY ON AGRICULTURAL PRODUCTION

Main Streams of Technological Development in Agriculture

The modern farmer has new machines, techniques, and knowledge to pit against the adversities of land and weather. The inventions which constitute

[3] 6,835,356 farm owners, tenants, managers, foremen, and laborers in an experienced civilian labor force of 58,998,943 as shown in the United States Census of 1950. See Bureau of the Census, *United States Census of Population: 1950,* Vol. III, Part 1 (Washington, Government Printing Office, 1953).

[4] See Chapters 7 and 8, which describe social effects of motion pictures, radio, and television.

modern agricultural technology may be summarized under five headings. These are:

1. Invention, improvement, and use of machinery and power.
2. Introduction, adaptation, and improvement of plants and animals.
3. Increased ability to control insects, pests, and diseases.
4. Increased knowledge relating to the use and replenishment of soils.
5. Improvement in managerial and marketing techniques.

Each of these will be briefly described in the next section.

Invention, improvement, and use of machinery and power. *a. Mechanization Before 1900.* Through countless centuries, agriculture was carried on by hand labor, with only a few simple tools supplemented to a slight extent by animal power. The New England farmer of colonial times was dependent upon tools of the most primitive sort. His chief farm tools were the harrow, a spade, and a fork, all made of wood and clumsily constructed. Few could afford a plow, and a town often paid a bounty to anyone who would buy a plow and keep it in repair. One plow would be used to do the work for a large territory.[5]

Between 1800 and 1850 three very important farm tools were added. These were iron and steel plows, seed drills for sowing grain, and the mechanical reaper.

The plow in common use in 1800 was a cumbersome wooden contrivance. In 1814 Jethro Wood patented a cast-iron model, but farmers feared soil poisoning and its adoption was temporarily delayed. However, by 1833 thousands were using iron plows and were ready to adopt the steel moldboard plow which appeared in that year. The rich, sticky, and heavily root-matted soils of the prairies would not yield to iron but required steel. John Deere, the blacksmith who perfected the steel plow and manufactured it, is given credit for making possible the successful cultivation of the prairies.[6]

Seed drills were introduced in the 1840's and shortly thereafter came the corn planter and corn cultivator. Perhaps the most significant of the inventions of this period was that of Obed Hussey and Cyrus H. McCormick, who produced the mechanical reaper between 1833 and 1845. It replaced many hands at that crucial point in grain production when the work must be completed quickly to save the crop from ruin. The threshing machine appeared in 1850.[7]

The inventions which followed in the latter half of the nineteenth century

[5] Harold U. Faulkner, *American Economic History*, 6th ed. (New York, Harper, 1949), p. 62. See also Percy W. Bidwell and John Falconer, *History of Agriculture in the Northern United States, 1620–1860* (Washington, Carnegie Institution of Washington, 1925), Ch. 3.

[6] Everett E. Edwards, "American Agriculture—The First Hundred Years," in *Farmers in a Changing World,* Yearbook of Agriculture (Washington, Government Printing Office, 1940), p. 229.

[7] Murray R. Benedict, *Farm Policies of the United States, 1790–1950* (New York, Twentieth Century Fund, 1953), p. 83.

were more numerous and impressive. Improvements in machinery for planting, cultivating, and harvesting appeared simultaneously. The most important of these was the invention of the binder used in harvesting. The climate in the wheat regions of the Middle West required rapid harvesting when the crop was ripe; thus the amount of grain planted depended on the amount of grain that could be harvested. In 1858, C. W. and W. W. Marsh patented the "Marsh harvester," a reaping machine which delivered grain upon a table where two men could bind it as they moved along. This reaper almost doubled the amount of grain that could be harvested in a given time. But in 1878 a still more remarkable development took place, namely, John F. Appleby invented the "twine binder which increased eightfold the speed in harvesting."[8] There were two effects of this invention. It not only increased the amount which a farmer could harvest, but also increased by that precise amount the quantity which he could profitably grow. At the end of the century, the steam threshing machine worked a revolution in the separating of grain from the husk. The corn harvester and corn husker made their appearance and transformed the handling of the corn crop. As these machines were adopted, horses replaced men as the motive power for agricultural implements. The number of horses used as draft animals increased rapidly with the increase of such implements as the plow, the grain drill, the haymower and rake, the reaper, and the thresher.

In the Cotton Belt, the cotton gin was greatly improved and the development of a cotton picking machine was begun. The cotton seed planter, fertilizer distributor, cotton stalk cutter, and various specialized plows and harrows were introduced. Dairying too became mechanized with cream separators and churns.[9]

b. Mechanization Since 1900. The nineteenth century produced greater changes in agriculture than had occurred in thousands of years prior to 1800. Even greater changes in agriculture were to take place during the first half of the twentieth century.[10] They revolved chiefly about the substitution of mechanical power for horse power. The improvement of the internal combustion engine made possible a successful gasoline tractor first introduced by Benjamin Holt in 1903. The automobile truck was soon widely used for hauling. Together the tractor and truck spelled the end of horses and mules as efficient sources of motive power in the agricultural process. By 1953 there were 4.4 million tractors and 2.5 million trucks working on American farms.[11]

The tilling of land has been vastly improved by the steel gang plow and the disc-harrow combine drawn by the gasoline tractor. The planting of land

[8] Faulkner, *op. cit.,* p. 427.

[9] E. E. Edwards, *op. cit.,* p. 231.

[10] Martin R. Cooper and Glen T. Barton, "A Century of Farm Mechanization," *The Agricultural Situation* (March-April, 1948), Vol. 32, No. 9 (Washington, Bureau of Agricultural Economics).

[11] J. Frederick Dewhurst and Associates, *America's Needs and Resources, A New Survey* (New York, Twentieth Century Fund, 1955), p. 784.

Courtesy of E. I. DuPont de Nemours

THE IMPRESSIVE MECHANIZATION OF A MODERN FARM

may be done by fleets of large grain drills. Harvesting of grain is now done almost exclusively by the combine which cuts, threshes, cleans, and bags grain all in one process. Corn harvesters of far greater capacity have been invented.[12] The cotton picker now widely adopted is producing marked changes in Southern agriculture, one of which is the displacement of hand pickers who have been largely Negroes, Mexicans, and Indians. California has recently joined the cotton producing states with the most highly mechanized production in the world. Over 1,400 cotton picking machines were used on the million acres which California had in cotton in 1952.

Electric power, an important part of farm equipment, is available to about

---

[12] John A. Hopkins, *Changing Technology and Employment in Agriculture* (Washington, U. S. Government Printing Office, 1941), pp. 70–72. Cf. R. R. Gray "Some New Farm Machines," in *Science in Farming,* Yearbook of Agriculture, 1943–1947 (Washington, Government Printing Office, 1947), pp. 815–817.

nine-tenths of all farms.[13] A picture of some agricultural implements used on a mechanized modern farm appears on page 329. The farmer is John D. Burkholder of Lititz, Pennsylvania, who operates 84 acres. He grows corn, wheat, hay, tobacco, and potatoes. For his work he uses such machine tools as tractor, truck, tractor plow, disc harrow, corn planter, hay rake, hay baler, manure spreader, combine harvester, elevator, milking machine, and others.[14] An English productivity team found 28 different machine implements on a typical American family-size cereal farm of 160 acres.

Introduction, adaptation, and improvement of plants and animals. *a. The Improvement of Crop Varieties.* The improvement in crops by breeding and selection is made possible by application of the science of genetics. This science is only about fifty years old, but already it has made many contributions to agriculture. Agronomists and horticulturists have brought about some remarkable improvements in yielding ability and in quality. Plant breeding has made possible the development of strains resistant to diseases and pests. Varieties of some crops have been developed to permit production under different climatic conditions.

The most spectacular example of yielding ability is undoubtedly that of hybrid corn. Records kept since its introduction after 1930 show that a 15–30 per cent increase in per-acre yields has been secured. These yields provide each year an extra 35 pounds of pork for every person in the United States.[15]

The development of species resistant to disease have saved many wheat, oat, and cotton crops. Ninety-one varieties of wheat were distributed between 1909 and 1934. Resistance to the deadly black stem rust was bred into our common wheats through research involving crosses with related species.[16] Fifty-seven improved varieties of oats have been distributed in the United States since 1909.[17] In addition, 125 superior strains have been selected for such characteristics as resistance to disease and to cold. A radical change in cotton varieties was caused by the spread of the boll weevil.[18]

Recently, geneticists have become especially interested in micro-organisms, especially molds, yeasts, bacteria, and viruses which are of considerable importance in the field of medicine; the Penicillium mold is an outstanding example of this.

[13] Dewhurst, *op. cit.,* p. 784.

[14] Productivity Team Report, *Productivity in Farming* (London, Anglo-American Council on Productivity, 1951), p. 34.

[15] U. S. Department of Agriculture, *Research and Related Services in the United States* (Washington, Government Printing Office, 1951), p. 2.

[16] E. P. Sears, "Genetics and Farming," in *Science in Farming, op. cit.,* p. 245.

[17] T. R. Stanton, *Superior Germ Plasm in Oats,* Yearbook of Agriculture (Washington, Government Printing Office, 1936), pp. 381–387.

[18] W. C. Holley and Lloyd E. Arnold, "Changes in Technology and Labor Requirements in Crop Production—Cotton" (Washington, W.P.A.-N.R.P. Report No. A-7, September, 1938), pp. 64 ff.

Some persons have supposed the new varieties of yeasts and fungi might be bred to replace soil-grown plants as sources of food. There is very little indication that this development will soon, if ever, take place.[19]

b. The Improvement of Livestock. Technological changes have brought about the development of healthier, more productive animals. These changes involve (1) the improvement of various breeds to bring about greater efficiency in converting feed into milk, pork, or beef; (2) discoveries in animal nutrition; and (3) the control of animal diseases.

Improvement of Breeds. Fifteen million head of beef cattle are slaughtered every year in the United States to provide for a per capita consumption of 70 pounds.[20] Unfortunately, there has been no formula developed for making all cuts tender. However, pronounced progress has been made since 1900 in breeding and selecting livestock for greater production. The breeder uses three basic tools to bring about the genetic improvement of animals. These are *selection, inbreeding,* and *crossing.*

Cattle breeders use *selection* as the chief tool to improve their stock. Selection is based on the performance of the breeding animal. This method has been more successful in raising production. Further gains have been achieved by determining the ability of breeding stock to transmit high-producing capacity to their offspring, and then using the offspring of proved stock for further breeding. Although "test tube breeding" did not begin in the United States until 1935, a total of 4 million of the nation's 24 million dairy cows had been bred artificially at the beginning of 1952. Since artificial insemination enables a bull to father 2,000 calves a year instead of the normal 40, it permits a more intensive use of well-proved sires. A more rapid improvement of herds and milk production is thus secured.[21]

Inbreeding, the second of the breeder's tools, increases the chances that animals will pass on their traits to their offspring, and it is useful in maintaining a high relationship of stock to an especially desirable ancestor. *Cross breeding* for the production of market animals takes advantage of the increased productivity owing to the hybrid vigor that frequently results from the crossing of distinct types and breeds.[22]

All three of these methods of breeding recognize that improvements in heredity play a large role in production. It has been estimated that from 40 per cent to 50 per cent of the variation between individual cows in milk production and between 60 per cent and 70 per cent in butterfat production is attributable to differences in heredity.[23] The remainder comes largely from feeding and environment.

[19] Sears, *op. cit.,* p. 255.
[20] Ralph W. Phillips, "Producing Better Beefsteaks," in *Science in Farming, op. cit.,* p. 61.
[21] *Farm Journal* (February, 1953), p. 64.
[22] Phillips, *op. cit.,* pp. 33–60.
[23] J. W. Gowen, *Milk Secretion* (Baltimore, Williams and Wilkins, 1924), pp. 153–336.

Discoveries in Animal Nutrition. Great progress has been made in economical animal production through the discovery of the needs of animals for proteins, minerals, hormones, and vitamins. Livestock feeding seeks to provide a balanced ration of all these needed growth elements. This has brought about healthier and more productive animals.

Control of Livestock Diseases. Considerable progress has been made in eradicating diseases affecting animals. Tuberculosis is estimated to have caused losses among livestock in the United States of $40 million a year before systematic eradication work was begun.[24] Tick fever was estimated to cause an annual loss of $40 million in 1906 to beef cattle producers. Hog cholera, the most serious disease of swine, has caused heavy losses for many years estimated at $50 million per year.[25] Vaccination and immunization have reduced all of these more serious diseases, but this has been accomplished at a heavy cost of time and money.

Increased ability to control insects, pests, and diseases. Man is engaged in a constant battle against insects, weeds, rodents, and plant diseases. It is estimated that the American farmer in 1952 lost $5 billion worth of crop to weeds, $4 billion to insects, $4 billion to plant diseases, and $2 billion to rats and other rodents—a grand total of $15 billion.[26] The most serious of crop enemies is the insect. Fortunately, modern chemical technology has developed many insecticides to fight off the ravages of insects upon food crops. The farmer finds a growing list of insecticides on the shelves of the local feed store. The older insecticides were arsenicals, lime-sulphur mixtures, nicotine sprays, and pyrethrum dusts. The newer insecticides are organic compounds specially synthesized for specific tasks. DDT is widely known for its high killing power and long residual effect against many insects. Others are marketed under such names as methoxychor, chlorodane, TEPP, BHC, Toxaphene, Parathion, aldrin, dieldrin, and allethrin. Each has its special effectiveness against a range of insects ranging from tiny orchard mites and aphids to grasshoppers and roaches. The dream of the insecticide business has been to produce a systemic insecticide: something which after a single application would enter the sapstream of the plant and make every part of it poisonous to any insect feeding on it. Only one has been certified by the United States Department of Agriculture as ready for market. This is Systox, a complex organic chemical, which is used on cotton for the control of aphids and mites.[27]

Weed killers have appeared to cut both crop loss and crop labor. In 1953

[24] Alexander E. Wright, "Eradication of Tuberculosis Among Livestock in the United States," *Proceedings of the Twelfth International Veterinarian Congress,* II, Section I (1934), pp. 33–34.
[25] M. Dorset and U. G. Houck, *Hog Cholera,* rev. ed. (Washington, Department of Agriculture, Farmer's Bulletin No. 834, 1928 and 1937).
[26] Eric Hodgins, "Farming's Chemical Age," *Fortune* (November, 1953), p. 153.
[27] *Ibid.,* pp. 206–208.

it is estimated that the airplane was used by American farmers to chemically treat 30 million acres of crop land in order to kill weeds.[28] Spraying by airplane permits a rapid application of weed killers over large acreage.

Plant diseases are being successfully fought by new organic compounds and the old-fashioned copper salts and lime-sulphur mixtures. The three most important diseases caused by fungi are apple scab, potato blight, and stem rust of wheat. In addition, fungi and bacteria attack seeds. Treatment of seed with disinfectants has become highly important since 1920.[29] Seed disinfectants are now protecting the relatively expensive hybrid-corn seeds. Millions of bushels of wheat, oats, grain sorghum, and barley are also being saved yearly by protecting the seed from fungus attack. Cotton, also subject to seed-borne disease, has witnessed an increase of seed disinfecting.

Increased knowledge of the use and replenishment of soil. The nutrition of man (and of all other animals) begins with the soil. The variety of foods that comprise the normal diet should provide enough of essential minerals and vitamins to meet our needs. But many of the soils on which food crops are grown do not supply the plants with sufficient minerals to meet our needs or to enable the plants to synthesize the vitamins in sufficient quantity. It is now known that there is an interaction among the nutrient elements: when one is reduced, the plant responds by accumulating an increased quantity of other elements and vice versa. This is especially noted in the interactions between the three principal nutrients: potassium, calcium, and magnesium. The occurrence of a deficiency is brought about by the relationship or balance between a critical element and the levels of all of the other elements in the leaf. The other elements may include besides the three principal bases such nutrients as nitrogen, phosphorous, iron, manganese, zinc, copper, and boron—all of which must be accumulated in the proper proportions to one another if satisfactory crop production is to be maintained.[30]

This knowledge of plant growth raises two considerations regarding the soil. The first has to do with increasing the yield and the second with improving the nutritive quality of the crops. Many chemicals are now available to help attain both of these objectives. These can be described as *fertilizers, growth regulators,* and *soil conditioners.* Fertilizers now have the role of providing to the soil the balance of nutrients needed.[31] Growth regulators like 2,4-D and many others permit selective plant growth. They have taken on such tasks as thinning out the blossoms on fruit trees to produce better fruit without handwork, to delay fruit budding until danger of frost is past, to produce fruit without seeds, to alter the shape of plants, to accelerate

[28] John Strohm, ed., *The Ford Almanac* (New York, Simon & Schuster, 1954), p. 91.
[29] Hopkins, *op. cit.,* p. 87.
[30] C. B. Shear and H. L. Crane, "Nutrient—Element Balance," in *Science in Farming, op. cit.,* p. 594.
[31] Kenneth C. Beeson, "Better Soils, Better Food," in *Science in Farming, op. cit.,* p. 497.

ripening, and so on. Soil conditioners first went on the market in 1952. Their function is to make the soil more friable and by so doing to prevent surface baking and crusting and to increase absorption and retention of water. At present, the price of soil conditioning chemicals is high and the value of soil conditioning is not proved.

New practices in the use of the soil have added to productivity and conservation of the soil. These include crop rotation, protecting the soil with trees and grasses, practicing contour cultivation, strip cropping, terracing, pasture furrowing, and basin listing.[32]

Improvement in managerial and marketing techniques. Efficiency in farm production depends on two kinds of managerial decisions. The first involves questions of *what* and the second questions of *how*. Initial decisions include what crops and livestock to produce, what to feed the animals, what fertilizers and insecticides to apply, what kind of farm equipment to invest in, and so on. Once the "what" is decided, then a number of "how-to-do-it" decisions must be made. Farm work can be greatly simplified if the easiest, most effective, and economical ways to do a job are systematically developed.[33] The revolution in farm techniques demands more managerial and executive capacity in farm operators. Today's farmer is an applied scientist, machine operator, and manager. Constant efforts are being made to assist farmers in improving their methods.[34] In late years, the United States has been spending about $100 million a year for agricultural research in the United States Department of Agriculture and the land-grant colleges. Another $75 million a year for teaching new methods is expended by the Extension services.[35]

The county agricultural agent and home-demonstration agent are continuously available to farmers for teaching, advice, and access to the latest research publications in agriculture. In a North Carolina study, E. A. Wilkening found the most frequent sources of information about eight improved farm practices were as follows:[36]

[32] D. B. Krimgold, "Managing Surface Runoff," in *ibid*, p. 537.

[33] E. C. Young and L. S. Hardin, "Simplifying Farm Work," in *ibid.*, p. 817.

[34] A primer on Advanced Farm Practices published by a farm machinery company gives an indication of the kind of knowledge now being made freely available. The topics listed are: Diversification of Farm Products, Livestock Farming, Pasture Management, Pond Construction, Proper Tillage, Stubble Mulch Tillage, Modern Seeding, Weed Control, Surface Cultivation, Contour Farming, Terrace Building, Manuring—Fertilizing, Soil Building Rotations, Timely Harvesting, Ensiling Feed Crops, High Protein Hay Production, Machine Selection, Machine Care, Safety, Record Keeping. —*Advanced Farm Practices*, 4th ed. (Racine, Wis., J. I. Case Co., Inc., 1947), p. 2.

[35] Lauren Soth, *How Farm People Learn New Methods* (Washington, National Planning Association, 1952), p. 3.

[36] E. A. Wilkening, "Sources of Information for Improved Farm Practices," *Rural Sociology*, Vol. 15 (March, 1950).

Other farmers 28%
Extension Service 26%
Dealers 16%
Vocational Agriculture Teacher 11%
Soil Conservation Service 9%
Farm Journals 5%
Other farm agencies 2%
Radio 2%

Summary of technological development. The technology which supports agriculture today draws upon such basic and applied sciences as metallurgy, engineering, chemistry, physics, plant and animal physiology and pathology, entomology, forestry, genetics, scientific management, geography, and marketing. In this section we have described briefly the history of farm mechanization, the improvement of plants and animals, the control of insects, pests, and diseases, soil use, and managerial techniques. Agricultural technology has been described in the following terms:[37]

[It is] science, art, and invention. It is tractors, combines, cornpickers. It is the testing and breeding of animals and the conquest of diseases. It is hybrid corn, new kinds of wheat, soy beans, and lespedeza. It is the way to feed cows, plants, and men. It is road building and rural electrification. It is contour plowing, conservation of soil, management of forests, protection of wild life. It is marketing and distribution. It is a race between insect pests and ways to kill them. Technology is the workshop, barn, grove, field, and home.

Agricultural Technology: Evolution of Machines

The agricultural technology parallels the four-stage pattern set out in Chapter 11 which traced the evolution of industrial technology. These are the stages called the *modern craft age,* the *machine age,* the *power age,* and the *atomic age.* They are ages which may be said to have emerged about 1000 A.D. with the craft age and which have succeeded one another in the sense that new key inventions have altered the ways of producing goods and services. The changes which have accompanied each age have not obliterated all traces of the preceding ages. On the contrary, vestiges of almost every technological age can be found in any community. Karl Mannheim used the phrase "the contemporaneity of the non-contemporaneous" to refer to culture traits left by each age even as the new emerges and becomes dominant. The important elements in the technology which shape a pattern are:[38]

Power	Material
Tools	Transportation
Work skills	Communication

These are shown for each of the four stages in the following table.

[37] Special Report of the United States Department of Agriculture, *Technology on the Farm* (Washington, Government Printing Office, 1940), p. 3.

[38] I am indebted to Lewis Mumford, *Technics and Civilization* (New York, Harcourt, Brace, 1934). Mumford proposes a series of stages called eotechnic, paleotechnic, and neotechnic.

FOUR AGES OF AGRICULTURAL TECHNOLOGY

Important Determiners of Technology in Dominant Ages		Modern Craft Age 1000–	Machine Age 1830–	Power Age 1920–	Atomic Age 1960–
Power		Human and animal muscle	Multiple horse teams and steam	Gasoline and electricity	Atomic energy used to produce electric power and heat
		Man, horse, and mule Use of wind	Man, horse, and steam tractor	Motorized tractor, truck electric motors	Alcohol burning tractors
		Hand wrought	Machine wrought	Multiple machine tools	Automatic radar-directed machines on fields
Tools		Wooden plow, cradle, scythe, horse collar.	Iron and steel plow, mower, reaper, grain drill, self-binder, thresher, cream separator.	Increasingly, self-propelled such as combine, corn harvester, cotton picker; and electrified machines such as milking machine.	Automated farm and biochemical production of food in factories.

Work Skills	All-around subsistence farm skills.	Specialized in diversified farming.	Skills of mechanic and machine operator, and electrician.	Highly trained engineers as designers are required.
Material	Wood, iron, bronze	Steel, copper	Alloyed steels, light alloys, aluminum	Super alloys, use of new metals, plastics
Transportation	Walking, use of animals via dirt road.	Steam train, horse and buggy	Auto, diesel train, airplane	Rocket and helicopter via stratosphere
Communication	Word of mouth, newspaper, messenger.	Mail moved faster by rail and water; newspaper printed on steam press. Telephone, Telegraph.	AM and FM radio, movies, television, microfilm, and magnetic tape	Televised telephone, talking book or newspaper, universal two-way radio communication, electronic machine, magnetic tape photography, voca-typewriter

Modern craft age. Until the nineteenth century A.D., colonial American farmers used the same methods and tools as the food raisers of 3000 B.C.[39] The only significant advances were the cradle and scythe—first seen in the United States in 1790—and the horse collar. The horse collar, introduced about 1000 A.D., is claimed by some historians to be of basic importance. Before that time, farmers had tried harnessing horses to the plow in place of oxen but had failed because the harness strap pressed on the horse's windpipe and cut off his breath. The horse collar, which left the animal's windpipe free, increased fourfold the motive power at the farmer's command. The tandem harness and the horseshoe were invented about the same time and the use of animals was increasingly facilitated.[40]

The machine age. Starting in the second third of the nineteenth century, an outpouring of inventions transformed agriculture and the face of the country. A description of this remarkable period of invention was given in the discussion of mechanization before 1900. It will be remembered that in quick succession came first the cast-iron plow, then the steel mold-board plow, the mower, reaper, grain drill, threshing machine, and the twine binder. These remarkable inventions, forged from the new steel, produced an industrial revolution in agriculture just as machine tools were bringing the factory and mass production to manufacture.

Although steam tractors were used on large prairie farms soon after the invention of steel plows, they were not altogether satisfactory because of their weight and the difficulty of providing fuel and water. It was not the tractor but the horse which dominated motive power for agricultural implements until 1920. The steel implements were strong and teams composed of as many as 20 to 24 horses or mules might be hitched together to implements placed in tandem, increasing production and reducing manpower.

The power age. The power age is characterized by the widespread adoption of the tractor and the electrification of the farm. The motorized general-purpose tractor was introduced in the 1920's and proved so satisfactory that horses and mules were widely displaced. The use of inanimate energy in agriculture was delayed, since the steam engine was never entirely suitable for farming, especially family-size farming. However, in the power age, the farm caught up technologically with manufacture. Electric and motorized power became widely used.

The combine is an outstanding agricultural example of the multiple machine tool which has proved so useful in industry. It cuts, reaps, threshes, and bales. Some clean, sack, and weigh the grain. Another multiple implement is the two-row corn harvester which cuts the stalks, picks the ears, husks, and discharges the corn into a wagon while the stalks are shredded. Several new tillage machines plow, disc, and harrow a seed bed in one operation. One new potato harvester will dig, pick, and sack potatoes in any kind of soil. Increased versatility is being built into the tractor and its equipment.

[39] Faulkner, *op. cit.,* p. 234.
[40] R. J. Forbes, *Man, the Maker* (New York, Schuman, 1950), p. 110.

The new alloys have made it possible to produce lighter tractors and implements while retaining strength. Aluminum is being used increasingly as a building material, especially for barns and sheds.

The airplane is playing a growing role in the transport of perishable fruits, flowers, and vegetables.[41] It is also being increasingly used for such jobs as crop dusting, spraying with insecticides and herbicides, fertilizing, seeding, and defoliating.[42]

The atomic age. Agriculture is destined to undergo vast changes in the years ahead. Achievements in the field of synthetic chemistry promise better utilization of farm products and the creation of artificial foods by purely chemical methods. Since 1913, the University of California has been investigating a water-culture technique for growing plants without soil.[43] Soilless agriculture is a technique of growing plants with their roots in a solution containing the mineral nutrients essential for plant growth. Yields from soil-grown and solution-grown plants are about equal under similar conditions. Some commercial development has been attempted in vegetables like tomatoes, celery, and asparagus. The California scientists believe the water-culture method has commercial possibilities in the growing of special high-priced crops, particularly out of season in greenhouses in localities where good soil is not available or when maintenance of highly favorable soil conditions is found too expensive.[44] Recent experiments at Cornell University dealt with sheep fed in the conventional way with natural grains and grasses, and with others which were raised exclusively on synthetic laboratory products. The latter were definitely superior in weight, wool, and other important points. The Department of Agriculture has announced that piglets fed synthetic sow's milk made with terramycin weigh 10–35 pounds more than animals fed natural sow's milk.[45]

Further mechanization of agriculture may mean the use of radar-controlled tractors. It has been demonstrated that on level land the tractor, utilizing a simple guiding apparatus, can plow a field without a human operator. The pilotless tractor is no more impossible than the pilotless aircraft that is now an actuality. The agricultural complement of the automatic factory may turn out to be either a chemical food factory or automatic, tractor-propelled tillage, cultivating, planting, and harvesting equipment. The power for this equipment might be alcohol made from grain, although alcohol from farm products cannot now compete successfully with petroleum products as a fuel. Atomic energy may be used to supply electric power. If farm man-

[41] W. Wilcox, *op. cit.*, p. 297.

[42] *The Ford Almanac, op. cit.*, p. 91.

[43] D. R. Hoagland and D. I. Arnon, "The Water-Culture Method For Growing Plants Without Soil," Circular 347 (Berkeley, Calif., Agricultural Experiment Station, 1938), p. 1.

[44] *Ibid.*, p. 16.

[45] U. S. Department of Agriculture, *Research and Related Services in the United States* (Washington, Government Printing Office, 1951), Vol. I, p. 16.

agers, professional specialists, and farm labor were centralized in a village, small town, or city, atomic energy might also be a principal source of heat. Modern means of transportation and communication can be expected to continue urbanization of all social life. The "farmer" may become indistinguishable from the urban worker in personal outlook and in his way of life. If the family-size farm should disappear and industrialization of agriculture should extend to its technological conclusion, industry would come to signify a common set of productive operations for all that part of economic life which was once known as agriculture.

THE INFLUENCE OF TECHNOLOGY ON INTERNAL ORGANIZATION OF THE FARM

Influence on Size of Farms

The present character of American agriculture. Agriculture in the United States is essentially an industry of small units. There were 5.4 million farms in 1950, ranging from under 3 acres to over 1000 acres, with 75 per cent of the farms under 180 acres. The table below shows the total number of farms by size in the United States in 1950.[46]

TOTAL NUMBER OF FARMS BY SIZE IN THE UNITED STATES IN 1950

Acres	Number of Farms
Under 3	76,606
3–9	408,308
10–29	853,608
30–49	624,242
50–99	1,047,801
100–179	1,102,562
180–259	487,325
260–499	478,084
500–999	182,264
1000 acres (and over)	121,362
Total farms	5,382,162

In 1945 the largest 8.7 per cent of the farms in the United States produced 45.5 per cent of the gross value of all farm production. The largest one-third of our farms produce about four-fifths of all our farm products for market.[47]

Clearly, the smallest two-thirds of the farms in the United States are producing only 20 per cent of all agricultural commodities. Millions of small family farms, not well equipped or very productive, are barely providing a "living" for the operators. Full advantage of technological advances requires in most areas that each farm family on a full-time farm must operate more

[46] *Statistical Abstract of the United States, 1953* (Washington, Government Printing Office, 1954), p. 615.
[47] Department of Agriculture, *United States Census of Agriculture, 1945* (Washington, Government Printing Office, 1947), p. 8.

land, use more machinery, and in livestock areas, handle more livestock. The far greater efficiency of the new machinery renders any successful competition of the archaic farmer with mechanized farming out of the question. Technology delivers this imperative: more land and capital need to be associated with each farm worker.[48] The full adoption of technological changes portends sweeping readjustments in every phase of rural existence. Indeed, they threaten the very future of the family-size farm, a matter which will be discussed in the last section of this chapter.

In 1930, the average acreage per farm was 156.8; in 1945 it was up to 195 acres; in 1950, 215 acres.[49] Between 1910 and 1945 the farms of 1000 acres or more increased in number from 50,135 to 112,899, and the acreage in these larger farms increased from 167 million to 460 million; by 1945, these farms contained over 40 per cent of all farming land (a considerable portion being ranch and pasture land).[50] The development of larger equipment may continue to stimulate the consolidation of farms and a still further displacement of labor. However, the relationship between technology and farm size must be interpreted in terms of the specific crop. What is large for vegetable farming is very small for livestock.[51]

The 1945 census found that the average acreage for various types of farms was as follows (in acres):

Livestock	610
Forest Products	208
General	179
Dairy	143
Vegetable	83
Fruit and Nut	81
Poultry	70
Self-sufficing	61
Horticulture-specialty	49

These acreages do not necessarily represent the land required for maximum efficiency. They simply make apparent that size of farm varies greatly with the specific crop.

Influence on Agricultural Employment

There is perhaps no effect of technology which reveals so quickly the extent of social change than the drop in the proportion of the nation's workers engaged in agriculture. Farm workers engaged in agriculture made up 72 per cent of the total labor force in 1820, 53 per cent at the end of the Civil War, 27 per cent at the end of World War I, and about 14 per cent at the end of World War II.[52] As reported earlier in this chapter, the United States Census listed 12 per cent for 1950. It is primarily the technological develop-

---

[48] Sherman E. Johnson, "Farm Science and Citizens," in *Science in Farming, op. cit.*, p. 931.

[49] W. S. Woytinsky and E. S. Woytinsky, *World Population and Production* (New York, Twentieth Century Fund, 1953), p. 488.

[50] Department of Commerce, *Census of Agriculture, 1945* (Washington, 1948), p. 3.

[51] *Ibid.*, p. 28.

[52] W. S. Woytinsky and Associates, *Employment and Wages in the United States* (New York, Twentieth Century Fund, 1953), p. 370.

ments, such as the replacement of animal power by motor power and the accompanying shifts from hand to machine operations, that have shifted labor from farms to the city. A realistic projection of future agriculture employment requires an extension of past trends with allowances for new influences. The Bureau of Agricultural Economics taking these factors into account stated: "Mechanization and other technological developments have been releasing farm workers for other work for many years, and by 1975 they may reduce the number of farm workers needed by another 15 to 20 per cent despite a substantial increase in total farm output."[53]

In 1950, the experienced labor force in agriculture numbered 6,835,356 workers out of 59 million in the total experienced labor force. They were distributed as follows.[54]

Farm owners and tenants	4,285,462
Farm managers	35,114
Farm foremen	17,143
Farm laborers, wage workers	1,569,112
Farm laborers, unpaid family workers	918,898
Farm service laborers, self-employed	9,627

Mechanization has affected not only the number of workers engaged in farm work but it has also changed the kind of work they do. Farm owners and tenants, who constitute the overwhelming majority of farm workers, have found that machinery has released them from many arduous tasks and has probably shortened their working day. Machinery has enabled many a farm operator who once employed a year-round hired hand to get along without help except for seasonal workers at harvest time. As a consequence, work opportunities for year-round labor have been reduced. In recent years, only about a seventh of the hired farm working force have been regularly employed on one farm for the greater part of the year.[55] Seasonal farm workers have also declined drastically in wheat areas with the introduction of combines. The size of the army of migrant workers who followed the harvest each year from Texas to Canada numbered nearly a million at the time of World War I. Within ten or fifteen years, tractors and combines displaced this labor; now this type of agricultural employment has been almost entirely replaced.

The most spectacular development which lies ahead is the potential mechanization of cotton harvesting. Cotton picking occupies a third of the hired farm workers in the United States during the fall.[56] A shift to mechanical cotton pickers could greatly reduce the proportion of hired farm workers.

[53] *Long Range Agricultural Policy,* A Study of Selected Trends and Factors Relating to the Long Range Prospect of American Agriculture, Committee on Agriculture, House of Representatives, prepared by the Bureau of Agricultural Economics, 1948.

[54] *Statistical Abstract of the United States, 1953,* pp. 198, 202.

[55] W. S. Woytinsky and Associates, *op. cit.,* p. 374.

[56] *Surveys of Wages and Wage Rates in Agriculture,* Report No. 19, Bureau of Agricultural Economics, July, 1947.

Other dramatic changes are occurring in the harvesting of sugar beets, where mechanization is being rapidly introduced. It is also underway in the harvesting of sugar cane, produced mainly in Louisiana. These changes indicate a further decline in farm labor.

The effects of agricultural technology on agricultural employment may be summarized as follows:

1. There has been a decline in the proportion of all farm workers (including owners, tenants, and wage workers) in the labor force from 72 per cent in 1820 to less than 12 per cent in 1950.

2. A continued decline in the proportion of all farm workers is anticipated and will continue until further increase in labor saving is no longer attained. Much more mechanization is possible now and the end of labor saving is not in sight.

3. The number of year-round hired "regular" workers appears to be declining. Only about a third of the year-round workers, or 5 per cent of all farm workers, are employed throughout the year on farms.[57]

4. Most farm wage workers are seasonal workers who live in the neighborhood in which they work or near enough to return home each night. These workers are only casually attached to agriculture and spend the greater part of the year in some other occupation.[58]

5. Migratory workers have made up about a fifth of the hired farm working force in recent years.[59] These workers have declined in number, and there is a prospect for further rapid decline with the growing mechanization of cotton picking and sugar-beet harvesting.

INFLUENCE OF TECHNOLOGY ON THE ECONOMIC AND SOCIAL ORGANIZATION OF RURAL LIFE

The Economic Organization of Farming

The widening gap between types of farms. The advances in agricultural technology have brought into question the future of the family-size farm. The day of the small farm is coming to an end in many areas. In cereal and cotton farming the trend is toward large-scale operations using the newest and most efficient machinery. The marked increase of large farms of 1,000 acres and over has been pointed out. Outside of cereal and cotton farming, the trend is likely to be toward specialized agriculture, such as fruit raising, vegetable growing, and dairy farming. While these cannot be mechanized as completely as cereal farming, larger-sized farms may be indicated.[60]

There is a widening gap in general well-being between farmers who are able to apply modern technology and those who cannot. A classification of

[57] W. S. Woytinsky and Associates, *op. cit.*, p. 379.
[58] *Ibid.*, p. 380.
[59] Louis J. Ducoff, *Migratory Farm Workers in 1949,* Agriculture Information Bulletin No. 25 (Washington, Government Printing Office, 1950).
[60] Robert Brady, *Technology and Planning,* mimeo. manuscript (Berkeley, University of California Bookstore, 1950), p. 16.

farms based on type and value of products shows the wide range of farm organization:

NUMBER OF U. S. FARMS BY ECONOMIC CLASS, 1950[a]

(number in thousands)

ECONOMIC CLASS	CLASS INTERVAL (VALUE OF PRODUCT SOLD)	NUMBER	PER CENT
ALL FARMS		5,382.1	100.0
Commercial farms			
Class I	$25,000 and over	105.5	2.0
Class II	$10,000 to $24,999	386.1	7.2
Class III	$ 5,000 to $ 9,999	725.6	13.5
Class IV	$ 2,500 to $ 4,999	882.3	16.4
Class V	$ 1,200 to $ 2,499	895.9	16.6
Class VI	$ 250 to $ 1,199[b]	707.7	13.1
Other Farms			
Part-time farms	$ 250 to $ 199[c]	642.1	11.9
Residential farms	Under $250	1,032.4	19.2
Abnormal farms[d]		4.5	.1

SOURCE: *The Agricultural Situation,* Bureau of Agricultural Economics, March, 1952.

a Preliminary census data; totals obtained by adding state or county census releases.

b With the operator working off the farm less than 100 days and farm sales greater than other family income.

c With the operator working off the farm 100 or more days and/or other family income exceeding farm sales.

d Chiefly public and private institutional farms.

It can be observed in the table above that at one end of this range stands the large-scale farms and the more prosperous family-commercial farms. At the other end of the scale are Class V and VI family-commercial farms of a marginal and subsistence type on which the farmer is barely making a living. Note also the part-time and residential farms which require the operator to have nonfarm income in order to maintain a farm. A number of questions are raised by this trend. Should agriculture strive for maximum efficiency in production with larger and larger units, more concentrated ownership and management, and eliminate the two million or more small, substandard farms? Should it seek to support a larger population wtih small incomes, maintaining or increasing the number of farms by using a public subsidy program if necessary? Should it seek some middle ground in which larger and more efficient "family farms" are encouraged and protected so that they can compete with large commercial farms?

Murray R. Benedict observed recently that "there is as yet, however, little in the way of a well-defined national policy in regard to it [the small farm problem]. Still less is there a clearly developed position with respect to the large farm problem. Neither of these problems has bulked large in the policy proposals of the major farm organizations."[61] What will happen eventually may rest as much on social and political considerations as technological and

61 M. Benedict, *op. cit.,* p. 518.

economic ones. The family farm is more than an economic unit; it is a way of life cherished as tradition and prized as an American heritage. But even traditions fall before technological fact, and the full scope of the challenge must be faced.

Alternative Socioeconomic Farming Patterns

Seven patterns of farming have emerged to compete for economic dominance and social survival. These patterns include:

1. Subsidized and restricted production
2. Self-sufficient proprietorship
3. Part-time farming
4. Efficient family size commercial farms
5. Co-operative farming
6. Corporate farming
7. Collective farming

All of these patterns have emerged in this country and their co-existence makes up the composite structure of the agricultural industry. Each has implications for economic organization, for political institutions, and for a way of rural life.

Subsidized and restricted production. Agricultural surpluses are now the main problem of the American farmer. Increase in food production has outstripped population growth, and the chief problem faced by the farmer is how to dispose of his crop profitably. The present government policy is based on a parity principle by which the purchasing power of farm products is determined on the basis of their previous purchasing power at a period which was relatively favorable to the farmers.

The government system of price support operates in three ways: (1) acreage allotments and marketing quotas on certain farm commodities; (2) crop loans to farmers, in which case the government holds the crop as collateral until such time, if ever, that it can be sold on a favorable market; (3) outright government purchases of farm products to maintain the general price level of any farm product.

This system of government-administered prices, in contrast to competitive prices, has a twofold result: (1) Higher farm income for all farmers producing protected crops, and (2) the support of the two million or more small substandard farms which might otherwise be eliminated. This policy is justified by its proponents on economic, social, and political grounds. As a working policy, it has made the farmer dependent on government. The former vigorous individualism of the American farmer and his opposition to government interference in business and to government aid to individuals has diminished. The government is now the greatest storage agent of food in the world. An inventory in the summer of 1950 showed the Commodity Credit Corporation had 516,250,000 bushels of wheat and corn stored up—enough to fill a freight train reaching halfway around the world; some 3,600,000 bales of cotton, or enough to make 90 million bedsheets; 88 million pounds of dried eggs—all that the bakers of the country would need for eight years; 99 million pounds of butter; 316 million pounds of dried milk; and a large supply of cheese, soybeans, tobacco, dried fruit and peas, cottonseed meal, and similar items.[62] Surpluses continued to mount, and in 1955 farm experts said: "Storage facilities are full to bursting in spite of the large increases in capacity that have been and are being made. Storage alone is costing the government in excess of half a million dollars per day."[63]

Self-sufficient proprietorship. M. L. Wilson of the Department of Agriculture suggests that vast numbers of farm people could produce a much higher standard of living with self-sufficient practices. Diversity of production to include a supply of their own consuming needs would have the effect of reducing the need for cash outlay and would decrease the surplus of crops which now stand in the way of a good price. It is argued that "there is nothing retrogressive about a family supplying its own food from its own acres by means of progeny-tested hens, blooded sires, hybrid corn, pressure cookers, glass jars, electric refrigeration, and quick freezing. It is precisely by such applications of modern technology that subsistence practices can be made most effective."[64]

This pattern is undoubtedly followed in part by millions of farm families, but a cash income is usually necessary. The practice of mixed or diversified farming and the raising of livestock have increased farm returns and produced more steady returns. It removes dependency on the precarious nature of one market crop.

Part-time farming. Many farmers cannot diversify their farm sufficiently to provide for their food needs and the cash income necessary for other needs. In the year 1949, 13 per cent of all farm operators reported nonfarm work as their major occupation; and an additional 14 per cent reported some non-farm work but said farming was their main occupation. If to these two groups are added the farm operators who spent part of the year at hired farm work on other operators' farms, then almost two-fifths of all farmers devoted part of their time to gainful work other than operating their own farms.[65] Millions of hired workers move back and forth between industrial and agricultural work on a part-time basis. The automobile makes part-time farming increasingly possible if the worker can live within travel distance of an industry which needs his skills. Decentralization of industry will also facilitate this possibility. If service enterprises were established to meet the need of farmers on mechanized farms, considerable nearby nonfarm work

[62] Harry E. Barnes, *Society in Transition* (New York, Prentice-Hall, 1952), pp. 373–374.

[63] Committee Report of the Twentieth Century Fund, found in Murray R. Benedict, *Can We Solve the Farm Problem?* (New York, Twentieth Century Fund, 1955), p. 403.

[64] M. L. Wilson, "Beyond Economics," in *Farmers in a Changing World,* Yearbook of Agriculture (Washington, Government Printing Office, 1940), p. 933. Cf. Ralph Borosodi, *Flight from the City* (New York, Harper, 1933).

[65] W. S. Woytinsky and Associates, *op. cit.,* p. 372.

could be made available for workers who are not needed in agriculture. The pattern of part-time farming and rural living combined with nonfarm work can be expected to grow if these conditions develop.

Efficient family-size commercial farms. Although advances in technology tend to lead toward larger full-time commercial farms, there is no evidence to indicate that the competitive position of the efficiently operated family farm is weakened by this change.[66] Mechanical power and farm machinery have been made economically adaptable to family-size farms. However, an increase in size of farms and in the amount of machinery is indicated if family-size farms are to maximize production and compete with the largest-scale farms. The total investment per farm becomes higher and the management job becomes more involved. The tractor and electric power equipment eliminate most of the drudgery of both field and home work on the efficient farm. The real income per farm and per family is larger, and more time is available for other things such as education, recreation, and increased leisure. The marked rise of farm income during the past fifteen years has enabled many family farms to increase their size and competitive position. Following the depression of the 1930's, the number of farms declined steadily and the average size of the family farm increased.[67] The moderate-sized family farm continues to be the common producing unit in most sections of the country. However, the number of both smaller and larger units is growing while the number of moderate-sized units is declining.[68]

Co-operative farming. Co-operative farming is not common in America.[69] There is some common ownership of farm equipment but little else. The "threshing ring" was well known when the large thresher was required. Groups of neighboring farmers would buy and manage jointly the threshing equipment, all on a nonprofit basis. Needless to say, the rings died with the advent of the small combine. In contrast, farmers marketing and purchasing associations are now big business—over $5,545,000,000 worth of annual business, 4,505,000 farmer members, more than 10,150 associations.[70]

The co-operative principle in farming means that ownership remains in the hands of those who operate family-size farms but within a co-operatively managed enterprise which has a pool of machinery, equipment, farm build-

[66] Sherman E. Johnson, *op. cit.,* p. 932. Dr. Johnson is chief of the Bureau of Agricultural Economics.

[67] Walter W. Wilcox, *The Farmer in the Second World War* (Ames, Iowa State College Press, 1947), p. 303.

[68] *Ibid.,* p. 304.

[69] The history of 15 co-operative corporation farms which the Farm Security Administration sponsored from 1940 to 1944 is instructive. See Joseph W. Eaton, *Exploring Tomorrow's Agriculture* (New York, Harper, 1943), p. 80; A. Whitney Griswold, *Farming and Democracy* (New York, Harcourt, Brace, 1948), pp. 167–172. *Cooperative Living* (Winter 1953–1954) lists eleven private communities in the United States following co-operative practices.

[70] The 13th Annual Report of the Farm Credit Administration (Washington, D. C., 1947), pp. 118–119.

ings, and handling.[71] Farmers own their own small tools, tractors, cultivators, seeders, and fertilizer placers. But the pick-up balers, forage harvesters, and such machines which operate most economically in large sizes are owned co-operatively. The co-operative can own and service such costly machines as sugar-beet harvesters, cotton pickers, airplanes for dusting and defoliation, and other large equipment.

Corporate farming. A corporate farm is usually a large commercial farm or chain of farms operated by a manager with a corps of labor under corporate organization. A. Whitney Griswold has pointed out that "of late years, technology and commerce together have given such an impetus to large-scale commercial farming as to suggest a modern American enclosure movement that would swallow up family farming as it did in England."[72]

The farming corporation may buy up a large tract of land or lease and unite many small farms. Once the land has been acquired, the most advanced types of farm machinery are applied in the most complete utilization that can be achieved. A farm manager and farm labor are hired to provide the appropriate utilization of man power. From a purely economic view, the large farms are often more efficient in production, and in use of man-power units. The effect of such large-scale mechanized farming on personal and social relationships contrasts markedly with that of small-scale family-size farming. A study by the Bureau of Agricultural Economics contrasted a large-scale farming area and a small-farm district in the San Joaquin Valley in California. General agricultural conditions and population make-up were virtually the same in the two areas. But personal relations, local business, and social services were far superior in the small farm district.[73] Such a comparison need not be taken as a blanket condemnation of large-scale farming, but it does show that problems of social organization accompany the installation of corporate farming.

Collective farming. The collective farm has been called the farm factory. The concept of the factory applied to agriculture means that all factors in production, including man power, are organized on the land as if they were operating under some huge shed of an industrial building. It is similar to the large corporate farm in this respect except that the corporate farm is privately owned and managed while the collective farm is under rigid state supervision. In Russia, since 1938, agriculture has been conducted on the pattern of the collective farm called *kolkhozy*, a "co-operative" society composed of all farmers in a village or a district. An agreement is signed by which the

[71] The Farm Column, *Fortune* (May, 1945),. pp. 158–164. Describes the Walker-Gordon System of co-operative farm management.

[72] A. Whitney Griswold, *op. cit.,* p. 131.

[73] See Carey McWilliams, "Small Farm and Big Farm," Public Affairs Pamphlet (New York, Public Affairs Committee, 1947) The primary report is to be found in *Small Business and the Community* (Washington, Small Business Committee of the United States, 79th Congress, 2nd Session, December 23, 1946).

locality pledges to conduct its collective economy according to a plan prescribed by state authorities. The president is usually a communist party functionary and all decisions made by members of the *kolkhozy* must be acceptable to the party. Land, farm livestock, implements, stables, barns, even seed and forage supplies are collectivized. State-owned machine tractor stations serve the collective farms. Members of the *kolkhozy* are paid in proportion to the number of days they work. The work day is the unit of payment, but each job is evaluated on the basis of piece work.

Government quotas for grain and other agricultural products must be delivered and all expenses taken care of before the members of the collective farm are paid for their services. Each member is conceded the right to work a tiny plot of about one acre, the produce of which is his own. At the beginning of 1940 Russia had more than 236,000 *kolkhozy* with 371 million acres and about 4000 huge state farms with 4.7 million acres.[74] The collective and state farms represent agricultural industrialization pushed to an extreme of technological rationalization. The large state farms take the socialized factory as a model. The means of production are owned by the state and operated by the state. Workers receive salary and wage returns for specified amounts of labor.

The American Farm Outlook

The central American farm policy has been based on adherence to the family-size farm. Modern technology poses a genuine challenge to this policy. Griswold summarizes the American problem in the perspective of British and French experience:

The British experience shows us that it is possible to reduce the farm population to an irreducible minimum, and small, owner-operated family-size farms virtually to extinction, and still have democracy. The French contrast shows us that it is possible to maintain a maximum farm population and carry family farming to its extreme logical conclusion, and all but lose democracy in the bargain. In the most recent phases of our public policy for agriculture, we have been fumbling and groping for a mean between these two extremes. . . . Out of the confusions and contradictions of the past ten years, one central purpose has crystallized—in theory. We have resolved to achieve an optimum farm population whose characteristic unit of production is an efficient family-size farm. Whether the resolution can be made effective remains to be seen.

CONCLUSION

Technological advances in agriculture are bringing about many social changes which are comparable to those occurring in manufacturing industry.

Among the most marked changes may be listed the following:

1. The increased use of inanimate energy in the tractor, truck, and auto-

[74] W. S. Woytinsky and E. S. Woytinsky, *op. cit.,* p. 499.

mobile has resulted in sharply increased crop production and has drastically reduced man hours of labor required.

2. The average farm size has increased and the trend is clearly toward larger farms where full-time farming is pursued.

3. The largest one-third of our farms are producing about four-fifths of all of our farm products for market.

4. There is a marked decline in the proportion of workers who are employed in agricultural production. Farm workers now make up less than 12 per cent of the experienced labor force. It is believed that the utilization of the best technological advances on the farm lands which are presently least productive would reduce all farm workers by at least one half.

The central American farm policy has been adherence to the family-size farm. Modern technology poses a genuine challenge to this policy.

ANNOTATED BIBLIOGRAPHY

BENEDICT, Murray E., *Farm Policies of the United States, 1790–1950* (New York, Twentieth Century Fund, 1953). An excellent history of farm policies followed by the United States from 1790 to 1950. The significance of the family farm policy is emphasized.

DEWHURST, J. Frederick, *America's Needs and Resources, A New Survey* (New York, Twentieth Century Fund, 1955). Contains a thorough recent review of agricultural technology and capacity.

GRISWOLD, A. Whitney, *Farming and Democracy* (New York, Harcourt, Brace, 1948). Reviews French, British, and American experience in organizing farming and relates the various patterns to democratic aims and methods.

HOPKINS, John A., *Changing Technology and Employment in Agriculture,* (Washington, Government Printing Office, 1941). This is a summary and appraisal made by workers in the Department of Agriculture covering changes in agricultural technology and employment.

LOOMIS, Charles P., and BEAGLE, J. Allan, *Rural Social Systems* (New York, Prentice-Hall, 1950). A rural sociology text. Part III, "Social Strata as Social Systems," is especially valuable in appraising the internal organization of the farm population.

SCHULTZ, Theodore W., *The Economic Organization of Agriculture* (New York, McGraw-Hill, 1953). Surveys the economic organization of agriculture in the United States as an industry and traces the history of research support for agriculture.

United States Department of Agriculture, *Farmers in a Changing World,* 1940 Yearbook of Agriculture (Washington, Government Printing Office, 1940). Contains comprehensive social and technical history of American agriculture. Seventy-two experts contribute chapters on such subjects as agricultural production, conservation, farm organization, and farm policy. Part 5, "What Some Social Scientists Have to Say," contains chapters by Robert Redfield, W. Lloyd Warner, and Rensis Likert. Carl Taylor has an authoritative statement on the contribution of sociology to agriculture. The Appendix contains a brief chronology of American agricultural history.

———, *Science in Farming,* 1943–47, Yearbook of Agriculture (Washington, Government Printing Office, 1947). A comprehensive report of new developments in farm science.

WOYTINSKY, W. S. and WOYTINSKY, E. S., *World Population and Production* (New York, Twentieth Century Fund, 1953). This is a monumental source book of world needs and resources. The chapters on agriculture deal with production, farm organization, size of farms, and rural population. Gives an excellent coverage of the United States followed by a treatment of other countries in the world.

CHAPTER 15

INFLUENCE OF
TECHNOLOGY ON WAR

■ *Francis R. Allen*

As the weapons of war change, so does the character of war change, . . .

MAJOR GENERAL JOHN F. C. FULLER (1932)

Modern science has utterly changed the nature of war and is still changing it.

VANNEVAR BUSH (1949)

IF THE recently-drafted army recruit or the combat veteran of Normandy, Guadalcanal, or Porkchop Hill were asked to state his beliefs regarding the influence of technology on war, he might respond with some colorful profanity—or with a snort of disgust—or possibly with a blank stare. It sounds very abstract and academic in contrast to the red-blooded experiences of war. Sooner or later, however, he would be apt to comment on his army rifle or the wonders of the bazooka, or the new jet planes, or possibly the atomic cannon, or guided missiles. If he is an *old* soldier, he might compare a recent campaign with a former one and recall differences in weapons and in methods of fighting. He might be impressed with the many changes that have taken place due to new weapons and other technological innovations.

The social scientist has a different perspective, which may or may not be related to personal experiences. He is interested in war as man's foremost social problem and is likely to study the evolution of wars as carefully as possible, noting how wars have changed over the centuries. Striving for objectivity in his study, he is interested in making generalizations which apply to all wars if such generalizations may be validly made. He will observe the factors that all wars have in common and also the significant differences between various wars.

The objective of the present chapter is to show the influence of technology on war over the centuries of history and to make conclusions as to such influence. Thus attention is focused on one element related to war, and this technological factor will be described from early wars (as of the Greeks

352

and Romans) down to World Wars I and II and the "limited war" in Korea. The saying goes that "war is war." But *was* war the same during the Middle Ages as it was in 1865; and was the latter approximately the same as World War II? Some people will maintain that over the centuries war has become vastly different, and that the difference is largely owing to the nature of weapons used—in short, to the influence of technology.

Such is a thesis, in fact, of this chapter, although this view should be carefully examined rather than glibly accepted. The interests of this chapter, however, extend further. Preliminary appraisal suggests that not only has the technological influence on war been tremendous but advancing technology appears to be the precise variable most closely related to the changing character of war. As one changes, so does the other. It is suggested that this relationship may properly be stated in the form of an hypothesis. Technology is, to be sure, not the only factor related to changing warfare.[1] Other influences include the factor of military leadership; number and composition of personnel (both combatants and workers on the "home front"); morale of personnel, their courage or lack of it; their training, supplies, information regarding the enemy (intelligence); geographical and climatic conditions, and others.

Over the long span of years these other factors tend to function as *relative constants* with respect to the changing nature of war, whereas the factor of technology is the clear-cut, outstanding *variable* of importance. For example, military leadership is a vital factor in war. Leaders will decide the strategy and tactics to be used; it should be observed, however, that the latter will be significantly related to the weapons available. Leaders will have charge of the mobilization, organization, and training of troops. They will make all-important decisions as to the development and use of weapons. Yet the question arises whether leaders—a Napoleon, Wellington, Eisenhower, or Von Rundstedt—change appreciably the nature of war. Are not the functions of leadership in all armies strikingly similar? Moreover, is not the inherited ability for leadership about the same today as it was during the Middle Ages? We conclude that differing types of leadership have not had decisive influence on the nature of warfare—that this factor operates over the long run as a *relative constant* in the equation of war.

Similarly with the factors of morale and courage of combatants and of home forces. In a particular battle or campaign, high morale and magnificent courage may tip the scales in favor of victory, and the opposite may spell doom. The refusal to concede defeat—the "they shall not pass" determination at Verdun or the "Nuts!" defiance at Bastogne—may be an important element leading to victory. Nevertheless, over the centuries of time this factor, like that of leadership, is thought to be a *relative constant* in warfare.

[1] See relevant discussion in Hans Speier, "War and Peace," *Bulletin of the Atomic Scientists*, Vol. XI, No. 9 (November, 1955), pp. 346–349. This essay constituted a part of the Columbia University Bicentennial lecture series, "Man's Right to Knowledge," and was broadcast over the CBS radio network on November 21, 1954.

War does not appear to have changed markedly because of the factors of morale and courage, important as they are in specific situations. It is granted that the unbudging, resolute attitude may be partly related to feeling of adequacy in weapons and other military considerations. Indeed, this attitude may lead to slaughter of one's side if there is not adequacy of equipment.

So with other factors—supplies, intelligence, geographical and climatic conditions. These may be decisive in determining the outcome of specific battles or campaigns. Again, we suggest that they tend to be *constants* in their net effects over the long-range trend of warfare itself. They do not appear to have brought dominant changes in the character of waging war.

It has been pointed out in Chapter 2 that changes in any phenomenon are not explained by constants related to the occurrence; a variation must be explained, on the other hand, by some factor which itself varies. One such variable is believed to be the technological factor in warfare. The present objective, at any rate, is to marshall facts concerning this variable which seemingly has brought decisive changes and which now threatens tremendous destruction and even casts doubt upon human survival.

If one grants the decisive influence of technology on war, one must not fail to grasp the implications of this for the future. Present-day technological trends will undoubtedly be extended. If one is interested in assessing the nature of future warfare—assuming that wars will continue to be fought— one can hardly do better, according to this view, than examine the trends of war technology.

With this brief orientation, attention is directed to the central topic of discussion—advancing technology in relation to war as both have changed over the centuries of history.

HISTORICAL DEVELOPMENT OF WEAPONS OF WAR

Let us trace the development of war weapons according to various stages of history, following in the main the stages set forth by Professor Quincy Wright in his monumental work, *A Study of War*.[2] Wright outlined four historical periods; the writer has modified the last one.[3]

The Weapons of Preliterate Peoples

The war weapons used by preliterates do not require lengthy discussion, for the weapons are in general simple and war among such people is fairly

[2] Quincy Wright, *A Study of War* (Chicago, University of Chicago Press, 1942), Vol. I, p. 30.

[3] Wright's subperiods of history are "the periods of experimental adaptation of fire arms and religious war (1450–1648), of professional armies and dynastic wars (1648–1789), of industrialization and nationalistic wars (1789–1914), and of the airplane and totalitarian war"—(1914 to present).

As used in this chapter, the last period is divided into two parts: 1914 to 1938, and 1939 to the present. The year 1939 is assumed to mark the beginning of World War II.

rare—if one accepts a commonly-used definition of *war;* anthropologists carefully distinguish between warfare and feuds, raids, and other limited operations of short duration.[4] Demographic considerations alone, observes Herskovits,[5] forbid a small people to have an "army." Nevertheless, many primitive tribes *have* carried on war in every sense of the word. These include the Zulus, Ashanti, and Dahomeys of Africa; the Aztecs and Incas of Central and South America; the Iroquois of North America, and various other peoples.[6]

Simplicity is the keynote of the war weapons used by preliterates. The striking weapons are confined to arm-, foot-, and mouth-propelled instruments.[7] These weapons run the gamut from sharp stones, slings, spears, javelins, bow-and-arrow, dart-thrower, the blowgun (favorite of jungle tribes of South America as well as of tribes in Indonesia and southeastern United States[8]), the war club or skull crusher, the tomahawk (a development from the war club), the throwing-stick or hurled war club (used by Australian aborigines) to all sorts of knives. Weapons of more limited use include the Australian *boomerang* and the South American *bolo.* Of the weapons used by preliterates, the bow-and-arrow appeared to be the most efficient or "deadly."[9] However, the hurling spear, declares Hoebel, was the "truly heavy artillery of early primitive man."

In using their weapons, primitive warriors generally have a simple military organization. There are no separate categories of fighters, specialists, and the like. All the men pitch in and hurl spears or throw clubs and boomerangs at the opposing fighters; most American Indians fought with bow-and-arrow and club. As society and culture became more complex, specialties appeared, the number of warriors became greater, organization was clear-cut, and an "army" became more the usual thing.[10] The various branches of service gradually developed—what are now called the infantry, artillery, engineers, ordnance, and other branches.

[4] Turney-High states that a *war* is marked by tactical operations, by definite command and control, by ability to conduct a campaign in order to defeat the enemy, by large-group (rather than family or individual) participation and by an adequate supply of forces in the field. As quoted in Melville J. Herskovits, *Man and His Works* (New York, Knopf, 1948), p. 344. Regarding the distinction between a *war* and lesser operations, see also E. Adamson Hoebel, *Man in the Primitive World* (New York, McGraw-Hill, 1949), p. 393.

[5] Herskovits, *op. cit.*

[6] The Zulus are a good example of a truly warlike people. It has been claimed that King Chaka of Zululand "kept a force of 100,000 men under arms, one half of which was on constant call."—Harry H. Turney-High, *Primitive War* (Columbia, University of South Carolina Press, 1949), pp. 250–251.

[7] Wright, *op. cit.*, Vol. I, p. 81.

[8] Hoebel, *op. cit.*, p. 395.

[9] Turney-High, *op. cit.*, p. 6; Hoebel, *op. cit.*, p. 394.

[10] Eliot D. Chapple and Carleton S. Coon, *Principles of Anthropology* (New York, Holt, 1942), p. 349; also Wright, *op. cit.*, Vol. I, p. 144.

War Weapons of Early Civilization: Battle-axe, Ballista, Bow

The period of early civilization—from approximately 4000 B.C. (the approximate date of the beginning of written language) until the middle of the fifteenth century A.D.—saw the gradual development of more complex war weapons. Weapons were first made of bronze (instead of stone and wood). This occurred first in the Egyptian, Mesopotamian, Hittite, Greek, and Roman civilizations; it spread later to central and western Europe. The Bronze Age was at its full development around 3000 B.C.[11] As bronze-casting developed, the sword was used by foot-soldiers and horsemen, while helmets and shields were used for protection. The supply of bronze was not, however, plentiful; usually only the noblemen and guards had good bronze weapons.[12] The Iron Age began in the Asia Minor region about 1400 B.C. A larger supply of this metal was available, and by 800 B.C. iron was used for such standard fighting equipment as swords, helmets, and shields.[13]

Weapons developments of the 4000 B.C.–1450 A.D. period were in the beginning like those of primitives. Typical weapons of the Ancient Egyptian, Assyrian, Greek, Macedonian, and Roman civilizations included the spear, javelin, sword, sling, bow-and-arrow, and battle-axe, with helmets and shields for protection.[14] The pike (a long wooden shaft with a pointed iron head) was used in Greece about the time of the Persian Wars (roughly 500 B.C.); the typical soldier, in fact, was the *hoplite* or armored pikeman, with archers, slingers, and javelin men serving as auxiliaries.[15] The pike was also used in the Macedonian nation about 370–180 B.C., and in Rome both during the early years and after the time of Christ.

Beginning three or four centuries (perhaps more) before the time of Christ, and developing markedly after that, extensions of some of the simple primitive ideas began to assume more importance. Impressive siege weapons, using principles of mechanical elasticity, torsion, and momentum, were devised which were far superior to the use of human muscle power.[16] Instead of throwing rocks, a warrior could now use one of these inventions, for example, the *catapult,* which was operated on a winch and twisted-rope system; with this, he could throw huge rocks a considerable distance.[17] A hundred or more

---

[11] A. L. Kroeber, *Anthropology,* rev. ed. (New York, Harcourt, Brace, 1948), pp. 705–706. Kroeber estimates that use of bronze had spread to Hungary by about 1900 B.C., to Czechoslovakia, central Germany, and Italy by around 1800 B.C., and to France and Britain by about 1700 B.C.

[12] R. J. Forbes, *Man the Maker, A History of Technology and Engineering* (New York, Schuman, 1950), p. 56.

[13] Kroeber, *op. cit.,* p. 725.

[14] Oliver L. Spaulding, Hoffman Nickerson, and John W. Wright, *Warfare, A Study of Military Methods from the Earliest Times* (Washington, The Infantry Journal, 1937), pp. 17–18, 23–24, 76–77, 107–108, 154, 245. See also Lynn Montross, *War Through the Ages* (New York, Harper, 1944), Ch. 1–6.

[15] Spaulding and others, *op. cit.,* p. 42.

[16] Wright, *op. cit.,* Vol. I, pp. 145–146.

[17] George M. Chinn, *The Machine Gun* (Washington, Government Printing Office, 1951), pp. 5–8; Spaulding and others, *op. cit.,* pp. 314–315; Forbes, *op. cit.,* pp. 82–84.

of these catapults could produce a heavy bombardment of forts, castles, and other fortified structures. Catapults were not very accurate, but a battery of them could pound a wall or fort to dust in a few days.[18] A similar innovation was the *trebuchet,* which depended for its power upon use of a heavy counter-weight. These siege engines threw not only stones but flaming projectiles, objects such as a dead horse, even at times live men. "Roman siege engines were built to throw stones weighing up to six hundred pounds distances up to a thousand yards. Archimedes is said to have made a machine for the defense of Syracuse which could throw stones weighing one thousand eight hundred pounds, . . ."[19]

Another war weapon of this period was the *ballista,* essentially an exaggerated crossbow with its tension increased by use of winches;[20] with this a soldier could throw a long spear or javelin some 450–500 yards with great force and considerable accuracy. Such shots could not penetrate walls but were useful against men or other objects beyond the range of other throwing weapons. There were various types of catapult and ballista.

New types of the bow-and-arrow were also invented, such as the *crossbow* and the *English longbow,* which brought greater accuracy of fire at longer range.[21] At the Battle of Hastings in 1066, which was decisive in the Norman conquest of England, use of the crossbow was prominent. It was believed to have been invented by Norman artisans. Some archers were equipped with a mechanical bow arrangement that could discharge several arrows at one time.[22] The crossbow was widely used in Europe, although Pope Innocent II called it in 1139 a "most barbarous and cruel weapon." It had, however, the blessing of the Church for use against infidels, and King Richard the Lion-hearted greatly admired the weapon; on his crusade against the unbelievers he took a thousand crossbowmen with him. After this time the weapon was used all over Europe. A simpler and more powerful bow was, however, the English longbow.[23] This was widely used during the fourteenth century, and was considered to be the highest development of the bow.[24] Suits of body armor, such as are sometimes now shown in modern museums, were worn

[18] Chinn, *op. cit.,* p. 5.

[19] Wright, *op. cit.*

[20] Chinn, *op. cit.,* p. 8; Spaulding and others, *op. cit.*

[21] Chinn, *op. cit.,* p. 10; Abbott P. Usher, *A History of Mechanical Inventions* (New York, McGraw-Hill, 1929), pp. 82–84.

[22] The Battle of Hastings, illustrative of war during the eleventh century, is well described in Spaulding and others, *op. cit.,* pp. 304–310.

[23] Chinn, *op. cit.,* pp. 9–10; Tom Wintringham, *The Story of Weapons and Tactics: From Troy to Stalingrad* (Boston, Houghton Mifflin, 1943), pp. 68–69.

[24] The Battle of Crecy, fought on August 26, 1346, was a notable "weapons victory" for the English using the longbow. Though outnumbered four to one, the English army routed and nearly annihilated the French army.—Chinn, *op. cit.;* Spaulding and others, *op. cit.,* p. 374–379.

during this period as protection against the shafts from the crossbow and English longbow.[25]

In spite of these developments, one is impressed with the very slow and gradual change in weapons during the long period from approximately 4000 B.C. to 1450 A.D.,—a period of some 5500 years. After this time, developments took a different turn.

Weapons Used Between 1450 and 1914

The period since 1450 may be regarded as the time of modern technology. It begins as the first use of printing and the era of world contact were inaugurated.[26] The beginning of this period, moreover, coincided rather closely with the occurrence of the Renaissance, which brought a new flowering of culture; this included the making of significant inventions that had a real effect on war. The whole period is characterized by a great increase in annual number of inventions made in pure and applied science.

In particular, this period of modern technology saw the development of the use of gunpowder and of guns. Thus a new era began in the history of warfare. Preliminary (though inconsequential) use of gunpowder began before 1450. Indeed, it is not known exactly when and by whom gunpowder was invented. It has been alleged—though never proven[27]—that the Chinese or Mohammedans invented it long before this time. What is known is that Roger Bacon (1219–92) wrote of gunpowder as early as 1242 (some say 1248), reporting that it was *already known* in his time.[28] A German monk, Barthold Schwartz (1310–84), has also been credited with discovering gunpowder, but available evidence indicates that he did some work in mixing explosives and that is all. Chinn declares that Schwartz, in addition to the above, invented a system of casting bronze cannon in his Venice workshop; while the latter "never claimed to have originated gunpowder or firearms, . . . he did attempt to improve both."[29]

Although the actual inventor of gunpowder is unknown, data has been recorded as to its early uses. During the tenth and eleventh centuries it was used to set fire to enemy warships at Constantinople and in China, but not

[25] But this answer to the bow did not always bring a favorable outcome. The French at Auray, in their suits of armor, lost disastrously to the English (1365) because the former were weighted down and could not move around. The English, finding at first that their arrows bounced off the French armor, finally bludgeoned the French with battle-axes.

[26] Wright, *op. cit.*, Vol. I, p. 32.

[27] Spaulding and others, *op. cit.*, p. 406; Forbes, *op. cit.*, pp. 118–119; Walter H. B. Smith, *Rifles* (Washington, National Rifle Association of America, 1948), pp. 3–5.

[28] Spaulding and others, *op. cit.;* John U. Nef, *War and Human Progress* (Cambridge, Harvard University Press, 1950), pp. 23–25; Montross, *op. cit.*, p. 176. Montross seems to favor the claim of Bacon rather than Schwartz, but if Bacon stated that gunpowder was already known in his day, any claim staked in his behalf would seem to be disposed of.

[29] Chinn, *op. cit.*, pp. 11–12.

to propel a bullet, cannon ball, or other projectile.[30] Renn states that "The first historically substantiated occasion when gunpowder was used to fire a projectile was in the reign of Alfonso the Wise, King of Castille (1221–1284), . . ."[31] Chinn maintains that the beginning of the use of artillery weapons fired by gunpowder occurred at the Battle of Crecy in 1346. While the long-bow was the decisive weapon in this battle, gunpowder had been exploded in a cannon for the purpose of frightening the horses; it was known at the time as "stampede cannon."[32] Be this as it may, this important milestone of pro-pelling a projectile through a tube by a force generated by gunpowder seems to have first occurred somewhere during the 1275–1340 period. However, gunpowder was not much of a factor in war for at least a century. During the Hundred Years' War, from the mid-fourteenth to the mid-fifteenth century, cannon were used very little. Following 1450 the use of gunpowder increased gradually and as it did so the nature of war changed tremendously. The bombard (a cannon-type piece) and the cannon were the first weapons to be developed which used gunpowder as a missile propellant. Not only could the knight-in-armor be put out of battle by a musket or cannon ball before he could strike a blow—which was partly responsible for unhorsing the knight[33] —but that medieval citadel of feudalism, the castle, could be blasted to its foundations. The feudal lord and his people were no longer secure behind their fortifications.[34] From this time on, except for use by Indians and other primitives, the bow-and-arrow and its type of fighting was on the way out.

The bombard and the cannon gradually replaced the earlier siege artil-lery—the catapult, ballista, and trebuchet. The bombard could "lob" pro-jectiles in a high trajectory over walls. It is stated that Mohammed II recog-nized the value of the bombard in his siege and conquest of Constantinople in 1453.[35] Cannon were used as flat-trajectory weapons for a direct fire against, say, walls. With their long barrels, cannon were at first heavy and clumsy to handle; they tended to develop more slowly.[36] After the gun was fired, a long period of inactivity followed. But improvements suggested by Leonardo da Vinci (1452–1519) and others were steadily made.[37]

[30] Spaulding and others, op. cit.; Chinn, op. cit. It is agreed that both Bacon and Schwartz thought of gunpowder as an explosive, neither as a propelling agent.

[31] Ludwig Renn, Warfare, The Relation of War to Society (New York, Oxford Uni-versity Press, 1939), p. 122.

[32] Chinn, op. cit.

[33] The weapon that had an even greater influence in "unhorsing the knight" was the English longbow. However, as use of firearms increased and became more accurate, it completely sealed the fate of the knight-in-armor.

[34] Wright, op. cit., Vol. I, p. 294; Wintringham, op. cit., p. 80.

[35] With this conquest it was conceded that gunpowder had revolutionized military engineering.—Spaulding and others, op. cit., pp. 406–407. Regarding the bombard, see also Montross, op. cit., pp. 178–181; and Albert Manucy, Artillery Through the Ages, bulletin (Washington, Government Printing Office, 1949), pp. 3–4.

[36] Chinn, op. cit., p. 44; Wintringham, op. cit., p. 96.

[37] Chinn, op. cit., pp. 14–15; Forbes, op. cit., pp. 144–146; Nef, op. cit., pp. 46–48; Usher, op. cit., Ch. 7.

Other developments of this time included the discovery by Kuttner in 1540 that a spirally grooved or "rifled" barrel imparted to the bullet a spinning motion which improved accuracy of fire. This method of constructing gun barrels gave the rifle its name.[38] During the sixteenth century the idea was conceived of placing the multi-barrels of a gun in a circle so that they would revolve as the gun was discharged. Thus a revolving type of firearm came into being.[39] More basic improvements occurred as the result of advances within the field of metallurgy itself. These included the discovery that iron ore (like bronze) could be reduced to a liquid, and that the cost of wrought iron could be lessened by the introduction of certain new techniques.[40]

During the 1648–1789 period, weapons developments included the innovations of the bayonet and of the grenade. The former innovation was responsible for the elimination of the pikemen, who had protected infantrymen (musketeers) in event of close-quarters fighting.[41] The grenade—a shell with fuse burning that is fired at close range into the ranks of the enemy—was introduced about 1435, but it was not regarded as safe and dependable until about 1600.[42] Grenadier companies were formed in each regiment; this was a specialist job. The work was regarded as somewhat hazardous, and the word *grenadier* was a title of honor.

During the 1789–1914 period—a time associated with the rise of nationalism, of democracy, and of industrialization—war *really became mechanized*. Steam power was increasingly used for land and water military transportation; ordnance for army and navy developed significantly in range and accuracy, in particular the rifle, machine gun, and larger artillery pieces; the coming of steam power, the screw propeller, iron-hulled vessels, and heavy guns were important developments for the navy, as were the mine, torpedo, and submarine.

Important industrial advances lay behind such weapons achievements noted above. In particular, the rise of mass production and the inauguration of improved methods of making steel were most important in their effect on war weapons. The advent of mass production is a long story in which prominent parts were played by Richard Arkwright in the early years and Henry Ford during the twentieth century.[43] A significant milestone in the manufacture of military weapons occurred about the year 1800 when Eli Whitney, inventor of the cotton gin, saw the possibility of making muskets in quantity —which had not been accomplished up to this time.[44] Whitney, operating a factory in New Haven, Connecticut, emphasized the standardization of parts

[38] Forbes, *op. cit.*, pp. 119–120.

[39] Chinn, *op. cit.*, p. 16.

[40] Nef, *op. cit.*, pp. 35, 38.

[41] Spaulding and others, *op. cit.*, pp. 528–530.

[42] Forbes, *op. cit.*, p. 121; Wintringham, *op. cit.*, p. 118.

[43] Roger Burlingame, *Backgrounds of Power, The Human Story of Mass Production* (New York, Scribner, 1949), p. 47.

[44] *Ibid.*, Ch. 5 (esp. pp. 79–89).

of the weapon. Then he established patterns, guides for tools, and machines such that firearms production could be performed by any capable worker—not necessarily by a gunsmith. He demonstrated in Washington before ordnance experts and even the President of the United States the interchangeability of parts of weapons—after which he assembled the weapons and fired them.[45]

It was recognized that with the coming of mass production there was a greater need than ever for steel. The "Bessemer process" of making steel was invented independently by two men about the middle of the nineteenth century—William Kelly in the United States in 1846 and Henry Bessemer in England in 1856. With important improvements made by Alexander Holley, William R. Jones, and others, Bessemer steel made available for the first time a strong, wear-resistant, tough, and reasonably inexpensive metal.[46] This was vital for the munitions industry. The statistics of steel production after 1870 in the three leading steel countries of the world—the United Kingdom, the United States, and Germany—reflect these advances in making steel.[47]

The remaining need was for improved design of weapons themselves. Forward strides here were preceded by improvements in the ignition system of firearms—a crucial item. Important discoveries were made during the early 1800's by Berthollet, Howard, Rev. John A. Forsyth, and Joshua Shaw.[48] The use of cartridges was gradually developed after 1850. With these prerequisites attained, a veritable outpouring of models of rifles, pistols, and machine guns resulted.[49] In general, all of these guns have had a long period of development; for example, crude rifles and muskets were manufactured in Pennsylvania, Kentucky, and other areas as early as 1732. Usually the significant advances were made after 1850 and, more particularly, after 1900. The same is generally true of artillery pieces, such as cannon, mortars, and howitzers. The development of modern artillery came with the wide use of steel, the advent of smokeless powder and high explosives, and the innovation of more efficient sighting.[50]

Within a few years of the turn of the century five inventions were made which were of utmost significance to war—and four of these were of major

[45] Chinn, op. cit., p. 21; Jeannette Mirsky and Allan Nevins, The World of Eli Whitney (New York, Macmillan, 1952), Chs. 13–14, 18.

[46] See "Steel, The Bessemer Process," The Encyclopaedia Americana, Vol. XXV (1946), pp. 563–566; "Iron and Steel," Encyclopaedia Britannica, Vol. XII (1949), pp. 649–674 (esp. pp. 655–656, 673).

[47] Meredith Givens, "Iron and Steel Industry: History and Present Organization," Encyclopaedia of the Social Sciences, Vol. VIII (New York, Macmillan, 1932), pp. 296–297.

[48] Chinn, op. cit., p. 20.

[49] For details, see George M. Chinn's definitive work, The Machine Gun, to which reference has already been made many times; Walter H. B. Smith, Pistols and Revolvers (Washington, National Rifle Association of America, 1946); and Smith, Rifles (Washington, National Rifle Association of America, 1948).

[50] Albert Manucy, op. cit., pp. 17–21.

importance for civilian life as well. These inventions were the radio-telegraph, the perfecting of the internal combustion engine, the marine turbine engine, the perfecting of the submarine, and the first flight by humans in an airplane.[51] The first invention, by Marconi, was to revolutionize the communications systems of armies and navies; and radio communication was fundamental in aviation when the airplane was developed. The second one led to such vehicles as the truck, jeep, tank, and other armored vehicles which revolutionized transportation in war. It brought the possibility of rapid mobility of troops, the new concept of motorized infantry, and that new branch of the army, the armored force. The third and fourth inventions revolutionized naval warfare. The epoch-making flight of the Wright Brothers in their crude plane at Kitty Hawk, North Carolina, in 1903 brought a new dimension to warfare; and, again, an entirely new branch of the military service developed from the invention. This one, the air force, was one of the most crucial changes to occur to war during the latter's long history. With these and other inventions, the trend toward mechanized war was to be accelerated. Unquestionably, the most arresting technological influences were yet to come.

Weapons Used Between 1914 and 1939

The entire period from 1914 to the present emphasized the airplane, totalitarian war, atomic energy, and other elite technologies. The subperiod 1914 to 1939, dominated by World War I and its aftermath, the world depression beginning in 1929, and the aggressions by Japan, Italy, and Germany beginning in 1931, saw the use of machine gun and barbed wire; early use of tank and airplane; chemical agents; and accelerated use of artillery. In the land fighting of World War I the machine gun weapon and the practice of using barbed wire together brought the struggle to a quick stalemate. The machine gun so increased firepower that the defense was immensely strengthened. As a result of this, the trench system developed. In these circumstances, neither side could dislodge the other until some new element was introduced; for a year or more both sides were forced to wallow in muddy trenches like cattle.[52]

The new element that finally broke the deadlock was the tank. The same basic mechanical processes that produced the machine gun, artillery, and barbed wire brought forth the tank; and the same internal-combustion engine that powered automobiles and trucks moved the tank. The tank was able to knock down the barbed wire, and men could follow. Tanks first went into action during the Battle of the Somme on September 15, 1916, but their use was premature and ended as a fiasco. They were more successfully used at the Battle of Cambrai from November 20 to December 1, 1917. Their greatest success came on August 8, 1918. This time the new weapon was used

[51] John F. C. Fuller, *Machine Warfare* (Washington, The Infantry Journal, 1943), p. 12.

[52] Vannevar Bush, *Modern Arms and Free Men* (New York, Simon and Schuster, 1949), p. 11.

according to the plan of those who had conceived and developed it. On that day 456 Allied tanks moved toward the enemy lines, crashing through barbed-wire entanglements and irresistibly rolling right over trenches—with the infantry following. There was no stopping the tanks. It is said that they even surprised the German General Staff at breakfast.[53] It was eventually realized that the tank, which had been vigorously opposed at first in official military circles, was a mobile fortress that could revolutionize the art of land war.[54]

Use of the airplane in war was inaugurated during World War I. While the airplane was used mostly for reconnaissance purposes at this time[55]—it did not bring great advantage to either side—its potential value was nevertheless realized. At first planes were not even armed; British pilots were instructed to take along some sort of weapon (for example, a rifle). Finally machine guns were mounted on planes. Then rapid-fire killing was applied to the air arm, for a plane could swoop down on marching troops and the gunners inflict numerous casualties. Anthony H. G. Fokker, a Dutchman, conceived the idea during the early part of the war of gearing the machine gun to fire through the rotating propeller blades; the latter controlled the firing of the gun, and bullets could be released only between blades. Fokker sold his invention to the German air command. After this, German planes used the synchronized machine gun with telling effect. Soon a Fokker-equipped plane was brought down behind the Allied lines, and the French and British learned and adopted the device. Today, guns fire from the wings, fuselage, and nose of the military plane.[56]

Another development of World War I was the use of chemical weapons. The idea of using poison gas was far from new; as an invention, it is older than gunpowder.[57] During the war between Sparta and Athens in the fifth century B.C., the Spartans soaked wood in a mixture of pitch and sulphur and burned it under the walls of Greek cities; it released sulphur dioxide and other smothering gases. The first use of gas in World War I was apparently made by the French, who fired rifle grenades containing tear gas during August, 1914. When they again used a lachrymator a few months later, the

[53] General Ludendorff later testified that German morale cracked on that day in August, 1918. See George W. Gray, *Science at War* (New York, Harper, 1943), pp. 102–106.

[54] Wintringham, *op. cit.*, pp. 174–175. It is interesting that even after the immensely successful use of the tank during the latter part of World War I, many military officers had little appreciation of it as a weapon. This was especially true in the English-speaking countries. It was not until Nazi Germany formed her panzer divisions and showed in Poland and other countries the power of the armored force, that finally England and America awoke to the importance of this branch of the army. See Bush, *op. cit.*, p. 11; also Foreword by Lt. Col. S. L. A. Marshall to John F. C. Fuller, *Armed Warfare* (Harrisburg, Pa., The Military Service Publishing Company, 1943).

[55] Bush, *op. cit.*

[56] Gray, *op. cit.*, pp. 87–89.

[57] *Ibid.*, pp. 159–160.

Germans charged a technical violation of the Hague Pact. The Germans decided to use gas after they were stopped at the Marne and the static trench warfare had set in. On April 22, 1915, at Ypres they used chlorine. After the greenish yellow clouds drifted to the Allied lines with the spring breeze, men were coughing, choking, running away—terrified. Within an hour, declared Field Marshall French, the whole position had to be abandoned. Twenty thousand men were rendered helpless, and some five thousand of them died. Thus mass inflicting of casualties was obtained via the chemical route. But the Germans appeared to be surprised by the turn of events and acted slowly. Meanwhile the Allies hastily re-established their line. Within a few days, the British and French had improvised simple but effective gas masks. More elaborate masks came later. Germany's opportunity to gain even greater advantage was now gone.[58]

Following this, the German command took gas warfare seriously, as did the Allies too. The former then used a more dangerous gas, phosgene—a lung irritant. But British intelligence was aware of the plan, and the Allies were ready with masks. During the remainder of the war both sides used gas many times.[59] The most effective gas used by either side during World War I was mustard gas. More powerful gases, adamsite and lewisite, were available at the time of the armistice but were never used. After World War I other dangerous gases were invented, such as the nitrogen mustards. These have neither color nor odor, hence are likely to escape detection.[60] To combat this, special chemical paints which change their color when poison gas is in the atmosphere have been devised for use on vehicles and other objects.

Mention should also be made of the increased use of artillery in World War I. Artillery preparation became more and more an important part of each battle. At the Third Battle of Ypres (1917), said Fuller,[61] the preliminary bombardment alone used 4,283,550 shells, which cost $110 million and weighed 107,000 tons. Wintringham believes that artillery was the dominant weapon in 1914–18 because "it killed most enemy soldiers and did most damage to their defenses and was the most effective weapon for hampering movement behind the front line."[62]

It was clear that by the end of World War I mechanized war was in gear— ready to move ahead. Vannevar Bush declared:[63]

[58] With sufficient troops, says Gray, the Germans could have swept to the channel ports; it is even conceivable that they might have won the war in a bold stroke on that April day.—Gray, *op. cit.*, p. 161.

[59] For an authoritative summary and discussion of gas attacks which were made by both sides during World War I, see Augustin M. Prentiss, *Chemicals in War* (New York, McGraw-Hill, 1937), pp. 662–667.

[60] *Ibid.*

[61] *Machine Warfare*, p. 17.

[62] Wintringham, *op. cit.*, p. 168.

[63] Bush, *op. cit.*, p. 16.

When the First World War ended there were thus in existence nearly all the elements for scientific warfare. The principal devices had been tried out in practice. There were automatic guns, self-propelled vehicles, tanks, aircraft, submarines, radio communication, poison gases. . . . The petroleum, automobile, chemical, and communication industries had approached maturity; thousands of men had become skilled in techniques. . . . The world was fully launched on mechanized warfare. For all the technical devices that were later to be used in the second war, except only atomic energy, practically every basic technique had appeared, waiting only construction and development.

After 1930 there was considerable development of the air and armored forces, especially in Germany (after Hitler rose to power). However, the rise of peacetime aviation in the United States was phenomenal. Because production of the modern war weapons was so related to industrial development and because air war increasingly threatened the bombing of enemy cities and production centers, the concept of *total war* emerged. No longer was war just a matter for military personnel; civilians, industrial workers, transportation workers and facilities, and other vital war facilities were now, in effect, brought into the war zone. Military organization now had to be geared with the agricultural, industrial, and professional population for a total national effort.[64] As expressed by General Marshall a few years later, "Wars in the twentieth century are fought with the total resources, economic, scientific, and human of entire nations. Every specialized field of human knowledge is employed. Modern war requires the skills and knowledge of the individuals of a nation."[65]

From 1939 to the Present

The period from 1939 to the present, emphasizing World War II and its aftermath, was the time of fully developed, ultra-scientific, sometimes spectacular, mechanized war. By 1939 the new, high-gear military force was primed—especially in Germany—and Hitler gave the orders to roll. The Nazi panzer divisions literally raced through Czechoslovakia and Poland. Stuka dive-bombers removed the few nests of antitank guns that sometimes impeded an advance. All was co-ordinated by radio communication. In addition to the blitzkrieg tactics, the world was to see from time to time the curtain lifted on new elite weapons developed by various nations, not the least of which was the United States. Many of these new secret weapons were applications of modern physics, so much so that World War II has been called the physicist's war.

Here it is proposed to discuss briefly certain highlights of the recent war technology: (1) further development of tank and antitank weapons, (2) further developments of the airplane, (3) radar, (4) guided missiles, (5) the

[64] Wright, *op. cit.*, Vol. I, pp. 305–307.
[65] George C. Marshall, *General Marshall's Report* (New York, Simon and Schuster, 1945), p. 118.

atomic and hydrogen bombs, (6) further developments in chemical warfare, and (7) biological warfare.

Tank and antitank. Germany took the lead in developing the tactical uses of the tank. The Nazi victories of 1939–40 made a deep impression on the English and American military. The tank was now regarded as an important weapon of the day, a view held formerly by only a minority among army leaders. The results of this realization were chiefly two. First, the English and American armies hastily built up armored forces of their own. The latter, indeed, were active during the remainder of World War II, especially in North Africa, France (following the Normandy invasion), and in Germany. Secondly, various nations, especially the United States, rushed the development and production of antitank weapons. The bazooka, antitank mines, antitank artillery, and rocket-carrying planes were all effective in combating the tank. Before the end of World War II the tank was no longer regarded as the invincible weapon of August, 1918 (in the hands of the Allies), or of 1939–40 (as used by the Nazis against Poland and France). American armored divisions, led by General Patton and others, were, to be sure, impressive and dramatic in the 1944 sweep across France. By war's end, however, it was perceived that antitank weapons amounted to just about a match for the tank. The bazooka's rocket is deadly and is quite capable of smashing a tank.[66] Just as deadly are the rocket-carrying planes and certain artillery pieces such as the 105-millimeter gun. The tank dealt out much punishment to the enemy, and it was perfectly suited to the flat terrain of Poland, North Africa, and France. But the tank itself increasingly absorbed punishment and eventually its offensive threat was fairly well checked. Unquestionably, the tank functioned best when well co-ordinated with air power and with the infantry—when planes or infantry could knock out nests of antitank guns and when planes radioed word of what lay ahead of the tank.[67]

Aviation and war. The airplane has revolutionized warfare. It was enormously improved between World Wars I and II.[68] The airplane not only brought the attack to enemy soldiers and ships but to the civilian population, industry, key installations, and other structures vital to the war effort as well. It lessened the effect of geographical barriers and minimized the factor of distance.[69] The English Channel, for example, had been in earlier wars a protective moat of importance for the British, but in air war it was no barrier at all. As for distance, planes are now able to fly nonstop around the world— and bombs can be dropped at any desired point. In the battle zones, airmen may bomb or strafe enemy troops, key installations, supply depots, trans-

[66] Bush, *op. cit.,* pp. 31–32; Gray, *op. cit.,* p. 76.

[67] General Fuller called the latter "eyes" for the tank: "Without the tank, the rear of the air (force) is largely uncovered, and without the airplane the front of the tank is largely blind."—*Machine Warfare,* p. 86.

[68] See Chapter 9.

[69] William F. Ogburn, "Aviation and International Relations," in Ogburn, ed., *Technology and International Relations,* pp. 86–89.

portation junction points, naval vessels (including the submarine), and of course attack enemy planes. They may, if desired, release poison gas from the plane. Machine guns and rockets mounted on planes provide considerable firepower, and a new form of attack—that of the airborne infantry and parachute troops—may be launched. All this increases the swiftness of attack and helps to bring about a mobile, fast-moving type of war.

Near the beginning of World War II (in 1940, to be exact) a striking demonstration of modern air warfare was provided in the "Battle of Britain." Germany sought to knock out the (British) Royal Air Force and after that to force the island nation to surrender. For twelve weeks the German Luftwaffe tried to bomb the English into submission. Almost continual air warfare was fought at heights of from three to six miles. This is likely to be reckoned as one of the decisive battles of history, for if Hitler's forces had destroyed Britain at this time, they would have conquered all Europe—leaving the United States isolated. The German Air Force, as we know, finally absorbed such losses in planes and personnel that it was forced to call off the attack.[70] The defensive victory of the British, as Gray points out, was probably due to two principal factors: (1) the courageous fighting of the Royal Air Force, and (2) use of the new secret weapon, *radar* (called the "radiolocator" by the English). This device emits radio waves that are reflected back from any object (for example, an airplane or ship), hence one can detect the presence of the approaching object long before it is visible or before its motors may be heard with microphones. The aircraft warning system developed from this. Also, using guns with radar controls, one can tell precisely where to fire even though he cannot see the approaching object.

The development of the airplane even during the period of World War II was amazing. Greater speed, cruising radius, and bomb-load capacity were recorded.[71] During the latter part of the war, the jet, turbojet, and ramjet engines were developed. The destruction wrought by the great Allied bombing raids over Berlin, Hamburg, and other German cities was tremendous, and undoubtedly constituted one of the important reasons for the gradual weakening of Germany. The immensity of many of these raids, involving from five hundred to a thousand or more planes, was also one of the reasons why some of Germany's secret weapons were never produced. So impressive were the mass bombing raids that some enthusiasts spoke of "victory by air power," which echoed the sentiments of General "Billy" Mitchell expressed during the early 1920's. But the conclusion that finally emerged was that important as air power is and tremendous as its influence has been on war, it

[70] Gray, *op. cit.*, pp. 17 ff; Montross, *op. cit.*, pp. 806–810.
[71] See remarks of the late General H. H. Arnold, Commander of the U. S. Air Force during World War II, which are quoted in General Marshall's Report, *op. cit.*, p. 5. See also Gray, *op. cit.*, p. 99, for discussion of that technological device, the *bombsight* —a special optical and computing device for aiming the missiles so as to have greater accuracy in hitting the target.

does not win wars by itself.[72] It cannot alone crush an enemy nor can it secure enemy territory that has been conquered. Ground troops are still necessary for the latter.

By early 1954, American military policy came to rely strongly on air power coupled with the ability to use nuclear bombs if needed. This policy was known as the "New Look," and it embodied a change from the former "balanced forces" concept wherein military expenditures were evenly split between the Army, Navy, and Air Force. Hence the role of the Air Force became more dominant.[73] Some observers likened its influence to that of the British Navy during the nineteenth century.

It must be reported, on the other hand, that air power has been partly countered by anti-aircraft artillery, use of radar, use of the proximity fuse, and of guided missiles.[74] It may be that the losses of attacking planes will be higher in the future, although it seems likely that *some* of the attacking planes will be able to break through the defensive forces. If one plane, carrying an H-bomb, penetrated the defense, it could no doubt accomplish the mission of the attack. (See further discussion in Chapter 10.)

Aviation, moreover, presents a constantly changing picture; new developments are occurring all the time. The U. S. Navy announced during January, 1955, that new fighter planes can "take-off" vertically, thus having a new tactical advantage.[75] Shortly thereafter officials of the Bell Aircraft Corporation also announced progress on a new jet-propelled, vertical-rising airplane —no runway is needed—calling it "the most significant single development in aircraft flight since the Wright Brothers."[76] General Nathan F. Twining, Air Force Chief of Staff, and others have stated that before many years airplanes are likely to be nuclear-powered.[77]

Before leaving the subject of military aviation, mention should be made of the helicopter, since the latter was most successfully used during the Korean War of 1950–53. Helicopters proved themselves in the battle areas by moving combat troops and hundreds of tons of supplies over difficult terrain in short periods of time. They were frequently able to move personnel and materiel to commanding mountain heights which were inaccessible by other means of transportation. They were useful for generals and other high officers

[72] The ending of the Pacific part of World War II may seem to refute this. But the Navy, Army, and Marine Corps had played prominent roles in this war theater. It is generally acknowledged that Japan was well along the road to defeat before Nagasaki and Hiroshima were A-bombed. The latter, it is true, brought the final surrender.

[73] See, for example, *Aviation Week*, Vol. LX, No. 11 (March 15, 1954), pp. 45–46.

[74] Bush, *op. cit.*, p. 52.

[75] *New York Times*, January 16, 1955.

[76] *New York Times*, February 4, 1955.

[77] *New York Times*, January 28, 1955; *ibid*, June 9, 1955. The McKinney Report also notes that "technical prospects for military aircraft with atomic propulsion are considered good, . . ." See *Peaceful Uses of Atomic Energy*, Report of the Panel on the Impact of the Peaceful Uses of Atomic Energy to the Joint Committee on Atomic Energy, Vol. I (Washington, Government Printing Office, 1956), p. 82.

who wanted to inspect the front areas. The assertion is attributed to ranking Marine Corps officers that the helicopter, all told, was the foremost tactical innovation of the Korean War.[78] "Lost battalions," as in 1917–18, appear to be phenomena of the past; it was stated that in Korea cut-off units would soon hear the "chop-chopping" of helicopters and would be amazed to have supplies deposited at their feet. Moreover, the Signal Corps used helicopters in messenger service and in laying field telephone wire; and the Medical Corps had airlifted by the time of the armistice (July, 1953) over 16,000 casualties from the battlefield. By this time the Army had established regular transportation helicopter companies, with twenty-one cargo helicopters operated by each company.[79] Marine Corps enthusiasm for the helicopter persists for the additional important reason that Marine leaders see it as an invaluable aid in beachhead assaults despite use of nuclear weapons by the enemy. Marine strategists recognized in 1955 that massed ships ready for an assault, as at Iwo Jima during World War II, could be wiped out with one atomic blast. However, a scattered fleet with helicopters to carry the troops ashore and place them where needed presents more successful prospects. Even landing craft offer a lucrative target for nuclear weapons. Helicopters do not.[80]

Guided missiles. A technological innovation that held promise during the 1950's of revolutionizing war was the guided missile. Men have hurled missiles at one another for many centuries.[81] However, to *guide* the missile to its target was something new, made possible by advances in physics. The maneuverings of many of these missiles can only be described by the word *fantastic*. In the race between offense and defense, guided missiles were developed for three main reasons: (1) airmen sought greater bombing accuracy, with less exposure to anti-aircraft fire, (2) ground forces needed improved anti-aircraft weapons if the air attacks were to be more devastating, and (3) development of an improved missile used by ground forces brought the need of an anti-missile missile. The general types are generally known as the air-to-surface, surface-to-air, surface-to-surface, and air-to-air missiles.[82]

Beginning with the preset system, as in the V-1 buzz bomb and the V-2 rocket used by Nazi Germany during World War II (in which cases man had no control once the missile was launched), guidance systems have become more complicated. The missile may be guided by remote (electromagnetic) control into the target. An operator may guide the missile to its target by use of television. The missile may be guided by long-range radio navigation. The

[78] Lynn Montross, *Cavalry of the Sky, The Story of the U. S. Marine Combat Helicopters* (New York, Harper, 1954).

[79] *Aviation Week*, Vol. LX, No. 11 (March 15, 1954), p. 69.

[80] Claude Witze, in *Aviation Week*, Vol. LXII, No. 11 (March 14, 1955), "22nd Annual Inventory of Airpower," p. 298.

[81] Bush, *op. cit.*, p. 71.

[82] Nels A. Parson, Jr., *Guided Missiles in War and Peace* (Cambridge, Harvard University Press, 1956), pp. 7–12.

missile may be slaved to a light, radar, or other energy beam which is trained on a target, hence the missile follows the beam to the target. Finally, there is the target-seeking missile, in which a "homing" mechanism takes charge of the missile and directs it to the target even though the latter may be moving.[83]

The following missiles are now in use or are being developed by the U. S. armed forces:[84]

Missile	Type	Approximate Range (mi.)	Approximate Speed
Nike	Army antiaircraft	30	Supersonic
Terrier	Navy ship-to-air	6–10	Twice speed of sound
Rascal	A.F., air-to-surface	100	Supersonic
Sparrow	Navy air-to-air	4–8	Thrice speed of sound
Matador	A.F. ground-to-ground	500	Subsonic
Corporal	Army ground-to-ground	100	Supersonic
Regulus	Navy ship-to-surface	500	Subsonic
V-2 with WAC Corporal	Research	250 (altitude)	5300 mph

One may already discern some of the influences of guided missiles on strategy. One is that the theater of war will be further widened, tremendously so when the intercontinental missile has been perfected (a probable development). We have seen that the area of combat was small in early times. It was enlarged by use of long-range guns and of airplanes; no longer did bodies of water or mountain ranges afford protection. As a reasonable degree of accuracy and reliability of the intercontinental missile is attained,[85] it will be possible to attack transoceanic targets with nuclear explosives. It is clear that a revolution in warfare will occur with this development. Estimates vary as to how many years will pass before this "grand-daddy" missile will fly reliably for thousands of miles when used operationally.

Another effect of the guided missile on strategy and tactics is that ground troops and materiel will henceforth need to be increasingly dispersed. Indeed, a future technique may be to force the enemy to mass, to reveal the location of his main effort, then to subject him to guided missile attack which will use the nuclear warhead. In fact, a sustained and definable front in future warfare may be, as Major Parson declares,[86] "abnormal rather than normal."

A third effect on strategy and tactics is to increase the military significance of the submarine; as with the preceding item this effect ensues actually from the combined use of the guided missile and of atomic power. While the submarine has been a potent weapon even before these developments, the

---

[83] Ibid., pp. 54–58.

[84] Hanson W. Baldwin, "Awesome Era of Fantastic Missiles," New York Times, Magazine Section, Sunday, August 29, 1954. See also Parson, op. cit., Chs. 7–9; "Story of the 'Push Buttons': Latest on New Weapons of War," U. S. News & World Report (August 12, 1955). The latter comprised an interview with Donald A. Quarles who, a few days after this article was published, became Secretary of the U. S. Air Force.

[85] Parson, op. cit., pp. 98–100.

[86] Ibid., pp. 134–135.

Lifting the Redstone guided missile into position on a test stand.

Three guided missiles set on launchers. From the left, Honest John, Nike, and Corporal.

**GUIDED MISSILES: POTENT WEAPON IN MODERN
TECHNOLOGICAL WAR**

The Matador, Air Force guided missile.

Honest John rocket just leaving the launcher.

Launching a Terrier missile from the USS "Boston."

Launching a Regulus missile from the USS "Princeton."

atomic-powered sub (already in use) will become more independent of its base; it will be able to stay submerged for months at a time if necessary. It has extraordinary possibilities when armed with guided missiles. It will be able, for example, to move within target range underwater, surface, then fire at ship or shore targets hundreds of miles away, and disappear again even before the missiles have reached their destination.[87]

Up to the present time, guided missiles have largely aided the defense. But it is clear that with such developments as are noted above, these weapons are likely to more and more be of benefit to the offense. Many persons regard the development of the intercontinental ballistic missile as especially crucial. The United States is developing at least three types of intercontinental missiles: the Snark, a pilotless plane with transoceanic range and high subsonic speed; the Navaho, a pilotless plane with transoceanic range and supersonic speed; and the Atlas, a ballistic guided missile capable of crossing the ocean in minutes. These are estimated to be available for use roughly between 1958 and 1965.[88] However, the American effort has been accelerated during 1955–56, owing to Russian success in developing the middle-range missile (and other military weapons). Concern in various American quarters has been expressed lest the Russians forge ahead in certain of these developments, particularly that of the intercontinental guided missile.[89]

The A-bomb. Many people have generally regarded the atomic bomb as the greatest single technological innovation of the present period, and the term *atomic age* (or *nuclear age*) has been widely applied to the present era of man's existence. Since nuclear energy has been specifically treated in Chapter 10, the discussion here will be brief.

The influence of the atomic bomb on war can be clearly indicated. First, the destructive possibilities of war are tremendously heightened by the use of this new weapon. An estimated 71,000 persons killed and 68,000 persons injured as a result of the explosion of one bomb, such as happened at Hiroshima, Japan, on August 6, 1945, must be regarded as terrific[90]—even to one who may be hardened to battle casualty figures. The explosive force of the Hiroshima bomb has been estimated to be approximately equal to that of 20,000 tons of TNT. The world has seen many wars, but it had never seen before 1945 such destructive capabilities as this! Second, it was realized within a few years after 1945 that even though the A-bomb explosion was tremendous, the bomb should not properly be regarded as an "absolute

[87] *Ibid.*, pp. 112–114.

[88] Hanson W. Baldwin, "Guided Missiles: Progress Report," *New York Times,* March 13, 1955.

[89] See, for example, Senator Henry M. Jackson, "The Increasing Threat of Ballistic Missiles," *Bulletin of the Atomic Scientists,* Vol. XII, No. 3 (March, 1956), pp. 90–92; *Aviation Week* (March 12, 1956), "23rd Annual Inventory of Airpower," pp. 70–71, 78–79, 98–101; Charles J. V. Murphy, "Defense: The Revolution Gets Revolutionary," *Fortune* (May, 1956), pp. 101 ff.

[90] R. E. Lapp, *Must We Hide?* (Cambridge, Addison-Wesley, 1949), pp. 18–19.

weapon," namely, one so overpowering that it makes all other methods of waging war obsolete or that it guarantees victory.[91] Third, even more powerful atomic bombs have been made during the years since 1945. The A-bomb tested at Bikini in 1951, for example, has been estimated to have been two-and-one-half times as powerful as the Hiroshima bomb.[92] Fourth, it was clear by 1950 that the coming of atomic energy had brought not just one weapon (the bomb), but the new force could be applied to a host of land, sea, and air weapons. The latter included atomic artillery (the 280-millimeter cannon), radioactive dust, atom-powered submarines, atomic torpedoes, atomic depth charges, and similar weapons. Lastly, it was soon realized after 1945 that the A-bomb could be used to detonate the much more powerful "thermonuclear" or "fusion" device, the hydrogen bomb. United States' forces tested small H-bombs during 1951 and on November 1, 1952; the Russians claimed to have tested one during August, 1953.[93] Then American forces detonated large hydrogen bombs during March, 1954, at the Pacific proving grounds. These explosions had a force in the megaton range—a megaton being equivalent to one million tons of TNT. The force of these blasts was said to be about 600 to 700 times those of the A-bombs that destroyed Hiroshima and Nagasaki. Admiral Lewis L. Strauss, Chairman of the Atomic Energy Commission, declared that now any city (even New York) could be "put out of commission" by one bomb blast. He further stated that hydrogen bombs could be made of any desired size.[94] Devastating as this was, the American public was informed, after a delay of several months, of the problem of radioactive fall-out—a further menace. This critical problem has been discussed in Chapter 10 and is further discussed in Chapter 16.

With puny man having such enormously destructive forces at his disposal, one can only imagine the consequences of a future war. In the attempt to grasp the tremendous influence which technology has had on war, one may contrast atomic-hydrogen-guided-missile war with, say, the Battle of Crecy, fought in 1346 with the bow-and-arrow as the main weapon. One may recall that the English won at Crecy because they developed a "new weapon"—the longbow—which was superior to the crossbow used by the French. Was there much similarity between war during the 1950's and Crecy, Bunker Hill, or Gettysburg, aside from the one fact that they all involved killing and destruction?

[91] *Ibid.*, p. 5; Bush, *op. cit.*, p. 90.

[92] Hanson W. Baldwin, "What Kind of Defense in the Atomic Age?" *New York Times*, Magazine Section, May 17, 1953.

[93] *New York Times*, August 9, 1953; AEC Press Releases, November 16, 1952 and August 20, 1953.

[94] See *Sixteenth Semiannual Report of the Atomic Energy Commission*, July, 1954 (Washington, Government Printing Office, 1954), pp. 15–16; AEC News Release, August 5, 1954 (Address by Lewis L. Strauss, Chairman, U. S. Atomic Energy Commission); *New York Times*, April 1, 1954; and *U. S. News & World Report* (April 9, 1954).

Chemical warfare. Discussion of nuclear energy does not, however, end this appraisal of developing war weapons; two other classes of weapons remain to be considered. The first one is that of chemical warfare, a field in which notable advances have been made. Interestingly enough, chemical weapons were not used by either side during World War II, although both sides were well prepared for it. The Germans did not have large stocks of advanced war gases until the time when they had lost control of the air.[95] They were aware of the Allied power to retaliate, hence wisely refrained from using gas. The Allied side had apparently adopted the policy of not using chemical gas unless the Germans did so first.

Whether or not chemical gas will be used in a future war is anybody's guess. But if not, it will not be because potent gases are not available. More toxic chemical gases have now been produced and they can be made in large quantities. Also, nerve gases, especially the deadly tabun that was produced by German research, are now available. Gases in the tabun series are virtually odorless, and they persist in an area for weeks. Much is known about the effects and treatment of nerve gases.[96] Use of atrophine and other therapy provides effective treatment against this gas. The symptoms are serious, however, and treatment must be given quickly. Widespread education concerning this gas is desirable for all military personnel and for civilians located in places where such gas might be used in event of war. Since some of the symptoms are alarming, "military commanders and medical officers must give serious consideration to the possibility of panic among combat personnel in nerve-gas attack and take all possible steps to prevent or control it."[97] Futhermore, says Baldwin,[98] experiments since World War II regarding all gases have indicated that it is now "theoretically possible" to produce new gases as much as one thousand times more poisonous than previously known agents.

Germ warfare. Biological warfare is another possible type of weapon which might be used in future war. From what is publicly known about this subject—which is not extensive in view of security requirements—one may reach several conclusions. (1) Biological warfare is no mere subject of "conjecture" or of "fanciful sensationalism" but is a realistic possibility in event

[95] Bush, *op. cit.,* p. 140. Brig. General Charles E. Loucks, Deputy Chief, U. S. Army Chemical Corps, reported that when the Allied armies entered Germany toward the end of World War II they found 250,000 tons of German-made gas and gas bombs which had been available for use.—*New York Times,* January 23, 1952.

[96] A mimeographed bibliography entitled "Suggested Unclassified References to Nerve Gases," dated August 7, 1953, has been sent to the writer through the courtesy of Captain Malcolm M. Semple (U. S.) Army Chemical Corps, Office of the Chief Chemical Officer, Washington, D. C. This bibliography lists 41 titles and 73 references in bulletins, journals, and newspapers.

[97] John R. Wood, Paul F. Dickens, Jr., John Rizzolo, and M. W. Bayliss, "Treatment of Nerve-Gas Casualties," *U. S. Armed Forces Medical Journal,* Vol. II, No. 11 (November, 1951), pp. 1609–1617.

[98] Baldwin, *op. cit.,* pp. 70–71.

of future war. Germs could be released by sprays, or the water or food supply could be contaminated. Water- and food-borne epidemics of typhoid fever have been, indeed, common in the past without anyone intentionally trying to infect the water or food. (2) Advances in biological science have produced extremely poisonous germ weapons. Specific germ agents now available for use include anthrax; botulinus toxin (botulism is perhaps the most lethal poison known to man); tularemia (rabbit fever); psittacosis; typhus fever; bubonic plague; and pneumonic plague. Many agents could, however, be used.[99] (3) New microbe detectors do offer hope for the defense. The U. S. Army Chemical Corps perfected around 1950 a revolutionary detection device around which a "workable defense" can be built. It consists of a new filter which permits the identification of germs within 15 hours, or one-sixth of the time previously needed. Still speedier tests for all biological agents are being sought.[100] (4) The concept of "super virulence" of certain germs, sometimes alleged as a "BW" possibility, is *not* regarded as valid by reputable authorities on the subject.[101] It is believed, on the other hand, that germs which would be used in a war would be the usual ones known to medical officers everywhere. And lastly, (5) "BW" has never been used much in war as yet.[102] Its significant development, says Rosebury,[103] is largely a product of work performed during World War II.

It is important to have the fundamental view that "BW" is, essentially, public health and preventive medicine *in reverse*.[104] Except for new methods of deliberately spreading germs during a war, nature has waged this kind of war against man for thousands of years; and modern public health practice has produced effective defenses against it. During wartime an enemy might use germ weapons against cattle and crops—in the attempt to destroy man's food supply as well as himself.

It must be conceded that since "BW" has not been significantly used as yet in war, it remains something of an unknown quantity. Presumably this type of attack could be launched by means of shells, airplanes, or submarines. The latter could rise to the surface near a coastal city, and the submarine per-

[99] Theodor Rosebury, *Peace or Pestilence, Biological Warfare and How to Avoid It* (New York, Whittlesey House, 1949), Chs. 5–7; Baldwin, *op. cit.*

[100] Mimeographed copy of address entitled "Biological Warfare" delivered by Brigadier General William M. Creasy, Commanding Chemical Corps Research and Engineering Command, before the American Chemical Society on October 23, 1951. The writer is again indebted to Captain Malcolm M. Semple, Office of the Chief Chemical Officer, U. S. Army, for sending this mimeographed copy of address as well as other unclassified material. Biological warfare in the U. S. Army comes under the jurisdiction of the Army Chemical Corps.

[101] *Ibid.*

[102] Baldwin, *op. cit.*, pp. 71–75. See also George W. Merck, "Report to the Secretary of War on Biological Warfare" (1946), which has been published in *Bulletin of the Atomic Scientists*, Vol. II (October 1, 1946), and has been condensed in the *New York Times*, January 4, 1946.

[103] Rosebury, *op. cit.*, p. 14.

[104] Mimeographed copy of address, General Creasy, *op. cit.*

sonnel could disperse the germs with use of sprays. It is clear that this subject of use and defense against biological weapons needs to be given extremely careful consideration. It may be that the best defense against germ attack is the threat of retaliation—which is also perhaps true with regard to the A- and H-bombs and chemical warfare.

NET EFFECTS OF TECHNOLOGY ON WAR

In tracing the influences of technology on war over the centuries, we have explored in the preceding section many, though not all, of known influences. The subject of danger of exterminating the human race by use of radioactive clouds has not been underscored in this chapter since it has been discussed elsewhere in this volume. Other technological influences have been omitted because of limitations of space.[105] Nevertheless, it is thought that the coverage has been complete enough to permit us to establish certain *net effects* of technology on war and then to make conclusions on the basis of the facts cited.

Some of the *net effects* on warfare, considered as briefly as possible, are these:

1. The developing technological devices have brought an increasing trend of war casualties. More efficient killing power has been, indeed, the prime objective of the new weapons. The machine gun was a much more "successful" killing agent than the bow-and-arrow; but the former was rather trifling as compared with the atom bomb—surely a triumph in mass killing though itself now dwarfed by the possibilities of the hydrogen bomb.

Specific figures showing the upward trend of war casualties over the centuries have been presented in Chapter 3, hence will not be repeated here.

2. The newer technological weapons have brought not only an increase in mass killing of war combatants but, it may be noted, of noncombatants as well. When a city is bombed, there is no distinguishing between soldiers and civilians; there is no wish to make such a distinction. Modern large-scale war means total war. The objective is to knock out the enemy nation in any and all ways—by defeating its professional soldiers, destroying its cities, denying its access to raw materials, bombing its factories and transportation lines, destroying its ports, killing off as much of the civilian population as possible, and sapping the will to resist of the living population by propaganda and other psychological measures. Women and children become the targets of the

105 For example, discussion has been omitted of ordinary (non-nuclear) bombs which followed the invention of dynamite made by Alfred Nobel during the 1860's; the sensitive RDX bombs; developments concerning the submarine as the "schnorkel" and the long-range torpedo; antisubmarine devices as *sonar* and *MAD* (magnetic airborne detection); the development of magnetic and other mines; new Signal Corps (communications) devices including radio and radar; new quartermaster advances including new types of foods and clothing; and, lastly, new developments of the Transportation Corps as the "Duck" (or "DUKW") of World War II and the huge "BARC" (an amphibious vehicle capable of carrying a medium tank and a 35-ton crane at the same time and landing them even in a roaring surf) of around 1950.

new mass-killing weapons as much as soldiers. The "Battle of Britain" is an example of this, as is the bombing of Hiroshima and Nagasaki. While some noncombatants have doubtless been killed in all wars, many more tend to be killed when modern technological weapons are used.

3. The financial cost of waging war has vastly increased as a result of use of the modern technological weapons. The economic cost of slingshot or bow-and-arrow during earlier centuries was negligible. The musket of colonial times seems to have had a comparatively low cost. The cost of arms has steadily risen since the latter part of the nineteenth century; at the present time it is staggering. The cost of outfitting one infantry or armored division is tremendous,[106] as is that of building one cruiser, aircraft carrier, battleship, or atom bomb. In general, the cost per unit of producing war vehicles and equipment (tanks, trucks, airplanes, etc.) is reduced as mass-production methods are used and as the workers gain experience; the required man-hours of labor per unit tend to decrease in most cases. Typical costs of arms and military equipment during recent years are included in the following table:[107]

Article or Vehicle	Cost for What Year	Estimated Cost (per unit)
1. M-1 Garand rifle, standard U. S. Army rifle	1954	$ 70.00
2. 75-millimeter anti-aircraft gun (known as the "Sky-sweeper")	1954	500,000.00
3. F-94 A/B airplane	1955	281,260.00
4. Navy plane, aver. cost	1954	814,450.00
5. Mobile search radar set	1950	782,798.00
6. U. S. Navy aircraft carrier (Forrestal type)	1954	208,000,000.00

The total expenditures of the modern military services are stupendous, but much of this is spent on salaries, labor costs, and other items which are not necessarily related to the influence of technology.[108]

[106] It has been estimated that in June, 1950, the initial equipment of a full-strength infantry division (U. S.) costs about $80 million. Costs of equipping an armored division are listed as more than double that of an infantry division. See "The Price of a Division," *Fortune* (December, 1950), pp. 74 ff.

[107] Data from *Department of the Army, Appropriations for 1954, Hearings before the Subcommittee of the Committee on Appropriations, House of Representatives, 83rd Congress, First Session* (Washington, Government Printing Office, 1953), pp. 1336, 1328–1329; same for *Department of the Air Force, Appropriations for 1955,* p. 817; *Department of the Navy, Appropriations for 1955,* pp. 24, 419.

[108] For example, the total military financial request for the fiscal year ending June 30, 1955 (when the U. S. was not engaged in an active war) amounted to $29,842,000,-000. Of this total sum, $8,211,000,000 was requested for the Army; $9,870,000,000 for the Navy; $11,200,000,000 for the Air Force; and $561,000,000 for certain inter-service expenditures. *Department of Defense, Appropriations for 1955, Hearings before the Subcommittee of the Committee on Appropriations, U. S. Senate, 83rd Congress, on H. R. 8873* (Washington, Government Printing Office, 1954), p. 9.

The fantastic expense of modern technological war is made vividly clear when one considers two things: (a) Many military vehicles or planes when fully outfitted with modern technical gadgets are much more expensive than the unequipped truck or plane. Hunsaker observes,[109] for example, that when the F-86 fighter plane is completely rigged out with power plant, radar, guns, sights, and spare parts, the cost is about twelve times that of the bare airplane. (b) The extent of destruction of arms and vehicles in battle is huge. The testimony of General J. Lawton Collins concerning the Korean "local war" reveals that between June, 1950, and December 31, 1952, United States forces had destroyed or used up more than 800 tanks, more than 40,000 trucks, and more than 19,000 battlefield radios. Ammunition used included 600,000 tons of 105-millimeter ammunition; 300,000 tons of 155-millimeter ammunition; 75,000 tons of 8-inch howitzer ammunition; and 80,000 tons of 4.2-inch mortar ammunition.[110] The above does not mention losses of airplanes, ships, and many other items. Yet the above consumption was small as compared with that during World War II.

Hanson Baldwin comments as follows regarding the all-around cost of modern war:[111]

The new technology is frighteningly expensive; the "garrison state" can easily become the "bankrupt state." A pilot model of a modern bomber now may cost $20,000,000 to $30,000,000; guided missiles with their intricate propulsion and guidance systems will be ten to a thousand times more costly than the shell which they will largely displace. The basic facilities for the development and testing of the new weapons—wind tunnels, proving grounds and laboratories—will require the expenditure of billions even *before* a single intercontinental super sonic weapon has been tested.

In providing for modern military needs a sum like one million dollars seems to shrink visibly. Certainly when equating it with capacity to outfit an armored division or produce a modern bomber or aircraft carrier, one soon tends to add such diminutives as "paltry" or "measly"—and maybe to end up (as suggested in *Fortune*) with a reference to "peanuts." Unfortunately, the million as a standard economic unit in assessing military costs has already been more or less superseded by the billion. One only hopes that the next expression to take root will not be "a paltry billion."

4. The influence of technology on war has brought various changes in the branches of military service. To mention briefly effects that could be discussed at considerable length, modern technological war has led to: (a) the virtual replacement of the Cavalry by the Armored Force; (b) the dominant position of the Air Force; (c) decreased power of the Navy, associated

---

[109] Jerome C. Hunsaker, *Aeronautics at the Mid-Century* (New Haven, Yale University Press, 1952), p. 106.

[110] *Department of the Army, Appropriations for 1954, Hearings before the Subcommittee of the Committee on Appropriations, House of Representatives, 83rd Congress, First Session* (Washington, Government Printing Office, 1953), pp. 10–11.

[111] Baldwin, *op. cit.*, p. 289.

especially with the rise of air power, for even large aircraft carriers may now be A-bombed. The Navy is still important, though relatively not as much so as formerly.[112] The Air Force, allied with the use of A- and H-bombs, has a new position of military importance comparable to that of the British Navy during the nineteenth century. And (*d*) the supply services (the Quartermaster and Transportation Corps) are increasingly using helicopters for carrying troops and cargo in mountainous and other areas of rough terrain. In such areas helicopters are likely to replace the use of trucks.

5. Technological influence has brought an expansion of the area of fighting. A major war is no longer likely to be a localized one. Tanks, airplanes, and other innovations tend to dictate a war of movement—to extend the area of operations. What formerly would have been a battle of Paris would now likely be a battle of France, with armored divisions racing over a wide area. Actually, an important, modern war is more and more likely to be world-wide in scope, since planes like the B-36 have a range of over 10,000 miles and can attack almost any place in the world. Future use of long-range rockets or high-trajectory guided missiles would emphasize this even more. The ultimate is likely to involve excursions into interplanetary space, with one's side and the enemy rivals in establishing space stations in some location for military observation.

6. A modern, large-scale war is now fought by industrialized nations; mass production of weapons and equipment is important. Little nations or ones without significant steel production cannot fight modern wars. They may, however, ally themselves with "great powers." Industrial strength is more or less of a requirement for the fighting of modern mechanized conflicts.

7. The influence of technology has brought the decline, though not the complete end, of personalized war. While the infantry and certain other forces have personal, hand-to-hand combat with the enemy, the increasing tendency is to wage war at a distance. Artillerymen, firing their shells, do not usually see the enemy. The aviator releasing bombs will often be flying so high as to neither see nor be seen by the enemy. Modern scientific war thus becomes depersonalized. The earlier notion of "withholding fire until one sees the whites of their eyes" is likely to be replaced by the more modern "fire when the radar screen indicates the presence of an enemy plane"—a plane which, probably, one can neither see with one's own eyes nor hear with one's ears.

[112] The Navy's general position is ably stated in Bernard Brodie, *Sea Power in the Machine Age* (Princeton, N. J., Princeton University Press, 1941); also pertinent comments are found in his chapter entitled "New Techniques of War and National Policies" in W. F. Ogburn, ed., *Technology and International Relations* (Chicago, University of Chicago Press, 1949). The role of individual services may need to be reassessed as major innovations are made. We have pointed out that the use of guided missiles coupled with atomic power seems likely to bring about a more major role for the submarine.

8. Fighting wars becomes more and more a matter of using technical, scientific skill, less and less one of muscular strength. Scientific brains are increasingly needed, not the brawn of a Goliath; physical strength is probably more needed in the infantry than in other branches of service, but even here the successful infantryman is likely to be adept in the use of modern gadgets. One may note that elaborate, highly-advanced training is often needed for military tasks. A bomber pilot, says Hunsaker,[113] needs as long a training period as a doctor of philosophy. This longer training is also costly. Former Secretary of the Air Force Harold Talbott states that the United States spends $14,600 on each airman during his initial enlistment; and a B-47 pilot (cross-trained as a bombardier, navigator, and radar operator) represents an Air Force investment of $210,000 for training only.[114]

9. In considering *net effects* one may note, finally, that certain derivative effects of modern technological war may be of great consequence. With all-around high costs, one such derivative effect is to bring the risk of financial bankruptcy to a nation engaged in war or in circumstances where war is threatening.

CONCLUSIONS

It seems to this writer that certain solid conclusions emerge from the data presented in this chapter. These are felt to be sturdy truths that must be considered in making further reckonings with respect to war.

The first and most important single conclusion of the chapter is that war has now become so astoundingly destructive that man must control it if he expects to survive. Early war, with man using tomahawk, bow-and-arrow, or musket, was tragic and bloodthirsty enough. Since man's brute impulses may now be expressed with use of H-bomb, radioactive cloud, germs, chemical agents, and other destructive devices, he is faced with a clear-cut issue: he either controls war or he is likely to perish as a living species.[115] Nuclear scientists have themselves been most concerned over the destructive power of their own creations, and many other thinkers have shared this concern.

Man's situation about mid-1956 was, however, complicated. With the United States and Russia both possessing great nuclear and air potential, this fact itself provided a potent deterrent to further large-scale war. A condition of nuclear stalemate was at hand. While this "deterrence by the threat of nuclear air terror" amounted essentially to an uncordial deadlock which could hardly be comfortable for any length of time, it was conceded that it

---

[113] Hunsaker, *op. cit.*, p. 107.

[114] *Department of Defense, Appropriations for 1955, Hearings before the Subcommittee of the Committee on Appropriations, U.S. Senate, 83rd Congress, on H. R. 8873*, p. 74. Testimony of Mr. Talbott, Secretary of the Air Force.

[115] In the words of the nine noted scientists (led by Bertrand Russell) who drew up a statement during July, 1955, "there is a very real danger of the extermination of the human race by dust and rain from radioactive clouds."—*New York Times*, July 10, 1955.

might provide a rational basis for permanent peace; that is, the latter might grow out of this circumstance. The stalemate of the mid-1950's was precarious for the further reason (as Hanson Baldwin remarked[116]) that the great powers needed to maintain capacity for a devastating nuclear strike, yet also be able to win small wars without permitting them to turn into large ones. This was by no means easy to do.

The plain fact is that war, with man using the implements of modern technology, no longer pays. As Spaak sagely observed,[117] wars have been fought throughout history because people thought that by fighting and winning a war they could solve their problems. This no longer obtains. With a modern nuclear attack followed by "massive retaliation," it is clear that everybody loses.

The second conclusion made here is that the rate of change in war technology is clearly accelerating. The gradual change in weapons has been shown—from clubs and spears to H-bombs. The simpler weapons were used for many centuries; the elite ones are recent products. This accelerated rate of change in war technology, which is similar to that found for general culture, has tremendous import for the future. Man, recently gaping in amazement at radar, rockets, and the A-bomb, can expect even more startling war innovations in the future.[118] Further war applications from advances in physics, chemistry, biology, and other fields will undoubtedly be made. This principle has been well stated by Hart.[119] Thus it would be expected that increasing sentiment would develop in favor of the general control of war if, indeed, further motivation is needed.[120]

The third conclusion to be drawn is one suggested early in this chapter: That technology is the variable having a close—probably the closest—association with the nature of war; for as one changes so does the other. In its influence on the character of warfare, technology "calls the play." Thus in the age of bow-and-arrow technology, the combatants fought a bow-and-arrow type of war whether they were Englishmen at Agincourt or Indians in the Mohawk Valley; whether their leader had the personality of a certain Indian chieftain, an English nobleman, a Patton, or an Eisenhower. In World War I, trench warfare grew out of the use by both sides of the machine gun and of barbed wire. The mobile, high-speed land campaigns of World War II were based on use of the tank and the tactics applying to armored divisions.

[116] Hanson W. Baldwin, "The New Face of War," *Bulletin of the Atomic Scientists,* Vol. XII, No. 5 (May, 1956), p. 157.

[117] Paul-Henri Spaak, "The Atom Bomb and Nato," *Foreign Affairs,* Vol. 33, No. 3 (April, 1955), pp. 353–359.

[118] As Donald Quarles declared, as of August, 1955, the U. S. Armed Forces had some seven thousand to eight thousand different research and development projects at various stages of completion. Scarcely any weapons field "from the rifle on up" was untouched by new developments.—*U. S. News & World Report* (August 12, 1955), p. 59.

[119] See Chapter 3 of this volume.

[120] Ogburn, *loc. cit.*

In a similar way, atomic, chemical, biological, and electronic weapons place their own special stamp on the character of a war. If one is interested in the nature of a *future* war, it follows that one may well keep a watchful eye on the developing technological weapons—and if possible project these trends of development into the future.[121]

The fourth conclusion which is drawn here is that technology is a major factor in *success* in war. Other factors are, to be sure, leadership, number and training of troops, morale, adequate materiel, able intelligence work, home industrial production, and doubtless others. All such factors are important and necessary. Nevertheless weapons, and tactics based on weapons, are of basic importance and may make the difference between winning or losing a war. In 1939–40, to take an example, the German defeat of Poland and France was a clear-cut victory of tanks and planes and of lightning-war tactics over slow-moving, static, nonmechanized tactics.[122] There is no reason to believe that the Poles were less brave or courageous than the Germans. In this chapter, many other examples showing the association of some technological innovation and victory or near-victory have been cited. There was, briefly, the submarine which threatened to give victory to the Germans in both World Wars I and II; the German V-1 and V-2 missiles which threatened to knock out England during the latter part of World War II; the use of the improved tank in 1918 which was the final element that made the Germans crumble; the use of radar by the British in 1940 which was a basic factor in winning the "Battle of Britain"; and lastly the use of the atom bomb by the United States in 1945 which caused Japan to surrender, although the latter was gradually losing the struggle. This by no means exhausts the list of examples of weapons occupying a prominent, if not decisive, role in some war victory.

General Fuller makes the following statement:[123]

Tools, or weapons, if only the right ones can be discovered, form 99 per cent of victory. . . . Strategy, command, leadership, courage, discipline, supply, organization, and all the moral and physical paraphernalia of war are as nothing to a high superiority of weapons—at most they go to form the one per cent which makes the whole possible.

In war, more especially in modern wars, in which weapons change rapidly, one thing is certain, and this is—that no army of fifty years before any date selected would stand a "dog's chance" against the army existing at the date. . . .

121 In concluding that the factor of technology is the variable having a markedly close association with the character of war, it is admitted that no attempt has been made here to compare this technological influence with, say, that of leadership, nationality or race of combatants, or other influences. This chapter, concentrating on the effects of technology, concludes, then, that this factor bears a close relation to the nature of wars as they are fought—not that it is X per cent more important in influence than factor A or factor B (if such could be proved).

122 See Fuller, *Machine Warfare*, pp. 44–51.

123 *Ibid.*, pp. 61–62.

Possibly the above estimate of 99 per cent may seem to be extreme.[124] One should add that the development of new weapons and devising of tactics for the use of the weapons is surely a function of leadership; the production of the weapons is a matter of industrial organization, possession of technical "know-how," and development of the fundamental scientific base. Mass production is especially important in modern warfare. The ability to turn out tanks, planes, guns, ships, in large quantities for the huge armies of a "great power" is essential, as it is also for the replacement of arms and vehicles which have been destroyed in combat; finally, training of the men to use the weapons skillfully is a function of military leadership and organization. Thus to some extent the various factors are interrelated.

It is to be noted that new weapons do not always win wars. Their use may be countered in time, as in the case of the submarine; they may be gradually destroyed, as in the instance of the V-1 and V-2 missiles in 1944–45; adequate protection may be devised, as in the case of chemical gases during World War I; or the other side may also adopt the new innovation, as was true of various airplane devices including the Fokker shooting-between-the-propellor-blades device of 1916–18 which was of great aid to accuracy of fire. Adoption of an innovation by both sides tends to nullify any advantage for either. How much damage is done to one's successful prosecution of a war depends on how soon the innovation of the enemy is countered or neutralized.

The fifth and final conclusion is, in essence, a corollary of the last one: As long as wars continue to be fought it is practically essential for a nation to keep up in arms development with potential enemies. The needed armament expenditures in modern times are likely to be staggering, hence every effort should be made to keep down grandiose and unnecessary expenses and to avoid downright waste.[125] But for a nation to permit potential enemies to forge ahead in weapons development is to invite military disaster. Arms preparedness may not bring real security, as Einstein stated,[126] and an arms race is likely to seem both extremely expensive and foolish—especially when viewed from the long-term, world perspective. It may further be pointed out that it is difficult to achieve peace when nations are constantly preparing for a possible future conflict. Nonetheless, the conclusion is clear that arms preparation is necessary as long as nations live in an atmosphere of hostility or suspicion. The possibility of arms reduction, on the other hand, must be allied with confidence in other nations, their willingness to reduce arms,

[124] Even if the weapons factor constituted 75 per cent of victory it would be, in this writer's judgment, impressive. Fuller's idea, it is argued here, is more important than his specific percentage.

[125] Baldwin, *op. cit.,* pp. 290–291.

[126] Albert Einstein, "Arms Can Bring No Security," *Bulletin of the Atomic Scientists,* Vol. VI, No. 3 (March, 1950), p. 71.
This statement was written following the announcement by former President Truman that the United States would proceed with the development of the hydrogen bomb.

and/or the all-around control of war. To reduce arms without any of the above could well be catastrophic.[127]

SUMMARY

Over the centuries of history, man has wrought remarkable developments of war weapons and technologies. Beginning with simple weapons like stones, spears, slings, and bow-and-arrow, he has produced mechanical devices and "siege engines" such as the catapult, trebuchet, and ballista; gunpowder to use in propelling bullets and cannonballs; specific firearms technologies and industrial methods, for example, that of mass production which aided in weapons production; the trend toward mechanized warfare which began with World War I; and finally fully-matured mechanized war—a phenomenon of World War II and thereafter which emphasized the use of the airplane, tank, submarine, radar, guided missile, atom and hydrogen bomb including the effects of radioactive fall-out (the latter not as yet used in war), other miscellaneous electronic devices, chemical agents, and the possible use of germ agents.

Various "net effects" and conclusions resulting from the influence of technology on war have been drawn from the data of the chapter. These are: (1) that the rate of change in war technology is shown to be accelerating; (2) that the destructive power of war weapons has tremendously increased—so much so that man must control war now if he wants to have adequate expectation of surviving; (3) that advancing technology is a variable having a close association with the *nature* of war, for as one changes, so does the other; (4) that technology is a major factor in *success* in war; (5) that the new military technology is enormously expensive, is a tremendous financial drain on governments; and (6) that a nation nevertheless needs to maintain proper arms, scientific, and technological development so that it does not lag behind that of potential enemies—as long as wars remain uncontrolled. To do otherwise in times of international hostility is the supreme military sin; it invites disaster.

ANNOTATED BIBLIOGRAPHY

BRODIE, Bernard, *Sea Power in the Machine Age* (Princeton, N. J., Princeton University Press, 1941). Thorough review of impact of technology on sea power up to 1940. Excellently done.
Bulletin of the Atomic Scientists, Vol. XII, No. 5 (May, 1956) and No. 6 (June, 1956). These issues contain a series of thought-provoking articles on the theme "Science and Military Strategy." The authors include Sir John

[127] In this connection it is well to recall that one of General George C. Marshall's chief recommendations at the end of World War II was for the United States to have a program of intense scientific research and development for the future. He also emphasized that this nation was almost completely unprepared at the beginning of both World Wars I and II, and reminds his readers of the "nearness of defeat" in 1942.—*General Marshall's Report, op. cit.,* pp. 1, 6, 95.

Slessor (Marshall of the Royal Air Force), Hanson W. Baldwin, C. W. Sherwin, Richard Meier, Warren Amster, and others.

BUSH, Vannevar, *Modern Arms and Free Men* (New York, Simon and Schuster, 1949). Valuable discussion of war innovations developed during World War II by the (then) Director of Office of Scientific Research and Development. Discussion of the submarine, radar, proximity fuse, guided missile, A-bomb, and chemical warfare is especially recommended.

FULLER, John F. C., *Machine Warfare, An Inquiry into the Influence of Mechanics on the Art of War* (Washington, The Infantry Journal, 1943); *Armored Warfare* (Harrisburg, Pa., The Military Service Publishing Company, 1943). Forward-facing volumes by a British general who was alert to the changing conditions of war. Author was an exponent of armored, mechanized war. Ably written.

GRAY, George W., *Science at War* (New York, Harper, 1943). Rewarding discussion of the effect of various fields of science on war—up to the nuclear age. Nontechnical.

HART, Hornell, "Social Science and the Atomic Crisis," *Journal of Social Issues,* Supplement Series, No. 2 (April, 1949). This bulletin (which won the E. L. Bernays Atomic Energy Award for 1948) analyzes the current war crisis and presents a full-scale program designed to meet it. The author sees the crisis as basically due to a lag of social science behind the powers of destruction.

MILLIS, Walter, *Arms and Men* (New York, Putnam, 1956). Chapters 5, "The Scientific Revolution," and 7, "The Future of War," are especially recommended. The author (like Mr. Spaak) questions man's further use of the institution of war, modern weapons being as destructive as they are.

OGBURN, William F., ed., *Technology and International Relations* (Chicago, University of Chicago Press, 1949). Expert discussion of many influences of technology (as steam and steel, airplane, A-bomb, and the mass-communications inventions) upon international relations. Authors include the editor, H. Hart, R. Leigh, A. P. Usher, W. T. R. Fox, B. Brodie, and Q. Wright.

PARSON, Nels A., Jr., *Guided Missiles in War and Peace* (Cambridge, Harvard University Press, 1956). The clearest, most comprehensive summary-statement on guided missiles that this writer has seen (as of Nov., 1956). The author, a U. S. Army major, is Chief of Review and Analysis Branch, Headquarters, Continental Army Command, Fort Monroe, Virginia.

SPAULDING, Oliver L., NICKERSON, Hoffman, and WRIGHT, John W., *Warfare, A Study of Military Methods from the Earliest Times* (Washington, The Infantry Journal, 1937). Thorough account of early wars which describes, but does not emphasize, the influence of technology. Discussion ends with year 1800.

WRIGHT, Quincy, *A Study of War* (Chicago, University of Chicago Press, 1942), 2 vols. The best single, all-around work on the subject of war. Discussion extends up to World War II. Recognizes importance of technological influence.

CHAPTER 16

TECHNOLOGY AND THE PRACTICE OF MEDICINE

■ *Francis R. Allen*

IN CONSIDERING the influence of advancing technology on the practice of medicine, it is well to bear in mind an observation made by the dean of medical historians, Henry E. Sigerist.[1] Dr. Sigerist commented that the evolving practice of medicine is intertwined with two other phenomena: the changing picture of disease, and the general evolution of all social thought and ideas. These latter phenomena will be noted as much as possible in the present chapter, although the treatment must necessarily be brief. Technological advances are, at any rate, likely to bear relationship to the diseases which are prevalent at the time, as they are also to the ongoing stream of social thought, particularly to developments within the basic sciences. On the latter the specific techniques of medical practice will largely rest.[2] Therefore, the development of medicine and medical technology can profitably be viewed in relation to evolving human societies, their changing social ideas, their conceptions of disease, and their struggles against disease. Such might be called a sociological view of the practice of medicine.

In appraising the technological influence on the practice of medicine over the centuries, we may further remind ourselves of the definition of *technology* stated in Chapter 1. We ordinarily relate technology to the state of the industrial arts which may or may not permit the making of some artifact or instrument; in doing this we tend to associate technology with material culture. We may speak of a rudimentary or handicraft state of technological development, and contrast it with a highly advanced state which may use nuclear power and electronic devices. During modern times it is noted that the methods and findings of science tend to underlie the artifacts and other

---

[1] Henry E: Sigerist, *A History of Medicine* (New York, Oxford University Press, 1951), Vol. I, Ch. 1; also see Sigerist, "The History of Medical History," Ch. 5 in New York Academy of Medicine, *Milestones in Medicine* (New York, Appleton-Century-Crofts, 1938), pp. 171–181.

[2] It may be observed that the same developments in physics, chemistry, biology, and other basic sciences may constitute root ideas which may be applied for medical, military, or other purposes.

productions of technology, as a vaccine, x-ray apparatus, or electrocardiograph machine. It is useful and of consequence in connection with the subject of medicine to add, however, that the term *technology* also includes principles, methods, techniques, customs, and skills related to the artifact or instrument.[3] The vitamin capsule as a technological product can hardly be divorced from scientific knowledge of vitamins as well as the "know-how" to synthesize the product; nor can it be separated from the concept of vitamins as an element in nutrition. Stern has commented that sometimes medical instruments are constructed for which there is little use until valid concepts relating to the subject have been formulated.[4]

We may even carry the meaning of the term one step further. Since technology is linked with applied science, it is felt to be entirely proper to use the term in connection with nonmaterial elements as well. In discussing medicine this is significant because nonmaterial items, such as a principle of nutrition or of mental illness (for example, Freud's doctrine of the unconscious mind and its relation to mental illness), will hence be included. As noted in Chapter 1, a broad use of the term *technology* is assumed. With this preliminary word we turn to the influence of technology upon the practice of medicine as both have evolved over the centuries.

BASIC ADVANCES IN MEDICAL TECHNOLOGY

Until 1800

Here the discussion centers on the nature of medical practice in primitive societies and during early times (defined as up to the year 1800); brevity will be emphasized. This period may be compared with the bow-and-arrow stage of war weapons, noted in the previous chapter.

First of all, it is worth while to observe that no matter how old or how rudimentary in living standards a civilization may be, there has always been the need of medical skill and service. As Sigerist reasons,[5] early man had diseases and injuries; he was occasionally involved in accidents like his modern counterpart. Early skeletal remains show evidences of disease.

In primitive societies, medical care involved a combination of empirico-rational ideas and practices (including use of some effective herbs, roots,

[3] See John P. Gillin, *The Ways of Men* (New York, Appleton-Century-Crofts, 1948), Ch. 17.

[4] The microscope is an example of this. While the microscope is today regarded as a most valuable, indeed indispensable, medical instrument, it was neglected (though it had been invented) throughout the eighteenth century; it was not until the germ theory of disease had been established and there was need to identify microorganisms that the great value of the microscope was realized. Similarly the whole development of vaccines depended on the principle of the germ causation and the notion of stimulating antibodies.—Bernhard J. Stern, *American Medical Practice in the Perspectives of a Century* (New York, Commonwealth Fund, 1945), p. 41.

[5] *A History of Medicine,* Vol. I, pp. 38–44.

and drugs[6]) and of ideas and practices related to magic and religion; the latter usually dominated the treatment. Generally, primitive man has been and is highly suggestible. The medical practitioner—medicine man or shaman—ordinarily explained disease in terms of the magical beliefs, that is, action of the deities, spirits, demons, taboos, and "evil powers." The shaman, frequently a master of legerdemain, was likely to be inventive in explaining why the sick person was stricken. In prescribing treatment he resorted to magic once more. The family of the sick individual must placate the gods, "chase away the disease" (often done symbolically with sticks), and implore the spirits at ceremonials to remove the evil element. If the patient should die, then his or her soul departs. As long as body and soul are together, the person is regarded as in sound health (a forerunner of psychosomatic medicine?). If the soul starts to depart, perhaps the family or tribe can influence the gods to intercede and bring the return of the soul. Death may mean, however, that the gods refused to intercede; perhaps a strong taboo had been broken or a totem animal killed. Incidentally, when herbs or drugs are prescribed by the shaman, this is unlikely to be any simple act (the equivalent of purchasing some product in a modern drug store); the shaman will feelingly conduct religious rites, imploring the gods and the spirits to restore an individual's health.[7]

In early societies (nonprimitive) up to the year 1800, it is clear that the general level of medical practice was low in the sense that little was known about medicines and medical treatment. Nevertheless, some noteworthy accomplishments were made, some of them well before the time of Christ. Since they have been frequently discussed in the medical literature, they will be treated briefly here.

1. The discovery of *opium* as a pain-killer was made during early Egyptian times—around 1550 B.C. The exact discoverer is unknown.[8] The Mesopotamians knew of the drug, as did the early Arabians, and the latter are believed to have brought it to India and China.

2. Use of the medical compound *mercury* for leprosy and other skin diseases was made by the early Arabs. Syphilis was at the time not distinguished from leprosy, hence it was used for the former too.[9]

3. Another early medical preparation was *Cinchona bark* from a tree found in Peru (hence "Peruvian bark"), used in the treatment for fevers. This was brought to Europe following the discovery of America, and quinine was

[6] Sigerist writes: "Most astonishing is the sometimes very considerable knowledge of drugs that primitives possess. . . . We should remember that we owe many effective drugs to primitive and folk medicine, such as opium, cocoa, cinchona, ephedrine, caffeine, cascara sagrada, chaulmoogra, digitalis, ipecacuanha, podophyllum, pyrethrum, and squill, to mention only a few."—*Ibid.*, pp. 203–204.

[7] *Ibid.*, Ch. 2.

[8] David Riesman, *Medicine in Modern Society* (Princeton, N. J., Princeton University Press, 1939), pp. 18–19; Sigerist, *History of Medicine*, Vol. I, p. 341.

[9] Riesman, *op. cit.*, p. 20.

isolated from the crude bark in 1820.[10] Although this is a specific only for malaria fever, the value of the drug was recognized long before malaria was distinguished from other fevers.

4. An outstanding achievement occurring in 1628 was the first demonstration of the *circulation of the blood* by the English physician William Harvey. Based on simple but convincing experiments showing the role of the heart in pumping blood, this discovery is often regarded as a starting point of modern medicine, certainly of physiology.[11]

5. *Digitalis* or *Foxglove,* reportedly first used by William Withering, an English physician, in 1775, is a valuable remedy for certain forms of heart disease. It improves the strength and tone of the heart muscle.[12]

6. The *principle of vaccination* was introduced during the 1700's. In 1749 Edward Jenner was impressed with the statement of a milkmaid that she would not develop smallpox since she had had cowpox. Recognizing the significance of this general belief of dairy people, he sought to test out the vaccination thesis. On May 14, 1796—a milestone date—he inoculated a boy with material from the arm of a milkmaid who had had cowpox. Then on July 1 of that year he inoculated the boy with smallpox virus; the boy had developed immunity. In several pamphlets he described his method of vaccination, and within a few years the procedure had spread throughout the world.[13]

7. The invention of the *microscope* was made about the year 1600, although the value of lenses as an aid to eyesight had long been known; the eyeglasses (spectacles) business may be traced back to the time of Euclid (300 B.C.). The science of optics made considerable progress around the sixteenth century, and Antonius von Leeuwenhoek in 1674 ground single lenses with which micro-organisms could be seen. Zacharias Janssen, another Dutch spectacles-maker, had previously (1590) combined convex lenses in a tube to form an instrument for magnifying minute objects; hence the microscope. Galileo, hearing about the Dutch achievements, invented a microscope of his own.[14] Unfortunately, the microscope was not used much for many years, and Leeuwenhoek's methods were generally ignored. With the

[10] *Loc. cit;* Richard H. Shryock, *The Development of Modern Medicine* (New York, Knopf, 1947), p. 162.

[11] Bernhard J. Stern, *Society and Medical Progress* (Princeton, N. J., Princeton University Press, 1941), pp. 50–51; Michael Foster, "Vesalius and Harvey: The Founding of Modern Anatomy and Physiology," in Samuel Rapport and Helen Wright, ed., *Great Adventures in Medicine* (New York, Dial Press, 1952), p. 124.

[12] Withering used it successfully in his practice, and in 1785 published his *Account of the Foxglove*—regarded as a medical classic.—Riesman, *op. cit.,* p. 23.

[13] *Ibid.,* pp. 24–25; W. H. Woglom, *Discoverers for Medicine* (New Haven, Yale University Press, 1949), Ch. 5. Controversies over smallpox vaccination did rage later, as during the early part of the twentieth century in the United States. See B. J. Stern, *Should We Be Vaccinated? A Study of the Controversy in Its Historical and Scientific Aspects* (New York, Harper, 1927).

[14] Stern, *Society and Medical Progress,* pp. 53–55; Shryock, *op. cit.,* p. 23.

bacteriological triumphs of the 1870's (which will be noted shortly), the microscope really was fully utilized.

8. Another clinical aid was the *thermometer,* which permitted the precise diagnosis of fever. Galilei had taken human temperatures during the early seventeenth century, and in 1659 Bouillian made a thermometer of mercury in a glass tube. Gabriel D. Fahrenheit (1686–1736), originally of Danzig, was responsible for the more general use of mercury thermometers. The centigrade scale of measurement which was eventually used in most scientific work was developed about 1742 by Celsius and Stromer.[15] However, after its invention the thermometer had a fate similar to that of the microscope. It was not extensively used until after the middle of the nineteenth century. It was only in 1867 that thermometers were first generally used in English hospitals, while it was reported that during the Civil War, only about a half-dozen thermometers were used in the largest Union Army hospitals.[16] As the years passed the size of thermometers was reduced, the reading was made more exact, and the instruments have become standardized for accuracy.

Advances During the Nineteenth Century

Medical technology continued its state of leisurely advance during the first part of the nineteenth century, while the field of medicine was emerging (as Shryock tells us[17]) from a period of confusion into the relatively clear atmosphere of modern science. Laennec invented the *stethoscope* in 1810. This instrument, however, met with the same reception as did the microscope and thermometer: it was promptly ignored. As another indication of cultural lag one records the fact that use of the stethoscope was first mentioned in the Catalogue of the Harvard Medical School in 1868–69.[18] Presumably it was not used significantly in a Harvard medical education until that time.

At about the period 1835–40 we figuratively "stop the clock" momentarily in order to assess the condition of medical practice and medical technology as of that time. This period is chosen because impressive strides in medicine were to occur *after* this time. The average American physician, who was in 1835–40 practicing in a primarily rural nation, visited his patients on horseback or in a gig or buggy; he prescribed the few available drugs largely on the basis of speculation and unproven theories;[19] and he did much to mitigate pain and undoubtedly helped both the patient and his family. It appears accurate to say that at that time he had neither the tools nor the proven knowledge to diagnose[20] and cure most medical problems. The medical doc-

[15] Shryock, *op. cit.,* p. 123; Riesman, *op. cit.,* p. 69.
[16] Stern, *Society and Medical Progress,* pp. 73–74.
[17] Shryock, *op. cit.,* Ch. 9.
[18] Stern, *Society and Medical Progress,* p. 190.
[19] This is not stated by way of criticism but as an estimate of the available historical facts. A similar appraisal would be made of social science, for example, during its early period of development.
[20] As we have seen certain diagnostic tools were available (that is, they had been invented), but were not generally used.

trines of the time tended to center on a few simple "clinical pictures" like "dropsy," "inflammation of the lungs," and "fevers."[21] Approved treatment frequently involved bloodletting, sweating, or use of cathartics or diuretics with the objective of ridding the body of its "ill humors." Finally, many medical cults flourished, and their practitioners vied with each other and with "regular" physicians.[22]

After this time the medical picture changed abruptly. Some basic and extremely valuable developments in medical technology occurred: (1) the invention of anesthesia, a boon to surgery; (2) the development of antisepsis, also of vital consequence to surgery; (3) the establishment of the germ theory of disease; (4) the development and use of antitoxins; and 5) establishment of the transmission of certain diseases by insects.

Anesthesia, a great blessing to humanity and a technical aid to surgeons, since they could thence proceed more deliberately during operations, was first used during the 1840's. Dr. Crawford W. Long of Georgia used ether in 1842 in order to abolish pain during a surgical operation, but did not pursue his discovery nor did he publicize it.[23] Dr. W. T. Morton of Hartford, Connecticut, suggested the use of ether as an anesthetic after he had watched Dr. Horace Wells, a dentist, extract teeth after administering nitrous oxide. Dr. J. C. Warren of the Massachusetts General Hospital, Boston, acted on Dr. Morton's suggestion, performing a history-making operation on October 16, 1846, after administering ether. This event served to introduce the use of ether into surgical practice in both America and Europe.[24] In 1847 Sir James Simpson of Edinburgh, Scotland, used chloroform as an anesthetic. Many improvements in administering anesthesia have been made in recent years.[25]

Antisepsis, along with anesthesia, has brought enormous progress and many outstanding triumphs in surgery. Before the late 1840's operations had led to rather high mortality because of blood poisoning (septicemia), erysipelas, tetanus, and hospital gangrene. Semmelweis in Vienna and Joseph Lister in England (both surgeons) were concerned with the mortality that had followed operations and urged scrupulous cleanliness in the operating room; Lister had been acquainted with Pasteur's early researches concerning the

---

[21] Stern, *American Medical Practice in the Perspectives of a Century,* pp. 22–26.

[22] There were, for example, the Irregulars, Broussaisians, Sangradoarians, Morrisonians, Beechitarians, Botanics, Thomsonians, Reformed Thomsonians, Diplomatical Homeopathians, Rootists, Herbists, and others.—*Ibid.*

[23] Shryock declares that Long was fearful of public censure for using a "dangerous procedure."—Shryock, *op. cit.,* p. 175.

[24] *Ibid.,* p. 176.

[25] Variations have been adopted as giving the patient a sedative in advance before general anesthesia (which takes away last-minute tension and may even lessen the amount of anesthetic required), and administering nitrous oxide gas first which will be followed by ether. Local anesthesia and spinal anesthesia are also available for use.—Riesman, *op. cit.,* pp. 26–28.

role of bacteria in fermentation. Eventually the emphasis of these surgeons made a deep impression on the whole Western world. The antiseptic methods of Lister have in recent decades undergone change, and now surgeons emphasize *asepsis,* that is, keeping germs entirely away from the operative field rather than trying to destroy germs that are present.[26] Operations, it could now be said, were relatively safe as well as relatively painless.

The germ theory of disease, which was established during the latter half of the nineteenth century, was a tremendous medical achievement—another of the great medical discoveries of all time. Initial work in establishing the doctrine of germ causation of communicable diseases was performed by Pasteur, Koch, and Klebs in their researches concerning anthrax. But it was quickly perceived that this advance provided a method of attack against many other diseases as well. The concept of specificity was now established (i.e., a disease may be caused by a specific bacterial agent), methods of finding the cause were defined, microscopes were available for use, and detailed techniques (staining, freezing, etc.) had been devised. Koch and his coworkers were particularly skillful in developing staining and other techniques.[27] At any rate, bacteriology moved to the center of the medical stage. One micro-organism after another was identified as the specific cause of various diseases.[28] Knowledge of causation was the first solid step in the conquest of disease; control was to follow.[29] While these bacteriological triumphs of the 1870's, 1880's, and 1890's have been cited many times before, it must still be realized that they constituted epochal milestones in the history of medicine. A tremendous achievement it was to have identified for the first time the cause of such killers as tuberculosis, cholera, bubonic

[26] Hence the use of sterilizers, gowns, caps, masks, rubber gloves, and the meticulous scrubbing of hands and arms by surgeons and nurses before operations. See Shryock, *op. cit.,* pp. 280–281; Riesman, *op. cit.,* pp. 29–30.

[27] It is frequently stated that Pasteur was the bacteriological pioneer, while Koch excelled as the perfecter of technique. See Louis I. Dublin, Alfrd J. Lotka, and Mortimer Spiegelman, *Length of Life,* rev. ed. (New York, Ronald Press, 1949), p. 148; Shryock, *op. cit.,* p. 282; Riesman, *op. cit.,* pp. 32–33; Stern, *American Medical Practice in the Perspectives of a Century,* pp. 32–35; and Rapport and Wright, eds., *op. cit.,* pp. 262–292.

[28] The main list is as follows: The bacillus of relapsing fever was identified by Obermeier in 1873; the gonococcus by Neisser (1879); the typhoid bacillus by Eberth and Gaffky (1880); the leprosy bacillus by Hansen (1880); diplococcus of pneumonia by Sternberg, also Pasteur (1880); the protozoon of malaria by Laveran (1880); the tubercle bacillus by Koch (1882); the erysipelas bacillus by Fehleisen (1883); the cholera bacillus by Koch (1883); the diphtheria bacillus by Klebs and Loeffler (1883), the tetanus bacillus by Nicolaier (1884); the meningococcus by Leichtenstern (1885); the bubonic plague bacillus by Kotasato and Yersin (1894); and the spirochaeta pallida (syphilis) by Schaudinn and Hoffman (1905). See Stern, *American Medical Practice* . . . , p. 34; Shryock, *op. cit.,* p. 286.

[29] Pasteur was the first to visualize a world in which man would be master of the epidemic diseases through knowledge of their causes. The development of vaccines, etc., also of "pasteurizing" milk, came later.—Dublin, Lotka, and Spiegelman, *op. cit.,* p. 148.

plague, diphtheria! Mankind could indeed be thankful that these scourges were gradually tamed!

Another medical landmark was the discovery of the *transmission of various diseases by insects,* a development of the latter part of the nineteenth century. That flies carry diseases, especially typhoid fever and dysentery, was officially confirmed by new bacteriological insights and techniques. In 1893 Theobold Smith demonstrated that the cattle disease *Texas fever* was caused by a protozoan conveyed from sick to healthy cattle by the bite of a tick. This in turn led to the demonstration by Manson and Ross and Grassi that malaria was transmitted by the anopheles mosquito. Then, at the turn of the century Walter Reed and his associates established that yellow fever, another scourge of the nineteenth century, was spread by a different species of mosquito (the stegomyia). Finally, Rocky Mountain spotted fever and typhus fever were shown to be conveyed by the bite of a tick and a louse respectively.[30]

Another significant medical landmark of the late nineteenth century was the *discovery of the x-ray* by Roentgen in 1895.[31] This provided a powerful diagnostic instrument of precision, bringing the internal, hidden parts of the body to scrutiny. It provides invaluable information regarding the lungs, gastro-intestinal tract, gall bladder, kidneys, the teeth. It can reveal the presence of tumors and other abnormalities in the skull. It is unsurpassed as a means of discovering fractures of bones. Finally, x-ray is effective in treating certain diseases (as some cancers). In many cases it will destroy healthy as well as diseased tissue, but it cures some cancers without damage to the surrounding areas.

Other instruments of precise measurement that were developed during the nineteenth century may be briefly mentioned. The *blood-pressure apparatus* for use on man was invented by S. S. K. Von Basch in 1887. The *electrocardiograph,* another basic and valued instrument, makes photographic records of the electric currents flowing in the heart. It is of major benefit in understanding normal heart action as well as irregularity of the heart beat. Sanderson and Page of Oxford, England, demonstrated in 1878 that an electric current is generated when the heart muscle contracts. To record the currents was a considerable problem, but Einthoven of Leyden solved it in 1902; he used a galvanometer in devising the electrocardiagraph.[32] The *basal metabolism* instrument, which measures a person's use of food and oxygen, was perfected and used in clinical medicine during the closing years of the nineteenth century. It is of special value in detecting disturbances of the thyroid gland.

Other instruments of considerable value include the ophthalmoscope and otoscope for examination of the eye and ear respectively (invented during the 1850's); the laryngoscope (1855); the stomach tube (1867); the cysto-

---

[30] Shryock, *op. cit.,* pp. 287–290; Riesman, *op. cit.,* pp. 35–36.
[31] Riesman, *op. cit.,* pp. 70–71; W. H. Woglom, *op. cit.,* Ch. 12.
[32] Riesman, *op. cit.,* pp. 71–72.

DR. JONAS E. SALK
University of Pittsburgh medical scientist whose
polio vaccine was declared in April, 1955, to be
highly effective.

scope for examining interior of bladder (1879); the bronchoscope (1898); the
respiration calorimeter (1905); also the gastroscope for examination of stomach; the dermatherm, which measures skin temperature; the photometer,
which measures night blindness; the audiometer, which measures hearing;
the hemacytometer, which counts blood corpuscles, and others.[33] Finally, a
valuable medical tool may be mentioned, namely, the *hypodermic syringe*.
This was first used in the administration of drugs in 1845 by Francis Rynd
of Dublin. It is now used for many purposes, as in withdrawing blood for a
Wassermann test (syphilis), in making blood transfusions, in withdrawing
spinal fluid, and for administering vaccines and antitoxins.

Advances During the Twentieth Century

The development of immunology grew out of the identification of germs
or viruses as specific causes of different diseases, in short, to the fundamentals established by Pasteur, Koch, and other workers. Many vaccines, containing weakened or dead bacteria, are currently available as protective
agents against various diseases.[34] As is well known, the vaccine stimulates
the activity of antibodies that provide protection against the disease.

[33] Stern, *American Medical Practice* . . . , p. 42; S. McKee Rosen and Laura Rosen,
Technology and Society (New York, Macmillan, 1941), Ch. 6.

[34] The list includes typhoid fever, smallpox, tetanus, typhus fever, yellow fever,
diphtheria, whooping cough, rabies, and cholera. "BCG" tuberculosis vaccine has been
administered to millions of persons, mostly in Europe and Asia.

The latest disease for which protection is provided is poliomyelitis. Announcement was made on April 12, 1955, that the anti-polio vaccine developed by Dr. Jonas E. Salk of the University of Pittsburgh School of Medicine is "safe, effective, and potent."[35] This vaccine protects the individual against crippling effect of the three types of virus known to cause polio—the Brunhilde, Lansing, and Leon strains. It provides immunity by stimulating production in the bloodstream of three types of antibodies, each specific for one of the three strains mentioned above.[36]

While the prediction was made that by 1959 the Salk vaccine will have conquered paralytic polio[37] just as other vaccines have tamed smallpox, typhoid, yellow fever, and other diseases mentioned in footnote 34, there is further promise in the Salk achievement. It may pave the way for similar efforts concerning other diseases, even that "ever-present and menacing urchin among diseases, the common cold." Indeed, by the end of 1955 U. S. Public Health Service scientists had already developed a vaccination against certain kinds of colds.[38]

Advances in nutrition. Many outstanding accomplishments have been made in the study of diet and nutrition during the twentieth century, nutrition here being viewed as "the science concerned with the relation of foods to health and disease."[39] Although there are still gaps in our knowledge, a tremendous amount is now known about nutrition. Some of this goes back as far as the eighteenth century, when scurvy was empirically found to be a nutritional deficiency disease, but the larger proportion of nutritional knowledge has been amassed during the present century, especially that pertaining to the minerals, vitamins, most deficiency diseases, relation of

[35] *New York Times,* April 13, 1955.

[36] In honoring this accomplishment on the part of Dr. Salk it is proper to add the names of others who aided in the process of developing this vaccine; indeed, Dr. Salk has himself suggested that this aid be recognized. Prior developments necessary for the final success included: the discovery in 1949 by Dr. John F. Enders and associates at the Harvard Medical School that polio virus could be grown in test tube culture on monkey tissues of nonnervous origin (which was regarded as the first major breakthrough on the poliomyelitis front); the discovery in 1952 by Dr. William M. Hammon of the University of Pittsburgh that relatively small amounts of antibodies in the human blood stream could protect against paralytic polio; and the discovery made independently by Drs. David Bodian and Dorothy M. Horstmann that polio virus circulates in blood only briefly before symptoms of disease appear. *Ibid.*

[37] This prediction—that "paralytic polio will be completely eliminated as a threat to children and adults" by 1959—was made by Dr. Salk and by Dr. Leonard A. Scheele, at the time Surgeon General of the U. S. Public Health Service, before the membership of the American Medical Association in June, 1956. See *New York Times,* June 12, 1956, article by William L. Laurence.

[38] "Interview with Dr. Joseph A. Bell—'New Vaccine Helps Prevent Colds,' " *U. S. News & World Report* (November 25, 1955). Dr. Bell is chief of the epidemiology section of the National Microbiological Institute, a division of the U. S. Public Health Service.

[39] Frederick J. Stare and others, "Nutrition," Ch. 6 in Morris Fishbein, ed., *Medical Progress: 1953* (New York, Blakiston, 1953), p. 85.

diet to body weight, relation of diet to condition of teeth, food allergies, and so on. Only an abbreviated summary can be presented here.[40]

The term *vitamin* was introduced about 1911 by Casimir Funk to describe active food elements essential for normal body metabolism.[41] The various vitamins and their functions—so well known that they will not be listed here —were isolated during the years following, beginning with vitamin A.[42] One of the most recent vitamins to be added to the list is B_{12}, isolated in 1948. It is a specific for pernicious anemia, a disease in which the red blood cells do not mature normally. This vitamin is found in liver extract.[43] Most if not all the vitamins are now made synthetically.

While the field of nutrition has many current research interests, the following subjects appear to be among those emphasized:[44] the effects of infections and trauma on protein utilization; various aspects of food intake in relation to obesity (the latter a condition associated with various degenerative diseases); and the dietary factor in cardiovascular disease, especially the relations (if any) between diet and atherosclerosis. The latter subject has proven to be a knotty though important one.[45]

Chemotherapy. Another area of major medical advances during the twentieth century has been that of chemotherapy[46] and the antibiotics. The era of chemotherapy was ushered in with Paul Ehrlich's preparation of salvarsan in 1910 as a remedy against syphilis. Since salvarsan contains a large proportion of arsenic, the use of which involved certain technical difficulties, Ehrlich pressed on for a more satisfactory solution. In his 914th chemical preparation (salvarsan had been his 606th) he felt he had the perfect agent with which to kill the spirochete; he called this neosalvarsan.

While hopes of cures by use of chemical agents ran high after Ehrlich's discovery, the world had to wait almost twenty-five years for the next major advance in chemotherapy.[47] Suddenly the age of the sulfonamide drugs

[40] For more extensive treatment, see Margaret S. Chaney and Margaret Ahlborn, *Nutrition,* 5th ed. (Boston, Houghton Mifflin, 1954); L. Jean Bogert, *Nutrition and Physical Fitness,* 6th ed. (Philadelphia, Saunders, 1954); Clara Taylor and Florence MacLeod, *Rose's Foundations of Nutrition,* 5th ed. (New York, Macmillan, 1956).

[41] Shryock, *op. cit.,* p. 312.

[42] Stern says: "The vitamin hypothesis was established between 1912 and 1915. By 1926, the distribution of vitamins A, B_1, B_2, C, D, and E was known, the effect of their absence in the diet could be demonstrated, and theurapeutic treatment of consequent disease states was established."—*American Medical Practice* . . . , p. 39.

[43] Donald G. Cooley, *The Science Book of Wonder Drugs* (New York, Pocket Books, 1954), Ch. 8, "Vitamins, Miracle Drugs in Foods," esp. pp. 200–203.

[44] F. J. Stare and others, *op. cit.*

[45] See Steven M. Spencer, *Wonders of Modern Medicine* (New York, McGraw-Hill, 1953), Ch. 3.

[46] "Chemotherapy" is assumed to mean the administration of a chemically-prepared substance (as distinguished from a biological antibody or serum) which is designed to attack specifically the invading organism or virus, with a minimum of toxic action upon the patient.—Dublin, Lotka, and Spiegelman, *op. cit.,* p. 151.

[47] Perrin H. Long, "Infectious Diseases," Ch. 3 in Morris Fishbein, *op. cit.,* esp. pp. 37–38.

dawned. The curtain raiser was the announcement of the discovery of sulfanilamide in November, 1936.[48] Although enormously successful against many infections,[49] this "wonder drug" was soon followed by other sulfas that were regarded by physicians as even more effective: sulfapyridine, sulfathiazole, sulfadiazine, sulfaguanidine, sulfamethazine, and others. The latter brought greater potency under various circumstances and less toxicity. In considering the sulfa drugs it is interesting to note, as does Shryock,[50] that they were used in medical practice almost immediately; there was no time lag, as happened in the case of other procedures and instruments.[51]

The field of medicine and the lay public had hardly become used to the sulfa group when a new amazing drug was announced: penicillin. This drug inaugurated the era of the antibiotics; it involves the principle of setting one type of organism against another. A signal event occurred in 1928 when Dr. Alexander Fleming of London was performing some research with antibiotics. One of his cultures became contaminated with penicillium mold, and he observed empirically that it was highly effective in combating certain pathogenic bacteria. But here events bogged down. Team research was necessary in order to be able to produce the drug synthetically and in quantity; drug companies co-operated in the project. Finally the end result was achieved in 1946.[52] Penicillin is used against the same kind of infections generally as are the sulfa drugs. However, the former is regarded as more effective and less toxic than the sulfas. Penicillin has little effect, on the other hand, against the tubercle bacillus, nor does it appear to have much value against viruses.[53]

Other antibiotics are available in addition to penicillin. Dr. Selman Waksman isolated the substance now called *streptomycin* from a soil mold. This drug is happily effective against the tubercle bacillus, and mortality from that disease is being lowered with its use.[54] There is also *bacitracin, polymyxin,* and the "general purpose" antibiotics, *chloramphenicol (chloromycin)* and

[48] D. G. Cooley, *op. cit.,* p. 30.

[49] As pneumonia, scarlet fever, childbed fever, ear infections, septic sore throat, the venereal diseases, and others.

[50] Shryock, *op. cit.,* pp. 448–452.

[51] One important reason for the absence of lag was that the discovery was made in a world in which the mass media of communication were actively functioning, hence knowledge of the sulfa drugs was rapidly diffused. There is likely to be, as Shryock maintains, stronger interest in developments relating to *cures* rather than to preventive measures (concerning which the public is often indifferent).

[52] Shryock, *op. cit.,* pp. 452–453.

[53] *Loc. cit.*

[54] The crude death rate for tuberculosis (all forms) in the United States amounted to 45.9 per 100,000 population in 1940. It had been reduced to 22.5 in 1950; 15.8 in 1952; and 10.2 in 1954. The latter are the latest figures available at this time of writing. See "Deaths and Death Rates for 64 Selected Causes: United States, Each Division and State, 1954," *Vital Statistics—Special Reports,* National Summaries, Vol. 44, No. 12 (September 14, 1956), National Office of Vital Statistics (Washington, Department of Health, Education, and Welfare), p. 270.

the *tetraclycine* group (aureomycin, terramycin, achromycin, etc.), which are effective in varying degrees against virtually all bacterial diseases and also those produced by the Rickettsial group of micro-organisms and by certain viruses.[55] Dr. Long comments as follows:

Striking changes in mortality rates of infections have occurred even in the fifteen years following the introduction of the sulfonamides and antibiotics. The mortality rate from hemolytic streptococcal infections has had a tenfold decrease, that from staphylococcal infections, lobar pneumonia, and appendicitis a fivefold decrease, and that from peritonitis a threefold decrease. Gonorrhea can be cured in a matter of hours, and syphilis in a few days. Many of the forms of bacterial meningitis are curable promptly, and in epidemic meningitis the case fatality rate has been lowered in large series of patients to four per hundred patients. Debilitating and prolonged infectious processes such as undulant fever are now controlled quickly, while epidemic typhus, which in the recent past had killed by the hundreds of thousands or even millions, is cured rapidly by any one of the general purpose antibiotics.[56]

The net results of the antibiotics in saving human lives are, needless to say, tremendous.

Hormone therapy. Another conspicuous area of medical advance during the present century is that involving hormones. These hormones, which are chiefly secretions of the endocrine glands, may bring difficulties either because of over- or under-secretion. Glandular extracts may be used to make up for deficiencies from which some persons suffer. Thyroxin, for example, is the hormone produced by the thyroid gland, adrenalin by the adrenal gland, and insulin by the pancreas. These secretions are essential to normal life. Glandular preparations have been dispensed as needed for some decades;[57] many diabetics are able to live normal lives with regular injections of insulin.

The subject of hormones was made dramatically prominent in 1949 by the announcement of the accomplishments of the "wonder hormones" cortisone and ACTH. Cortisone (produced by the adrenal cortex) appeared to be remarkable for at least two reasons: the suddenness of its cures and, secondly, the wide variety of diseases that yielded to it. It brought successful and immediate results when used for rheumatoid arthritis, bursitis, severe systemic infections, asthma, hay fever, and certain skin diseases; nor did that exhaust the list. It removed the symptoms of rheumatoid arthritis like magic. As the news concerning cortisone traveled swiftly and more and more

[55] Perrin H. Long, *loc. cit.*

[56] *Ibid.*

[57] Stern summarizes as follows: "Adrenalin, the hormone of the adrenal medulla, was demonstrated in 1894, isolated in 1901, and prepared synthetically in 1906. . . . The active principle of the thyroid was prepared in the form of crystalline thyroxin in 1915 by Kendall, . . . The treatment of endocrine disorders made greatest progress with the discovery of insulin in 1922 by Banting and Best, and its isolation was achieved in 1924. The male sex hormone was isolated in 1931 and prepared synthetically in 1934; and the hormone of the corpus luteum was isolated in 1934. . . ."—*American Medical Practice* . . . , p. 40.

physicians tried it out on eager patients, a second phase of some disillusionment developed. It sometimes produced objectionable side effects, and in some instances it failed to hold early gains made by the patient. Nevertheless, it brought much relief to many arthritis patients and was a powerful weapon against the other ailments. It is still regarded by many as one of the most significant medical discoveries of the present generation, and Drs. Edward C. Kendall and Philip S. Hench of the Mayo Clinic were awarded the Nobel Prize for developing cortisone.[58]

ACTH (adreno-cortico-tropic-hormone) brought similar effects. It is a hormone of the pituitary gland which stimulates the adrenals to produce a larger amount of natural cortisone. It achieved miraculous results in relieving arthritis symptoms, but sometimes produced distressing side effects also—growth of hair on face, pads of fat on shoulder blades and hips, depression psychosis. The hormone is now administered more temperately, with smaller doses; frequently both cortisone and ACTH are prescribed for patients who do not respond to other types of treatment.[59] Further study of cortisone and ACTH has brought the conclusion, moreover, that the beneficial results of these hormones tend to be temporary. In themselves they do not bring curative action; they suppress pathologic reactions while a disease such as acute rheumatic fever runs its course.[60] These hormones are being tested further, and new hormones of a similar nature have been and are being developed.

Then, there is the possibility of administering sex hormones—*testosterone* which is produced by the male sex glands and *estrogens* produced by the female glands. Favorable results have often resulted from administering sex hormones of the other sex when there is a cancerous growth related to the sex organs; that is, a woman who has a cancer of the breast is given male sex hormone, whereas a man with cancer of sex organs is given the female sex hormone. In such cases the cancerous growth may recede.[61]

Psychiatry. Another medical area in which considerable progress has been achieved during the twentieth century is that of mental hygiene and psychiatry. This field, like many other branches of medicine, has had a long history. Psychiatry before 1900, however, was markedly influenced by ideas of magic (demons) and of theology. The sensible idea finally gained currency that the mentally ill are simply sick people who should be treated according to their needs by whatever medical techniques are appropriate.[62]

The contributions of Sigmund Freud around the turn of the century are well known and scarcely need elaboration here. The social invention of

[58] Steven M. Spencer, *op. cit.,* p. 163.
[59] *Ibid.,* p. 171.
[60] Edward W. Boland, "Rheumatic Diseases," Ch. 5 in Morris Fishbein, ed., *op. cit.*
[61] Cooley, *op. cit.,* pp. 138–140.
[62] See Shryock, *op. cit.,* Ch. 17, "A Delayed Advance Against Mental Disease"; Albert Deutsch, *The Mentally Ill in America* (New York, Columbia University Press, 1949).

psychoanalysis, based on the significance of the unconscious mind in relation to mental disorders, is probably about on a par with Pasteur's doctrine of the germ causation of infectious diseases. More recent contributions to the Freudian doctrine have been made by Adler, Jung, Meyer, Sullivan, Horney, Fromm, and others.[63]

The major technique in treating mental patients is still psychotherapy, involving face-to-face discussion between patient and psychiatrist; this may be of the Freudian type (emphasizing Freudian concepts and doctrines) or it may emphasize the ideas of other psychiatrists named above. Group therapy is often used, when conditions are suitable, for patients having essentially the same sort of problems; encouragement may result from the group contacts and social relationships are fostered. Various somatic treatments may be added to the above if they are necessary or seem appropriate. Shock treatment is frequently used for serious cases—either electric shock or use of insulin or a drug like metrazol. Also for serious cases (psychosis) surgical treatment such as prefrontal lobotomy may sometimes be recommended. New drugs regarded as extremely valuable in mental illness are *chlorpromazine* (a recent French discovery) and *rauwolfia* (a drug extracted from a root grown in India). Neither the new drugs nor shock nor surgery is, however, a substitute for psychotherapy. Their essential function is to make it possible to approach the patient for psychotherapy.[64] Braceland states that during and since World War II psychiatry has tended to turn away from the somatic emphasis of the 1930's (shock therapies, etc.), and has intensified its interest in the psychoanalytic contributions to psychotherapy.[65]

Impact of nuclear energy on medicine. Another major development during the twentieth century—indeed, since World War II—has been that of the impact of use of nuclear energy on medicine. This major advance in basic science, providing a new important source of energy, has affected and is affecting many fields as has been shown in other chapters of this book. It has chiefly influenced medicine in three ways: (1) in providing a new technique of medical investigation—use of radioactive isotopes as tracers; (2) by the use of nuclear substances in treating various diseases; and (3) in caus-

[63] See volumes by these psychologists or psychiatrists or consult standard texts in these fields such as William C. Menninger, *Psychiatry* (Ithaca, Cornell University Press, 1948) or Franz Alexander, *Fundamentals of Psychoanalysis* (New York, Norton, 1948).

[64] The content of this paragraph has been largely based on Leonard Engel, "Survey of the Present State of Psychiatry," *New York Times,* Magazine Section, Sunday, February 20, 1955.

Concerning shock treatment and psychosurgery, see also Paul R. Hawley, *New Discoveries in Medicine* (New York, Columbia University Press, 1950), pp. 70–94. Concerning recent use of drugs for mental illness, see "Year's Review in Medicine," *New York Herald Tribune,* January 1, 1956; Harold E. Himwich, "The New Psychiatric Drugs," *Scientific American,* Vol. 193, No. 4 (October, 1955), pp. 80–87.

[65] Francis J. Braceland, "Psychiatry and Psychosomatic Medicine," in Morris Fishbein, ed., *op. cit.,* Ch. 10 (esp. p. 146).

ing a new major medical problem to develop, namely, injury through radiation.

The use of radioactive isotopes as tracers has provided a valuable new method of medical investigation which may be compared in importance with the development of the x-ray or the microscope.[66] When the radioactive material (salt, iodine, phosphorus, etc.) is administered to the patient, its progress throughout the body may be followed by use of a Geiger counter. Consequently if there is an obstruction due to tumor (benign or malignant), the location of the tumor is indicated. Isotopes have also been found to be valuable in locating brain tumors.[67] Hence a new key is available for acquiring knowledge in internal medicine.

Isotopes are also important for other research or theurapeutic purposes. They are used for tracing the circulation of blood within the heart; studying or treating hyperthyroidism, cancer of the thyroid, and certain blood diseases as leukemia; treating certain cases of angina pectoris; acquiring knowledge concerning hardening of the arteries, cancer as an over-all problem, virus infections, and other diseases; and adding to the stock of knowledge (using isotopes) about the assimilation of proteins, enzymes, fat compounds, and cortisone. Undoubtedly new uses are continually developing.

It seems reasonable to conclude, however, that the most important consideration of all relative to the use of radioactive isotopes is that stated by Dr. John C. Bugher, Director of the Division of Biology and Medicine of the Atomic Energy Commission:[68]

We merely stand on the threshhold of a new era of knowledge. Phenomena and concepts of which today we do not even speculate, surely lie in the future before us. . . . Future medical study will likely emphasize the dynamic characteristics of intra-cellular reactions which can be observed in the living state without injury to the individual.

Anticipating that within the next fifty years the infectious diseases will no longer be a major threat to life and health, man will study increasingly prob-

[66] Spencer comments: "Radioactive atoms are today illuminating every pathway of research. They constitute a flexible and precise tool for almost any task a scientist can think up. As a means of extending man's perception the isotopes have, in fact, been called the greatest advance since the invention of the microscope. They can penetrate into hidden corners of plant and animal anatomy and telegraph out step-by-step reports of the most complex chemical and physiological reactions. They can measure ingredients millions of times too small in quantity to be detected by the most delicate chemical analysis."—Spencer, *op. cit.,* p. 86.

[67] Use of radioactive isotopes for this purpose has now been successful for some seven or eight years. At the Massachusetts General Hospital, Boston, investigations are currently reported in which a new isotope, *arsenic 74,* is used. When this isotope is administered intravenously, it concentrates largely on cancerous tissue. Special detection instruments and techniques then locate the site of the tumor.—*Fifteenth Semiannual Report of the Atomic Energy Commission,* January, 1954 (Washington, Government Printing Office, 1954), p. 42.

[68] AEC Press Release dated March 23, 1955. Remarks of Dr. John C. Bugher before the National Health Council, New York City.

lems of the physiological limitations of life and of the effect of environmental factors on the population. The indications are that man is now in the early period of great advances in biochemistry. The techniques of radiobiology now being developed are likely to point the way in this new trend.[69]

On the other hand, a staggering new problem—injury through radiation—is at hand. One may momentarily reflect on Dr. Sigerist's observation, noted early in this chapter, that medicine develops in relation to the evolving pattern of disease and the changing general ideas and thought of mankind. Surely this is an apt illustration. The onward sweep of advancing science brought the nuclear age; with it came the hitherto unknown medical problem of radiation and radioactive fall-out, both as a wartime phenomenon and a peacetime one. The field of medicine, and also that of public health, is inevitably compelled to deal with this problem. One would expect this to be a stupendous problem in event of future large-scale war involving nuclear weapons. Even during times of semi-peace the American-conducted test H-bomb explosions in the Marshall Islands (Pacific) during March, 1954, resulted in significant problems of radiation exposure to some 31 American personnel, to 236 Marshall Island natives, and to Japanese fishermen on a trawler that happened to be in the vicinity at the wrong time.[70]

Radiation injury may be assumed to have two aspects:[71] (1) immediate, somatic damage to people affected; and (2) genetic effects—damage to the germ cells which may show itself in future generations. The former damage is likely to relate basically to the central nervous system, the blood-forming organs and tissues, and the gastro-intestinal tract. Symptoms may manifest themselves within a few minutes if the radiation dose is large or in several weeks if the dose is small. If there are approxmiately four hundred roentgens of immediate gamma radiation from the nuclear bomb, a death rate of about 50 per cent of the population is to be expected. Exposures to the amount of about two hundred roentgens of whole-body gamma radiation may cause such a depression of white cells that antibiotics are required to block secondary infections. Moreover, the joint Japanese-American studies of the casualties at Hiroshima and Nagasaki showed that there was an appreciable incidence of cataracts among the survivors. Finally, some shortening of life expectancy due to radiation exposure was indicated, although not positively proven.[72]

[69] *Ibid.*

[70] *Major Activities in the Atomic Energy Programs* (January–July, 1954), pp. 51–54.

[71] Here the writer is indebted to the discussion by Dr. John C. Bugher, Director of the Division of Biology and Medicine, U. S. Atomic Energy Commission. See AEC Press Release, September 23, 1954.

[72] This has been shown for animals, and is indicated for man. No specific cause of death seems to be related to this; it is apparently a general acceleration of the aging process.

Radiation, including radioactive fall-out,[73] may also affect the germ cells and alter the genes upon which inheritance depends. It appears that there is a linear relation between the amount of radiation and the frequency of gene changes. Quantitative studies of radiation have been made using mice and the fruit fly. But the effect of radiation on human beings comprises the all-important question, especially since the possibility of radiation injury has caused much concern among biologists and other scientists.[74] Accordingly a report on this subject based on a year-long survey made by the National Academy of Sciences, the leading scientific body in the United States, was eagerly awaited. The report of six committees of the NAS, announced during June, 1956, has been called "the most comprehensive U. S. effort to determine how the future of the human race might be affected by the unleashing of nuclear power."[75] Both civilian and military radiation effects were discussed.

Some of the conclusions of the committees of the National Academy of Sciences were: (1) that radiation, no matter how small the dose, shortens life to some degree; (2) that all-out nuclear war conceivably could make the earth uninhabitable; (3) that radiation causes mutations or harmful changes in the genes or germ cells of the reproductive organs of a person receiving (a) background radiation due to cosmic rays and other natural sources, (b) radiation from use of medical and dental x-rays, and (c) radiation from weapons tests; the committee on genetics predicted that harmful effects of radiation would cause a slow, almost imperceptible deterioration of the human species over the decades which would manifest itself in a shortening of the life span, reduced ability to produce children, and sometimes but not often birth of deformed or freakish offspring; (4) that the American public was currently using up about one-third of its (radiation) safety limit in medical and dental x-rays; (5) that nuclear weapons tests are the least harmful source of radiation from the individual's point of view; (6) that a national system of personal records should be instituted whereby every American would know his total amount of radiation exposure; (7) that the effect of this exposure is

[73] "Radioactive fall-out" has been defined as "the radio-activity which falls out of the atmosphere after the explosion of a nuclear weapon." See AEC Press Release, June 3, 1955.

[74] Ralph E. Lapp states: ". . . [relative to the fall-out problem] geneticists are worried over the impact of a thermonuclear war upon the continued existence of *homo sapiens*. There is a thousandfold difference between a test program and a war involving weapons developed by these tests."—*Bulletin of the Atomic Scientists*, Vol. XI, No. 5 (May, 1955), p. 200. Also see Lapp, "Strontium Limits in Peace and War," *ibid.*, Vol. XII, No. 8 (October, 1956), pp. 287–289, 320.

Other statements appearing in the press are as follows: On March 16, 1955, Professor Linus Pauling of the California Institute of Technology, Nobel Prize chemist, warned that radiation from atomic tests could be potentially fatal to persons whose resistance to cancer is low. And on March 21, 1955, Professor Frederick Soddy, British Nobel Prize physicist, said that hydrogen bomb explosions "are fouling the air with radioactivity and it is nonsense to say it is harmless."

[75] *New York Times*, June 13, 1956, article by Anthony Leviero.

cumulative no matter how long the period over which it is experienced; and (8) that disposal of atomic wastes should be most carefully performed and buildings housing atomic reactors should be sealed.[76]

The above summarizes some of the major conclusions of certain of the committees. It is apparent that the conclusions of the committee on genetics most emphasize the hazards from radiation. Other reports will undoubtedly be made, despite the high standing of the NAS scientists and their report; one by the British Medical Research Council has already been issued.[77] It is likely that these vital radiation problems will be discussed for many years. Gaps in man's knowledge regarding radiation will gradually be filled. Eventually one may expect a consensus among world scientists on these important matters.

With this discussion of the impact of nuclear energy on medicine, this section on progress in medical technology during the twentieth century is concluded. Consideration of other worth-while developments has had to be omitted.

EFFECTS

The following are regarded as valid effects of advancing technology on the practice of medicine and on related phenomena:

1. *The medical profession has been able to provide more accurate diagnosis and more skillful, more efficient treatment in virtually all branches of the field as a result of advancing medical science and technology.* One may compare the high-quality service in a modern hospital, or in a physician's office, utilizing x-ray, microscopic technique, use of potent antibiotic drugs or hormones, and perhaps radioactive isotopes, with the medical service of a few decades back. The oldtime physician may have been natively bright and a constructive-minded, helpful practitioner who, indeed, relieved the pain of patients and generally made them feel more comfortable.[78] But he often did not have the available techniques at the time for an accurate diagnosis and effective treatment. Certainly, to mention a drastic contrast, the most able physician in 1850 could do little with severe infectious diseases as typhoid fever or smallpox; today if cases of these diseases developed at all (which itself would be unlikely), the average physician would have little difficulty in stopping them abruptly with modern drugs.

---

[76] The above has been summarized from the full report in the *New York Times,* June 13, 1956, and from *Science,* Vol. 123, No. 3208 (June 22, 1956), and following issues.

[77] For comparison of content of British and American reports, see Bentley Glass, "The Hazards of Atomic Radiations to Man—British and American Reports," *Bulletin of the Atomic Scientists,* Vol. XII, No. 8 (October, 1956), pp. 312–317.

[78] The latter should not be underrated either, although more personalized attention undoubtedly may be correlated with the more rural living of past generations. It is possible that the modern, efficient, big-city hospital may provide an "objective" environment in which "feelings" for the patient sometimes get lost.

EXPECTATION OF LIFE AT BIRTH, IN YEARS, 1879 to 1954
INDUSTRIAL POLICYHOLDERS, METROPOLITAN LIFE INSURANCE COMPANY*

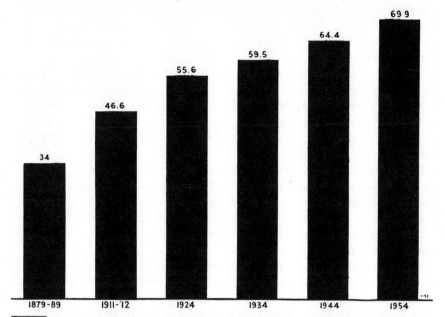

*Weekly and Monthly premium-paying business combined for 1954; Weekly alone in prior years. *Note*—Excludes deaths from enemy action.

Source: Metropolitan Life Insurance Company, *Statistical Bulletin*, Vol. 36, No. 1 (January, 1955), p. 6.

This development of skillful, efficient medical care shows itself in the declining death rates of the nation and in the corresponding rise in average life expectancy; other factors are also responsible as we shall shortly see. In Chapters 3 and 19 are figures citing the accelerating rise in life expectancy, hence it seems unnecessary to repeat here similar figures. However, the progress experienced in combating disease-mortality is indicated in the figure above.

It is admittedly difficult to build an airtight case that would establish the crucial effect of advancing medical technology on mortality, since the latter rates also reflect (as pointed out in Chapter 3) the increasing standard of living,[79] improved health education, rise of the public health movement, improved consumption of food, trends in governmental expenditures, international co-operation in health matters, and doubtless other influences. Yet, with all this, there can be little doubt that the occurrence of, for example,

[79] As concluded by Professor Ogburn, the standard of living in the United States has approximately doubled during the first half of the twentieth century. See William F. Ogburn, "Technology and the Standard of Living in the United States," *American Journal of Sociology*, Vol. LX, No. 4 (January, 1955), pp. 380–386.

declining pneumonia death rates at the precise time that the highly-effective sulfa drugs and penicillin came into use is a correlated phenomenon of great significance; correlation in such a case would be high. A similar instance was the sudden halt in typhoid fever and smallpox cases as vaccination techniques were adopted. The relationship between these two sets of facts is apparent to most observers.

2. *The modern physician needs to be proficient in many technical skills— use of many machines, x-ray, many different kinds of gadgets.* Of the various professions, medicine has probably been influenced to a greater extent by modern technology than any of the others except engineering. Whether the physician is engaged in research, in general practice, or in a specialty, he would be lost today without use of his machines.

3. *The influence of technology has made it necessary for the modern physician to purchase expensive machines before he can practice.* To launch oneself on a medical career is, in short, a costly matter, unless one is attached to a large-scale research organization or similar institution where machines will be provided. A certain amount of gadgetry will be regarded as necessary "tools of the trade" for the physician.

4. *The invention of technical instruments bears on the formation of medical specialties.* It is admitted that there are other influences which promote specialties too. The development of instruments of diagnosis along with concepts dealing with them—microscope, x-ray, use of isotopes, and so on— fosters the development of a field. In general, knowledge remained in a crude and undeveloped state until such instruments were used. Around the 1830's, as has been observed, physicians spoke simply of "fevers"—a vague and generalized concept. When the microscope was constructed and the concept of germ causation grew, bacteriologists identified specific germs and knowledge of epidemiology and immunology grew apace; the content of medicine expanded. So it is with other instruments. As medical science expanded, no person could master the whole field and specialties became a necessity. To be sure, competence was needed to master the instruments of the specialty too. The eye-and-ear man was not generally competent to use the machines of the heart specialist or urologist and vice versa. Moreover, the findings of each medical area required skilled interpretation. Then, as more and more specific techniques were used, the stock of knowledge in each medical branch grew. Gradually even the specialties had a wealth of information to be mastered.[80] Progress in medicine has been accelerated by specialization. However, technological advance has an underlying connection with the entire specialization trend.[81]

5. *The present chapter has, up to this point, documented the generaliza-*

---

[80] It is granted that other influences outside of the field of medicine had influence on the development of specialties too—for example, the increasing size of city populations, also the income level of the population.

[81] Stern, *American Medical Practice* . . . , pp. 45–47.

tion that the nature of medical practice (i.e., how the physician proceeds with his work) has been vastly changed by advancing medical technology. The coming of anesthesia, antisepsis, the sulfa drugs, antibiotics, hormones and new surgical techniques has made the practice of medicine a different thing from what it was during, say, the early 1800's.[82] A non-M.D. would imagine it to be something of a task to "keep up" with all the latest developments; other fields, however, have the same situation, though not always to quite the same degree. This widespread change is in a sense the basic thesis of this entire volume. At any rate, highly regarded treatment for a certain disease at the present time may be considerably different from what it was fifteen to twenty years ago. We have noted the conspicuous changes in treating the infectious diseases and the outstanding successes achieved during recent years.

Henri Péquignot, well-known French physician, declares:[83]

To borrow a device dear to the hearts of novelists, one could say that a doctor who had gone to sleep in 1940 and woke up in 1954 would no longer recognize either prognosis or the methods of diagnosing and treating the most common complaints, and would think he was faced with constantly recurring miracles, apart from the necessity of starting afresh his medical studies.

At all events, modern diagnosis of disease is likely to include laboratory examinations, x-ray examinations, and electric recordings, and sometimes use of isotope tracers. It may involve a team of specialists. As compared with earlier medical practice, it will likely be both amazingly precise and complex.

6. *The technological influence on medicine has brought an over-all increase in the costs of medical care for the patient.* This is in part related to the two preceding effects, but it is more than that. The fact that modern medical care often involves a "team,"[84] with the main physician or surgeon in charge but with high-priced specialists in consulting capacity, itself increases the cost. Other members of the team include nurses, dentists, x-ray technicians, physical and occupational therapists, dieticians, and others. All must be highly trained. Standards have been raised in these occupations, and the training period has been extended since the tasks have become more technical. Higher qualifications, standards, and periods of preparation lead eventually to higher salaries.[85] Hospital care is expensive, especially if private nurses

[82] Changes in other types of technology—transportation inventions as the automobile, communication inventions as the telephone, newspaper, and radio,—have in various ways (directly and indirectly) had an impact on the life of the physician.

[83] Péquignot, "Scientific and Social Aspects of Modern Medicine," *Impact of Science on Society,* Vol. V, No. 4 (December, 1954) (Paris, UNESCO), p. 211.

[84] Frank G. Dickinson, "The Medical Care Team," *Annals of the American Academy of Political and Social Science,* Vol. 273 (January, 1951), pp. 25–33. Also see, by the same author, *Is Medical Care Expensive?* (Chicago, American Medical Association, Bureau of Medical Economic Research, Bulletin 60, 1947).

[85] Péquignot, *op. cit.,* pp. 221–222.

are needed. The costs of new medicines and drugs are often high. These various costs must, of course, be borne by the patient.

The subject of the costs of medical care is an extensive one, but word may be added on at least one other matter, namely, that the very efficiency of modern medicine means that the patient is likely to live to an older age, hence be a candidate for other diseases—which will bring further cost. Thus the youthful patient who is cured becomes a future potential patient of heart disease, cancer, or other post-maturity disease. Since the objective of the medical profession is to prolong life, this may seem to be an objectionable, even cruel, remark to make. One merely points out that while the medical objective is more and more being attained by modern scientific procedures, the fact is that over-all medical costs rise as an accompaniment of this result. Moreover, older people usually require a large amount of medical care.

7. *The technological influence on medicine, bringing more efficient medical care, has led in turn to a growing desire for medical service on the part of the general population.* Medical cures, sometimes remarkable, have been responsible for the increased demand. This is, indeed, one aspect of the "socialized medicine" problem. In the event of illness, almost everyone wants medical service—while not everyone is able to pay for it. In earlier times, for example, when the death rate was high following operations, it may be presumed that the demand for medical service was not so insistent. At any rate, current interest in health insurance, hospital care plans, and other plans dealing with the economic aspects of medical care are partly based on this development.

Three other subjects may be mentioned at this point. While these subjects are technically outside the scope of this chapter, they represent important derivative effects of the technological influence on medical practice and should not be omitted from consideration. They are as follows:

1. *Advances in medical technology have been influential in dictating the activities and dominant emphases of the public health field.* Public health workers, applying medical practices in the community, perforce can only use what is known; and of course evolving social objectives have also been a factor in directing various preventive health activities. Quarantine practices, to take an example, have been based on what is regarded at the time as correct notions of how diseases spread and how they may be controlled. So also with protection of public water supplies, milk sanitation, mosquito control, venereal disease control, and other endeavors. The sequence of events, then, is something as follows: (*a*) occurrence of medical discovery, (*b*) use of discovery in private medical practice and public application of idea by public health workers, both after a time lag in many cases.

Earlier in this chapter mention was made of the bacteriological triumphs of Pasteur, Koch, and others in isolating the specific germ causes of various infectious diseases; many of these were achieved during the 1870's and 1880's. Public health departments began to emphasize epidemiological work on these bacteriological discoveries around 1900. Bacteriological laboratories were established for the identification of germs. Communicable disease control via vaccination and like methods was also emphasized at that time. Similarly, venereal disease control was emphasized by public health workers during the 1930's and 1940's when effective drugs were available for their treatment.

During the next 10's it appears reasonable that certain changes might be made in public health activities due to the possibilities of injury from exposure to radiation and radioactive fall-out. This problem comes to the fore as a major challenge.

The U.S. Bugher, previously cited, states the following:[86]

As the uses of atomic energy for industrial and scientific purposes multiplies, so increases the responsibility for insuring that the environment and the biological systems upon which human life depends, shall not be contaminated to a level of population hazard. In general, this requires that the environmental contamination must be maintained at levels considerably below those considered significant as hazards to individuals.

That development means that the sanitary engineer and the public health worker, not only now but especially in the years to come, must give increasing thought to the control of radio-active substances in the environment and the manner in which such substances may enter the various life cycles that constitute our food chains. It requires diligence and a redirection of public health education.

2. *It must be recognized that the successes of medicine and public health in controlling infectious diseases have, in turn, comprised one element that has made possible the rise of the large city.* Although much emphasis has rightly been placed on industrialization, advances in transportation, and an increasingly productive agriculture as factors in the growth of cities, the health factor should not be overlooked. Since during earlier times epidemics of yellow fever, cholera, typhoid fever, smallpox, and other diseases killed off large numbers of urban dwellers and caused considerable disruption of normal community life, it is doubtful if the modern metropolis could have developed as it has, without adequate health protection. The city's continued well-being still depends, it might be added, on that protection. Epidemic diseases spread rapidly amid congested urban populations. They must be held in check.

There is no particular reason, however, to be concerned about this problem today. On the contrary, large city populations are well protected today from the epidemic diseases by effective medical and public health techniques. Prevention of a smallpox epidemic in New York City in 1947 afforded a convincing demonstration of how a potential epidemic may be suppressed in

[86] AEC Press Release, March 23, 1955. Address of Dr. John C. Bugher, National Health Council, New York City.

modern times. Infectious diseases are currently well controlled, especially with recent developments in antibiotics. These diseases are in general retreat. This is a matter of some importance, however, for city dwellers.

3. *The successes of medicine and public health in controlling infectious diseases have likewise affected the population structure of the nation.* This is a major matter; but since it has been alluded to previously and is widely discussed in the literature on population,[87] it may be briefly treated here. The enormous reduction in death rates from such infectious diseases as, diphtheria, typhoid fever, scarlet fever, and tuberculosis has meant that many people live to mature and advanced ages who in earlier decades would have died young. The average length of life has increased. With more and more people living on to older ages, the age composition of the population is thus affected; the United States has a gradually aging population. This has brought social, economic, political, recreational, educational, military, and other consequences.

In particular, more facilities of all sorts are needed for older people. Hauser has asserted that the number of persons age 65 and over will continue to grow until it reaches between 17 million and 20 million in 1975.[88] The state of mind and activities of the nation in all respects are likely to reflect this gradual aging of the population.

CONCLUSION

This chapter is concluded with the statement of a hypothesis which is similar to the one expressed at the end of the preceding chapter on war. It is believed that the facts of the present chapter affirm the tremendous influence of advancing technology on the practice of medicine. The changes in medical practice have been both noteworthy and beneficial to mankind. *The hypothesis is that the most significant variable associated with changing medical care over the centuries is the factor of applied science and technology.* Practitioners of medicine may be regarded as a constant factor in the picture. They will differ in interests (within the profession) and in abilities. They will have different types of personalities as do lawyers, teachers, and others. Granting such variations as these, however, physicians of the 1850's are not dissimilar from those of the 1950's as a professional group. It is in this sense that physicians may be considered as a *constant* in the equation. Medical education will be another variable; it will be affected by advancing technology and science. Medical organization is still another one, though it may be af-

[87] See, for example, Paul H. Landis and Paul K. Hatt, *Population Problems*, 2nd ed. (New York, American Book, 1954), Ch. 5; Rupert B. Vance, *All These People* (Chapel Hill, University of North Carolina Press, 1945), Ch. 5; T. Lynn Smith, *Population Analysis* (New York, McGraw-Hill, 1948), Ch. 15.

[88] Philip Hauser, "Demographic Aspects of Our Aging Population," unpublished paper read at the Northwestern University Centennial Conference, June 7, 1952; see also Paul H. Landis and Paul K. Hatt, *op. cit.,* Ch. 5.

fected in part by technology too. There may be other factors in the situation.

In this chapter the data has not been directed toward comparing the influence of applied science and technology on the practice of medicine *with other influences*. Admittedly testing of the hypothesis proposed here would probably be difficult, perhaps even impossible at the present time.

If the present hypothesis should be substantiated at a later time, the results would be of real significance. The future of the practice of medicine could be estimated, in such an event, on the basis of changing science and technology. The latter would thus constitute an important key in appraising changes to come.

SUMMARY

This chapter is based on the assumption that the evolving practice of medicine is related both to the changing picture of disease and to the general development of all social thought; basic science particularly has had a strong influence on medicine. The influence of technology as an application of science on medical practice is then traced as follows: (*a*) major developments on medicine in primitive societies and in nonprimitive ones up to the year 1800; (*b*) major advances of medical technology during the nineteenth century; and (*c*) outstanding developments during the twentieth century.

Advances in the field of medicine during the present century which are discussed include the development of vaccines and antitoxins, including the Salk vaccine for poliomyelitis; various advances in nutrition; advances in chemotherapy and in antibiotics; advances in hormone therapy, including cortisone and ACTH; advances in psychotherapy; and the influence of nuclear energy on the practice of medicine, especially the use of radioactive isotopes as tracers, use of nuclear substances in treating certain diseases, and the development of the new medical problem of injury through radiation.

Effects of advancing technology on medicine are appraised. These include provision of more accurate diagnosis and more skillful treatment on the part of practicing physicians; the need of modern physicians to be proficient in technical skills and in use of machines; aid to the trend of developing medical specialties; significant change in the manner of conducting medical practice (that is, what the physician does and why); decisive changes in the activities of public health workers; the virtual conquering of infectious diseases, which has in turn brought fundamental changes in the population structure—in particular, the gradual aging of the American population. This, further, has had many different consequences affecting most activities of the nation. As a general over-all conclusion of the chapter, it is hypothesized that the factor of applied science and technology is the most significant variable associated with the changing practice of medicine in the United States. It may be regarded as a major key to further changes in medical practice in the future.

ANNOTATED BIBLIOGRAPHY

DUBLIN, Louis I., LOTKA, Alfred J., and SPIEGELMAN, Mortimer, *Length of Life,* rev. ed. (New York, Ronald Press, 1949). A rewarding volume. Excellent source on the life table. Chapter 8 is especially appropriate for present discussion.

FISHBEIN, Morris, ed., *Medical Progress:* 1953 (New York, Blakiston, 1953). An annual review of medical advances. Somewhat technical but excellent. Contributions are by leading authorities—Paul D. White, Charles W. Mayo, Perrin Long, Irving H. Page, F. W. Stare, and others.

Medical Research: A Midcentury Survey, The American Foundation (Boston, Little, Brown, 1955), 2 Vols. Vol. I, "American Medical Research," discusses medical research in the perspective of the basic sciences, trends and agencies of research. Vol. II, "Unsolved Clinical Problems," is concerned with cancer, infertility, arteriosclerosis, the viruses, alcoholism, and schizophrenia. Worthy of thorough study.

"Mental Health in the United States," *Annals of the American Academy of Political and Social Science,* Vol. 286 (March, 1953). Especially recommended are articles by Boudreau, Felix and Kramer, Gruenberg, and Frank.

RAPPORT, Samuel, and WRIGHT, Helen, ed., *Great Adventures in Medicine* (New York, The Dial Press, 1952). Selections concerning or by well-known medical personages: from Hippocrates to Pasteur to Alexander Fleming. A stimulating collection of readings.

RIESMAN, David, *Medicine in Modern Society* (Princeton, N. J., Princeton University Press, 1939). A wise and insightful book.

SHRYOCK, Richard H., *The Development of Modern Medicine* (New York, Knopf, 1947). A splendid volume on the all-around interrelationships between the development of medicine and other scientific and social factors. Well-assimilated material.

SIGERIST, Henry E., *A History of Medicine,* Vol. I, *Primitive and Archaic Medicine* (New York, Oxford University Press, 1951). This first volume of the contemplated eight-volume series on the history of medicine, by the dean of medical historians, covers the subjects of primitive medicine and medicine in Ancient Egypt and Mesopotamia. Shows an enormous range of knowledge. Definitive.

SPENCER, Steven M., *Wonders of Modern Medicine* (New York, McGraw-Hill, 1953). Informative, solid writing on such subjects as arteriosclerosis, cancer, antibiotics, hormones, polio, and diabetes. Nontechnical. Author is a journalist who has been especially trained for medical writing.

STERN, Bernhard J., *American Medical Practice in the perspectives of a Century* (New York, Commonwealth Fund, 1945). The author, a sociologist, has written "an historical exposition of the reciprocal interplay between the social, technological, and economic forces and medicine." An able job. Covers the expanding field of medicine, specialization, the supply of physicians, and other subjects.

————, *Society and Medical Progress* (Princeton, N. J., Princeton University Press, 1941). Medicine seen as related to socioeconomic conditions, not as an isolated field. Helpful material on medical progress, role of medical schools, and development of the modern hospital.

PART IV

Rapid Social Change and Social Problems

CHAPTER 17

THE HYPOTHESIS OF CULTURAL LAG: A PRESENT-DAY VIEW

■ *Hornell Hart*

THE CRISIS of our civilization might be epitomized by a hydrogen bomb poised in the air over the United Nations building in New York City. The bomb represents the towering upsurge of military technology—the vastly multiplied power of destruction which modern science has placed in the hands of the Soviet as well as of the American government. The glass-faced building of the United Nations symbolizes the frail structure of international law and order, groping upward, uncertain and as yet feeble—yet embodying the best aspirations and collective achievements of mankind until now in our struggle to bring collective intelligence to mastery over colossal brute force. Quite evidently, the growth of world law and order is lagging disastrously behind the upsurge of destructive technology. Can that lag be overcome?

Collective intelligence operates most effectively and most swiftly when it achieves the form of science. Our crisis may well be formulated in terms of the lag of social science behind material science. But if we are to have any realistic hope of bringing social science to bear effectively on the solution of the world crisis, it is necessary that we obtain first at least some small degree of scientific understanding of the nature of cultural lag itself.

The concept was first set forth by William F. Ogburn, in his book *Social Change,* published originally in 1922. Since that date cultural lag has been the subject of many articles, and it has been discussed in practically all the major textbooks in general sociology. Let us begin our present discussion by examining the concept in one of its simpler forms.

LAG AFTER A SINGLE INVENTION

Stuart Chase popularized cultural lag in a simplified and easily understandable form which may be called *The Tandem Theory:*[1]

[1] Stuart Chase, *The Proper Study of Mankind* (New York, Harper, 1956), p. 115.

Inventions are usually accepted into culture in two stages. To begin with, people change their day-by-day behavior to accommodate the new device. . . . Then, considerably later on, people change their institutions and belief systems to allow for the invention, and arrange means for controlling its effects in the interest of society. The time between the first and the second stages is known as the cultural lag, a term invented by Ogburn.

Under this Tandem Theory, culture is regarded as being technologically determined. Major mechanical inventions disturb cultural adjustments. When the steam engine, or the automobile, or the airplane, or the atomic bomb upsets our social processes, we must work out such readjustments as will fit our social life into the new technology. According to the Tandem Theory, the technological innovation comes first, and the readjustment always takes time. The time interval available for making those adjustments becomes shorter and shorter. Society took thousands of years to adjust to the invention of the bow and arrow, and hundreds of years to adjust to the invention of gunpowder and artillery. But the bombing plane did not permit Poland, England, and Germany hundreds of years to adjust to its menace and its destruction. And the atomic guided missile, or the radioactive fog, or the ultra-deadly virus, or the hydrogen-uranium-lithium metropolis-smasher will not allow its victims decades—or even years—to make social adjustments.

Hitherto, social leaders have waited until the steam engine, or the bombing plane, or the atomic bomb has been invented and has precipitated a social crisis. Then, in the face of the resulting Industrial Revolution, or the resulting urban demolition, or the resulting threat to civilization, social adjusters have gone to work by trial-and-error fumbling to patch up some sort of remedy. It is becoming more and more obvious that that process can no longer safely be trusted. The magnitude of the required social adjustments becomes larger and larger; the time available for the adjustment approaches closer and closer to zero. If the unmodified Tandem Theory of social change were correct, civilization would certainly seem to be doomed. The sinister implications of this theory offer no argument either for or against its validity. But they do underline the importance of determining verifiably whether such a theory is sound.

THE TENSION THEORY OF CULTURAL LAG

The Tandem Theory focuses attention on the effect of a single invention, presenting it as a one-two-three kind of sequence. Actually the process is much more complex. We might begin to get a more adequate idea by thinking of a wire hoop with rubber bands stretched across it in various directions, and with a network of criss-cross bands knotted to these strands at many different points. Now let us suppose that one end of a new rubber band is fastened into the network at some point and then is pulled. This new band may be thought of as a new invention. If all the bands were perfectly elastic (though of different degrees of size and strength), the ways in which the whole network is stretched and twisted by the pull of the new band might be taken as a greatly simplified and idealized representation of the cultural adjustments called for by a new invention or discovery.

If the new rubber band is a small one and if, after it is tied in, it is pulled slowly and gently, and is tied to other strands which it crosses, we may think of the new invention as having been assimilated into the culture, with relatively minor adjustments. But suppose that a large and strong rubber band is tied into the network and then is jerked suddenly and powerfully. The old network will then be twisted and stretched in much more violent ways. This represents what happens whenever social change of a swift and powerful nature takes place. But the principle of cultural acceleration (which was pointed out in Chapter 3) means that larger and larger changes occur faster and faster. In our world today, therefore, the network of cultural adjustments is being stretched and strained to a very high degree. Other chapters in this book have provided a number of examples.

For purposes of simplification, we have thought of the strands of existing culture and of new inventions as being perfectly elastic. But this, obviously, would misrepresent the facts. Some strands are young and frail, whereas some others are old and rotten. They break down under the stresses of innovations. Other strands are strong and inelastic. Other strands are more like tigers' tails which, when jerked, produce powerful reactions. Still others are like lanyards on great guns which, when pulled, set off far-away explosions. And the transmission of the invention's pull takes time. The strands may be like new vines which have to grow and put forth leaves, or like the network of fire hoses which need to be connected up and brought to bear in a great conflagration. Complications like these involve cultural lags.

CULTURE HAS THREE DIMENSIONS

Every culture may be regarded as made up of many culture complexes. Our modern Western culture, for example, contains (among many others, and with variations) the following: the monogamous, democratic family; the automobile complex; the free public school system; parliamentary government; and Protestant Christianity.

A culture complex is a functional combination of closely interrelated traits within a culture. For example, the up-to-date family includes such traits as the TV set, the use of contraceptive techniques, ideas and attitudes about dating, and some method of managing family finances.

Without attempting even to suggest any comprehensive list of culture complexes, it should be noted that they can be grouped into the six broad institutional categories, as follows: (1) economic, such as railroads, coal mines, department stores, and advertising; (2) family, such as the patriarchal, matriarchal, democratic, and Hollywood moving-picture-actor family types; (3)

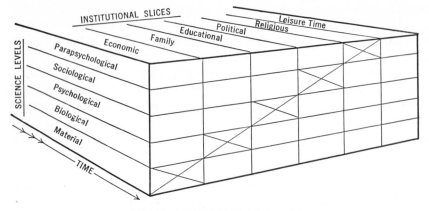

THE THREE DIMENSIONS OF CULTURE

educational, such as nursery schools, kindergartens, primary grades, high schools, colleges, and universities; (4) political, such as city, state, and national governments, juvenile courts, political parties, and elections; (5) religious, such as the Methodist Church, the Christian Endeavor Society, and Revivalism; and (6) leisure-time, such as baseball, radio, amateur dramatics, and singing societies. Obviously culture complexes (as thus conceived) might be classified, differentiated, and subclassified in innumerable ways.

Culture complexes of the six basic types combine with each other in an almost infinite number of ways to create the general culture fabric of a society. Medieval European culture, for example, combined such complexes as a dominant Catholic religion, feudalistic political institutions, household industries, the patriarchal family, horse transportation, and the like. Each of these broad institutions included a vast variety of culture complexes.

This complex culture structure may be grasped more easily if we think of it in terms of a three-dimensional diagram—something like a vast five-layer cake, stretching back infinitely into the past, and sliced from front to back in six institutional slices. The above chart sketches the idea.

Vertically, culture traits may be classified into five levels, corresponding with the five layers of the cake. Each of these five layers is closely related to the sciences which have primary concern with them. On the material level are those culture traits dealt with primarily by physics, chemistry, geology, and other sub-biological sciences. On the biological level are those traits dealt with primarily by such sciences as zoology, botany, anatomy, physiology, and the medical sciences. On the psychological level are those traits dealt with primarily by psychology, functional psychiatry, educational science, and the like. On the sociological level are those traits dealt with by sociology, cultural anthropology, political science, and the like.

Checking back to the chart, it will be noted that each of the first five institutional slices is primarily related to one of the science levels, but that each also has aspects closely related to each of the other four levels. Economic institutions are concerned primarily with the material world. The family is primarily a biological institution, concerned with reproduction. Education is primarily psychological. Government is primarily sociological. Religion is primarily spiritual. And leisure-time institutions are related to all five science levels.

Every culture complex involves traits on at least all the lower four science levels. The automobile complex, for instance, consists (1), on the material level, of such items as the automobiles themselves, the factories and shops in which they are manufactured and repaired, and the machinery specifically designed for building them. (2) On the biological level, the automobile complex consists of the organisms of the individual drivers and passengers who use them, the workmen who build them, the engineers who design them, the salesmen who sell them, and the like. (3) On the psychological level, the automobile complex consists of such elements as the skills, interests, and attitudes of the people just enumerated, the literature about automobiles, including textbooks and instruction books for building and using them, and the special vocabulary developed in connection with automobiles. (4) On the social level, the complex consists of the organizations concerned with automobiles—such as manufacturing and sales corporations, automobile clubs, and highway police organizations. To the social level belong also the laws and rules controlling the driving, regulation, and sales of automobiles.

Every culture trait is dependent on a host of others. When a new invention is adopted into a culture complex, that adoption means the forming and modification of innumerable functional relationships with other traits and complexes. The TV set, for example, could be invented only by virtue of relations between electronic theory, glass-manufacturing techniques, the radio-broadcasting complex, electric-power-supplying systems, and so forth. Its adoption involved immediate adaptive changes in manufacturing and sales techniques, family habits of spending, use of leisure time, arrangements of furniture, appearance of the roof of the house, and so on. After its adoption, the TV complex precipitated changes in children's attention to their school work, public attendance at movies, dramatic techniques at studios, Congressional investigative procedures, political campaigning, advertising, religious propaganda, and so on.

CULTURAL LAG IS ALSO THREE-DIMENSIONAL

The wire hoop with the rubber bands stretched criss-cross on it provides a two-dimensional diagram of cultural lag. But actually we need three dimensions. We must think of culture interlaced with tensions, up and down, side to side, and past to present to future. Such a conception of culture is in accord with this statement by Ogburn: "The parts of civilization move forward or backward at different speeds. The strain which exists between two correlated parts of culture which change at unequal rates may be interpreted as a lag."[2]

Where the present analysis goes beyond Ogburn's is with respect to the inescapable complexity of cultural structure, and with respect to the importance of scientific thinking as compared with mechanical invention in causing social change. Dr. Ogburn said: "Inventions are of two kinds—mechanical (or technological), and social (or nonmaterial). We are inclined to favor the hypothesis of the greater importance of the sequence of technology causing social changes than of social conditions bringing about mechanical inventions."[3] Instead of merely two levels (mechanical and social), we seem quite clearly to need the five science levels. And instead of technology being the basic cause of change, our analysis regards creative thinking as primary.

It is true that creative thought has tended to produce inventions most prolifically on the mechanical level, and that these developments in technology have usually been the initiating factors in cultural tensions, with psychological, political and other social aspects requiring a considerable time lag before making the obviously needed adjustments. Yet a good many instances can be cited in which the leading factor has been political or sociopsychological. In other words, some striking forms of cultural lag emerge from the development of nontechnological innovations.

One example is the growth of grafting on the part of public officials and corruption on the part of citizens in connection with payment of income taxes. The progressive income tax may be regarded as a definite social invention, nontechnological in character. It is located on the sociological level of the political slice. Economists and other social scientists, studying the problem of taxation in relation to capacity to pay, and in relation to social values in general, came to the conclusion that persons with large incomes could pay to the government a larger percentage of those incomes with no more suffering or sacrifice than is involved in the payment of much smaller percentages by persons who receive smaller incomes. As a result of this development (which is actually a phase of social ethics rather than merely of economics or political science), elaborate legislation providing for progressive rates of taxation for larger and larger incomes has been developed. This means that persons with incomes of over $300,000 a year (for example) may pay as much as 88 per cent of their annual net income to the government.

In order to calculate the exact amount of income tax due, elaborate forms of bookkeeping are required, and a great many decisions have to be made as to the specific application of the statute to this or that kind of situation. To administer such regulations it is necessary to have a large staff of income-tax

[2] William F. Ogburn and Meyer F. Nimkoff, *Sociology* (Boston, Houghton Mifflin, 1940), pp. 859–860, 865, 885–886, 889–890; *ibid.*, 1950, pp. 561–563.
[3] *Ibid.*

collectors and agents. But since the amounts of money involved are often measured in thousands and quite frequently in hundreds of thousands or even millions of dollars per individual, the inducement to find some fraudulent method of escaping from part or all of the payment becomes intense. Unscrupulous receivers of large incomes are likely to try to find employees of the Revenue Service and of the Attorney General's department who can be bribed, directly or indirectly, to allow illegitimate deductions, to fail to prosecute illegal evasions, or to make unwarrantably generous settlements of tax claims.

The cultural lag in this case is the time interval between invention of progressive income taxation and the (still not completely achieved) development of adequate social controls to prevent tax frauds and to maintain honest tax payments.

Another instance of cultural lag resulting from nontechnological causes is the situation of elderly people in the United States at present. Indirectly, the increasing proportion of persons over the age of 65 can be traced back to the increasing expectation of life of the population, and this in turn is a result compounded from the great successes of medical science in preventing and curing disease, the rising standard of living resulting from the Industrial Revolution, and the progress in the application of science to manufacturing, agriculture, mining, and commerce. But the immediate development precipitating this particular instance of cultural lag is simply the change in the age distribution of the population, with a larger and larger number of persons over the age of 65, each of them (recently) having a longer and longer expectation of life. This social change, on the biological level, ramifies into all the six institutional slices.

Another social trend which has combined with this progressive aging of the population has been the development of industrial insurance plans. Employers have increasingly adopted programs under which benefits are paid to workers who are sick and in some cases to the survivors of workers who have died. Compensation for victims of industrial accidents has been another phase of this program. Insurance costs tend to rise steeply in the upper age brackets. The rates paid by employers for these insurance protections are lower if the average age of the employees is kept down. This puts a premium on discharging workers when they reach the age of 60 or 65 and on refusing to hire them after they reach 45. But the combination of the longer and longer life of the population with the increasing reluctance of employers to hire persons in the later decades of life has brought about a larger and larger reservoir of retired workers who suffer from a series of acute financial and emotional needs. Most persons beyond the age of 60 have no source of continuing income from their past labor period. A considerable fraction of these older people are taken into the homes of their married children, but this tends to create tensions, to burden the rising generation, to create domestic friction, to make both the old and the young people unhappy. These unemployed elderly people not only feel impoverished for lack of the opportunity to earn a living, but they also feel acutely their lack of useful occupation, their essential neglect and loneliness, and their feeling that they have been discarded as no longer useful.

This great body of more or less maladjusted old people creates major pressures for various forms of innovation. One striking product of the situation has been the movement for old-age pensions. The Townsend Plan became almost a national epidemic at one stage of this agitation. The "ham and eggs" plan proposed an extravagantly lavish program for old-age pensions. The Federal social security program has been progressively liberalized to pay larger and larger stipends to persons beyond the age of 65, and various other insurance schemes, both public and private, have been developed as partial answers to the need. Various programs for recreation and for social activities on the part of elderly people have grown up. But all of these developments have been slow and inadequate, with the result that this cultural lag is still with us and has no immediate prospect of being removed.

At the other end of the age-distribution problem, the recent rapid increase in child population has created several types of cultural lag. One example is our failure to construct school buildings fast enough to take care of the expanding school population. Closely related, but not entirely explainable in terms of child population, is the lag of school teachers' salaries behind wages in comparable occupations. The lag of educational curricula behind the established knowledge and demonstrated practices of modern education is another example.

Many other instances of cultural lag in the sociopsychological and political fields could be cited. One outstanding case is the failure of Europe to achieve a federated union of the democratic countries or even a customs union. Another is the lag in the treatment of African, Asiatic, and Oceanic peoples by the dominant democracies, as compared with the principles avowed in the constitutions and the collective pronouncements of these Western powers.

WHAT, THEN, DO WE REALLY MEAN BY CULTURAL LAG?

In the light of the above analysis, *cultural lag* may be defined as consisting in a time interval between two phases in the development of a culture complex or of two different culture complexes, where the length of the interval requires shortening in order better to promote generally accepted social ends, and where such shortening is regarded as potentially possible through social planning. When specific examples are studied, it becomes evident that two extremes must be distinguished.

One of these is implied by Stuart Chase's theory and may be referred to as *tandem lag*. In this sense, cultural lag consists in the time interval between a specific invention and the achievement of a specific adjustment called for by that invention. An example would be the lag between the invention of the automobile and the development of radar speed-timing.

The second type may be referred to as *complex lag*. This consists in the time interval between emergence of a stated social need (as the result of the development of a stated culture complex) and the meeting of that need by the development of adequate adaptive complexes. An example is the gap between the accelerating development of mass-destructive military technology and the lagging development of the international-law-and-order complex. A more generalized example is the lag which has often been pointed out between technology and social science.

Once the contrast is stated, it becomes evident that tandem lag and complex lag merge into each other. To regard the automobile as a single, specific invention is an obvious over simplification. Traffic accidents are the result of the developing highway-speed complex and of the lagging highway-safety complex. On the other hand, specific developments in the mass-destruction complex, such as the invention of the atomic bomb, have provided focal points of evident need for adaptive social inventions.

THE VALUATION ASPECTS OF THE LAG CONCEPT

One of the most frequent objections raised against the cultural-lag concept is that it inherently involves valuation. The issue reduces really to this question: "Can the value judgment implied in the term *lag* be reduced to objective and verifiable facts?" In considering this issue it is essential to recognize that all cultural behavior is dynamic, that most if not all invention is goal-directed, and that valuational aspects therefore cannot be excluded. Social change results from the dynamics involved in valuational behavior. The process can be understood only when this valuational behavior is dispassionately and fully understood, and when the problems involved are worked out along appropriate dynamic lines.

Any legitimate objection to the valuational implications of the cultural-lag concept may be eliminated by stating, explicitly and objectively, the value frame within which the lag to be investigated is conceived. A comprehensive study of the attitudes of sociologists toward value judgments has led to the formulation of certain conclusions which seem to be practically universally accepted. Among these is the proposition that it is entirely proper, scientifically, for applied sociology, having discovered what human purposes are most fundamental, or what ones are most widely accepted as ideal, to seek and disseminate knowledge as to how these purposes may be more adequately fulfilled.[4]

For example, it is almost universally conceded that the killing and maim-

4 Hornell Hart, "Value Judgments in Sociology," *American Sociological Review*, Vol. 3 (December, 1938), pp. 864–865.

ing of human beings through automobile accidents is undesirable. When technological progress increased the speed of automobiles, there was at first no concomitant increase in methods for preventing accidents. Granted that resulting rises in traffic death rates are contrary to the general welfare, it is a proper function of social science to work out methods for curing this particular form of lag.

THE MEASUREMENT OF CULTURAL LAG

One of the criticisms of loose uses of the cultural-lag concept has been that quite frequently a quantitative variable was implied but never actually defined or measured.[5]

The seriousness of this difficulty becomes increasingly evident when one attempts to reduce to actually quantitative terms some of the purportedly quantitative formulations of cultural lag. For example, how might one measure the "strain which exists between two correlated parts of culture which change at unequal rates," which strain constitutes cultural lag as defined by Professor Ogburn?

One method of measuring lag is in terms of a gap between two indexes using the same units. For example, one phase of the recent biological phenomenon of a rising birth rate is the increase which is now going on in the number of children of school age. This biological aspect of the family complex calls for an expansion in the material level of the school complex. But there is a marked lag in such expansion. The leading development can be measured in terms of the number of children needing places in school buildings, and the lagging variable can be measured in terms of the number of places available in the appropriate schools. The resulting lag variable has two dimensions—time, and number of places lacking in schools.

A second method of measuring cultural lag is to find a quantitative index of the unprevented or potential damage resulting from the innovation for which adaptive measures are lagging. Examples of this kind of lag-measurement are to be found in the chart on page 478.

THE LAG BETWEEN PHYSICAL SCIENCE AND SOCIAL SCIENCE

When expressions of concern on the part of social scientists and social thinkers in general are collected, it becomes evident that they are thinking of the problem in terms of complex lag rather than of tandem lag. A sampling of statements on the subject may serve to bring out this fact into clearer relief:

Dr. Sidney B. Fay, Professor Emeritus of History at Harvard, asserted on

[5] E.g., John Mueller, "Present Status of the Cultural Lag Hypothesis," *American Sociological Review*, Vol. 3 (June, 1938), p. 320.

December 28, 1946, as retiring president of the American Historical Association:[6]

Natural science has far outstripped social science. Our social skills have not kept pace with our technical skills. . . . We have discovered how to split the atom, but not how to make sure that it will be used for the improvement and not the destruction of mankind.

President Frank P. Graham, of the University of North Carolina (subsequently appointed United States Senator), said on February 6, 1946:[7]

Social mastery lags behind scientific knowledge, and the social conscience lags behind technological power.

Philip H. Hauser, Assistant Director of the Bureau of the Census, said, in August, 1946:[8]

Man's almost fantastic advances in harnessing the forces of nature can in large measure be traced to the laboratories of the physical and natural sciences. No corresponding connection can be traced between our social, economic and political institutions and the social sciences. . . . Although we have not yet managed to achieve social institutions in keeping with our present physical world, we stand at the threshold of a new physical revolution, alongside which the 'industrial revolution' as we experienced it, may well appear as a ripple on the tides of history.

Dr. Margaret Mead, Associate Curator of Anthropology of the American Museum of Natural History, said:[9]

Civilization has long been in an unbalanced state due to the different rates of progress in the social and physical sciences, but now that the atomic age has arrived, the situation is becoming dangerous.

William C. Menninger, President of the American Psychiatric Association, said:[10]

We have learned to eliminate space and to annihilate people, but we still lag far behind in learning how to get along with each other.

Gordon W. Allport wrote:[11]

Our plea is for an accelerated development of social engineering based on social research, to the end that we may overtake and control the ravages of a rampant and amoral technology.

The above six quotations all imply that the understanding and control of the material environment is one phase of cultural development, while the

[6] *New York Times,* December 29, 1946, p. 12, col. 3.
[7] *Durham Morning Herald,* February 7, 1946, p. 5, col. 5.
[8] *American Sociological Review,* Vol. 11 (August, 1946), p. 379.
[9] *New York Herald Tribune,* June 16, 1946, pp. 10, 11.
[10] *Time* (June 2, 1947), p. 74.
[11] For references to this and additional citations of similar import, see Hornell Hart, "Atomic Cultural Lag: 1. The Value Frame," *Sociology and Social Research,* Vol. 32 (March, 1948), p. 768.

understanding and control of social relations is another; and that progress in the material phase is rapid, whereas progress in the social phase has been disastrously slow.

NUCLEAR-AGE CULTURAL LAG

Recognizing cultural lag as a time interval between two phases in the development of culture complexes, and recognizing that such lags often consist of tensions between major aspects of culture, resulting in social damage or danger which can be measured, let us turn to the most outstanding example of menacing cultural lag in our world today: the accelerating development of the technologies of mass killing and destruction as contrasted with the vastly slower development of the means of international social control by which World War III might conceivably be prevented.

The fact that destructive technologies are accelerating more steeply than any other major aspect of human culture has been brought out in Chapter 3. The specific threat of paralysis raids, capable of causing the death of the United States as a nation, has been brought out in Chapter 10. These are the leading aspects in atomic cultural lag. What are the *lagging* factors?

One way in which the present danger from the accelerating technology of destruction has been measured, in Chapter 3, is in terms of the growth of the area in which human beings can kill each other from a given base. For comparison, some index is needed of the development of man's power to control such agencies of destruction. That power is vested in governments. A government (so long as it holds sway) exercises legal, political, and if necessary police power—imperfectly, but on the whole successfully—to suppress, arrest, restrain, and prevent would-be rebels who attempt to damage or destroy persons or property within its domain. Externally, a government exercises similar power by diplomacy, and if necessary by military force, to repel and expel invaders. The growth of the areas controlled by a unified government from a central capital provides an index to compare with the growth of destructive power, as represented by the expansion of the killing areas.[12]

The principle of cultural acceleration applies to political institutions as well as to mechanical inventions. Social organizations, as well as machines, are developed through the uniting of previously existing elements into new working combinations. The validity of this theory may be verified by checking it against the facts of political history.

Taking the history of Western civilization as a whole, the over-all trend of political growth has clearly been accelerating. Some intimation of this fact

[12] Size of territory is, of course, an imperfect index of governing power. It is used because it is directly related to the problem of civilian deaths from bombing, and because it is the only index for which it has been found possible to obtain reasonably dependable quantitative data to measure trends since ancient times.

can be caught from a comparison of the maximum size attained by each of three famous world empires:

Date	Empire	Maximum Governmental Area (sq. mi.)
1450 B.C.	Egyptian	690,000
117 A.D.	Roman	2,050,000
1940 A.D.	British	13,500,000

The accelerating expansion of governmental areas is clearer when the gains per 1,000-year period, in the maximum area ever ruled by a single government, are compared:

Period	Growth (in sq. mi.) per 1,000 Years
2000 B.C. to 1000 B.C.	440,000
1000 B.C. to 0 B.C.	1,630,000
0 A.D. to 1000 A.D.	2,060,000
1000 A.D. to 1950 A.D.	9,120,000

This evidence shows that the power to govern (as measured by maximum areas controlled) has grown more than four times as much in the past 1,000 years as in any previous 1,000-year period. Continuously uniform acceleration is by no means inevitable, as is indicated by the slackening of the rate during the Dark-Age period between 0 and 1000 A.D. But the over-all trend is unmistakable.

The development of governments among human beings has fallen into four eras: (1) the prehistoric; (2) the historic land-borne; (3) the sea-borne; and (4) the air-borne. The prehistoric era has been dealt with in another study.[13] That inquiry concluded that during the 50,000 years just preceding the dawn of history, the maximum areas controlled by any one people increased at accelerating speed.

The second period in the expansion of governmental areas was the historic land-borne. After history began, in the areas around the Mediterranean and also in China, the records of expanding political units became definite enough to estimate with reasonable accuracy the areas held by successive empires. During the major part of recorded history the greatest kingdoms and empires were conquered and maintained with little or no assistance of sea or air power. For the historic land-borne empires of the Western and Eastern worlds, the successive increases in record-breaking areas controlled by any single government (as estimated from the most reliable historical maps) are shown by the terraced lines in the chart on page 430. Like many other kinds of social trends, the growth of maximum land-borne empires was composed of subsurges, made up (in this case) of the growth of the successive, record-breaking areas. Any given point, on any terrace in the left-hand portion of

[13] Hornell Hart and Donald L. Taylor, "Was There a Prehistoric Trend from Smaller to Larger Political Units?" *American Journal of Sociology*, Vol. 49 (January, 1944), pp. 289–301.

GROWTH OF RECORD-BREAKING LAND-BORNE EMPIRES

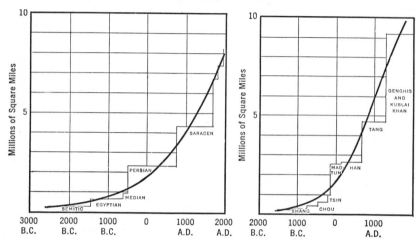

Western World (Centered in the Near East,   Eastern World (Centered in China)
North Africa, or Europe)

SOURCE: Hornell Hart, "Logistic Growth of Political Areas," *Social Forces,* Vol. 26 (May, 1948), pp. 398–405.

the chart, represents the largest land-borne area which up to that date had ever been ruled from a single capital in the Western world. Corresponding meanings apply to the points on the terraces in the right-hand portion of the chart.

The curved lines running through these terraces represent mathematically fitted trends. Such well-marked trends as these two cannot be dismissed as mere results of random fluctuation. Statistical analysis establishes, beyond any reasonable doubt, that a real accelerating trend has existed in each case.[14]

The growth of land-borne empires since 2400 B.C. has followed a 4,000-year-long-trend. If the horizontal time-scale is expanded to show the period since 1400 A.D., as in the chart on page 431, the land-borne-empire trend is a gently upward-sloping, almost straight line. The growth trend of Russia broke through this long-time slope at about 1735 A.D. For a little over 100 years, the land-borne realm of the Czar was the largest unit which had ever been governed from a single capital in the Western world. Then the greatest sea-borne empire of all history—the British—took the lead. American world leadership cannot be measured adequately in terms of square miles, but it does exemplify the fourth great era of world power—air-borne. The over-all record of man's growing power to govern (as measured rather crudely by the maximum territory under any single government at a given date) is shown by the top of the curves in the chart.

[14] Hornell Hart, "Logistic Growths of Political Areas," *Social Forces,* Vol. 26 (May, 1948), pp. 398–399.

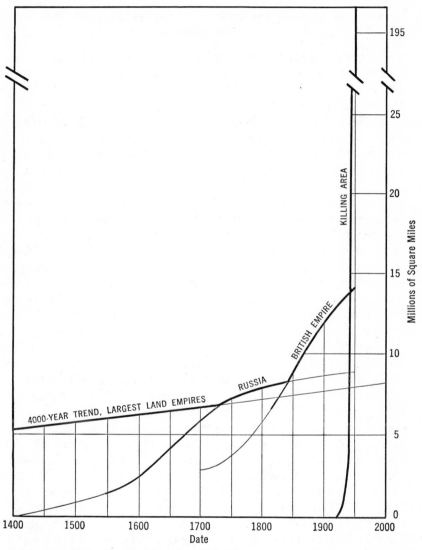

SOURCE: Hornell Hart, "Atomic Cultural Lag: II. Its Measurement," *Sociology and Social Research*, Vol. 32 (March, May, 1948), p. 847.

**THE SLOW INCREASE IN GOVERNING AREAS COMPARED WITH THE PRECIPITATE
GROWTH OF KILLING AREAS**

MEASURED LAG OF THE POWER TO GOVERN BEHIND THE POWER TO DESTROY

In spite of the acceleration which has just been pointed out, the political growth summarized above has evidently been lagging far behind the swift expansion in destructive technology summarized in Chapter 3 and epitomized by the growth of the killing area.

In atomic cultural lag, the leading variable is the maximum area within which, at any given date, people could be killed from a given base. The lagging variable is the ability to prevent this accelerating power from damaging or destroying the kind of civilization which is valued within the accepted frame of values. The "Largest Land . . . ," Russian, and British curves in the previous chart represent the best available index for this purpose. They show the growth of the maximum areas within which any single government has exercised police and defense power up to the given dates. Just as the steepest curve (at the right) represents growth in areas over which destruction can be waged from a given center, so the more gradual curves represent growth in areas over which legal, political, and defensive control has been exercised from a given center. Up to the date of this writing, neither the League of Nations nor the United Nations has developed effective authority to arrest, restrain, or forcibly prevent would-be destroyers of life and property, except in minor conflicts where no great power has felt its vital interests to be menaced by the control. If the United Nations did develop adequate international control, its area would then have to be included in the index.

Although the killing area had been growing with slow acceleration since before the dawn of history, the chart shows that in 1900 it was still almost negligible compared with the governing area. Indeed, as late as 1912, the longest recorded range for projectiles was 11.4 miles, giving an area of approximately 408 square miles. From that date onward, however, the killing area increased precipitately. In 1944 it surpassed the size of the largest governing area ever attained. In 1948 the "tactical radius" for bombing was 3,900 miles, giving a killing area of approximately 45,000,000 square miles.[15] The development of refueling in the air, and the development of bombers of still greater range, have extended the potential killing radius to globe-encircling dimensions.[16] The lag in 1954 was then measurable in the ratio between the maximum governing area attained at that date (approximately 13,500,000 square miles) and the 197,000,000 square miles of the earth's surface, to which the killing area has now expanded.

The slowness of growth toward world government, in contrast with the swiftness of our plunge toward world destruction, has been summarized graphically in the last chart. It can be depicted also in another way, as in the following chart. The relative sizes of four circles show the relationships

---

[15] *New York Herald Tribune,* March 21, 1948, p. II 9.
[16] See "Gas Stations in the Sky," *Science Digest,* Vol. 26 (December, 1949), pp. 23 ff.

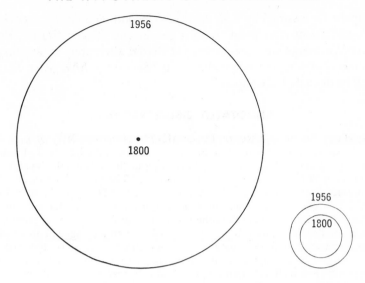

**GROWTH IN MAN'S POWER TO KILL COMPARED WITH GROWTH
IN MAN'S POWER TO GOVERN**

Left: Growth in the largest area within which men could be killed from a single base,
1800–1956.

Right: Growth in the largest area within which men have been governed from one central
capital, 1800–1956.

between these two rates of growth. Look first at the two on the right. These
represent, for the past century and a half, the growth in man's power to
govern as measured by the largest land area controlled by any single government. In 1800 Russia held the record, with a little under 8,000,000
square miles; by 1950 Great Britain had pushed the record up to 13,500,000.
The power to govern *had* been growing. But compare that growth with the
increase in the power to kill. On the left, the dot at the center represents the
largest area, in the year 1800, within which one man could kill his fellows
from a given base. With the best artillery available at that date, the maximum
killing area was approximately 4.5 square miles. But while the governing
area has somewhat less than doubled, the killing area has increased at least
40,000,000-fold. With the aid of refueling in the air, bombing planes now
in use, taking off from a given base, have the potential power to kill anyone
anywhere on the entire surface of the earth. In 1800 the maximum killing
area was a minute fraction of the maximum governing area. But today the
area of slaughter far exceeds any area of control. This, then, constitutes one
index of the concrete meaning of atomic cultural lag.

MUST THE CULTURAL-GAP KEEP GROWING WIDER AND WIDER?

If technology inevitably develops faster than social science, then the problems of social control will become ever more huge, while the means of control

will progress far less rapidly than the need. Uncontrolled destructiveness on a vaster and vaster scale points toward greater and greater disaster. But is this Ever-Widening-Gap Theory correct? Before attempting an answer, we must consider an alternative hypothesis—*the Successive Emergence Theory.* This will be discussed in Chapter 21.

ANNOTATED BIBLIOGRAPHY

BARNES, Harry Elmer, and RUEDI, Oreen M., *The American Way of Life: Our Institutional Patterns and Social Problems,* Englewood Cliffs, N. J., Prentice-Hall, 1942 and 1950), Ch. I, "Cultural Lag in the Twentieth Century: Institutional Windmills in an Age of Dynamos." The keynote of this book is contained in the following sentences from page 5: "The expression, 'cultural lag' . . . refers to the fact that in modern times material culture has changed far more rapidly than the social setting. Progress in economic, political, and social relationships with our fellow men has lagged behind progress in science and technology. . . . Our institutions have changed far more slowly than our technical equipment. Why is there such determined opposition as we all too often find to social reforms? The reasons are numerous and diverse. . . ."

MERRILL, Francis E., and ELDREDGE, H. Wentworth, *Culture and Society, An Introduction to Sociology* (Englewood Cliffs, N. J., Prentice-Hall, 1952), pp. 512–529. A recent textbook develops some of the implications of Ogburn's theory of cultural lag.

ODUM, Howard W., *Understanding Society: The Principles of Dynamic Sociology,* (New York, Macmillan, 1947), Ch. 12: "The Folkways, the Mores, the Technicways," pp. 225–239; Ch. 20: "The Technicways in Modern Society," pp. 363–374. Odum's concept of "Technicways," as related to the folkways and the mores, presents a stimulating different view of the inter-relations of various aspects of social change.

OGBURN, William F., *Social Change* (New York, Viking Press, 1922, 1928, 1950), pp. 200–280. This is the first source of the cultural-lag concept, published originally in 1922, and reissued by the publishers in 1950, with a supplementary chapter by Dr. Ogburn.

SCHNEIDER, Joseph, "Cultural Lag: What Is It?" *American Sociological Review,* Vol. 10 (December, 1945), pp. 786–791; HART, Hornell, "Atomic Cultural Lag: I. The Value Frame; II. Its Measurement," *Sociology and Social Research,* Vol. 32 (March, May, 1948), pp. 768–775, 845–855. These two articles constitute the nearest approach to a definitive summary of discussions of cultural lag up to 1948.

SIMS, Newell LeRoy, *The Problem of Social Change* (New York, Crowell, 1939), pp. 260–262, 290–296. Cultural lag is discussed, with fairly extended comments on the Ogburn theory. Cultural acceleration, however, appears not to be mentioned.

CHAPTER 18

MAJOR PROBLEMS ARISING FROM RAPID SOCIAL CHANGE

■ Hornell Hart and Francis R. Allen

As HAS BEEN SHOWN in Chapter 17, lag is inherent in the very nature of any change in culture. Because of the interdependence of culture traits and of culture complexes, every new invention is certain to upset to a greater or less degree the existing adjustments and is likely to create tensions calling (1) for the correction of damage done, and (2) for the development of further inventions which have been made possible by the newly introduced trait or complex. Many adjustments are likely to be needed in other parts of culture.

In this chapter we examine various broad types of lags or of other problems which are related to times of rapid social change. We consider (1) the lag of the general public behind the experts in knowledge of various fields; (2) the lag of many government officials' actual knowledge of the social science fields, which have been rapidly expanding; (3) problems of university instructors as related to times of rapid change; (4) women's problems in relation to the present era of rapid social change; and (5) problems of nations arising from the fact that some nations have industrialized rapidly and have high standards of living, while others are "underdeveloped" and have low living standards.

LAG OF THE PUBLIC BEHIND THE EXPERTS

The swiftest cultural changes which we have found in the preceding chapters have been those developing from technological inventions. Underlying these inventions, and basic through the whole problem of accelerating social change, has been the increasingly rapid growth of the sciences. This scientific knowledge, by its very nature, becomes the possession of a relatively small body of experts. This is true for two fundamental reasons. First, the achievement and development of scientific knowledge require specialization. The higher the level of culture, the greater the specialization required; and this is particularly true in the field of science. The second reason why experts are needed is that the capacity to master scientific knowledge varies immensely.

The development of expert knowledge is reflected in the growth of higher education. The greater the progress in these advanced fields of education, the greater the gap between the trained experts and the people who drop out in the grades, in high school, or in undergraduate college. When Einstein announced his theory of relativity, it was said that there were only twelve men in the world who were capable of understanding the mathematics on which that theory was based.

This development of rarefied scientific specialties is accompanied by the fact that the great rank and file of the public is entirely incapable of grasping what the specialists are thinking, talking, and writing about—and to a very great extent are incapable even of appreciating the importance of what the experts are doing. Fifty years ago it used to be taken for granted quite widely that everybody (if given a proper education) would want to read newspapers like *The New York Times,* magazines like the *Atlantic Monthly* and *Scientific American,* novels produced by the top level of literary genius, and plays written by the greatest dramatists. But about that time William Randolph Hearst discovered moronia. He and other "yellow journalists" found that they could swiftly build up immense circulations by concentrating on such interests as sex, horror, money, and funnies.[1] These same four basic thrill interests proved to be the open sesame to treasure trove in the publication of pulp magazines and cheap books. They also became the keynote for moving pictures, radio, and television.

If the moron cares to go to the polling place, his vote counts just as much as that of an Einstein. Moreover, the trend of our economic development is determined by the way in which people spend their money. Purchasing power is not very closely correlated with intelligence. The kind of movies produced depends upon "box-office"; the kind of TV shows put on the air depends upon the Trendex rating, indicating how many potential purchasers are listening to the commercial to which the program is hitched. Book manuscripts find difficulty in getting published unless they have an appeal to mass purchasing power. In other words, votes and dollars represent the basis for a large part of the power in democracies, and the experts are not usually able to make their wisdom effective in guiding the ways in which power from these sources is used. Various types of cultural lag develop as a result of the factors which have just been summarized.

Restriction versus Encouragement of International Trade

For generations, experts in economics have been pointing out the advantages of international trade. Every nation has a relative advantage over other nations in the production of certain goods and services, but suffers disadvantages in the production of certain other goods and services. Ideally, the citizens of each nation can attain the highest standard of living by specializ-

---

[1] See Susan M. Kingsbury, Hornell Hart, and others, *Newspapers and the News* (New York, Putnam, 1937), pp. 3–39.

ing in producing the former, and then exchanging these for the goods and services in producing which they are at the greatest relative disadvantage. Economists have long known that no nation can really get rich by selling its goods and services for money and credit certificates without taking goods and services in return from other nations. Yet the hallucination that the wealth of a nation consists in its "favorable trade balance," and in the pile of gold or the stack of certificates of indebtedness which it or its citizens accumulate, has repeatedly and persistently dominated the Congress of the United States and the policies of our political parties. The failure of the public to assimilate the basic facts about international trade is compounded by the rapid evolution which has taken place in international finances and in the development of techniques for interfering with international trade—such as quota systems and the manipulation of currencies.

Part of the difficulty consists in the fact that uneconomic industries get built up under tariff protection, and then the very livelihood of the owners and the workers in those industries comes to depend upon the maintenance of these high tariffs—or even on a still further increase of the protection. The sugar-beet growers and processers, the sheep herders and wool spinners and weavers, found themselves in a situation where lowering the tariffs would ruin their industries and put tens of thousands of people out of work. These interests were vital to them, whereas the extra cost of sugar and of wool clothing to the general public, while even greater in total amount than the advantage to the protected industries, was spread out so thinly that the average citizen—even if he had realized his loss—could not afford to take the time and put forth the effort necessary to protect himself against high tariffs.

Not only consumers but also exporters suffer as a result of high tariffs. The interests of the exporters are more concentrated and more intense than the interests of the consumers and hence tend to be more effective—though the pressures are not in general so crucial as those upon groups who feel that their economic status would be ruined by lowering the tariffs. However, the economists and statesmen who looked at these problems from the standpoint of national welfare gradually developed such mechanisms as the Reciprocal Trade Agreements Act, and gradually succeeded in opening up the channels of international trade for a freer exchange of goods, with resulting benefit to both the United States and foreign nations.

Public Attitudes toward the United Nations

The problem of international organization has been studied by two major groups of experts. The first group consists of political scientists, historians, international lawyers, and other academic specialists who have been gathering library information on the subject. The second group consists of the diplomats—the foreign offices of the various governments, the representatives (such as ambassadors and consuls) which they have exchanged with one another, and the delegates of the various nations to international conferences and to the United Nations. The second group has been accumulating actual operational experience in international collaboration and has been accumulating its own type of library material in the form of reports and other documents.

The growth of expert knowledge, understanding, and skill in the field of international relations seems at first view to have been lethargically slow in comparison to the acceleration in the military technology of destruction. But if one considers the developments which have occurred since 1800, the accelerating progress in this field becomes evident. The rapid growth of international arbitration between 1820 and 1900 may be gathered from the following figures:[2]

Dates	Instances
1820–1840	8
1840–1860	30
1860–1880	44
1880–1900	90

The above figures show marked acceleration, even in that early stage in the development of international law and order, comparable to that which was occurring at about that time in mechanical inventions. As in the case of mechanical inventions, the idea of the establishment of a permanent tribunal for the pacific settlement of international disputes had been put forward long before its realization—by Jeremy Bentham toward the close of the eighteenth century, and by James Mill in the middle of the nineteenth century. The permanent court of arbitration at The Hague was established in 1899 as the outcome of a conference summoned on the initiative of the Czar of Russia. The establishment of the League of Nations after World War I and of the United Nations after World War II represent further developments of increasing magnitude and importance toward international organization and the achievement of international law and order.

The swift growth of theoretical and practical knowledge about international co-operation, which is reflected in the above developments, presents a striking example of the lag of general public knowledge and sentiment behind the knowledge of the specialists. Two major groups of people give evidence of marked failure to keep up with the knowledge of the experts. The first group has been made up of the various movements which have proposed to establish world government by some sudden short-cut.[3] These movements, in general, have been carried away by oversimplified ideas which seemed to their adherents to be the key to a world solution. For ex-

[2] *Encyclopedia Britannica* (1929), Vol. 2, p. 222D.
[3] For a detailed review of leading movements of this sort see Hornell Hart, ed., *Toward Consensus for World Law and Order,* a Cooperative Project, lithoprinted, June, 1950.

ample, Ely Culbertson had a formula for armament ratios which he felt would insure the world against aggression. Clarence K. Streit proposed a Federal Union of the democracies, with power sufficient to overwhelm any aggressor. (The North Atlantic Treaty Organization may be regarded as to some extent an embodiment of this idea in more realistic terms.) The World Constitution movement, centered at the University of Chicago, drafted an idealistic and highly socialistic constitution for world government, with the apparent hope that it might be adopted by the nations of the world. The United World Federalists have a plan for a minimum world organization adequate to prevent aggression, but leaving other functions as far as possible to individual governments. Quakers operate on the faith that pacificism, based on brotherly love, would be an adequate solution. All of these plans, and other one-idea solutions, have ignored the basic fact that communism regards world conflict as inevitable until communistic dictatorship (as they hope and plan) takes possession of the earth.

The second major group which has failed to assimilate the findings of the experts consists of those who are such intense nationalists that any idea of supra-national government—or even of action through the United Nations— appears to them to be hateful treason. In the United States, the *Chicago Tribune* has been an outstanding vehicle for such ideas. The American Legion and various "100-per cent American" organizations and movements have been vociferous in their propaganda against the UN and UNESCO. Senator Joseph McCarthy, of Wisconsin, also sponsored this view repeatedly.

Insofar as the advocates of world government and the anti-UN agitators have stirred up discussion, they have undoubtedly contributed toward a better understanding of the realities with which mankind must come to grips if world law and order are to be established and preserved. But it seems increasingly clear that in the area of international relations—as in every other field of complex human problems—there is an inescapable need for systematic, rigorous, and increasingly operational research by expert specialists, and that only on the basis of science (as thus interpreted) can genuine and sound progress be achieved.

One critic has objected that the above paragraph seems to him to overlook the democratic process. But democracy does not consist in every citizen becoming equally expert on every possible subject. Democracy consists in government by consent of the governed. The experts must win the confidence of the people whose lives are affected by their expert decisions. That means, in the long run, that they must deserve that confidence, and that they must win as high a degree of popular understanding as practicable. But the rank and file of the public will be more and more incapable of understanding the technical problems of government, in proportion as the advancement of science makes those problems more and more complex and specialized.

Summary on the Lag of the Public Behind the Experts

1. To a greater or less degree, the lag of public opinion behind the knowledge of the specialists is inevitable. In every field—including the systematic study of social problems—the specialists are bound to acquire knowledge and skills which are inaccessible to the general public who lack the time and may lack the ability or interest to master such fields.

2. Part of the difficulty lies in the misconception that democracy consists in equality. If we could re-educate our citizens to accepting the fact that democracy consists in government by consent of the governed, and that this consent often must be based upon willingness to accept the conclusions reached by experts, our democratic institutions might become more effective.

3. Another part of the difficulty, in connection with cultural lags of the kind discussed in this section, is the fact that pure intellectual search for truth is obstructed and often misdirected by the pressures of intense emotional needs and desires. The success or failure of one's economic activities, the snatching of one's son, husband, or lover into far-off wars, the venting of one's indignation against shocking crime—and even the expression of one's fanatical enthusiasm for some pet idea—may make the public blind to basic truths which (to dispassionate experts) seem indisputable.

4. One of the urgent responsibilities of behavioral scientists is to come to grips with the kinds of problems represented by the above illustrations. Granted that mankind will enjoy richer, more abundant, and more secure living if the wisdom of specialists is adopted and made use of by the voters and their chosen representatives, the behavioral-science problem then reduces to questions (1) of how such lags as those described in this book could be cured or averted if expert opinions could be adopted, and then (2) of how the expert solutions can be brought into effect.

LAG OF GOVERNMENT BEHIND SOCIAL SCIENCE

In the preceding section we have reviewed some areas in which the general public has lagged behind the knowledge of specialists with respect to specific social problems. The present section deals with what is really a subdivision of that broad topic, namely, the lag in information and knowledge on the part of government officials at all levels—in the legislative, judicial, and executive branches of government. Of course, some government officials *are* experts. Hence it should be made clear that in this section we are not referring to expertly and technically-informed specialists such as those employed by the Bureau of the Census, by the Department of Agriculture, Department of State, Department of Commerce, and so on, but to others in the various governmental categories as noted in the following pages: (More will be said about administrative specialists presently).

Some Reasons for Lag in Senatorial Efficiency

Consider, for example, the situation of a United States senator. It must always be remembered that the first requirement for the incumbent of an elective office in a democratic government is the capacity to get elected. The senator may often go to Washington with no special preparation for deciding national and international problems aside from "social studies" and history courses which he had in high school, and perhaps a few elementary college courses in such subjects as economics, psychology, sociology, or political science. When he is established in his office in the Senate Building, he finds that a quite large share of his time is occupied by demands from his constituents for special favors. In order to build his reputation, he of course wants to be on important senatorial committees, and he finds that a great deal of his time when he attends meetings of these committees is occupied in hearing the rambling and often irrelevant testimony of witnesses who are frequently ill-informed and who are frequently interrupted by captious and ill-considered questions. Much of the real acomplishment of such committees is contributed by employed experts who do the research and draft the reports.

With this sort of background and with such demands constantly crowding upon and frittering away his time, the senator is expected to become informed on a series of crucial and involved questions—such as tariffs, taxation, racial segregation, juvenile delinquency, organized crime, freedom of the press, aviation, the warlike and peaceful uses of nuclear energy, higher education for GI's, social security payments for the aged, whether professional women should be allowed to deduct the cost of baby-sitters in figuring their income taxes, the bearing of price-support payments on each of scores of different branches of agriculture, the research program of the agricultural department relative to the canning of peaches; the proper functions, powers, budgeting, and selection of personnel for the UN; whether Chiang Kai-shek's hold on two small islands off the coast of China shall be defended by the United States of America; whether to negotiate with the Soviet government about each of a long series of world problems, and, if so, on what basis; what to do about radioactive fall-out; how to keep Israel and Egypt from starting a war—and so forth and so forth and so forth.

Unquestionably, eminently qualified individuals do sometimes get elected or appointed to the Senate. For example, Professor Paul H. Douglas, from the University of Chicago, who was an expert on unemployment and other economic questions, has repeatedly been elected United States Senator from Illinois. Dr. Frank P. Graham, former President of the University of North Carolina, was appointed United States Senator from that state—but failed to be re-elected. Sometimes eminent newspaper men, with broad backgrounds of knowledge of national and international affairs, are elected to the Senate. Sometimes senators have had a long and more or less effective apprenticeship in the House of Representatives or in state legislatures. But if a senator is well qualified in any one subject with which Congress must deal, that means ipso facto that he cannot have spent enough time on other subjects to become expert in these other lines. It is not a question of dereliction of duty on the part of our elected representatives; it is simply a question of the basic limitations in the amount of attention which the human mind can pay to given subjects in a given period of time, and of the basic acceleration which has been taking place in our culture. New knowledge has been proliferating so rapidly, and new complexities have been piled so monumentally upon old complexities, that it has become more and more absurd to expect any single human being to have even the background of knowledge necessary to comprehend the questions upon which public decisions must be made.

In the United States Senate and the House of Representatives (and similarly in state and local legislative bodies), it usually happens that certain individuals become specialists in lines in which they have some initial interest. Thus, one senator gets to know a great deal more than other senators do about income taxation, whereas another informs himself to an unusual extent about international trade. Another becomes interested in labor problems, and another in agriculture. These specialists are listened to with more or less respect by their colleagues. They have more voice than others do in the framing of legislation in their special fields. Undoubtedly, only the devoted activities of such specialists prevent our government from making even more disastrous blunders than those which often emerge from the decisions of Congress and of administrators and judges.

Lag in the Executive Branch

Persons appointed to office in the executive branch of the government are, of course, far more likely to have specialized in the fields to which they are appointed. But the special skills required for these various offices are often subordinated to political considerations—such as the amount of help which the individual or his friends gave in the election of the President of the United States or of senators and congressmen who recommend their appointment.

One of the major functions of officials in the executive branch is to advise members of Congress in connection with the framing of legislation. When competent specialists from government offices are summoned before Congressional committees, and when the hearings are intelligently conducted, much specialized knowledge can be brought to bear upon problems before the committee. But many chairmen and committee members make use of their power at such hearings for purposes not conducive to the public interest. Because of the appropriating and appointing powers, members of Congress can often intimidate administration witnesses and can suppress what a disinterested expert might want to say, thus forcing the hearing into line with the prejudices or special interests of the senator or representative. The hysteria about internal security has been exploited by various senators and representatives who have gained national notoriety by harassing witnesses. The persecution of experts—particularly the most vitally needed experts in fields of nuclear energy, of military technology, taxation, international relations, and other crucial fields—has made it increasingly difficult to secure the services of competent men and women in appointive positions.

All of these difficulties are intensified by the swiftness of cultural change. It would be hard enough for our legislators and government executives if they merely had to become acquainted with the ramifications of our national life at the present moment. When what they learned a year or two ago may be obsolete and misleading today, the task of intelligent government becomes still more difficult.

Lag in the Legal Branch

In the judicial field, adjustment to current problems has special difficulties. To become a lawyer competent enough to be elected or appointed to an important judgeship requires that a man spend long years of very intensive study of legislation and judicial decisions. Laws are based upon a highly developed and very specialized system of thought. Under the Anglo-American legal system, laws are applied by judicial interpretation. What judges think, and how much judges know about the world of ordinary men, is of prime importance in making the legal system fit that ordinary world. Decisions tend to be derived from the brief of one attorney or another. The working attorney is even busier than the judge, and his view of the social and economic problems he deals with may be even more limited.

One striking example of the resulting archaism of the law is the legal definition of insanity, which was laid down by the Law Lords in England in the early nineteenth century, and which legislators and judges all over the United States still attempt to apply, overruling the insistence of psychiatrists who point out that this legal definition has little or nothing to do with the medical facts.

The volumes of national and state legislation, and of court decisions based on that legislation and on common law, multiply so rapidly that law libraries find difficulty in keeping abreast. Lawyers and judges do well if they are able to keep up their reading in the legal field. This makes it extremely difficult for members of the legal profession to find time to become acquainted with new developments of thought in such fields as economics, political science, psychology, and sociology. The legal system itself has an immense inertia, and its basic methods of thinking were evolved long before the behavioral sciences had even been born. As a result, our legal system tends to be riddled with archaic ideas and practices.

Problems of University Instructors as Related to Rapidly Changing Times

The vast majority of public servants doubtless endeavor to execute their job faithfully and to the best of their ability. Often they do not have the time to acquaint themselves with expanding knowledge in academic fields. Probably many of these very officials wish more than anyone else that they could be better informed as to relevant social-science knowledge that might aid them in their tasks.

How about the college or university instructor whose primary obligation is to acquaint himself with the expanding knowledge of his specialty, to teach it to his students, and if possible to add to this knowledge himself? If the government worker cannot be expected to "keep up" with abounding knowledge, surely (the outsider might think) this would be relatively easy for the professor. The fact is that in times of rapid social change and swift accumulation of knowledge, even this is much more of a problem than the uninitiated might think. In the various social science fields (including international relations) and in virtually all of the physical sciences—to cite a few areas—this can be a difficult problem indeed. In fact, the modern college teacher is likely to be just about as harried on the average as the government man.

Even though keeping abreast of developments in his field is positively expected—it is "his job"—nevertheless the professor knows full well that this means "keeping up" with a vast outpouring of books off the presses, a large volume of research projects, dozens of new developments which may be described at professional meetings, considerable journal reading, many governmental reports and documents, and other miscellaneous developments. To keep up with the annual outpouring is not easy, but the conscientious professor will at least try. Moreover, he may be burdened with a full teaching schedule—which, after all, is the main activity of the college or university. He may also be loaded with administrative and other duties.

The average college teacher usually learns soon that he cannot keep up properly with a whole field of knowledge like sociology, economics, physics, or chemistry, in times of rapid accumulation of ideas as the present. Thus he usually tries to narrow the field and specialize in a subfield such as (in sociology) population, the family, race, or social change. Here there is a better chance of keeping abreast of developments. However, even in many subfields the literature will be profuse. Nevertheless, keeping up in one's specialty is clearly expected in the teaching occupation, and most teachers will achieve it in one way or another. They will, for one thing, learn to distinguish consequential developments in the area from the more trivial, and should certainly be informed as to the former.

There are other problems related to the effects of rapid change on education, such as that of endeavoring to keep textbooks up-to-date. In some specialties as nuclear physics, a new textbook may be *really* out-of-date by the time it is issued from the presses. A further matter is the impact of social change on whole fields of study. In Chapter 9 the effects of aviation on various disciplines were discussed. Concerning the many effects of social change on education, further comment is impossible here.

WOMEN'S PROBLEMS IN THE FACE OF RAPID SOCIAL CHANGE[4]

A large majority of all the productive processes which used to be women's responsibility in the home have been transferred, in Western nations, to factories. The woman who presided over a home in colonial times had a crowded life, in which she occupied a position of economic importance and even of necessity to her husband and children. But in our shrunken modern homes, only a small fraction of the older activities are still conducted.

One of the best ways to live richly and usefully is to commit one's life to at least a few major projects. Men still find satisfying life projects in the careers to which they devote themselves, in marriage, in hobbies, in sports, and in civic interests. But how about women? How have technological developments and the resultant transfer of functions from the home to outside centers affected their fulfillment of life? Several different lines of solution have been adopted.

1. A gradually increasing proportion of our women are engaged in paid occupations. The percentage of married women working outside of their homes increased from less than 5 per cent in 1890 to over 27 per cent in 1953.[5]

2. Many women have made use of the release from drudgery which technology has given them to concentrate on the more creative and leisurely aspects of homemaking.

3. Being freed from household drudgery has given many women an opportunity to engage more fully in civic, philanthropic, and religious activities.

4. To a large and perhaps unrealized extent, women have turned attention to fantasy activities. TV, pulp magazines, paper-bound novels, and moving pictures have provided vast channels for fantasy experience.

5. Some of the leisure increasingly provided through technological inventions and through the resulting shrinkage of family responsibilities has undoubtedly been turned into dissipated and unsocial if not antisocial forms.

How has the increasing amount of education of modern women affected their status and functioning? In the Middle Ages, education was the monopoly of a very small group of monks and other privileged individuals, almost all of whom were men. In American colonial days, education beyond the three R's was the monopoly of a small male minority. Since 1880, high-school and college education has rapidly been extended—first to a larger and larger proportion of men, and then (with relatively slight lag) to a larger and larger proportion of women. For example, in 1910, only 43 per cent of persons aged 16 and 17 in the United States were enrolled in school; but by 1950 this had jumped to 74 per cent.

[4] Cf. Nelson N. Foote, "Changes in American Marriage Patterns and the Role of Women," *Eugenics Quarterly*, Vol. 1 (December, 1954), pp. 254–260.

[5] *Statistical Abstract of the United States, 1954* (Washington, Government Printing Office, 1955), pp. 194, 204.

Cultural lag has been evident in the slowness with which curriculums have adjusted to the actual needs of modern life. This has been less true in secondary than in higher education. High school girls now almost universally take courses in domestic science, and courses in courtship and marriage are increasingly prevalent. Business courses also provide many girls with skills in stenography, typewriting, and bookkeeping. Social studies courses in high school are more and more adapted to putting adolescents into touch with the realities of modern life and with their responsibilities and opportunities as citizens as well as consumers.

Colleges have been relatively resistant to shifting from traditional education to studies having practical bearing upon success in modern living. Ancient and foreign languages, pure mathematics, philosophy studied as an intellectual exercise having little connection with practical problems, laboratory sciences divorced as much as possible from practical applications—such courses have occupied and still do occupy large places in the so-called education of women as well as men. Professional schools have become more and more realistic in their training of men for earning a living and succeeding in their vocations. But women are still kept to very small minorities in such schools. And many if not most colleges of liberal arts pride themselves upon being purely intellectual, and avoiding any sort of course which would be useful in later life aside from training the individual for mental activity for its own sake.

Modern college girls manage, to a considerable extent, to escape from this sterility. They swarm into courses on marriage and the family, child psychology, child welfare, sociology, social work, politics, art, drama, literature, music, and other courses from which they may obtain real help toward successful living as individuals and as citizens.

One of the anachronisms of modern life is the way in which education (as well as many other of our social institutions) has been allowed to stumble and fumble along, operating still on the momentum of the Renaissance and adapting only blindly and short-sightedly to urgent pressures from current modern life. Perhaps if the behavioral sciences really achieve operational validity, education may be viewed in a far more realistic and functional manner, and some daring innovators may develop methods of training both women and men in ways which will be closely and deliberately connected with their actual needs and desires.

INDUSTRIALIZED NATIONS AND "UNDERDEVELOPED" ONES

Another problem resulting from rapid social change has been the disparity between the standard of living found in certain nations of the world and that found in other nations. The United States, for example, has experienced a rapid rise in its living standards during the first half of the twentieth century, owing largely, one may add, to the influence of technology. Ogburn has concluded, on the basis of three sets of data, that the standard of living of the American people in terms of what money buys has doubled during this time period.[6] On the other hand, the standard of living has not risen appreciably in other areas in the world, and in some instances is distressingly low. The latter are frequently known as "underdeveloped areas." Fairfield Osborn has divided the nations of the world into three groups based on their standard of living. He declares:[7]

The first (group) consists of most of Western Europe, of North America, and of Australia and New Zealand. This group contains about one-fifth of the world's population and is characterized . . . as having low birth rates, low death rates, high average food supply . . . and a population increasing less rapidly than the world average.

The second group, containing another one-fifth of the world's population, consists of Eastern and Southeastern Europe, Spain, a few South American countries like Brazil and Argentina, and finally Japan. This group can be described as having a moderate and rising industrial activity, a high but falling birth rate, and a medium but falling death rate. . . .

The third group can be described as the truly critical one—and rightly so. It contains three-fifths of the world's population and takes in most of Asia and some of its adjacent islands, most of Africa as well as major portions of South and Central America. Its population of almost one and a half billion people lives at or near a starvation level, with an estimated two thousand calories or less per day for each individual. It has, in general, a high birth rate, a high but widely fluctuating death rate, which drops when harvests are good and there are no epidemics, and soars under opposite conditions. . . .

To have a high and increasing standard of living in some nations while other populations live more or less at the poverty level presents problems. First of all, people in the latter nations are likely to develop an unwholesome envy of the people whose standard of living is high. Travelers or official representatives from the wealthier nations may tend to show off and strut with their luxurious possessions before the eyes of the misery-ridden Asiatics and Africans. Such conditions skew not only the economy but human relations, as Stuart Chase has pointed out.[8]

The present is no time, moreover, to have foreign economies and human relations skewed. America and other economically advanced nations need all possible friends in the world. In view of the world struggle with communist Russia which probably has not abated despite the Geneva Conference of July, 1955, America has no wish for "unwholesome envy" to exist in the minds of millions of foreigners. Certainly in a "cold war" world, the United States does not want millions of underprivileged peoples to embrace

[6] William F. Ogburn, "Technology and the Standard of Living in the United States," *American Journal of Sociology*, Vol. LX, No. 4 (January, 1955), pp. 380–386.

[7] Fairfield Osborn, "Their Need—Our Obligation," *Bulletin of the Atomic Scientists*, Vol. X, No. 3 (March, 1954), Technical Assistance Programs: Part I, p. 73.

[8] Stuart Chase, "New Energy for a New Age," *Saturday Review* (January 22, 1955), p. 36.

communism; the loss of China was severe enough. Yet it is known that want and misery are the breeding ground of social and political unrest, and communism has great appeal under such conditions. On the other hand, what *is* wanted—cordial, constructive global relations—can hardly prosper when millions of people have empty stomachs and uneducated minds. Hence this problem of underdeveloped areas is related to the world power struggle and, further, to the possibilities of world peace.[9]

Then, many American citizens and government officials and those of other economically advanced nations may have genuine sympathy toward the millions of misery-ridden, starving people of the world and desire to see an improvement in living conditions in these underdeveloped areas *for its own sake*. Cynics are likely to question this. However, motives of altruism, generosity, humanitarianism, and religion do exist in the world. This is not to say that the above sentiments may not be tinged with some self-interest too. The altruistic spirit may be diluted.

The general answer to the problems of underdeveloped areas has been, at any rate, the various activities of the "Point Four" program. The original idea of this program was stated as the fourth major point in the foreign policy part of President Truman's inaugural address delivered on January 20, 1949. "Point Four," since administered by the Department of State, was designed to remove some of the huge gap between the standard of living in economically advanced areas and that in underdeveloped areas. As Bingham observed,[10] the term *Point Four* is a convenient shorthand for such a large linguistic mouthful as the following: "a program of technical co-operation plus capital investment to help the underdeveloped areas of the world help themselves to develop their resources and raise their standard of living." The *real start* of "Point Four" occurred on October 30, 1951, when the Congress appropriated a substantial sum for it under the Mutual Security Act of 1951.[11] "Point Four" was, however, not the only program of this kind to be established; there was also the United Nations program for technical assistance and the Colombo Plan of the British Commonwealth.

This is not regarded as the proper place for an extended discussion of "Point Four" activities and of results achieved thus far. Suffice it to say that the program emphasizes *self-help*. Its officials insist that it is not a "giveaway" program but a co-operative sharing with peoples of less developed areas of the knowledge and skills they need in order to develop their abilities and resources. Economic aid, financial grants-in-aid, and so on have at times been regarded as advisable for various nations and have been given; but they are not regarded as the essential emphasis of the program, which

---

[9] See Jonathan B. Bingham, *Shirt-Sleeve Diplomacy, Point 4 in Action* (New York, John Day, 1954), pp. 8–9; Omar B. Pancoast, Jr., "The 'Point Four' Policy," *Bulletin of the Atomic Scientists*, Vol. X, No. 3 (March, 1954), p. 87.

[10] Bingham, *op. cit.,* foreword.

[11] *Ibid.,* p. 24.

is the distribution of *knowledge*. The "Point Four" viewpoint is, however, relatively new for the world. Even if self-interest is mixed with the generous idealism, this program may be viewed as a revolutionary development of modern times. Arnold Toynbee has commented as follows:[12]

Our age will be remembered chiefly . . . for its having been the first age since the dawn of civilization . . . in which people dared to think it practicable to make the benefits of civilization available for the whole human race . . . the sudden vast enhancement of man's ability to make nonhuman nature produce what man requires from her has . . . made the idea of welfare for all a practical objective.

"Point Four" has been related to improvement of agriculture, resources, health conditions, sanitation, fostering industry, capital formation, education, population problems, and other subjects.[13] While all of these activities are important and are interlocking in many ways, the emphasis on industrialization is a key one. Future industrialization of these areas, asserts Harrison Brown,[14] is not only basic but is perhaps the most formidable task confronting mankind today. Doubtless enormous investments of materials, labor, and capital are needed before goods can be produced and used. The present low incomes in underdeveloped areas mean that outside financing is necessary in the initial stages of industrialization; indeed the most difficult part of the industrialization program may be in getting started. Yet the need is tremendous. It appears that world stability as well as regional self-sufficiency will be much the gainer if a higher standard of living is achieved for underprivileged peoples. It is conceded that at this time of writing "Point Four" has made only a slight start in industrialization, and that a long-term program is in order.

The various "Point Four" activities have not all, of course, met with success since the expanded program began late in 1951. Much of this work has involved interrelations between American personnel and the natives of the underdeveloped nations. Various experiences in many places have been regarded as highly successful; others have encountered difficulties.[15] In some instances personality difficulties have brought failure, in others health problems of the area, educational problems, local customs, and so on have led to frustrations. Much has been learned, indeed, about how to perform such jobs —and how not to try to perform them. In spite of some individual failures and the financial cost involved, the program itself is still regarded as eminently

12 *Ibid.*, p. 16; originally published in the *New York Times* Magazine Section (date unstated).

13 See excellent discussion in Eugene Staley, *The Future of Underdeveloped Countries* (New York, Harper, 1954); see also J. Bingham, *op. cit.;* O. Pancoast, Jr., *op. cit.*

14 Brown, *The Challenge of Man's Future* (New York, Viking Press, 1954), pp. 243–246.

15 Richard Wohl, "Technical Assistance—Retrospect and Review," *Bulletin of the Atomic Scientists,* Vol. X, No. 3 (March, 1954), pp. 75–80.

worth while.[16] To the peoples of underdeveloped areas, the realization that economically advanced Americans appreciate the hopes, strivings, and critical problems of their poverty-level existence may be itself a positive force of no little importance. So maintains Dr. Charles Malik, Chairman of the Delegation of Lebanon to the United Nations General Assembly.[17]

SUMMARY

In this chapter we have considered certain problems which may be regarded as characteristic of periods of rapid social change. These problems are viewed basically as "lagging situations." They are not the ordinary type of social problem which might be discussed in textbooks on that subject, such as economic depressions, crime, and divorce. They present in typical form examples of people who for some reason or reasons have not "kept up" with the advancing tide of change or where there are at least marked disparities between rates of change.

We have discussed the following: (1) the increasing gap between knowledge of the experts and that of the general public; (2) the gap between the rapidly increasing knowledge in various fields (especially social science) with that known to the average governmental official; (3) the problem of even the educational specialist trying to "keep up" with rapidly accumulating knowledge in his field during the present period of rapid change; (4) the gap between the rapid changes in the "social world" of women and the average educational preparation of women for living in that world; and (5) the gap between the high standard of living in the United States, due largely to technological advances, and that in other "underdeveloped areas" of the world.

Many other major problems arising from rapid social change could have been discussed. One may conclude (1) that it is inevitable that problems will develop in times of rapid change, and (2) that typical problems of "changing times" will in turn cause other problems to develop. Thus it is likely that other problems will develop, for example, from the gap existing between knowledge of the experts and that of the general public. Similarly, a continuing gap between the standard of living found in various nations might lead to a trend toward communism or it might lead to the starting of wars. There is need, therefore, to fill such gaps as quickly as is possible.

ANNOTATED BIBLIOGRAPHY

NATIONAL AND INTERNATIONAL GOVERNMENT

DAHL, Robert A., and LINDBLOM, Charles E., *Politics, Economics, and Welfare* (New York, Harper, 1953). The authors make joint use of the tools of

[16] The program has, however, its strong, though not numerous, critics. See Eugene W. Castle, *Billions, Blunders, and Baloney* (New York, Devin-Adair, 1954).

[17] Charles Malik, "Some Reflections on Technical and Economic Assistance," *Bulletin of the Atomic Scientists*, Vol. X, No. 3 (March, 1954), p. 96.

political science and economics. They recommend rational calculation and effective control as tools for social planning.

DOUGLAS, Paul H., *Ethics in Government* (Cambridge, Harvard University Press, 1952). A study of corruption in government, by a college professor who became a Chicago alderman and then a United States Senator.

LIE, Trygve, *In the Cause of Peace: Seven Years with the United Nations* (New York, Macmillan, 1953). "The questions which concerned me most during seven years as Secretary-General of the UN."

MANGONE, Gerard J., *Short History of International Organization* (New York, McGraw-Hill, 1953). Traces the development of international organization along constitutional lines. Emphasizes the role of power politics in relation to organized efforts to cope with the problems of world society.

CHANGING LIFE PATTERNS OF WOMEN

BRITTAIN, Vera May, *Lady into Woman: A History of Women from Victoria to Elizabeth II* (New York, Macmillan, 1954). A study of the changing role of woman in Britain and throughout the world during the struggles from which emerged greater equality of the sexes.

GRUENBERG, (Mrs.) Sidonie, and KRECH, Hilda Sidney, *The Many Lives of Modern Women* (New York, Doubleday, 1952). Has been called "the most logical analysis yet available of the development of the American Woman's life pattern."

"UNDERDEVELOPED AREAS" OF THE WORLD

BINGHAM, Jonathan B., *Shirt-Sleeve Diplomacy* (New York, John Day, 1954). One of the best books to date on the "Point Four" program. A well-written, full account—pro "Point Four." Author was deputy administrator of the Technical Cooperation Administration of the State Department, 1951–53.

Bulletin of the Atomic Scientists, Vol. X, No. 3 (March, 1954). This issue is largely devoted to technical assistance programs, including "Point Four." Articles by Fairfield Osborn, R. Richard Wohl, Omar Pancoast Jr., and Charles Malik are valuable.

COTTRELL, W. Fred, *Energy and Society* (New York, McGraw-Hill, 1955). Discusses societies from standpoint of high and low energy systems and resulting effects on social structure. An ably written book, of interest to all the social sciences.

Economic Development and Cultural Change (quarterly journal), published by Research Center in Economic Development and Cultural Change at the University of Chicago. Contains significant articles on underdeveloped areas and on the effects of technological and other changes.

GOLDING, E. W., "Local Energy Sources for Underdeveloped Areas," in *Impact of Science on Society,* Vol. V, No. 1 (Spring, 1954) (Paris, UNESCO), pp. 27–46. The author, a British engineer, discusses the possibilities of developing local energy sources. Recommended.

HATT, Paul K., ed., *World Population and Future Resources* (New York, American Book, 1952). Concerning underdeveloped versus economically-advanced nations, see chapters by Warren S. Thompson, Kingsley Davis, Irene Taeuber, and Joseph J. Spengler.

STALEY, Eugene, *The Future of Underdeveloped Countries* (New York, Harper, 1954). Recommended.

PART V

Social Change, Planning, and Social Control

CHAPTER 19

PREDICTING FUTURE TRENDS

■ *Hornell Hart*

MORE THAN a century ago, Comte epitomized the purpose of social science in a French pun: "Prevoir pour pouvoir"—to predict in order to control. For many years that Comtian statement of the role of social science was widely accepted. But of late a controversy has been raging as to whether social prediction is actually possible. Let us tune in for a moment on the debate.

Pauline V. Young, author of one of the most widely used textbooks on social research, has said:[1]

In the early 1920's American sociologists, committed to the belief that prediction is a function of social science, began to develop methods by which they could reliably predict the outcome of behavior on the basis of current tendencies and past trends.[1]

Professor George A. Lundberg, a leading sociological operationist from the University of Washington, has said:[2]

Our every-day adjustments to our fellow men are carried out on the basis of highly reliable predictions of what other people will do. The task of science is to develop more formal and generally reliable methods of such prediction. Encouraging progress has already been made in this direction. . . .

Speakers on the negative in the debate included Spahr and Swenson, authors of the textbook on *Methods and Status of Scientific Research:*[3]

It has been urged repeatedly that the chief function of science is to predict. . . . But *accurate* prediction is confined almost solely to those fields of the exact sciences in which the ability of human beings to control or affect the results is negligible is not entirely absent. . . .

A somewhat sensational repudiation of prediction by a famous columnist is the following excerpt from one of Dorothy Thompson's releases:[4]

[1] Pauline B. Young, *Scientific Social Surveys and Research* (New York, Prentice-Hall, 1949), pp. 101–102.
[2] George A. Lundberg, *Social Research* (New York, Longmans, Green, 1942), p. 22.
[3] Walter Earl Spahr and Rinehart John Swenson, *Methods and Status of Scientific Research* (New York, Harper, 1930), pp. 22–23.
[4] Dorothy Thompson, "Not Predictable," *Durham Morning Herald,* November 9, 1954, Sec. 1, p. 4, col. 3.

Whenever the expert election predicters fail this column rejoices and takes out a new lease of faith in Democracy. For if human behavior were predictable according to patterns of past behavior as assembled by the so-called "social scientists" and fed into the computing apparatus of an infallible mechanical brain, there would be no sense in elections at all. The "social scientists" could assemble their pattern and a robot throw the switch.

We put "social scientists" in quotes because we don't think there is such a thing as social or political "science." Human thoughts, reactions, responses, feelings, desires, and choices are not measurable with scientific exactitude. . . .

Charles A. Beard, famous historian, elaborated as follows the difficulties of social prediction:[5]

A genuine political science would deal with known tendencies projected in time; it would be in some indeterminate measure prophetic. . . .

It certainly would deal with the future. Reasoning from the vast and cataclysmic changes of the past and from the tendencies of the present, it could scarcely escape prognosticating changes for the near future, greater changes for the more distant future, and something volcanic for the coming millennium. . . . Such changes will of necessity . . . shake to its foundation one or more prodigious interests: the church, the state itself, property and labor. . . .

Let us assume, for example, the possibility of such a political science in Virginia in the year 1850. If it had been scientific and not merely descriptive (correctly speaking an impossibility), then it would have been compelled to place at the center of its prognosis the destruction of the slave system of this commonwealth. Could it have been safely taught at this University to the scions of the old aristocracy? . . .

Of course such a science of pronostication is impossible. Nobody could foretell in October, 1928, whether Mr. Smith or Mr. Hoover would be elected President, and yet we are asked to plot the social trajectory of the United States until the end of the century. . . . All such prognostications are hazardous intellectual adventures, with the chances perhaps a thousand to one, against correctness.

A striking phenomenon in the history of social thought is the frequency with which people take great pains to prove that something is impossible, while at the same time others are actually doing the "impossible" thing. One example has been provided in the publications of Simon Newcomb, a highly distinguished astronomer and mathematician. Between 1901 and 1906, while Langley and the Wright brothers were actually building the first successful airplanes, Newcomb published articles with the following conclusion:[6]

The demonstration that no possible combination of known substances, known forms of machinery, and known forms of force can be united in a practicable machine by which men shall fly long distances through the air, seems to the writer as complete as it is possible for the demonstration of any physical fact to be.

In considering to what extent and with what degrees of accuracy social scientists may be able to predict the future, the scientific procedure would

[5] Charles A. Beard, "Political Science," in Wilson Gee, ed., in *Research in the Social Sciences* (New York, Appleton-Century-Crofts, 1949), pp. 273–275.

[6] Simon Newcomb, *Side-Lights on Astronomy and Kindred Fields of Popular Sciences: Essays and Addresses,* 1906, p. 345.

seem to be to gather actual data about attempted predictions and the degrees to which they have been fulfilled, studying the conditions favorable and unfavorable to accuracy of forecast. When the problem is approached in that way, the first fact which becomes apparent is the one noted in the above quotation from Lundberg. Instead of prediction of social behavior being impossible, "our every-day adjustments to our fellow men are carried out on the basis of highly reliable predictions of what other people will do." All train schedules, announced times of meals, of meetings and of marriages, all schedules of school and college classes for coming semesters, all announcements of future radio, TV, and movie performances, and all other announcements of times when future human actions are to take place—all are based on predictions. Many such schedules are not carried out with "highly reliable" accuracy, but the average precision of fulfillment of some train schedules (for example) is amazing, when one considers the intricacies of the co-operative actions required to perform them. Moreover, contracts and agreements involve implied or asserted predictions. All tax legislation is based on more or less crude—but more or less reliable—predictions as to yields. Advertising campaigns and professional fund-raising drives are based on specific forecasts of yields to be expected. The above are only samples; the general facts are inescapable.

Since predictions of human behavior are thus not only practicable but commercially feasible and indeed indispensable, Lundberg would seem to have a valid point when he says that "the task of science is to develop more formal and generally reliable methods of such prediction." Proceeding, then, in an inductively scientific rather than a dogmatically futilitarian way, let us explore some specific examples of attempted predictions which go beyond the types involved in the ordinary scheduling and planning of social activities.

PREDICTING SOCIAL TRENDS

In the first three volumes of his *Social and Cultural Dynamics,* Professor Sorokin, of Harvard, nineteen times reiterated in one form or another his denial of the existence of any "perpetual main linear trend in history and most of the social processes." It is obviously impossible to prove the existence of any *perpetual trend,* for much the same reason that it is impossible to prove a universal negative. But Sorokin appears to be using this logical truism in an attempt to demonstrate quite another proposition: that the history of human culture consists simply in oscillations between "ideational," "idealistic," and "sensate" cultural phases. The invalidity of his attempt to formulate a universal nonlinear generalization about culture history is evident from his own data as to the relationship between "empiricism" and "materialism." During the 2,500 years from 600 B.C. to 1920 A.D., according to Sorokin's own indexes,[7] materialism has declined from being more than twice as prevalent as empiricism to being less than one-third as prevalent, and (if Sorokin's indexes are reliable and valid) this decline has been practically linear. But Sorokin's generalization is nullified also by the basic trends reviewed in Chapter 3 of the present book, and by the conclusions reached by such scientists as Ogburn, Chapin, Lowie, Kroeber, Lewis H. Morgan, James Harvey Robinson, and other outstanding social thinkers whose views have been referred to at other points in the present volume.

The sociological law on which descriptions of past social trends and tentative predictions of future social trends may be based has been developed in Chapter 3 of this book. It may be restated as follows:

Over the long sweep of time, man's power to carry out his purposes has been increasing with steeper and steeper acceleration, but with stagnations and setbacks.

The usefulness of the general law stated above can be tested in terms of practical demonstrations of valid predictions. The following examples must be considered as being in the nature of pilot studies, suggestive of the possibility of more trustworthy results if past methods are critically reviewed and systematically improved.

PREDICTING THE TREND OF WORLD SPEED RECORDS

An example of fairly successful prediction of a trend is found in speed records. Even in 1931, the fact of age-long acceleration in human speed was inescapably clear:[8]

The curve of progress in maximum human speed . . . shows the same accelerating upward tendency which has appeared in the indexes previously reviewed. During the past 10 years a greater increase in man's maximum swiftness has been achieved than in all the previous 1,000,000 or more years since the Dawn Man was chipping flints in Britain. Ninety-five per cent of all human progress in speed has been won within the past century and a quarter. This acceleration, however, is seen to be the result of successive inventions, each of which brought a temporary upward spurt, only to slow down and be surpassed by another invention. . . .

If the airplane, like the human sprinter, the horse, the locomotive and probably the automobile, should begin to approach its maximum speed, further major increases would have to be achieved by some new invention. The candidate most frequently mentioned for this position is the rocket-ship.

At the time when the manuscript of *The Technique of Social Progress* was being prepared for the printer, the maximum speed record was less than 300 miles per hour. But before the book could be gotten through the press, a new

---

[7] *Social and Cultural Dynamics,* Vol. II, as summarized by Hornell Hart, "Sorokin's Data versus His Conclusions," *American Sociological Review,* Vol. 4 (October, 1939), p. 638.

[8] *Technique of Social Progress,* 1931, pp. 77–78.

record of 358 m.p.h. had been made, and the curve was extended, at the upper right-hand corner, through the chart's previous ceiling. More recent aviation speeds have been noted in Chapters 3 and 9 of the present volume.

During the million or more years of cultural development up to 1931, when the generalization about accelerating progress in speed records was first published, mankind had increased human speeds from about 3 to 358 m.p.h.; during the 22 years between 1931 and 1955, human speed records increased from 358 to over 1,600 m.p.h. The confirmation of the accelerating trend is obvious.

The above prediction was merely that speeds would continue to increase acceleratingly. No specific speeds were predicted in the 1931 textbook. But the present writer has been attempting, at various dates since 1943, to predict future world speed records. The methods used have (it is believed) been of decreasing degrees of crudity, though still leaving much to be desired. The resulting successive forecasts have been as follows: On July 15, 1943, a manuscript predictive curve was drawn, indicating a speed of 675 miles per hour for the year 1953. In June, 1946, an article was published containing a prediction, made in November, 1945, that the maximum speed in 1953 would be 1,110 miles per hour.[9] On January 13, 1949, a manuscript predictive curve was drawn which indicated 1,226 miles per hour as the 1953 speed. The actual record, established on December 6, 1953, was over 1,600 miles per hour.

Perhaps the most outstanding fact about the above forecasts is the persistent tendency to underestimate future speeds, in spite of progressive improvements owing to acquisition of more and more recent data and to refinements in mathematical procedures.

PREDICTING PASSENGER MILES FLOWN

A discussion on this topic between the present writer and Dr. Ogburn was published in the *American Sociological Review* in February, 1949. That discussion included a graph entitled "Passenger Miles Flown by Domestic Airlines," showing data from 1930 to 1948, with a fitted exponential trend. That graph is reproduced here on page 460, with subsequent data-points inserted. Dr. Ogburn's forecast for 1953 (published in 1946)[10] is indicated by the double-headed arrow.

The actual data for the years 1949 to 1953 show an increasing downward departure from the exponential trend, which confirms in a striking way a prediction suggested in 1949 by Dr. Ogburn. He said then:

[9] The 1945 forecast was published in "Technological Acceleration and the Atomic Bomb," *American Sociological Review*, Vol. 11 (June, 1946), pp. 285–287; the other two forecasts were recorded in manuscript only. The record of 1953 is to be found in *Facts on File*, 1953, p. 424 G2.

[10] William F. Ogburn, *Social Effects of Aviation* (Boston, Houghton Mifflin, 1946), p. 119.

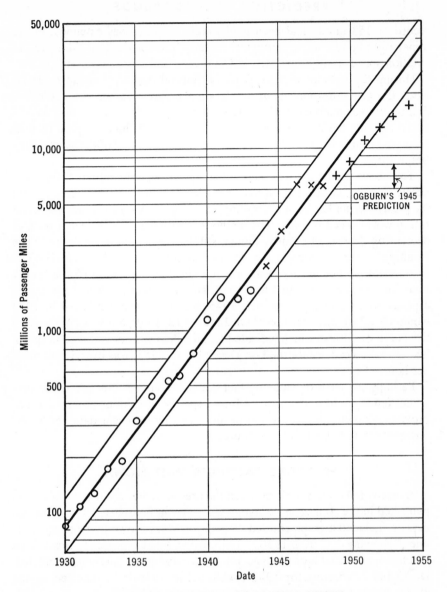

PASSENGER MILES FLOWN BY DOMESTIC AIRLINES

The trend was fitted in 1949 on the basis of the O's and X's. Ogburn's prediction of 1945 was based on the O's only. The +'s represent data which become available after the trend was fitted.

Professor Hart extrapolates his exponential curve which fits so well up to 1948, up to 1955, and gets a figure of passenger miles flown which is three times the total Pullman traffic today. I don't know where all that traffic is coming from. I wonder if the slow growth of population and income, the competition of railroads, and possibly a business recession won't make his straight line trend (on log paper) bend downward before 1955.

The trend *did* bend downward before 1955. The passenger miles flown for the year 1954 were 4.5 standard errors below the exponential prediction for that year—a deviation which would not occur by mere chance once in 100,-000 times.

THE ACCELERATING GROWTH IN PER CAPITA REAL INCOME

For speed records and passenger miles flown, definite predictions were made in past years on the basis of established trends, and in the preceding sections these predictions have been reviewed in the light of subsequent data. With respect to per capita real income, J. Frederic Dewhurst and Associates, under the auspices of the Commonwealth Fund, have published two elaborate studies of *America's Needs and Resources,* one in 1947 and the other in 1955. Those studies made predictions in many areas of American life. But the one which seems to have been most central and fundamental in these studies had to do with per capita real income in the United States. On the basis of data through 1944, the Dewhurst report (1947) predicted that per capita real personal income in 1950 would be 26.2 per cent greater than it had been in 1940. Actually the increase (as reported in the 1955 study) was 42.0 per cent—more than half again as great as had been predicted eight years earlier. Also, the 1947 report predicted that per capita real income in 1950 would be 15.8 per cent less than it had been in 1944. The 1955 report showed that the 1950 figure was only 4.5 per cent lower than 1944—a drop less than one-third as great as that forecast in the earlier report. Both predictions were in the right directions but, like my own forecasts of world speed records, Dewhurst underestimated the degree of acceleration in the trend.

Closely related to real income is national product per man-hour. An eight-year prediction of this trend was made in Dewhurst's 1947 report. His forecast for the year 1950 was an increase of 14.2 per cent over the average of the 1940 and 1944 rates. Actually the mean of the years 1948 to 1952 inclusive showed a gain of 25.4 per cent over the mean of the 1940 and 1944 product per man-hour, as shown in the 1955 report. Here again, Dewhurst's forecast was only a little over half of what the actual rate proved to be. The significant thing, however, is not that his predictions proved to be somewhat conservative. The significant fact is that this group of social scientists set seriously about the task of social prediction, developed valid techniques in their 1947 report, improved those techniques in their 1955 report, and brought forth indicators which provided social guidance in the right direction.

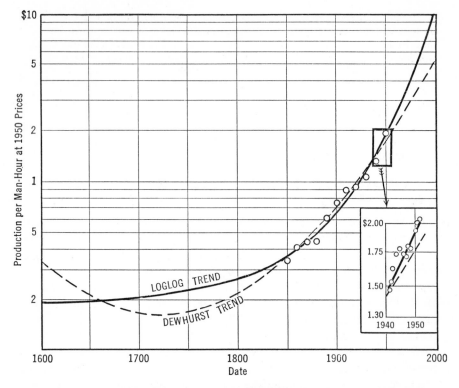

PRODUCTION PER MAN-HOUR IN THE UNITED STATES AT 1950 PRICES, SHOWING BOTH DEWHURST AND LOGLOG TRENDS

THE PAST AND FUTURE TREND OF PER-MAN-HOUR PRODUCTION

Dewhurst's forecast of the 1950 per-man-hour production has already been referred to. But Dewhurst went beyond mere forecasting. He fitted a hyperbolic trend to the decennial data and noted that the deviations were all less than 12 per cent. This marks an advance toward more reliable prediction, but Dewhurst's curve is open to two basic criticisms which are illustrated in the chart above. First the Dewhurst trend, which is indicated by the dotted curve, becomes irrational if projected back of about 1725, since it reaches a minimum at about that date and starts back upward as earlier and earlier dates are selected.[11] The loglog trend, which is indicated by the solid curve, is rational, no matter how far carried back, since it rises from a baseline of 17.8 cents per man hour, at 1950 prices. Second, the Dewhurst curve, while

[11] The formula for the Dewhurst trend line is:

$$\text{Log } Y_c = 1.837 + .071x + .002x^2$$

where x represents the number of decades after or before (—) 1900. The loglog trend has the formula:

$$\text{Log } Y_c = 1.250 + 10^{9.701} + .00521 \, (d_a - 1890)$$

where d_a is any assigned date.

giving a fairly close percentage fit to the decade data from 1850 to 1940, provides a relatively poor fit from 1942 onward. For example, the Dewhurst curve predicted $1.94 per man hour (at 1950 prices) for 1955. The loglog curve, based on data through 1952, predicted $2.15. The actual figure was $2.15.[12] Thus, the loglog prediction was exactly right, whereas the Dewhurst curve was 10 per cent too low. From 1930 to 1955 the loglog trend fits with less than one-third the percentage variance around the Dewhurst curve.

The closer fit of the loglog trend suggests that Dewhurst's forecast of future man-hour production, sensational though it appears to be, may prove to be too conservative.

PREDICTING THE TREND OF EXPECTATION OF LIFE

That the average length of human life (expectation of life at birth) has been increasing with accelerating speed was shown in Chapter 3 of this book (page 34). But could that trend be used as a basis for predicting future gains in expectation? A venture in that direction was made in a paper which was presented before a section of the American Sociological Society in New York City on December 30, 1925. The abstract of that paper, as it appeared in the proceedings, was as follows:[13]

The expectation of life has steadily increased at an accelerating rate until now, for the registration area, it is about 58 years. If the line of gains in life expectancy should follow a regular curve along its present tendencies, the expectation of life at the year 2000 would be much over 100 years. The plausibility of such continued increase is based on the general tendency toward acceleration of man's power to control his environment, the rapid recovery of the loss in expectation of life resulting from the war, the success of medical science in coping with diseases of later life, and the continued activity in medical research.

The *New York Times* for December 31, 1925, reported this prediction in a story with the headline "Life Mean in 2000 Set at 100 Years." This item was followed up by a feature story on February 28, 1926, under the headline "The Expectation of Life of Babies Born in the Year 2000 Will Be Over 100 Years."[14]

Five years later, Dr. Louis I. Dublin, Actuarial Vice President of the Metropolitan Life Insurance Company, took issue with this prediction in an article entitled "Can We Extend the Life Span?" Dublin made this statement:[15]

I drew up a hypothetical life table a few years ago which represented the maximum expectation of life, assuming that mortality could be reduced to the

[12] *New York Times,* August 21, 1955, p. E7, col. 4.

[13] Hornell Hart, "Urban Expectation of Life in 2000 A.D.," *Publications of American Sociological Society,* Vol. 20 (July, 1926), pp. 118–122.

[14] *New York Times,* December 31, 1925, p. 6, col. 3; *ibid.,* February 28, 1926, Sec. VII, p. 16, col. 1.

[15] *Harper's* (May, 1930), p. 770.

very limit of present-day knowledge. . . . Our hypothetical life table forecasts an expectation of life of about 65 years at birth.

The prediction that the accelerating increase in expectation of life would continue was reiterated in a textbook, *The Technique of Social Progress,* which was published in 1931:[16]

Life expectation increased 20 years from 1550 to Pasteur's discoveries in 1865, and there was a gain of 15 years from 1865 to 1925. The average rate of gain before Pasteur's discoveries was .6 years per decade; since Pasteur it has averaged 2.5 years per decade. The general shape of the curve is, therefore, one of accelerating rise. It will be noted, however, that the curve has had plateaus. . . .

The progress of life-span extension seems to have reached a stage comparable to that of bridge spans before the cantilever or suspension principles had been discovered, or to human speeds just before the development of propulsion by gasoline engines. The next step in invention is apt to be thought of as impossible just before it is achieved. It would be strange if man's accelerating progress in the power to carry out his purposes should suddenly halt before the present obstacles to further major extensions of human life. To suppose that past acceleration in life-extension will continue seems absurd: but so did steel bridges, automobiles, airplanes and antitoxins before they were invented.

Here then, a quarter of a century ago, were two general predictions about trends in length of human life. The distinguished actuary, on the basis of then-available medical knowledge and insurance experience, set a fairly low ceiling as the probable limit of future gains. The sociologist, on the basis of the underlying law of cultural acceleration and the long-run trends of length of life, made a fairly incredible forecast, covering the next three-quarters of a century. In one sense, the two predictions were not as different as they might at first seem. Dr. Dublin did not deny that scientific knowledge might progress in matters of life extension. He merely ignored that possibility and wrote as if even the full application of medical knowledge then available was unlikely. He stressed the seemingly safe, conservative side of the picture, while the sociological forecast predicted an upsweeping trend, based on the recently discovered law of cultural acceleration.

Since 1925, more than 30 of the 75 years of the prediction span have now elapsed. Which of the two predictions has thus far been most nearly justified? To test this question, let us now draw the accelerating curve which fits the data up through 1925, and which passes through the 100-year-expectation point in the year 2000. Let us then plot circles to represent the actual expectations of life for the United States as a whole from 1925 through the last year available at the time of this writing[17] The results are presented graphically in the following chart. Note first that Dr. Dublin's ceiling of 65

---

[16] *Op. cit.,* pp. 491–500.

[17] The 1925 prediction was made in a paper dealing with *urban* expectation of life. Data are available only for expectations for the country as a whole, including both rural and urban populations. Urban expectations have been increasing at a much steeper rate than rural. Hence, if the rate for the country as a whole reaches 100 years in the year 2000, the urban rate should be much above that figure.

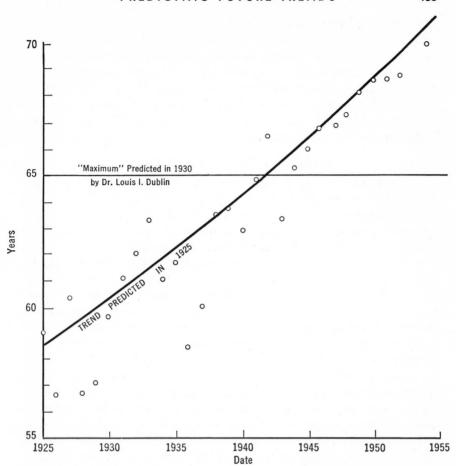

TREND OF EXPECTATION OF LIFE PREDICTED IN 1925 COMPARED WITH SUBSEQUENT DATA FOR THE TOTAL POPULATION OF THE REGISTRATION STATES

years was broken through in 1942, only 12 years after he had made it, and that the rate has remained above that ceiling ever since 1944, being now five years above it. Note also that the circles representing the annual returns have clustered closer and closer to the trend line.

Dr. Dublin revised his 65-year ceiling twice within the next 12 years. In 1933 he raised it to 70 years.[18] In 1942 he suggested 71 years as being "based entirely on reasonable assumptions." But he queried: "Does this set the limit for the future?" and he answered: "Decidedly not."[19]

Dr. Dublin's earlier actuarial predictions failed to take into account the underlying laws of cultural acceleration. The swiftly accelerating progress

[18] Louis I. Dublin, "Longevity in Retrospect and Prospect," in Edmund V. Cowdry, ed., *Problems of Aging* (Baltimore, Williams & Wilkins, 1942), p. 101.

[19] *Id.*, "How Many Years Will You Live?" *American Mercury* (July, 1942).

of biological research, the persistently exponential increase in real incomes per capita in the Western world, and the demonstrated super-acceleration of expectations of life during recent decades—all these point to the conclusion that a revolutionary change is impending (unless the accelerating increase in destructive power cancels out other major trends). Disease and death are being defeated in our society to a degree and an extent which promise to transform radically the character of our population and the basic problems of the lives of our grandchildren.

PREDICTING POPULATION TRENDS

Raymond Pearl and L. J. Reed published in 1924 their conclusion that the logistic curve provided a basis for predicting future populations.[20] But Palmer Putnam, after reviewing the available evidence, concluded: "Population growth may often, perhaps always, follow a logistic. [But] the logistic is valueless as an independent means of forecasting population growth."[21]

In their statistics text published in 1940, Croxton and Cowden fitted a logistic trend to the population data for the United States for 1790 to 1930.[22] The maximum error of the logistic prediction was that relating to the population estimate for October 1, 1955 (25 years after the last data point used in fitting the curve), when the data exceeded the forecast by 10 per cent.

Another method of forecasting population has been used by Whelpton.[23] He pointed out that the future population depends upon four major factors: (1) present population; (2) future fertility rates; (3) future mortality rates; and (4) migration. He discussed considerations involved in forecasts of these factors. As a result of his explorations, he offered predictions that (on various assumptions) the population of the United States in 1975 might be as low as 151 or as high as 185 millions. The date 1975 is 28 years beyond the last data point used by Whelpton. His error (whether based on the average of his two extremes or on Croxton and Cowden's logistic value for that date) is about 10 per cent, or almost exactly the same as the demonstrated error of the logistic curve for a similar length of forecast.

WITHIN WHAT LIMITS CAN PREDICTION OF TRENDS BE DEPENDABLE?

Major doubts as to use of past trends in order to predict the future have been raised by Kurt Lewin:[24]

[20] Raymond Pearl and L. J. Reed, "The Growth of Human Population," in Pearl's *Studies in Human Biology* (Baltimore, Williams and Wilkins, 1924).
[21] Palmer Cosslett Putnam, *Energy in the Future* (New York, Van Nostrand, 1953), p. 282.
[22] Frederick E. Croxton and Dudley J. Cowden, *Applied General Statistics* (Englewood Cliffs, N. J., Prentice-Hall, 1940), p. 454.
[23] P. K. Whelpton, *Forecasts of the Population of the United States, 1945–1975* (Washington, Bureau of the Census, 1947).
[24] Kurt Lewin, "Psychological Ecology," in Dorwin Cartwright, ed., *Field Theory in Social Science: Selected Theoretical Papers* (New York, Harper, 1951), pp. 171–172.

Numerous attempts have been made to forecast the future on the basis of "social trends"; we know now that their value for prediction is very limited. Not infrequently, they are misleading.

There are several reasons why technical advice for bringing about changes cannot, as a rule, be based on the study of historical trends:

1. Even if the sampling method is perfect for securing both reliable and valid data, the prediction for the future is a probability statement which presupposes that the situation will remain stationary, or that it will change at a known rate in a known direction. The crux of the matter is that conditions frequently do change radically from one day to another.

2. There is no definite way to judge from historical trends the degree of difficulty for bringing about a change in a certain direction. A long duration of a group habit does not necessarily mean that this habit is rigid. It may mean merely that the related conditions happen not to have changed during that period. It may well be that food habits which remained rigidly upheld for a long time can be changed more easily than habits which in the past have shown a fair amount of flexibility.

3. No amount of descriptive data will settle the question of what techniques are efficient in bringing about desired changes. For instance, no amount of data about what people eat or have eaten can tell whether advertisement, or lecture, or school education will be most effective.

That trends may have an extraordinary regularity is illustrated by the use of a logistic trend to detect an error which had gone uncorrected through 21 yearly editions of the *Statistical Abstract of the United States*.[25] Striking as are the regularities of many logistic and loglog trends, however, it is clearly a fact that such curves often change their character suddenly, without advance warnings which can as yet be reliably identified.[26]

A second major difficulty with trends as a basis of prediction is that even when the trends are regular and persistent, variations around or from the trend are often of major importance, and are often unpredictable, or capable of being forecasted only within wide margins of error. This is strikingly the case in relation to national income.

In spite of the difficulties just stated, one fundamental fact has been established in the present chapter: that the trend toward accelerating increases in man's power to carry out his purposes is so basic that broad predictions have been demonstrated to be practicable in various subfields—specifically in relation to expectation of life, speed records, air travel, and per capita real income. The validity of such broad predictions is of central importance in the nuclear crisis.

In several instances, a tendency to underestimate the actual amount of future acceleration has been evident. This tendency has already been noted in connection with my own predictions of world speed records (see page 459). A

---

[25] Hornell Hart, "Depression, War, and Logistic Trends," *American Journal of Sociology,* Vol. 52 (September, 1946), pp. 113–116.

[26] Cf. Palmer Cosslett Putnam, *op. cit.,* pp. 277–282.

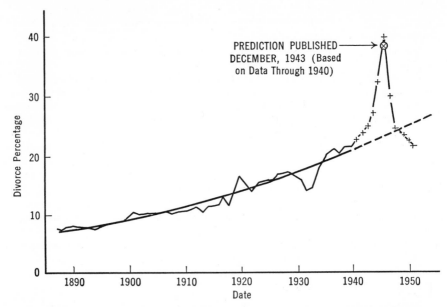

PREDICTION PUBLISHED⟶⊗
DECEMBER, 1943 (Based
on Data Through 1940)

DIVORCES PER 100 MARRIAGES DURING THE AVERAGE OF THE PREVIOUS TEN YEARS, 1887 TO 1952, WITH LOGISTIC TREND BASED ON DATA FROM 1888 TO 1940

similar tendency toward under-forecasting has been found in a study of forecasts of U. S. petroleum production.[27]

PREDICTIONS OF DEVIATIONS FROM THE DIVORCE TREND

Most of this chapter, up to this point, has been devoted to exploring the extent to which social *trends* can be predicted. A second type of statistical prediction has to do with the forecasting of *deviations* from trends which have been established within reasonable degrees of future probability. This type of prediction may be illustrated by the experiment in which Miss Henrietta Bowne, under the direction of the present writer, predicted in the December, 1943, number of *Social Forces* the divorce rate for the United States in the year 1946.

The first basic step in Miss Bowne's procedure was to establish the trend of American divorces from 1888 to 1940. She fitted a mathematical curve which accounted for 92 per cent of the variance in the divorce rate during that period.[28] The chart above embodies the basic prediction developed in

[27] Robert E. Wilson, "Oil Prophecies and Realities," in Paul K. Hatt, ed., *World Population and Future Resources* (New York, American Book, 1952).

[28] Hornell Hart and Henrietta Bowne, "Divorce, Depression, and War," *Social Forces,* Vol. 22 (December, 1943), pp. 191–194. For a revision, see Hornell Hart, "Logistic Social Trends," *American Journal of Sociology,* Vol. 50 (March, 1945), p. 341.

the Bowne study, but it makes use of the latest National Office of Vital Statistics revision of the data involved, with the logistic trend and with the supplementary data from 1941 through 1952.

The prediction, made in 1943, from data which extended only through 1940, was as follows:[29]

On the basis of the foregoing factors, we may venture a tentative prediction as to the divorce rate in the United States in the year 1945 (or whenever demobilization reaches its peak). The predicted rate for 1945 (if that should prove to be the maximum year after World War II) is 38.3. . . . It thus seems safe to estimate that the maximum divorce rate after this war will be between one-third and one-half of the marriages.

The average number of persons in military service actually reached its peak of 11,608,000 in 1945, dropping to less than 4,000,000 in 1946 and to less than 2,000,000 in 1947. That makes the year of maximum demobilization 1946 instead of 1945. If the year 1946 instead of 1945 had been substituted in the predictive equation, the forecast would have been .6 higher, or 38.9 per hundred marriages.

The actually predicted value of 38.3 is indicated by the circled "X" on the chart. The actual rate for that year proved to be 40.0, as indicated by the plus mark in the year 1946. The error of the actual prediction was thus 1.7.

In appraising this forecast, it should be noted that the predicted value deviated 15.3 above the trend value (which was 23.0 for that year). The predicted deviation was 6.8 standard errors above the trend—a deviation which would not occur by chance once in 100 billion times.[30] In the data up to 1940, the largest previous deviation from trend was 3.1 in 1920, which was only 1.4 standard errors. After the predictive article was published, the divorce rates for 1944, 1945, 1946, and 1947 all deviated farther above the trend than any deviation previous to 1944.

The deviations for 1949, 1950, and 1951 (as will be seen from the chart) are all below the predicted trend, but the largest of these deviations is only 1.7 standard errors. The largest previous negative deviation from the trend was 1.7 standard errors in 1932, during the depth of the depression.

Relative to the factors determining the long-run trend in divorce rates, the Bowne article said:[31]

[29] *Op. cit.,* p. 194.

[30] Professor Ogburn has pointed out that if the deviations subsequent to the date of prediction were included in calculating the standard error of estimate, that standard error would be somewhat greater, and hence the significance of the deviation would be slightly less. That method of calculation would not alter appreciably the above-stated conclusions. But the present author believes that the prediction constituted the statement of a sociological law, and that part of that law consisted in the error of estimate based on data from which the law was derived. The prediction was made in the face of the fact that the predicted amount of deviation from the trend was wildly improbable if merely the previous deviations were taken into account. The soundness of the forecast should be appraised in the light of the conditions under which it was made.

[31] *Op. cit.,* p. 194.

The outstanding feature of the divorce rate during the past half century has been the accelerating increase which has persistently appeared. The causes for this are not evident in our study, but sociologists will doubtless consider such factors as increasing urbanization, increasing mobility, transfer of functions from the home to other institutions and agencies, increasing economic independence of women, weakened religious sanctions, decreased rigidity of divorce legislation and administration, decreasing birth rates, and increasing sexual promiscuity.

Of the factors listed, the only ones which appear to have changed direction since the Bowne article was published are birth rates and possibly functions of the home. The development of TV may perhaps involve an intensification of home entertainment in comparison with the movies and other outside activities. Whether this will affect the divorce rate requires further investigation. The birth rate has stopped declining and has started increasing. Possibly this may account for the divorce rate being below the normal trend in 1949 to 1951, in spite of the fact that these years were prosperous. In relation to these factors, the deviations of the divorce rate from the trend during the period of demobilization of troops which were fighting in Korea should be of interest.

BUSINESS FORECASTING INVOLVES PREDICTING DEVIATIONS

Some of the best-known systems of business forecasting during the past few decades, such as the Babson system, the chart of business conditions developed by Leonard P. Ayers for the Cleveland Trust Company, and the chart "Business Trends and Progress" issued by the Crescent Insulated Wire and Cable Company, of Trenton, New Jersey, all have been constructed on the assumption that there is a normal trend of business conditions, with fluctuations above and below the normal. From time to time these charts revise their definition of the "normal trend," so as to have it constitute a sort of moving average of the indexes employed.

A different conception of business trends and fluctuations has been suggested by Dr. Albert Gailord Hart, Professor of Economics at Columbia University:[32]

"Cycles" in Perspective. These statistics exhibit the familiar "peaks and valleys" of "business cycles." But peaks and valleys are not the best geological metaphor. The curves look more like the profile of a gradually sloping plain eroded away in parts—like the Great Plains of our West.

The evidence suggests strongly that when production is high, it comes up against a rather clear-cut ceiling—but a ceiling which itself rises through time. This limit is evidently the limit of available manpower. Its rise reflects the growth of the working force plus the growth of productivity which comes with improvement of productive methods, education of the workers, and so forth.

There is no "floor" corresponding to this ceiling. Industrial-commercial output can drop to very low percentages of potential, and seems to have dropped below 60 per cent at the bottom of the Great Depression of the 1930's.

[32] Albert Gailord Hart, *Money, Debt, and Economic Activity,* 2nd ed. (Englewood Cliffs, N. J., Prentice-Hall, 1953), p. 275.

The prediction of deviations—whether from a central trend or from a potential-output ceiling—has been a subject to which immense effort has been devoted—without achieving closely reliable results. Professor Gordon sums up past attainments as follows:[33]

Even during the 1920's the leading forecasting services were able to predict the important cyclical turns with only a fair degree of success. Then came the stock-market crash in 1929 and the Great Depression of the thirties. The business fore-casters of that period were unprepared for the catastrophic decline in business activity and stock prices which occurred. . . .

More recently there has been a revival of interest. . . . These new forecasting techniques have had a mixed record. There have been some spectacular failures. . . .

In spite of the wide margins of error in even the best business forecasting methods, business executives have come to appreciate the importance of forecasting in their operations.[34] As in the case of elections forecasts, the specialists seem to feel that past failures are due to defective theories and techniques rather than to any inherent unpredictability of social phenomena. Researchers are hard at work in both fields, seeking methods for reducing the errors of estimate in such predictions.

PREDICTING FUTURE SCHOOL NEEDS

The upsurge of the birth rate since the end of World War II has created an acute shortage of school facilities. With respect to the need for grade-school rooms and teachers for a period six years in the future, the social prediction can be about as simple and reliable as in any area.[35] Since attendance in grade schools is compulsory, the need for such schools depends simply on the future population of school age and the number of children assigned per teacher. The death rate of children is now so low and so accurately predictable that as soon as a generation is born, its need for grade-school facilities six years later and throughout the compulsory school years can be quite accurately predicted.

For young people in high school and college the proportions attending, out of the population of suitable ages, have been increasing, but the trends have been quite clearly marked and the forecasting can therefore be fairly accurate. Here, then, is a problem in connection with which social prediction is obviously important and can be made highly reliable.

[33] Robert Aaron Gordon, *Business Fluctuations* (New York, Harper, 1952), pp. 450–451.

[34] *Business Forecasting: A Survey of Business Practices and Methods* (Controllership Foundation, Inc., 1950).

[35] Cf. J. Frederic Dewhurst and Associates, *America's Needs and Resources, A New Survey* (New York, Twentieth Century Fund, 1955), pp. 75, 406–410.

CONCLUSION

The facts reviewed in the present chapter seem sufficient to refute the defeatism of those social thinkers who have denied the possibility of social prediction. It must be recognized that the prediction of social phenomena is a difficult and hazardous process. However, instances cited in the present chapter show that a number of quite specific predictions have been fulfilled. Not only is all social scheduling based upon routine forecasts of human behavior, but specific and fairly complex events and trends can (in some cases) be predicted within reasonable margins of error. If sociology is to become a science worthy of the name, the energies of its practitioners might better be directed toward improving the techniques of prediction rather than toward demonstrations that prediction is impossible.

ANNOTATED BIBLIOGRAPHY

BIRD, Caroline, "Prophets Can Be So Wrong!" *This Week Magazine,* April 18, 1954, pp. 7, 22, 55. A popular discussion of the limitations of social prediction.

DODD, Stuart C., "Predictive Principles for Polls," *Public Opinion Quarterly,* Vol. 15, No. 1 (1951), pp. 23–42. This is a basic and fairly thorough theoretical analysis in this field.

DOLLARD, John, "Under What Conditions Do Opinions Predict Behavior?" *Public Opinion Quarterly,* Vol. 12, No. 4 (1948), pp. 623–632. A good analysis of the problems involved in such predictions.

DUBLIN, Louis I., LOTKA, Alfred J., and SPIEGELMAN, M., "Forecasts of Mortality and Longevity," in *Length of Life* (New York, Ronald, 1949), pp. 167–187. This presents the problem as it appears to life insurance actuaries.

ELDERSVELD, Samuel J., "British Polls and the 1950 General Election," *Public Opinion Quarterly,* Vol. 15, No. 1 (1951), pp. 115–132. An informative review of a successful experiment in political prediction by the opinion-poll method.

HART, Hornell, "Expectation of Life—Actual versus Predicted Trends," *Social Forces,* Vol. 33 (October 1954), pp. 82–85. This article checks up on the first twenty-five years of a seventy-five year prediction relative to expectation of life at birth in the United States.

———, "Logistic Social Trends," and "Depression, War, and Logistic Trends," *American Journal of Sociology,* Vol. 50 (March, 1945), pp. 337–352, and Vol. 52 (September, 1946), pp. 112–122. These two articles summarize available information about logistic social trends, with fairly comprehensive bibliographies. They also contribute some new general principles in this field.

HODGINS, Eric, "Pollsters and the Dopesters," *Saturday Review* (January 3, 1953), pp. 7–8 and 63–64. A popularized but penetrating presentation of the controversy about opinion-polling predictions, in the light of difficulties in predicting preceding elections.

HORST, Paul, *The Prediction of Personal Adjustment,* A Survey of Logical Problems and Research Techniques with Illustrative Application to Problems of Vocational Selection, School Success, Marriage, Crime (New York, Social Science Research Council, 1941). This is the definitive study, up to the time of its publication, of the types of prediction dealt with in the latter part of the present chapter.

KAPLAN, A., SKOGSTAD, A. L., and GIRSHICK, M. A., "The Prediction of Social and Technological Events," *Public Opinion Quarterly*, Vol. 14, No. 1 (1950), pp. 93–110. An outstandingly important experiment in social prediction.

LUNDBERG, George A., *Social Research* (New York, Longmans, Green, 1942), pp. 1–44. This opening chapter on "The Theory and Planning of Social Research," has a highly significant section on "Predictability of Social Behavior."

OGBURN, William F., "How Technology Changes Society," *Sociology and Social Research,* Vol. 36 (November, 1951), pp. 75–83. In this article the outstanding leader in sociological thinking about social change presents his basic conception of the part played by technology in social change, and hence of the ways in which technology must be taken into account in predicting the future.

————, "On Predicting the Future," in his *The Social Effects of Aviation* (Boston, Houghton Mifflin, 1946), pp. 32–57. A thoughtful review, by the most famous expert in the field, calling attention to a series of considerations which need to be born in mind in attempting social forecasts.

CHAPTER 20

PLANNING IN THE ATOMIC CRISIS

■ *Hornell Hart*

THE NATURE OF THE ATOMIC CRISIS

Previous chapters in this book have already set forth in considerable detail the nature of the atomic crisis. The essential conclusions already reached on this subject in this text are as follows:

1. Acceleration in technological mastery is one of the most fundamental tendencies of cultural development.

2. The acceleration in the technologies of destruction has now reached a point where the menace to civilization is increasing with almost incredible speed.

3. Within a decade, atomic weapons may be expected to be developed in Argentina, Australia, Belgium, Brazil, Canada, France, India, Netherlands, Norway, South Africa, and Sweden.[1]

4. To safeguard civilization against the pulverizing of its cities and the decimation, paralysis, and starvation of its nations through nuclear and bacteriological warfare requires an immense acceleration from past progress toward the development of world law and order based on consent and scientific insight.

The Atomic Crisis in Historical Perspective

Social planning involves the application of systematic thinking—and if possible of scientific findings—to the solution of social problems. Science can be applied only to phenomena which recur (or crucial elements of which recur) repeatedly in identifiable forms. If social planning is to be applied to the atomic crisis, it is necessary to identify that crisis as a special case of a recurrent type of social phenomenon, or as involving identifiable recurrent elements. Previous chapters (and especially Chapter 17) have shown that the atomic crisis is a highly acute example of menacing cultural lag. Once the category of "damaging or menacing cultural lags" is identified, it becomes

---

[1] *Bulletin of the Atomic Scientists,* Vol. IX (September, 1953), p. 243.

evident that a long series of such lags has been occurring down through history.

Innovations usually have negative as well as positive effects upon values. They not only facilitate the carrying out of various purposes and the satisfying of various needs and desires, but they also are likely to damage or menace the structures and the functioning of various individuals and organizations. These damages and menaces may be classified into two broad groups: (1) those which occur through the careless, unguarded, or inadequately organized uses of newly invented powers or facilities; and (2) those which occur through deliberately exploitive or destructive uses. Without attempting an exhaustive inventory, the table below contains a list of casually collected instances which may be clarifying.

SOME EXAMPLES OF DAMAGING OR MENACING CULTURAL LAGS CREATED BY TECHNOLOGICAL ADVANCES

The Technological Advance	Menaces Created (or Accentuated)	
	Accidental	Deliberate
Fire	Burns; conflagrations	Arson
Poison	Accidental poisoning	Murder
Knives; daggers; cutting tools	Accidental cuts	Mayhem; murder
Slavery	Race problems	Enslavement
Explosives	Accidental explosions	Bombardments
Pistols, revolvers, machine guns	Accidental shootings	Murders, hold-ups; robberies; gangsterism
Paper currency; bank credit	Loss or destruction of hoarded currency	Counterfeiting; embezzlement; fraudulent securities
Insurance	High costs due to inefficient administration	Fraudulent collection of benefits
Coal mining	Explosions, fires, cave-ins	Nation-paralyzing strikes
Manufacturing by machinery	Maiming; occupational diseases; deaths; slums; unemployment	Sabotage; child-labor; absentee landlordism
Railroads	Collisions, derailings, manglings, etc.	Sabotage; financial frauds; rail-rate collusions
Automobiles	Accidental injuries and deaths	Gangsterism; murder; auto thefts; kidnapping
Airplanes	Crashes	Aerial bombings
Radio, movies, cheap printing, and other modern technologies of communication	Psychological damage to the immature; flights from reality	Exploitive propaganda; fraudulent advertising; pandering to sensationalism
Bacteriology	Infections of laboratory workers	Bacteriological warfare
Nuclear energy	Radiation poisoning; disasters of all sizes	Devastation of civilization

The Accidental Type of Cultural Lag

Mankind has been exposed to accidental disasters since long before the dawn of history. Indeed, even before men created their own technological menaces by new inventions, they encountered accidental dangers from high cliffs, wild animals, bacteria, storms, and earthquakes. With the introduction of fire, poison, and cutting tools, man-made accidents multiplied.

Forms of cultural lag which are due to accidental maladjustments (such as death rates from storms, spontaneous epidemics, railroad, automobile and air catastrophes, and industrial diseases involve primarily problems of mechanical and biological adjustment, in which the difficulties are largely technical. A certain amount of resistance is to be expected from individuals who have to change their habits and attitudes in order to apply new safeguards, but the major problem consists in solving questions of natural science.

The Exploitive Aspect

In contrast with accidental cultural lag, a second type of lag consists in problems created by the fact that certain groups of individuals make a financial profit, gain political power, or otherwise strengthen themselves through the deliberate exploitation of new inventions and discoveries; and that the elimination of the unfavorable consequences has to be accomplished in the face of the opposition of those who benefit by the maladjustment. This is the obverse of the resistance to innovation which develops from vested interests that would be damaged by adoption of a new invention or discovery. The exploitive use of new inventions brings up basic questions of social control. For example, the invention of bank checks made it possible for forgers to profit at the expense of the banking system or of depositors. The development of steam-powered factories made it possible for employers to exploit child labor, women's labor, and unorganized adult male labor. The development of the "blitz" type of air-tank warfare made it possible for Hitler to conquer Poland, France, and other large areas, and to exploit them militarily, politically, and economically. The discovery of certain pain-relieving drugs and of other "patent medicines" has made it possible for unscrupulous manufacturers to exploit persons who become habituated to such drugs. To overcome cultural lags of these exploitive types requires not merely that technical devices be developed, but also—and primarily—that methods of social control be perfected whereby the power to exploit is taken away from possessors of these new inventions and the new developments are assimilated into constructive or at least harmless functions in the culture. One of the basic difficulties about dealing with nuclear bombs and with bacteriological and chemical forms of warfare is that these resources, in the hands of unscrupulous dictators, become potential instruments for international blackmail and for political conquest and aggression.

The Problem of the Aggressor as Related to Cultural Lag

In addition to the technological problems of adjusting to new inventions, and the problems of social control raised by exploitive types of cultural lag, the phenomenon of aggression introduces special difficulties. Whenever a new invention has increased the power of individuals over other individuals and groups, certain persons have seized upon that invention as an instrument for exploitation. Examples given in the table above include poisons, firearms, methods of swift transportation, and the new war technologies. The unscrupulous exploiter can gain at least a short-run advantage by *sudden* use of such discoveries—particularly before safeguards have been developed. For example, the possessor of a revolver who is unscrupulous, and quick on the draw, can rob and otherwise coerce individuals with whom he comes into contact until the posse, or the police, or the FBI catch up with him. Similar principles apply to the use of poisons, the use of burglar tools for cracking safes, the use of rapid means of transportation to provide get-aways for criminals, and the like.

These principles apply with particular effect to the use of the modern technologies of destruction by dictatorships. Dictatorships have an opportunity to execute sudden aggressions which cannot be undertaken by democratic countries without sacrificing the essence of the democratic system. To be specific, the Japanese launched the Pearl Harbor raid without any warning. Similarly, it is theoretically possible for the Kremlin to launch a paralyzing raid against American cities without any warning. But in the case of the nuclear raid, the consequences in devastation and paralysis would be as immensely greater than the Pearl Harbor effect as hydrogen weapons are greater than TNT bombs.

This advantage of the unscrupulous aggressor gives him a time interval which is determined quite largely by the efficiency of the policing systems for preventing crime and for capturing criminals and making them harmless. There is always (in our cities) a residuum of unprevented crime—burglary, robbery, arson, rape—through which innocent and law-abiding citizens are exploited, damaged, or even killed. But in the event of a paralysis raid against the United States, this aggressor's margin can mean to the nation not a merely inconvenient, painful, or damaging effect of social imperfection but a fatal disaster which (if it could be recouped at all) would at best reduce human standards of living abysmally, for centuries.

The above factors summarize, in a brief way, the major aspects of the atomic crisis resulting from atomic cultural lag. The rest of the present chapter seeks to explore the possibilities for deliberate and constructive social action in response to that challenge.

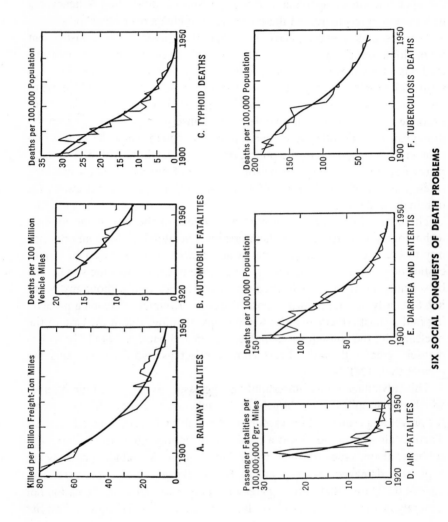

Killed per Billion Freight-Ton Miles

A. RAILWAY FATALITIES

Deaths per 100 Million Vehicle Miles

B. AUTOMOBILE FATALITIES

Deaths per 100,000 Population

C. TYPHOID DEATHS

Passenger Fatalities per 100,000,000 Pgr. Miles

D. AIR FATALITIES

Deaths per 100,000 Population

E. DIARRHEA AND ENTERITIS

Deaths per 100,000 Population

F. TUBERCULOSIS DEATHS

SIX SOCIAL CONQUESTS OF DEATH PROBLEMS

CAN SOCIAL PLANNING DEAL WITH ACCIDENTAL CULTURAL LAG?

Ward versus Sumner

Sociologists have differed widely as to whether deliberate and systematic social effort can produce effective solutions of such problems as those listed on page 475—or, indeed, whether collective purposeful action can have any constructive effect whatever. Without taking space for a theoretical discussion of this issue, the extremes may well be exemplified by the positions of Lester Frank Ward on the one hand and of William Graham Sumner on the other. One of the most distinctive things in Ward's social philosophy was his passionate affirmation of the possibility of intelligent social progress. He believed that society can direct or at least greatly modify its own evolution for the benefit of man.[2] In contrast, Sumner's laissez-faire philosophy was summed up in his essay on "The Absurd Effort to Make the World Over."[3]

The scientific way to attack a controversial question of this kind is to examine factual instances and gradually to build up inductively operational principles on which successful social policies may be founded. As a start in this direction, let us first examine a series of cultural lags which may be classified in the accidental group. The conquest of six such problems is represented by the indexes shown graphically in the chart on page 478. Each of these six problems involved high death rates due to cultural lag.

Air-Travel Killings

One of the clearer cases of the lag of social adjustment behind technological progress is represented by Graph D, in the lower left-hand corner of the chart, representing the trend of air-passenger death rates in crashes of regularly scheduled domestic carriers. (The date scales on all the charts are the same.) The trend of airplane fatalities, like that of railroad fatalities, has been steeply downward. Reduction of airplane fatalities has been far steeper than that for steam travel: the railroad death rate required fifty years to be reduced to one-tenth of its 1890 level, whereas the airplane death rate was cut to one-tenth of its 1930 level in fifteen years. This comparison fits into the general principle that social change is taking place at faster and faster rates. In view of the critical need for accelerated reduction in the military death rate, this accelerating improvement offers hope.

Automobile Fatalities

As a measure of the amount of exposure to automobile accidents, the number of vehicle-miles traveled is used here (since the number of passenger-

[2] Charles A. Ellwood, *A History of Social Philosophy* (Englewood Cliffs, N. J., Prentice-Hall, 1938), p. 547.

[3] William Graham Sumner, *War and Other Essays* (New Haven, Yale University Press, 1919), pp. 196–210.

miles cannot be estimated reliably). The death rate of motor-vehicle acci-dents, per hundred-million vehicle miles, has been decreasing along a reversed exponential trend, as illustrated in Graph B. The proportional de-crease, from 1920 to 1953, was intermediate between that achieved in rail-way deaths and in airplane deaths. This has been accomplished in spite of the fact that the proportion of passenger automobiles traveling over 50 miles per hour has increased from 38 per cent in 1942 to 53 per cent in 1952, while truck-speeds have shown a corresponding increase.[4] The decline in auto-mobile fatalities has been achieved by the enforcement of highway safety laws, an intensive campaign of public education, improvements in the strength and dependability of automobiles, and improvements in highway design.

Baby Deaths

Graph E in the chart shows the conquest of diarrhea and enteritis. In this case, again, although the problem presents itself as a medical one, the actual origin is closely related to the ancient invention of securing milk from cattle, to the more modern invention of the nursing bottle, and particularly to the de-velopment of slum conditions in the cities which grew up after the Industrial Revolution, in which outhouses and open sewers provided breeding places for flies that systematically conveyed bacteria from sick babies into the food of well babies. The overcoming of cultural lag in this example involved an even greater achievement of social and political organization than in the conquest of typhoid (discussion of which has been omitted here for lack of space). The carrying out of elaborate statistical studies to determine the causes of infant mortality,[5] the carrying forward of campaigns to eliminate unscreened outhouses and other sources of contamination, the battle against the housefly, the development of clinics in which mothers were instructed how to save their babies' lives—and above all, the pasteurization of milk and the inspection services to enforce the elimination of the sources of disease—such measures were responsible for cutting this death-rate to a level only one-twentieth as high as it was fifty years ago.

The progressive conquest of railway accidents is shown in Graph A of the chart; that of typhoid fever is shown in Graph C, and that of tuberculosis in Graph F. The factors involved are sufficiently similar to those already dis-cussed so that comments may be left to the reader.

The Significance of Cultural Acceleration in Relation to Accidental Lags

The success of collective endeavors to reduce the death rates resulting from the three types of traffic accidents and from the three types of civiliza-tion-aggravated diseases graphed in the chart might seem to promise suc-

[4] *Highway Statistics, 1952* (Washington, Department of Commerce, 1953), p. 60.
[5] E.g., Robert Morse Woodbury, *Causal Factors in Infant Mortality* (Washington, Children's Bureau, 1925).

cessful conquest of all the types of accidental cultural-lag menaces listed in column 2 of the table on page 475. But one aspect of that series is disturbing when confronted searchingly, namely, the significance of the acceleration factor.

The principle of acceleration applies to the accidental consequences of technological inventions as it does in other aspects of innovation. First, the size of accidental disasters has been correlated with the magnitude and power of the structures, tools, chemicals, and other inventions involved. The gash resulting from the accidental slippage of a flint blade is only a tiny fraction of the damage to human bodies which results, say, from a major explosion in a modern factory. Moreover, technological progress has involved the concentration of larger and larger numbers of people, with the result that modern disasters tend to kill and maim more people than primitive disasters did. The overturning of a canoe means a smaller loss of life than the sinking of an ocean liner; the burning of a primitive grass hut causes less damage to human beings than such disasters as the Chicago or San Francisco fires. Both the amount of damage per individual and the number of individuals involved increase. These dangers are further swollen by growth in the sizes of cities, factories, crowds, ships, trains, and other units subject to damage.

But now consider the conclusion from a syllogism which emerges from the facts about acceleration in the magnitude of disasters. The major premise is that the number of people killed and the amount of property destroyed in accidents resulting from inadequately controlled technological inventions has tended to increase with the increase in the power of the inventions and in the size and richness of the groups and structures subject to being damaged. The minor premise is that the power of nuclear-energy releases and the richness of the target areas likely to be damaged by nuclear bombardment are both increasing with accelerating speed. The conclusion is that nuclear accidents are becoming more and more menacing as potential sources of world catastrophe. The accidental radiation-burning of Japanese fishermen by fallout of radioactive material from the fusion-bomb explosion in March, 1954, is a very minor example of the kind of thing to be expected. In April, 1954, William L. Laurance, science commentator of *The New York Times,* wrote:[6]

[It is now] certain that the most dreaded weapon of all—the cobalt bomb— . . . can be successfully built. This is the type of hydrogen bomb of which Albert Einstein said: "If successful, radioactive poisoning of the atmosphere and hence annihilation of any life on earth, will have been brought within the range of technical possibilities."

The most elaborate safety precautions are taken to prevent nuclear accidents. Yet the accident to the Japanese fishermen *did* occur. And as the potential size of such accidents goes on skyrocketing, it will not be enough

[6] William L. Laurance, "Now Most Dreaded Weapon, Cobalt Bomb, Can Be Built," *New York Times,* April 7, 1954, p. 4, cols. 4–6.

merely to reduce the *rate*. One or two of the kind of accidents looming as possibilities in the near future might be fatal to civilization—or to the human race.

SOLVING EXPLOITIVE AND AGGRESSIVE CULTURAL LAGS

Social Reform versus Social Planning

Social reform differs from social planning in several respects. First, social reform is ordinarily motivated by strong emotional revulsion against some form of cultural lag. Personal experience of one's own suffering from social maladjustment, sympathy with other sufferers, indignation at obstructionists who ignorantly or conservatively resist the advocated social change—such motives as these are prominent, with the result that the reform movement is likely to take on the character of a crusade involving verbal, legislative, and sometimes physical attacks upon the opposition. When the problem is created by aggressors or is maintained by exploiters who are profiting by the cultural lag, the indignation of reformers is likely to be intensified. Social planning, on the other hand, stresses much more dispassionate appraisal of the social needs involved and much more systematic application of research and of established scientific knowledge to the development of techniques for meeting those needs.

Second, social reform is ordinarily concerned more with altering the existing structure of specific social institutions, particularly in legislative ways, whereas social planning is ordinarily concerned more with administrative problems related to applying existing laws and to improving the functioning of existing social organizations.

Third, social reform usually must acquire the power to act by electing a slate of candidates, passing legislation, or the like, whereas social planning is usually based on authority already acquired and is concerned with the wise utilization and application of that power.

In spite of the above three differences, social reform and social planning merge into each other; they may be regarded as two phases of the same continuum, differentiated merely with respect to the ratios between emotional drive and scientific procedure, between legislative modifications and administrative improvements, and between the acquisition and the utilization of social power.

The six examples of successful reduction in death rates produced by cultural lags each involve (in varying degrees) both social reform and social planning. The reduction of infant mortality and of motor-traffic deaths have both engaged the activities of social reformers—as, indeed, have all the other four forms of death-conquest summarized in the chart on page 478. But each of the six has also involved extensive social planning.

Child Labor Reduction as a Social Reform Movement

Closely related to the movement for the reduction of infant mortality has been the series of campaigns for the reduction and progressive elimination of child labor. Many of the same organizations were involved in both of these movements. The infant mortality problem may be regarded as an example primarily of the accidental type of cultural lag. Various incidental forms of social exploitation were involved, but the fundamental problem was the quite unintentional increase in infant mortality which was brought about by the growth of urban congestion and other factors which have already been reviewed. The child-labor problem, on the contrary, provides an outstanding example of social exploitation. The problem developed when (in the early stages of the Industrial Revolution) the builders of factories discovered that various types of machinery could be operated by children who could be hired at very low rates of pay. Not merely machine processes, but also mass production in general, opened up the possibility of exploiting children and reaping financial profits by purchasing juvenile services at low rates. For example, the development of sugar-beet farming created types of agricultural labor which could be performed on a mass-production basis by children; this resulted in a form of agricultural child labor which social reformers regarded as very damaging. The development of city newspapers with huge circulations provided other channels through which child labor was exploited in the sale of papers. The use of children to sweep chimneys in England and elsewhere was cultural lag related to the invention of chimneys and of soft-coal-burning grates. It was not due to the invention of machinery, but on the contrary was actually eliminated ultimately by the invention and utilization of chimney-sweeping machines. On the other hand, the vast bulk of child labor in textile mills, glass-blowing plants, coal mines, and the like may be ascribed (1) to the development of the factory system, and (2) to the introduction of semiskilled machine processes on which children could be employed at low wages.

The movement for legal regulation of child labor began at the close of the eighteenth century in Great Britain. An international labor conference in 1890 discussed child labor among other problems. In the United States, the National Consumers League was organized in 1899 and was led for many years by an enthusiastic social reformer named Florence Kelley. In 1904 the National Child Labor Committee was created and was led vigorously for years by another social reformer named Owen R. Lovejoy.

In 1924, the National Consumers League reported:[7]

In 1900 less than a dozen states were seriously attempting to limit the labor of children in mills, mines, factories or stores, in sweatshops or street trades. Such laws as existed were chiefly unenforced, and all were lamentably meagre.

[7] *Encyclopedia of Social Sciences* (New York, Macmillan, 1937), Vol. III, p. 418B.

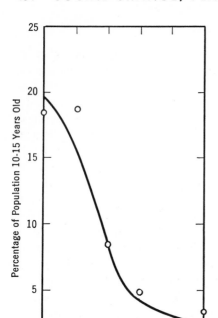
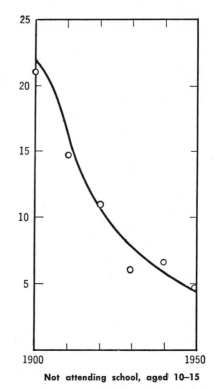

Gainful workers under 16   Not attending school, aged 10–15

TWO INDEXES OF THE DECLINE IN CHILD LABOR

. . . At the present [1924] all but two states have adopted a nominal age minimum of at least fourteen for full-time employment in industry and usually in some if not all other occupations.

Attempts to secure federal legislation to restrict child labor were marked outstandingly by repeated defeats. The first Federal Child Labor Act, passed in 1916, was declared unconstitutional in 1918. The second Federal Child Labor Act, passed in 1919, was declared unconstitutional in 1922. A Child Labor Amendment to the federal Constitution, approved by Congress in 1924, was acted on adversely by more than three-quarters of the states. It was not until 1938 that Congress actually provided legal restraints on child labor by passing the Fair Labor Standards Act, applying a basic 16-year minimum age for employment in industries producing goods for interstate commerce. ·

In spite of the repeated rebuffs between 1900 and 1938, the percentage of children 10 to 15 years of age reported as being gainfully employed decreased as indicated in the chart above. The percentage dropped from 18.4 in 1910 to 1.8 in 1940. The logistic trend line shows a decline of 88 per cent between 1905 and 1950.

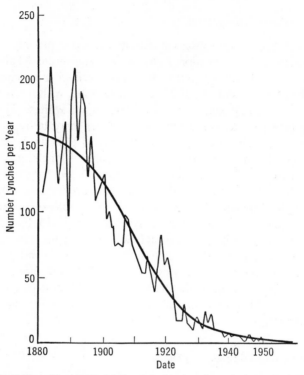

SOURCE: Hornell Hart, "Logistic Social Trends," *American Journal of Sociology*, Vol. 50 (1945), p. 353, supplemented with subsequent data.

NUMBER OF PERSONS LYNCHED IN THE UNITED STATES PER YEAR, 1882–1951, WITH LOGISTIC TREND

Closely related to child labor is the percentage of children aged 10 to 15 not reported as attending school. (That index is shown at the right of the chart.) The movement to raise the age of compulsory school attendance, to extend the number of days of tuition provided per year, and to enforce truancy laws effectively was co-ordinated with the movement to raise the minimum age for employment of children and to enforce such provisions by adequate inspection.

These two movements were thus teamed up to apply social control to the use of children's time—negatively to forbid gainful employment and positively to require school attendance. Both movements made basic use of statistical research—by the Census, the Bureau of Education, the Children's Bureau and other governmental agencies, and by private organizations. Their joint success has been achieved not by any single, dramatic enactment but rather by the cumulative effects of various bits of legislation and the gradual transformation of social attitudes and administrative policies of national, state and local governments.

Reduction of the Lynching Rate

Whereas child labor illustrates exploitation, lynching provides an example of a problem involving aggression. Like the problems discussed above, lynching results from cultural lag; but in this case the instigating cause is to be found in the development of the African slave trade, with the resulting cultural clashes and status tensions between Negroes and whites. (The lynchings of white persons, which contributed to the total, may be regarded as the product of similar status-tensions, arising out of ill-assimilated economic and ethnic developments.) The persistent decline of lynching (as shown in the chart on page 485) is especially significant for our present purpose in view of two facts. First, the essential remedy has been not so much new legislation as the development of greater understanding, tolerance, and readiness to accept law and order. Long after the lynching rate had dropped to a small fraction of its one-time height, reformers were still trying, unsuccessfully, to get a federal anti-lynching law through Congress. A second point of high significance is the fact that the lynching rate fluctuated more widely than any of the indexes shown in the chart on page 478, and that the lynching problem is thus still further parallel to the problem of dealing with international warfare.

An Amendment to Cultural-Lag Theory

The facts brought out in the preceding sections, about the social conquest of death rates due to cultural lags, bring up for re-examination a proposition of Ogburn's which appears at the top of page 422 of the present book: "The strain which exists between two correlated parts of culture which change at unequal rates may be interpreted as a lag." The implication of this statement is that the rapidly changing aspect of culture creates problems more swiftly than the slowly changing aspect of culture can correct them; hence unsolved problems tend to accumulate. The most glaring example is the multiplication of destructive menaces connected with the extreme acceleration in military technology, combined with the very halting and seemingly ineffective developments of international law, international security arrangements, adjustments of relations between the wealthier, better-educated, and otherwise more prosperous nations as interacting with the poverty-stricken, ill-educated, and backward nations, and the like.

Theoretically, it seems quite plausible that technological invention should proceed much faster than political and sociopsychological adjustments. It is far easier to measure success in the development of more and more powerful explosives or of swifter and swifter projectiles than it is to measure success in developing international democracy, justice toward weaker peoples, sincere good will between nations, and the like. But when one seeks for specific illustrations of this apparent truism, one encounters the fact that in one field after another, the initial lag caused by swift technological development is (sooner or later) overcome. Thus the death rates from automobile accidents and from airplane crashes continue to decline in spite of the fact that safety regulations, adequate inspection of equipment, enforcement of speed laws, and the like, are sociopsychological in character and presumably must develop at slower rates than the technological developments which create the problems.

When this actual triumph of the apparently halting and tortoise-like sociopsychological, political, and attitudinal developments is recognized, the theory of cultural lag would seem to be in need of further revision. Speed of development would seem to be only one dimension of the problem. The multiplication of remedial factors may (apparently) overcome the inherent slowness of individual steps. To take a specific example, the rate of progress in the amount of power delivered per pound of automobile engine would seem to be inherently more rapid than improvement in legislation relative to safety on highways. The former is subject to accurate measurement, controlled experimentation, and clear definition of objectives, whereas the legislative process appears to take place by a series of more or less blundering conferences, deals, amendments, political pressures, and other not readily measurable social processes, activated by confused and more or less contradictory motivation. And yet the net effect of the combined efforts of various agencies to reduce the automobile traffic death rate per million passenger miles has been succeeding. The rate of such success, however, may or may not be sufficient to save the lives of given individuals or to prevent the occurrence of peak numbers of deaths on week-end holidays.

Similarly, feasible processes in international relations may or may not be sufficient to prevent such cataclysms as the hypothetical paralysis raid on American cities discussed in Chapter 10. But the crucial fact to recognize is that the fundamental principles of cultural lag are *not* such as to make defeat inevitable. First, as has been brought out in Chapter 21 (page 514), the Comtean theory has actually been working out in relation to social thinking. In the successive emergence of scientific method on more and more complex levels, the social sciences are now showing clear signs of following the upsurges in the prerequisite sciences out of which such momentous developments in the culture of the Western world have taken place. Second, the cumulation of social reform and social planning activities, focused on problems which have come to be recognized as crucial, has actually resulted in the solving of such lags as those which have just been reviewed in this chapter.

Civilization, therefore, is not doomed merely because of the slow and blundering processes of social control. Conceivably, these processes may be improved and speeded up to a point where the apparently overhanging disaster of nuclear World War III can be averted permanently. But it seems at the present time to be a touch-and-go possibility.

DEMOCRATIC VERSUS THE DICTATORSHIP CULTURE AREA

The Democratic Culture Area

A systematic study of past wars by Professor Quincy Wright, of the University of Chicago,[8] has brought out a fact of such major significance that all further planning for world law and order needs to be built on that foundation. The fact is this: twelve nations have demonstrated, during the past century and a third (1815 to 1956), that it is possible for democracies to work out their reciprocal national relations without war, and with major advantages in terms of their mutual prosperity and security. These twelve countries include the five English-speaking nations: the United States, Great Britain, Canada, New Zealand, and Australia. They include three Scandinavian countries: Sweden, Norway, and Denmark. They also include France, Switzerland, Netherlands, and Belgium. These countries form the nucleus of a common Democratic Culture Area.[9]

The culture-area concept regards the Western democracies as a special case of a fairly highly integrated group of cultural traits and complexes, the development of which does (it is true) conform to basic laws which have been adumbrated by sociology and anthropology, but which must be analyzed, interpreted, and dealt with in accordance with the distinctive characteristics which this particular area displays. These distinctive traits of the Democratic Culture Area may be summarized as follows:

1. **Democratic government.** Each of these twelve nations has a constitution which recognizes the people, acting through their elected representatives, as the supreme authority. This democracy is the product of centuries of experiment, experience, and evolution.

Governments in these countries are avowedly for the public welfare. In the democracies in general, the rights of minorities have on the whole been recognized and defended.

2. **Education** has been provided, in these twelve democracies, for larger and larger proportions of those able to profit by it.

3. **Free growth of science.** All of these countries have shared in the accelerating growth of science, interchanging their inventions and discoveries, and the applications of these to industry, agriculture, health, amusements, and other interests—particularly to military destructiveness. Science, like government, industry, and religion, has been strongly competitive but, as in those other fields, organized co-operation is increasingly taking the place of individualistic competition.

[8] Quincy Wright, *A Study of War* (Chicago, University of Chicago Press, 1942), Vol. I, pp. 644–646.

[9] This concept needs to be considered in relation to (1) that of "The Atlantic Civilization," or "The Atlantic Community"; and (2) the conception of civilizations in general as recurrent phenomena of a standard basic type. The former has been developed by Michael Kraus, in *The Atlantic Civilization: 18th Century Origins* (Ithaca, Cornell University Press, 1949). The oscillating theory is one which has been presented in various forms by Sorokin, Arnold Toynbee, Flinders Petrie, and others.

4. **The quest for verifiable truth.** The emphasis on scientific thinking has had a powerful influence toward exalting the ideal of verifiable truth as a basis for planning and for action. This same regard for verifiable truth extends into the legal systems of the democracies, and it undergirds business accounting, engineering, and reputable journalism in the democracies. Where it fails to so do, citizens of these countries recognize that to that extent their social system is showing dangerous weaknesses.

5. **Competitive capitalism, evolving toward state socialism.**[10] All of these twelve countries have based their economic life on private property, more-or-less free competition, and individual initiative. But in all of them, the size of industrial and financial organizations has been increasing with accelerating speed, economic power has tended to gravitate into the hands of more-or-less monopolistic interests, labor unions have gained increasing power, government regulation has grown, welfare activities have developed, governmental functions and budgets have expanded acceleratingly, and free competition has more and more been superseded by governmental and private collective action.

6. **The standards of living** in these twelve countries are the highest in the world, and have been increasing more rapidly than in other nations. Death rates are lower, and expectations of life higher, than anywhere else.

7. **Protestantism and religious toleration.** All these countries have had overwhelmingly more Christians than members of any other religion, and in practically all of them (except France and Belgium) Catholics have formed only a minority of the Christians in recent decades.

8. **Warless co-operation with other democracies.** International relations between these twelve democracies have tended toward voluntary co-operation. None of them has engaged in warfare against another of this group for over 135 years.[11] Except for countries maintaining neutrality, and countries occupied by enemy armies, all of these nations allied themselves together in World War I and World War II against militaristic and dictatorial aggression. Practically all of them have been active participants in the League of Nations and the United Nations. America has given tens of billions of dollars for lend-lease, for relief, and for Marshall-Plan and other foreign-aid grants to former enemy nations as well as to its allies. The leading democracies are now acting through the United Nations and the North Atlantic Treaty Organization (NATO) to guard against threats to their respective and collective interests.

9. **Imperialism, evolving toward commonwealth.** Toward weaker, less educated, and economically less developed nations, the democracies first developed exploitive policies, but they gradually modified their relations in the

[10] Cf. Calvin B. Hoover's summary in his "Institutional and Theoretical Implications of Economic Change," *American Economic Review,* Vol. 44 (March, 1954), p. 14.

[11] The Civil War in the United States, the Boer War and Irish Rebellion in the British Commonwealth, and the Sunderbund War in Switzerland involved hostilities *inside* democratic nations, See Quincy Wright, *op. cit.,* pp. 644–646.

direction of co-operative commonwealth, as exemplified in the freeing of
the Philippines by the United States and of Eire and India by Great Britain.
How swift this progress has been since the UN Charter was signed is shown
by the following tabulation:[12]

Date	Total Population of Non-Self-Governing Colonies of Western Democracies
June, 1945	700,000,000
December, 1954	170,000,000

10. **Freedom as the key to Western culture.** The nine characteristics just
reviewed involve, over and over again, the basing of social relations upon
regulated competition and regulated conflict, as means whereby personalities and organizations may be given maximum freedom to function in accordance with their own purposes and characteristics, subject (theoretically)
to only such restrictions as may be necessary to prevent intereference with
the functioning of other personalities and organizations. This cultural development appears to have had its roots in the Reformation as a struggle for
liberation from the religious regimentation imposed by the Catholic Church
and in political revolutions against the feudalism which regimented political
life. The Industrial Revolution also represented a swift emergence of individuals, firms, and corporations which took over the libertarian ideals developed in political revolutions. The idea of free competition with a minimum
of state interference was rationalized by Adam Smith and the other classical
economists, and received intellectual reinforcement in Darwin's theory of
evolution through survival of the fit in the struggle for existence.

The democracies have set up fulfillment of life for the individual as the
goal of social activity, but have conceived of this as something which has
to be achieved through competitive struggle, with such regulation as may be
found to be necessary in order to prevent the growth of new tyranny through
monopolies.

The Soviet-Dictatorship Culture Area

That at least twelve nations belong to a living and expanding area of international democracy seems clear from the evidence reviewed in the preceding section. But the world struggle is due to the fact that a rival culture
area has also been expanding—namely, the area of communistic dictatorship. The present section will be devoted to reviewing outstanding characteristics of this antagonistic culture.

Soviet Russia is inhabited by diverse ethnic groups, speaking scores of
different languages and dialects. In many respects, therefore, the culture of
the peoples ruled by the Soviet dictatorship is anything but homogeneous—
particularly when such conquests as China, East Germany, Czechoslovakia,

---

[12] "Decline of Colonialism . . . ," map accompanying article by Sydney Gruson,
" 'Colonialism,' a Continuing Issue," *New York Times,* December 19, 1954, p. E5,
cols. 3–6. Cf. *ibid.,* April 24, 1955, p. E5, cols. 3–8, and December 11, 1955, p. E5,
cols. 3–8.

and so forth are included. Yet when the communistic system, in the historic cultural setting of the Land of the Czars, is contrasted point by point with the basic cultural features of the Western democracies, the dictatorship is found to differ radically and fundamentally in traits which either are already shared by the Russian people as a whole or are being imposed systematically upon all those who are absorbed into the U.S.S.R.

1. **Dictatorship by communist leaders.** The Soviet government has been developed out of centuries of experience with absolute monarchy, censorship, suppression of political parties, and imprisonment or death for all who oppose the government. All power in the Soviet Union has been concentrated in the hands of a small group of dictatorial leaders in the Kremlin.[13] This dictatorship maintains its power by forbidding all rival political parties and other organizations which it does not dominate; by rigid censorship of the press, radio, education, and international travel; by purging, imprisoning, or liquidating incipient opponents; and by maintaining a secret police with sweeping powers to enforce such measures. Russian communism has based its whole system on the proposition that the welfare of the common people can be achieved only through a violent revolutionary struggle against all private owners of productive wealth in all the world, that this struggle can succeed only by a dictatorship centered in the Kremlin, and that individual citizens or organizations can have no freedom and no rights except such as the dictatorship regards as favorable to the communistic revolution.

2. **Education of the people, as inmates of a dictatorship,** has been provided by the Soviet regime. But education and journalism in the Soviet culture area are used as instruments for promoting the dictatorship. History, current events, and even science and art are all distorted—and often directly falsified—in order to promote the current purposes of the Communist party leadership.

3. **Science** is also made the servant of dictatorship. Science and art, like education, are regarded as instruments to promote the Soviet communistic program. Scientists are encouraged to carry on researches leading toward the saving of Russian soldier lives, the development of atomic and hydrogen bombs, and pure scientific knowledge such as may produce results useful to the government. But it would be highly dangerous to any investigator to delve into social, political, or economic problems unless the results were guaranteed in advance to conform to the party line (i.e., to the theories and policies currently accepted and promoted by the Soviet authorities).

[13] "The Change Going on in Russia," *U. S. News & World Report,* Vol. 36 (February, 26, 1954), pp. 17–20. This digest of the views of "the top specialists of U.S., Britain and France" reported that three men, Khrushchev, Malenkov, and Molotov, formed a dictatorial committee that dominated the Presidium of the Communist Party Central Committee, which was "the real power in Russia." See also Harry Schwartz, "Communism: The Promise and the Reality," *New York Times* Magazine Section, May 2, 1954, pp. 9, 76, 77.

4. **Soviet "truth"** consists in whatever the Kremlin regards as expedient for promoting the policies of the Communist party.

Soviet court trials are not agencies for bringing out impartial truth but propaganda devices for proving to the public that the accused is guilty as charged.

Soviet statistics have been so falsified by the communists that only by indirect inferences can economists arrive at even plausible guesses relative to Russian development. Such falsifications are defended by communists as justifiable means to highly desirable ends.

5. **The Soviet economic system is communism,** evolving (apparently) toward a new exploitive class system.[14] Just as the political dictatorship in Russia has evolved out of centuries of Czaristic tyranny, so too the economic dictatorship has evolved out of ages of serfdom.

Russia's economic life has been swiftly going through the industrial revolution which Europe and America experienced a century ago. But in Russia all the factories, mines, railroads, and other means of production are owned and operated by government agencies. Even the farms are collectivized and operated as great government plantations. Instead of individual initiative, all industrial and agricultural production is carried out under five-year plans, which are imposed by government officials. Industrial managers who fail to conform to the plan are treated as criminals.

In the early years of the communist revolution, the ideal was to reduce economic inequality to a minimum. Increasingly the government officials, army officers, engineers, scientists, artists, and other powerful or valuable individuals have been given rewards and privileges more and more exceeding those of the rank and file.

6. **The standards of living** in Soviet Russia are among the lowest in Europe.[15] Until recently, the general scale of living of the common people is reported to have been as low as under the Czars—indeed, it is so low that the Russian rulers dare not allow their people to know how much better off workers and peasants are in neighboring countries. Partly this is due to the waste and destruction of two world wars. But it is also due to the extremely low efficiency of labor and of management under the Soviet regime, and to the large fraction of the Soviet national income which is devoted to military purposes. The expectation of life at birth in European Russia in 1930 was approximately 46 years, as compared with 60 years in the democratic countries. Life expectancy in Russia was lower than in any other European country.[16]

---

[14] Cf. Calvin B. Hoover, *op. cit.,* p. 2; Harry Schwartz, *op. cit.,* p. 76.

[15] Colin Clark, "Levels of Real National Product per Man-Hour," *Review of Economic Progress,* Vol. 1 (April, 1949), pp. 1–3.

[16] Derived from data in the Metropolitan Life Insurance Company's *Statistical Bulletin,* Vol. 31 (March, 1950), p. 2. That the Russian death rate dropped from 20 per 1,000 in 1938 to 8.9 per 1,000 in 1953 was claimed by Soviet Deputy Premier Anastas J. Milsoyan (*New York Times,* May 16, 1954, p. 31, col. 1). If true, this would mean a spectacular rise in Russian expectation of life.

Stewart Alsop reported the following findings on the basis of a recent trip to the Soviet Union:[17]

(*a*) By our standards, the Soviet citizen "is dully fed, badly housed, hideously clothed, lacking in the rudiments of freedom, and ruthlessly exploited by the State. By his standards he is better fed, better housed, better clothed than he remembers ever being. By his standards, moreover, he is almost intoxicatingly free from fear for the police terror has unquestionably been greatly muted since the death of . . . Stalin."

(*b*) The younger generation in Russia, born to the misery of war, wholly isolated from the world, and knowing only a slow but steady alleviation of misery, quite genuinely share the conviction that the Soviet system is superior to that of non-Communistic countries, and that the triumph of Communism is inevitable. As one young Russian expressed it to Alsop: "Your world is dying."

(*c*) Some economists claim that the Soviet economy is expanding at a rate double that of the United States; others that it is expanding only half again as fast. But no informed economist doubts that the rate of Soviet economic expansion, as measured in the production of steel and other indices of economic growth, is markedly greater than that of the Western nations. The Soviet workers are being ruthlessly exploited, but because they do not know it they do not resent it.

(*d*) The Soviet citizen has been trained to the conviction that any war can result only from imperialistic, capitalistic aggression, and that the "breakers of the peace" must be punished with a ruthlessness terrible enough to fit the terrible crime. The Red Army could march on Western Europe tomorrow, and the rank and file of Russians would respond in their millions to the call to arms against "the unspeakable capitalistic aggressors."

7. **Religion as the "opiate of the people."** Whereas the democratic nations have been preponderantly Protestant, with relative freedom from dogma and from ecclesiastical authority, Russia was dominated for centuries by the Eastern Orthodox Catholic Church. The Soviet repudiation of religious dogma has meant not a new freedom but a transfer to a new dogma and a new hierarchical domination.

Communists believe that all aspects of culture (including government, art, and religion) are determined by the ways in which people make their living. To them, Christianity is simply a propaganda agency, utilized by capitalism as a means of keeping the masses acquiescent while the capitalists exploit them. The Communist party in Russia has been aggressively atheistic. Even when religious toleration has been avowed, the revived Russian Orthodox Church has been used as an agency to promote Soviet policies, both in Russia and in other countries.

8. **The Soviet foreign policy is imperialism,** avowedly paternalistic, but expanding by fear, force, fraud, and secrecy. Russia has taken armed possession of Esthonia, Latvia, Lithuania, Poland, Czechoslovakia, and Rumania, and of parts of Finland. By armed occupation and otherwise she has fostered the imposition of communistic dictatorships in Yugoslavia, Bulgaria, Albania, Sinkian, and Outer Mongolia. In Hungary and in Austria the

[17] Stewart Alsop, "Those Smug, Smug Russians," *Saturday Evening Post* (December 31, 1955), pp. 66–67.

communists were "snowed under" in elections in November, 1945, but communism is not stopped by election defeats. Russia's military occupation of her sector of Germany has been used to quench liberty and impose communism there. Communists dominate China and North Korea. Through the Chinese dictatorship, communism seeks to subjugate all of Asia. Russia has been threatening Turkey, demanding control of the Dardanelles, and seeking strategic holdings in Northern Africa. Russia proclaims her interest in the poorer farmers and the masses of the workers and has taken property away from rich landowners and business groups (including a number of American corporations holding property in her zone of power), and she has been illegally seizing and taking to Russia vast amounts of machinery, food, and other property from countries occupied by her troops. She has encouraged various peoples subject to her to teach their own native languages in their schools and to cultivate local autonomy in some other ways, but she dictates their basic economic, political, and international policies.

9. **Their program is world domination.** "The Soviet leaders," said John Foster Dulles,[18] "consider peace and security to depend upon eradicating the non-Soviet type of society which now dangerously divides the one world into incompatible halves. . . . They consider the Soviet type of proletariat dictatorship, originated to promote the welfare of the masses and to end the exploitation of man by man, to be the ideal kind of government." Stalin, in his *Problems of Leninism,* quoted with approval the following statement by Lenin:[19]

It is inconceivable that the Soviet Republic should continue for a long period side by side with imperialist states. Ultimately one or the other must conquer. Meanwhile a number of terrible clashes between the Soviet Republic and the bourgeois states is inevitable.

On February 9, 1946, Stalin reiterated his belief that wars are inevitable so long as the capitalist system exists. While Russia apparently has not been ready for all-out war, her avowed program calls for using the agencies of democracy to destroy democracy. No basic change in these objectives appears to have developed since Stalin's death. Whether de-Stalinization will lead to mitigation of the Soviet drive toward world conquest is a question to be studied searchingly as the process develops.

Many documented studies of Soviet policies have reached essentially the above conclusions, as to the nature of the communistic culture area.[20] The

[18] "Dulles Sees World Conquest USSR Goal," *New York Times,* March 14, 1950, p. 2, col. 3.

[19] J. Stalin, *Problems of Leninism* (Moscow, Foreign Languages Publishing House, 1940); see also William C. Bullitt, *The Great Globe Itself* (New York, Scribner, 1946), pp. 96 and 98.

[20] One outstanding study of this kind has been made by the chairman of the Lebanon Delegation to the Fourth Session of the UN General Assembly, Dr. Charles Malik, in his statement before the Political Committee of the General Assembly, November 23, 1949, published by the National Committee for Free Europe, 301 Empire State Building, New York 1, New York.

facts are matters of common knowledge among intelligent people who are familiar with history and with current events. They do deserve detailed exploration, which they are receiving from many contemporary students of comparative culture. The admitted contrasts have some very practical bearings on the question of how the Soviet government can or cannot be dealt with successfully in the atomic crisis.

ANNOTATED BIBLIOGRAPHY

BAUER, Raymond Augustine, and others, *How the Soviet System Works; Cultural, Psychological, and Social Themes* (Cambridge, Harvard University Press, 1956). An attempt to assess the social and psychological strengths and weaknesses of the Soviet system on the basis of interviews with hundreds and questionnaires administered to thousands of refugees from the Soviet Union.

CUBER, John F., "Social Problems and Social Valuation," in his *Sociology: A Synopsis of Principles,* 3rd ed. (New York, Appleton-Century-Crofts, 1955), pp. 615–635. The author of a widely used sociology text comes to grips with the basic problem of social values.

HINDUS, Maurice, *Crisis in the Kremlin* (New York, Doubleday, 1953). The "Kremlin leaders," declares Mr. Hindus, "do not want war, cannot afford it, and can only dread it." The Kremlin, he thinks, is "too property-minded" and "too production-conscious to welcome or risk the destruction of its industrial accomplishments."

LUNDBERG, George A., SCHRAG, Clarence C., and LARSEN, Otto N., "Social Change," in *Sociology* (New York, Harper, 1954), pp. 667–710. Lundberg has been a leading exponent of operational sociology. He has stressed quantitative, factual, rigorously objective social science.

ROBERTS, Henry Lithgow, *Russia and America; Dangers and Prospects* (New York, Harper, 1955). A select study group, sponsored by the Council on Foreign Relations, supported by the Ford Foundation and chaired by John J. McCloy, has here produced what has been called "a citizens' national security council report."

CHAPTER 21

HUMAN ADJUSTMENT AND THE ATOM

■ *Hornell Hart*

EIGHT GRADUAL solutions of cultural-lag problems have been reviewed in Chapter 20. Three of these have been the progressive reduction of traffic accidents—train, air, and auto—to small fractions of the rates which once caused slaughter of American travelers. Three more victories have been registered in collective struggles with infant mortality, typhoid fever, and tuberculosis. All these six were conquests over types of cultural lag which result from ignorance and carelessness rather than from greed and violence.

The analysis of the atomic crisis has shown it to be a specific example of the aggressive and exploitive type of menacing cultural lag. In the past chapter, exploitation as a cause of cultural lag has been shown to have been prominent in the child-labor problem. Violence, vengeance, and aggression played their part in the lynching problem. Concerted social effort has thus been effective, not only in the first six problems, but also in the exploitive and aggressive cases. Do we then have precedents here for solving the crucial lag of the atomic crisis?

THE PEACE MOVEMENT, THUS FAR, HAS FAILED

Acceleration in the harvest of *war* deaths has been set forth in Chapter 3 (page 44). It will be recalled that the death rate of civilians from wartime bombings in England increased 120-fold during the 28 years from World War I to World War II. In Chapter 3 is a chart that shows the trend of military casualties. The reader is asked to turn back now to that chart (page 45) and review it in relation to the charts of descending death rates which have been analyzed in Chapter 20. During the 400 years from the thirteenth century to the seventeenth, the number of soldiers killed or wounded in battle increased from 5 to 37 per thousand of population per century—more than a sevenfold increase. Moreover, this increase showed a fairly typical accelerating rise. From the seventeeenth century to the first half of the twentieth, the increase was from 37 to 310 per thousand of population per century—an 8.4-fold increase in less than 400 years. This accelerating rise in this index of war severity is the primary significance of the chart in Chapter 3 mentioned above.

However, a second aspect of this chart is almost as significant and deserves close investigation, namely, the fact that for the 363 years from 1650 to 1913, the war casualty rate was actually undergoing a sharp and persistent decline. What is the meaning of that decline?

The persistent endeavors of social reformers and social planners to achieve world peace constituted a movement quite comparable in many ways to the movements which brought about the reduction of the traffic accident casualties and the disease death rates graphed in the chart on page 478, and are even more closely comparable to the social movements responsible for the reduction of child labor and of lynching. The emotional urge of peace advocates has surely been adequate. Personal bereavements suffered by fathers, wives and children of soldiers killed in war, the experiences of bombed populations, the poverty, inflation, and disorganization which have resulted from war, the violation of deeply cherished ideals—these and other sources of emotional protest have operated powerfully to generate movements for world peace, disarmament, and world government.

Historically, three plans for the federation of states for the maintenance of peace have been oustanding in the influence which they exercised upon the evolution of modern conceptions of world law and order. These are Abbe de St. Pierre's *Projet Pour Rendre la Paix Perpetuelle en Europe,* published in 1713; Jeremy Bentham's *Plan for a Universal and Perpetual Peace,* published in 1789; and Immanuel Kant's *Zum Ewigen Frieden,* published in 1795. The first international gathering for discovering means to maintain peace was The Hague Conference held in 1899, at which 26 states participated. The Second Peace Conference at The Hague was held in 1907. Tolstoy, the great Russian disciple of peace, lived from 1828 to 1910; Jane Addams, the great American peace advocate, lived from 1860 to 1935. The five individuals just enumerated are only outstanding examples from an innumerable throng of idealists and intellectuals who discussed, investigated, and agitated with a view to the mitigation and, if possible, the abolition of war.

These intellectual and reformist movements were not the only—perhaps not even the most important—factors contributing to the decline in war casualties from 1650 to 1913. Policies of the British government undoubtedly contributed in fundamental ways to the decline of the war spirit (though, in other ways, British policies may have been major precipitating factors in the outbreak of World War I). In any event, the trend during these three and a half centuries may be epitomized in the fact that following the Napoleonic Wars, Great Britain and France, after having suffered war casualties in almost every decade from 1630 up to 1815, both experienced 99 years (from 1815 to 1914) with almost none.[1] But then followed 1914 to 1945, with higher war casualties per thousand of population per decade than either country had ever experienced. In terms of war casualties, the 99 years had represented a close approximation to general peace for the Western democracies. If that achievement could have been maintained and still further improved, the problem of war might have been regarded as solved by social planning and social reform in a way comparable to the solutions of such problems as air-travel casualties, child labor, and lynching in the United States.

THE ENGINEERING APPROACH TO THE ATOMIC CRISIS

The present chapter is concerned with social planning as applied to the atomic crisis. Social planning involves (1) formulating clearly the values to be sought; (2) ascertaining what types of behavior patterns or lines of action are most likely to produce the desired results; and (3) considering what means of social control will best promote adoption of the necessary behavior patterns and programs of action.

The goals to be sought seem to be universally accepted in broad principle: negatively, the prevention of nuclear world war and in general of the destruction of civilization by the use of the swiftly increasing technologies of mass killing and devastation; positively, the attainment of richer and richer life through creative co-operation. Our earlier analysis of the atomic crisis indicates that what we are confronted with is a specific example of that general type of problem which may be described as a menacing cultural lag involving exploitation and aggression. In such a situation the desirable objectives can be made quite specific: (1) to reduce and ultimately eliminate the exploitation which Soviet Russia is at present exercising over her own people and the peoples of the satellite countries; (2) to reduce the likelihood of, and as far as possible prevent completely, the aggressive use of nuclear energy and other means of mass destruction on the part of the Soviet government and of any other governments disposed so to use them; (3) to reduce, and ultimately eliminate, the exploitation and coercion of the peoples of less-developed countries by leading powers among the Western democracies, so as to reduce the drive toward communism which results from antagonisms generated in Asia, Oceania, South America, Africa, and other areas by Western imperialism and colonialism. In their essence, the above objectives are identical with the objectives of the peace movements which (up till now) have so signally failed.

This brings us to the second step in the engineering approach, namely, to determine what programs of action and behavior are necessary. As a start

[1] Quincy Wright, *A Study of War* (Chicago, University of Chicago Press, 1942), Vol. I, pp. 658–660. In the case of France, a relatively minor exception (in terms of casualties) was the Franco-Prussian War of 1870–71.

on this second step, let us ask why the peace movements of the Victorian Age and since then have failed.

At the cost of a good deal of oversimplification, it may be pointed out that this movement broke down because a series of tensions related to political and economic power had been building up between the leading nations and were exploded by the outbreak of war in the Balkans in 1914. Britain, Germany, and other nations had been bitter rivals over the partition of Africa. Britain and Germany had been engaged in an intense naval rivalry from 1880 to 1914.[2] France and Germany had been engaged in a feud extending back to the Napoleonic wars. France and Russia had become allies in resistance against the rising dominance of the German empire. Austro-Hungary, itself a mass of unresolved tensions, had allied itself with Germany in the struggle against France and Russia. Italy had joined Germany and Austria to create the Triple Alliance, while England achieved an understanding with Russia and France to create the Triple Entente. Since the agreements which temporarily compromised these conflicts were based upon no genuine merging of purposes, the rivalries and suspicions were ready to burst into warfare when the assassination at Sarajevo occurred.

In the struggle to settle these conflicts, the two rival theories of government and social order became more and more clearly focused. Napoleon, Bismarck, the Prussian Junkers, Mussolini, and Hitler all belong in one evolving tradition of dictatorship. Magna Carta, the Hague Peace Conferences, the League of Nations, the United Nations—all these belong to an evolving tradition of reaching voluntary international agreements by creative discussion and achieved consent. The breakdown of the peace movement and the resulting upsurge in war deaths have thus been the outgrowth of an increasing contrast between two radically different conceptions of civilization, of government, and of international relations. In the current world crisis, this has taken form in a struggle between two great culture areas. That this is the crux of the atomic crisis was shown in Chapter 20.

THE LONG-RUN SOLUTION

If the entire world shared the essential characteristics which the twelve countries of the basic democratic culture area have demonstrated during the past century and a third, the atomic crisis could be resolved constructively with relatively little risk of disaster. Fundamental progress could then be made toward eliminating war, much as progress has been achieved toward eliminating child labor and lyinching. World peace, world disarmament, and a world commonwealth would become possible. None of the leading nations in the democratic culture area has any serious fear that any other nation in this group will commit armed aggression against any other member—let

[2] Hornell Hart, "The Logistic Growth of Political Areas," *Social Forces*, Vol. XXVI (May, 1948), pp. 405–406.

alone drop nuclear bombs on the cities of another. These nations have shown that they can resolve their difficulties by diplomacy, and if necessary by arbitration or by reference to the World Court.

The problem, then, is how to extend to the rest of the world the security-by-consent which has already been achieved among the twelve democracies. This would not imply the imposing of identical culture patterns on the rest of the world. In spite of the fact that the twelve democracies all belong to one general culture area, they use five different national languages, and include a far greater number of foreign-speaking minorities. Though they are predominantly Protestant, they include two Catholic countries; they defend the religious freedom of Catholic and non-Christian minorities. Though their governments are all democratic, they range through a wide diversity of constitutional systems. Though their economic tradition has been that of private initiative and competitive capitalism, they peaceably contain numerous varieties of socialistic, co-operative, and welfare institutions; and marked trends toward the welfare state, and even toward state socialism, have appeared in most of them. Though they all conform in general to the monogamistic family, they differ widely in their laws relating to marriage and divorce. The only characteristic which would have to be adopted by other nations is to learn to adjust differences by means of discussion, reciprocal education, co-operation, and (where other methods fail) by compromise, or by legal adjudication. This is the essence of traits 1 to 4 and 8 in the inventory of the traits of the democratic area in Chapter 20.

Broadly speaking, the essence of democracy consists in government by consent of the governed, whereas the essence of dictatorship consists in the exercise of power by means of fear, force, and fraud—that is, by means of psychological coercion, physical coercion, and deception. It is true that democratic countries do frequently employ psychological coercion, physical coercion, and even deception as means of social control. Insofar as democracies are true to their avowed basic ideals, however, they seek to maximize the application of voluntary consent by means of the four co-operative methods of social control—enlightenment, facilitation, inducement, and contagion—and to minimize the use of fear, force, and fraud. The dictatorships make extensive and intensive use of contagion as a technique, probably more consistently and more effectively in general than do the democracies. The dictatorships also use enlightenment where it fits their purposes, though the systematic and deliberate use of deception is characteristic of the dictatorial technique. Censorship, the suppression of all opposition, the use of blackmail, the use of court trials as methods of proving accusations rather than as methods of seeking justice—these and other dictatorial techniques are simply variations on the fundamental fear, force, and fraud procedures.

The exercise of democratic social control by means of enlightenment is based fundamentally upon discussion as a means of reaching agreements voluntarily acceptable to all parties. The enlightened person does voluntarily the things which he has come to realize are in his own best interests as well as in the interests of others. This enlightenment is gained through public education in our democratic school system. That necessarily involves a good deal of indoctrination. But enlightenment comes also through discussion. Much of this discussion is competitive, taking on the character of debate between opposed viewpoints. Some of it is antagonistic. Some of it is co-operative and creative, achieving high levels of intellectual team work. But all discussion (short of criminal libel, slander, and incitement) is safeguarded by civil liberties. These are vital to democracy because they are so essential in social control by enlightenment.

At its best, such discussion is creative in the sense of being based upon genuine and sincere intellectual co-operation in the search for truth and justice. However, democracy can and frequently does succeed by means of competitive and antagonistic discussion—provided that the fundamental rules of parliamentary procedure and of civil liberties are maintained. Democratic discussion is also valuable in preparing the way for facilitation, inducement, and contagion.

In international relations, democracy consists in reaching agreements between nations by consent. And here the discussion process is the very core of the technique for winning free and voluntary co-operation between nations. Whether the discussion is done by diplomats, by international radio and television broadcasts, by international journalism, or by debates in the United Nations, the progressive functioning of world democracy depends crucially upon the effectiveness of our processes for arriving at international working agreements by enlightened consent.

THE AGGRESSOR NATIONS ARE NOT SINCERELY DEMOCRATIC

The preceding section might make the solution of the atomic crisis seem to be encouragingly simple. Merely expand the democratic culture area to include the entire world, and the problem is solved. Indeed, the advocates of the League of Nations, and more recently many of the enthusiasts about the United Nations, have proceeded as if they believed that exactly that kind of program would be adequate. Indeed, the Charter of the United Nations virtually states such a program as its basis. But such assumptions are at best oversimplifications.

One of the greatest sources of fallacious thinking about relations between dictator nations and the Western democracies has been the uncritical assumption that the dictatorships in general, and Soviet Russia in particular, really belong to the same democratic culture area as the United States, and that if we will only be more friendly and fair toward such nations, the war-breeding conflicts will disappear. Cultural anthropology has been making social scientists aware of the fact that peoples belonging to different cultures are likely to have radical differences in their goals and in their mental and social processes.

The naive thinker about international relations takes it for granted that other peoples share the same great fundamental values, ideals, ideas, and methods which he has acquired from his own culture. But such assumptions can lead to catastrophic mistakes in international policies.

Essential to democratic discussion are the basic principles of intellectual integrity and fair play. But here we reach a basic obstacle in the attempt to apply constructive methods of social control in dealing with the atomic crisis. The essence of dictatorship is a repudiation of the indispensable conditions for democratic discussion. The State Department made an investigation (for example) of treaty agreements entered into by the Soviet government. The Foreign Affairs Committee staff of the House of Representatives made a study of 16 international agreements or groups of agreements made during World War II, or immediately after and closely connected with the war agreements. It found that at least 37 provisions of these agreements have been violated, and that, in most instances, these violations have been persistent and recurrent.[3]

DEMOCRATIC METHODS FAILED TO CONTROL WEAPONS OF MASS DESTRUCTION

Between the Western democracies, the four constructive methods of social control—enlightenment, inducement, facilitation, and contagion, applied through free discussion and negotiation—have proved effective in abolishing inter-democratic wars. But the inadequacy of those means of social control in relation to the communistic dictatorship has been demonstrated by the endeavors to control atomic and other weapons of mass destruction.

In June, 1946, Mr. Bernard Baruch offered proposals for the international control of atomic energy which became a basis for protracted discussion in the United Nations.[4] The unrealism of those proposals, in view of the actualities of the struggle between the democratic and the dicatorship culture areas, may be made vivid by supposing that the situations of the United States and of the Soviet Union had been reversed, and that the Soviets had offered to us, in the UN, the exact replica of the plan which we proposed to them in 1948. This would have involved the following conditions:

1. That the Soviet Union was in possession of a supply of atomic weapons approximately ten times as large as those possessed by the United States and its allies;

[3] House of Representatives, Foreign Affairs Committee staff, under direction of John M. Vorys, "World War II International Agreements and Understandings Entered Into During Secret Conferences Concerning Other Peoples," (Washington, Government Printing Office, March 12, 1953), p. v. For an earlier systematic list of charges, and particulars of violations by the Soviet government of international treaties, agreements and assurances, see William C. Bullitt, *The Great Globe Itself* (New York, Scribner, 1946), Appendix I, pp. 219–232.

[4] Division of Public Liaison, Office of Public Affairs, Department of State, "Comparison of the United Nations Plan of Atomic Energy Control with the Soviet Control Proposals," October 11, 1949.

2. That the Soviet Union and its satellites had developed such control (or such leadership) in the United Nations that it consistently outvoted the Western democracies five or ten to one;

3. That the UN, by an overwhelming majority led by the Soviet Union, adopted a plan whereby

   a. An international atomic-energy control agency would be appointed (with an overwelmingly Soviet-sympathizing majority);

   b. That this agency would have powers of inspection limited only by decisions of Soviet-controlled courts;

   c. That this agency would be empowered (without restriction by veto) to report to the UN and to the member nations any "violation" which it found, and to recommend appropriate self-preservative action.

If such a plan were proposed, under the conditions stated, what would be the probability that the delegation from the United States would approve it, or that, if it were so approved, the Senate of the United States would ratify such an agreement? The answers are so obvious that any thoughtful social scientist might be expected to ask the question why our UN diplomats spent eight years, from 1946 to 1954, proposing and arguing for this kind of plan (in reverse) as the best solution to the Atomic Crisis. This appears to be a clear-cut case of diplomatic cultural lag. There is no likelihood that the Soviet government, so long as it remains essentially a communistic dictatorship, will ever sincerely and voluntarily accept any non-communistic program for the control of nuclear weapons or any other program of world law and order which, without the safeguard of a veto, would seem to the Russians to put communistic nations at the mercy of anti-communistic majorities.

Note that the basic reason for the unrealism of the UN control proposals is the life-and-death struggle between the Soviet and the democratic culture areas. If the nations voting for the majority plan in the UN were the only ones which had to be considered, it seems likely that such a program might not only have been adopted but might also have been put into effect. Quite possibly such action would have stimulated strongly the growth of world government. The precedents of successful international agreements in the democratic culture area indicate that this would have been a normally-to-be-expected development. But the fact which the UN negotiators appear to have overlooked is that the dictatorship culture area is based upon fundamental repudiation of the principles which are indispensable to reaching voluntary and effective international agreements on vital matters.

REPRISAL WAR, AS A METHOD OF CONTROLLING AGGRESSORS, IS LIKELY TO PROVE DISASTROUSLY UNSUCCESSFUL

The failure of attempts to achieve international agreements by consent between the democracies and the Soviet dictatorship tends to increase the pressure toward the use of fear and force. Back in March, 1949, George Fielding Eliot, military and naval analyst of the *New York Herald Tribune* and of the Columbia Broadcasting System, was advocating preventive war.[5] But the first Soviet atom bomb was exploded in August, 1949. The expansion of Russian power to destroy America has transformed the problem. The threat is now reciprocal. The discussion has thus shifted from preventive war to reprisal war, and to "graduated deterrence."

An integral part of America's containment program to prevent Soviet world conquest has been the policy of deterrence. On January 12, 1954, Secretary of State Dulles announced that the National Security Council had formally adopted a further extension of that policy. He said:[6]

> If we can deter such aggression as would mean general war (and that is our confident resolve) then we can let time and fundamentals work for us. . . . The way to deter aggression is for the free community to be willing and able to respond vigorously, at places and with means of its own choosing. . . . The basic decision [by the National Security Council] was . . . to depend primarily upon a great capacity to retaliate instantly by means and at places of its own choosing.

The Dulles announcement raised a series of questions:

1. Just what did this retaliation threat mean? Did we really intend to bomb Russia if she should invade Iran or Yugoslavia—or if the communists won a major election in Italy and took over that country—or if Chinese communists should invade India via Tibet—or if France should be induced to enter into an effective alliance with Russia, instead of with the Western democracies?

2. Did this reprisal threat constitute a blanket ultimatum which, in spite of its vagueness, might have precipitated the paralysis raid of which Chapter 10 has shown the possibility? If we had really intended to carry out our threat, and if we had made that intention clear to the Soviet government, would we not have given the rulers of the Kremlin an adequate excuse to launch their own paralysis raid against us before we could launch our reprisal war against them?

3. If, on the other hand, we were merely bluffing, may not our dependence upon this fake threat have left the way open to the Kremlin to continue its march of triumph across Asia and across the world?

4. If we did launch a reprisal raid, how much destruction of the democratic countries would result?

5. What assurance is there that we could have won the war which would certainly have resulted if we carried out óur threats of "instant retaliation by means and at places of our own choosing"?

6. To what extent would the democratic way of life be destroyed by an attempted reprisal war against Russia?

7. Would not a nuclear attack on Russia mobilize against us not only the

---

[5] George Fielding Eliot, *If Russia Strikes* (Indianapolis, Bobbs-Merrill, 1949).

[6] See "Text of Dulles' Statement on Foreign Policy of Eisenhower Administration," *New York Times,* January 13, 1954, p. 2.

full might of the Russian people but also the horror, resentment, and fear of much of the rest of the world? Would it not destroy America's capacity to lead the world toward a better civilization?

The above seven questions all involve practical problems of social control. If social science has any operational validity, it should be able to shed light on such problems of social interaction.

WHAT ARE THE PROBABILITIES THAT THE SOVIETS WILL REFRAIN FROM NUCLEAR WARFARE?

The "Summit" conference at Geneva in July, 1955, between the heads of the Big Four governments, has been interpreted widely as having reached only one significant result, namely, the renunciation of nuclear warfare by both the Soviet and the Western governments, on the grounds that all-out war with modern weapons of mass destruction would be utterly disastrous to all concerned. To what extent can the alleged renunciation be counted on as a certainty?

From the American viewpoint, the purported agreement would seem to be an explicit cancellation of the reprisal threat discussed in the preceding section. President Eisenhower has repeatedly assured the world that the United States will not take the initiative in resorting to nuclear weapons. But how about the reliability of the Soviet renunciation of such warfare?

Such a question involves the basic problem of the possibility of forecasting human behavior. This question has been discussed, in some of its more quantitative phases, in Chapter 19 of this text. Our national departments of State and of Defense devote vast resources to attempting to estimate in advance the probabilities for and against such alternatives. A genuine upsurge in social science should increase the reliabilities and validities of such predictions in much the same way in which improvements in meteorology have been increasing the trustworthiness of weather predictions.

DID THE DOWN-GRADING OF STALIN MEAN PROGRESSIVE DEMOCRATIZATION OF THE SOVIET UNION?

On February 25, 1956, Kruschev made a two-and-a-half hour speech to a secret meeting of inner-circle Soviet leaders, denouncing Stalin. On June 4, the State Department of the United States released a transcript of this speech which had been obtained through Secret Service channels.[7] This denunciation and the repercussions which followed it raise a crucial question: To what extent does this official repudiation of Stalinism indicate a genuine transition in Soviet policy from dictatorship toward democracy?

Obviously, any generalization on that topic must be subject to wide margins of possible error. But if the public statements by the communists and other authenticated events related to this de-Stalinization are analyzed in

[7] New York Times, June 5, 1956, pp. 13–16; but see Life (January 14, 1957) p. 37.

relation to the points of contrast between the democratic and the dictatorship culture areas, as outlined in Chapter 20 and in the early portion of the present chapter, considerable light can be obtained.

Consider in particular the broad distinction as to methods of social control employed by the two types of government. Communistic dictatorship has made systematic use of fear, force, and fraud, while democracy seeks to achieve government by consent of the governed through enlightenment, facilitation, inducement, and contagion. Kruschev's denunciation of Stalin analyzed the dictator's crimes in terms of the use of fear, force, and fraud. Take the following passage as a decisive example.

> Stalin originated the concept "enemy of the people." This term automatically rendered it unnecessary that the ideological errors of a man . . . be proved; this term made possible the usage of the most cruel repression, violating all norms of revolutionary legality. . . . This concept . . . eliminated the possibility of any kind of ideological fight for the making of one's views known on this or that issue. . . . The formula "enemy of the people" was specifically introduced for the purpose of physically annihilating [those] who opposed the party line. . . .
>
> Berea's gang outdid itself in proving the guilt of the arrested and the truth of materials which it falsified. . . . How is it possible that a person confesses to crimes which he has not committed? Only in one way—because of the application of . . . tortures . . . deprivation of his judgment, taking away of his human dignity. In this manner "confessions" were acquired.
>
> [In the 1937–38 purge] of 139 members and candidates of the party's Central Committee who were elected at the 17th Congress, 98 persons (i.e., 70%) were arrested and shot. . . . The same fate met . . . the majority of the delegates at the 17th party Congress. Of the 1,966 delegates with voting or advisory rights, 1,108 persons were arrested. . . .
>
> Monstrous are the acts whose initiator was Stalin. . . . [Take for example] the mass deportations from their native places of whole nations. . . .

Note that, even in this brief excerpt from Kruschev's address, fear, force, and fraud are specifically designated as the essence of criminal Stalinism, and that while the emphasis was upon the use of these methods against Russian communists, and against officers in the Soviet army, the denunciation of mass deportation broadens the denunciation to apply also to international relations.

Government by consent—and international co-operation by international consent—are achieved basically by means of co-operative discussion, or more often by competitive discussion. Civil liberties have as one of their main functions the protection of freedom of discussion. What effect has de-Stalinization had at this point?

Under the Stalin dictatorship no free discussion was possible except in deep secrecy. To express an opinion deviating from the party line was to invite exile to Siberia or sudden death. But Kruschev's speech opened a chasm in the dam. A *New York Times* reporter said:[8]

---

[8] Jack Raymond, "Stalin's Image Fades But Slowly in Soviet," *New York Times,* June 17, 1956, p. E3, cols. 3–5.

Qualified persons report that the people have found their tongues, not only on the merits or demerits of Stalin. A new mood of critical approach is developing. Observers who have lived here continuously in recent years say the trend began with the death of Stalin in 1953. . . .

As for the repressions and injustices of the Secret Police and rigged courts, they are referred to in the press and by periodicals from time to time. . . .

That increased freedom of discussion is actually encouraged by the government is suggested by the reprinting in Pravda of the critical editorial by U. S. communist leader Eugene Dennis, editor of the *Daily Worker,* and by the publicity given in Russia to criticisms by communists in various other countries. Among other things, Dennis said: "Nothing can justify the use of tortures and rigged trials, large-scale deportations, provocative and chauvinist actions as in the case of Yugoslavia, the persecution of Jewish doctors. . . ."

Togliatti, Italy's veteran Communist leader, urged "the ruling group to take the initiative in the field of ideas, and in practice, and to be inquisitive, to engage in lively debate to attain . . . full independence of judgment and character."

As to the extent to which this increased freedom of discussion may be implemented in democratic parliamentary institutions, large questions arise. *Izvestia,* in June, 1956, contained an article by the anti-communist French statesman, Leon Hamon, arguing the merits of a well-informed parliament "where opinions were voiced publicly and everyone could be called on to state his personal views." Moscow dispatches reported widespread discussion of the possibility of permitting more than one candidate to run for seats in the local assemblies. "At the same time," Jack Raymond reports, "government officials have emphasized repeatedly that desanctification of Stalin must not be construed as a bid to people to institute procedures for opposition."

Democracy finds fullfillment in proportion as decisions are reached by consent based on enlightenment. The question is how far the flood of light let in by Kruschev's speech may lead the Russian people to securing more and more truth about their government, and about the policies which might lead to their destruction or to their increasing achievement of peace and high prosperity.

How Serious Is the Food Crisis in the Soviet Union?

A significant sidelight thrown on the Russian problem by Kruschev's address is contained in the following sentence:

All those who interested themselves even a little in the national situation saw the difficult situation in agriculture.

The Polish writers in Pozan in the summer of 1956 cried out for bread. *Newsweek* summed up the situation thus:[9]

[9] *Newsweek* (July 9, 1956), p. 45.

All the long way from China's famine-plagued coast to East Germany's potato lines, hunger hangs over the Communist world.

Bungled agricultural planning, peasant resistance to collectivization, and continued blind insistence on guns before butter have produced churning unrest in the satellites and in Russia itself.

If fear, force, and fraud are inherently unsound and ineffective methods of social control, the Soviet government may be expected to break down in one way or another sooner or later. In the summer of 1956, current discussion suggests that the military efficiency of the Soviets has been brought up to a high point under the dictatorship. Ultimately, the whole question may boil down to the relative survival value of the democratic and the dictatorial way of life and of government.

EXTENDING THE DEMOCRATIC CULTURE AREA

The world is not completely apportioned into the democratic and the communistic-dictatorial culture areas. A vast intermediate zone exists, into which both the democratic and the communistic ways of life are seeking to expand. The long-run social-planning problem of the Nuclear Age is: How can the democratic expansion be promoted, and the dictatorship expansion be restricted?

Four basic factors may be recognized as fundamental in the past growth of the democratic group of nations:

1. A series of political, religious, and economic revolutions broke down old tyrannies and laid foundations for the institutions of freedom. Magna Carta, the Reformation, the American Revolution, and the French Revolution are the outstanding examples. Less violent, and still revolutionary in its contribution to the emergence of democracy, has been the extension of education, from the tiny male oligarchy who first monopolized it, to the great rank and file of both men and women. The recent development of the welfare state, with its expansion of the proportion of the national income going to the working classes, also belongs in this category.

2. The settlement of vast territories formerly occupied by hunting people, including North America, Australia, New Zealand, and some parts of Africa, has been a second method whereby the democratic area has grown. The dominant settlers in those areas were from countries belonging to the democratic bloc, and they brought with them the institutions of their fatherlands. Spanish America and most of Africa appear to be intermediate between the democratic and the dictatorship areas.

3. The third fundamental method has been inter-diffusion among the twelve countries. The religious freedoms achieved by the Reformation in Switzerland and Germany diffused to other countries; the political freedoms and the parliamentary institutions achieved in Great Britain and the United

States also were absorbed by the other nations. Educational and economic progress has readily passed from one nation to another.

4. The fourth method is diffusion to other countries outside the original twelve. Modifying gradually the internationally aristocratic attitudes of imperialism, the colonizing countries have increasingly diffused their concepts of liberty and democracy to such countries as India, Pakistan, the Philippine Islands, Indonesia, and other areas of the world.

Of the four methods, all are available today except the second.

Diffusion, however, does not take place merely as one-way traffic. Up to 1914, most students of international relations would have classified Germany among the democracies. Germany participated in the Protestant religion, the development of a vigorous parliamentary system, women's suffrage, the extension of secondary and higher education to at least a considerable fraction of the population, the development of social-welfare legislation, the observance of civil liberties, and various other characteristics which seem to have included most of the essentials of the culture shared by the other democracies. But peaceful relations between Germany and the other Western nations broke down; after her defeat she succumbed to the diffusion of the Nazi police-state pattern, similar to that of Italy, Russia, and Germany's own Nietzschean thinkers. After World War II, West Germany appears to have been restored to the democratic area.

It is a notable fact that China, up until World War II, seemed to be moving fundamentally and fairly rapidly into the democratic culture area. The educational and humanitarian work of the missionaries; the education of Chinese leaders in democratic countries, facilitated by the use of the Boxer indemnities to send Chinese students to America; the swift expansion of trade between China and the West; and the democratic ideals of the Sun Yat-sen revolution in 1911–12—all pointed toward the progressive incorporation of China in the democratic world. The loss of China to communistic dictatorship is a tragic reversal, due to causes too complex to review here, but reflecting fundamentally the lack of adequate education and training of the Chinese people to support and participate in genuinely democratic government.

The Cold War may well be regarded as an intensified struggle between the opposed diffusion currents of dictatorship and democracy. The police-state pattern and the freedom-and-justice pattern each seeks to extend its area in the world. The crucial issue is whether the democratic nations, by the utilization of concerted intelligence, systematically applied to the problems of democratizing the world, can turn the tide and promote world-wide growth of co-operation-by-consent.

Under the condition that Soviet communism either (1) breaks down, or (2) becomes too weak to menace the world, or (3) remains at its present or even greater strength but refrains from launching a nuclear aggressive attack, the immediate problem of the atomic crisis becomes that of cultivating, on a more and more nearly world-wide scale, an improvement on the kind of international relations which have existed during the past century and a third between the twelve democracies.

If it be granted that our international problem is essentially of the character which has been described above, the steps for actually expanding the world area of co-operation by consent hinge essentially upon the development of certain attitudes on the part of strategic decision-makers. The task would seem impossibly difficult if it actually involved the immediate raising of the educational levels of the rest of the world (including the peoples of China, India, and Africa, and of the Soviet Union as soon as they become accessible) to the level which already prevails in the democracies. While such an educational process is highly desirable and should be promoted as rapidly as feasible, it is not prerequisite to the establishment of co-operation by consent.

The people of the United States would react violently to the bombing of an American city, to the dramatic assassination of some prominent American in a foreign country, or to some other event which captured their imagination or aroused their resentment. But so far as the detailed conduct of our international relations is concerned, the rank and file of the American people generally accept the policies formulated by their elected representatives and by appointed government officials—or react irrationally to the incitement of demagogues who use real and imaginary international menaces as exciters to stir up political power. If American leaders follow a soundly constructive policy which is in line with the basic beliefs and mores of the people, that is all that is required.

Similarly, the effective participation of India and Pakistan in international co-operation by consent does not need to wait upon the solving of the problems of illiteracy in those countries. The leaders of India and Pakistan are far more intelligent about international relations than the average college graduate in the United States. Those leaders may have to discover ways in which they can gain and hold the support of the masses of the people in their countries, but those methods, again, do not have to wait upon the adequate education of the rank and file.

Since the winning of active consent on the part of national leaders is the essential problem, we are confronted with a type of project which is becoming increasingly familiar to large bodies of the practitioners of applied psychology—in the professions of education, advertising, salesmanship, personnel management, and the like. The more expert (at least) of our advertisers can lay out with a great deal of confidence the kind of program which will induce the public to purchase a previously unfamiliar product. Public relations experts have developed methods by which they can change popular ill-will into popular good-will—at least within fairly wide limits. Educators are beginning to discover how to create in the minds of school children and of high school and college students the insights and the skill required for given social purposes. The development of our air force during World War II was a spectacular demonstration of the effectiveness of applied psychology when used systematically and energetically for the achievement of a nationally essential end.

The agencies through which these processes of applied psychology can be brought to bear upon the creation of a world-wide area of co-operation by consent are provided by the United Nations. UNESCO has been specifically created with a view to long-run achievement along this line. When it is protested that the United Nations has been relatively feeble and ineffective in accomplishing international understanding and co-operation, the rejoinder is not that the task is impossible but that our efforts have been too half-hearted and too lacking in the use of the best available techniques and resources. Sociopsychologically, it is entirely practicable to achieve the required goal—if World War III can be prevented.

It must be recognized, of course, that national interests at present often seem incompatible with each other. But similar incompatibilities have often arisen among the twelve democratic nations. Such conflicts have proved, during the past century and a third, to be soluble without going to war about them. Peaceful international co-operation is possible if the best available methods are used. The United Nations provides an opportunity to cultivate such methods.

In the process of building up the economic welfare, the intelligence, and the capacity for democratic government in the areas of the world intermediate between the Soviet bloc and the democratic culture area, it should be remembered that the positive methods of social control are the ones most likely to succeed. Instead of resorting to fear, force, and fraud in our attempts to win adherents among the so-called backward nations, the progress toward a world solution can be hastened by employing enlightenment, facilitation, inducement, and contagion. These processes are implicit in and indispensable to the programs of economic and technological assistance which were proposed in President Truman's "Point Four" program, and which have been carried forward (on a rather meager and inadequate scale) by the United Nations and by the United States government. In a report made to Congress in the winter of 1953–54, Dr. Raymond W. Miller listed 27 specific recommendations for strengthening that program.[10]

A specific example may help to point up the significance of creative co-operation between the Western democracies and the intermediate nations:[11]

[10] Dr. Raymond W. Miller, "Making Point Four Work," *Harvard Business School Bulletin* (Winter, 1954). Cf. discussion of Point Four in Chapter 18 of the present text.
[11] Howard A. Rusk, M.D., "U. S. Health Aid Abroad," *New York Times,* December 11, 1955, p. 24, col. 5.

In Iran, for example, the incidence of malaria in 13,000 villages with a population of more than 4,000,000 dropped from 90 to 10 percent following DDT spraying.

Most health projects achieve dramatic and significant results at a low unit cost. Within three years the incidence of yaws in Haiti was reduced from one in six of the population to one in 3,000 at a cost of 30 cents per capita, of which 20 cents was provided by Haiti. . . .

Joint Health projects in Latin America have reached more than 25,000,000 persons. . . .

Health projects . . . increase national productivity and ability to purchase goods produced in the United States. Following malaria control programs, industrial absenteeism in the Philippines dropped from 33 per cent a day to 4 per cent. The average gross income of families in certain districts of Greece doubled as the areas they cultivated increased 50 per cent. Rice production in one area of Bengal increased 543 pounds to the acre.

THE COMING UPSURGE OF SOCIAL SCIENCE

Since the first atomic bomb was exploded in 1945, one after another of the outstanding leaders of our Western world has reiterated the conclusion that our civilization has a chance of avoiding colossal smash-up—but only if the lag between the towering acceleration of destructive technology and the lethargic and groping development of international law and order can be overcome. The future of civilization depends upon the invention of better methods of social invention, or, in other words, a radical speed-up in the development of genuine social science.

Science Generates Progress

Four instances may be cited in which unprecedented upward surges in man's power to carry out his purposes have taken place in fields in which man has begun to use accurate and systematic forms of thinking.

The first instance is the discovery of the Western world. Popular history glorifies Christopher Columbus and Americus Vespucius. Actually, courageous and farsighted though they were, these explorers made their discoveries by virtue of centuries of scientific progress in navigation. During ancient times ships had to hug the coasts because they had no method for steering any extended course over the open sea. The invention of the magnetic compass, the development of various instruments for making astronomical observations, and the improvement of mathematical techniques for calculating latitude and longitude made it possible for these navigators to plow directly across the Atlantic and to open up the new world.

The second illustration is the Industrial Revolution. That revolution was the result primarily of the application of science to the development of power for running stationary machines and for transportation—combined with the invention of machines suited to be run by such power.

A third illustration of the upsurges which have resulted from systematically accurate thinking, as applied to practical problems, is the increase in expectation of life which has taken place during the past 150 years.

The fourth illustration of the impact of science upon social change is the accelerating power of human beings to destroy each other's lives and wealth.

Now if science can have produced these four surges in human power to carry out purposes—the opening up of the Western world, the doubling and quadrupling of real income in America, the adding of a quarter century to the human life span within a hundred years, and the sudden engulfing of practically the whole globe within the ranges of our death-dealing weapons—why might not science be applied with equal effectiveness to preserving the peace in the Atomic Age?

Comte and the Theory of Successive Emergence

It was Auguste Comte who first suggested the Successive-Emergence Theory of intellectual progress. Comte argued that the order of emergence out of the theological and the metaphysical stages into the positive stage is determined by the relative simplicity of the various sciences and by their dependence upon one another. Physics and chemistry emerged relatively early, because of the readily measurable and verifiable character of their data. But later, when living organisms were studied systematically, with the aid of the microscope developed by physics and of the substances and the techniques developed by chemistry, biology emerged into its scientific stage. When psychology borrowed the experimental methods, the mathematical devices, and the rigorous procedures of its predecessors, it too became scientific. Each of these sciences, in turn, made giant strides as soon as its specialists learned to think systematically and rigorously. This conception would suggest at least the possibility that scientific methods of thinking, which have emerged successively in such fields as physics, chemistry, biology, economics, and psychology may become effective in the areas of social relations and may develop sufficient control over social behavior to provide a creative solution for nuclear cultural lag.

If the Successive-Emergence Theory is sound, two factual verifications should follow. First, the history of science should show upsurges of development in one phase of human thought after another, in something the order indicated by Comte. Second, evidence should now be appearing that social thought is beginning to take its turn in emerging into the scientific stage.

As to the first of these possible verifications, some pertinent evidence has been published by Lehman.[12] Reading from his charts, the approximate dates at which 25 per cent of the total progress up to now was reached by certain of the basic disciplines were as follows:

[12] Harvey C. Lehman "The Exponential Increase of Man's Cultural Output," *Social Forces,* Vol. 25 (March, 1947), pp. 281–290; "National Differences in Creativity," *American Journal of Sociology,* Vol. 52 (May, 1947), pp. 475–488.

Science	*Year*
Philosophy	1640
Medicine and pathology	1680
Mathematics	1735
Geology	1762
Chemistry	1810
Genetics	1852

In the above list, philosophy, mathematics, geology, chemistry, and genetics would seem to be in about the relative positions called for by Comte's theory. Medicine and pathology, however, reached their 25 per cent level 172 years ahead of genetics. This is probably due to the urgent need which our ancestors felt for trustworthy knowledge to aid their struggle against disease and death.

Lehman's study did not provide quantitative data on the growth of the scientific aspects of social thought. Such data, however, are available, and when they are analyzed they show that social research in general, and experimental social psychology and business-cycle theory in particular, have had upsurge dates later than any of those in the above list—as the Successive-Emergence Theory has predicted. Evidence on this point is found in four bibliographies on social research published in 1936, 1937, 1944, and 1945.[13] These all reflect clearly an upsurge, between the two world wars, in the number of articles and books published about behaviorial and social research in general, and about social psychology and business cycles in particular, all of which follow the same general trend.

But Social Science Has Lagged

Upsurges in science consist not merely of articles and books published, nor merely of distinguished men listed in biographical dictionaries. Rather, this surge of science has consisted in the growth of a vast series of culture complexes, involving laboratories, equipment, research funds, intensively trained people, publications, increasing social interest and attention, and progressively developing skills and bodies of knowledge.

One index of the swift growth of this culture complex has been the mounting curve of college graduates. Another is the growing appropriation for research. But when the swift and massive growth in the science complex in general is broken down into types of sciences, we are confronted with a preponderance of attention and resources being devoted to the earlier-upsurging sciences as compared with social science. The comparative memberships

---

[13] Dorothy Campbell Culver, *Methodology of Social Science Research—A Bibliography* (Berkeley, Calif., University of California Press, 1936); Ernest Greenwood, *Experimental Sociology—A Study in Method* (New York, King's Crown Press, 1945), pp. 147–154; Gardner Murphy, Lois Barclay Murphy, and Theodore M. Newcomb, *Experimental Social Psychology* (New York, Harper, 1931 and 1937), pp. 1057–1103; Harold M. Somers, "Classified Bibliography of Articles on Business Cycle Theory," in *Readings in Business Cycle Theory* (American Economic Association, 1944), pp. 446–487. For a more detailed analysis of these trends, see Hornell Hart, "The Pre-War Upsurge in Social Science," *American Sociological Review*, Vol. 14 (October, 1949), pp. 599–607.

in learned societies gives some measure of the relative activity.[14] For example, sociology—the science with the nearest claim to be investigating the basic principles of social relations—has less than one-fortieth the number of members in the engineering organizations. Government expenditures for research in the natural sciences and technology were multiplied eighteenfold between 1938 and 1948; but government expenditures for social sciences and statistics increased less than threefold during the same ten years. In 1948, the government was spending nearly 15 times as much for natural sciences and technology as for social sciences and statistics.[15] The total picture would seem to be one of relatively minor availability of financial resources for social research, compared with gifts for immediate philanthropy and for research in "natural" sciences. In the light of the urgent necessity for an upsurge of social science to deal with the atomic crisis, this comparatively slender financial support would seem tragic were it clear that a sufficient supply of worth-while projects in social research would develop if the funds were largely increased. Demonstration of valid and significant results must interact with increased financial support if the needed upsurge is to be achieved.

The Scientific Study of Social Science

If social science is the most promising instrument for speeding up the development of democratic international controls, is not a valid science of social-science methods the most promising instrument for improving science? All that we know of scientific method should be brought to bear upon our present stumbling and inadequate techniques, in order that we may build up intellectual capital. Our factories produce with almost incredible abundance because our captains of industry built machines for the purpose of building machines. Social science is urgently in need of such an investment of intelligence toward promoting intelligence.

We need to make use of the keenest powers of organized human thinking to discover how those powers may be made more effective, swifter in discovery, more reliable in prediction, and more realistic in their judgment as to the actualities of the collective life of humanity. We need to explore experimentally the methods by which scientific experiments can be applied to the progress of the atomic age. We need searching studies as to the methods whereby the most able minds of the rising generation of scientists can be recruited for social research and can be so stimulated, facilitated, and rewarded that they will make their maximum possible contributions. We need to study swiftly and without delay methods whereby social research can

[14] *The World of Learning,* 1954, *passim.*

[15] New York Times, December 7, 1952, p. 1, col. 2; Frank Emerson Andrews, *Philanthropic Giving* (New York, Russell Sage Foundation, 1950), p. 219; Porter McKeever, Director of Ford Foundation Office of Reports, letter to Hornell Hart, dated June 30, 1954. For a discussion of the Rockefeller Foundation's gifts to social science, see Raymond B. Fosdick, *The Story of the Rockefeller Foundation* (New York, Harper, 1952), pp. 192–236.

be speeded up, the present intolerable procrastinations and delays eliminated, and intelligent decision reached in time to be of use in the urgent crisis of this Atomic Age.

ANNOTATED BIBLIOGRAPHY

CHAPIN, F. Stuart, *Experimental Designs in Sociological Research,* rev. ed. (New York, Harper, 1955). A critical collection of case studies of research into causes, by one of the outstanding pioneers in social research.

CHASE, Stuart, *The Proper Study of Mankind,* rev. ed. (New York, Harper, 1956). A popular and dramatic account of some of the achievements of social science.

DODD, Stuart Carter, *Systematic Social Science (A Dimensional Sociology)* (Beirut, American University of Beirut, 1947). This is one of the most comprehensive collections of quantitative sociological research studies. The "S Theory" should be examined critically rather than accepted unquestioningly.

FESTINGER, Leon, and KATZ, Daniel, eds., *Research Methods in the Behavioral Sciences* (New York, Dryden Press, 1953). This is a symposium by outstanding research workers in various social sciences.

GIROD, Roger, "Social Progress and the Organization of Social Research," *International Labour Review,* Vol. 65 (May, 1952), pp. 555–577. Describes the organization of social research in France and in the United States, and the relation between such research and social action.

HART, Hornell, "Social Research Methods: A Consensus," *Sociology and Social Research,* Vol. 34 (November, 1949), pp. 91–96. Presents agreements about social research among 32 outstanding treatises published during the preceding two decades.

LUNDBERG, George A., *Can Science Save Us?* (New York, Longmans, Green, 1947). A leading crusader for scientific sociology, reacting to the threat posed by the first atomic bombs, summarizes the promise and limitations of sociology as a natural science applied to the regulation of human affairs.

YOUNG, Pauline V., and Associates, *Scientific Social Surveys and Research* (Englewood Cliffs, N. J., Prentice-Hall, 1955). This has been one of the most widely used textbooks in this field.

INDEX

COM